STATE
AND
SOCIETY
IN
WESTERN
EUROPE

Percy Allum

Polity Press

First published in 1995 by Polity Press in association with Blackwell Publishers.

Editorial office:
Polity Press
65 Bridge Street
Cambridge CB2 1UR, UK

Marketing and production:
Blackwell Publishers, the publishing imprint of Basil Blackwell Ltd
108 Cowley Road
Oxford OX4 1JF, UK

Basil Blackwell Inc.
238 Main Street
Cambridge, MA 02142, USA

A CIP catalogue record for this book is available from the British Library.

Library of Congress Cataloging-in-Publication Data
Allum, P. A.
　State and society in Western Europe/Percy Allum.
　　p.　cm.
　Includes bibliographical references and index.
　ISBN 0–7456–0409–9 (acid-free paper).—ISBN 0–7456–0410–2 (pbk: acid-free paper)
　1. Europe—Politics and government—1989–　2. Comparative government.　3. European federation.　I. Title.
JN94.A2A45　1995
320.94'09'049—dc20

94–13288
CIP

Typeset in 11 on 12½ pt Times
by Wearset, Boldon, Tyne and Wear
Printed in Great Britain by Hartnolls Ltd, Bodmin, Cornwall

This book is printed on acid-free paper.

Contents

List of Figures

List of Tables

Preface

And what should they know of England who only England know?
Rudyard Kipling, *The English Flag*

Hobbesian laws, no; Machiavellian maxims, yes!
Slogan

History without political science has no fruit
Political science without history has no root.
J.R. Seeley, *Introduction to Political Science*

The debris is settling after the great upheaval in world politics of the early 1990s. The euphoria that seized Western Europe in the late 1980s, awakened by the promises of the Single European Act and culminating in the fall of the Berlin Wall in 1989, has now given way to a certain disenchantment as the economic recession has deepened. The Maastricht Treaty, far from being a further staging post on the road towards European union, has more the appearance of a terminus. As the dust settles, the more prominent landmarks are beginning to show up. The first is the international context: bipolarity and the rigid division of the continent have given way to fragmentation and a looser configuration of states. The second is that the nation-state remains the basic political unit in Europe because it alone, at present, is able to exercise the essential functions of political organization and legitimacy. The third is that in spite of the aspirations of many Europeans, public opinion is still shaped primarily by the structures of the national states. In the final analysis, the priorities of all West European states are national rather than European. The last is the collapse of actual socialism, which, in consigning the simple ideological and partisan dichotomy between democracy and socialism to the dustbin of history, has stimulated a long overdue and dispassionate re-examination of the precepts and working of Western democracy. This is of particular relevance to Western Europe also because it now concerns the European Union where the question of the 'democratic deficit' has become an issue in the current political debate. In these circumstances, a study of Western European politics today must not only start from the national structures of the West European states, even if their international dimension should never be lost to view, but also take account of their actual democratic practice. Such are the intentions of this study.

Before we proceed, however, two preliminary points are in order. The first concerns the states under study. They are, in fact, Britain, France, Germany and Italy – the four principal West European states. The choice is not accidental since we believe that size is an important, if often neglected, factor in contemporary comparative political analysis. It is well known that it was held to be significant in the eighteenth century: both Montesquieu and Rousseau in Europe and Madison et al. in America discussed it at length. The former shared the classical notion that a republic must be small if it was to be democratic; while the latter adopted the representative principle to justify the idea of popular, if not democratic, government in a large country.

Nonetheless, our interest in the problem of size is inspired by another consideration: the question of comparability. There are too many political studies of Europe based on ten, fifteen, twenty states which take no account of their different sizes. Some exclude Iceland and Luxembourg, but most include Denmark, Ireland and Norway and analyse them on a one-for-one basis with France and Germany.[1] This is misleading, as Thucydides asserted when he observed that: 'great states do what they may; tiny states do what they must.' The fact that smaller states, as Barrington Moore (1966) noted, depend economically and politically on the big and powerful means that the decisive causes of their politics usually lie outside their borders. The result is that their political problems are not really comparable with those of the big states. The big states in Western Europe are the four states[2] studied in this book. Moreover, they are more or less directly comparable in terms of the principal socio-economic (territory, population,[3] economic development) and political (representative democratic regimes) factors.

The second point is theoretical (more epistemological than methodological) and regards the approach adopted. We do not share the idea of an objective political science founded on Hobbesian laws. This presupposes a mechanistic conception of political and social activity which does not really correspond to human experience. Human beings are characterized by their capacity to reflect, both individually and collectively, on their experience and behave accordingly. For this reason, this study is largely descriptive and interpretative, but grounded in theoretical paradigms that seek to establish rough generalizations and *not* causal laws. The approach is based on the meanings which men and women attribute to their actions, and this relates to the direct experience of the actors (politicians, civil servants, ordinary citizens) so as to give the reader the feel of European politics. In other words, as an old Oxford friend of many years ago, Alasdair MacIntyre, has observed:

> the logical form of generalizations – or lack of it – turns out to be rooted in the form – or lack of it – of human life. We should not be surprised or disappointed that the generalizations and maxims of the best social science share certain of the characteristics of their predecessors – the proverbs of folk societies, the generaliza- tions of jurists and the maxims of Machiavelli. (1981, p. 105).

MacIntyre explains the 'scientization' of the social sciences in terms of the rulers' need to have a pool of scientific knowledge to justify their role as experts capable of understanding and managing industrial society in an age of scientific and technological progress; and this vindicates their claim to authority, power and money. We do not have such con- cerns or presumptions; hence, we have no difficulty in admitting that the approach adopted in this study is not scientific according to the neo-posi- tivistic canons of much North American political science. 'After so many failed prophecies,' Albert Hirschman (1982, p. 1483) has questioned, 'is it not in the interest of social science to embrace complexity, be it at some sacrifice to its claim to predictive power?'

It remains true, nevertheless, that as Seeley (1894, p. 77) observed a century ago, 'some compass, we must have in a sea of facts', and this is provided by a number of key concepts of social and political theory. Starting from such a premise, this study seeks both to ground itself in his- tory and to exploit the perspectives of contemporary political thought. But, in seeking a grounding in history, it ends up by being theoretically eclectic. It requires to be grounded in history for the simple reason that all political problems are historically determined in the sense that none starts from a *tabula rasa*. The state of every question has its 'archaeol- ogy', as Foucault (1969) has taught us to recognize. In order to under- stand a concept, it is necessary to take account of its genesis and its historical development, its displacements, its persistence and its transfor- mations. If the social sciences are the 'historiography of the present', his- tory largely dictates current problems. This is the sense we attribute to the Seeley quotation used as an epigraph to this preface.

Our study is theoretically eclectic because we are convinced that no one paradigm is sufficiently developed and coherent to enable us to dis- pense with all the others. Unfortunately, 'there is', as Dearlove and Saunders (1991, p. 10) observe of Britain, 'no simple key to open the door of the complex reality' that is the politics of West European states; thus, none of the paradigms dominant today – neither liberal pluralism, nor neo-Marxism, nor neo-conservative public choice – is able to provide satisfactory answers by itself. Hence, in what follows we will employ a plurality of paradigms and theoretical perspectives in the hope of being able to illuminate as many aspects of the politics of West European states as possible because, as often happens, the various perspectives invest different areas of politics which, far from being incompatible, are often complementary.

It is also true that these theoretical perspectives can help us only so far along the way because, as Brother William of Baskerville, the hero of Umberto Eco's (1980) celebrated novel, *The Name of the Rose*, observed to his disciple Adso, paraphrasing Wittgenstein: 'the order that our mind imagines is like a net, or a ladder, built to attain something. But afterwards you must throw the ladder away, because you discover that, if it was useful, it was meaningless' (p. 492). In short, theoretical perspectives are an instrument that we employ to understand reality but we must beware of imputing to them a power that they do not have. The aim, then, of this study is simply to provide a reasonable theoretically informed discussion of West European politics illustrated as far as possible with a wide range of relevant concrete examples to communicate the feel of European politics alluded to above.

For the rest – we would add – political analysis is a field which is inevitably cultivated by moralists because, in Lacan's pertinent formula, 'le réel c'est l'impossible.' In other words, it is impossible for analytical instruments to grasp reality in all its diversity.

A study such as this, above all in view of the time it has taken to complete, builds up debts of gratitude too numerous to acknowledge individually. Colleagues and friends, particularly those in the Venetias, knowing what I owe them, will accept, I feel sure, my thanks without my naming them personally. However, I must mention Gianni Riccamboni. His was the initial invitation that led to the book and only his personal persuasion first convinced me of the utility of the project and later obliged me to finish it. He was responsible for the Italian edition after the rash decision to write the first version in that language. He can take credit for any of the qualities that the study may have, but must be absolved of all its shortcomings. I should also like to thank my friend and former colleague, Peter Campbell, for reading the English manuscript in draft and for his many helpful suggestions and criticisms, and Marjorie McNamara for expertly organizing the material on disk.

Finally, special thanks are due to my family for their forbearance over many, not always easy, years, for a task that, at certain moments, they feared had turned into the labour of Sisyphus.

Acknowledgements

The author and publishers wish to thank the following for permission to use material.

Cambridge University Press for material from R. J. Morris, 'Voluntary Societies and British Urban Elites, 1780–1850: An Analysis', *Historical Journal*, 26, 1 (1983); G. Sartori, *Political Parties: Organization and Power* (1976); R. Rose, *Public Employment in Western Nations* (1985); T. Skocpol, *States and Social Revolutions* (1979); and with *Government and Opposition* for material from G. Parry and G. Moyser, 'A Map of Political Participation in Britain', 25, 2 (1990) reproduced in *Political Participation and Democracy in Britain*, CUP (1992).

The City University of New York, Graduate School and University Center, for material from J. A. Webman, 'Centralization and Implementation: Urban Renewal in Great Britain and France', *Comparative Politics*, 14 (October 1980).

Hamish Hamilton Ltd and P–E/Inbucon Management Consultants for material from John Ardagh, *Germany and the Germans*, Hamish Hamilton 1987, revised edition Penguin Books (1991). Copyright © 1987, 1988, 1991.

Harvard University Press for material from Joel D. Aberbach, Robert D. Putnam and Bert A. Rockman, *Bureaucrats and Politicians in Western Democracies*. Copyright © 1981 by the President and Fellows of Harvard College.

Harvard University, John F. Kennedy School of Government, for material from G. Satori, 'Political Development and Political Engineering', *Public Policy*, 17, 3 (1968).

Macmillan Publishers Ltd for material from H. Heclo and A. Wildavsky, *The Private Government of Public Money* (1974).

Methuen & Co. for material from M. Duverger, *Political Parties* (1954); M. Dear and A. J. Scott, eds., *Urbanization and Urban Planning in Capitalist Society* (1981).

New Left Review for material from G. Therborn, 'The Rule of Capital and the Rise of Democracy', *New Left Review*, 103 (1977).

Oxford University Press for material from B. Hogwood, *From Crisis to Complacency: Shaping Public Policy* (1987); K. C. Wheare, *Modern Constitutions* (1951); and J. E. Lane, D. McKay and K. Newton, *Political Data Handbook: OECD Countries* (1991).

Princeton University Press for D. Bayley, 'The Police and Political Development in Europe' in C. Tilly, ed., *The Formation of National States in Western Europe* (1975).

Routledge for material from J. J. Richardson, ed., *Policy Styles in Western Europe*, Allen & Unwin (1982); R. Rose, 'From Government at the Centre to Nationwide Government' in Y. Meny and V. Wright, eds. *Centre and Periphery Relations in Western Europe*, Allen and Unwin (1985); and A. Williams, *The Western European Economy: A Geography of Postwar Development*, Hutchinson, (1987).

Sage Publications for material from S. Rokkan, 'National Building: A Review of Models and Approaches', *Current Sociology*, 19, 3 (1971); A. Melucci, 'The New Social Movements: A Theoretical Approach', *Social Science Information*, 19, 2 (1980); A. Melucci, 'An End to Social Movements?', *Social Science Information*, 23, 4/5 (1984); J. Blondel, *Government Ministers in the Contemporary World* (1985); and R. Rose, *Understanding Big Government* (1984).

Social Research for P. C. Schmitter, 'Properties Distinguishing Pure Pluralist and Pure Corporatist Modes of Intermediation', *Social Research*, 50, 4 (1983).

Universitetsforlaget and Elizabeth Rokkan for material from S. Rokkan, *Citizens, Elections, Parties* (1970).

Weidenfeld and Nicholson for material from R. Miliband, *The State in Capitalist Society* (1969).

Every effort has been made to trace all the copyright holders, but if any have been inadvertently overlooked the publishers will be pleased to make the necessary arrangement at the first opportunity.

Introduction

Analysis of the politics of the major Western European states can usefully start from a historical paradox: the conviction of both classical liberals and Marxists that coexistence between capitalism and democracy was impossible, while their successors accept it as a natural and self-evident state of affairs. The political regime born of this match is liberal democracy, or, to employ a phrase with very different overtones, actual democracy.

There is no need to examine the reasons why Tocqueville (1835–40), J.S. Mill (1861) and many other nineteenth century liberals feared the extension of the suffrage to include the propertyless or why Marx and Engels (1848) welcomed it. They are well known. Suffice it to recall that the former were convinced that the tyranny of the majority would lead to political despotism and the despoiling of property; and the latter that the extension of the suffrage would strengthen the working class and aggravate social contradictions, so hastening the proletarian revolution. For the same reason, it is unnecessary to examine contemporary assertions, be they those of liberals such as Hayek (1944) or Milton Friedman (1962), for whom only the free market could secure freedom and democracy; or of Marxists for whom, in Lenin's phrase (1918), 'parliamentary democracy is the best possible shell for capitalism.'

Actual democracy

Since our object is the analysis of actual democratic politics in Western European states, it is more profitable to understand why such a change occurred than to debate the rights and wrongs of liberal and Marxist arguments. An obvious preliminary, but often neglected, point concerns changes in the meanings of the concepts. This is particularly significant in the case of democracy, always an ambiguous and controversial notion: is it a substantive conception or merely a procedural one?

Until the eighteenth century democracy was understood as a substantive concept, that is to say as government by the people and so incompatible with the existence of the state, for the reasons which even Rousseau (1762) himself felt obliged to spell out: 'there never has been a real democracy, and there never will be. It is against the natural order for the many to govern and the few to be governed' (book III, chapter IV). He outlined the conditions that he thought necessary for democracy – a very small polity, great simplicity of manners, a large measure of equality in rank and fortune, little or no luxury – and concluded: 'were there a people of gods, their government would be democratic. So perfect a government is not for men.'[1]

Nearly two centuries later, drawing on the lessons of Weber (1922) and Mosca (1895), Schumpeter (1942) spelled out the consequences of Rousseau's observation that men are not gods, reducing democracy from a substantive to a procedural notion: 'a mere method of government'. He defined it as 'that institutional arrangement for arriving at political decisions in which individuals acquire the power to decide by means of a competitive struggle for the people's vote' (p. 269).[2] The people do not rule for the simple reason that they cannot rule because the state is necessarily organized on the basis of a division of labour between rulers and ruled in an asymmetric relationship. The people only elect the politicians, who rule them in their (the people's) name.

For Schumpeter, therefore, democracy can only be a government of competing elected elites ('democracy is the rule of the politician': p. 285). In consequence, we can speak of the rule of the people only as a result of a definitional sleight of hand. In fact it is an oligarchic form of government legitimated by universal suffrage: 'democracy only means that people have the opportunity of accepting or refusing the men who are to rule for them' (p. 285). His model is often called the 'competitive theory of democracy' but, given its substantive limitations, is it proper to call it 'democracy'? It is surely no coincidence that one of the major liberal democratic theorists, Robert Dahl (1971), prefers to use the word 'polyarchy' to define the political systems of the advanced Western capitalist countries; others talk, instead, of 'pseudo democracy' (Green, 1985, chapter 2). This procedural conception is, for better or worse, the theoretical basis of actual democracy.

On the other hand, post-war European capitalism too is no longer the classic version analysed in Marx's *Das Kapital* (1867), characterized as it was by the unequal distribution of power and income between employer and employee, and the resultant dependence and exploitation of the working population, including women and children. Even more threatening for the existing social order, as Marx himself foresaw, were the recurrent economic crises or depressions that threw millions of people out of work. They promoted the conviction, not only of Marx and Engels but also of Weber and Schumpeter, that capitalism could not survive. And yet it has, thanks above all to the Keynesian revolution.

At the same time, changes in the structure of the capitalist system – like Burnham's *Managerial Revolution* (1941), which denoted the passage of economic power from the individual capitalist to a professional managerial bureaucracy (together with the assertion of the 'social responsibility of management') – have raised questions about the proper definition of capitalism. The more so since the mechanisms of the Keynesian revolution with their smoothing out of the business cycle and the attenuation of mass unemployment have reduced the hardship and despair associated hitherto with the operation of a capitalist economy. As Galbraith (1991) said of the East European revolutions of 1989: 'What the countries of Eastern Europe see as the alternative to socialism … is not capitalism. Were it capitalism in its classic form, they would not for a moment want the change. The alternative they see is the modern state with a large, indispensable mellowing and stabilising role for government' (p. 68).

In making these points we have only partially explained the transformations which occurred between the nineteenth and twentieth centuries. In other words, it is not just a terminological question about the meanings of the words 'democracy' and 'capitalism'. There is also a political problem of substance that can be formulated as follows: why did what the classical liberals feared and the classical Marxists predicted not happen?

Firstly, the ruling classes of the European countries resisted the extension of the suffrage as long as they could. None of the four states – neither France, nor Germany, nor Italy, nor even Britain – could be described as democratic on Schumpeter's own definition before the Great War, and three out of the four have been so only since World War II.[3] Secondly, once universal male suffrage was conceded – paradoxically more for politico-military reasons than from a desire for emancipation – no electoral majority has ever voted into power a party committed to the abolition of private property and a regime of social equality. This raises the question, discussed by certain utilitarians (John Mill, 1825), as to whether the subordinate classes have ever really been interested in equality. Whatever the truth of the matter, whenever capitalism and democracy have clashed, it was not democracy that suppressed capitalism, but capitalism democracy, as happened in Italy and Germany between the wars. Thirdly, the extension of the suffrage was accompanied by the economic and social reforms of the welfare state that have modified the operation of the capitalist economies significantly during the present century.

If these are some of the reasons which explain why what the classical liberals feared did not happen, the tensions and contradictions inherent in the relationship between capitalist society and liberal democratic state still remain. We have noted that what the classical liberals were frightened of was that the extending of the suffrage would lead to class rule and so to a social 'St Bartholomew's Day Massacre'. Not surprisingly, therefore, they theorized a clear distinction between the private and the public spheres, between economics and politics, between society and the state. They foresaw the supremacy of the public over the private in the eventuality of the extension of the suffrage and claimed that this would lead to an invasion of the economic by the political, the market by the state. Hence they raised the spectre of the tyranny of the majority as a prelude to socialism, which they were convinced was merely a new form of political despotism.

On the other hand, the Marxists criticized the liberal perspective for being both abstract and spurious: for them the public sphere was merely an extension (the visible part) of the private sphere, which conditioned the former. The political was in thrall to the economic, the state to society. It seems clear today, on the contrary, that the two spheres interpenetrate in such a way that in analysing the one, it is necessary to take account of the other, and vice versa. This is something that both the classical liberals and the classical Marxists overlooked. Polanyi (1944) has shown that the liberal conception of the separation of the state and the economy was, in fact, the expression of a precise class interest, and thus that liberal politics was nothing more than a special kind of state intervention. The latter became the *condicio sine qua non* of the historical formation of the market. For Polanyi, therefore, the history of capitalism must be interpreted as the interaction between state initiative and dominant economic interests.[4]

The classical liberals were not really prepared to take account of the fact that while extending the suffrage certainly did give the subordinate classes a political instrument to defend their interests, it did not place them on an equal footing with the property-owning classes. And this for the reason just mentioned, namely the interpenetration between state and society. The subordinate classes found themselves, in fact, participating in a political system which was already structured to their detriment (chapter 4). It suffices to note that the upper class exploited its private resources, whether economic, social, organizational or cultural, to its own advantage. The only resource which the subordinate classes had was their number – Tocqueville's 'unlimited freedom of association' – but initially this was largely theoretical given that it required organization (time and money) to make it effective (chapter 5).

However, even if the people had wanted to introduce a regime of social equality by means of universal suffrage, they would have had great difficulty. In addition to the limits imposed by electoral procedures (secret ballot, prohibition of mandating[5]), there was the mechanics of political competition itself resulting from the extension of the suffrage in the late nineteenth century which, as Weber (1922) was one of the first to appreciate, radically transformed the nature of partisan politics, separating elected members from electors, party leadership from rank and file party membership. In this way, parties quickly found themselves at the centre of the political stage as the principal actors, so that Kelsen (1929) was able to assert that 'modern democracy is totally based on political parties; the wider the democratic principle, the more important the parties'.

This transformation was the product of the organizational logic of party apparatuses which was responsible for two crucial developments. Firstly, the elector was reduced to the status of passive consumer,[6] by restricting the alternatives available and thereby further strengthening the position of a small elite inside the party apparatus (the professional politicians) who controlled the party and its representatives in parliament and local government. This was because the mediation between individual and collective interests on the one hand, and party and state decision centres on the other, rapidly and necessarily became a specialist activity. The result was Michels's (1911) well-known 'iron law of oligarchy' which states that 'it is organization which gives birth to the domination of the elected over the electors, of the mandatories over the mandators, of the delegates over the delegatees. Who says organization, says oligarchy' (p. 365). Secondly, the nature of party competition in the electoral market drives parties towards the centre of the party spectrum – because it is most advantageous as an electoral tactic representing the 'common good' – and encourages a politics of patronage, thereby reducing their capacity for political innovation and blunting class conflict. In this way, MPs lose their independence *vis-à-vis* their own party apparatus and that of the state (in particular the civil service).

Universal suffrage, far from subverting the social system, has shown itself, in fact, to be an instrument of social stability. In allowing the subordinate classes to express themselves – or at least giving them the illusion of expressing themselves – universal suffrage has acted, in Duverger's opinion (1972, p. 100) as a safety valve, and this, so the argument runs, explains the rareness of social crises. If it is the case, however, one might well ask whether voting can change anything and thus pose once more the question asked over a decade ago by Rose (1980): *Do Parties Make a Difference?* Whatever the reply, we must emphasize that the party system is the visible centre of gravity of West European political systems today: parties have become the visible link between society and the state; hence the basis of the latter's democratic legitimation.

The success of party competition endorsed by elections in reconciling capitalist society and the mass representative state in Western Europe can be gauged both from the institutionalization of the role of parties in post-war constitutions and from the form of contemporary government, namely party government. All of this, however, has not suppressed the tensions between state and society for the simple reason that there is a fundamental contradiction at the heart of this type of regime: the need to mediate class conflict without being able to eliminate it altogether. We need only recall, for instance, the French May 1968 and the Italian Hot Autumn of 1969, theorized by the celebrated trilateral commission as *The Crisis of Democracy* (Crozier, Huntington and Watanuki, 1975).

Nonetheless, this political mechanism has not prevented the introduction of the important economic and social reforms that were responsible for the creation of the Keynesian welfare state.[7] The class accommodation theorized by Keynes (1936) meant a very significant change in the working of the capitalist system because it justified theoretically state, and hence open political, intervention in the economy. Keynes recognized the need to limit the 'invisible hand' of the market in order adequately to regulate structurally hostile class relations. In essence, the Keynesian accommodation involved, according to Bowles and Gintis (1986), a series of mutual concessions by capital and labour. Capital agreed to accept: (1) the integration of the trade unions into the economic and political process; (2) the guarantee of a minimum standard of living; (3) full employment; and (4) the right of the workers to a share of productivity gains. Labour accepted: (1) profitability as the recognized criterion of resource allocation; (2) capitalist (that is private) control of production and investment; and (3) free capital mobility and international trade.

Crucial changes were introduced. The first was the management of aggregate economic demand which, through the use of certain economic mechanisms, ensured low levels of unemployment and a control of the business cycle unknown before World War II. The second was the established and active presence of labour organizations – parties and unions – in the decision-making process which led to the creation of a genuine welfare state: social security, care, health, education and housing benefits as of right and not as charity. This, in turn, considerably reduced the dependence of working people on the labour market for material security. The third was an end to the workers disputing the right of employers to control the workplace. The fourth was a commitment to relatively unimpeded capital mobility and an open international market which strengthened capitalist control of investment and development. It also furnished them with a weapon – the investment or capital 'strike'[8] – to thwart and paralyse governments thought dangerous to property and profit.

It is easy to understand, in the conditions which prevailed in Europe in 1945, why the Keynesian accommodation succeeded in reconciling capitalism and liberal democracy, market economy and the representative state. All the social partners benefited – workers from the security of employment and employers from economic stability and previously unknown profit levels – and the Western economies experienced unprecedented growth in the various 'economic miracles' (chapter 1). It was an excellent example of the positive-sum game. All the elements combined to reinforce one another: an active policy of public intervention stimulated economic growth; the increase in tax revenue, resulting from this growth, financed the expansion of social and welfare benefits while, at the same time, continued growth limited the resort to them by those who were entitled to them. As a result the political struggle became less focused on non-negotiable questions of principle – *choix de société* – and concentrated more and more on distributional, or rather redistributional, problems. Hence arose the thesis that the working class had, after due consideration, chosen the status quo, for the simple reason that, in the short and medium term, a redistributive capitalism was more in its interest than some hypothetical transition to socialism with all its attendant costs and the uncertainty of any long-term benefits. The success of the Keynesian accommodation, however, in resolving some problems, like that of the management of aggregate demand in a specific historical period, merely created others, such as, for instance, a new social stratification. It seemed an intrinsically unstable accommodation which was unable to resolve in the long run the tensions inherent in the coexistence of capitalism and liberal democracy. These tensions reappeared in the 1970s and became increasingly visible in the 1980s.

For a proper understanding of the welfare state in a political science perspective, it is necessary to grasp the problematic of 'citizenship' which lies behind it and which moulds it to a large degree. This was the object of a famous Cambridge lecture by T.H. Marshall (1950) in which he highlighted the unceasing struggle between 'class' and 'citizenship rights'. He claimed that class was the principal source of inequality in capitalist societies while citizenship, on the contrary, was a source of equality, and this was because to be a citizen of a national community means enjoying universal rights shared by all other members of that community. Marshall distinguished three basic types of citizenship rights in the modern state: civil, political and social. Civil rights refer essentially to individual legal rights (personal freedom, freedom of speech and of worship, the right to private property). Political rights refer to the rights of members of the political community to participate in the exercise of political power (as voter or elected representative). Finally, social rights refer to the right of every individual to enjoy certain minimum living standards, including welfare, social security and education.

Marshall's thesis argues that the three aspects of citizenship developed sequentially[9] at different rates over the last 300 years: civil rights came first in the eighteenth century, followed by political rights in the nineteenth century, and finally social rights in the twentieth century, so that each served as a sort of platform for the expansion of the others. It was only with the creation of the welfare state in the post-war period that the three types were fully achieved. In consequence, only in the post-war period did the development of citizenship rights come seriously to challenge the inequality of social class: 'in the twentieth century,' he wrote in an oft-quoted phrase, 'citizenship and the class system have been at war'

(p. 29), but he did not designate a winner. Indeed, citizenship cannot dissolve class division; all it can do is to mellow the tensions of class conflict. The 'war' can only produce a negotiated truce and not an unqualified victory for either side.

The political question raised by Marshall's analysis concerns the limits of reformism, that is to say how far democratic rhetoric can be given concrete substance. It is, moreover, a question that has taken on some urgency since the failure of actual socialism in Eastern Europe. It would appear, however, that Marxists have not really gone beyond the old Second International dispute between the revisionist Eduard Bernstein (1899) and the revolutionary Rosa Luxemburg (1899). For the former, liberal democracy would gradually evolve into socialism without the need for revolution: democracy 'was not only the means but the substance' of socialism (p. 142). For the latter (who shared Lenin's opinion on this point, although for other reasons), capitalism could not be reformed without a revolutionary break. Hence parliamentary democracy was a bourgeois masquerade: revisionism was 'not the realization of socialism but the reform of capitalism ... the suppression of the abuses of capitalism instead of a suppression of capitalism itself' (p. 50). As a result revisionism was denounced as anti-Marxist and no orthodox Marxist was prepared to accept that an accommodation of the sort achieved 40 years later under Keynes's intellectual aegis was either possible or desirable. In this perspective, 'Marxist science' lost credibility and its political strategies were increasingly irrelevant.[10] Despite this, some neo-Marxist problematics still have a contribution to make to contemporary political analysis.

As far as the classic liberals are concerned, the problem of the democratic reform has been largely irrelevant, given that liberal democracy was, for them,[11] a synonym for democracy; it was, *pace* Schumpeter, the only one we can have. Hence, it is easy, although rather facile, for them to claim that the development of the market and free trade is an indispensable safeguard for democratic politics, even if some of its consequences, like Galbraith's (1958) 'private affluence and public squalor', lack of political participation, manipulation of public opinion, and clientelism, would have shocked Tocqueville and Mill.

On the other hand, Marshall (who was a reformist) was convinced that the struggle for the extension of citizenship – far from being a waste of time and energy as many Marxists still believe today because it leaves capitalist society largely unchanged – seriously restricts capitalism. Indeed, the conquest of a larger space for citizenship means greater popular participation and a corresponding reduction in the decision-making space and autonomy of the ruling groups, which are obliged to take account of aspects of civil and political society which they could previously ignore. It suffices to compare the life situation of the peoples of Western Europe in the last 30 years with that of 100 years earlier to note an enormous improvement, even for the lower classes. The progress made in actual democratic regimes in the last 40 years – economic development and widespread affluence as well as ample margins of personal liberty – should not be underrated (even if they are generally taken for granted) above all in the light of what has happened in the actually existing socialist regimes of Eastern Europe. However, the 'broken promises', to use Bobbio's (1984) phrase, of actual democracy – political apathy, invisible power, widespread inequality, the abnormal influence of organized interests, the survival of oligarchies – should not be disregarded either.

Moreover, we should not forget, as Marshall[12] himself did not, that the 'war' between citizenship rights and the capitalist class system is never finally won, nor are reforms ever completely secure. 'The undertaking of transforming slaves into subjects and subjects into citizens', Veca (1990) wrote recently, 'is a never ending task both in the rich OECD countries and in the poor countries racked by famine and absolute scarcity' (p. 13). Everything can be undone, as in the case of certain social entitlements in Europe recently. This explains why politics is a struggle and, for reformers, calls also for 'eternal vigilance'. In this connection, it also explains why civil and political rights play an essential role in this struggle, if only because set out in a constitution, that is in a formal system of norms, they are more difficult to undermine at the first change in the wind. As regards the idea dear to many Marxists that what is needed to make progress down the road to democracy is a real shift in power, this is certainly desirable – 'the character of society is determined less by abstract rights than by practical powers;' R.H.Tawney (1931) asserted, 'it depends not on what its members *may* do if they can, but upon what they *can* do if they will' (p. 110) – but is not of itself sufficient. Unfortunately, Lord Acton's famous dictum – 'power tends to corrupt, and absolute power corrupts absolutely' – is still true, as the actual socialist regimes of Eastern Europe reminded the world in 1989. So long as the state exists, we are faced with Dunn's (1979) dilemma: 'democracy is the *name* of what we cannot have – yet cannot cease to want' (p. 27). Nonetheless, what we can have in the meantime is an active civil society which not only promotes pluralism in all its forms but also acts as a permanent channel of public contestation.

At the close of this discussion, it remains to say that legally organized competition for the exercise of political power constitutes the reality of actual democracy in Western European states today. Indeed, the political constitutions of Britain, France, Germany and Italy are founded on three basic principles: (1) political power is derived from popular sovereignty and so government authority issues from free and contested elections; (2) the organization of the state is based on political pluralism and a certain institutional separation of powers; (3) political power is limited by law. In other words, there is legal protection of a certain number of political and civil rights regarded as fundamental. But, since these constitutions operate within capitalist economic structures, one must stress once more the economic origin of much of the conflict between rulers and ruled. Political power, in fact, derives not only from popular sovereignty but also from the control of economic resources.

This coexistence of capitalist society and democratic constitutional state led Duverger (1972) to coin the expression 'pluto-democracy' to define this type of regime. In so doing, he focused attention on two important aspects. Firstly, the economic power of certain individuals, organizations and classes confers political power on them in these states. Secondly, this type of political regime is the preserve of wealthy societies: Britain, France, Germany and Italy are all members of the group of seven (G7) richest and most industrialized countries in the world as well as former imperial powers.

The analytical framework

In the light of the preceding discussion the problem posed in analysing concretely a nation-state's politics is the interrelation between political events and structures on the one hand, and economic and social ones on the other, that is to say state and society. Western political science has adopted one of two contrasting approaches to this problem: the state-centred or institutional approach (the causal logic running from state to society); and the society-centred or political sociological approach (the causal logic moving from society to the state). The former was the traditional approach and dominated the study of politics in Europe and North America in the early decades of the century: the focus was on the key state institutions (executive, legislature and judiciary) and the constitutional rules regulating relations between them. Little attention was paid to other institutions (except parties) before the First World War. The method was essentially descriptive and had a strong legal bias since it was more attentive to norms than performance.

This approach came under strong attack in the inter-war years, particularly in North America owing to its lack of realism, that is its bias towards the formal and visible and its neglect of informal relationships. It has often been pointed out that it was in these years (the 1930s) that a whole series of new social science techniques (social survey, probability theory) were developed in sister disciplines like psychology and sociology. The result was the so-called 'behavioural revolution' in the social sciences that saw a decisive shift in political science towards the society-centred approach. The shift was from the study of institutions to that of individuals and groups: politics was seen as reflecting the forces operating in the social structure. While it increased knowledge about how people see politics and behave politically – it investigated voting behaviour, group activity, the communication role of the media – it ran the risk of 'structural determinism', that is to say of political phenomena being treated as functions of the structure of society (Lane and Ersson, 1987). This is incidentally a danger which is also present in certain 'functions' that neo-Marxists attribute to the state.

Not surprisingly, in this perspective, attention has swung back to the state-centred approach – the notion that politics has a logic of its own, expressed in political institutions – in the last fifteen years. This new political institutionalism is concerned with the organization of institutions and the way they maintain themselves over time, irrespective of their socio-economic context. The state is thus crucial to this new institutionalism – but it is also a very different state from that of the institutional movement of the early decades of the century. The basic tenet of the new approach is that the structuring of the state has to be understood in terms of itself, that is as an active agent shaping and reshaping society. Here, the danger is of 'social indeterminism', meaning that the social context of politics is either ignored or dismissed out of hand, which would be patently absurd (Lane and Ersson).

The requirement is, then, for a framework that is complementary: that takes account of both contributions, the societal and the institutional, without falling into the twin traps of structural determinism or social indeterminacy. Politics, after all, occurs in a socio-economic context (place or locality that is not just physical but also socially constructed, and so cultural). Hence, the social dimension cannot be neglected. At the same time, however, some account has to be taken of the specific logic of political institutions which include both state apparatuses (governments, parliaments, administrations, armed forces) and autonomous social organizations (social movements, parties, groups).

Our point of departure is the conception of the political system as a system in which institutions, organizations and social forces (state and society) form parts of a structured and coherent whole, and in which they are articulated and interact. The problem is to determine, with some approximation, the relations between the parts and the interactions between them. An instrument that can facilitate this task is David Easton's (1953) famous 'input–output' or flow model. It can be used to represent systemically (figure 1) the relations between the various political institutions in Western European parliamentary regimes and help identify the two contrasting logics at work: the symbolic (constitutional) and the substantive (actual). These are the 'dignified' and the 'efficient' in Walter Bagehot's (1867) celebrated formulation: 'first, those which excite and preserve the reverence of the population – the *dignified* parts … and next the *efficient* parts – those by which it in fact works and rules' (p. 61).[13] The constitutional logic claims that power arises from the population (or electorate) to the state through parties, elections, parliament and government to descend down to the population again via public administration, public agencies and pressure groups. In other words, as regards input the people elect parliament by universal suffrage from party lists at general elections, and parliament controls the government

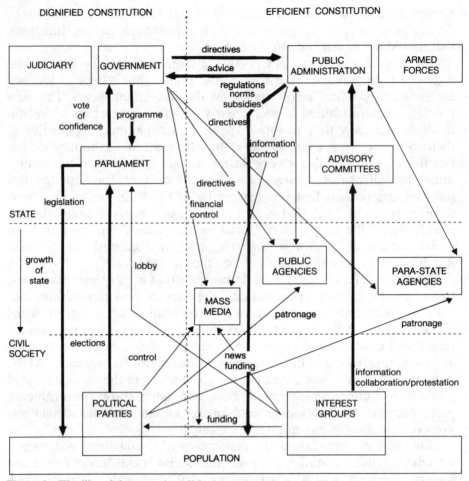

DIGNIFIED CONSTITUTION   EFFICIENT CONSTITUTION

Figure 1 The liberal democratic political system
Source: Allum, 1980, p. 1054

by means of votes of confidence: the government, in its turn, directs the
public administration. At the same time, however, the people organized
in interest and pressure groups communicate demands and information
to the public administration; the latter collates and transmits them to the
government in the form of legislative proposals and advice. In terms of
output, parliament discusses, amends and passes bills while the public
administration issues regulations and distributes public funds: the government coordinates the various policies and programmes it has undertaken. Finally, there is an input–output communications relationship
provided by the mass media which connects all the institutional actors in
a single system.

    Figure 1 helps to illustrate the two logics (symbolic and substantive)
underlying the working of the system. Constitutional theory states that
the decision-making process begins with the people (the holders of
national sovereignty) and arrives at the state (in the left-hand column) to

end back with the people again; the population expresses its demands (input) and the government implements its programmes (output). The rationale behind this logic is to show that the government, as the emanation of parliament, really does represent the people because, thanks to party political activity and periodic elections, it is the state institution which has the support of the people, from whom it draws the necessary legitimacy for the political system to operate consensually.

The model enables us, however, to apprehend a second logic that we have defined as substantive. In this the constitutional logic is turned on its head: instead of the government and parliament formulating policies and having them implemented by the public administration, it is organized groups that impose policies and measures on the government. If true, it means that the constitutionally sovereign institutions merely act to legitimize the outcome of substantive political processes. This is the pluralist thesis and above all that of the group theorists (chapter 6). They single out organized groups as the basic element of political analysis. According to them, the state only plays a limited role in policy formulation and its decisions merely reflect the power relations between groups in society at any given moment. An alternative version of this approach – 'neo-corporatism' – theorizes the emergence of an alliance between certain strategic groups (industrial corporations and unions) and state institutions (public administration) that secures the former a privileged position.

If the institutional flow model is a useful tool for studying the political processes of West European states, it is not very helpful in specifying the societal limits within which they operate because of the conceptual separation of the political system from the social structure that it implies. As already noted, West European states operate within capitalist economic structures – private appropriation of resources – that furnish a context and a series of opportunities and constraints that cannot be ignored. Hence it needs supplementing, and it is here that certain neo-Marxist discussions of state theory (Offe, 1972; Habermas, 1973) are helpful: first, in determining the state's role; and second, in specifying the properties of state action.

The state's basic role is simple: maintain public order and secure the reproduction of existing (that is, capitalist) society. In addition, since the state is composed of a legal order structured in a set of institutions separate from society with the ability to use force legitimately, it acts as a selective filtering system that seeks to ensure the prevalence of interests compatible with its basic objectives: public order and the reproduction of society. The latter has to include today 'sufficient provision for a certain level of collective goods' (McLennan, 1989, p. 229) (figure 2). State policy is constrained not because it is capitalist in any metaphysical sense, but for the simple reason that the state's material existence (including military capacity) depends on taxation revenue, and this in turn depends, in an industrial society, on successful accumulation: no economic surplus,

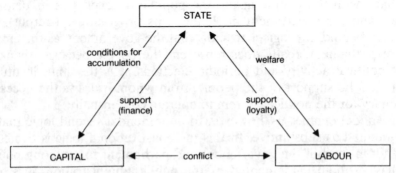

Figure 2 The interventionist state model
Source: Clark and Dear, 1981, p. 56

no fiscal resources. Furthermore, successful capital accumulation in this kind of society requires periodic democratic legitimation because of universal suffrage. Hence, the state's action is devoted to securing the conditions for capital accumulation *and* to seeking popular consensus for its policies through parliamentary elections.

In this perspective, much state activity can be viewed, according to Habermas and Offe, as strategies of crisis avoidance made necessary by class antagonism. Crises result from the contradiction between the needs of capital accumulation – from which, as mentioned, the state derives its own material resources – and the private appropriation of resources, on the one hand; and on the other, the need to conserve confidence in the state as an impartial arbiter of class interests, so as to ensure the legitimation of its own power.

One need not subscribe to a neo-Marxist orientation to accept the relevance of the Habermas-Offe argument and the determinants of state action that they postulate: the promotion both of a reasonable level of economic activity *and* of political consensus. Events in Eastern Europe since 1989 have amply demonstrated the perils that political regimes run when they fail to secure either of these conditions. The problem is knowing before the event where the critical thresholds for particular regimes lie. We suggest that it is much higher for the actual democratic regimes of Western Europe than it was for the actual socialist regimes of Eastern Europe. If this surmise is correct, it means not only that Western European governments have to be more sensitive to these conditions – which they surely are – but also that these conditions have a more direct relevance, as determinants of state action, than is commonly supposed. In other words, they are not the abstract parameters of state action that they would appear to be at first sight.

To complete the analytical framework it is necessary to integrate the institutional flow model (figure 1) with the Habermas-Offe paradigm (figure 2). However, in doing this we need to replace the rather generic notion of society used so far with the twin levels of the economy (productive and distributive systems) and civil society (social relations) in

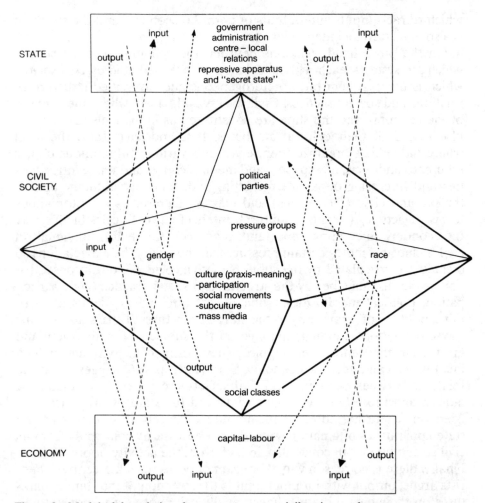

Figure 3   Model of the relations between economy, civil society and state

order to propose a three-level schema – economy, civil society and state (figure 3) – along the lines suggested by Urry (1981). Thus, if the three levels are separate, they are also interlinked and overlapping. The economy comprises the spheres of production and exchange (basis of surplus value and class conflict); civil society[14] comprises the spheres of reproduction and struggle (domestic and associative life, political mobilization); while the state, on the contrary, has the power to intervene in all four spheres, but does so intermittently. The crucial level for politics in advanced industrial societies, which are also parliamentary regimes, is civil society and its interdependent relations with both the economy and the state. It is worth noting, however, that certain areas of civil society pre-existed the formation of industrial society. This means that civil society is already structured (chapters 2 and 3), but, at the same time, it is the product of present-day conflict (that is to say is modelled by it: chapter 4). For this reason, it can be conceived, as in figure 3, as a prism which refracts inputs and outputs of both the economy and the state but is also in its turn an independent source of inputs.

On the other hand, relations between the economy and the state – which are systems, each with its own logic – are mediated by civil society which is not a system but a heterogeneous and diversified structure of relations and social practices. Civil society is the level where the subjects of the economy and the state are constituted as individuals in flesh and blood with all their cultural attributes. It is, moreover, also the level where individuals organize themselves into various autonomous bodies (churches and sects, newspapers and media, schools and universities, parties and interest groups, not forgetting independent voluntary philanthropic and civic associations) and express themselves in autonomous forms of activity (religious, cultural, intellectual, political). In this way the economy, in creating opportunities and constraints for individuals in civil society, promotes certain pressures on the state. The expectations so created are articulated by the subjects of civil society and transposed (or not, as the case may be) by the structures of social practice (civic participation, political mobilization, subcultures) into inputs (demands, petitions, political programmes) to the state apparatuses. Thus, state outputs (laws, regulations, funding) impinge on the subjects of civil society and are transformed into other impulses (new forms of activity and behaviour) which can affect the economy. Urry (1981, p. 116) suggests that the relations between economy and civil society are generally mediated by money, and those between civil society and the state by law (including coercion).[15] Furthermore, all the impulses, conceived as inputs of the state apparatuses of a nation-state, do not necessarily come only from its civil society; they can come also, in fact, from the activity of other states. Finally, there is no reason why there cannot be, as the state-centred theorists argue, output without input, that is to say action of the state apparatuses on their own initiative, hence analytically not as a response to an input of civil society or another state.

The international context: the European Union

The discussion has been limited so far to outlining the framework for analysing the politics of the Western European states from a national perspective as though each existed in isolation. However, as Otto Hintze (1906) pointed out long ago, a state's politics is determined as much by external factors – 'the external ordering of states – their position relative to one another, and their overall position in the world' (p. 183) – as by their internal structures. Indeed, the latter were often determined by the former, particularly in Europe where the European states' system had a significant impact on state formation and domestic politics from the seventeenth century (chapter 7). For the moment, we are concerned with the international influences on domestic politics, which can be said to operate at four levels: war, ideology, economy and organization. We do not really need to consider each individually in any detail here since they are self-evident and examples are mentioned in the relevant chapters. At all events, illustrations abound and the effects are obvious: whether they be those of the two world wars or more recently the wars in the Gulf or the Balkans; or those, in terms of ideology, of the Cold War and its end, the collapse of communism. Again, the domestic impact of international economic trends like capital flows, raw material prices (oil) or the activities of transnational corporations (TNCs) (chapter 6) has been considerable, as a casual reading of the financial press discloses. As regards the role of international organizations (UN, NATO, OECD, EC, WEU, ESCE), it is generally acknowledged to have grown since the war and become increasingly significant in foreign affairs (chapter 10).

This said, it is nonetheless necessary to look at the European Union (EU) a little more closely because it has become impossible to study the domestic politics of Britain, France, Germany and Italy – all EU member states – without reference to the institutionalized interstate cooperation represented by the EU. Indeed, since the Single European Act (SEA) and the Maastricht Treaty, EU politics and national politics are more than ever institutionally intertwined, so that 'the context of national policy-making has thereby been fundamentally transformed' (Reynolds, 1992, p. 26). This raises the question of the nature of the EU. Jacques Delors, former president of the Commission, has described it, somewhat humorously, as an 'unidentified political object' ('objet politique non-identifié'), since it has become a complex institutional structure that defies all traditional definitions. It is argued that it is something more than a mere international organization – it has a more complex institutional structure and greater policy responsibilities (it makes trading policies for twelve nations) – but something less than a 'supranational' federal state, because national governments (and bureaucracies) still play a crucial role in EU decision-making. Indeed, it rests on a set of 'intergovernmental bargains'. Recently, Keohane and Hoffmann (1991) have suggested that the EU 'is best characterized as neither an institutional regime nor an emerging state but a network involving pooling sovereignty' (p. 10).[16] Hence, its originality as a political system results from 'the extent to which it involves states engaging in *joint* action to formulate *common* policies to make *binding* decisions' (Nugent, 1991, p. 387: italics in original).

The institutional structure consists of a set of five institutions: the Commission, an independent executive body of seventeen commissioners appointed by member governments and assisted by a permanent staff of civil servants (the 'Brussels bureaucracy'); the Council of Ministers, the decision-making body composed of the representatives of member governments; the European Council, a periodic (twice yearly) summit meeting of heads of government and the commission president, responsible for strategic decisions and future development; the European Parliament (EP), a directly elected parliamentary assembly, exercising advisory powers; and the European Court of Justice (ECJ), a supreme court appointed by member governments, responsible for interpreting the EU treaties and law. To these the so-called 'comitology', the structure of advisory, regulatory and management committees – the Economic and Social Committee (ESC), the Committee of Permanent Representatives (COREPER), the new Regional Committee, the Court of Audit – have to be added. In the initial formulation of EU decision-making, the Commission was responsible for preparing draft proposals and the Council of Ministers for making the principal decisions. However, if the Council effectively made the decisions – unanimously – it did so in close consultation with the Commission and the EP. In fact, the latter aspect was reinforced by the SEA which – recognizing a 'democratic deficit' – introduced a 'cooperative procedure' giving the EP limited powers of codecision with the Council of Ministers (now on the basis of qualified majorities) over a range of important policy issues. As a result there has been an increase in consultation and indirect contact between the EP and the other institutions (including private organizations). Finally, once the decision is taken it is for the Commission to ensure its execution, but since it lacks an executant role in member countries, it is dependent on national (and subnational) civil servants for the implementation of individual regulations and directives.[17]

The significance of the EU for the national policy of member states is multiple. Firstly, the areas of the EU's competence are not the traditional ones of international organizations – foreign affairs and security (so-called 'high politics') – but internal affairs such as trade, agriculture, coal and steel, transport, energy, industry, research and technology (so-called 'low politics'). This means that EU regulations and directives have a direct effect on the daily life of citizens and companies of member states as producers and consumers.

Secondly, EU regulations take precedence over national laws and regulations in cases of conflict. Indeed, not only has the ECJ asserted the obligation of member states to implement national legislation consistent with EC directives, but that obligation has been followed to a remarkable degree. It is claimed that the national courts and administrations in fact implement EC law as effectively as national law. To this extent we can say that it has already created a form of 'EU citizenship'. In this connection, it is worth noting that implementation has been facilitated in the 1980s by a landmark ruling (*Cassis de Dijon* 120/78) in which the ECJ established the principle of 'mutual recognition', thereby creating a simple standard for resolving trade disputes that has had far-reaching consequences (for instance, by making the SEA and the Maastricht Treaty possible). Whereas before, the laws of the individual member states had to be harmonized and made identical in their effects and consequences, now each state is simply required to accept as legitimate the laws of other member states as long as certain European-wide health and safety standards are satisfied. The result is that the EU can simply move to the lowest common denominator among national laws. Incidentally, this has greatly accelerated the movement towards the single market since the Commission was able to codify the lowest common standard in one domain after another.

Thirdly, as mentioned, member governments still play a dominant role in the EU decision-making process, yet they do so not autonomously but in common. Policy is sectorially fragmented, although there is a great deal of informal coordination between the EU and national personnel, whether civil servants, politicians, interest group leaders or experts. This is where the innumerable advisory committees, working parties and groups of experts preparing the Commission's proposals and the Council of Ministers' decisions come into their own. It makes for a policy style of bargaining and coalition formation that has to take account of the contrasts between the domestic interests on the one hand, and the supranational interests on the other, of member states. Finally, the execution of the Council of Ministers' decisions by the Commission is closely supervised by committees of national civil servants. All in all, the EU forms an integral part of the policy process of member states; and, moreover, it has become increasingly difficult to disentangle national policies from EU policy and vice versa.

Conclusion

Our study of West European politics starts from the historical connections between democracy and capitalism. This is because the actual democratic regimes of Western Europe developed within capitalist economic structures. We noted how both notions have changed over the last 150 years: democracy from a substantive to a procedural notion; capitalism from a largely competitive form to a largely corporative one. In consequence, the incompatibility that the nineteenth century liberal social theorists feared was replaced by a certain affinity. One of the unforeseen instruments of this was the extraordinary success that the development of the party system had in taming the democratic implications of equal manhood suffrage. Furthermore, it did not prevent the important economic and social reforms that were responsible for the creation of the Keynesian welfare state which can be understood as an exercise in class accommodation.

However, tensions persist; they are considered in the light of Marshall's concept of 'citizenship' (the basis of the welfare state) and its antonym 'class' (the basis of capitalist society), and the ceaseless struggle between them. The political question this poses is the possibility of reformism and the responses of the major theoretical traditions – Marxism, liberalism and reformism. We argue that only the last has made any substantial contribution. The conclusion, nonetheless, is that the reformist struggle is never won; but the price is worth paying because until, if ever, the state is transcended, democracy must remain in Dunn's (1979) phrase 'the *name* of what we cannot have – yet cannot cease to want'. Legally organized competition for the exercise of political power is the reality of actual democracy in Western Europe today.

In developing the framework of political analysis the problem is how to avoid the twin dangers of the two general contrasting approaches in contemporary Western political science: the social reductionism of the society-centred or political sociological approach much in vogue in the post-war decades; and the social indeterminacy of the more recent state-centred or new institutional approach. Our solution is to propose a framework that synthesizes a certain number of paradigms. It uses Easton's input–output flow model to represent systemically the relations between the major institutions operating in Western European parliamentary regimes. This enables us to identify two contrasting logics at work – the symbolic (democratic) and the substantive (oligarchic). At the same time, however, the Western European states operate within capitalist economies: hence we need to incorporate the flow model within realistic socio-economic parameters. These are supplied by the Habermas-Offe paradigm of the interventionist welfare state. It helps to define the state's role – to maintain public order and secure the reproduction of existing society – and its properties, that is the set of institutions separate from society with a coercive capacity. The limiting factors are the state's need to ensure a reasonable level of economic activity (because of its material dependence on taxes) on the one hand, and to secure political consensus (to guarantee legitimacy) on the other.

The overall framework consists of integrating the two models, that is to say in placing the institutional 'flow' model within the Habermas-Offe paradigm. The result is a three-level schema – economy, civil society and state – in which civil society is the key level as it mediates relations between the economy and the state (both of which are systems with their own internal logics), while being a separate source of action in its own right.

This analytical framework tends to privilege the domestic political perspective of Western European nation-states as though they existed in isolation. This is certainly not the European experience; indeed, for at least three centuries, international factors have been as significant as national ones in state formation and domestic policies. The principal supranational actor in Western Europe today is the EU. It is not a supranational (federal) state because member governments still dominate EU decision-making, but the political novelty is that individual states act not autonomously but in common. Moreover, since the EU's competencies are mainly in the fields of domestic politics (trade, agriculture, industry, transport, energy) and EU regulations are binding on member states, we can conclude that the EU forms an integral part of the policy process of member states.

In the following chapters, we explore the gap between the rhetoric and the reality of actual democracy in Western Europe and seek to illustrate the way the major components of the political process operate. This enterprise is facilitated by the similarity – common history, political traditions, constitutional arrangements – of the major Western European states that has prompted the question: 'is there a European political model?' (Quermonne, 1990). Whatever the proper answer, the discussion proceeds in terms of the three levels (economy, civil society, state) indicated in figure 3 of the four principal Western European states (Britain, France, Germany and Italy). The first part of the study examines the economy from a dual point of view: economic structures and post-war economic development (chapter 1). The successive five chapters are devoted to analysing a civil society where a plurality of social forces is active and forms the basis of political life in the four states. They start with the main factors that structurate civil society: class, gender and race (chapter 2); and political cleavages and the historical roots of national cultures (chapter 3). Subsequently, the major actors and their activity are examined: citizen participation, social movements, subcultures and mass media (chapter 4); parties and party systems (chapter 5); and groups and interest intermediation (chapter 6). This brings us finally to the role of the state and its various institutions: government and executive power (chapter 7); public administration and the policy process (chapter 8); subcentral government and centre–local relations (chapter 9); and the dual state of diplomacy, the armed forces and the secret services (chapter 10). We conclude with a discussion of the major debates on actual democracy in Western Europe since the war and an appraisal of the possibilities of reformist politics in the present recessionary climate (chapter 11).

Further Reading

R. Alford and R. Friedland (1985), *Powers of Theory: Capitalism, the State and Democracy* (Cambridge: CUP).

G. Almond and G. Powell (1978), *Comparative Politics* (Boston, Mass.: Little, Brown, 2nd edn).

J.M. Barbalet (1989), *Citizenship* (Milton Keynes: Open UP).

A.H. Birch (1993), *The Concepts and Theories of Modern Democracy* (London: Routledge).

N. Bobbio (1989), *Democracy and Dictatorship* (Cambridge: Polity).

H. Daalder (1987), 'Countries in Comparative European Politics', in *European Journal of Political Research*, 15, 3–21.

R.A. Dahl (1989), *Democracy and its Critics* (New Haven, Conn.: Yale UP).

R. Dahrendorf (1988), *The Modern Social Conflict: Essay on the Politics of Liberty* (London: Weidenfeld & Nicolson).

P. Dunleavy and B. O'Leary (1987), *Theories of the State: The Politics of Liberal Democracy* (Basingstoke: Macmillan).

J. Habermas (1976), *Legitimation Crisis* (London: Heinemann).

D. Held (1987), *Models of Democracy* (Cambridge: Polity).

D. Held et al. (eds) (1983), *States and Societies* (Oxford: Robertson).

C.P. Macpherson (1977), *The Life and Times of Liberal Democracy* (Oxford: OUP).

C. Offe (1984), *Contradictions of the Welfare State* (London: Hutchinson).

G.-F. Poggi (1990), *The State: Its Nature, Development and Prospects* (Cambridge: Polity).

K. Tester (1992), *Civil Society* (London: Routledge).

D. Zolo (1992), *Democracy and Complexity: A Realist Approach* (Cambridge: Polity).

On Europe

M. Dogan and R. Rose (eds) (1971), *European Politics: A Reader* (London: Macmillan).

Y. Mény (1993), *Government and Politics in Western Europe* (Oxford: OUP, 2nd edn).

G. Smith (1989), *Politics in Western Europe* (Aldershot: Gower, 5th edn).

On Britain

J. Dearlove and P. Saunders (1991), *Introduction to British Politics* (Cambridge: Polity, 2nd edn).

P. Dunleavy, A. Gamble, I. Holliday and G. Peele (eds) (1993), *Developments in British Politics 4* (Basingstoke: Macmillan).

On France

J.E.S. Hayward (1983), *Governing France: The One and Indivisible Republic* (London: Weidenfeld & Nicolson, 2nd edn).

V. Wright (1989), *The Government and Politics of France* (London: Unwin & Hyman, 3rd edn)

On Germany

G. Smith (1986), *Democracy in West Germany* (Alderdshot: Gower, 3rd edn).

K. von Beyme (1985), *The Political System of the Federal Republic of Germany* (Farnborough: Gower).

On Italy

P. Furlong (1994), *Modern Italy* (London: Routledge).
D. Hine (1993), *Governing Italy: The Politics of Bargained Pluralism* (Oxford, OUP).

On European Union

D. Dinan (1994), *Ever Closer Union? An Introduction to the European Community* (Basingstoke: Macmillan).
B. Laftan (1992), *Integration and Cooperation in Europe* (London: Routledge).
C. Tugendhat (1986), *Making Sense of Europe* (New York: Viking).

Relevant academic reviews

West European Politics
Government and Opposition
European Journal of Political Research
Comparative Politics
Comparative Political Studies
American Political Science Review
British Journal of Political Science
Revue française de science politique
Rivista italiana di scienza politica
Political Studies

PART I

The Economic System

1 Mixed Economies

Introduction

It is generally agreed that the industrial revolution marked a break in world history: Marx saw it as the triumph of capitalism, others as the birth of the modern world. Although general syntheses are usually dangerously simplistic in view of the complexities of individual societies, the contrast between pre-industrial (agrarian) societies and industrial societies is a useful one if only because the latter were the first to become self-consciously aware of the possibilities of economic growth and development. Of course, Western European societies are industrial societies (that is dedicated to the production of goods): after all, the industrial revolution first occurred in their midst.

For Raymond Aron (1962a), who endowed the notion of industrial society with a specific meaning in a famous course of lectures at the Sorbonne in the 1950s, it was 'simply defined as a society in which large-scale industry, such as found in the Renault and Citroën enterprises, is the characteristic form of production' (p. 97). From this definition, he inferred a series of features which he claimed were representative of Western societies: the separation of enterprise and family; an advanced division of labour; the accumulation of capital; rational economic calculation; a desire for growth; and a changed distribution of labour (concentration of workers in factories and their families in cities). The final feature is of major political significance: the proximity of workers and their families facilitated their organization in unions and parties as a direct challenge to property ownership. The result, Aron (1964) claimed, was that the capital/labour conflict structured the whole of society.

If Aron's definition of industrial society is an approximate description of certain key features of Western society in the 1950s and 1960s, it must nevertheless be pointed out that the giant industrial enterprise was not, as he was aware, the only form of productive organization in these societies. Indeed, it never employed the majority of the active population. In so far as the manufacturing sector ever employed the majority of the active population – very rarely the case – the larger part usually worked in small firms and handicraft workshops. The factory worker was not, in fact, ever the most common type of worker; a higher proportion of wage-earners has always worked in agriculture and the service sector. Moreover, Aron's industrial society was predicated on the basis of self-perpetuating economic growth and better (that is to say, fairer) distribution of wealth. He was persuaded that growth would continue unabated because it was an essentially technical and progressive feature: 'the key to modern economic history', he argued, 'is technical progress' (1962a, p. 174). The application of scientific discoveries and their technical application would be sufficient to ensure economic growth and wider distribution of wealth. On this latter point, his analysis was increasingly found wanting in the economic crises of the 1970s and 1980s.

We should add, however, that changes, particularly in employment patterns, emerging by the 1970s – rapid expansion of the tertiary sector (distribution and services) and decline of traditional manufacturing industry – led to the formulation of the notion of 'post-industrial society' (Touraine, 1969; Bell, 1973). To the extent that, in terms of employment, Western societies had become 'service societies', the notion was more representative than Aron's earlier characterization. The only problem is what specific features the notion was intended to convey other than the suppression of the 'manufacturing era'. For Bell, author of the most comprehensive account, *codified* knowledge (systematic, coordinated information) has replaced the production of goods as the driving force of progress; scientists and technologists have replaced industrialists and entrepreneurs as the key social groups. The consequence is a shift away from the 'work ethic' towards a freer, more hedonistic lifestyle. The work discipline and organization of industrial society is giving way to the pleasure-seeking and spontaneity of post-industrialism. The theory, however, seems somewhat suspect. Ralf Dahrendorf (1988), in fact, has caustically observed: 'as one rereads Bell's book, one is struck by its tone, which is very much that of an industrial society, albeit one which has progressed beyond manufacturing to information-led economic growth' (p. 137). Many service sector jobs contribute, in fact, to the production of goods, and hence are really to be considered part of the industrial sector; indeed, it is claimed that they are as much integrated within manufacturing production as displacing it.

It is not necessary to decide here on the ultimate validity of these theories. As so often, they contain important features of the current era, helping to explain a number of developments while misleading on others. What is important, however, is to stress the continued centrality of the production of goods in Western societies. Without successful production, there is no surplus value; and without surplus value all the other features of contemporary Western European societies (welfare provisions and ultimately actual democracy itself) are at risk. In this chapter, we will outline the basic te tures of the economic structure and after that we will present a synthesis of West European economic development since the war. The object is to set out the economic context of post-war politics.

The economic structure

West European economies are 'mixed economies': this means that, despite the domination of private capital and the logic of the market, they are characterized by Keynesian intervention[1] (that is to say by a guided market) and a substantial public sector (larger in France and Italy, smaller in Germany, and even smaller in Britain).[2] We must bear in mind, however, that the relations between the logic of the market and state regulation can change over the years as they can differ between individual countries. Thus, state guidance was greater in the immediate post-war decades than in the 1980s; and much greater in France than in Britain, with Germany and Italy following a more middle course.

A second major structural feature is the growing internationalization of the European economies. This has followed a specific pattern – trade, capital, production. The production phase has seen TNCs (American and Japanese as well as European) setting up branch companies in different countries to respond to changing marketing and production needs. One of the principal factors in this has been the movement towards European economic integration starting with the Coal and Steel Community in 1951 and the Common Market in 1956 (with subsequent enlargements) to the SEA in 1985 and the single market in 1992. Not only has the EU been responsible for the emergence of new economic groupings within Europe and changing relations with outside economic powers (USA, Japan, newly industrializing countries), but its policies have come to dominate Western European economic development today (the European monetary system and moves to monetary union).

A third feature is the wide disparity of economic conditions in the four countries, despite similar demographic structures. Britain, France, Germany and Italy had populations of similar size until 1990 (table 1.1) when German unification suddenly undermined this similarity. Thus, per capita income varies widely between them (table 1.2), as it does between regions inside individual countries (table 1.3). However, European economic integration with its enlargement of the market has increased the division of labour, promoting greater automation of productive processes and larger units of production (the latter usually the result of concentration), the whole stimulated by greater competition. These developments required large capital investment and the introduction of

Table 1.1 Resident population (millions)

	1946	1960	1970	1980	1990
Britain	49.0	52.5	55.8	56.0	57.2
France	40.3	45.7	51.0	53.7	56.4
Germany	44.2	53.2	61.8	61.6	62.0
Italy	45.5	49.6	54.7	57.0	57.5

* With German reunification the population rises to 79.1 million.
Source: OECD

Table 1.2 Per capita income (1975 dollars)

	1950	1960	1970	1980	1980/1950 (%)
Britain	2377	2988	3784	4482	188.6
France	2485	3547	5486	7409	298.1
Germany	2228	4323	6260	8858	397.6
Italy	1185	1749	3176	4111	346.9

Source: OECD

Table 1.3 Regional per capita GDP, 1982 (EC average = 100)

National average		Richest region		Poorest region	
Britain	98.2	South-east	108.5	Northern Ireland	81.4
France	114.7	Île de France	162.0	Limousin	90.3
Germany	122.6	Darmstadt	153.0	Luneberg	82.6
Italy	70.5	Valle d'Aosta	101.8	Calabria	42.0

Source: Williams, 1987, p. 245

new and more sophisticated technologies (for instance, information technology), but they resulted in a doubling of the per capita income in Western Europe between 1950 and 1970 thanks to gains in productivity. This in turn displaced consumption from agricultural products to consumer goods and services. In consequence, employment in agriculture fell dramatically while that in industry peaked and then declined, and that in the service sector expanded rapidly (table 1.4). Thus, if the service sector is dominant today in all four countries, agriculture still retains importance in France and Italy, while the industrial sector is strongest in Germany (where it supplied half the gross national product in the late 1980s) and weakest in Britain (which has suffered particularly severe deindustrialization: for example, the number of persons employed in industry fell over 30 per cent, from 7 million to 4.5 million, in the 1980s).

The evolution of the occupational structure in West Europe has followed, several decades later, the pattern of the United States: a fall in agriculture; an expansion of industry up to the 1970s, and a subsequent accelerating decline; and a rapid growth of services. Mandel (1972) has defined this process as 'the third technological revolution' and it formed,

Table 1.4 Labour force employed in economic sectors (per cent)

		Britain	France	Germany	Italy
1950	Agriculture	6	32	25	42
	Industry	48	35	43	31
	Tertiary	46	33	32	27
1960	Agriculture	4	22	14	33
	Industry	48	38	49	37
	Tertiary	48	40	37	30
1970	Agriculture	3	14	9	20
	Industry	45	39	49	44
	Tertiary	52	46	42	36
1980	Agriculture	3	9	6	14
	Industry	39	36	45	38
	Tertiary	58	55	49	48
1990	Agriculture	2	6	3	9
	Industry	29	30	40	32
	Tertiary	69	64	57	59
1950–90 variations	Agriculture	−4	−26	−22	−33
	Industry	−19	−5	−3	+1
	Tertiary	+23	+31	+25	+32
1970–90 variations	Agriculture	−1	−8	−6	−11
	Industry	−16	−9	−9	−12
	Tertiary	+17	+18	+15	+23

Source: OECD

as noted, the empirical basis of theories of post-industrial society. A similar American pattern is discernible in the individual sectors of industrial activity. For example, the traditional sectors (textiles, leather goods, clothing, foodstuffs) and the older industrialized countries (like Britain) grew much less rapidly in the post-war period than the newer sectors (chemicals, petrochemicals, electronics) and the more recently industrialized countries (like France and Italy). The significant exception is West Germany, an older industrialized country which had the most rapid and prolonged industrial development of the post-war period (even if here specific reasons – Nazism and military collapse – played their part).

These tendencies of industrial growth led to a movement of manpower from the outlying provinces to the industrial centres, from agriculture and the traditional industries (coal, iron, shipbuilding and textiles) to the new industries (chemicals, electronics, information) and services. The energy crises of 1974 and 1980 gave added effect to the transformations that were taking place. Increases in the cost of energy and raw materials as well as of labour favoured industries which produced goods with a 'high-tech' content and a high added value. On the other hand, traditional industries were unable to meet the competition of the newly industrializing countries (NICs) of South East Asia, resulting in deindustrialization in the old industrial centres (like northern England, Scotland and north-eastern France). Finally, if the effects of population redistribution were absorbed positively in quantitative terms until the beginning of the 1970s (the growth in jobs in the four countries was about 1 million overall in the 1960s), the cost in qualitative terms was enormous. We have only to recall the 'biblical' exodus from southern Italy, or immigration in France and West Germany, to see that population movements are one of the principal causes of serious social tension (social struggles in Italy; racial riots in Britain, France and now Germany). Unemployment in Europe ran at around 10 per cent of the active population (10 million people) for much of the 1980s; part-time and temporary employment are also on the increase in all West European countries.

The fourth feature is the division of industrial activity into three sectors (O'Connor, 1973). The first sector is the competitive sector which consists of an ensemble of productive activities and services in which the physical capital-to-labour ratio and output per worker (or productivity) are low. Growth of production depends less on physical capital investment and technical progress than on exploitation of labour (low wages). In consequence, this sector comprises small firms, active in traditional industrial sectors (clothing, leather goods, furnishing) but also in commerce (drug and grocery stores, restaurants and service stations). Wages are low because of competition, and turnover is high in terms of both firms and jobs, which are often casual, seasonal or part-time, so the workers are usually non-unionized.

The second sector is the monopoly sector and embraces most big industrial firms, many of which are TNCs. They are characterized by a high physical capital-to-labour ratio and a high output per worker (physical productivity) since production is large scale, usually subject to technological innovation, and markets are national or international in scope. Firms are generally of such a size that they can dominate the national – and even world – economy in their sector and so the politics of their country of origin (like the oil companies, or Fiat in Italy and Siemens in Germany). They operate in the capital goods (oil, steel, copper) and consumer goods (cars, electrical appliances, soap products) sectors. Their oligopolistic[3] market situation and the need for long-term planning, owing to the large amounts of fixed capital invested, create stable industrial structures with relatively stable labour relations and high wages. This explains the social conditions of production, which are highly controlled, thanks also to powerful and legitimate trade unions. Firms of this type are able to pass the cost of technological investment on to their customers. It is a position which some are losing because of the increased international mobility of capital.

Finally, the third sector is the state sector, which falls into two categories: production of goods and services organized by the state itself (like Rhône-Poulenc, Usinor-Sacilor, SNCF in France; British Coal in

Britain; IRI, ENI, FFSS in Italy; VW in Germany); and production organized by industries under contract with the state (military equipment and
supplies, capital and highway construction). The ratio of capital to
labour, productivity and productivity growth are relatively low because
they are usually unrelated to profit maximization. Wages are relatively
high and the workers are unionized with a high level of job security. In
any event, state industries are subject to political shifts: costs are borne
by the state budget, so politicians decide according to their political priorities. Recently, there has been a move to privatize the public sector
(sale of public utilities in Britain in the 1980s; public groups in France
and public holdings in Italy in the 1990s) to promote efficiency and cut
public expenditure.

The three sectors coexist in all four countries. However, it is difficult to
specify the particular relations between them in individual countries, the
more so since they are continually changing. The competitive sector is
the most widespread in terms of employment in all four countries, and
most significantly in Italy; the monopoly sector is very strong (size and
capitalization) in Germany and Britain; while the state sector is still
important in France and Italy. Despite the imprecision, these indications
suggest nonetheless an important observation.

This regards the geographical location of development, whose continental centre of gravity is presently situated in the so-called 'golden triangle' formed by the cities of Lille, Hamburg and Stuttgart, and in the
three regions placed round it of London, Paris and Berlin. The Italian
'industrial triangle' represents an intermediate area half-way (not only
geographically but also economically) between the golden triangle and
the poorest regions of the EU, like southern Italy, rural Portugal, Spain
and Greece, and now East Germany. In this perspective, the German
economy is the core economy of Europe, while the British and Italian
economies are substantially peripheral, with all that this means socially
and politically.

More interesting from a sociological point of view is Bagnasco's (1977)
hypothesis that these three sectors (competitive, monopoly and state)
can be geographically localized and have specific socio-cultural bases.
With regard to Italy, Bagnasco has shown that while the monopoly sector
has tended to be concentrated in the industrial triangle of the north-west
of the country to form a 'core' economy, the competitive sector has
spread above all to north-east and central Italy to constitute a special
type of 'peripheral' economy. On the other hand, the state sector has
developed particularly in the south in the absence of endogenous industrialization alongside a 'marginal' agrarian economy. We believe that it is
possible to extend Bagnasco's model to the other three countries and
identify similar regional economies of the core, peripheral and marginal
types. Moreover, if these geographical areas have regional historical traditions (that is to say different subcultures structured at the level of civil
society), as in Italy, it is clear that a territorial/cultural dimension is

added to the functional/economic one which has significant political consequences (repository of votes for certain parties).

O'Connor's industrial sectors (suitably integrated with Bagnasco's sociological regions) permit the identification of different economic logics with specific social and political consequences that explain certain conflicts. The analysis draws attention, for example, to a significant, but often neglected, dimension of conflict situated alongside the major conflict in industrial societies (capital/labour). This is the sectorial dimension (between different categories of industrial and service producers) that can have territorial bases and so reinforce, or cut across, traditional economic conflicts (agriculture/industry, town/country, between regions) in European societies. It helps to explain why the major industrial conflict has never really structured the whole of these societies, as Aron's industrial society model hypothesized, as well as to illuminate some of the social mechanisms now moving centre stage, like, for example, 'marginality'.

Post-war economic development

The post-war period can be divided very schematically into three phases. The first, reconstruction, was a brief and very intense phase which was completed around 1950. The second phase, that of the economic miracles (*les trente glorieuses*), ended around 1973–4. The third phase, still in progress,[4] has been marked by two energy crises and the 1990s depression.

Reconstruction: the context

Before discussing the major aspects of the three phases, we need to fix the context. Firstly, there is the division of Europe into two blocs until 1990, with Britain, France, Italy and West Germany in the Western bloc. This meant that not only the type of society, and so the economic organization, was underwritten by NATO, but also the type of economic development (namely the production and export of capital and consumer goods) was conditioned by the international division of labour. A necessary condition of this economic order was the creation of a stable international monetary system around the dollar at Bretton Woods in 1944 that was guaranteed by a number of international institutions (IMF, OECD, GATT) which sanctioned American domination resulting from the Second World War. Given that the United States market was the largest consumer market in the world, it was natural that the European economies were closely tied to it. Hence the phrase: 'When the US sneezes, Europe catches a cold.' This economic order had a number of consequences for European countries: stagnation and decline in Britain, rapid growth in West Germany, Italy and France. Finally, the European economies were subject, as noted, to a growing internationalization of the market from the 1960s onwards, stimulated by the creation of the EEC.

Secondly, during the boom years, the European economies were subject to economic cycles, initially attenuated in the 1950s, becoming more accentuated in the 1960s, leading to depressions in the 1970s and slumps in the 1980s and 1990s. The periods of recession were relatively brief in the 1950s while those of recovery and growth were correspondingly longer. But the situation began to change in the 1960s and continued into the 1970s, with ever longer recessions and ever briefer expansion. This was due to the fact that in the 1950s the different economies found themselves at different moments of the economic cycle, so there was a push–pull effect, with the expanding economies acting as a locomotive to pull the contracting economies out of recession. The worsening of the recessions, complemented by the crisis of the international monetary system, led inexorably to the progressive alignment of the economic cycles of the Western countries. The energy crisis of 1973–4, moreover, contributed decisively to this trend which, by forcing up inflation, obliged the governments of the principal Western states to introduce inflationary packages which led to a depression (table 1.5).

Thirdly, to understand the boom, we need to remember the low base line of departure. West Germany was physically destroyed, France and Italy badly disrupted by war and foreign occupation. Their populations had suffered deportation and hardship, and so were prepared to work long hours and make sacrifices. In addition, there was enormous unused productive capacity. Hence, not surprisingly, European economic development was based on export-led growth. Britain alone was unable to instigate such a mechanism: its development was much more modest – 2.7 per cent against a minimum of 5.2 per cent per year for the other three economies between 1950 and 1970 – and was based on import-led growth which explains its 'stop–go' (deflation–reflation) economic policy.

Les trente glorieuses

If we ask what were the reasons for the greatest and longest economic boom (*les trente glorieuses*) that Europe has ever known (and which nobody foresaw), we are bound to reply that there is no single explanation. If at all, we can talk of a concourse of circumstances, some willed and others fortuitous. In addition to the new international monetary system created at Bretton Woods and strong domestic demand due to postwar reconstruction, an ensemble of factors was responsible (*inter alia*, the resumption of world trade, strong technological development, high levels of industrial investment, abundance of cheap labour, European

Table 1.5 Trends of the European economies, 1950–1986

	GDP (annual average variation)	Inflation rate (annual average variation)	Employment rate (annual average variation)	Investments (%)	Unemployment rate (%)	Balance of payments (annual average $ million)
Britain						
1950–64	2.9	3.3	0.8	15.6	2.5	270
1964–73	3.0	5.9	—	20.3	3.2	116
1973–79	1.3	15.6	0.1	18.8	5.1	−2691
1979–86	1.2	8.2	−1.5	20.4	10.5	3471
France						
1952–59	4.2	3.3	−0.2	16.8	2.0	67
1959–69	5.7	3.9	0.7	22.2	1.8	−288
1969–73	5.6	6.2	0.9	24.3	2.6	45
1973–79	3.0	10.7	0.3	22.5	4.5	−1699
1979–86	1.6	8.7	−0.2	21.0	8.7	−3414
Germany						
1950–60	8.0	1.9	2.1	22.5	3.8	838
1960–70	4.7	2.6	0.1	24.0	0.6	760
1970–79	2.9	4.5	−0.5	22.2	2.4	3609
1979–86	1.4	4.4	−0.5	20.8	6.7	8328
Italy						
1951–63	5.8	2.7	0.1	24.4	6.7	65
1963–69	5.3	3.4	0.4	24.2	5.3	1919
1969–79	3.3	12.2	0.6	21.1	6.2	471
1979–86	2.2	13.7	0.7	22.6	8.8	−3928

Source: OECD

integration and specific government policy). Without wishing to examine these factors in any detail, it is worth recalling a few aspects. The first concerns the Marshall Plan, generally considered, certainly at the time, a primary factor. However, Milward (1984) has shown that it played a much less crucial role than was thought: economic recovery in many countries had already begun before the funds' arrival and they did not serve to remove the European countries' balance of payments deficit with the USA. Nonetheless, the $13 million were used to buy essential raw materials and technological imports (machine tools and capital goods) which allowed a more rational programme of economic development.

Furthermore, if the Marshall Plan was a generous gesture by the USA, it was not a disinterested one. It was necessary, in order to relaunch the American economy in peacetime, to develop international trade, and this required markets for American products. Hence, reconstructing the destroyed European economies and favouring their integration was a logical step for the USA to take. It implied a free market policy on the part of Europe (already agreed at Bretton Woods) and, hence, the opening of its markets, something which was not achieved without serious problems (failure of the Havana Charter in 1948, replaced by GATT). In this way, the USA succeeded in securing a free market base (the economy of the 'free world') to underpin its defence strategy (Atlantic alliance, NATO).

The second aspect regards the question of cheap labour which Kindleberger (1967) believes was the crucial factor in keeping production costs low and profit rates high. War disruption created a vast mass of unemployed labour. For instance, in West Germany there were 1.5 million unemployed in 1949 and full employment was reached only in 1960 in the middle of the economic miracle. This mass of unemployed labour came largely from German-speaking displaced persons fleeing from Eastern Europe who continued to arrive until the building of the Berlin Wall in 1962. They were usually skilled workers and qualified technicians who had suffered hardship, first under the Nazis and then under the Soviets, and so were prepared to go anywhere and do anything. This offered German industry the advantage of both geographical and sectorial labour mobility that did not exist elsewhere in Western Europe. In Italy, in addition to the temporary unemployment caused by the war, there was a vast 'reserve army' of unemployed in the underdeveloped but overpopulated south. The emigrants who left the south in the period 1955–70 have been estimated at 2.6 million, an exodus of truly biblical proportions. Not surprisingly, the famous 'southern policy' (land reform of 1950, creation of the Cassa per il Mezzogiorno) was interpreted as a policy of 'stabilization', intended not to tie the surplus peasants too strongly to the land, but to ensure a continuous flow of migrants to the developed regions. In consequence, tendential 'full employment' was reached in Italy at the beginning of the 1960s only among the most skilled categories of labour.

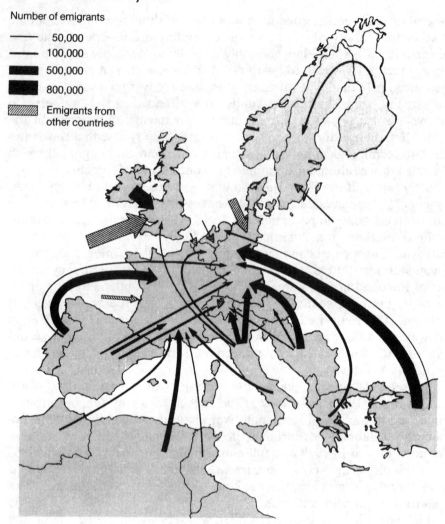

Number of emigrants

——— 50,000
——— 100,000
▬▬ 500,000
▬▬ 800,000
▨ Emigrants from other countries

Figure 1.1 Principal migratory movements in Europe in the post-war period
Source: Williams, 1987, p. 62

Although caused by the need for cheap labour, the question of emigration and immigration in Western Europe is not solely an economic problem, as the displays of racism in the 1970s and 1980s have so vividly illustrated (chapter 2). Europe was traditionally a continent of emigrants – for example, the mass transoceanic emigration of the late nineteenth and the early twentieth centuries – but in the post-war period the situation has been dramatically reversed and Europe has become a continent of immigrants (some 8 million between 1950 and 1980). This reversal of the traditional pattern was due to the policy of the principal European countries (but not Italy), worried about the lack of manpower after the post-war economic take-off: in Britain and France, the immigrants came from their former colonies; in West Germany, they were *Gastarbeiter* originating from Southern Europe (figure 1.1). The economic advantages for the host country were substantial: to overcome the manpower short-age, permit economies of scale, maintain high investment levels, reduce labour costs and, in this way, sustain profit rates, and thus to contribute to export-led growth by controlling inflationary thrusts and so the need for deflationary policies. Moreover, the social costs of reproduction were lower for the *Gastarbeiter* than for indigenous workers (educational and training costs as well as welfare and social security were borne by the state of origin). Some states maximized the economic advantages accru-ing to them from the presence of *Gastarbeiter* by imposing administra-tive measures (for instance only issuing six-month work and residence permits) in order to maintain a high level of manpower flexibility.

After the first energy crisis, a turning point occurred in the immigra-tion policy of European countries, that was anticipated in Britain in the previous decade as a result of its economic weakness (Commonwealth Immigration Acts of 1962 and 1968). The rise in unemployment during the 1970s, backed by a fall in labour demand, provoked political tensions and pressures (racial riots in Britain and France) in support of anti-immi-gration measures. The decisive factor was probably the fact that the eco-nomic advantages accruing to the host country from immigrant labour began to decline, because the costs in terms of social investment (health and education for immigrant children) rose considerably. The real costs of foreign manpower had, in fact, begun to increase before the demand for foreign labour fell. Moreover, immigrants were no longer prepared to accept the marginalized situation in which they were kept, above all once they had learnt the local language and started to be socially inte-grated. It has been estimated that in the period 1974–8 some 1.5 to 2 mil-lion foreign workers lost their jobs in Western Europe.

West Germany and Italy

The different economic policies pursued by the governments of the dif-ferent countries explain in part their different levels of success. The Federal Republic and Italy depended almost exclusively on monetary instruments (Erhard's *Soziale Marktwirtschaft* and the Einaudi line). Production was relaunched by an apposite currency devaluation (1949 in the FRG) or deflationary policy (1947 in Italy), followed by tight credit control to force industrialists to export. This combination of measures was very successful: economic take-off was very rapid and in less than ten years both West Germany and Italy were in the middle of economic miracles. There were, however, significant differences in economic policy in the two countries. Both could have chosen, within the free market framework adopted, between two alternative strategies: (1) a growth strategy in which consumption was controlled and resources oriented towards capital goods production and, hence, reinvested to expand production and increase capital formation; and (2) an international market-guided growth strategy with the expansion of consumer goods production (destined for the middle classes) and severe wage compression. The result of the former was the growth of the working class, with a limited rural exodus towards the industrial rather than the service sector: the effect of the second was, instead, a delayed development of the working class accompanied by a massive rural exodus and rapid growth of the service sector and so of the middle classes. Not surprisingly, West Germany chose the former strategy and Italy the latter, with important consequences for the subsequent economic and political development of the two countries.

France

French policy was different again: the government made economic growth an absolute priority, and chose a *dirigiste* approach, using 'indicative planning' as the instrument to pursue it. France, like Britain, but in contrast to Germany and Italy, found itself on the side of the victors, in spite of Vichy and German occupation. This had a number of consequences. Firstly, the French people felt that they were victims and not responsible for the war and so were less ready to make sacrifices than the Germans; hence, manpower mobility was less. Secondly, the governments of the Fourth Republic lacked the political will to impose the modernization of the productive apparatus, a task which was entrusted to the administration, via planning (Monnet Plan), and which was to bear fruit fifteen years later. Moreover, France, like Italy, had an important agricultural sector which could not be ignored for electoral reasons. Thirdly, France had an imperial heritage (Indo-China, North Africa) which soaked up energy and resources in colonial wars, resources that in West Germany and Italy were used for economic growth. Significantly, economic take-off (mainly controlled by the state) followed almost immediately on the resolution of the colonial question. Fourthly, defence spending for a policy of independent defence (*force de frappe*) was responsible for a higher proportion of GDP devoted to it than in West Germany and this even after the latter's integration into NATO.

It is significant from a political standpoint that French economic growth was linked to the change of regime in 1958 and the policy then pursued (devaluation of the franc, credit control), even if, as noted, the take-off had been prepared by the post-war planning policy. French economic growth in the 1960s was stimulated also by the creation of the EEC. The latter was founded, in fact, on Franco-German agreement: Germany needed markets for its industrial products – one of the causes of Nazi expansion in the Balkans between the wars – and France sought financial support for its backward agriculture, the basis of the country's political stability. The Common Agricultural Policy (CAP) (financed largely from German resources) enabled the French government to invest the surplus value of economic activity, previously used to support the agricultural sector, in the restructuring and modernizing of industry – a policy which the Gaullist regime accomplished successfully in the 1960s.

Britain

Britain's situation was also different: it had certain problems in common with France – a war victor, decolonization, military expenditure – but in a rather different context. The first country to industrialize in the nineteenth century, Britain had constructed an imperial system which was founded, on the one hand, on the domination of finance capital (the City) and, on the other, on protected markets. In addition, the war compromise was based on a combination of full employment and the welfare state. Decolonization, starting with India in 1947, meant the end of protected markets. Sterling's international role required the defence of the currency while the City's interests favoured financial intermediation (investment abroad rather than in domestic industry), and this resulted in the ageing of the industrial apparatus. Moreover, the policy of full employment linked to the corporative strength of the unions also constituted an obstacle to industrial modernization. All these elements fostered a policy of stop–go and the progressive decline of the country's industrial base. This meant Britain's exclusion from the continent's great post-war boom, as the import-led growth mechanism made clear. The British crisis occurred before the onset of the 1970s depressions as a result of specifically British factors (weakness of national capital, which saw its position worsen inexorably throughout the post-war period).

At the end of the 1950s, Europe was in the midst of the economic miracles: the boom received a further stimulus from the creation of the EEC which helped it overcome the American recession of 1957–8. Two points are worth noting. Firstly, there was a widespread myth that, thanks to Keynesian techniques, capitalist economies had overcome the economic cycle and the danger of economic crises. There was no reason, according to Samuelson (1960), Aron (1962a) and others, why economic growth should not continue indefinitely into the future. The instrument was credit control: expanded to increase demand in periods of recession; restricted in periods of overheating to reduce demand. This technique did not suppress the cycle, it only attenuated the consequences. Furthermore, it fed an inflationary tendency: sustaining demand every six years meant encouraging quickening inflation that already threatened the international monetary system. At this point the technique lost its efficacy and recessions became depressions. Secondly, this kind of economic growth, strongly assisted by the creation of the EEC, implied strong horizontal rather than vertical integration, that is to say the development of trade and investment between European industrial economies instead of between imperialist economies and their colonies, as before the war.

French May and Italian Hot Autumn

In the 1960s, despite the economic miracles, or perhaps because of them, came the first difficulties: between 1963 and 1966 there were the first post-war economic crises. Accelerating growth with high-level capitalization and the revival of worker combativeness thanks to tendential full employment provoked a fall in profit margins. Industrialists found themselves confronted with the classic problem of capital valorization: wage rises in Italy, France and Germany caused a series of balance of payments difficulties. Each government responded with a classic deflationary package (Giscard d'Estaing's *Plan de stabilisation* in 1963 in France; the July 1964 crisis – *golpe* De Lorenzo – and deradicalized *centro-sinistra* in Italy; government/trade-union accord and Grosse Koalition in West Germany in 1966). In France and Italy, the workers – in Germany, the *Gastarbeiter* – paid the price of the crisis; this fact more than any other explains the violence of the 1968–9 crisis. In Italy, growth was relaunched during 1965 thanks to an increase in productivity without investment, that is an increase in work rhythms and, hence, industrial accidents. Similar techniques were used in France and West Germany: there was much talk on the shop floor of military methods and discipline. Not surprisingly, the principal working class demands of the French May and the Italian Hot Autumn were for improvements in working conditions. The governments and employers responded with wage rises in both countries.

The French government resorted to a judicious devaluation (August 1969), exploited the weakness of the working class – which it was able to isolate thanks to the constitutional mechanisms of the Fifth Republic - and was able to launch a new phase of economic growth. In Italy a similar manoeuvre was unsuccessful because the Italian government found itself confronted by a working class that had taken control of the shop floor and imposed its own work rhythms, but which also enjoyed considerable institutional support thanks to the political strength of the PCI. The boom mechanism – based on high productivity and high profits – was shattered. Italian economic growth henceforth became ever more irregular and dependent on small-business activity. Even in West Germany, despite the change in political majority in 1969 which strengthened the government/union accord and encouraged a limited recovery, profit margins fell, putting an end to the great period of rapid German growth.

The event which marked the change in the post-war economic climate was the suspension of the convertibility of the dollar (August 1971); it decreed the end of the international monetary order created at Bretton Woods in 1944 which had constituted one of the necessary conditions for *les trente glorieuses*. Its significance can be understood if we recall that the American balance of payments had been in deficit since the late 1950s and could not be rectified because the fixed parity of the dollar – a pillar of Bretton Woods – did not permit devaluation. Up to 1971 international trade was financed by American gold reserves; initially this was no problem given the vastness of these reserves, but later heavy expenditure on the Vietnam War reduced them to a level that put too great a pressure on the dollar. The fixed exchange rate system was replaced with a more flexible one of floating exchange rates that permitted two devaluations of the dollar (8 per cent in 1971 and 10 per cent in 1973), but it introduced a further world inflationary element. The 1972 recovery, in fact, was largely stimulated by currency speculation and thus characterized by strong inflationary pressures.

First energy crisis

The recovery of the two most important Western economies (USA and FRG) was already on the wane when the world was hit by the first energy crisis of 1973–4 and the fourfold rise in the oil price provoked by the Arab oil embargo (figure 1.2). The energy crisis was not the cause of

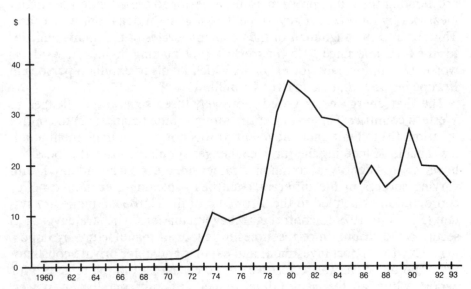

Figure 1.2 International oil price, 1960–1993 (dollars per barrel)
Source: OPEC

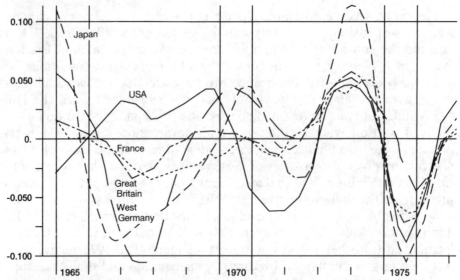

Figure 1.3 Synchronization of economic cycles, 1965–1976
Source: Grjebin, 1986, p. 150

the 1974–5 depression, even if it did make things worse. It was, nonetheless, the most serious post-war depression up to then, and the first which saw a drop in international trade. The crisis had already begun and was due principally to a fall in profit margins resulting from overcapitalization and excess labour. The energy crisis accentuated, as it were, tendencies already at work. By reinforcing inflationary pressures and accelerating the fall in profit margins, it hastened the adoption of similar measures by all Western governments – a general deflationary package. This ensured the alignment of the economic cycles of the main countries for the first time since 1945 (figure 1.3), thus making the negative effects worse. Unemployment, for example, which involved 3 million persons in Europe in 1969–70, rose to over 4.5 million.

The first energy crisis posed, however, three separate challenges to Western countries: (1) to correct the foreign trade balance; (2) to control inflation; (3) to limit unemployment. It was not easy to implement a policy capable of meeting the three challenges simultaneously. It is possible, however, to identify a common strategy in the policies adopted with varying success in the different countries – including economic policy coordination, which led to the setting up of the European monetary system (EMS)[5] in 1979 to control currency fluctuations. The strategy was to secure a redistribution of resources in favour of manufacture by imposing a levy to support investment and exports and deter private consumption. The objective was to reserve an increasing part of manufacture for export while at the same time reducing family purchasing power. Moreover, to prevent social and political tensions that such a levy might

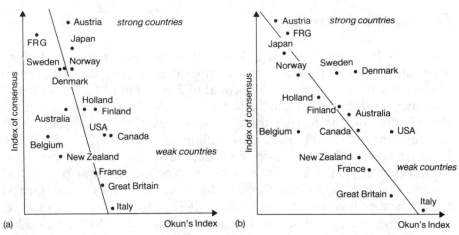

Figure 1.4 Consensus and macro-economic performance: (a) 1968–1973 (b) 1980–1983. The index of consensus is a weighting of three factors: level of political and ideological consensus (cooperation between unions, employers and government); effective wage bargaining; regulation of labour conflicts. Okun's index is the inflation rate plus the unemployment rate
Source: Grjebin, 1986, pp. 143–4

provoke, special welfare packages were introduced to aid the worst-hit social groups.

In the countries with a strong economy, like the FRG (figure 1.4), such a strategy quickly proved successful: the levy on wage-earners' real purchasing power more or less 'paid for' the increased oil bill. In return, the deficit on the balance of payments was corrected quickly and inflation brought under control. Hence the German government was able to relaunch the economy in 1975 and ensure a strong, non-inflationary, recovery by 1976–7.

In the countries with a weak economy, which included Britain and Italy, and France to a lesser degree, it was, on the contrary, much more difficult to apply this strategy successfully, above all because of the combativeness of the working class. In this situation, wage-earners' purchasing power was maintained, and even rose, so that business enterprises 'paid for' the increased oil bill, despite a difficult cash-flow situation, made worse by rising labour costs and falling output. Thus, in a first phase (1974–5), the governments gave priority to the fight against inflation without much success; in a second phase (1975–6), confronted with a rapid rise in unemployment, they changed policy and relaunched the economy. The result was that the economy recovered but had not been 'purged' of either inflation or the trade deficit. Once again, the governments of these countries were forced to change direction and introduce, under IMF pressure, an economic squeeze (1976 in Britain, 1977 in Italy). This explains why these countries found themselves in a situation of zero growth on the eve of the second energy crisis, with high unemployment (6–8 per cent), high inflation (15–20 per cent) and foreign trade deficits.

Second energy crisis

The second energy crisis of 1979–80 (brought about by the Iranian Revolution) had similarities with, but also differed from, the first. The oil price rise was of the same order (equal to 2 per cent of GDP of OECD countries) and the inflationary effect was similar (about 3 per cent); the deficit effect on the foreign trade balance was also of the same order ($75 billion in 1979–80 against $26 billion in 1973–4). The differences, however, were: (1) the oil price rise occurred in stages, so was more easily absorbable; (2) the new rise was less destabilizing because people had got used to living with inflation; (3) the economic cycles of the OECD countries were less synchronized than in 1973–4. The consequences were, nonetheless, even more severe this time. In the early 1970s, the OPEC countries were unable to absorb internally the new foreign exchange income, so large quantities of capital had to be recycled through the international banks in the Western countries, thus contributing to the economic recovery of the later 1970s. At the end of the decade, the OPEC countries were better able to absorb new investment internally, so there was far less recycling of petrodollars. The result was a slump – the most serious since the great depression of the 1930s – which extended to all Western European countries and was accompanied by a doubling of unemployment (10 per cent, or over 10 million people).

The reaction to the second energy crisis was more varied than that to the first: it went from the free market liberalism of Thatcher in Britain and Reagan in America to the socialism of Mitterrand in France. The free market liberalism found its inspiration in a common critique of post-war Keynesian policies, condemned for their 'laxism' in the name of a real 'conservative revolution'. The objectives were: the defeat of inflation; the elimination of the foreign trade deficit; the reduction of the role of the state, judged excessive; and support of profit and free enterprise. Full employment was abandoned as an economic priority. The neo-liberal inspiration (Hayek) relied on the market as a regulator and favoured monetary policy as the policy instrument in keeping with the economic doctrine of Friedman and the Chicago school. It rejected Keynesian intervention and its policy instruments, like budgetary and fiscal policies.

British free-market liberalism

In considering Thatcherite economic policy, we must bear in mind that Britain became, between the two energy crises, an oil producing country, thanks to the discovery and exploitation of North Sea oil, which represented 3 per cent of world reserves. From the end of the 1970s Britain was thus in the privileged position of energy self-sufficiency (petrol and natural gas). It meant that for almost all the 1980s one of the fundamen-

tal constraints on the British economy – the balance of payments deficit
– did not operate. This fact goes a long way to explaining Thatcherite
economic policy which would not otherwise have been politically possible. Initially, a pure 'monetarist' policy was applied because, according to
the canons of the Chicago school, to control inflation it was sufficient to
control the money supply. But it was a policy which revealed itself, over
time, to be totally inadequate. In practice, the principal elements of the
economic policy turned out to be a high exchange rate for sterling (now
a petrocurrency) and an extremely restrictive budgetary policy. They
provoked a very severe slump, which was responsible for the destruction
of a quarter of the country's industrial capacity, more than 3 million
unemployed (13 per cent) and a fall of 3.6 per cent in GDP. Inflation,
however, did fall from 20 per cent to 3–5 per cent in the mid 1980s.
Moreover, workers' combativeness was undermined by the high level of
unemployment, special anti-union legislation[6] and an authoritarian policy of 'law and order' (increase in police numbers and extended powers).

As a result of the slump's severity, the recovery, when it came, started
from a lower base than in any other post-war economic cycle; and, even
if it did give rise to the longest post-war period of uninterrupted growth,
the boom was founded on financial intermediation (deregulated credit),
supported by North Sea oil revenue, and not on industrial production.
However, inability to control wages in the private sector, in spite of trade
union weakness, and lack of industrial investment followed by the
decline of oil revenues, led to a new, more serious balance of payments
deficit and a resumption of inflation at the end of the 1980s. Great
Britain, then, despite the unexpected gift of North Sea oil found itself at
the end of the Thatcherite decade with the same problems as before: the
danger of a renewed stop–go policy. Nonetheless, the Thatcher government felt sufficiently confident to enter the EMS in autumn 1990.
However, entry coincided with German unification and the rate of sterling against the Deutschmark was too high, so its stay was short-lived
and its exit in September 1992 was inglorious; and the Major government
was left without an alternative economic policy.

At all events, Thatcherite policies contributed significantly to the creation of a dual economy (the so-called 'two-thirds, one-third society':
Therborn, 1989): on the one side, certain sectors (financial, but also high-
tech) and regions (the south-east) prospering; on the other side, many
sectors (traditional and heavy industries) and regions (north, north-west,
Scotland) marginalized and being run down. It is the logic of a dual society: the rich get richer and the poor get poorer. In this connection, the
most original element in the Thatcherite programme (imitated by the
Chirac government of 1986–8 in France, and by the Amato government
in Italy in 1992–3) was the privatization of public assets, which had three
objectives: (1) reduce the role of the state; (2) create a shareholding
democracy (6 million shareholders claimed today); (3) finance public
expenditure in order to reduce direct taxation.

French socialist economics

In discussing French economic policy, we must bear in mind that the left came to power in the midst of the slump triggered off by the second energy crisis (May 1981) with a programme of fighting unemployment and instituting economic and social reforms (reduction of inequalities, redistribution of work and nationalization of the big industrial and financial groups). The strategy pursued was based on stimulating a modest recovery through a rise in the SMIG (guaranteed minimum wage) and selected social benefits which should, in turn, have stimulated popular consumption. This should have relaunched domestic output and encouraged new industrial investment. The policy was predicated on a favourable international conjuncture so that the growth in exports would have sustained the domestic recovery and corrected the foreign trade deficit. Unfortunately, not only was there no international recovery in 1982, but the slump worsened. The result was that imports grew, the domestic manoeuvre aborted and the foreign trade deficit got worse. The external constraints were such (EMS) that the Socialist government was forced to review its whole policy radically and to introduce an economic squeeze in an effort to reduce the foreign trade deficit – devaluations of the franc in June 1982 and March 1983 – and to fight inflation. The objective was partially attained by the time of the 1986 elections, won by the right.

To achieve these results, however, the Socialist government was obliged to adopt, *malgré lui*, certain policies of its predecessor (Barre government, 1976–81). This explains, according to Mossé (1989, p. 183), a paradox: 'the Socialist experiment succeeded best where it was least expected (price control, wage disindexation, reconstitution of profit margins, reduction of the foreign trade deficit); but its main objective, substantially reducing unemployment, was far from being achieved.' Certain orientations of the Socialist government were not abandoned, nonetheless: (1) the public sector remained dominant and retained its pilot role; (2) social solidarity was maintained, particularly through fiscal policies; (3) the 'social treatment' of unemployment (*travaux d'utilité collective*) was stepped up.

Germany and Italy

Finally, the economic policies of Germany and Italy did not experience the radical policy changes of Britain and France. The Kohl government, after its arrival in power in 1982, pursued a more market-oriented policy than its social-democrat/liberal predecessors, without ever going to the Reagan and Thatcher extremes. The overall balance appears positive, but it faces very serious problems today in the wake of German unification in integrating the former East German economy. In Italy things went on much as before, in the sense that economic policy was bedevilled by the inability of the government, for political reasons, to control public expenditure deficit, now running at 10 per cent GDP. The Craxi government succeeded in abolishing wage indexation (*scala mobile*) – despite a referendum in 1985 – and in securing a reasonably favourable monetary and financial climate for business. However, it was the vitality of the industrial sector (big and small firms) above all that enabled the country to overcome the growing constraints of the foreign trade balance.

There was a general recovery in Europe in the mid 1980s, stimulated after 1986 by the fall in the oil price – owing to the energy conservation measures introduced during the slump years – and by unrestricted credit. However, the boom was fragile because American economic growth was based on deficit financing (tax reductions, unlimited credit) giving rise to a large public expenditure and balance of payments deficits. Moreover, the generalized deregulation of stock markets as part of the move to complete the single European market provoked a massive movement of speculative capital which resulted in the October 1987 stock market crash (general 30 per cent fall in share prices). Although the catastrophic consequences feared at the time were avoided – thanks to the coordinated action of the principal Western governments and economic operators – the economic situation worsened at the beginning of the 1990s as a result of the consumer debts[7] incurred, provoking the worst slump since the 1990s (unemployment in the EU had risen in 1992 to 12 per cent or 15 million people). This grim situation was compounded by the economic consequences of German unification: costs escalated with the collapse of the East German economy in 1991. Moreover, the German government, having promised that unification would not necessitate raising taxes, resorted to borrowing which promoted inflation. The Bundesbank responded by raising interest rates, thereby provoking a European monetary crisis, given that the Deutschmark is the anchor currency in the EMS. Britain[8] and Italy were forced to abandon the EMS on 'Black Wednesday' (16 September 1992) and accept effective devaluation of their currencies, as did Spain some weeks after. In July 1993 the French franc also came under speculative attack in the money markets and the EMS was saved in name, if not in substance, by widening considerably the bands of permitted fluctuation. In the meantime (autumn 1993), all the major West European economies were in deep recession, although signs of recovery were discernible in America and Britain.

However, two major problems still beset the Western European economies in the mid 1990s: relatively slow growth and massive, rising unemployment in most countries. It is not easy to see how they can be overcome given the unattainable fiscal policy targets enshrined in the Maastricht Treaty and the widespread belief in European policy circles that markets know best, despite the accumulating evidence to the contrary. Indeed the problems, and particularly unemployment, are likely to get worse. As Boltho (1993, p. 75) has observed: 'It took rearmament and World War II to eliminate hysteresis from the European labour markets of the 1930s. It is difficult to see what can achieve a similar feat in Europe in the 1990s.'

Conclusion

This chapter has discussed the economic context of post-war West European politics. We began by outlining two models, Aron's industrial society and Bell's post-industrial society, which stressed certain key features – the giant industrial enterprise and codified knowledge – and their supposed implications. However, the important point is the continued centrality of manufacture, because without successful production there is no surplus value – and without surplus value the other features of contemporary Western European societies are at risk.

West European economies are mixed economies: this means that although they are dominated by private capital and the logic of the market, they are also characterized by Keynesian state intervention. Other structural features are internationalization, of which European integration was both a stimulus and a consequence; widely disparate economic situations inside each country in spite of the similarity of demographic structures; and finally, the division of industrial activity into three sectors, competitive, monopolistic and state. These sectors have different logics with specific social and political consequences which help to explain why the major industrial conflict between capital and labour has never really structured the whole of these societies, as Aron's industrial society model suggests it should.

Post-war European economic development was analysed in three phases: reconstruction (1945 to 1950); the boom years (1950 to 1970–5); and the depression years (1970–5 to the present). The analysis highlighted the major features of each phase and the general factors determining the way it developed. At the same time, attention was paid to each country's individual specificity, whether in terms of special factors or policy options. However, this exposition of the complex, and often tortuous, processes that have characterized the post-war developments of the major European economies is intended to suggest some general points of use in subsequent political analysis.

Firstly, it demonstrates the interconnection that exists between economic and political processes. It is impossible, in fact, to discuss European economic development without referring to political actions and events. Economic growth in certain countries was the direct result of the economic policy adopted, in the same way as policy choices in other fields were conditioned by the general economic situation and the relation of social and political forces. For example, as noted, reconstruction policies in Germany and Italy as a result of their alternative strategies had differing economic and political outcomes. Similarly, the logic of capital accumulation in conditions of dependence on the world market forced all western countries to adopt simultaneously deflationary policies in the mid 1970s, even if local factors were responsible for the timing and the success of such policies nationally. Economic and political factors, both national and international, then, explain the modalities, the success or failure of the British neo-liberal and French socialist experiments in the 1980s. At all events, it goes to show that political analysis of a specific state requires accurate knowledge of all the processes that concern it.

Secondly, the discussion highlights the importance of the diachronic dimension in any analysis. This has two aspects. On the one hand, economists, like sociologists and political scientists, are often slow to draw all the implications for their analytical models of changes in collective behaviour, such as the decline in the propensity to save in the 1970s, a recessionary period with high interest rates; or again the effects of the plastic credit debt on consumer spending in spite of a drop in interest rates at the beginning of the 1990s. On the other hand, certain policies are possible in certain conjunctures but *not* in others. To take a notorious recent example, if Mrs Thatcher's policies were intellectually contemplatable in post-war Britain before the 1980s thanks to Hayek, they were certainly not politically viable without North Sea oil revenues.

Further reading

P. Armstrong, A. Glyn and J. Harrison (1988), *Capitalism since World War II* (Oxford: Blackwell, 2nd edn).

R. Aron (1967), *Industrial Society* (London: Weidenfeld & Nicolson).

D. Bell (1974), *The Coming of Post-Industrial Society* (London: Heinemann).

A. Boltho (ed.) (1982), *The European Economy: Growth and Crisis* (Oxford: OUP).

D. Dyer (ed.) (1992), *The European Economy* (London: Longman).

D. Dyer (ed.) (1992), *The National Economies of Europe* (London: Longman).

G. Therborn 1986), *Why Some People are More Unemployed than Others* (London: Verso).

A.M. Williams (1987), *Western European Economy: A Geography of Postwar Development* (London: Hutchinson).

PART II

Civil Society

2 Class, Gender and Race

Introduction

Civil society, as noted in the introduction, is a crucial area of analysis of Western European politics because, in advanced industrial societies with representative parliamentary regimes, it is the site where men and women are constituted as subjects in flesh and blood with all their cultural attributes. It has been defined as a part of society distinct from and largely independent of the state, comprising a complex of autonomous organizations – households and markets, churches and sects, newspapers and electronic media, schools and universities, parties and interest groups, philanthropic and civic voluntary associations – which mediate the relations of the individual with the state. In other words, civil society furnishes the necessary link between the economy and the state in the sense that the latter set the parameters (money and laws) of individual and collective political options, while the former determines (through political activity and ideology) the actual action undertaken.

In such a perspective, we must take account of three aspects. Firstly, civil society is made up of an ensemble of practices that are neither unified nor homogeneous, but 'structurated'. By 'structurated', we intend that the practices have acquired a persistence that their meaning is taken for granted, that is to say they are understood by a group, a community or even society without the need to be made explicit. Secondly, this structuration necessarily has a historical dimension resulting from collective understandings of the group's, community's or society's past experience. Thirdly, and furthermore, it is not static, that is fixed once and for all. In fact, granted that civil society is the site where individuals are constituted as social subjects, it is also the site of political conflict. And political conflict over the distribution of scarce resources, modifying social and political relations, necessarily changes the structuration of civil society. Indeed, the goal of certain contemporary social movements (chapter 4) is precisely that of changing social and political relations and so the structuration of civil society.

In discussing civil society, we propose to start from the structural factors – what Harry Eckstein (1966) has termed 'objective social differentiation' – and proceed to the principal actors operating in civil society. Hence in this chapter we examine class, gender and race, and in the next the historical roots of national cultures. Subsequent chapters are devoted to the organizations active in cultural change, namely voluntary associations, social movements, subcultures and the communications media (chapter 4), parties (chapter 5) and groups and interests (chapter 6).

Class

Division of society into social classes[1] is a basic feature of industrial societies. Certainly, class has played a fundamental role in the politics of Western Europe for the last century and a half. Indeed, not only was a major social theory – Marxism – built on it, but so also were two major types of political party – the social democrat and the communist. Moreover, even many liberals who contest the Marxist analysis of capitalism as a class society accept the notion of social stratification. They resort to the image of the ladder to represent the social hierarchy: it is intended to communicate the idea of individual social mobility, that is the facility with which a motivated person can get to the top whatever his social origin. The supporters of class theory use, in contrast, the image of the pyramid to represent capitalist society in order to emphasize the fact that it is the privileged few who sit at the top of the pile and the deprived masses who find themselves at the bottom.

These two images are the visual expressions of the two major traditions of class analysis – the Weberian and the Marxist – from which the contemporary debate derives. The importance of this debate turns largely on the 'problem of the middle classes'. Do intermediary classes really exist? If so, what are their bases? Are they growing or declining? The middle classes are of special interest because, whilst Marxist theory predicates the progressive disappearance of intermediary classes as capitalism develops, many liberals share the conviction that a substantial middle class is a necessary requisite for a functioning representative democracy: 'a large middle class tempers conflict by rewarding moderate and democratic parties and penalizing extremist groups' (Lipset, 1959, p. 61).

However, despite the importance of the concept of class in the social theories of Marx and Weber, there is surprisingly no systematic treatment of the topic in their works. Marx died at the very moment when he was embarking on writing the unfinished chapter LII of volume III of *Das Kapital* and left less than 50 lines, while Weber's two theoretical texts are also both incomplete. Hence, disagreements and confusions have dogged understanding of the use of the concept. It has been suggested, in fact, that two different conceptions of class can be found in the works of both writers: (1) an abstract model applicable to all class systems; (2) specific analyses of concrete historical situations.

The Marxian model

This is a dichotomous model: all class societies are characterized by the existence of two fundamental classes in an asymmetrical relationship. A minority of non-producers own the means of production and extract from the majority (the producers) the surplus product which is the source of their wealth and power. Classes are thus defined on the basis of the relations of individuals to the means of production in that type of society: patrician/slave in ancient society; lord/serf in feudal society; bourgeois/proletarian in capitalist society. It is a relation of exploitation because the minority owns the source of wealth in society and the majority is deprived of access to it. In capitalist society, the proletarian sells his labour to the capitalist, but the capitalist buys something more: labour power, which is the labour capacity of the worker for a defined period. This means that labour power combined with capital has a unique capacity: it creates new value. The capitalist is obliged, in order to survive and prosper, to get the worker to produce, in the labour time contracted, a greater value (in terms of commodities/services) than the exchange value of the labour contracted (the wage). This is the basis of the exploitative nature of the relationship which neither capitalist nor worker can avoid. Its significance is twofold: (1) the capitalist, through ownership of the means of production, retains control of the product and so the use of the surplus product (profit); (2) if the capitalist and proletarian contract in the market, this is only one face (visible) of their relationship, the other (invisible) being consummated in the creation of surplus value. For Marx, the latter is fundamental for the simple reason that the production and the use of surplus value determine the prosperity and the conditions of life in that society, until such time as the true producers of surplus value (the proletariat) are able to control directly its creation and distribution (through socialization, and *not* nationalization, of the means of production).

Already, it is clear that it is axiomatic in the abstract Marxian model that political domination is tied to economic domination. Ownership of the means of production ensures political control: the capacity to dispose of surplus value. The class division of society is a division of society which concerns power as much as property: exploiters and exploited, oppressors and oppressed, privileged and deprived. Class relations are conflictual and necessarily unstable: the dominant class seeks to secure its position and general social stability by means of a legitimating ideology that justifies its economic and social domination and explains to the subordinate class why it is subordinate and why it should accept its subordinate position. Class struggle, which the classes cannot avoid, except at the cost of their disappearance, provides the motor of history. Classes express for Marx the fundamental identity of a type of society. Thus a fundamental change in class relations provokes an inevitable change in social organization and so the type of society: ancient, feudal, capitalist, socialist.

The problematical elements of the Marxian model are numerous and derive in part from the application of the abstract model to concrete situations. How, for example, can one conciliate the dual-class model with the plurality of classes that Marx himself analysed in his historical writings on Britain, France and Germany? One way which both Marx and Engels adopted was to suggest that certain 'transitional classes' – like the peasantry in France or the aristocracy in Britain – were the class residues of an earlier social formation (feudal society in this case). They also recognized that the two principal social classes can be split into what they called 'class factions': for instance, financiers and industrialists among the bourgeoisie, stably employed and long-term unemployed among the proletariat. These arguments, however, do not really explain the rise of the new middle classes – or white-collar petty bourgeoisie – over the last 100 years. The more so since Marx predicted the inevitable deepening of class antagonism under capitalism and so the progressive disappearance of the middle class. This is not what has happened, which doubtless explains why the neo-Marxist Olin Wright (1985) speaks of 'the embarrassment of the middle classes' (p. 13).

Behind this failure of prediction lie, nevertheless, much more serious problems. The first is the veracity of Marx and Engels's assertion in *The Communist Manifesto* (1848) that all hitherto existing societies were class societies. Certainly, there are difficulties in considering feudal society a class society in so far as it was ordered as much by relations between 'estates' (social factor) as ownership of the means of production (economic factor). Moreover, if the Marxist analysis of feudal society is faulty it raises doubts – of which the rise of the middle classes is a symptom – about the accuracy of the Marxist definition of the nature of capitalist society. This leads on to the conclusion that class is not necessarily the basic division of advanced industrial society. It may be that other divisions – gender and race, for example – are just as, or even more, important.

If this reasoning is founded, then it undermines the credibility of the Marxist model as a tool of political analysis. Doubts about the class position of a significant class make it impossible to identify reliably – 'scientifically' in Engels's language – its class interest. Further, doubts about the importance of class as a fundamental social force mean that there may be no such thing as specific class interests. And inability to know class interests with certainty prevents the proper determination of 'correct' political action. This does not mean that Marxist class analysis is devoid of interest – Olin Wright's (1978; 1985) analyses of the middle classes on the basis of 'contradictory class locations' are undoubtedly of value – but it does mean that it cannot deliver its major promise: class as the key to politics (Hindess, 1987).

The Weberian model

This is a multidimensional model developed in opposition to the Marxian model and above all to counter what Weber believed was Marx's economic determinism. Thus, although Weber was prepared to accept the concept of class as a division of society based on economic conditions, he did not limit it to the ownership of the means of production; he considered that market power is just as important. This was because his concept of class is based on the notion of 'life chances' (*Lebensmöglichkeit*). People may share similar life chances because they own property (which can be made to earn a profit) or because they have skills and credentials or qualifications (that can command high salaries on the labour market – managerial and professional occupations). Hence, for Weber, there can be both positively and negatively privileged occupational or 'commercial' classes as well as 'property' classes.

However, Weber does not limit social stratification to the sole economic dimension (class), but considers that the social and political dimensions are just as important. Thus, prestige and esteem, just as their absence, can create what he calls status groups (*Stände*) based on 'lifestyles' (*Lebenstile*) that may be independent of class divisions. One thinks, for example, of the prestige of titles in many European (including republican) societies.[2] Moreover, once again status groups can be positively or negatively privileged; as regards the latter, one thinks of pariah groups of which the Jews were the exemplar for so long in Europe. Finally, Weber was sensitive to the autonomy of the political dimension which he believed could influence, through the agency of party and access to the state, stratification independently of class and status. Here again, there are groups that can be positively or negatively privileged politically, like, for instance, Mosca's 'political class' in the former case, and 'racial minorities' in the latter case. In this connection, we need to bear in mind that Weber, unlike Marx, considered class and status groups *a priori* to be social aggregates and *not* social forces. They can become social forces to the extent that they are organized politically, usually by a party. Whether they have become social forces is, for Weber, an open question for empirical investigation in each case.

On the basis of the summary exposition, it is clear that Weber's model permits a complex typology of classes, groups and strata which Marx's not only does not envisage, but positively denies. Indeed, the possible combinations of factors (property, skills, prestige, party; positive and negative in each case) are numerous. This means that the Weberian model is better equipped than its Marxist rival to analyse the nature of the middle classes. In addition, it helps to explain other social phenomena, like gender and race, in a way that Marxism cannot because it is able to show that people in identical class positions may, nevertheless, enjoy very different status positions (black and white factory workers; male and female lawyers) and so form the basis of what has been dubbed 'the fragmentary class structure' (Roberts, Cooke and Semeneoff, 1977). Finally, the Weberian model has been criticized, above all by Marxists, for its structural limitations and hence its dismissal of the fundamental nature of class antagonisms, but since it is essentially classificatory in intent – that is as guidelines to identify the various bases of collective action – it does not pretend to furnish the political conclusions that the Marxian model does. Hence, it is not open to the kind of attack on political grounds that the latter is and has been.

However, having vigorously criticized the centrality that Marxism traditionally accords to the concept of class, we do not wish to deny it all political relevance. After all, advanced industrial societies have a structural dynamic founded on the logic of capital (the need to accumulate to survive and prosper) and of labour to resist it (the need to defend jobs and wages). The logic of capital is thus part and parcel of the everyday life of a large mass of the population. In this situation, it is understandable that the political forces which organize capital, like those which organize labour, have historically played a decisive role in the European political struggles of the last 100 years. In fact, improvements in the general economic condition of the working class and the achievement of some fundamental citizen rights, culminating in the establishment of the Keynesian welfare state – which contributed to a significant change in the character of Western European societies – were the result, in large measure, of these, often hard-fought, political struggles. So, if class conflict between capital and labour, bourgeoisie and proletariat, does not have *a priori* that centrality that Marxists have always accorded it – other conflicts, religious and national, sexual and ethnic (to which we turn below), also count – it still plays a role, if only because major political forces (parties, employers' associations, trade unions) are still largely organized on the basis of that conflict.

To conclude: Marxists and Weberians identify two basic classes in advanced industrial societies – a small, propertied upper class and a large propertyless working class – with an intermediate grouping, the middle classes, of differing social origins and locations. As hinted, much of the polemic in this area regards the criteria for identifying the nature of this intermediate grouping: exploitation, domination, occupation, credentials, lifestyle, individual social mobility? Argument in this area is likely to continue as it has done intermittently for decades because definitive agreement is as improbable today as ever, granted the different theoretical perspectives of the protagonists.

Gender

It has recently been argued that industrial societies are as much 'gender structured' as 'class structured'. It is certainly true that inequalities of gender – that is the subordination of women in terms of wealth, power and prestige – are more deep-rooted historically than class systems. Indeed, as feminists have not been slow to point out, there are few if any known examples of societies in which women are more powerful than men. This observation poses two questions. (1) Why should patriarchy – or male dominance – be so universal? (2) Are patriarchy, and gender relations generally, an autonomous dimension of the social structure, or simply class dependent?

In answer to the first question, the key appears to be 'mothering'. Women give birth to children and nurture them. This initial physical necessity leads readily into a prolonged 'caring' role which women have adopted in all societies. This mothering role forces women to become absorbed in 'domestic' activities and hence they normally inhabit the 'private' domain of civil society. Indeed, Carole Pateman (1988) has drawn attention to the dual nature of civil society and its consequences for women. It is divided into two opposing spheres, the public realm and the private domain, each with its distinctive and contrasting mode of association. Patriarchy is consigned to the private domain and hence appears to have no relevance for the public realm. But, as she argues, this is grossly misleading: patriarchal right extends throughout civil society since the two spheres are at once separate and inseparable. Yet, by focusing attention on the public realm alone, women, who are in no way inferior to men, either physically or intellectually, find themselves obliged to suffer male domination in 'official' silence ('It's a man's life'). In Simone de Beauvoir's (1949) insight, fundamental to the feminist concept of gender: 'one is not born, but rather becomes, a woman' (p. 301).

Before the development of birth control, women were at the mercy of their biological condition. Frequent pregnancies and continuous children-rearing made them dependent on men for their material provision. The suggestion is that as a result of modern contraceptive techniques women have gained some measure of control over their bodies and lives, and have started to revolt against their subordinate condition to the extent that feminism has become a major influence throughout the world: for instance, demands for easier divorce, free contraception, abortion on demand, equal pay for equal work, equal opportunities and education, free child care.

The second question is more complex: the tacit assumption until recently was that class inequalities explained gender stratification. The reason for this was that it was felt that only if gender disadvantages overwhelmed class differences would it make sense to consider gender as a dimension of the social structure in its own right. Indeed, Goldthorpe (1980) believed that women had limited relevance to the class structure, arguing that the class position of women is simply that of their husbands or fathers. This widely held view has recently come under critical attack. Firstly, it has been argued that a large number of women are now in paid employment in European societies and so it is patently absurd to treat men and women differently for the purposes of class analysis. The more so since, for a substantial number of households, the woman's income is vital to the family's economic position and lifestyle. Moreover, women's work can have significant consequences for voting and other behaviour of family members that cannot be accounted for simply by referring to the husband's class position.

Finally, there are families where the wife's occupation may set the standard of the family's situation. One thinks, for example, of the case where a semi-skilled worker is married to a school teacher, as occurred with D.H. Lawrence's parents and artistically depicted in his novel *Sons and Lovers* (1913). In these circumstances, why should the male work situation be given precedence over the domestic domain in defining class structure? Gender may, therefore, be an important factor in social stratification. Moreover, the proportion of one-parent families, in which the woman is the sole breadwinner, is growing, and in this situation she, and *not* her father, former husband or companion, is the determinant of her own class position. The conclusion must be that the class position of a woman can no longer simply be, as it once was, assimilated to that of her husband or father. The result of women becoming more central to the class system, it has been claimed, is nothing less than to introduce a more fluid form of stratification and hasten the general process of class decomposition, noted by many observers.

At all events, recent research suggests that the labour market is indeed segregated by gender, and further that gender divisions are just as significant within occupational groups as between them (table 2.1). In pre-industrial European society, every member of the family worked and women were not confined to a domestic role, even if married. This was possible because productive work was carried on in the home – cottage industry – and there was no distinction between domestic and productive labour. The separation of home from work, consequent upon the setting up of factory production, made it increasingly difficult to combine the two activities. Contemporaneously, and not coincidentally, the notion of the woman's 'rightful' place in the home was voiced.[3] Economic independence for married women, so it was claimed, would undermine the institutions of marriage and the family, lead to child neglect and even impair the birth of healthy children! The result was the exclusion of

Table 2.1 Proportion of men and women in selected occupations in Britain, 1981 (per cent)

	Men	Women
Professions		
Judges, barristers, advocates, solicitors	85	15
Administrators, national government	80	20
Administrators, local government	67	33
Medical practitioners	76	24
Economists, statisticians, system analysts, programmers	80	20
Accountants, valuers, finance specialists	90	10
Scientists, engineers, technologists	88	12
Marketing, sales, public relations etc.	84	16
Teachers in higher education	74	26
School teachers	37	63
Nurses and nursing administrators	8	92
Non-professional occupations		
Clerks	30	70
Shop sales staff and assistants	16	84
Secretaries, typists, receptionists	12	88
Domestic staff and school helpers	2	98
Cleaners, window cleaners, chimney and road sweepers	18	82
Total in employment (millions)	13.77	9.15
	(60)	(40)

Source: calculated from 1981 Census data, quoted in Garrett, 1987, p. 101

women from certain fields of activity – navvying, construction, transport, mining as well as certain skilled work such as spinning in the cotton industry – and a sexual division of labour in the labour market similar to that in the family. In addition, women were excluded from the professions, civil service and scientific trades. Indeed, in the mid nineteenth century, women were to be found in four main fields: domestic labour, child care and training, distribution and retail trades, and certain specific areas of manufacture (textiles). Today, they are found in the semi-professions – teaching, nursing and social work – and certain manual occupations in service industries and in food, textiles and footwear production (Garrett, 1987).

The position of women in the labour market has remained remarkably stable over the years, despite – or perhaps because of – the increase of married women in the labour force in the last 40 years, and fully justifies Ann Oakley's (1972) observation that 'in all industrialized societies there is a marked differentiation by gender of most, if not all, occupations.' Men are not only more likely than women to be employed, but also 'command the majority of jobs carrying high prestige, high skill and high income' (pp. 152–3). The white-collar occupations provide a perfect illustration: the expansion in numbers and the feminization of the workforce have led to a marked decline in the conditions and status of clerks. In the nineteenth century, they were highly esteemed and relatively well-paid men who often carried out many management tasks; today not only have the status, wages and responsibilities of this work declined dramatically, but so also has the proportion of men. Crompton and Jones's (1984) study of clerical work shows that the higher the position, the greater the number of men holding it. The authors contend that the possibilities of promotion are monopolized by men. Hence, the clerical occupations are fractured along gender lines. Women are concentrated in the lower grades; and this is because the white-collar career structure was constructed in such a way that women cannot hope to meet the criteria of merit which male-dominated managements lay down. Breaks for child-birth and domestic commitments as well as difficulties in moving around for career purposes all mean that women are defined, when it comes to promotion, as less experienced, less responsible and above all less committed – they are prone to take days off work for illness – than their male colleagues. The conclusion is that significant areas of the class system, like the lower middle class, are gender based.

Race

Race is a relatively modern concept, even if the conflicts to which it gives rise are not. Prejudice and ethnic hostility have a long history. Thus, although racial and ethnic relations are often treated in parallel, it is customary to distinguish between them: race in principle refers to biological characteristics, such as skin colour, body hair and certain physical features; ethnicity, in contrast, refers to cultural characteristics of various kinds. While there is no scientific basis to the widespread notion that there are different racial types based on genetic differences – indeed, the genetic diversity within populations that share certain visible physical features is as great as that between groups – nonetheless the visible physical (phenotypical) differences are believed to be biologically, and hence socially, significant. For instance, there are stereotypes that attribute inherited behavioural and personality characteristics to individuals of a particular physical appearance. The difference, then, between race and ethnicity is that while ethnic groups can hope to be assimilated into the mainstream of the host society because their difference is cultural (that is to say more changeable), racial groups are unlikely to be because their difference is phenotypical (that is less changeable). Indeed, John Rex (1986) notes that in Britain, 'in a strange popular usage black and Asian people were regarded as "immigrants" whereas actual immigrants from Europe, Ireland and the white Commonwealth were not' (p. 18). Perhaps this was because most black–white encounters in the modern world have been conflictual, resulting from the colonial experience in which exploitation and ethnocentric attitudes ('white man's burden') were dominant among the European colonists. Certainly, racist views of the superiority of whites over blacks became a central trait of European culture, as evidenced by Gobineau and the Nazis.

However, the persistence of racial and ethnic conflict in advanced industrial societies goes against the thrust of both liberal modernization theory and Marxism. Both postulate the displacement of 'primordial' loyalties such as race and ethnicity by more universal modern identities such as class and citizenship. The idea was that the extension of the market would erode racial and ethnic identities because they have no direct relevance to market transactions and so would lose their social meaning. This has clearly not happened. Indeed, the increasing complexity of society, far from undermining the particularism of racial and ethnic identity and solidarity, has acted to reinforce it. This is because it furnishes an easier criterion for recognizing friends from enemies than is the case with the more universal, but less obvious, criteria of class, occupation or even party. Such tendencies have been further strengthened by the fact that the benefits and costs of modernization have not been equitably distributed across society. Hence, racial and ethnic solidarity is a better bet for the individual of a minority population than subordinate assimilation into the mainstream.

Race and ethnicity as components in the structuration of society refer, according to Rex, to situations in which minority groups find themselves confronted by the following elements: (1) severe conflict, discrimination, exploitation or oppression; (2) clearly distinguished categories of people who cannot move at will from one category to the other; (3) a system of subordination justified by some sort of deterministic theory, usually a biological or genetic one. He indicates that there are two major theories of ethnicity: the 'primordial' and the 'situational'. According to the former, racial and ethnical ties cannot become too involved with, or dependent upon, the class system; they simply cut across it. Moreover, it is suggested that if the group's evaluation of its position is based on race or ethnicity, it will not be altered by external pressures, which will be judged negatively. Race and ethnicity, it is claimed, have their own dynamic independent of other elements in the political process. However, there is no reason why racial and ethnic groups should not exist for primordial reasons *and* also form part of the class system. According to the latter, the appeal of race and ethnicity can be a vehicle of general class mobilization, but it also has a more contingent function, that is to say primarily as a resource – 'black consciousness', 'black pride' – that can be activated to attain political goals or left latent as the situation dictates. Of course, the opposite is also true, namely that racial and ethnic appeal is not only a resource but also a 'stigma'[4] – 'wogs', *bicots*, – that other groups can, and have not hesitated to, use for denying rights and privileges.

The problem that these theories pose is the racial and ethnic populations' relationship to the structure of society as a whole: is there one social world or several? Lloyd Warner (1936) suggested long ago that white America and black America both had their own separate class systems, and defined the relations between black and white as one of caste. Moreover, the increase in the black upper class did not breach the caste barrier, it merely tilted it so that the status of the black upper class was more akin to, though separate from, the white middle class. This view was contested by the Marxist O.C. Cox (1970), who suggests that the relations between black and white are those of exploited and exploiter and hence of class. He claims that what is going on within black and white groups is status striving, whereas the relations between the two races are those of economic class. As Rex has noted, there is no reason why the relations within the black and white communities should not also be of economic class conflict; and, if they are, what are the relations between the black and the white working classes? The latter observation lends credence to Lloyd Warner's notion of a caste-like racial barrier. The implication is that there are several social worlds in a multiracial, multicultural society and that the struggle between classes in it is also part of a struggle between castes, namely that it is political as much as economic, legal as much as social.

As already noted, foreign immigration is a recent phenomenon in Western Europe; before 1945 most nations were more or less racially and ethnically homogeneous. This is now no longer the case (table 2.2) and so, in the light of the American discussion, the question is whether racial and ethnic minorities in European countries are incorporated in a single class system or whether they live in different social worlds. The latter implies a dual labour market in which two kinds of workers (black and white) are not in competition with each other at all. This extreme situation rarely exists; what is much more likely is that there are types of low-paid, dirty and insecure jobs which are unattractive to natives, whose educational system has led them to aspire to white-collar and skilled employment, and therefore open to any comer. It is here that the racial and ethnic minorities are likely to be concentrated. The colour bar does not necessarily operate at the lowest level, but it is a different matter when it comes to promotion to skilled and supervisory work, or in other fields like social security, welfare and housing. On the basis of research in Britain, Rex claims that there is 'no total and complete separation of immigrant minorities on a class basis'. Moreover, he notes that:

> Some do obtain desirable jobs, stay out of unemployment, get good suburban housing and good education for their children, as well as enjoying the protection of the police. But statistically speaking the chances of a family not enjoying these rights are overwhelmingly greater for immigrant minorities than they are for the host community. It is this majority who form the immigrant underclass (1986, p. 73).

Table 2.2 EC and non-EC immigrants, late 1980s (thousands)

Country	EC immigrants	Non-EC immigrants	Total
Britain	765	1110	1875
France	1578	2100	3678
Germany	1276	3213	4489
Italy	90	205	295

Source: EC

Finally, he points to an important difference between most European immigrant situations and Britain which is worth mentioning. Many of the immigrants in France and Germany are from Southern European countries, whose culture has much in common with the host countries. But Turks in Germany and Arabs in France share many of the problems of the Asians and West Indians in Britain. He suggests that the situation of Southern Europeans in France and Germany is one of immigration only (like the migration of southerners to north Italy: see chapter 1), while that of the Turks, Arabs, Asians and West Indians is one of immigration *and* race relations. Immigrant communities may expect their descendants to be absorbed into the host society and culture in three and four generations. The prospects for the more geographically and culturally distant immigrants, and especially those who are racially distinguishable, are less hopeful. They are likely to remain distinct for a much longer period and even become a culturally disorganized and deprived underclass of a more permanent kind.

The European social structure

In view of the foregoing discussion and bearing in mind the economic and demographic realities, it is reasonable to consider the West European class system as a regional dimension of a continental structure rather than a series of different national structures. Such a proposition is intended to suggest that industrial France (or Italy) is today more like industrial Germany (or Britain) than rural France (or Italy), and vice versa. Perhaps Britain – an island – constitutes an exception, if only because the British peasantry were expelled from history at the beginning of the nineteenth century. At all events, Naville (1971) was surely right when he observed that 'the situation prevailing in France is merely one aspect of the development of classes in Western industrial Europe' (p. 223). The conclusion is that national class structures are losing their peculiarities and an alternative classification founded on transnational regional bases would be more appropriate. Unfortunately, adequate empirical research does not exist to allow this to be done. Indeed, data are available only on a national basis (table 2.3), and are very fragile and

Table 2.3 Class structure (per cent)

	Britain		France		Germany	Italy	
	1966	1982	1968	1982	1975	1971	1983
Ruling class (bourgeoisie)	6	5	3	4	5	3	3
Middle class, of which:	44	53	52	55	45	49	54
Salaried middle classes	35	45	27	39	27	17	26
Independent petty bourgeoisie	6	6	22	14	15	29	24
Special categories[a]	3	2	3	2	3	3	4
Working class, of which:	50	42	45	41	50	48	43
Stable workers	34	29	28	23	35	26	26
Precarious workers	16	13	17	18	15	23	17
Underclass	nd	nd	nd	nd	nd	nd	nd
Active population	46	42	41	40	42	36	37

nd: no data.
[a]Includes clergy and military.
Sources: Sylos-Labini, 1975, p. 164 and 1986, p. 227 for France, Great Britain and Italy; Claessens, Klonne and Tschoepe, 1978, p. 300 for FRG.

not necessarily homogenous, so must be considered only as an indication of general trends.

Middle class societies

If the class system in Western Europe is posited as structurally polarized between a relatively small upper class (bourgeoisie) and a vast working class (proletariat), this is not borne out by the data. The two major classes representing capital and labour have always been separated by significant intermediary strata (middle classes). Indeed, one of the areas of major contention, discussed above, concerned the growth of the middle classes and the emergence of what have been called 'middle class societies'. As noted, this development is politically very significant because it has been argued that a substantial middle class is a necessary basis for a stable parliamentary democracy. It is certainly true, as far as the historical data exist (Sylos-Labini, 1975), that all Western European societies governed by parliamentary regimes based on universal suffrage have been characterized by the existence of a substantial middle class (never less than 45 per cent and generally around 50 per cent). Thus the socialist premise that the proletariat was the vast majority of the population seems to have been false, undermining the Second International's strategy of organizing the workers so that with the introduction of universal suffrage in the various countries the socialist parties would win power on the basis of absolute majorities.

More interesting than discussing the global figures as such are the general trends they underwrite. The first is the increase in numbers of the upper class that represents a change in its composition and partially in its nature: the replacement of individual entrepreneurs and bankers by corporate groups of so-called 'technocrats' – directors and executive managers – with large-scale shareholdings. The second is the contraction, both absolutely and relatively, of the mass, male, industrial working class and the consequent decline of the traditional labour movement in its organizational forms (trade unions and party) (chapters 5 and 6) that it portends. The third is the aforementioned growth of the middle classes, though this was the product of a double movement, the relative decline of the traditional middle class (small-owning peasantry and artisans) and the rapid expansion of the new middle class (private sector industrial and public service white-collar workers; new professionals). This was one of the effects of the development of administration in both private companies and the welfare state, anticipated by Weber. Finally, there are consequences for the social structure of the rapid and sustained growth in the post-war period. This has meant above all two things: (1) full employment (at least until the 1970s) and a higher and more generalized level of affluence and standards of living for most people, thanks to productivity gains and the two-income family; and (2) an influx of foreign workers to undertake the 'dirty', precarious and poorly paid jobs that the native populations shunned, resulting in the persistence of areas of poverty among immigrant workers and other marginal groups (old, infirm and disabled).

Despite the generalized diffusion of wealth, it would appear that the relative positions in the income hierarchy (table 2.4) have not changed all that much. Indeed, the evidence of the concentration of wealth in Western Europe suggests that it has remained largely unchanged since the beginning of the century. In Britain, it is summarized in the figures '7/84',[5] namely that 7 per cent of the population own 84 per cent of the wealth. Figures for income are similar, though not quite so striking: in 1985 the top 5 per cent of earners received 16 per cent of total income; and the top 20 per cent got 42 per cent of the total, which is less disparate than before the war. Aron (1968) believed that the really important thing, politically and socially, is the general rise in well-being – the 'affluent society' syndrome – arguing that 'even if relative inequality has not been changed appreciably, the general increase in wealth has narrowed the gap between different modes of living. If the basic needs are provided in an approximately similar way, what real difference is made by great fortunes or huge incomes?' (p. 11). It was part of his general contention that the class struggle in industrial societies was gradually giving way to a 'semi-peaceful competition' between social groupings (*catégories sociales*), a necessary basis for stable 'democratic' politics.

This argument sounds less convincing, however, when it is realized that great fortunes still procure disproportionate political power, as the recent careers of Bernard Tapie in France and Silvio Berlusconi in Italy testify. It can be argued, moreover, that the maintenance of great inequalities in the distribution of wealth and income (which appear to have increased in the 1980s) is in itself a token of the success of the capitalist class in conserving its dominant economic position. One reason for this success, recently defended by Galbraith (1992), is the contention that the price of prevention of any aggression against one's own income is tolerance of the greater amount for others. Advocacy of redistribution of income of the very rich by tax opens the way for taxes for the comfortable, but less wealthy, middle classes; and taxes are the last thing that the middle classes want. As he writes: 'The plush advantage of the very rich is the price the contented electoral majority pays for being able to retain what is less but what is still very good' (p. 26).

With regard to social mobility, data on movement from one class to another of single individuals (intergenerational) or between father and son (intragenerational) are somewhat contradictory. Heath (1981, chapter 7) argues that the mobility rate is less in the 'old' conservative societies of Western Europe than in either Eastern European 'socialist' societies or North America. He claims, moreover, that the range of social mobility is limited, that it is usually over a short distance between closely

Table 2.4 Salary differentials of certain occupational groups, 1986 (sterling: parentheses show ratios to unskilled worker)

	Britain		France		Germany		Italy	
Managing director	23,900	(3.6)	43,800	(7.3)	38,600	(4.5)	28,000	(4.5)
Middle management	12,440	(1.9)	27,800	(4.6)	21,030	(2.5)	18,200	(3.0)
Skilled worker	10,750	(1.6)	10,200	(1.7)	13,800	(1.6)	10,140	(1.7)
Unskilled worker	6,650	(1.0)	5,900	(1.0)	8,440	(1.0)	6,140	(1.0)

Source: P-E Inbucon Management Consultants, London, quoted in Ardagh, 1988a, p.147

located strata, as, for instance, between worker father and teacher son. Finally, lower class access to the middle classes is naturally much more frequent than to the ruling class; in other words, there are many more children from working class homes who get white-collar jobs than who get big company directorships. Hence he concludes that social inequality in class life chances appears to have remained pretty stable in Western Europe during this century. However, this conclusion is disputed by Saunders (1990), at least as far as Britain is concerned. He believes that the fact that 7 per cent of the sons of working class fathers are now in the upper class is evidence of a relatively open class system. He argues that there are many more opportunities for working class people in Britain today than there were before the war because of economic expansion, which suggests that opportunities should have been greater in continental countries granted their records of economic growth.[6] Finally, while he is prepared to admit that working class children start life at a disadvantage, he claims that substantial numbers manage to overcome the obstacles and achieve significant upward mobility, but feels it necessary to add the rider that in the 1990s the penalty for failure may be higher than in the past in view of the high rates of working class unemployment.

Upper class

Turning now to the individual classes, it has already been noted that the upper class (capitalist class or bourgeoisie) has not lost its supremacy as regards both property and income, even if there are clear status differences between 'old' and 'new' money. Dahrendorf (1964) among others has suggested that education has replaced property as the key resource in post-war Western Europe. Even if this is so, then it can be shown that the upper class has adapted well to the technocratic era, ensuring that its offspring acquire the requisite education to succeed to paternal posts, both in business and in the state: civil service, army, university. University entry was greatly enlarged in the 1970s, but the proportion of workers' sons remained very low. Thus higher education remains the preserve of the middle classes; but, alongside the growth in general university places, special schools and postgraduate programmes like the top Parisian *lycées* and *grandes écoles* in France, public schools and Oxbridge in Britain, *Technischen Universitäten* and *Hochschulen* in Germany and the Università Commerciale Bocconi in Italy have maintained or increased their prestige.

In this way, the upper class perpetuates itself by passing on wealth, educational privileges – Bourdieu's (1971) 'cultural capital' – and occupational opportunities which ensure the continuing concentration of property ownership (through intermarriage and interlocking directorates), social prestige and power in few hands. It is suggested that only a small segment, a core of perhaps a few thousand top bankers, managers and directors of companies, takes the key economic and administrative decisions that directly determine the use of capital and direction of the political system, thanks to family ties and interlocking social networks.[7] Of course, there is some circulation of individuals and families between the upper and other classes,[8] but it does not appear to have increased as much in the last 100 years – except perhaps in Germany where the break caused by Nazism and World War II needs to be taken into account – as the so-called 'technicians' revolution' would have led one to suppose. One reason is that top managers are usually substantial shareholders. The upper class remains in all Western European countries relatively closed with notable generational continuity.[9]

Middle classes

The situation of the middle classes is different: they have known the greatest expansion in the post-war period. As already noted, this growth has been neither simple nor linear. In fact, it has masked a double movement: on the one side, the decline of the old independent petty bourgeoisie, in particular the small peasant farmers; on the other, the rise of the new salaried middle classes of executives, managers and professions, especially in the service sector, both public and private. Moreover, there has been further differentiation inside this double movement. Thus, for example, if the independent petty bourgeoisie has been declining, thanks to the rural exodus and the high turnover in small businesses, it is not disappearing as Marx predicted. In effect, in certain areas – and specifically those where the 'competitive' sector is dominant, like north-east and central Italy – this stratum has converted itself from rural petty bourgeoisie (peasant farmer of small farm) to industrial petty bourgeoisie (businessman of small family firm). In addition, the number of small shopkeepers and hoteliers has shrunk because they have been unable to compete effectively with large supermarket and hotel-restaurant chains, but not as much as many predicted. For many, the idea of 'working for yourself' continues to be attractive; hence there is a continual replenishment despite the insecurity. It is generally believed that small businessmen have a distinct political outlook, often supporting right-wing extremism, like Poujadism in France in the 1950s and the Lega in Italy in the 1990s.

The rise of the new middle class or 'service class' has been not only spectacular but characterized by numerous divisions. A first distinction is made between the upper middle class, composed of those holding managerial and professional positions, and the lower middle class, which broadly coincides with the clerical occupations (the original 'white-collars'), but includes sales representatives, teachers, nurses and others.

Most of the former have had some form of higher education – indeed, they are distinguished by their training and professional qualifications – and hence enjoy relatively secure careers, privileged work situations and high earnings (table 2.4); whereas many of the latter have only a compulsory education and summary training (they are engaged in routinized jobs with low-level technical skills, and in supervision as foremen), reasonable job security and work situation, but lowish earnings (often lower than manual workers). As noted above, clerical work has been increasingly feminized (today over 70 per cent of clerks are women concentrated in the lower grades) with significant effects on the stratification of this class.

A second distinction inside both the upper and the lower middle classes is made between the public and private sectors; it was above all in the public sector that the spectacular increase in the new middle classes occurred since the private sector usually stagnated. The growth in the welfare state meant an increase in educational, health and social welfare programmes in the 1960s and 1970s. In addition, this was often followed by reorganizations of the public services, which were occasions for creating jobs for teachers, social service professionals and technicians, and administrators. Public sector professionals thus had an interest in the maintenance and growth of public expenditure and this, not surprisingly, influenced their voting behaviour. They tended to vote for left (labour and social democrat) and Christian democrat parties in recognition of their greater commitment to state services. The rise in public sector union membership, whilst blue-collar unionism has been declining, is a clear token of this orientation, although the increasing number of women in these occupations has been seen as complicating the possibilities of consciousness and action. On the other hand, the private sector middle classes (to which the new professions like public relations (PR) and financial consultants, the so-called 'yuppies', should be added) continue to support overwhelmingly the centre and conservative parties as they have always done. Finally, those in the lower middle classes – the most heterogeneous stratum of all – often adopt reactionary social and political attitudes to differentiate themselves from the manual workers. 'Fragmentation and ubiquity', then, are the characteristics of the middle classes. Their members, according to Sylos-Labini (1975, p. 53), 'are the universal administrators; they condition basic choices – in many cases almost being able to exercise a kind of veto power – but they do not make them.' They make up the ranks of Galbraith's 'contented majority'.

Working class

Finally, post-war developments have changed the position of the working class, significantly. Technical progress has not only reduced the traditional mass male industrial proletariat but also transformed radically the relation of the worker to his work. Mechanization, according to Gorz (1980), has caused deskilling and fragmentation. It is no longer the worker who runs the machine, but the machine which runs the worker. The consequences are twofold. Firstly, work loses its interest for the worker (it becomes external to him) and he goes to work only to be paid. Working class demands are now those of mass consumer society. Secondly, the working class is divided into a number of categories like the middle classes. One such division is in skill levels: the upper or skilled working class – Lenin's 'aristocracy of labour', today's 'affluent worker' – consisting of fitters, bus drivers, printers and trained coalface workers, whose members have incomes (table 2.4), conditions of work and job security superior to those of their fellow workers; and the lower or semi-skilled and unskilled workers, made up of machinists, bus conductors, storekeepers, labourers, refuse collectors and cleaners, with lower incomes (table 2.4), inferior job security and little or no training. A second division concerns the economic sector in which the worker is employed: the 'monopoly' and 'state' sectors are considered 'core', while the 'competitive' sector is 'peripheral' – not to mention the 'informal' or 'black economy' sector which is 'marginal'. Not surprisingly, the upper working class (white and male) is found in the core sectors where unionization is high; and the lower working class in the competitive sector where not only is unionization low, but part-time work and unemployment are rife, and poverty is widespread. Finally, the passing of the mass proletarian model and the contemporary break-up of traditional, established working class communities spell the end of common experiences that gave rise in the past to collective forms of social organization and political action.

Underclass?

A third division (or rather demarcation) concerns race, the separation between the ethnic majority and the racial minorities. The question is: are the latter part of the lower working class or do they form a separate underclass, that is to say a separate social world? Saunders (1990) claims that an underclass has four key features: it suffers multiple deprivation; it is socially marginal; it is dependent on state welfare provision; and its culture is one of resigned fatalism ('dependency'). It is clear that racial minorities (West Indians and Asians in Britain, Algerians in France and Turks in Germany[10]) are disproportionately represented in such a definition. However, they are not alone; other marginal groups, like the infirm and the disabled as well as unmarried mothers, are also a part. So they do not form a separate world in the American sense: the poor have always been a permanent feature of competitive capitalism, even if their numbers have been rising in the 1980s and 1990s recessions. Finally, there is a suggestion that the situation might well get worse and englobe a significant part of the native population: Gorz (1980) has argued that a society of permanent mass unemployment is being created before our eyes in Europe as a result of the introduction of automation: in other words, a society made up of a growing underclass allied to a proletariat of precariously employed workers to do the 'dirty' jobs. The classical factory-based, mass male proletariat, as we have known it, is being consigned to history. The only alternative, in his view, is a big reduction in hours of work and a radical change in the means and ends of production.

Conclusion

Civil society is a key area of our analysis of West European politics because it is the place where individual men and women live out their daily lives. We argue that it is a distinct domain made up of an ensemble of largely autonomous institutions – households, markets, churches, parties, groups, associations, media – that mediate the relations of the individual with the state. It is, however, also a complex of social practices which are neither unified, nor homogeneous, but structurated. Of course, this structuration has a historical dimension but, at the same time, it is not static. Indeed, it can be, and is, modified by political conflicts which can, and do, change the meanings of social practices, although this is a process that usually requires time.

This chapter is devoted to discussing three of the factors that determine the structuration of civil society in advanced industrial societies: class, gender and race. The discussion started with the two major traditions of class analysis – the Marxist and the Weberian – which still dominate the contemporary debate. The Marxian model is dichotomous: all class societies are characterized by two fundamental, asymmetrically related, classes determined by their relationship to the means of production. This means that the relation is antagonistic and, indeed, it is class conflict over the control of resources that furnishes the motor of history. Classes for Marx express the basic identity of a type of society, and a fundamental change in class relations provokes an inevitable change in social organization and so type of society. The problematic elements of the Marxian model derive from its application to concrete situations: how to conciliate the dual-class model with the plurality of classes, and above all the rise of the new middle classes, existing in advanced industrial society. It fails to do this satisfactorily, which sorely undermines its credibility as a tool of political analysis.

The Weberian model is multidimensional: class is one (economic: market power as well as property) of a number of structural cleavages – others are status and political power – based on life chances. This means that it takes account of consumption patterns as well as production factors and so can explain the structural complexity of advanced industrial societies: phenomena like gender and race as well as the intermediary classes. It is a classificatory model intended to identify the bases for collective action and so is not open to attack on political grounds as is the Marxian model. Most class analyses of industrial societies identify two basic classes – a small propertied upper class and a large propertyless manual working class – and a growing intermediate grouping of middle classes with differing origins and locations.

Gender inequality is older than class inequality and is founded on a patriarchy that appears to be almost universal. The reason seems to lie in the mothering role of women underwritten by their biological condition in the pre-contraceptive age. The introduction of safe contraceptive methods in the last 30 years has given women a measure of control over their bodies and lives that has led them to question their systematic subordination (feminism). Until recently, moreover, women were considered to be irrelevant to the class structure because it was assumed that their position was that of their fathers or husbands. The rapid rise of women in paid employment has undermined this view, leading to a further complication (and fragmentation) of the social structure. However, despite this, the labour market remains segregated by gender with the result that women find themselves, when not excluded, in the lower-paid, and often more precarious, occupations.

Race introduces elements of inequality and discrimination additional to those of gender. While it has no scientific basis, the notion of racial behavioural and personality characteristics has remained both common and strong in Western Europe. This is certainly due to the colonial experience where most black–white encounters were antagonistic, and which gave rise to a definite racial ideology (Gobineau). In addition, the persistence of racial conflict in advanced industrial society contradicted both liberal modernization and Marxist theories that postulated its displacement by more universal identities such as class and citizenship. It is now argued that this did not happen because race and ethnicity furnish an easier – visual – criterion of identity than the more universal and abstract ones of class and citizenship. Finally, it appears as an independent dimension of the class system in so far as whatever the class position of a black person, his status is consistently lower than a white in the same class position: for instance, black and white workers. The proof is the existence of a more or less dual labour market in which the two kinds of workers are not really in competition. The result is that, like women, racial minorities are concentrated in the lowest grades and among the unemployed underclass.

A summary analysis of the class system in the major West European countries suggests that it is best conceived as a regional dimension of a continental structure, that of advanced industrial society. Moreover, the data reveal the statistical strength of the intermediary classes and so confirm the emergence of middle class societies. Furthermore, while the diffusion of affluence has been widespread, above all in the boom years, inequalities of wealth (if not of income) have remained largely intact. The discussion also pointed to the fragmentation and divisions of both the middle and working classes. The passing of the mass male industrial proletariat raises the question not only of the existence of a new under-class, but also of mass employment as a more permanent feature of West European society. Finally, as for the political relevance of the class system, we can subscribe to Sarre's (1989) general argument that unless we believe that 'economic class is an unimportant basis for politics, it seems arguable that economic class creates a variety of class positions which then interact with contingent factors in generating a system of self-conscious political parties' (p. 122).

Further reading

M.S. Archer and S. Giner (eds) (1971), *Contemporary Europe: Class, Status and Power* (London: Weidenfeld & Nicolson).

M.S. Archer and S. Giner (eds) (1978), *Contemporary Europe: Social Structures and Cultural Patterns* (London: Routledge & Kegan Paul).

S. Ardittis (ed.) (1994), *The Politics of East–West Migration* (Basingstoke: Macmillan).

J. Bailey (1992) (ed.), *Social Europe* (London: Longman).

S. Castles (1984), *Here for Good: Western Europe's New Ethnic Minorities* (London: Pluto Press).

S. Collinson (1993), *Europe and International Migration* (London: Pinter/RIIA).

R. Crompton (1993), *Class and Social Stratification: An Introduction to Current Debates* (Cambridge: Polity).

S. Garrett (1987), *Gender* (London: Tavistock).

B. Hindess (1987), *Politics and Class Analysis* (Oxford: Blackwell).

R. King and J. Raynor (1981), *The Middle Class* (London: Longman).

J. Lovenduski (1986), *Women and European Politics: Contemporary Feminism and Public Policy* (London: Wheatsheaf).

J. Rex (1986), *Race and Ethnicity* (Milton Keynes: Open UP).

P. Saunders (1990), *Social Class and Stratification* (London: Routledge).

S. Walby (1988), *Gender Segregation at Work* (Milton Keynes: Open UP).

E.O. Wright (1985), *Classes* (London: Verso).

3 The Forming of Civil Society

Introduction

Mention has already been made of the importance of civil society for the analysis of industrial societies as the site where men and women are constituted as social subjects. It has also been pointed out that social relations are neither unified nor homogeneous, but asymmetrically structurated. Elements of this structuration of civil society – class, gender, race – were discussed in the last chapter, but it was also recognized that they were not the only elements of structuration. Structuration, moreover, is not static, but subject to change over time. Indeed, its historical dimension was noted: this means that (1) some elements of structuration pre-existed, as it were, both industrialization and constitutional democracy; and (2) other elements change over time as a result of political struggles. In consequence, structuration not only conditions political conflicts, but is also the object of them. As Marx (1852) observed in a celebrated passage: 'men make their own history, but they do not make it as they please; they do not make it in circumstances chosen by themselves, but under circumstances directly encountered and transmitted from the past. The tradition of all the dead generations weighs like a nightmare on the brain of the living' (p. 247).

In other words, it is in the course of political conflict that ideologies and ways of life are grounded in practice and spread, becoming common sense and political traditions (Allum, 1991). Moreover, conflict occurs not in a vacuum, but in a specific historical context which gives it a meaning. Lastly, the groups which engage in conflict have access to different levels of resources, a factor which is responsible for further differences in strategy and opportunity. All of which helps to explain the diversity of structuration from one country to the next. It is not surprising, therefore, that the history of such conflict and its outcome is extremely complex, and often has no apparent logic at all.

This lack of logic is further fortified by the fact that political action often gives rise to unintended consequences, that is to consequences different from those proposed and pursued. To give a specific example: the extension of citizen rights – for many in Europe the most salient political fact of the present era – has not been a triumphal forward march from the French Revolution to the present day; it has, in fact, been a hard and often ambivalent journey, punctuated by about-turns – fascism is an obvious example – and large areas of uncertainty, for instance as regards social rights. All of which further highlights the complexity and ambiguity of European political development, which embraces a multiplicity of factors: from the religious to the national, from the demographic to the geopolitical, from the military to the institutional (table 3.1). It is because of this variety of factors that a study of one alone is incapable of demonstrating the importance of meanings in politics.

If history has no inherent logic, as surely it does not, this does not mean that attempts have not been made to provide a conceptual understanding of a phenomenon – European political development – which has been defined as 'unique'. It is unique in the sense that it has resulted, since World War II, in a type of regime that has made possible levels of personal freedom and social justice which may be judged as historically unprecedented. On the other hand, this uniqueness of European political development can be synthesized in a single word: 'pluralism'. The favourable premise for such a development was the existence of a geographical area – the size of a continent – of common civilization (Judaeo-Christian) that no single power has successfully controlled for very long since Roman times. Some elements that contributed to this state of affairs, such as the church–empire duality in the Middle Ages (see below) or the multitude of rulers – and the antagonistic, and often violent, relations between them – are well known; while others, like the role of civil society, are less so and hence are worth stressing. At all events, the result was a pluralism founded, over the centuries, on the real autonomy of economic and social groups, that set limits to even the most absolute rulers' arbitrariness.

This is not the place to discuss the different theses about European

Table 3.1 Parliamentarization of political regimes and extension of the suffrage

	Parliamentari-zation	Universal male suffrage	Universal female suffrage	Interruption of suffrage
Britain	1832–5	1918	1928	–
France	1814–30	1884	1945	(1940–5)
Germany	1918	1871 (Reich)	1919	1933–49
Italy	1861	1913	1946	1924–46

Sources: adapted from von Beyme, 1982, p. 7 and Therborn, 1977, p. 11

political development, from Hintze (1906) and Elias (1939) to Barrington Moore (1966) and Bendix (1964), Braudel (1979) and Wallerstein (1974), to name the most celebrated. Instead, we prefer to present Rokkan's (1970) stimulating geopolitical 'conceptual map' of Europe because it is a relatively simple tool for identifying the major cleavages that lie behind many of the political conflicts in West Europe today. Presentation will, of necessity, be schematic and limited to the essential elements of Rokkan's conceptual map necessary for an understanding of the structuration of civil society in Europe. After that, we shall outline the intellectual basis of contemporary political ideologies before discussing the particularities of British, French, German and Italian political experience and their cultural traditions.

Nation-states and socio-political cleavages

Rokkan's conceptual map of Europe

In his attempts to understand the major lines of European political development, Rokkan was always keenly aware of both the geopolitical and the historical dimensions of the problem. He was interested, like others before him, in the 'long term' (*longue durée*) because macro-phenomena tend to be durable. For instance, the process of nation-state formation – Europe's original experience in institutional and cultural organization – lasted for almost 1000 years, if it started, as he claims, with the fall of the Holy Roman Empire in the eleventh century and was concluded only at the beginning of this century with World War I. Rokkan noted, moreover, the persistence of political behaviour despite the disappearance of the factors that were initially responsible for it. Things happened, he observed, as though the original events were reinterpreted in the light of an almost unchanging frame or grid, resulting from a political tradition.

He identified the critical historical period for European nation-state formation in the Reformation era – the decisive moment for the definition of national identities in Europe – and that for the structuring of party systems in the period (early/mid nineteenth century) immediately preceding the extension of the suffrage, when the so-called 'law of first comers' applied. But it was above all in the European geopolitical logic of the Reformation and Counter-Reformation era that Rokkan found the crucial factors that structured the continent's political development, expressed in the concept of nation-state. This was a synthesis of two parallel, but often conflicting, territorial claims: political control (state) and cultural identity (nation). He presented these two factors as spatial, but

		State: state–economy dimension, east–west axis				
Territorial centres: City networks:		Weak Weak Seaward peripheries	Strong Strong Seaward empire-nations	Weak Strong City-state in Europe	Strong Weak Landward empire-nations	Weak Weak Landward peripheries
Nation: state–culture dimension, north–south axis	Territorially defined national church	Iceland Scotland Wales	←Norway Denmark England	Hause Germany	Sweden Prussia	Finland
	Mixed territories			Netherlands Rhineland Switzerland	Bohemia→	Baltic states
	Supra-territorial church	Ireland Brittany	France	Belgium	Poland→ Bavaria	
	Counter-Reformation		Portugal Spain	Catalonia Italy	Hungary→ Austria	

Italic: territories recognized as sovereign in 1648.
Arrows: changes in status from fourteenth to eighteenth centuries

Figure 3.1 Conceptual map of Europe in the sixteenth and seventeenth centuries
Source: Rokkan, 1971, p. 24

also analytical, axes, underpinning his conceptual map. The first axis is north–south and reflects the problems of the nation, while the second is west–east and invests those of the state (figure 3.1).

The north–south axis is essentially cultural, but touches a crucial political problem, namely the difficulties encountered by the rulers nearest to Rome in achieving their projects of national unification. This was because the Roman Catholic Church treated all attempts to re-create the Holy Roman Empire as a threat to its temporal power since it would subordinate the spiritual to the temporal. Thus the Reformation, with its rejection of the universal pretensions of the Catholic Church, was, in Rokkan's opinion, the first major step on the road to the definition of territorial nations. It was no accident, in fact, that the ecclesiastical organization of the new Protestant churches (Anglican, Lutheran, Calvinist) quickly became an integral part of secular national states (England, Prussia, Switzerland). Furthermore, the Reformation occurred only a few decades after Gutenberg: the state churches of the Protestant north became major agencies for the standardization of national languages (for instance, James I's authorized version of *The Bible* for the English language) and for the socialization of the masses into unified national cultures. In the Catholic south – that is in the Counter-Reformation countries – the Roman Church remained supraterritorial and never really became an agency of nation building in the way the Protestant churches did in the north.

Rokkan's conclusion was that for nation-state building to occur it was necessary that the spiritual power's opposition should not be too close at hand. This explains both why the first European states to be formed were those on the continent's periphery – west, in the first instance, namely Spain, Portugal, England, France, Sweden; east later, namely Prussia, Russia – and why Germany and Italy had such difficulty in becoming nation-states, succeeding only in the mid nineteenth century.

The second axis, west–east, is essentially politico-economic (chapter 7). Two elements were important on this axis for the consolidation of territorial centres: one was specifically economic and the other political. To appreciate the significance of the location of states on the west–east axis it is necessary to refer to the geopolitical structure of sixteenth and seventeenth century Europe, divided as it was into three zones: (1) the dominant city network of the politically fragmented trade belt between the Mediterranean and the North Sea (city-states of north-central Italy and the Hanseatic League); (2) the strength of the cities in the territories to the seaward side of this belt (London, Paris, Madrid, Lisbon); (3) the weakness of the cities in the territories brought together under the strong military centres on the landward marches (Berlin, Moscow, Vienna). Essentially this was a contrast between the levels of monetarization of the economy reached at the time of the decisive consolidation of the territorial centres: England, France, Portugal and Spain in the sixteenth century; Prussia and Russia in the seventeenth and eighteenth centuries.

In the west, the great surge of commercial activity made it relatively easy for the elite of centre builders to extract resources in easily convertible currency. In the east, the cities were unable to provide the essential resources necessary for the military apparatus of the new centres to accomplish this task, and it could only be done in a violent manner by reducing the peasants to serfs as was done by the *Junker* in Prussia. This contrast in economic resources goes a long way to explaining, according to Rokkan, the differences between the political systems of Western and Eastern Europe and the character of their mass politics. He emphasized, in addition, the fact that the city-state Europe of the central trade belt impeded the formation of nation-states in that area (Germany and Italy) for a long time, not only because of rivals' hostility – the papacy, above all – but also because no political centre had the economic resources to dominate the area stably.

To these elements of political economy, Rokkan added subsequently a more specifically political element: the distrust of the rulers of the periphery towards the bourgeois aspirations of the trading cities of the central belt. In other words, the nearer these states were geographically to the city-states, and their dangerous example, the more they armed themselves against the risk of possible contagion of self-government and the denial of monarchical authority. This would explain the centralized and authoritarian form of government of such states – Spain, France, but also Prussia – which also had to contend with the pressure of the Counter-Reformation Catholic Church, in contrast with the more distant countries (England, above all, but also Sweden), further from the city-states of the central belt as well as, for good measure, Rome, and which could therefore allow themselves less social control, less centralism and authoritarianism in state building.

Although these two axes were fundamental to Rokkan's explanation of the diversity of European political development, even he recognized that they did not explain everything. Thus he suggested two further variables that ought to be taken into account. The first, following Barrington Moore (1966), was that the bases of democratic development were determined by the outcome of the agrarian question and the relations of domination thus formed. On the basis of the kind of industrialization and the nature of class relations (landed aristocracy and industrial bourgeoisie; bourgeoisie and proletariat), Rokkan specified certain consequences in terms both of institution building (weak or strong parliaments, but also weak or strong executives) and of party formation (socio-political cleavages). The second was that, as far as the development of some central standard of linguistic communication was concerned, the *Völker-wanderung* (transmigration of peoples) and the conflicts of the Middle Ages created very diverse conditions for linguistic unification in the different territories of Europe. The Roman Empire left the heritage of Latin, but the alphabetic script allowed the vernaculars rapidly to become literary languages in their own right: this produced the linguistic fragmentation of the continent and generated a variety of conflicts between claims for territorial control and claims of national identity. Nowhere was there necessarily a complete fit between state and nation, and the conflicts between these two sets of claims were particularly violent in the central trade belt. They are not totally exhausted, as recent events in the Balkans illustrate all too vividly once again.

In the north, the processes of state building and nation formation proceeded together, but not without conflict, as, for instance, that between the Anglo-Saxons and the Celts. The result was the development of sufficiently uniform values and attitudes, that ensured a democratic development compatible with the maintenance of the general bases of existing socio-political structures. On the contrary, in the central trade belt which had inherited strong linguistic standards from the Holy Roman Empire (German in the north, Italian in the south) there was no corresponding political development because of the ideological control exercised by the Catholic Church in the Counter-Reformation territories – the role of the Inquisition, for instance – and the failure of any state to unite the area by conquest.

In this regard, Hermet (1986, p. 158) claims that France found itself as a half-way house: far enough away from Rome for the state to affirm its own authority, but too near to risk a violent break with the Catholic Church. The result was *gallicanisme*, by which the French church defended its own autonomy in relation to Rome, but was unable, because of the supraterritorial character of Catholicism, to offer the state that legitimation of national identity that the Anglican Church furnished the English state. Without a national religion, the French state, according to Hermet, was incapable of structuring an undisputed national identity; hence the age-old political instability of the French. However, the French state has never abandoned its attempt to create a definitive national identity. This would explain why France went furthest in linguistic standardization, for which the *levée en masse* and compulsory public education were the decisive agencies in the nineteenth century.

In this context, the contrast between Catholic Austria and Protestant Prussia was, according to Rokkan, striking. Whereas the former, in fact, extended the domain of its state apparatus far beyond the borders of the German-speaking community and acquired a multilingual empire, the latter, formed in the eastern marches, consolidated its strength in the west in the core areas of the ancient German nation. The Catholic power held on to the supraterritorial ideal while the Protestant power fought to acquire control over the one national community. The struggle between *Kleindeutsche* and *Grossdeutsche* was basically a struggle between a political (state) and a cultural (nation) conception of territorial community. Not unnaturally, Rokkan summarized his analysis of the two processes thus: 'the alphabet and the city decided the destiny of Europe: the emergence of vernacular standards of communication prepared the ground for the later stages of nation building at the mass level, and the geography of the trade routes made for differences in the resources for state building between east and west' (1973, p. 80).

Critiques of Rokkan

Stimulating as is Rokkan's map, it has been criticized, like all such macro-schemas, for having neglected certain aspects of European political development. Thus, for instance, Badie and Birnbaum (1979) claim that Rokkan, in using a very broad definition of the state, underplayed the impact of differences in state structures. They insist that he confused state building with political control of a territory. Otherwise, they ask, how does one explain that it was in the Catholic countries of the Counter-Reformation, and not the Protestant ones of the Reformation, as Rokkan maintained, that the processes of bureaucratization, of the differentiation of private and public law and the autonomy of political institutions – all fundamental elements of the state's development – were furthest developed? To clarify their criticism they propose a distinction between the notion of state on the one hand, and that of political centre on the other, that allows them to outline two contrasting models of European political development.

In the first model, 'state-led society' (society dominated by the state), the state develops autonomous authority structures over civil society and in certain specific cases (France and Prussia) it acquires sufficient legitimacy to lead the nation according to its system of values (meritocratic and secular in France; hierarchic and secular in Germany). Moreover, external factors as much as internal factors required the maintenance of an imposing military apparatus, that thus justified the development of a powerful state machine. The domination of civil society became such in these states that control of the state was soon the unique goal in politics. For the political forces, in fact, there was nothing outside the state, so that, for a long period, they were unable to imagine that social progress could be achieved without the state's direct intervention: for instance, as a result of direct negotiations between social forces without state mediation.

The second model, the 'political centre', is the opposite of the first. It is a case of 'society-led state', that is a network of specialized elites and institutions which have national legitimacy in place of the state: for instance, the 'establishment' and the 'crown in parliament' in Britain. In this model, the different segments of society are left relatively free to express their own aspirations without the tutelage of a strong state power. Politics lacks that pre-eminence which it has in the other model; indeed, in this one, it is considered a social activity like any other. Political influence is founded on social values and not on the forcible conquest of the state; and civil society is governed by the principle of 'self-regulation'[1] symbolized in the notion of the 'common law', which applies to everyone, including the state. Political conflicts are resolved by direct negotiation between social forces rather than in relations with the state: for instance, the British tradition of informal meetings.[2]

The origin of these two models of the social control of consensus, constructed on the binary couple between state and political centre – that distinguishes France, Germany and Italy on one side, and Britain on the other – lies in the different contextual situations of the four nations which have imposed all kinds of constraints on them: spatial, geopolitical, historical and so on.

A second criticism of Rokkan's conceptual map concerns the national or cultural axis. This time, the criticism is the opposite to that of the state, namely that his definition of culture is too restrictive because it is limited to linguistic structures and ecclesiastical organization, and thus neglects important aspects. One way of pointing up this problem is to look at Elias's (1939) schema in which he distinguished three models of the formation and propagation of national cultural norms: (1) the English model of an aristocratic-bourgeois culture; (2) the French model of a culture that is the product of state power (aristocratic before the revolution; bourgeois after); and (3) the German model of a bourgeois and academic culture.

In England, the 'courtly-absolutist' era was, in Elias's view, too brief to succeed in imposing a centralized courtly culture and in redefining the aristocratic conception of freedom and authority that had already dominated the elite since Magna Carta. In France, the opposite occurred, namely the centralizing effort of the monarchical state to impose the courtly culture was successful. In other words, the courtly-absolutist era lasted sufficiently long for the court of Versailles to leave an indelible mark[3] on French society. In Germany, the situation was different again: in a territorial area which lacked a central authority, bourgeois and academic culture developed as a reaction to the cosmopolitan nature of a myriad of small courts which were too weak to impose a national culture; in consequence, it was the German universities that developed, from the eighteenth century, a bourgeois cultural model in which nationalism was the chief unifying factor.

From such bases Elias derived the specifics of the national cultures within a common framework, that of European civilization: freedom and authority, tolerance and inequality, self-discipline and pragmatism in England; ideological intolerance and instrumentalism, authoritarianism and formalism (*le beau langage*) in France; authoritarianism, bureaucratism, discipline and conformism in Germany. He outlined, with a wealth of detail, the different mechanisms – loss of military role of the English aristocracy and consequent commercial alliance with the bourgeoisie in Britain; replacement of the court of Versailles by a bourgeois representative-bureaucratic state in France; the role of the *Volksgeist* and the aristocratic military-bourgeois bureaucratic alliance in Germany – that consolidated and propagated these national elite cultural traits among the people. Elements of them can still be found in political behaviour in these countries, and this despite the enormous social changes – alphabetization, mass education – that have occurred in the last 100 years. Examples include the mania for secrecy in public affairs among the British state elite; and the apocalyptic language of French politicians designed not only to denounce but above all to delegitimize political opposition. In conclusion, however, Elias's schema, like all those of a similar kind, remains very general and should be used with caution in specific analyses.

We must add that Rokkan's conceptual formulations were not limited to the nature of nation-state formation, but were also intended to identify the key elements of the countries' cultural structuration, that is their internal political development and outcomes. He distinguished two processes: the democratization or formation of mass political regimes on the one hand; and the rise of the principal political cleavages on the other. As regards the former, he hypothesized that democratization occurred as a result of a sequence of four critical phases: (1) penetration (political, cultural and economic integration at the elite level; control over territory): (2) unification (communication of a sense of identity from the elite promoting national unification to the people, via conscription and compulsory mass education); (3) participation (mass mobilization and extension of political rights, including the suffrage); (4) redistribution (creation and extension of social services). However, it has been noted (Therborn, 1977; Zincone, 1987) that democratic development does not always follow this sequence. For instance, social rights (redistribution) in Germany preceded political rights (participation). Indeed, it was because he feared the consequences of the concession of full political rights to a labour movement – considered too radical and dangerous – that Bismarck suddenly decided to extend social rights to German workers in the 1880s, thus creating the premises of the welfare state.

Recently, Zincone (1989) has pointed to the sequence of the last two phases (participation, redistribution) as the basis of two alternative elite strategies for integrating the subordinate classes, principally the labour movement. The first, defined as an 'indirect integration strategy', provides for negotiation with social organizations, the institutional centrality of oppositional organizations, and efforts to win mass consensus, either by means of a gradual, limited but real extension of the suffrage or through the delegation of social security and education to civil society organizations (as in Britain). The second, defined as a 'direct integration strategy', provides instead for the repression of oppositional organizations, the concentration of decision-making power in organizations outside oppositional elite control, and efforts at securing mass consensus directly, either by means of a rapid extension of the suffrage or through state control of social security and education (as, for instance, in Germany, but also in France and Italy).

The outcome of these two strategies, according to Zincone, are two different prototypes of the political system: (1) the society model, in which civil society oversees the state; and (2) the state model, in which the state controls and shapes civil society. The coincidence of these two models with those of Badie and Birnbaum is not accidental: it means that the decisive factors in the two strategies have a long history. However, the ambiguity in Rokkan's sequence merely serves to highlight once more the complexity of European historical development. Moreover, this development also disavows the view of those who, like Giddens (1983), believe that the welfare state was essentially a conquest of working class struggle.[4]

Critical junctures and socio-political cleavages

As regards the specific structuration of civil society in Europe, Rokkan identified a number of 'critical junctures' in European history in which the conflicts provoked mass mobilization and this, in turn, resulted in major long-term cleavages. The first and most significant was the Reformation and Counter-Reformation of the sixteenth and seventeenth

centuries, where the stakes were the control of ecclesiastical organizations and hence the conflict was responsible for a cleavage between
centre and periphery in the consolidation of state control of the national
territory. The second was the national revolutions of the eighteenth
and nineteenth centuries (French Revolution, 1848 in Germany,
Risorgimento in Italy), where the struggle was for the control of the so-
called 'ideological apparatuses' – and most specifically the national educational system – in a period of the expansion of mass communication
and gave rise to a conflict between church and state.

The third critical juncture was the industrial revolution, which was
responsible for two major conflicts: one in the *commodity* market
between industrial and commercial interests and agrarian interests over
tariffs (town against country, free trade against protectionism); the other
in the *labour* market between employers and workers over property
rights (class struggle). A fourth critical juncture can be identified in the
Bolshevik Revolution, which precipitated a conflict inside the labour
movement between revolutionaries (communists) and reformists (socialists) over whether to support the international revolutionary movement
or integrate the working class into the national state. Finally, some consider 1968 and the movements of contestation as a fifth critical juncture,
provoking a new cleavage over the ecological question, of which the
'new social movements' would be the major protagonists (the 'new politics': environment against development).

Naturally, in historical reality the various conflicts overlap and it is difficult to unravel each cleavage separately, given the variety of individual
situations. Nonetheless, Rokkan considered the first two conflicts were
ideological, the direct products of what he called the 'national revolution', whereas the third and fourth were direct products of the industrial
revolution. The fifth was in a certain sense a product of both; and the
sixth – if it is one – would appear to be the product of uncontrolled economic development, that is a prolongation of the industrial revolution.
At all events, it was Rokkan's claim that much of the history of Europe
since the beginning of the nineteenth century can be described in terms
of the interaction between these two processes of revolutionary change,
the one triggered in France (national revolution) and the other originating in Britain (industrial revolution); both had consequences for the
cleavage structure of each nation, but the former produced the deepest
and bitterest conflicts.

Rokkan's thesis was that the first three cleavages were responsible for
the differences between the European political systems, while the fourth
contributed towards their uniformity. The crucial differences between
the political systems appeared in the first phase of political competition –
in the mid nineteenth century before the phase of mass mobilization –
also as a result of the 'law of first comers': the political movements that
were able to establish themselves first enjoyed an incalculable advantage
over those which attempted to follow them, particularly if the latter's

ideologies were directed at similar social support. These differences related to fundamental divergences in the conditions and sequences of state building and in national economic structures at the moment of the industrial revolution. Rokkan's problem was to identify the nation-building elites' choices in each country at each critical juncture. To do this he proposed a series of typologies on a simple dichotomous basis ($2 \times 2 \times 2$) of the political alternatives open to them (figure 3.2) in order to reduce the bewildering variety of empirical material and cases to a 'set of ordered consequences of decisions and developments' at the three critical junctures.

The model spells out, as Rokkan himself stated, 'the consequences of the fateful division of Europe brought about through the Reformation and Counter-Reformation' (1970, p. 116). The outcomes of the conflict between church and state determined the structure of national politics nearly 300 years later in the era of democratization and mass mobilization. In Southern Europe, the Counter-Reformation consolidated the position of the church and tied its fate to the *ancien régime*. The result was a polarization of politics between a national radical secular movement and a Catholic traditionalist one (France and Italy). In Northern Europe, the sixteenth century settlement gave a very different structure to the nineteenth century cleavages. The Protestant churches did not stand in opposition to the nation-building elites but were, in fact, part of them; hence politics was less polarized and more concerned with economic than religious problems (Britain).

Thus, in Britain, there was a nation-building alliance between the national (Anglican) church and the landed gentry, opposed by Nonconformists, industrial interests and the Celtic fringe (conservatives versus liberals). In Germany, as a result of the large Catholic minority,[5] the opposition alliance to the nation-building elite (which was very similar to Britain) joined secular and Catholic interests (conservatives versus liberals and Catholics). In France and Italy, on the other hand, there was a very different situation, so the alliances were different: the nation-building elite in both countries was constituted by secular and urban interests, while the opposition alliance was formed of Catholic and agrarian interests (liberals and radicals versus conservatives and Catholics). We are aware that in placing France and Italy together in terms of political alliances, we must not forget that the two countries had different histories as regards national development. Even Rokkan noted that nation-building elites and opposition alliances have very different meanings in each country: for instance, real parliamentarianism in France after 1875; 'façade' parliamentarianism in Italy as a result of *trasformismo* before fascism.

The fourth cleavage – employers versus workers – modified substantially the previous situation of all the political systems, introducing an element of uniformity due to the logic of capital – the imperative of capital accumulation – and that of labour to resist it in the name of wages,

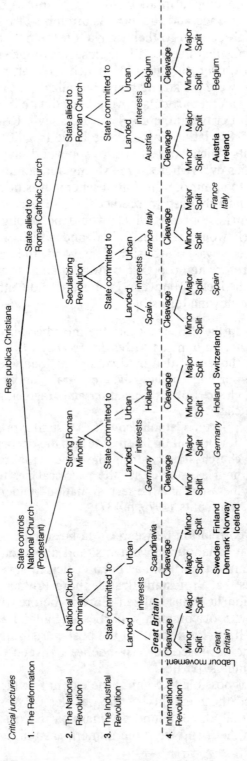

Figure 3.2 Cleavage structures: Rokkan's typological schema. Major powers in italics
Source: adapted from Rokkan, 1970, p. 116

jobs and conditions of work. In fact, labour movements and socialist parties developed in all European countries between the first extension of the suffrage and the various attempts at repressing party pluralism. The initial reaction to their arrival on the national political stage was for the old hostile forces to ally themselves to face the common enemy.

However, the question which Rokkan raised was different: he asked what were the strength and mobilization capacity of each national labour movement, particularly when faced with divisive tendencies, of which the fourth critical juncture – the Bolshevik Revolution – was the most decisive. The latter revealed the basic fragility of the various labour movements which were subject to splits and saw the foundation of communist parties everywhere, some strong and some weak. In this regard, Rokkan had to admit that his initial schema was not very helpful because it made it relatively easy to predict the rise of socialist parties in all European countries, but not which would be strong and which would be weak, which would remain united and which would be prey to splits. This, indeed, was quite simply beyond the schema's predictive capacity. Therefore he proposed, by way of an answer, a simple typology based on the distinction between Protestant and Catholic countries, formulated in the following terms:

> In the Protestant and the mixed countries the discriminating criterion appears to be the *recency of the nation-building process*: the less settled the issues of national identity and the deeper the ongoing conflicts over cultural standardization, the greater the chances of radicalization and fragmentation within the working class.
>
> In the Catholic countries a similar process seems to have been at work but in different terms: the deeper and more persistent the church–state conflicts, the greater the fragmentation of the working class; the closer the historical ties between the ecclesiastical hierarchy and the secular 'nation-builders', the less chance of left-wing splits. (1970, p. 137)

The correlation between Catholic countries, radicalization and fragmentation of labour movements, and above all Catholic culture and strong communist parties, has been criticized severely by Hermet (1986), who notes that Protestant Brandenburg Prussia was the strongest communist bastion in industrialized Europe before 1933, without mentioning the strength of communist parties in Finland and Iceland today. He claims that Italy – as a result of the post-war strength of the PCI – was the basis of the proposed correspondence between Catholic countries and strong communist parties.[6]

It is possible to confirm the extent to which these cleavages have penetrated the mentality of the peoples of Western Europe, both from the fact that all contemporary mass parties originate in one way or another from them and from the numerous studies of mass values and attitudes.

Table 3.2 Political cleavages and social bases of the vote, 1950s, 1970s and 1980s

	Religions			Rural/urban			Class		
	1950s	1970s	1980s	1950s	1970s	1980s	1950s	1970s	1980s
Britain	7	5	2	10	nd	nd	37	34	22
France	59	40	31	11	nd	nd	15	15	11
Germany	40	30	28	17	nd	nd	27	13	11
Italy	51	49	29	12	nd	nd	19	15	15

nd: no data.
Based on Alford's class index and Lijphart's religious index.
Sources: 1950s from Lijphart, 1971, pp. 14–15; 1970s from Inglehart, 1977, pp. 236, 258; 1980s from Inglehart, 1990, appendix A24

To take one well-known example, Inglehart's (1977) comparative study of attitudes in Western countries in the 1970s clearly shows that religion is the best predictor of the adult political identity of the French, Italians and Germans; for the British, it is social class. In fact, Inglehart concludes his analysis of the *Eurobaromètre* survey data, asserting that it is only in Britain and Denmark that the classic pattern of industrial cleavage is predominant, while pre-industrial cleavages remain secondary. In all of the other European countries (including France, Germany and Italy) pre-industrial cleavages are preponderant and, in some cases, post-industrial ones (namely, those based on 'post-material' needs). 'Among the countries we have analysed,' he writes, 'pre-industrial cleavages seem to dominate the scene, even today' (p. 256) (table 3.2).

Socio-political cleavages in history

There are numerous historical studies which document the origin of the major cleavages in a number of countries and which illustrate how specific events at Rokkan's critical junctures institutionalized them. A good example is Bois's (1960) classic study of the origins of the famous breach between the royalist west and the republican east in France. This derived from a latent antagonism in the *pays du bocage* between the closed and homogeneous peasant world and urban society, which was crystallized around 1790 by the impact of Parisian revolutionary politics. The outcome was the Chouannerie, a six-year civil war that forged a particular mentality (that of the *chouans*) and which, thanks to the support of the nobility and clergy, secured a mass base for a clerico-reactionary ideology. The peasant world in the Parisian area, less homogeneous and more open (*villageois*), was much more receptive to the revolutionary politics. The result was a red and black line of cleavage which lasted for more than 150 years, down to the present day. In addition, studies of several southern departments – for instance, Agulhon's (1979) study of the Var – have shown that the crisis of the Second Republic (coup of 2 December 1851) was decisive for implanting the republican tradition there.

On the other hand, Trigilia (1986) has identified similar processes in the formation of the red and white regions in Italy, namely the mobilization of a cohesive social structure in reaction to a crisis. It is no accident that the critical period was the post-Risorgimento: the immediate aftermath of the Italian national revolution. In the case of the white region (Venetia), a compact society of small peasant farmers, characterized by a strong Catholic tradition in the countryside and a weak secular tradition in the towns, was mobilized against the secular national state by the agrarian crisis of the 1880s, the full rigours of which the liberal-controlled state was unable, and unwilling, to minimize. The result was a mass exodus accompanied by the mobilization of the peasant population, the valorization of the existing religious identity and the church's entry into the socio-economic field which the state itself had refused to countenance. In the red region (Emilia-Romagna), a strongly polarized society of labourers in the presence of a weak clerical tradition in the countryside and a stronger secular tradition in the towns was mobilized to defend itself in the long end-of-century crisis. Once again, the liberal ruling elite was unwilling to remedy the marginalization of large masses of the population, and their defence was organized by the nascent socialist movement. The struggle crystallized a new socialist tradition which, once institutionalized, put down strong territorial roots. English (church and chapel: for instance Martin, 1967) and German examples can be added to this list.

Bois has written:

> ideological residues resist transformations that were believed to be critical ... Tradition survives long after its true nature has been forgotten; it survives even for a while after the decline of the economic and social structures that helped it to persist ... Ideology that is born one day, crystallizes in a neat and simple way a whole complex personality in asserting it against another personality. This ideology lasts as long as a new population or profound changes in the way of life have not distorted or obliterated the collective personality that it symbolizes. (1960, pp. 363–4)

The matrix of contemporary ideologies

Before discussing the specifics of the political experiences of Britain, France, Germany and Italy and their cultural legacies, we need to outline the intellectual basis on which the major contemporary European ideologies were formed. The significance derives from the fact that they are founded as a result of a sharp epistemological break with the cultural tradition of the medieval *res publica Christiana*. This was built on a theocentric view of the world: God was the author of all things and his will was therefore authority in all matters, animate and inanimate. Society was conceived as a divinely ordained moral organism in which everyone had their natural and predetermined place. In the words of the nineteenth century hymn: 'The rich man in his castle, / The poor man at his gate, / God made them, high or lowly, / And ordered their estate.' The world was as it was because God had created it thus and any attempt to change things was against nature and the right order of things, and so considered subversive. In this sense, God's representatives on earth, that is to say the universal church and princes, had the right to be obeyed in their respective spheres. Indeed, the fundamental political text of the Middle Ages was St Paul's Epistle to the Romans (13: 1–5): 'Let every soul be subject to higher powers: for there is no power but God, and the powers that be are ordained of God. Therefore he that resisteth the power, resisteth the ordinance of God; and they that withstand shall receive to themselves judgement.' Political participation, as we understand it today, was a product of the Enlightenment (chapter 4).

Behind this theocratic conception of the world, there lay, nonetheless, a dualistic vision of reality, split between the eternal and the temporal, the spiritual and the material, between divine law and natural law. The intellectual assumption was of a necessary correspondence between the natural and the divine, as two faces of the same reality, to wit the Aristotelian idea that the individual could perceive divine reality behind material appearances. Thus, if it was the church's responsibility to proclaim divine law, it was the king's – or civil government's – to realize temporal values, which were embodied in natural law, defined as 'what natural reason has established among all men' and summed up in the legal maxim 'Rex non sub homine sed sub Deo ac Lege'. This meant that if men were obliged to obey the king – and the civil government – there was a limit to the king's will and this was that it conformed to 'natural law'. In other words, there was a strong constitutional strain in medieval culture, which was affirmed in the continuing conflicts between the papacy and the Holy Roman Empire. An individual or community had the right to resist – or free themselves from – a tyrant, if he did not respect natural law: hence the many papal excommunications. In this way, Western Christianity, despite the conception of authority as directly constituted by God, recognized the importance of the principle of the consent of the political community, and this was an element that was to play an important role in the development of modern constitutionalism.

What eventually undermined the theocratic conception of the medieval world was the 'scientific revolution'. Its intellectual triumph was a long process of some 300 years which it is not necessary to detail here. It is enough to recall the changes mentioned above, and specifically the Reformation which, with the constitution of different national churches and the wars of religion (that sanctioned the principle 'cuius regio, eius religio'), probably gave the decisive push. At all events, the growing discrepancy between temporal reality and theological doctrine provoked the sixteenth century epistemological break. The scientific spirit was founded on the subjectivity of knowledge, synthesized in the Cartesian formula 'cogito, ergo sum', and pushed to its logical conclusion by Hume's (1740) claim that 'nothing exists, but sensation.' Nobody has any longer a monopoly of truth, that is to say, there are no ultimate demonstrable truths.

The outcome of this break was the formulation of a totally new world view in Europe, at least intellectually: secular instead of religious, anthropocentric instead of theocentric. Firstly, the source of public authority is conceived as coming from below and no longer from above, that is founded on the popular consent of the people, expressed through universal suffrage, instead of on God in the person of the king and royal proclamations. Secondly, the goals of human society are of this world and not of the next, to wit the pursuit of individual freedom and material well-being in place of the salvation of the soul. Thirdly, knowledge is founded on the capacity of human reason and on the idea that the individual is able to calculate rationally his own interest and act accordingly. This system replaced the earlier one based on divine will and the conception of the organic society. By extension, and combined with the conception of popular sovereignty, it meant belief in citizen participation as a civic virtue. This gave rise to the notion of popular mobilization. Finally, a purely political community, the nation, was created in place of the universal *res publica Christiana*. Its source, as we have seen, was cultural and it was usually constructed from an opportune selection of events and myths of a specific population in a given territory with the express intention of creating a common identity (see below), without which that population would be incapable of collective goals. Hence the term 'fraternity' in the French republican motto (the other two words refer naturally to aspects of political authority of the new social order that was intended to replace the *ancien régime*).

Despite the fundamental difference between the old and the new European *Weltanschauung*, the new one appropriated important elements of Christian practice, transforming them in the new intellectual climate. Thus, for instance, the Christian eschatology of the millennium that was to usher in the reign of the righteous was translated in terms of an earthly paradise or a secularized version of the kingdom of heaven. Examples are the liberal myths of 'scientific progress' and 'perpetual peace'; the communist post-revolutionary 'classless society'; and the Nazi 'thousand-year Reich'. In addition, the Christian myth of paradise was transmuted into the liberal dream of progress and was the basis of the dominant optimistic attitudes of nineteenth century liberal culture. In a similar way, the liberal concept of constitutionalism and limited power expresses clearly, albeit in a different form, the Christian idea of community control. Examples are the social contract tradition (renewed by Rawls, 1971), institutionalized in popular and periodic elections, and the detailed definition of fundamental human rights that characterize, for instance, the UN Charter (1946), the European Convention of Human Rights (1950) and many European constitutions.

At the end of this discussion of the intellectual tradition common to Europe as a whole, we now turn to the peculiarities of the political experience and cultural traditions of Britain, France, Germany and Italy.

National political experiences and cultural traditions

Britain

The distinctive aspect of the British political experience, particularly when compared with continental states, is its constitutional continuity. Britain, in fact, has not known a change of political regime or a constitutional break for more than 300 years, and this despite the world wars, the Irish Revolution and the loss of the empire. This history obviously colours the vision that the British have of politics and their constitution. One mythical, but still widespread, vision is the so-called 'Whig view of history' which can do justice to the country's political virtues in four lines of doggerel: 'A land of settled government, / A land of just and old renown, / Where Freedom slowly broadens down / From precedent to precedent.' The political genius of the British, according to this view, lies in their success in combining the maximum of advantages – political stability and efficacy with liberty and democracy – without the disadvantages of their continental neighbours. The truth or falsity of the Whig view is not very important, although continuous economic decline over the last century raises some very embarrassing questions. What is important in the European context is that British political development is based on the subordinate role of the state. Indeed, it was necessary to invent specific conceptions like 'society model' or 'civil society dominated state' to describe the British experience, a fact which confirms that it represents a deviant case in the history of European nation-state formation.

England enjoyed, in fact, an advantageous geopolitical position: dominating an island far from Rome, not too large in size but with easy access to trade routes which allowed it to establish a national identity very early without the need for a centralized state apparatus, either administrative or military. Moreover, the absence of such a state structure in the seventeenth century prevented the Stuarts from creating an 'absolute state'. It was also the first country to experience both a political revolution and the industrial revolution; hence its experience has remained unique and defied imitation. The European countries that followed Britain did not repeat the British experience, but attempted to learn the right lessons so that their political development was the result of a project based on a constitutional theory. Thus they developed something very different from the British: the abstract or 'impersonal state', that is a different and entirely distinct entity from civil society. It was on this basis that, from the seventeenth century on, British and European developments diverge: British developments became characterized by a confusion between state and civil society, with the latter dominating. This conception still influences British culture[7] today – for instance, in the role of voluntary associations in social self-regulation, in self-help, and so on – even if a state apparatus became necessary from the 1830s.

At all events, parliament, as the representative of civil society, is the heart of the British political system. Moreover, the fact that the outcome of the Glorious Revolution of 1688 established the consent of parliament as the basic principle of political authority in the country – and confirmed the crown in parliament as the site of national sovereignty – appeared to open the way directly to democracy. In one sense, it did: with the extension of the suffrage, parliament – or more precisely the House of Commons, which was always based on territorial representation and not on estates as in other countries – was eventually endowed with a democratic base in the twentieth century after some 200 years. But in another, more significant sense, it did not: the concept of the nation as state, and hence of the people as citizens and not as subjects, has never really been accepted by the British ruling class. Indeed, the development of democracy was so slow, with so many compromises and corrections, and shrouded in so many traditional forms, as to make many observers wonder whether a democratic spirit has every really existed in the country. Thus, for instance, Ralf Dahrendorf (1988) has recently suggested that perhaps 'Britain's secret was that it was not a democracy at all' (p. 65),[8] while Raymond Williams (1961) has argued that the problem in Britain has been to separate the principle of democracy from the habitual loyalty to the establishment: 'The symbols of democracy, in the English mind, are as likely to be institutions of power and antiquity, such as the Palace of Westminster, as the active process of popular decision, such as a committee or jury' (pp. 123–4). Even today, Britons are apparently content to describe themselves as 'British subjects'[9] who enjoy 'the liberties of the subject', where liberty means not rights in the sense of the French Declaration of the Rights of Man, but simply a permissive area in the margin of an unquestionable duty. That the English tradition contrasts with the French one was made clear, unconsciously, by Mrs Thatcher in a notorious published interview on the eve of the bicentenary celebrations of the French Revolution.

The settlement of 1688 was compatible, however, with a set of differing interpretations of the constitutional relations that formed the basis of the flexible and piecemeal development of the so-called 'English constitution'. In the eighteenth century, this was founded on the political balance between crown (king) and parliament (landed proprietors), but in ultimate analysis was controlled by the latter. In the nineteenth century, it was based on the supremacy of the commons (elected) over the peers (hereditary) in parliament, and the responsibility of ministers to parliament and no longer towards the crown. Finally, in the twentieth century, it was based on the party system as the instrument for integrating people, parliament and government. The basis of this progressive adaptation of the English constitution to the needs of popular sovereignty and democracy was on the one hand a series of 'political understandings' and 'conventions', and, on the other a social class, the establishment (Bagehot's *'chosen* people'), which really ruled the country. An integral part of the conventions was the division of labour between 'high politics' – Whitehall's business and the responsibility of the executive and treated as a private matter with minimum publicity – and 'low politics' – Westminster's business and the object of the political struggle between the parties and private interests. Bulpitt (1983) has defined this division of labour as the 'dual polity' (see chapter 9 in this book), which incorporated local self-government, indirect rule of the empire and an elitist vision of politics, in which the chosen people had not only the right but the duty to represent the people: 'leaders know best.' Indeed, the people's active political participation has always been discouraged in the English conception of democracy, and so it is no accident that the Schumpeterian model was theorized on the basis of British praxis.

As regards the establishment, it was formed in the seventeenth century by the landed proprietors, whom the local gentry quickly joined as did the urban bourgeoisie later in the nineteenth century. Moreover, an alliance between landed aristocracy and urban bourgeoisie was mutually advantageous because the English aristocracy lacked the privileges enjoyed by their French counterparts under the *ancien régime*; the English aristocracy have always been active in trade and the professions. In point of fact, a process of osmosis between these classes occurred quite rapidly which ensured the establishment's cohesion in the eighteenth and nineteenth centuries. It was quite happy to dominate in a decentralized and non-bureaucratic manner by using 'informal' mechanisms: so-called 'political understandings'.

At this juncture, two questions arise. Firstly, how was such a minimal state able to last so long, that is right up to the mid nineteenth century? Secondly, how was it possible to integrate the working class into the political system without a serious constitutional crisis? The short answer to the first question has already been given when referring to the success of the commercial and imperial strategy in fusing the various interests of the establishment with those of the rising middle classes, and which led to the industrial revolution. In fact, it was the very success of this strategy (clothed in traditional procedures and terminology) that ensured that the establishment did not require the strengthening of the state. The answer to the second question is more complex and implies a paradox:

working class integration was essentially political and constitutional and *not* social. In social and cultural terms, the British working class has maintained a distinctly separate character, 'them' and 'us', as Hoggart (1957) noted:

> 'They' are 'the people at the top', 'the higher-ups', the people who give you your dole, call you up, tell you to go to war, made you split the family in the thirties to avoid a reduction in the Means Test allowance, 'get yer in the end', 'talk posh', 'are all twisters really', 'never tell yer owt' (e.g. about a relative in hospital), 'clap yer in clink', 'will do y' down if they can', 'summons yer', 'are all in a click [clique] together', 'treat y' like muck'. (p. 62)

In short, it was the 'premature' bourgeois revolution of the seventeenth century that induced a similar 'premature' birth of the labour movement; and this 'precociousness' in turn is the key to its integration in a subordinate position. This resulted from its inability to contest the system – as other labour movements were to do afterwards – because it lacked both a working class philosophy (Marxism arrived much later in the British Isles) and winning alliances (feudal serfdom, the basis of bourgeois-subordinate class alliances elsewhere in Europe, had long since disappeared). The peasants (another element) were expelled from the land by the enclosures in the eighteenth and early nineteenth centuries. In consequence, after the defeat of the first political projects (Owenism, Chartism, both idealist and pre-socialist), the labour movement withdrew into a trade-unionist 'corporatism' in the second half of the nineteenth century. Indeed, it is through the trade unions that the British labour movement entered the political stage. As is well known, Britain is the country where the original model of the political organization of the labour movement moves from the trade unions to the party (that is to say, the unions are the sponsors of the Labour Party) and not vice versa, as on the continent. One consequence is that the British labour movement has always conceived participation in the political system as a pragmatic means for obtaining gradual economic improvements, and has never envisaged political revolution as a way of changing life once and for all. Its radicalism has always been more moral than doctrinal. Another consequence is that, in organizing itself in this way, it forced the upper and middle classes to form an alliance to defend their interests and privileges, so that the class cleavage became the principal political cleavage in Britain in this century (table 3.2). This also helps to explain, *soit dit en passant*, why the seventeenth century constitutional–religious conflict between parliamentarians and royalists (Whigs and Tories in the eighteenth century; Liberals and Conservatives in the nineteenth century) was transformed without a break into that between Labour and Conservative in the twentieth.[10]

In conclusion, it is not that other political cleavages do not exist in Britain, but rather that for a complex set of reasons their incidence has been minimal. Some of them have already been mentioned, like the country's geopolitical position and its particularly favourable access to resources. Perhaps the most significant fact is that, thanks to them, Britain has found itself in the fortunate situation of being able to face, at least in the past, the various critical junctures, having satisfactorily solved the problems posed by the previous ones. However, there are indications that this fortunate situation is a thing of the past. The British political system has been subjected to increasing tension in the last twenty years as a result of continuing economic decline and the loss of the empire: criticism of the constitution, peripheral nationalisms and urban riots are only some of the more obvious signs. But it will probably take a serious political crisis to reveal just how far the country has changed, because it remains, as Disraeli commented in 1881, 'a very difficult country to move'.

France

The French political experience is generally contrasted with the British one. Firstly, great emphasis is laid on constitutional instability – demonstrated by the sixteen political regimes since 1789 – and political dissonance, illustrated by the strength of 'anti-system' political forces (chapter 5). Secondly, reference is made to the omnipotent role of the state. Indeed, the French state is usually considered the ideal model of the modern European state; so it is no surprise that the categories used to define the French political system are the opposite to those used for the British political system, namely it is a case of the 'state model' or 'state-dominated civil society'. It is claimed, moreover, that the state is an independent apparatus, totally distinct from civil society, and that it created the French nation, the suggestion being that without the state there is no French identity. 'France only exists', de Gaulle declared in 1962, 'thanks to the state: France can only remain herself through it.'

The exemplary nature of the French political experience in the context of the formation of the European nation-state was also dependent on its geopolitical position, which was very different from the British one: a continental situation and much larger in size in the crucial period (fifteenth to seventeenth centuries), with enemies on three sides, at a lesser distance from Rome and with a reasonable access to the trade routes. Indeed, to create a viable political community – the French nation – in these conditions, the monarchy was obliged to build a centralized administrative and military apparatus capable of controlling the territory, an apparatus which in the seventeenth century created the 'absolute state' – absolutism, in this case, being defined by the French historian Robert Mandrou (1966) as 'a perfected bureaucratic organization'. In building the state, the French monarchy was assisted by the revival of Roman law which recognized the separation of *jus publicum* from *jus privatum*. More significantly, it accorded a privileged role to public authority and justified *raison d'état* on the basis of Ulpian's famous maxim: 'Quod principi placuit legis habet vicem.' In consequence, the French monarchy succeeded in institutionalizing, conceptually and actually, public power, the state, as both separate from and independent of civil society. Conceived initially in terms of military functions – France was the first country to provide itself with a standing army – the French state progressively extended its field of activity to territorial surveillance and administration, to the control of trade – mercantilism – and even manufacture. It even effectively subordinated the church of France, which defended the French monarchy against Rome (*gallicanisme*) without a breach of religious faith. State intervention reached such proportions that Tocqueville (1856) claimed that the French had never been kept under the tutelage of such a power since the fall of the Roman Empire!

At all events, the role of the French state in relation to civil society did not decrease as a result of the French Revolution as one might have expected. On the contrary, state power and centralization increased, as Tocqueville himself was the first to stress. What changed was less the state structures – the names of the institutions were changed (prefect in place of *intendant*, for instance) but not the hierarchy of command – than the conception of legitimacy. Popular sovereignty replaced the divine right of kings and with it the notion of the state as the incarnation of the nation founded on the people as citizens with universal rights. This directly opened the way to universal suffrage. In reality, however, there was a subtle displacement of meaning in an elitist direction from popular sovereignty to national sovereignty and so to the sovereignty of the national assembly. This is Furet's (1978) thesis: the revolutionary break was essentially political and cultural rather than economic and social, with the institution of a new style of government based on 'rule by opinion' and the power of the 'word'. He writes: 'The revolution replaced the conflict of interests for power with a competition of discourses for the appropriation of legitimacy', specifying that 'since the people alone had the right to govern ... power was in the hands of those who speak for the people' (p. 49). If Furet is right, this would explain why the post-revolutionary political struggle in France has been fought in Manichaean ideological terms, with each political force sure that it possesses the absolute truth. This aspect was so manifest that France fully deserved its reputation of being 'the world's ideological factory' (Finer, 1970, p. 260).

If there is little doubt that the state's predominance over civil society was strengthened by the revolution, the revolutionary break still has to be explained, the more so because it produced the deepest and most long-standing cleavage in French politics: that between republicanism and the *ancien régime*. In this, the emphasis is placed, firstly, on the dependence of the civil society elites (both aristocracy and bourgeoisie) on the absolute state. In fact, the French aristocracy was, in contrast to its British counterpart, tied to the king's absolute power by a double thread: on the one hand by its military role, which it retained in a situation in which war still played a role in the state's very existence; and on the other by its feudal and royal privileges, which replaced its lack of economic independence. At the same time, and secondly, the mercantilist system, which prevented the bourgeois class's independent commercial development, meant that the bourgeoisie were oriented towards administrative and political activities instead of commercial ones, which, in turn, increased the rivalry between the two classes. Finally, the inability of the French agricultural economy to produce a sufficient surplus to meet increased external military and economic pressures, without overburdening the peasantry more and more, meant that the *ancien régime* lived under the permanent threat of peasant risings. It was no accident, therefore, that economic and political reforms were impossible and corruption grew to the point that the royal (or rather state) finances collapsed under the strain.

The calling of the estates general in 1789, for the first time for over 150 years, dramatically posed the question of the state's form and the legitimacy of its structures. Since an alliance between aristocracy and bourgeoisie, as in Britain, was not possible, the bourgeoisie turned to the people for support to oust the aristocracy. This explains its appeal to Rousseau's egalitarian democratic ideology, expressed in the famous motto *Liberté! Égalité! Fraternité*! However, if the principal social spur came from the peasantry – rebelling against the heavy rents and taxes that forced the Constituent Assembly to abolish feudal rights and royal privileges and so eliminate the basis of the aristocracy's power – the alliance at the summit, that is the Jacobin one, was actually formed between the national bourgeoisie and various urban strata, and rapidly provoked a conflict between urban and rural interests. This conflict was a significant factor in both the reconstruction of a strong state on firmer foundations – national systems of legislation, taxation and education – and in deepening the cleavage between the two conceptions of the state's form, popular democracy or autocratic monarchy. Such a historical formation – unitary state and divided nation – was responsible, according to Barrington Moore (1966), for the notorious instability of French politics, in which the democratic development of the country, made up of bold advances but also of spectacular retreats, was scanned by periods of mass popular revolt (1830, 1848, 1871, up to 1968).

The integration of the subordinate classes into the French political system was achieved by the so-called 'republican strategy'. As regards the peasantry – the largest class, numerically – the instruments were compulsory education and conscription which secured both subordinate integration and forced indoctrination. In consequence, the radical governments of the Third Republic were able to use universal male suffrage in the provinces as a conservative weapon against the revolutionary activism of the Parisian proletariat. As regards the working class, the state employed a policy of systematic repression, instead, to marginalize it politically.[11] Indeed, the 20,000 executions of *communards* by Thiers and the Versailles government in 1871 deprived the French labour movement of its cadres, and left it in a position from which it took more than a generation to recover. These events go a long way to explaining the great difficulty that the French labour movement experienced in organizing itself politically, first in parties and later in trade unions, both of which have always remained relatively weak. When the labour movement re-emerged in the first decade of the century, parliamentary democracy was sufficiently strong to keep it marginalized as well as to avert, between the two wars, the danger of fascism.

In his well-known analysis of the 'republican strategy', Hoffmann (1963) contrasted its 'ideological formula', which included the extreme left but excluded the counter-revolutionary right, with its 'social formula', which, on the contrary, included the reactionary forces and excluded the revolutionary ones. In other words, the republicans, according to him, presented elections as a 'choice of regime' for or against the republic. But, once the votes were counted, they formed 'centrist' governments with conservative political programmes, that excluded the representatives of the labour movement, even though the latter formed part of the republican majority. This systematic 'ghettoization' of the labour movement contributed on the one hand to its internal divisions (multiple parties and union confederations) and on the other to its radicalization, initially libertarian and anarchist but later communist after the Bolshevik Revolution. The result was an ideologically divided and politically impotent labour movement.

Having located the republican/*ancien-régime* cleavage as the fundamental one in modern French politics, we need to outline the significant aspects. It comprises a set of polar conceptions – people/state, liberty/order, democracy/autocracy, secularism/clericalism – which have changed over time and which today can be summarized in the left/right opposition. In the nineteenth century, the two hostile traditions were represented by two opposing regimes. The republican was founded on popular sovereignty and identified with three fundamental constitutional ideas: (1) the need for republican institutions to secure liberty; (2) the inevitability of a sovereign national assembly elected by popular suffrage; and (3) recourse to the barricades as the final sanction of liberty against an over-mighty executive. In practice, the republican tradition has always led to assembly regimes in which the governments formed from it have done very much as they pleased. Unfortunately, they showed themselves to be either 'irresponsible' or impotent, which explains much of this tradition's obsession with political forms. Finally, there has always been a plurality of tendencies within the republican tradition (liberal, democrat, radical, socialist).

On the other hand, Bonapartism took over the *ancien régime* tradition in the second half of the nineteenth century and defended absolute state 'autocracy' and the concept of the supremacy of the national interest, expressed in *raison d'état*, but in a Caesarist and populist form.[12] In practice, this tradition was linked to regimes in which the executive dominated the legislature and the head of state established a direct and charismatic relationship with the people, institutionalized in the form of plebiscites and referenda at the expense of assemblies and parties. De Gaulle, who claimed the credit for having resolved the cleavage between these two traditions with the semi-presidential republican constitution of 1958 (chapter 7), personally expressed typically Bonapartist conceptions. For instance, he scandalized a former minister of justice by making comments such as: 'There is France. There is the state. And then, after the higher imperatives, and only in third place, there is the law.' Or again: 'Three things count in constitutional matters. Firstly, the higher interest of the country ... That has priority over everything else and I alone am judge of it. Secondly, a long way behind, come the political circumstances ... Thirdly, and very much further behind, come legal matters' (Hayward, 1983, p. 4). There is little doubt, therefore, that Gaullism is the contemporary heir to the Bonapartist legacy which includes, in addition to a strong, centralized but now republican government and the acceptance of a precise conception of national solidarity, also hostility towards parties and professional politicians. They are some of the aspects which distinguish it from the old counter-revolutionary and anti-republican right.

The republicans' appeal to anti-clericalism – above all in defence of the concept of secular education – has meant that the *ancien-régime*/Bonapartist tradition has enjoyed the support of the church, which hoped, at least until 1905, to recover some of its pre-revolutionary privileges. Hence this cleavage was lived in the villages of provincial France as a struggle between the *instituteur* (elementary school teacher) and the *curé* (parish priest). A further consequence of the church's allegiance to the right is that the church of France did not organize Catholics in an independent political movement in the nineteenth century as its counterparts did in Germany (Zentrum) and in Italy (Opera dei Congressi). It is no accident, therefore, that the clerical/anti-clerical cleavage still coincides with the right/left cleavage (table 3.2), as the mass mobilizations over the schools' issue in the 1980s demonstrated.

Political instability, as manifested in the periodic oscillation between two opposing types of regime in the two centuries since the revolution, has led to a strengthening of the role of the French state, inspiring an ambivalent attitude to it in most Frenchmen: either great dependence, or suspicion and contempt. The French know that the state is a source of protection and group privileges, but, at the same time, they fear it. Hence they are generally prepared to accept its impersonal and bureaucratic rules, particularly when they are advantageous, but they are in no way committed to them, so that they feel free to contest them when they find them detrimental. Politics, for the French, 'is a private question of individual conscience'; thus their political participation, voting apart, tends to be rather poor. However, they are prepared to exploit so-called 'parallel relations' (that is, personal relations) to solicit favours, but in private, because they are contrary to impersonal public rules. It is for these reasons, according to Crozier (1963) and Hoffmann (1974), that a specific style of authority has developed in France which discourages negotiation as a pragmatic method of problem-solving, but which prefers decision by decree instead, even if it provokes periodic crises. These are all the more frequent since they form part of a protest ritual practised by all groups, in which blackmail, direct action and violence are part of the *règles du jeu*. In the trial of force with the state, the group's goal is not to overthrow the government, as the foreign observer might be forgiven for thinking, but to gain concessions. If the state is unable to suppress the group it is forced to concede. Once the crisis is resolved, the state seeks to reduce the group to the rank of client again. Crozier is convinced that reform is impossible without a revolutionary crisis, because 'to obtain a limited reform in France, you are always obliged to attack the whole "system" which is thus constantly called into question' (p. 287).

In conclusion, if the emphasis has been placed on the importance of the state in the structuration of French society, this is because it has played a fundamental role. The contrast with Britain is striking. However, although France is an old nation, like Britain, and social and economic developments were slow up to World War II, the *trente glorieuses* triggered an accelerated cultural transformation which has involved the whole of civil society with the result that politics too has known rapid change. Many traditional structures are fast disappearing, leading, for instance, to the simplification of the French party system. But it would take much more to change the dominant role of the French state, even though certain, perhaps superficial, cracks have already begun to appear in its structure.

Germany

Discussion of the German political experience is inevitably coloured by the Nazi episode, as though it was the ineluctable result of a specific demon of the German psyche, like Adorno et al.'s (1950) 'authoritarian personality' syndrome. In categorically rejecting an approach based on the unique nature of German culture, we have to say, however, that German culture[13] has its own specificity which makes it different from both the British and the French. In contrast to these old nation-states, German unification came late – in the nineteenth century – and, moreover, lasted for a relatively short period (75 years). Indeed, Germany has been a nation-state only since 1871 with the creation of the Deutsches

Reich, under the impulse of Bismarck and the Prussian monarchy. From 1949 to 1990, Germany was again divided, this time into two states as a result of the Cold War (Federal Republic in the west and Democratic Republic in the east), and a large part of the territory that it had in the east in 1871 was lost at the Potsdam agreement (chapter 10). The division of Germany left its mark politically on the Federal Republic for at least three reasons. Firstly, the negative example of the Soviet model imposed on the Democratic Republic, and symbolized for almost 30 years by the Berlin Wall (1961–89), implanted a strong anti-communist bias in the population. Secondly, the separation of Protestant Prussia in an autonomous state meant that German Catholics found themselves equal, in terms of numbers, with Protestants in the Federal Republic, and this has healed one of the wounds of the Second Reich: the *Kulturkampf* and the fear of being oppressed as a minority. Thirdly, the division raised questions about the strength of the Prussian cultural legacy in the German political tradition, given the fundamental role played by the Prussian state in the building of the German nation. Chancellor Brandt's *Ostpolitik* and his successor's sensibility towards the east, culminating in unification, were in keeping with the Prussian cultural tradition that interpreted Germany's role as a bridge between east and west.

On the other hand, German politics, similar in this to French politics (and even Italian too), has been characterized by considerable discontinuity. The country has known, in fact, four different regimes in the last century: the authoritarian empire of the Second Reich (1871–1918); the liberal democracies of the Weimar (1919–33) and Bonn (since 1949) republics; and the totalitarian Nazi dictatorship of Hitler (1933–45). To this must be added the two lost world wars, in which Germany was one of the principal protagonists, and four years of Allied military occupation (1945–49), as well as the 40 years of Soviet regime in the east (1949–90). Despite this discontinuity and the wide diversity of political experiences, German society has been characterized surprisingly by considerable continuity, much more than the historical events and territorial changes would suggest.

Once again, the key to German political experience is to be sought in Germany's geopolitical position: a vast territory at the centre of the continent, namely the northern area of the old Holy Roman Empire that included in its western part the city-state trade belt (Hanseatic League). Thus, as Calleo (1978) has noted, 'geography and history conspired to make Germany's rise late, rapid, vulnerable, and aggressive' (p. 6). Indeed, none of the other European powers could afford to remain indifferent towards the building of a powerful nation-state in the heart of the continent, because it undermined the pre-existing geopolitical balance. It was for this very reason that the papacy had laboured for centuries to prevent such a possibility, and also because in so doing it helped secure its ideological control of the continent. It was no accident, therefore, that the Reformation broke out here (Luther's 95 theses nailed to the

Wittenberg church door in 1517). Indeed, this area became a frontier and war zone between Catholicism and Protestantism. The latter established itself in the regions furthest from Rome (Prussia and Saxony) while the former maintained its supremacy in the less distant regions (Bavaria).

At the same time, no political centre was able to dominate the entire area and build a state capable of uniting the German nation. Only from the seventeenth century did Prussia, situated on the infertile soil of the eastern borders of this territory, succeed in building a state with significant military power. However, given the lack of material resources, this effort was only possible thanks to the intensive exploitation of the peasantry, organized in regiments on the large *Junker* estates and reduced to bondage. Thus, the Prussian state was a state founded on coercion (not surprisingly called a *Polizeistaat* or barracks-state) and dominated by the army and the police. In the seventeenth and eighteenth centuries, the armed forces and civil service were entirely colonized by the *Junker* who, in turn, were subject to the monarch after the suppression of the estates general and the municipalities. Unlike the French absolute state, the Prussian state apparatus was not initially subject to public law, but only to the monarch's will, who used the 'right of despots', in accordance with Lutheran doctrine, to impose his own religion on his subjects. Hermet (1986) writes that: 'in Germany's case, the suspicion that there was a relationship between the exorbitant status accorded to power by Lutheran culture and the long-standing subordination of the German concept of citizenship to authoritarian and totalitarian values is well founded.' He argues that: 'the barracks-state of Frederick William [the Great Elector], then the Hegelian concept of the state as "the world which mind has made for itself ... [and that] man must therefore venerate as a secular deity ... [that] knows what it wills and knows it as something thought", found their chosen ground in this environment subjected to obedience through religious faith.' And he concludes: 'later on, Bismarckian authoritarianism, and above all the Nazi paroxysm, corresponded to this conditioning of a part of German society' (pp. 41–2).

Whatever the truth, in view of the backward nature of the agrarian sector, the Prussian state's ability to extract the necessary resources to maintain a standing army and an administrative apparatus depended, in the final analysis, on the army and administration themselves. At the same time, a strong state hindered the commercial development of agriculture, reduced capital accumulation and prevented the growth of a vigorous bourgeoisie. Hence, it was state interests that structured the development of the various classes, making subsequent industrialization dependent on state intervention. It is no accident, then, that the Prussian state – more powerful and efficient than its rivals – should become the instrument of German unification, which Bismarck carried to a successful conclusion in 1871 against his principal rival, the Habsburg Empire. It should not be forgotten that the West German states annexed by Prussia to form the Second Reich resembled France more than Prussia, characterized as they were by small landed property, an independent peasantry and a more active and emancipated bourgeoisie. This different social structure was responsible for a clear distinction between a more liberal and bourgeois west and a still feudal east that was mirrored to some extent in the division of the two Germanies between 1945 and 1990.

At this juncture there surfaces the delicate matter of Nazism and its contribution to the implantment of liberal democracy. There is an influential thesis linked to such famous names as Veblen (1915), Schumpeter (1919) and Gerschenkron (1943), and taken up by Dahrendorf (1965), according to which the German question – namely, the aggressive external policies that shook first Europe and then the world – was due to a peculiar combination of forced industrialization, authoritarian politics and reactionary society. In Veblen's view, imperial Germany combined a medieval institutional scheme with rapid, but borrowed, industrialization: 'the latest and efficient state of the industrial arts – wholly out of consonance with their institutional scheme, but highly productive, and so affording a large margin disposable for the uses of the dynastic state' (p. 249). The basis of the thesis was the discrepancy between modernizing economic development on the one hand, and traditional social values and political forms on the other. It was a direct consequence of the failure of the liberal-bourgeois revolution of 1848 and so of the 'revolution from above' carried out by the Prussian state under Bismarck's leadership.[14] According to Schumpeter, it was the attempt of a beleaguered elite (the Prussian *Junker*) that had created imperial Germany, to defend its privileges, exploiting its class speciality – war – to promote militarism and demagogic mass politics. This would explain both the forced industrialization – the need for military technology – and the *Sozialpolitik*. Dahrendorf (1988) is prepared to maintain that this 'authoritarian industrialization' ruthlessly carried out by the old ruling class, with largely feudal credentials, led to Nazism, following military defeat in World War I and the failure of Weimar, simply because 'welfare paternalism was unable to hold down the class struggle for ever.' His conclusion is just as disconcerting: 'it took Hitler's national socialism to complete the revolution of modernity for Germany. This thesis of mine ... has often been criticized, but I would still maintain its essence, which is that all the remaining premodern barriers of estate and church allegiance, of authoritarian benevolence without civic participation, were brutally destroyed by a regime which needed total mobilization to maintain its totalitarian power.' The instrument of this policy was the notorious *Gleichschaltung* (coordination law). 'But it meant', Dahrendorf claims, 'that in the negative sense of the absence of traditionalist obstacles, German democracy had its first real chance after 1945' (p. 69).

However, the new historiography has considerably reappraised the implications of this thesis. It does not deny the authoritarianism of Bismarck's politics, feudal residues or the *Junker*-bourgeois alliance.

What it contests is the significance of the so-called 'liberal' bourgeois revolution of 1848 because this implies that the bourgeoisie was by definition 'liberal', when this was not even true of the English and French bourgeoisies. Indeed, the new historiography even suggests that, in the famous alliance of 'rye and iron' (agrarian interests and heavy industry), the bourgeoisie was in the ascendancy and the *Junker* were no longer dominant, even though they still held, at least until World War I, a privileged position in the state apparatus. Calleo (1978) identifies the causes of the German state's collapse – which opened the way, between the wars, to the rule of a band of political adventurers – in Germany's geopolitical position, combined with late and forced industrialization (policy inimical to parliamentarianism), the threat of a strong socialist movement, and the lack of an adequate colonial empire. In other words, the German political system was unable to withstand, in the first half of the century, the intense pressures brought to bear on society from its external problems. Burckhardt (1906) had already noted with concern in the 1870s that: 'first and foremost, however, what the nation desires, implicitly and explicitly, is power ... its one desire is to participate in something great, and in this it clearly betrays that power is the primary objective, culture is at best a very secondary goal. More specifically, the desire is to make the general will of the nation felt abroad, in defiance of other nations' (pp. 85–6). The external problems arose from the fact that German unity had undermined the bases of the European system of states (chapter 10). The imperialism of the late nineteenth century was itself the consequence of expanding demands confronted by shrinking resources which the international system was incapable of peacefully composing, and which resulted in World War I. Domestic problems came from the labour movement which in Germany had built, for the first time, a powerful organization in which the union apparatus was subordinate to the party (SPD). Late unification and the novelty that this introduced into the international system were naturally the focal point of this tension, and the rest is history: World War I, Weimar, Hitler, World War II.

At all events, countries which arrive late at a critical juncture find themselves in greater difficulty in confronting the challenge of later crises, above all in the nineteenth century when they tended to accelerate. This was notoriously the case of Germany (and Italy) when compared with Britain. Imperial Germany had to face both the problem of the form of government – parliamentarianism – and that of the organization of the subordinate classes: the propagation of working class and socialist ideologies in Germany, in contrast to Britain, preceded the great drive to industrialize and the industrial concentration that accompanied it. It is no accident, therefore, that these problems were considered secondary and less urgent than those regarding the power of the state and the development of the national idea. This explains, on the one hand, façade parliamentarianism – 'a pseudo-constitutional absolutism',

Mommsen called it – and, on the other, authoritarian executive power, which reacted to the arrival of the social democrats on the political scene first with a state of siege and then with paternalistic welfare. However, what was tolerable initially because transitory, became intolerable when its permanence undermined its original justification. 'Nazi seduction', Hermet has asserted, 'should be understood, in part, in the light of this concatenation of events' (1986, p. 158).

If the new historiography appears more convincing than the old in explaining the significance of the imperial German experience, specific aspects still remain to be explained. And this is all the more important because many believe that the implanting of liberal democracy was assisted by the 1940s radical break, which was as much socio-economic as political. Dahrendorf defends the thesis that the social revolution accomplished by the Nazis through the *Gleichschaltung* created, unintentionally and for the first time, the basis for a real liberal democratic regime in Germany. In addition, the collapse of the German state in 1945 and four years of Allied occupation allowed the rules of party competition to be redefined and consolidated in new socio-political conditions. Indeed, the loss of prestige, as a result of the Nazi defeat, of the two historically most influential state institutions (civil service and armed forces) left a power vacuum that the parties (authorized, in the first place, by the Allies) were able to fill to their own advantage, and they were also able to preside over post-war reconstruction. In this situation, it has been suggested that the Federal Republic has become a 'liberal democracy on the Anglo-Saxon model'.

In addition to this last consideration, however, the parties' central role in the new constitutional order – the importance of party membership (*Parteibuch*) for appointment to and/or promotion in public institutions, the concrete services (clientelist) rendered to their members, and the identification of the main parties with the 'liberal democratic constitution' – has contributed to the development of a definition of the Federal Republic as a *Parteienstaat*, a symptom, among others, of the persistence of the Prussian state tradition, despite the 1940s break. In the same way, the parallel polemic over the *Sozialstaat* is linked to this tradition. Finally, Dahrendorf himself admits that 'even present-day West Germany has not been able to rid itself entirely of bureaucracy' (1988, p. 67), another element typical of the Prussian tradition.

If aspects of past experience have survived to influence contemporary German politics – the division of the labour movement at the beginning of the 1930s is an instance that comes to mind – the most significant element remains state supremacy. The Prussian-German state, like its French counterpart, is characterized by its primacy *vis-à-vis* civil society. So much so, in fact, that it is not just another case of Badie and Birnbaum's 'state model', but is a state with its own autonomy in relation to society, a fact confirmed also by the experience of East Germany. This suggests the hypothesis that if the Prussian state tradition has declined in

West Germany, as many claim, its disappearance is as much a result of the division of Germany, if only because 'the state-country of the east ceased to prevail only at that moment over the state-country of the west' (Hermet, 1983, p. 156). The Hanseatic and Rhineland-Bavarian territories were, moreover, always more regardful of socio-economic factors than of purely political ones.

The Prussian-German legacy can be understood also in a further aspect, that is to say authority in its bureaucratic version of the domination of law. This is perceptible in the juridical concept of expert-official (even ministers prefer to be regarded as technicians rather than politicians); in the use of legal means to prevent the propagation of radical opinions, for instance in declaring the neo-Nazi and communist parties anti-constitutional in the 1950s; in the *Berufsverbot* in the 1970s; and finally in the political use of the Bundesverfassungsgericht (constitutional court) through the technique of *abstrakte Normenkontrolle* (abstract review of legal rules).

To conclude, a by-product of the implanting of liberal democracy in the Federal Republic has been the tendency of political competition to degenerate into a pure conflict of interests between social groups and political organizations for short-term corporate advantages, lacking political substance for the most part. Indeed, despite the *Bürgerinitiativen* (the citizen initiative groups) in the 1970s and the *Grünen* in the 1980s, Offe (1984) has deplored 'the fact that, in the face of the exceptionalism of twentieth-century German history, *all* political parties, though especially the SPD, find it particularly difficult to relate to any consciousness of a collective identity, whether conceived in national, class or cultural terms' (p. 209). This is also because religious and class factors have become purely electoral variables (table 3.2) without mobilization capacity any more. The result, according to Offe, is an 'extremely statist politics' in which change is always conceived only in administrative and legal terms and where democracy risks becoming, in Hennis's phrase, 'almost emotionally irrelevant'. German modernization is yet again, in this view, 'an *external* process, one that has not been accompanied by a modernization of values, attitudes, and forms of political association' (Offe, 1984, p. 217).

Italy

The Italian political experience is also unique in the sense that it differs from all the other European countries in one essential fact: Rome has been for almost 2000 years the spiritual capital of Catholicism and the home of the papacy. It is easy, therefore, to understand that this fact alone has meant that the relations between church and state in Italy are different from those in all other European countries. Suffice it to recall that all the popes for 450 years, from Leo X in 1520 to John Paul I in 1978 – the period that saw the formation of the nation-state in Europe – were Italians, to realize why the church has always taken a 'special' interest in Italian affairs.

In such a situation, it is no surprise that Italian unity, like German, was achieved late: between 1861 and 1870. The surprise, if there is one, is that it succeeded at all. Moreover, it should be no surprise that once unity was achieved, Italian politics were characterized by considerable discontinuity. Thus although Italy, unlike Germany, did not suffer from significant territorial changes after unity – except for the annexation of the Trentino-Alto Adige after World War I and the loss of Fiume and part of Istria after World War II – it has known, like France and Germany, four political regimes in the last 100 years: the liberal monarchy (1861–1922); Mussolini's fascist dictatorship (1922–1943/5); the Allied military occupation (1943–1945/6); and the liberal democracy of the post-war republic (since 1946).

A discussion of united Italy's political experience means above all a discussion of the Catholic Church's role since it strenuously opposed the formation of secular and independent states in the territories of the former Holy Roman Empire: hence the struggles between Guelphs and Ghibellines in Italy. Indeed, the only kind of state that it was prepared to tolerate in the peninsula was that of a pluri-ethnic empire under a Catholic sovereign, that is a state whose power was potentially universal and sacred, and legitimated by the pope, in keeping with Catholicism's universal vocation; this role was filled formerly by the Spanish monarchy and later by that of the Austrian Habsburgs. Thus both the concept and the tradition of the independent, centralizing absolute state were lacking in Italy. Paradoxically it was a peripheral power, namely Piedmont, more strongly influenced by France – a centralizing state with a strong administrative tradition – that finally succeeded in uniting the peninsula with foreign support (France militarily and Britain diplomatically) and imposing on the new nation, as best it could, its own state system which was still in the process of institutionalization.

The new ruling class, however, met such strong resistance (Catholic *non expedit*, southern brigandage) that it was unable to create a really autonomous state. The result was not a 'modern state', as Gramsci (1949) charged, but 'something of a bastard', to wit a weak state apparatus incapable of controlling the territory over which it claimed to exercise the sovereignty that is the primary attribute of every real state. Gramsci commented that:

> the leaders of the national movement ... aimed at stimulating the formation of an extensive and energetic ruling class, and they did not succeed; at integrating the people into the framework of the new state, and they did not succeed. The paltry political life from 1870 to 1900, the fundamental and endemic rebelliousness of the

Italian popular classes, the narrow and stunted existence of a sceptical and cowardly ruling stratum, these are all the consequences of this failure. A consequence of it too is the international position of the new state, lacking effective autonomy because sapped internally by the papacy and by the sullen passivity of the great mass of the people. (p. 90)

In partial justification of the liberal ruling class of the new Italy – a tiny minority – was the complete hostility of the Catholic Church. Far from decreasing with unity, on the contrary, it increased because the new state deprived the papacy of its temporal power, its territory (with the exception of the Vatican) and church property. The Holy See, in fact, refused to recognize the Italian state and observed a policy of non-collaboration: the *non expedit* was implemented under the banner of *ne eletti, ne elettori* (no elected representatives, no electors), initially to dissuade, and later to explicitly forbid, Catholics from taking any part in Italian public life. This policy was a serious threat to the legitimacy, and so stability, of the new state if only because of the very high proportion of Catholics. Indeed, the church had endowed itself with wide popular support, particularly among the peasantry, as a result of its Counter-Reformation offensive against the Protestant heresies. It was during this missionary offensive that the parish clergy became Gramscian 'organic intellectuals' of peasant society thanks to a symbiosis with the rural masses made up of common customs and language. Moreover, it was only at the start of this century that the church changed its policy and initiated, with pope Pius X's encyclical *Fermi propositi* of 1905, its reconciliation with the Italian state that was officially sealed in the Lateran pacts of 1929. In the meantime, the church had organized militant Catholics in their own socio-political organizations (Opera dei Congressi, Azione Cattolica) which laid the institutional basis of a separate Catholic subculture.

The church's hostility was not the only major obstacle that the new liberal ruling class had to confront. More important in many ways was that implicit in Prince Metternich's famous definition of Italy as merely a 'geographical expression'. The reference was as much to the country's regional diversity – 'the dualism of civilizations' (Fortunato) – as to its general decadence. Even the poet Leopardi lamented in his youth that Italians not only lacked feelings for the nation as such but were also devoid of any sense of society.[15] It was an agricultural country dominated by latifundia (Gramsci's 'great social disintegration') and industrial backwardness (D'Annunzio's 'cities of silence'[16]). Hence, the problem was how to establish a liberal regime. The answer, according to Hermet (1983), was a 'fictitious' or 'façade parliamentarianism'. In united Italy, this type of regime had two components: one at the institutional level (that is, of the parliamentary elite), *trasformismo*; and the other at the level of society (to wit, MP–voter relations), *clientelismo*. *Trasformismo* is a parliamentary procedure in which the government requests the support of MPs individually (and independently of their ideological convictions) in the name of an ill-defined political solidarity. It was theorized by the Piemontese prime minister Depretis in 1882, in terms of the need to bring political procedures into line with the natural development of things – 'the general law of living things', in Minghetti's famous formulation – and of an appeal to parties to 'transform themselves' and so do away with ideological differences. It was a kind of lowest common denominator unifying principle which in fact cut the government off from the electorate.

Behind this parliamentary procedure, however, lay another practice, certainly more obstructive: *clientelismo* (that of MPs doing favours for their client-voters) which was the second component of Italian-style façade parliamentarianism. Individual MPs' support of the government was secured by patronage. The Italian parliament became a market for the distribution of favours,[17] that is, MPs gave precedence to the needs of their constituency over that of the country's general interest. This was the source of Mosca's (1895) famous observation: 'when we say that the voters "choose" their representative, we are using a language that is very inexact. The truth is that the representative *has himself elected* by the voters': he adds ironically, 'If that phrase should seem too inflexible and too harsh to fit some cases, we might qualify it by saying that *his friends have him elected*' (p. 154). As a Sicilian, moreover, he knew full well who were the friends of his island's MPs! However, two aspects need to be stressed. Firstly, there is the symbiotic relationship between *trasformismo* and *clientelismo*: the general opinion inclines to the view that *trasformismo* is, unfortunately, the most efficient, if not the sole, parliamentary procedure in a largely 'nepotistic' society. Secondly, the fact that *trasformismo* brought *clientelismo* right to the heart of the state is of great significance for the subsequent development of Italian politics because 'it conferred a sort of legitimacy on patron–client networks and stimulated "unscrupulous dealings" ' (Bollati, 1983, p. xi), and this led to its institutionalization. Galli (1974), in fact, has identified the thread of post-unity Italian history in *trasformismo* on the basis of the following sequence: '*connubio, trasformismo, giolittismo*, fascism, Christian Democrat "bloc of order", recent hypotheses of consociational republic and grand coalition' (that is, 'historic compromise': p. 21). The constant elements are mediation, compromises and general *ad hoc*-ism.

Clientelismo, as an integral part of Italian parliamentarianism, has an ambiguous face as well; that is, in addition to its obviously corrupting aspects, there is a legitimating aspect also. The southern 'notable' is simultaneously the protector of his 'clients' against the threats of the outside world, usually personified in the hostile state. Hence the patronage tie can assume, according to Hermet, that sacred aspect sanctioned by St Augustine,[18] and confirmed today in a widespread popular saying; '*Senza santi non si va in paradiso*' ('Without saints you cannot go to heaven'). The notable is the natural and respected guide of his clients and becomes 'the person through whom the "clientelist" vote ceases to be the product of a fraudulent and coercive artifice' (Hermet, 1983, p. 94). Façade parliamentarianism was, in all probability, a necessary stage in the development of Italian democracy, because neither the modern state nor the modern economy – full employment – ever reached the south. For many, as for Benedetto Croce (1928), it represented a necessary, but not excessive, price that Italy had to pay for a liberal regime: 'why should they [the Italians] not have been content with the ministries,' he asked himself, 'which, for all their instability, gave them on the whole such a measure of liberty, law and government as corresponded to their needs and was practically possible?' (p. 22). It is probable that it allowed the country to move towards unity, respecting the imbalance arising from regional dualism (summed up in the century-old 'southern question'), but at what price? The disagreement, in fact, is over the price paid. Some people, like Bollati, judge it excessive: 'where *trasformismo* (which is masked violence) fails,' he argues, 'it is replaced by open violence' (p. xvi). This raises the question of the relationship between *trasformismo*, fascism and Mafia (Catanzaro, 1988). Without wishing to discuss the merits of the question, we note that Bollati and others do see a link between them, claiming that Croce – for whom fascism was an 'unhappy parenthesis' (p. viii) – with his philosophic distinction between use and worth, the world of politics and the world of the spirit, ended by conferring on *trasformismo* a cultural dignity that it did not warrant.

At all events, as regards fascism there are other aspects of the price of *trasformismo* to be noted. Firstly, the granting of legitimacy to *clientelismo* quickly led to the institutionalization of arbitrary acts and abuse which undermined the state's authority. Intervention in the central administration by private interests and compromises with Mafia and Camorra in the provinces became the rule and left their mark. Secondly, *trasformismo* was a big obstacle to authentic democratization. On the one hand, it discredited parliamentarianism as a method of government in the eyes of the mass of the population: it created the illusion of a change without the substance. On the other, it meant the abandonment of the state's role as the organizer of a democratic society, with consequent socialization of the masses in an anti-state way by extra-parliamentary movements dedicated to destroying the system by means of either radical revolution or dictatorship, as actually happened in the case of fascism.

The façade parliamentarianism operated by the Italian liberal oligarchy (on the basis of that alliance between northern capitalists and southern landowners, baptized 'historic bloc' by Gramsci) was unable to meet the domestic political challenge on the morrow of World War I. In fact, it was undermined above all by two emerging processes: (1) the entry of the masses on the political stage through two mass parties (socialist and Catholic), thanks to universal male suffrage and war mobilization; and (2) the formation of fascist combat squads by demobilized soldiers disillusioned by the war and in favour of a strong regime, but also prepared to use violence as a political weapon. The outcome was inglorious: Mussolini's twenty-year fascist dictatorship. Italy, having reached, like Germany, the critical juncture of unity late, had to face the next junctures, those of participation and redistribution, one after the other. Lacking, unlike Germany, both a strong state tradition and a sufficient level of industrialization, Italy opted for the strategy of gradual participation, but it proved fatal to the liberal regime in the end.

The question at this point is the same as that concerning Nazism in Germany: whether the fascist dictatorship accomplished a similar modernizing social revolution to the one that Dahrendorf claims was the Nazi regime's great unintended legacy to its Western successor. Fascism certainly intended to create a modern nation-state. According to Mussolini: 'The dissonance is between nation and state. Italy is a nation. Italy is not a state.' Hence, the fascist effort was to achieve, through mass mobilization (in the ranks of fascist organizations), that nation-state which, in its view, the Risorgimento had not even attempted: 'Nothing without the state. Nothing outside the state. Nothing against the state.' Nonetheless, Mussolini's regime was less successful than Hitler's, even though it lasted nearly twice as long. This was principally due to the price that it had, like its *trasformista* predecessor, to pay for the series of compromises that it was obliged to make. Suffice it to recall, for instance, the conservative economic policy, the indiscriminate anti-labour repression and, above all, the pact with the church. Despite this, fascism was not totally without a legacy: in the field of political organization it created the first party machine (PNF) that embraced the whole national territory and secured its articulated presence in civil society as well as the state (exploiting, of course, the old patron–client networks). LaPalombara (1987) claims that the Fascist Party furnished not only the organizational model of the post-war mass parties (DC and PCI), but also that of the political process (*partitocrazia*), that is the notion that the parties could informally overcome the weakness of the state institutions.

The proof of fascism's lack of success in creating new enduring state structures was the re-emergence of aspects of pre-fascist, even pre-Risorgimental, Italy. 'Who could still represent Italy, after fascism,' Baget-Bozzo (1982) asked himself, 'if not the papacy?', commenting: 'The DC won the succession to the Risorgimento state just because it was the expression of that historical force, the church, which had never recognized it, and merely endured it. There are older memories, deeper motivations than those that come from immediate political events, which explain the Christian Democrats' accession' (p. 11). But, as Bollati observed, Croce, having furnished *trasformista* practices with a cultural dignity, ensured them 'in fact, unlimited survival as a way of thinking and acting politically that it shared with the postunity ruling class' (p. xviii) – something which has been much in evidence in the post-war period. Finally, fascist anti-labour repression contributed to the PCI's implantation; its discipline conferred it a primacy in clandestinity that ensured it a leading role in the resistance, which it was able to exploit subsequently, above all in the appropriation of the socialist subculture.

In conclusion, we would stress yet again the weakness of Italy's state tradition that did not succeed in liberating itself from the parties' embrace. They colonized the state (*sottogoverno*) as in Germany, where the practice has been called *Parteienstaat*, whereas in Italy it is known as *partitocrazia*, just because of the state's weakness, even if many of the political mechanisms in the two countries are similar. The *trasformista* practices have continued, but under new guises, while patron–client networks have spread everywhere (Cazzola, 1988), thus revealing a dangerous confusion between state apparatuses and private organizations (including the Mafia), between state and civil society, which often tends to camouflage certain deep cleavages and socio-political tensions that nonetheless exist (table 3.2).

However, we can note a qualitative change in the level of political participation since the 1960s. But, if the causes lie in the social movements and the great post-1968 social struggles, in economic development and secularization, it did not happen without difficulty, or in only one direction, as terrorism and the 'years of lead' (1974–9) demonstrated. Finally, the most significant advances in the post-war period are on the one hand the acquisition of a widespread legitimacy by democracy, combined with a loss of legitimacy by the political class and the political institutions, worsened by the *tangentopoli* (bribesville) scandal, and resulting in majority electoral reform in 1993; and on the other the progressive integration of the labour movement, leading to the dissolution of its principal expression, the PCI, in 1991.

Conclusion

Rokkan's conceptual geopolitical map of Europe is a useful tool for identifying the major political cleavages which structurate European civil society today. It is based on two parallel, but conflicting, territorial claims – political control and cultural identity – which provide a key to the continent's political development. He presented the claims as both spatial and analytical axes: north–south (cultural) and west–east (political-economic). The former touched a crucial problem: the difficulties encountered by rulers of the countries nearest to Rome in achieving projects of national unification owing to the universal pretensions of the Roman Catholic Church. Hence, the significance of the Protestant Reformation in the formation of the nation-state. The latter was concerned with the material resources required to build the state and their availability. Although these two axes were fundamental to Rokkan's explanation of the diversity of European political development, he recognized that other factors also played a role, for example the outcome of the agrarian question and the surfeit of linguistic fragmentation.

Rokkan's map has been criticized for neglecting significant aspects of European development such as using too broad a definition of the state and thus underplaying the impact of differences in state structure – for example between state-led societies (France) and society-led states (Britain) – or again, using too narrow a definition of culture and thus neglecting important cultural aspects, for example Elias's role of the court. Rokkan's map was not restricted to state formation, but was also oriented towards elite strategies in the area of the formation of mass politics. In this he identified a number of critical junctures in European history – Reformation/Counter-Reformation, national revolutions, industrial revolution, Bolshevik Revolution – whose outcomes determined the predominant cleavages in the various countries. Rokkan's thesis was that the early cleavages were responsible for crucial differences between the European political systems while the later ones contributed towards uniformity. The value of this thesis was illustrated from a number of significant historical examples.

Contemporary ideologies have a common intellectual matrix in the seventeenth century scientific revolution which undermined the theocentric vision of the *res publica Christiana*. God was replaced by the people as the basis of political authority. There are no longer any ultimate demonstrable truths. The result was the formulation of a totally new world view, at least intellectually: secular and not religious, anthropocentric and not theocentric. Despite the fundamental differences between the new and old world views, the former included several significant features of the old, but transformed in the new cultural climate, like the Christian kingdom of heaven which became the liberal dream of an earthly paradise or the communist dream of the classless society.

The British political experience and cultural tradition are characterized by their continuity, as much a reflection of Britain's geopolitical position and size as any specific feature of its population. Early unification in favourable circumstances meant that it did not need a centralized state structure until relatively late. Hence stability and autonomy became virtues. Moreover, parliament as the representative of civil society become the heart of the British political system and was slowly democratized over a long period. In addition, Britain's role as the first industrial nation and the centre of a great empire meant that it disposed of significant resources at the critical moment of the development of mass politics. Economic improvement became a feasible goal for the subordinate classes and so class became naturally the major political cleavage. It is not that other cleavages (religion, race) do not exist, but that their incidence has been limited hitherto.

The French political experience, in contrast to the British, is characterized by political instability, the result also of its geopolitical position, a much larger continental country with enemies on its land borders. The nation was built by the absolute state, defined as a perfected bureaucratic organization. Hence civil society was subordinate to the state. The French Revolution, the originator of the decisive cleavage in contemporary French politics, turned out to be essentially political and cultural rather than economic and social. The key was popular legitimacy, and he who spoke in the name of the people had power, so the political struggle was carried on in ideological terms: republic versus the old order. Political instability, as manifested in the oscillation between the two opposing types of regime, led to a strengthening of the role of the state. This inspired an ambivalent attitude in most Frenchmen towards it – either dependence, or suspicion and contempt – which merely serves to emphasize the state's fundamental contribution to the structuration of French society.

The German political experience has been marked by discontinuity, both territorial and political. A state of relatively late unification, like Italy, it has been subject to widespread territorial changes as well as five political regimes since 1870. In addition, the country has just been united after 40 years of political division. Again, like Britain and France, its geopolitical position – the largest country in the centre of the continent – has been a crucial dimension of its political experience, visible above all in the efforts necessary to create first the Prussian state and then the German. Moreover, the country embodies the Reformation religious divide (Protestantism versus Catholicism). The major historical experience of the present century was Nazism, and it is moot whether it was an aberrant experience due to late unification and forced industrialization or something more peculiarly linked to the German mentality. Dahrendorf holds that, whatever its causes, Nazism completed the revolution for modernity in Germany, thus creating the basis for liberal democracy. The question since the second unification is whether liberal democracy is sufficiently consolidated to overcome the economic difficulties that it has brought in its wake or whether it is just skin deep.

Finally, the Italian political experience is unique in that it is coloured by the fact that Rome is the spiritual capital of Catholicism and the home of the papacy. To this must be added late unification and significant political discontinuity (four regimes since 1870). Conflict with the papacy meant that the Italian political elite was forced to resort to administrative centralism and a façade democracy founded on *trasformismo* and clientelism in the liberal period. However, this did not survive the disruption of World War I when it collapsed and was replaced by Mussolini's fascist dictatorship. Moreover, fascism failed to achieve the modernizing social revolution that Nazism is credited with accomplishing in Germany, or even the creation of a strong state, mainly because it had to come to terms with the Catholic Church. The proof of fascism's lack of success was the re-emergence of pre-unification forces, above all the church as the dominant force in post-war Italian politics, and the continuing weakness of the state which resorted once again to *trasformismo* and clientelism, and even private criminal organizations (Mafia, Camorra). Its weakness was revealed by the ending of the Cold War when the traditional political forces came under attack for their mishandling of state finances, promoting constitutional reform to the top of the political agenda.

Further reading

G.A. Almond and S. Verba (eds) (1989), *The Civic Culture Revisited* (Newbury Park, Calif.: Sage).

S. Ashford and N. Timms (1992), *What Europe Thinks: A Study of Western European Values* (Aldershot: Dartmouth).

B. Badie and P. Birnbaum (1983), *The Sociology of the State* (Chicago: Chicago UP).

W. Bagehot (1992), *The English Constitution* (London: Fontana).

R. Barthes (1973), *Mythologies* (St Albans: Paladin).

G.A. Craig (1984), *The Germans* (Harmondsworth: Penguin).

R. Dahrendorf (1967), *Democracy and Society in West Germany* (London: Weidenfeld & Nicolson).

R. Dahrendorf (1985), *On Britain* (London: BBC).

A. Gramsci (1988), *Selected Writings* (London: Lawrence & Wishart).

S. Hazareesingh (1994), *Political Traditions in Modern France* (Oxford: Oxford UP).

G. Hermet (1986), *Sociologie de la construction démocratique* (Paris: Economica).

O. Hintze (1975), *The Historical Essays of Otto Hintze* (ed. F. Gilbert) (New York: Oxford UP).

S. Hoffmann (1974), *Decline or Renewal? France since the 1930s* (New York: Viking).

R. Inglehart (1977), *The Silent Revolution* (Princeton, NJ: Princeton UP).

R. Inglehart (1990), *Cultural Shift* (Princeton, NJ: Princeton UP).

J. LaPalombara (1987), *Democracy, Italian Style* (New Haven, Conn.: Yale UP).

G. Orwell (1982), *The Lion and the Unicorn* (Harmondsworth: Penguin).

S. Rokkan (1970), *Citizens, Elections, Parties* (Oslo: Universitetforlaget).

S. Rokkan (1971), 'Nation Building: A Review of Models and Approaches', in *Current Sociology*, 3, 7–38.

G. Therborn (1977), 'The Rule of Capital and the Rise of Democracy', in *New Left Review*, 103, 3–41.

T. Veblen (1966), *Imperial Germany and the Industrial Revolution* (Ann Arbor, Mich.: Michigan UP).

R. Williams (1971), *The Long Revolution* (Harmondsworth: Penguin, 2nd edn).

4 The Changing of Civil Society

Introduction

After the structuration of civil society in its historical dimension – nation-state formation and resulting national socio-political cleavages – we must turn our attention to the elements that determine the persistence and change of such structuration. The social struggles and political conflicts of generations of men and women are the motor of political change. It is these struggles that form the collective experience out of which the different ways of life of these countries are forged. It is through social struggles and political conflict that ways of life as ideologies become part of common sense[1] and political tradition.

This view poses the problem of the nature of political participation – an ancient but also very recent phenomenon. It is very recent in the sense that it is closely linked to the development of liberal democracy since universal suffrage was only achieved in the main West European states after World War II (table 4.1). However, the experience of political participation in the ancient world (leaving aside questions of its content) made such a historical impression that a whole tendency of Western political thought – identified with Rousseau – has seen in direct democracy not only a possible model for the organization of political power, but also its optimum form, to be pursued wherever possible.

Without wishing to discuss the merits of direct democracy – which would be largely abstract, in any case – it is clear that the concept of political participation is also of fundamental importance to liberal democracy. However, the concept is many-sided, not to say ambiguous: it includes on the one hand people, both specific groups (like political leaders and party members) and the whole population (that is all citizens); and on the other a whole range of extremely varied actions and activities. For this reason, we reject the traditional view of the concept because it tends to confine it to forms of participation associated with the state's constitutional activity. We prefer, instead, to follow Pizzorno's (1966) approach just because he emphasizes the importance of other forms of participation which principally concern civil society and its structuration. Pizzorno's analysis is useful, in fact, because it helps to situate two phenomena which have a primary role in the structuration of civil society in Western Europe: social movements and subcultures. Finally, the necessary premise of all forms of political participation is political communication because, as Barbagli and Maccelli (1985) have quite properly observed, 'it is not possible to follow what happens in politics without a certain level of information' (p. 15). The principal source of information in the West today is the mass media, which are also the main channel of political communication, and hence the most important connection between civil society and the state – even though, as Barbagli and Maccelli also note, 'it is in participating, even invisibly, that one acquires new information on political actors and institutions.'

Political participation

Pizzorno's typology

Pizzorno's (1966) discussion starts from an obvious, but often overlooked, observation: participation only became a problem in the modern world with the emergence of the notion of popular sovereignty, namely in the period after the French Revolution, when mandatory representation was replaced by free representation. Under the *ancien régime* there was an almost complete coincidence between the social and political positions of an individual because political participation was accorded to a specific social status (corps): those who had this status (that is, belonged to this corps – usually peers of the realm) participated automatically; and those who lacked it did not. Meaningful political participation only started when this automatic relationship ceased. The development of political participation in Europe was the result of two converging processes of opposing origins. The one was part of the class struggle and came from civil society (from below) and took the form of a demand for the expansion of political rights, above all the extension of the suffrage; the other was part of nation-state building and came from the state (from above) and resulted from the need of the ruling class to win a completely new kind of legitimation on the basis of popular sovereignty. Thus political participation in European societies has a double problematic: equality plus consensus. Moreover, it is no accident that it is defined by some of the same elements that Rokkan identified as forming the bases of the principal socio-political cleavages in Western Europe since it is an aspect of the same process.

Such processes were converging but contrasting, even paradoxical, because on the one hand the *egalitarian* demand from below actually benefited those citizens who were able to bring to the political process the weight of their private position in civil society (to wit their property, prestige and capacity to mobilize resources), while on the other the groups which already controlled the state were forced – in order to defend their privileges – to make alliances with the new popular forces. Indeed, when all citizens have the right to participate in politics, but not all are equal in civil society – because they differ with regard to their socio-economic and cultural positions – the privileged naturally do not hesitate to use their particular advantages. The response of the under-privileged to this socio-economic and political inequality can only take the form of political organization. This process creates, in turn, a new kind of inequality, this time at the level of the state, no longer on the basis of socio-economic or cultural privilege, but now in terms of num-bers in a regime founded on universal suffrage.

The political organization of European societies has historically taken two forms: one which wants to radically change society and its values (social movements) and the other which wants to conserve it, more or less, and its values (parties and pressure groups). Social movements are born in civil society on the basis of solidarity of the 'collective enthusi-asm' sort. As such they are precarious, which means that they either rapidly achieve their specific purpose (radical social or political change) and disappear, or are transformed and typically become parties or pres-sure groups. The history of political parties is a long and complex one, originating either as factions inside the state, or as movements in civil society. Once they were implanted in civil society – at the end of the last century – they became (with pressure groups) the principal institutional connection between civil society and the state.

If the permanent organization of parties and pressure groups gave substance and meaning to the widening of participation, it also induced processes which substantially limited its possibilities. Firstly, it encour-aged the formation of a professional political class which, according to Pizzorno, 'claims that its legitimacy derives from the fact that it repre-sents the forces of society, in other words private interests. At the same time, it gains autonomy by the development of a new kind of specializa-tion' (p. 34). This specialization derived from the experience of party organization, that is the capacity of the new class to organize popular consensus which gave it the right to lead the state. In this way, the politi-cal class conferred political legitimacy on the state (Mastropaolo, 1984). Secondly, the party became a structure that was an end in itself: it was not only an instrument of participation but the object or aim of partici-pation itself. Participation in organization (rather than participation through organization) appeared as distinct from political action. This development is responsible for two important contemporary phenom-ena. One is bureaucratization, namely political action that has as its goal the survival of the organizational apparatus as such, even if this means overlooking the original political goals: it becomes a 'political machine'. The other is political subculture, that is to say associational participation at the grass-roots level which becomes involvement in a closed circle of social relationships, expressing a sense of identity rather than of intervening in the state's political processes, but which can provide both material and moral resources for the latter.

Parallelly, Pizzorno argues that the bourgeois revolution, by bringing the system of private interests within the state sphere, also brought in the class struggle. The class struggle was born in civil society, but in an international context – that is to say, little influenced by the reality of national states – and, hence, as the carrier of universal values, initially bourgeois and later proletarian. If the class struggle was institutionalized to some extent in the course of the present century as a result of the extension of citizenship rights, a strong radical and universalistic element nonetheless survives. As Pizzorno points out:

> This complies with the historical legacy which the class struggle received from revolutionary bourgeois ideology and the Enlightenment concept of man – in the name of which the bourgeoisie had claimed power. This historical legacy also contained a contradiction … the value system had both to presuppose the possibility of universal equality and also the function of gauging the inequalities of individual positions, that is of private inequalities. Class ideology arises from this contradiction and attempts to overcome it. (pp. 36–7)

Historical analysis of participation makes it possible, according to Pizzorno, to clarify two further points. The first is that there are several kinds of participation. He identifies four: (1) professional political activity in state and party posts; (2) political participation as an expression of citizenship through voting, campaigning, organizing; political participation in closed associations, more or less separate from dominant structures, which can be either (3) in social movements or (4) in subcultures (figure 4.1). The second point is that if participation is not only a problem of consensus, but also one of collective action in an inegalitarian

Nature of goals		Nature of interests	
		Political solidarity prevails	Private solidarity prevails
	Negotiable within the state system	Political profession	Civic participation
	Non-negotiable within the state system	Social movement	Subculture

Figure 4.1 Types of political participation
Source: Pizzorno, 1966, p. 59

structure, then the word 'politics' must mean something wider than mere participation in the state's constitutional activities.

Moving from historical to rational analysis, Pizzorno asserts that the state and class, like the family and friendship groups, are *systems of solidarity* between actors; that systems of solidarity are opposed to *systems of interest*; and that both give rise to *systems of evaluation*. The general characteristic of a system of interests is that the criteria of evaluation are objectively and functionally shared by its members and do not give rise to feelings of identity with that system. The system of interests, in other words, creates a competitive situation among its own members to gain a relative advantage, thus becoming a source of inequality. The economic system is an example of such a system of interests. Systems of solidarity are characterized, on the contrary, by the criteria of identity between individuals and the system as well as by the separation from, and likely contrast and conflict with, other systems, with the aim of creating equality between members who want to be recognized as equal among themselves. Solidarity endeavours to overcome difference and achieve equality. Classes and the national state are, unlike the family and friendship groups and other systems of solidarity, systems of *political* solidarity, because they constitute systems of interest too, that is to say they are the basis of specific values which support a historically determined system of interests.

Finally, the element that distinguishes the two systems of solidarity, state and class, is that while state action is nationally limited by territorial considerations and the presence of other states, class action is potentially universal. On this basis, Pizzorno proposes the following definition: 'political participation is an act of solidarity with others in the ambit of the state or of a class, with a view to conserving or modifying the structure (and so the values) of the dominant system of interests' (p. 255).[2]

As should be evident, the concept of solidarity is the key to the analysis, and it presupposes an 'area of equality' as the basis of all collective action. This is also the case of the concept of 'citizenship' which is the base of the actual democratic state (see the introduction to this book). As regards class, the fundamental qualification for participation is the occupational position of its members: Marx's 'class in itself'. However, class solidarity only becomes effective with organization, as in social movements, trade unions and parties. Paradoxically, nonetheless, the latter is related to the system of self-interests and, thus, is a source of new inequalities. The point that Pizzorno wishes to stress is that every political organization must in the beginning be, of necessity, an association between equals. Indeed, the general proposition that emerges from his observations is that 'participation is only possible among equals'. This proposition is not only true in the case of socialist parties and labour movements, whose ideology asserts the common goal of equality, but equally so in the case of conservative and bourgeois parties. The organizational formula of different groups linked together in a loose union –

like the National Union of the British Conservative Party – made it possible to avoid contact or confrontation between gentlemen and workers who were members of these bourgeois parties,[3] and officially on an equal footing. In fact, each social group tended to form its own 'subarea of equality', which was, of course, more or less socially homogeneous.

In the course of his analysis, Pizzorno outlines two models of participation. The first, the 'class consciousness' model, is constructed on the general proposition that 'political participation increases with the increase in class consciousness.' This is helpful in explaining, *ex post facto*, certain upsurges in participation, such as collective enthusiasms that cause social movements, but not in predicting them, just because we are dealing, by definition, with unstable conditions. The second model, the 'centrality' model, can be summed up in the general proposition that 'the higher the social position of an individual, the more he participates in politics.' Research in European countries confirms this proposition, as regards both the recruitment of the political class and civic participation through voting, for instance. Both depend more or less explicitly on the relationship in European liberal democracies between the dominant system of interests in civil society and the state, that is the political position of an individual is one of the many possible attributes of his private position in civil society. Finally, the apparent exceptions to this proposition – for instance, that of militants in secondary organizations – can also be explained using the concept of 'centrality', but in terms of group relations: the more an individual is part of a homogeneous group the greater, all other things being equal, will be his degree of political participation. This is nothing more than an expression of an individual's identity with a certain social group and an example of 'subcultural participation'.

The usefulness of Pizzorno's typology for our purposes lies in the distinction he makes between the various kinds of participation most directly connected with cultural change and persistence – social movements and subcultures – and those concerned with the operation of the political system – professional politics and civic participation. In American studies, civic participation has become the synonym of political participation *tout court*, while 'professional politics' is not usually considered a form of participation, but a professional activity, that is to say 'as one specialization amongst others in the division of labour' (p. 59).

To conclude this discussion of participation, we need to note that Pizzorno's analysis, and above all his broad definition of political participation, has been criticized, and not only by those who defend the narrower American view. Melucci (1977), for instance, criticizes, like Pizzorno, the American tendency to limit participation to the recording of observable behaviour, in so far as this is only the 'direct transcription of interests in political demands and behaviour', since any reference to 'non-participation' (that is all demands that are not expressed, because excluded) is missing from this approach. At the same time, however,

Melucci argues that, in his attempt to demonstrate that participation is also the bearer of interests which are formed outside the political system, Pizzorno ends up by proposing too wide a definition that covers all forms of collective action, leaving them thus in a state of indeterminacy. Indeed, Melucci asserts that one must avoid both a very narrow definition, which becomes a justification of the status quo, and a very wide one which deprives the concept of any heuristic value.

For Melucci, then, the concept has two different meanings: on the one hand, it is 'recognition of belonging to the system, identification with the general interests of the community, action to promote common goals'; and, on the other, it is 'the defence of particular interests in a competitive situation, attempts to influence the distribution of power' (p. 119). This means, in an inegalitarian society like Europe, that participation in the first sense is always an assertion of dominant interests (identification with the system), because it is the rules of the system which lay down what one can or cannot have, and the representation of the subordinate classes is subject to these rules. Hence a subordinate class's identification with the system means accepting its own subordination. In the second sense, participation can mean an attempt to change the relations of forces in the political system: to increase one's own influence over decision-making. In other words, the problem of political participation for the dominant classes is simple: it is a way of asserting the primacy of their own interests and seeing their primacy recognized by other groups. For the subordinate classes, participation is more complex: it is a way of increasing their influence on political decision-making, *but* in a situation where their interests cannot, by definition, be fully represented. Hence, these interests are expressed in extra-constitutional activity, namely in ways that differ from traditional political participation. For this reason, Melucci proposes a narrower definition of the concept, limiting it to constitutional activity, while all those phenomena which concretely concern the political system, but in which there is a breach of the rules or an exceeding of constitutional boundaries, are analysed as social movements and not as political participation.

There is no need to take sides in this dispute: both positions have merits and defects. For our purposes, it is sufficient to take account of both the activity of social movements and that of subcultures. Such activity has had fundamental consequences for the functioning of West European political systems. The political regimes of the various countries would certainly be very different from what they are now without movements and subcultures. However, before discussing them, we must look at the constitutional forms of participation. The political profession will be examined in the discussion of the state in part III. For the moment, then, the analysis is limited to the basic aspects of civic participation, namely that set of political activities, orientations and processes typical of Western democracies: voting, party militancy, demonstrating, political group membership, political discussion, electoral campaigning, contacting political leaders and political propaganda.[4] Tables 4.1, 4.2 and 4.3 present some comparative figures, to be considered purely indicative as based on survey data.

Table 4.1 Levels of invisible political participation (per cent)

(a) Interest in Politics

		A great deal	Not much	Not at all	Don't know
Britain	1958	23	44	32	1
	1983	12	73	15	–
	1990	13	68	19	–
France	1958	nd	nd	nd	nd
	1983	11	62	27	–
	1990	7	61	31	1
Germany	1958	34	38	25	3
	1983	14	74	11	1
	1990	25	67	7	1
Italy	1958	11	26	62	1
	1983	4	54	42	–
	1990	6	59	31	4

(b) Exposure to information media

		Every day	At least once a week	Less often	Never	Don't know
Dailies						
Britain	1974	37	30	18	14	1
	1983	53	13	10	14	–
France	1974	nd	nd	nd	nd	nd
	1983	31	27	13	28	1
Germany	1974	46	27	19	8	–
	1983	61	26	7	5	1
Italy	1974	19	20	20	40	1
	1983	26	32	14	27	1
Television						
Britain	1983	84	13	2	1	–
France	1983	63	28	5	4	–
Germany	1974	64	31	3	1	1
Italy	1983	65	26	5	4	–
Radio						
Britain	1983	56	18	12	14	–
France	1983	49	22	10	18	1
Germany	1983	53	34	9	3	1
Italy	1983	29	20	16	34	1

Table 4.1 *Continued*

(c) Discuss politics with friends

		Often/ sometimes	Rarely/ never	Missing data
Britain	1958	70	29	1
	1974	47	52	1
France	1958	nd	nd	nd
	1974	nd	nd	nd
Germany	1958	60	39	1
	1974	43	56	1
Italy	1958	32	66	2
	1974	37	63	–

nd: no data.
Sources: Weber, 1986, pp. 147–52; Ashford and Timms, 1992, p. 158

Table 4.2 Levels of visible conventional political participation (per cent)

(a) Types of political activity (1974)

	Often	Sometimes/ rarely	Never	Don't know
Convince friends to vote as self				
Britain	3	14	81	2
France	nd	nd	nd	nd
Germany	6	39	54	1
Italy	7	23	69	1
Attend political meetings				
Britain	2	19	77	2
France	nd	nd	nd	nd
Germany	5	41	55	–
Italy	7	30	63	–
Work to solve community problems				
Britain	4	26	68	2
France	nd	nd	nd	nd
Germany	4	31	64	1
Italy	7	22	69	2
Contact officials or politicians				
Britain	2	23	73	2
France	nd	nd	nd	nd
Germany	3	24	72	1
Italy	7	22	70	1

Table 4.2 *Continued*

(b) Participate in associations (1983)

	Membership of an association	Work for an association
Britain	58	18
France	43	22
Germany	60	15
Italy	36	22

nd: no data.
Source: adapted from Weber, 1986, pp. 164 and 187

Civic participation

The democratic ideal presupposes a citizenry interested in public affairs, in touch with political events, informed about the principal national and international problems, capable of choosing between the different alternatives proposed by the various political forces and involved in direct and indirect forms of participation. Reality is very different. Not only is interest in politics very limited (about 20 per cent of the electorate state that they are very interested in politics, while about 50 per cent claim that they keep in touch with political events) but the level of information is very low: if a majority of the electorate know the head of the government's name, the percentage falls rapidly when it is a case of news about a specific event or project. Moreover, these two kinds of participation are strongly linked to the socio-economic characteristics of the population. As regards the most common – and for many the sole – form of political participation in Western societies, that is voting, the levels are high (averages between 75 per cent and 92 per cent: table 4.4), even though the act itself is not an unambiguous one: many people vote simply because it is the norm.

In fact, the figures show that the countries with the oldest and longest uninterrupted democratic traditions, like Britain and France, have a lower electoral turnout – the case of the USA is particularly notorious, with barely half the electorate voting in presidential elections – than those, like Germany and Italy, where the democratic tradition is more recent and discontinuous. On the other forms of participation, it is not possible to have reliable data for comparison. However, there is no reason to think that visible participation, constitutional or not, is higher in Germany and Italy than in Britain and France, as the data in the tables suggest. At all events, even if the 1980s figures suggest that the differences that existed in the decade after World War II are disappearing, we ought to be very cautious, because participation tends to follow a cyclical pattern linked to national social mobilization. Thus, while one country

Table 4.3 Levels of visible non-conventional political behaviours (per cent)

	1974	1990
Petitions		
Britain	22	75
France	nd	43
Germany	31	51
Italy	10	42
Lawful demonstrations		
Britain	6	13
France	nd	13
Germany	9	19
Italy	17	32
Unofficial strikes		
Britain	5	8
France	nd	9
Germany	1	2
Italy	1	5
Occupying buildings		
Britain	1	2
France	nd	7
Germany	*	1
Italy	4	6
Damage property		
Britain	*	
France	nd	
Germany	*	
Italy	*	

	1974	1990
Boycotts		
Britain	5	14
France	nd	11
Germany	4	11
Italy	1	9
Rent strikes		
Britain	2	
France	nd	
Germany	1	
Italy	2	
Painting slogans		
Britain	*	
France	nd	
Germany	1	
Italy	2	
Block traffic		
Britain	1	
France	nd	
Germany	2	
Italy	2	
Personal violence		
Britain	*	
France	nd	
Germany	*	
Italy	*	

* Less than 1 per cent.
nd: no data.
Sources: Weber, 1986, pp. 178–80; Ashford and Timms, 1992, p. 158

Table 4.4 Turnout in post-war parliamentary elections (per cent voting (number of elections))

	1945–55		1956–65		1966–75		1976–90		Median 1945–90	
Britain	79	(4)	78	(2)	75	(4)	75	(3)	76	(13)
France	80	(4)	76	(3)	81	(3)	74	(4)	78	(14)
Germany	82	(2)	87	(3)	89	(2)	86	(5)	86	(12)
Italy	92	(3)	93	(2)	93	(4)	90	(4)	92	(11)

can experience a period of high participation, a European partner can have a low one, as, for instance, Italy in relation to Britain in the 1970s. Finally, it is worth pointing out that there has been a revival and development of 'associationism' in Western Europe, particularly on the continent in the last two decades, which is certainly connected to the new social movements to be discussed below.

To conclude this section, we must emphasize the low level of civic participation which contradicts the widely held view that it is the basis of every democratic regime. The inactive and the indifferent outnumber the politically active many times over. This observation raises two questions. Firstly, is the population really divided between the vast majority of politically inactive and a tiny minority of 'completely' active, or is the situation more complex? On the basis of a large research project on Britain, Parry, Moyser and Day (1992) affirm that the politically active tend to specialize in certain fields (figure 4.2), that is to say some devote themselves to group activity, others to protesting, others again to electoral campaigning. The result is that the number of 'complete' activists is

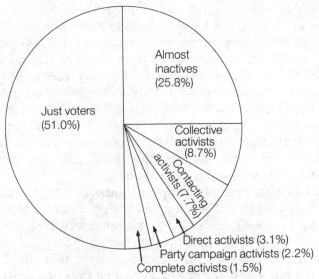

Figure 4.2 Types of political participation in Britain in 1985
Source: Parry, Moyser and Day, 1992, p. 229

extremely small (1.5 per cent of the electorate), but the total number of the politically active (23 per cent) is higher than generally accepted. The other question is more fundamental but also more delicate: what are the consequences of civic participation for the political system? Here, we can agree with Pasquino (1986) that this represents one of the most neglected areas of contemporary political science. In fact, he notes dryly that, more concerned with inputs (that is, individual motivations), political analysis has left 'the output side ... substantially in the shade' (p. 225). However, despite the organization of the subordinate classes in parties and trade unions, actual civic participation largely benefits the privileged and wealthy classes[5] – among whom the most active citizens are found – at the expense of the subordinate and disadvantaged classes, in majority inactive or not very active citizens because of their lack of individual and collective resources. The result is that policies more often favour particular participant groups and not a more general public interest for the simple reason that at the present time 'participation is a right that benefits those who use it – whoever they may be and for good or ill' (Parry, Moyser and Day, 1992, p. 418). They are the 'comfortable' and the policies favoured are those that Galbraith (1992) has dubbed 'the culture of contentment'.

Social movements

The importance of social movements in the forming of European society is universally recognized today. One need only recall the great movements for civil rights in the seventeenth and eighteenth centuries, or for political rights and economic and social justice in the nineteenth century, or for social and cultural liberation in the present century. In opposition to these emancipatory movements, authoritarian and populist movements (Catholic and fascist) have arisen either to defend the status quo or to establish a totalitarian society. However, theoretical reflection on social movements has remained fairly underdeveloped until recently. In fact, neither Marxism, with its concern to define the preconditions of revolution by examining the structural contradictions of the capitalist system, nor American 'structural functionalism', with its focus on the integrative mechanisms of institutionalized collective behaviour, paid particular attention to social movements.

For this reason, neither European Marxism nor American sociology have been able to shed much light on the peculiarities of such a complex phenomenon. Indeed, the students' movement of 1968 came as a severe shock to sociologists as neither major social theory had prepared them for the range and force of the social conflicts that shook the Western world in the late 1960s. Moreover, even a quarter of a century later there is still disagreement as to what a social movement is and what might distinguish it from a political party or a pressure group: whether it is to be seen in terms of an attempt to transform cultural patterns or merely as another actor in institutional politics. Alberoni (1968; 1976), for instance, conceives of it as a break: collective movements, he believes, are provoked by a discrepancy between expectations and achievements. He elaborated, in fact, an original theory about the appearance of collective movements, that of the 'nascent state' (*stato nascente*). It is a transitionary phase between two social orders, which differs from other forms of transformation, that is those that occur as a result of organized decisions, or of market changes, or again of collective processes – fashions, panics, crazes – because it is the only moment when new values are born. Further, Alberoni (1976) claims that 'no other social entity is capable of creating values'. He illustrates one of these moments:

> Let us begin by saying that in our country political, religious and cultural innovation occurs, as in the rest of the world, through spontaneous processes of small groups that, above all in their initial phase of 'nascent state', have common characteristics, like the experience that a radical revival, a renaissance, the start of a new history, is possible ... The participants live an exalting experience, in which the achievement of a new kind of life, a new kind of man and society appears possible ... there is enthusiasm, communism, a desire and need to tell the truth; an overall experience that causes an institutional crisis, makes everybody think and, to sum up, produces a great cultural transformation. Obviously, such periods do not last very long. (pp. 67, 57)

Why? Because to achieve the utopia to which they aspire, the actors are forced to give themselves a structure, in a word to institutionalize themselves. Institutionalization marks the end of the nascent state and the start of the 'movement' phase. This is a slow, difficult and often ambivalent process, and one which does not necessarily succeed. In fact, the institutional outcome – generating one's own institutional social formations, that is religious sects, small groups, parties, which are no more than the normalization of the new structured social order – is not the only outcome of the nascent state. It can be absorbed by existing institutions, as Alberoni (1977) appears to think is the case for the majority of Italian, and not only Italian, 1968 movements; or it can disappear altogether, defeated.

More recently, Alan Scott (1990) has suggested the following definition as a rough guide: 'A social movement is a collective actor constituted by individuals who understand themselves to have common interests and, for at least some significant part of their social existence, a common identity.' He adds by way of precision: 'Social movements are distinguished from other collective actors, such as political parties and pressure groups, in that they have mass mobilization, or the threat of mobilization, as their prime source of social sanction, and hence power. They are further distinguished from other collectivities, such as voluntary associations or clubs, in being concerned to defend or change society, or the relative position of the group in society' (p. 6). But this definition still leaves open the question of how they are to be understood. This can be done by examining the two theoretical paradigms that are now dominant in the field: (1) 'resource mobilization' theory (RMT: McCarthy and Zald, 1979; Tilly, 1978); and (2) 'identity-oriented' theory (IOT: Touraine, 1978; Melucci, 1989). The former, of largely American origin, focuses on the instrumentality of movement strategy; it is interested in the mechanisms by which movements recruit and mobilize and their effects on the social actors. The latter, of largely European provenance, focuses on how movements produce new historical identities for society; it is interested in the way in which macro-structural social processes are transformed into social movements. Both, however, make a number of common assumptions, for example that social movements involve con-testation between groups with autonomous associations and develop sophisticated forms of communication (networks, pamphlets, publics); or again that conflictual collective action is normal. More importantly, according to Cohen (1985), their insistence on the *prior* organization of social actors and on the *rationality* of collective contestation directly challenged the earlier theories of social movements.

Resource mobilization theory

RMT is particularly sensitive to the inherent constraints of collective action because it is based on economic models of human agency (or rational choice theory) and almost indifferent to the context and content of social movements. Rational choice theory postulates that individuals will only be induced to act in the collective interest where the group can distribute 'selective incentives', that is rewards commensurate with mem-bers' contributions. Where rewards remain purely collective, there is no incentive for the individual to participate because it is more rational for him to 'free ride', that is to accept the collective rewards without making sacrifices to obtain those rewards. For this reason, collective action is viewed as unstable, problematic and occasional. Indeed, because of the organizational constraints – the need to provide private benefits, the search for resources, the restricted demands that can be made on mem-bers – social movements are under pressure to institutionalize them-selves and pursue low-risk strategies. Hence,

> non-institutional collective action will tend to metamorphose into
> institutional action where the risks, for example of illegality, are
> lower. Furthermore, loose organization demanding high degrees
> of commitment from members will give way to tighter more for-

mal organization where the organizational burdens will be taken over by 'professionals' or quasi-professionals, and where demands on grass-roots membership will be restricted to occasional meetings, participation in collective action, etc. (Scott, 1990, p. 113)

The significance of RMT is that, unlike structural functionalism, it treats collective action as rational, actor-oriented activity. Moreover, it points up the problems facing social actors when they have to choose whether to involve themselves in collective action, rather than assume, as IOT does, that an adequately articulated critique of existing social relations will ensure mobilization. Hence it conceptualizes social change in terms of conflict resolution, and history becomes the unintended outcome of the strategic battles between organizations and movements. On the other hand, RMT's limits are that it assumes an impoverished view of human motivation which is reduced to mere instrumental rationality. Indeed, if this view were correct, it would paradoxically preclude the possibility of collective action. That it is not indicates that many people define self-interest not in terms of personal welfare but in terms of value orientation, like commitment, loyalty and so on. It disregards the idea that action can be its own reward; in other words, as mentioned above, it virtually excludes the notion that social movements are as much cultural as political phenomena, and that they can mould and modify people's perception of their interests and preferences and, hence, can completely transform an existing social order. Nonetheless, RMT is useful in stressing continuity between social movements, parties and pressure groups because, although it may exaggerate the extent to which activists are concerned to integrate themselves into existing power structures and employ social movements as the vehicle, this is, in fact, often what has happened, that is social movements end up by becoming parties and pressure groups, not only historically with the labour movement but even today with the greens.

Identity-oriented theory

IOT, as noted, inhabits a different intellectual world to RMT: it concentrates on substantive objectives, not motivations; on identity formation and how social movements produce new historical identities for society. Social movements were conceived as historical actors with their own projects. For Touraine (1978), the major theorist, the so-called 'new social movements' are the potential bearers of new social interests in a new historical era, that of post-industrial society; and their activity is seen as a prime mover of social change. They, and not individuals, are the new social actors. Hence they are to be analysed in terms of their projects and the processes and actions through which they attempt to achieve them, and not in terms of the motivations and strategies of their members. They are social subjects which create and perpetuate social relations. Indeed, society is conceived as the conflictual production of itself and social movements are the principal agents of this production. However, they do not produce it by themselves; rather it is shaped in encounters with other, antagonistic groups. In other words, modern societies are marked by what Touraine calls 'historicity': an outlook in which men and women use knowledge of social processes to reshape their conditions of existence.

To grasp the significance of this approach we must emphasize that although society has the capacity to develop and transform the way it operates, this capacity has never been exercised by society as a whole, but by a restricted group of innovator-dominators, the ruling class. The latter identifies itself with historicity, over which it assumes control, particularly with regard to the distribution of resources. The popular classes are subject to the ruling class to the extent that they are forced to accept the ruling class's socio-cultural dominance, while remaining rivals on the historical plane. In this sense, society is schematically formed of two opposing movements: one (the ruling class) which transforms historicity into order and power; and the other (the popular classes) which contests this order so as to 'rediscover the orientations and conflicts through *cultural innovation* and through *social movements*' (Touraine, 1978, p. 31). Social movements are, according to this logic, class conflict (but in a much wider sense than the Marxist, namely as much cultural as socio-economic) for the control of historicity in a given society. Hence, they are far from being rare and dramatic events; on the contrary, they lie permanently at the heart of social life, less formulators than propagators of culture.

The problem of analysis of social movements derives from the combination of collective behaviour (crisis – or aggressive – behaviour, crazes, panics, riots, speculative booms, and social deviancy) and conflict-based action (institutional political dissent, generally interpreted by parties and groups) that do not have the same social, cultural and political implications. As Touraine (1983) has noted: 'a social movement appears initially as a deviant act, a disorder, an assault on what is considered normal, that is expected behaviour' (p. 203). It then comes to recognize itself as a collective actor with a historical project through a process involving the interaction of three interconnected poles – totality, identity and opposition – and it forges its identity in a totality of a social field of action in opposition to a historical other. In poorer, if more comprehensible, language: 'If one is to fight, one should know in whose name one is fighting, against whom, and on what grounds' (Touraine, 1978, p. 81).

IOT theorists, further, maintain that the nature of social movements depends on the system of social relations in which the collective action is situated and to which it refers. Touraine, for example, identifies three systems of reference (that are levels of analysis and not concrete sites of social praxis): historicity, political system and social organization. The first system is the level of conflictual class relations: it defines the mode of appropriation and destination of resources, both material and symbolic, of a society. The second identifies the level of legitimate decisions. The third refers to the forms of social organization that secure the social equilibrium and society's adaptability to its environment. There is a hierarchy between the systems in the structure of Western society, in the sense that one system imposes on the others more constraints that it suffers: it goes from class relations (historicity) to organization, via the political system. Thus class relations fix the limits in which the political system can operate, and the latter, in its turn, lays down the rules of social organization.

On the basis of the systems of reference of social relations, which correspond to certain forms of collective action, Melucci (1980) – a former student of Touraine – has drawn up an articulated analytical framework (figure 4.3), using two of the analytical dimensions (conflict and breaking of system limits) which allow him to distinguish different types of collective action and situate the four principal forms (social movement, conflict-based action, crisis behaviour and social deviancy) and their modalities.

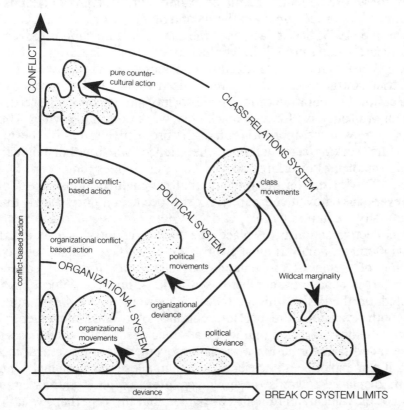

Figure 4.3 Melucci's analytical framework of collective action. Class movements cannot exist without mediation of the political or organizational system: pure class movements turn easily to counter-cultural action or violent marginality
Source: Melucci, 1980, p. 205

Types of social movement

The social movements of interest to our discussion are three: (1) organizational movements; (2) political movements; and (3) class movements. *Organizational movements* represent the minimum situation, namely when the collective action is situated at the level of a given social organization and is directed at the power governing a system of norms and rules, as, for instance, when working class action evades trade union control. In general, an organizational movement tends to transgress the institutional limits of the organization and go beyond its normative framework to invest the source of the norms. *Political movements* express conflicts that seek to surpass the limits of the political system, like the great nineteenth century struggles (Chartism in Britain) for extending political participation, or those less glorious for its suppression in Italy (fascism) and Germany (Nazism) between the two wars. *Class movements* invest the control of historicity, that is to say they pose directly and indirectly the question of cultural orientation: for what purposes, for whose benefit? The major example of this type of action is the European labour movement in the second half of the nineteenth century.

Touraine (1973) has, in fact, used the example of the labour movement to illustrate the nature of the conflict at this level. He argues that the working class shared the same cultural orientations as its adversary, the industrial bourgeoisie, that is it recognized the idea of progress as the basic cultural orientation of industrial society and encouraged the development of productive forces – machinery, work ethic and savings – but it bitterly opposed the appropriation of the productive forces by the ruling class. The working class defended the sciences which either helped the people (medicine) or offered society new possibilities (engineering), but rejected 'Taylorism' on the grounds that it benefited industrialists only. However, class movements rarely, if ever, occur in a pure state – that is without any mediation by the political system or by social organization – since collective action takes place in a specific country at a specific historical moment. Analysis must always, therefore, take account of a combination of elements: movements, but also other forms of collective action (crisis behaviour, conflict-based action). Finally, Melucci has formulated, on the basis of his analytical framework (figure 4.3), a number of hypotheses about the possible conduct of a class movement. For instance, he has suggested that in the absence of radical change in society or the failed transformation of a class movement into a political movement, it can explode and its class components lose their original content and be displaced towards the boundary areas of pure counter-cultural action or of 'wildcat' marginality. We opine that this is perhaps what happened to the two branches of the 1968 Italian student movement: Autonomia (counter-cultural marginality) and Brigate Rosse (wildcat marginality).

At this juncture, we need to point up the assumptions implicit in Touraine's IOT approach. These relate essentially to his understanding of contemporary society, namely that of a fundamental change in advanced industrial societies which has displaced social change from the socio-economic level (industrial society) to the cultural level (post-industrial society) with the result that 'new' social movements are fundamentally different from old 'historical' movements. Indeed, a major problem for IOT theorists appears to be identifying the new movements – predicated as capable of transforming society – from the old movements, capable only of defending their members. Not only is such a project teleological in the sense that it is the presumed post-industrial goals that determine the definition of a particular movement, but in fact the so-called new movements share many of the features of the old movements. Finally, Touraine predicated the rise of a movement representing the essential nature of post-industrial society and capable of synthesizing opposition to it into a single coherent oppositional force. He thought that he had found it in the anti-nuclear movement, but its failure to unify diverse ideological strands into such a single oppositional force capable of transforming society led him to opine that it was not a 'true social movement', that is a 'class movement', but merely a 'political movement'.

What is important, nonetheless, in the IOT approach is its emphasis on the normative character of movements and their capacity to effect cultural change: the invention of new norms, institutions and social practices in their struggle to redefine social identity. Naturally this concern with norms and identity over organization and the pragmatic context led Touraine and his followers to ignore the elements of calculation and self-interest that are the focus of the RMT approach. We should add that Touraine (1983), reflecting on the inability of the 1970 movements of contestation to effect the transformations he predicted, was reluctantly forced to recognize that he had earlier underestimated the importance of conjunctural factors in the decade's mass mobilization. In other words, he had overlooked that the flowering of the social struggles of that decade was also linked to economic expansion, with the result that the 1974–5 economic recession reinforced purely political action and thus reduced the space available to new social actors. A more pragmatic explanation is that the 'new' social movements were not so new (that is different from their predecessors) as Touraine had supposed. Collective social action always poses questions of leadership and organization. Indeed, it is no coincidence, as Melucci has noted, that movements are created where solidarity networks (such as associational links) and leaders already exist.

Social movements in history

One way of assessing the movement phenomenon is to focus on the actual social movements that have marked the life of West European societies in the last 100 years. The labour movement is the one which has most obviously stamped its imprint on the history of the period. It emerged in Britain in the first half of the nineteenth century and was subsequently formed in Germany, France and Italy in the second half of the century. It is often presented as a unified movement, which succeeded in dominating – at least, according to its adversaries – Western European political systems in the post-war period. This one-dimensional image obscures the movement's complexity and its history. As Hobsbawm (1975) has remarked:

> This process of emergence was a curious amalgam of political and individual action, of various kinds of radicalism from the democratic to the anarchist, of class struggles, class alliances and government or capitalist concession. But above all it was *international*, not merely because, like the revival of liberalism, it occurred simultaneously in various countries, but because it was inseparable from the international solidarity of the working classes, or the international solidarity of the radical left (a heritage of the period before 1848). (p. 135)

Thus its unity, far from being an indisputable fact, was always being challenged, in the same way that socialism was never accepted by the whole labour movement as the movement's 'organic' doctrine. The proof of this lies in the division of the movement which led to the split between communists and social democrats, on the morrow of the Bolshevik Revolution.

The struggle for control of the productive and labour processes is recognized today as the unifying element of the labour movement – which explains why the workplace, factory or office is the favoured site of labour conflicts and why a strong class consciousness developed – but class conflict has given rise to a multitude of forms of struggle (riots, strikes, marches, factory occupations) and class solidarity has found a plurality of organizational forms (trade unions, parties, cooperatives, friendly societies, cultural associations, working men's clubs). In this context, the experience of the British labour movement is particularly significant. It has recently been argued that an inversion of the economic conjuncture, linked to a move from cottage industry to factory organization – a change that opened a twenty-year period of economic expansion from 1850 to 1870 – coincided with a change in the form of labour struggles and organization. The change was from mass socio-political struggles to sectorial industrial ones and from the organization of great popular movements, like Chartism, to that of trade unions and other social bodies. Finally, it was only with another change in the conjuncture at the end of the century that the British labour movement rediscovered a political role: the Labour Representative Committee, forerunner of the Labour Party, was founded in 1900.

We should bear in mind that collective action, the activity and organizational forms of the European social movements, has been historically influenced by the nature of the political system and the structure of the society in which those movements found themselves operating. Firstly, the subordinate classes' right to create friendly societies was only recognized in most European countries in the late nineteenth century. The British trade unions were alone in enjoying a legal existence before 1850, while the legislation that authorized trade unions dates from 1884 in France and from 1890 in Germany, although a form of semi-legal tolerance existed in both countries from about 1860. Secondly, even if the right of social and political organization was legally secured, much depended on the political system's degree of openness. In Britain this openness was the result of a long period of political cooperation between the labour movement and constitutional political forces (Liberal Party). For this reason, theoretical socialism has never really been part of the British labour movement's cultural heritage. In Germany, France and Italy, on the other hand, the widening of the suffrage combined with the closure of the political system was accompanied by the subordination of social to political action, trade unions to the party. In other words, the unity of the labour movement was secured – but in cases like France, there was an anarcho-syndicalist split after the Commune of 1871 – by ideological means, that is to say the socialist idea, social revolution being achieved by political revolution. For instance, the German labour movement between 1880 and 1914 saw the SPD grow in strength as the principal opposition party in parliament – with about 30 per cent of the vote – and the creation of a whole network of social and cultural organizations to manage German working class life as a sort of counter-society. The same thing, on a smaller scale, occurred in Italy between 1890 and 1920. The British labour movement (around the cooperative movement) and the French (round the CGT) pursued similar policies between the two wars. They created a distinct culture (working class, red, labour) among the subordinate classes in certain zones, exploiting the fact that the working class was often territorially concentrated: working class districts, mining villages, landless peasant settlements. Finally, labour conflicts became progressively institutionalized after World War I with the creation of the welfare state. The result was to transform the labour movement into a political force, with the consequent development of its role as a political actor and the decline of that as social and cultural adversary.

The labour movement was not the only important social movement active in nineteenth century Europe. Around 1870, the Catholics in Germany and Italy created their own movement. In Germany, where they were a minority, Catholics identified Protestants as their adversary and it was Bismarck's *Kulturkampf* that provoked their mobilization between 1871 and 1879. In Italy, the adversary was the new secular, anti-clerical liberal ruling class of the Risorgimento, that had deprived the pope of his temporal power (20 September 1870). In both countries, Catholics united in a series of associations (peasant leagues, rural banks, cooperatives, professional groups, and later trade unions and party) on the basis of the ecclesiastical structure to create a society within society, a sort of institutional segmentation (*Verzeilung*) that, founded on Catholic social doctrine, sought to reduce to an absolute minimum Catholics' contact with the new secular state. In France and Britain this did not happen, either because, as in the former, the Catholics were politically divided (between monarchists and republicans) or, as in the latter, they were numerically insignificant, except in Ireland.

Even fascism can be considered a social movement. In fact, it has been interpreted as a movement of the middle classes that developed in a serious social crisis. Strata were mobilized to put an end to their position of *déclassé* groups, reinforcing their own collective identity and thus giving them a new social role. They identified their adversary in the labour movement: the fear of the socialist revolution was the basis of fascist and Nazi mobilization, which exploited nationalism as an ideology. Fascism was more a political movement than a class movement, in Melucci's terms, and succeeded in winning power in Italy in the 1920s post-war crisis and in Germany in the 1930s economic crisis. It did not succeed in France and Britain even though local fascist movements (Croix de Feu, Doriot's Parti Populaire, and Mosley's British Union of Fascists) were founded and developed in those years.

New social movements

As noted above, the IOT theorists believe that the social struggles of the last twenty years mark a new departure and are qualitatively different from the earlier ones. This assertion is based on the belief that a major social transformation has been taking place in Western countries, with the appearance of a new type of society, post-industrial society. The characteristic feature is social domination by giant technological apparatuses, and no longer that by industrial processes as in industrial society. The objects of the new social struggles are therefore the various, often state, apparatuses and systems that dominate large sectors of social life (university; large corporation; urban, educational, health and welfare systems; church) and exercise social control (prison, psychiatric hospital), involving the population in their quality of 'citizen' and not as a specific social category. A further consequence is the fragmentation of struggles – student, youth, women, ecology, health, anti-nuclear – without any visible unifying element. Touraine, as mentioned, saw in the anti-nuclear

protest and environmental movement the first signs of the anti-techno-
cratic movement that he was convinced was the new class movement of
post-industrial society. He believed that energy would play the same role
today as manufacture had in the industrial era. However, this has not
proved to be the case: hence, Touraine's subsequent change of mind.

Whatever the truth of the post-industrial society hypothesis – and we
have already expressed some scepticism (chapter 1) – another feature
has been advanced to substantiate the 'newness' of new social movements: this is their informal network-type organizational characteristics.
On the basis of research in Milan, Melucci (1984) has claimed:

> The normal situation of today's 'movement' is to be a network of
> small groups submerged in everyday life which require a personal
> involvement in experiencing and practising cultural innovation.
> They emerge only on specific issues as for instance the big mobi-
> lizations for peace, abortion, against nuclear policy, etc. The sub-
> merged network, although composed of separate small groups, is
> a system of exchange (persons and information circulating along
> the network, some agencies such as local free radios, bookshops,
> magazines providing a certain unity). Such networks ... have the
> following characteristics: (a) they allow multiple membership; (b)
> militantism is only part-time and short-term; (c) personal involve-
> ment and affective solidarity is required as a condition for partici-
> pation in many of the groups. (pp. 444–5)

This emphasis on informality is intended to contrast with the formal
hierarchical structure of the labour movement, organized as the latter
was by council and committee that ensured the effective subordination
of the rank and file membership. According to the Milan researchers,
this new organization represented a morphological shift in the structure
of collective action. However, although similar structures were found in
the other countries – the *Bürgerinitiative* groups in West Germany, CND
as an 'umbrella organization' for pacifist and feminist groups in Britain,
the ecological groups in France – the 'movement area' seems to have
been limited to four social areas: youth, women, environment and
counter-culture. In addition, it is claimed that it acts at two levels, the
latent and the visible. At the first, people experience directly new cultural models; at the second, they confront a political authority on a specific issue, and use this to demonstrate opposition not only to the issue,
but above all to the logic which leads to public policy decision-making.
At the same time, the public mobilization shows the rest of society that
the specific issue is connected to the general logic of the system, and also
that alternative cultural models are available. The action has above all a
symbolic function at the two levels. Melucci maintains that the two levels
are reciprocally correlated. Latency allows visibility in that it feeds the
former with solidarity resources and with a cultural framework for
mobilization. Visibility reinforces the submerged networks: it provides

energies to renew solidarity, and facilitates the creation of new groups and the recruitment of new militants attracted by public mobilization who then join the submerged network.

Donati (1984) has indicated the risks of antagonism: latency leads to expressive action and marginality; visibility leads to institutionalization (that is becoming a sect or a party). In both cases, however, the collective actor will cease to express conflictual demands, which, it is claimed, are the essence of the new social movements. This is because what distinguishes the new social from the old historical movements, according to IOT theorists, is that the former are social and active in civil society, forging new social norms and identities, while the latter are political and active in the institutional state system, promoting their members' interests. However, this is clearly not true since both, old and new, are active in civil society and the state system. As regards the new social movements, one need only think of the ecological movement in Germany. In 1972, the *Bürgerinitiative* groups (about 20,000 in 1977) created their own pressure group, the BBU, to coordinate their activity at the national level, and in January 1980 they joined with other groups in forming the Grünen party; in the 1983 German elections the party won representation in the Bundestag. The ecological movements in Britain, France and Italy followed a similar path with different degrees of political success. Despite the importance correctly given to cultural and normative innovation – central to the structuration of civil society – IOT disregards the political dimension and particularly the new social movements' political negotiation with parties and pressure groups in the political system. Indeed, the impact of the greens on left parties in Europe has been dramatic. One reason for disregarding the political dimension is that the non-negotiability of their demands – claimed to be a further distinguishing element of the new social movements – cannot, in the view of IOT theorists, be accommodated within the political structure of an industrial society. Once again, however, what is true in the initial stage of a social movement turns out to be much less true in the longer run: recent history shows that it adapts fairly rapidly to conventional forms of political influence. Indeed, the suggestion is that the newness of the new social movements is limited to articulating new issues, and in so doing they carry on the work of the older historical movements in a crucial area: opening up politics by creating 'public spaces for thinking new thoughts, activating new actors, generating new ideas' as well as forcing into the public domain issues previously confined to the private realm.

To terminate this section, it is worth repeating that there is no doubt about the important role of social movements in cultural change and thus in the structuration of civil society in West European countries. But, as Scott has concluded his discussion of both theoretical paradigms, 'approaches [RMT] which fail to incorporate the cultural aspects of social movements cannot account for mobilization and normative innovation; approaches [IOT] which confine themselves to cultural/life-style aspects fail to offer a realistic assessment of movement aims and possible effects' (1990, p. 133). The cultural remains primordial, but the political must not be disregarded.

Political subcultures

Unfortunately, there is no single unambiguous usage of subculture as a concept. It has been used to mean both spontaneous small groups' subversive lifestyle, as, for instance, that of the various mods, punks, rockers and skinheads, and specific organized communities' political tradition which can be territorial, like certain non-state nations (Scotland, Brittany, Bavaria), or ethnic, like certain immigrant groups in Europe (West Indians, Pakistanis, Arabs, Turks). Finally, it can also include the participant membership of institutionalized social movements. The second and third usages are of more interest to us than the first because, although the latter have similar origins, they usually result in a praxis which, after an initial panic, is fairly easily integrated in the national culture and thus rarely leaves a significant politico-cultural legacy. The politico-cultural identity of a group is, within certain limits, a function of the intensity of the struggles that it has to face: the more intense the group's struggles, the more politically and culturally cohesive is the group. This observation is particularly relevant to political subcultures. Indeed, the most enduring European political subcultures are all expressions of institutionalized social movements. In other words, they are the civil society legacy – manifest in specific forms of participation (the 'being together among equals' of working men's clubs noted by Pizzorno) – of the movement's struggles. Pizzorno differentiates between the two kinds of participation, on the basis of the values defended – alternative values in the case of social movements and marginal values in the case of subcultures – and of the goals pursued, which are universalistic for the former and particularistic for the latter.

   A subculture does not seek to change society according to a system of accepted values, but rather adapts its own value system and shuts itself away in social islands that profess a different system of values to the dominant national one. It is what Parkin (1971) has called a 'negotiated version' of the dominant value system: 'dominant values are not so much rejected or opposed as modified by the subordinate class as a result of their social circumstances' (p. 92). The most notorious example of a political subculture based on an institutionalized social movement is imperial German social democracy, as analysed by Roth (1963). He highlighted how the social isolation of the German working class within a class culture aggravated its social exclusion – encouraged by bourgeois society which treated workers as second-class citizens – but, at the same time, strengthened the SPD. His thesis is that the constitution of a separate society by the social democrat organizations – as a potentially new society within the old – explains that very special mixture of radicalism which rejected both reformist collaboration with the bourgeoisie and a real revolutionary strategy. There is no doubt that the social democrat subculture was a culture because the various organizations established were the institutional sedimentation of collective modes of thought and behaviour.

German social democrat subculture

It is perhaps worth pointing out that the identification of the German working class culture with the social democrat subculture – that is with the organized expression of the German labour movement – was much greater in imperial Germany than the similar identification in Victorian England. This was a consequence of the social and constitutional structure of the Second Reich, governed by the *Junker* who refused to give the German working class real civil and political rights. The social democrat movement thus devoted its organizational efforts to breaking down these structures with the aim of protecting the working class from the corrupting influence of bourgeois society. The associational network created for this purpose was really very imposing: clubs, trade unions, cooperatives, associations of all kinds (youth, women's, sporting and cultural, including choirs and theatrical groups), friendly societies, and journals that covered all aspects of members' lives 'from the cradle to the grave'. This goes a long way to explaining the growth of the SPD vote until 1920. Other factors, such as the communist split, the Nazi *Gleichschaltung*, the SPD's post-war decision not to reconstruct its socio-cultural network and finally the development of the mass media created a totally new situation after World War II. This new situation has led on the one hand to the progressive dissolution of the social democrat subcultural component in contemporary German mass culture, and on the other to the decline of class conflict that has fostered a more direct integration of the working class into German society.

British labourism

In Britain too, the working class had started to nurse alternative ideals in the early nineteenth century, under the pressure of government repression – Peterloo Massacre, Tolpuddle Martyrs, Poor Law – and to seek alliances with other social groups, organizing the People's Charter. Chartism represented an ideal which went beyond the terms of the single groups that comprised the movement. It was, as Raymond Williams (1961) has noted, 'more than an expression of democratic aspirations; [it was] also an assertion of an individual dignity transcending class ... it was also the claim to leisure, and hence to a wider life' (p. 79). At the same time, in developing its own organizations, the British labour movement made the most radical critique of all: the refusal of a society based on birth or money and its replacement by a society based on solidarity and cooperation. Yeo (1981) has described how British working class culture, in the crucial years between 1830 and 1850, was not only self-produced, but produced within its own organized social movement (figure 4.4). This culture took on a territorial dimension since the working class was forced to build its own working class halls because the middle classes refused to allow workers to use public buildings for their public activities such as meetings and concerts.

This experience implanted a sense of equality, solidarity, participation – for example, discussion – and democratic control: for instance, delegacy, not representation, became an unbending principle; moreover, procedures were continually being developed to make delegates accountable to local groups. The middle class response was interesting: after the failure of the policy of hostility and obstruction, the middle class practised, during the1850s, a strategy of 'civic vision', in which it furnished cultural resources (mechanics' institutes, free libraries, singing saloons) for use by the working class, but controlled by 'public figures', that is men from the middle class. Thus, in the second half of the nineteenth century, there was a great increase in the voluntary associations

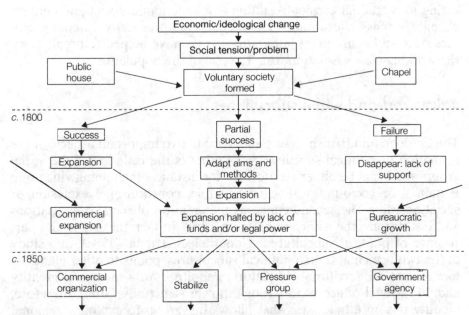

Figure 4.4 Development of voluntary associations in Britain, 1780–1850. Dates indicate broad time bands. Scheme should be appropriate for other waves of voluntary society formation
Source: Morris, 1983, p. 107

catering for working class leisure – music halls, popular comics – and provided by middle class money, with the accent placed on 'responsible' participation but without democratic control. However, Yeo concludes her study with the observation that the action of the British working class through its social movements not only helped change class relations and cultural forms by 1850, but also helped determine what shape they would take. Thus, although the working class suffered the political hegemony of the Liberal Party, the labour movement expanded its organizations, above all in the trade union and cooperative fields, creating a 'common style of life' which resulted in the creation of its own party at the beginning of the present century.

There is a tendency today to forget the importance of the concept of cooperation for the British labour movement. It was not merely a nineteenth century phenomenon (Robert Owen, the Rochdale Pioneers); indeed, the period of the greatest influence of the cooperative ideal was the first 30 years of the twentieth century. The labour militants' utopia until World War II was the so-called 'cooperative commonwealth' and their families were convinced cooperators. It is worth recalling that the cooperative movement was the central component of the labour movement (with 3 million members in 1914, groups in all sectors of activity and its own press). It is difficult to assess accurately how extensive was the labour subculture in this period. However, all observers agree on its 'social separation' and its somewhat 'corporate' class consciousness, noted in chapter 3. The whole edifice has declined in the post-war period owing to a gradual erosion resulting from economic, social and cultural changes – mass education, relative economic prosperity, Labour's welfare state and consequent integration – that have helped to break down the working class's isolation from the rest of the population.

Italian red and white subcultures

The German and British examples illustrate two important aspects of the formation of political subcultures. The first is the isolation of the social group which can be either territorial – for instance, the mining villages in Britain – or socio-political – for example, constitutional exclusion or social hostility. The second concerns the creation of social organizations and institutions: the associational network is, in fact, the key to the persistence of political subcultures.[6] Nonetheless, Trigilia (1986), in a study of the two principal Italian political subcultures, points to other elements too. Above all, territorial subcultures require both a territorial identity and a low level of access to national power structures. Often, therefore, identity has an ethnic basis that allows the group to exploit a regional language. These conditions did not exist in Italy; what existed, instead, was a particular relationship between centre and periphery – national government and provinces – based on weak national integration, a consequence of the process of national unification and the lack of a national myth. In this situation, in specific social contexts – fragmented class structure, low level of access to central power – factors like religion and political ideology (anti-clerical socialism) supplied a cultural identity for the political integration of the north-east and the centre of Italy on a subcultural basis. This form of political integration requires on the one hand a high and stable level of consensus for the dominant local political force, and on the other a high level of institutionalization, that is to say the necessary presence of a widespread institutional network that covers all social milieu. These elements were provided by the Catholic movement in the Venetias and the socialist movement in Emilia-Romagna. The event which provoked a break and made mobilization possible was the same in both cases: the agrarian crisis of the 1880s and its social consequences, pauperism and mass emigration. In the peasant areas of the Venetias, the crisis benefited the Catholics, while in the share-cropping areas of Emilia-Romagna, the socialists: the result in both cases was the formation of a political subculture, sustained by a strong associational network, and stimulated by the worsening social situation and the disinterest of the liberal national ruling class.

The re-emergence of the two subcultures after World War II – with the communists replacing the socialists in the red area – was encouraged by the Cold War and the mobilization that it provoked. Trigilia speaks of 'strong normative elements of delegation'.[7] However, it was sufficient, in view of the nature of Italian centre–periphery relations, to lead to the formation of real territorial subcultural political systems. As regards the present, Trigilia hypothesizes the gradual erosion of the 'normative (that is ideological) components' and the displacement of subcultural mediation on to instrumental bases:

> In fact, the ideological and traditional consensus was much freer from the satisfaction of particularist demands. These were aggregated within the framework of general reference furnished by communist ideology and Catholic culture and supported by the PCI and the church respectively. The decline of these elements, and the assertion in their place of a more specific assessment – influenced much more by pressure groups – of the PCI's and the DC's local policies, have generated tensions of a different nature in the two areas. In the red area, it is above all the industrialists, and a part of the salaried middle classes, who have begun to feel themselves not properly represented. In the white area, it is above all the workers, white-collars and some industrialists. (p. 308)

At all events, it is a fact that the persistence of political subcultures – at least, as measured in terms of electoral support for specific parties – is declining. Notwithstanding this, Bois has reminded us that ideologies and cultures are able to survive long after the original factors that gave rise to them have disappeared. On the other hand, Philippe Aries has drawn attention to the dialectical nature of cultural persistence which tends to evolve:

> the survival of a concept of life and of thought, if it triumphs over the momentary obstacles of history, does not produce dead forms, simple residues of the past. The preservation of a traditional element in a changing world determines a new structure, as different from the old structures from which it originated as from the more recent morphology whose consequences it has escaped.

Nevertheless, it remains to emphasize that political subcultures persist longer, even in a modified form, if they are sustained by an associational or institutional network. This is the element that gives consistency and continuity to the structuration of civil society of which they are a part. This said, however, the associational networks that sustained the major subcultural networks in West European societies have, as noted, tended to dissolve under the pressure of rapid social change, of which the development of the electronic media is surely the most important, if not the only, factor.

Mass media

The free flow of information has always been a basic concept of the liberal democratic tradition; so much so, in fact, that it is argued that there can be no democracy without a free press. Implicit in such an argument is the notion of political communication, to wit mutual communication in a plurality of directions: not only from the governors to the governed, but also from the governed to the governors, as well as among the governors and governed themselves. Now the term 'mass media', which refers to the modern communications systems, specifies communications and distributions systems that 'mediate' between small, relatively specialized groups of cultural producers and a mass of cultural consumers. In other words, they are one-way communications systems which do not allow direct and reciprocal relations between all the participants in the political system.[8] The mass media are a twentieth century phenomenon that more or less dominates political communication in Western European societies. They are part of what goes under the name of 'the leisure and entertainments industry'. This comprises a variety of sectors, of which the most important are: (1) publishing, (2) press, (3) cinema, (4) radio and TV, (5) cassettes and CD and (6) video (table 4.5). It is significant that all sectors are organized on industrial lines and behave according to a market logic, given that historically they are products of capitalist development. Thus it is no accident that a recurring theme in the

Table 4.5 Distribution of certain types of mass media

		Britain	France	Germany	Italy
Dailies					
(papers per 1000	1956	573	246	1277	107
inhabitants)	1965	479	247	326	112
	1977	410	96	423	97
Radio					
(sets per 1000	1957	280	229	272	123
inhabitants)	1965	348	315	337	204
	1978	360	328	363	236
Television					
(sets per 1000	1958	171	22	40	23
inhabitants)	1965	214	133	248	193
	1979	331	292	337	231
Cinema					
(visits per	1957	14.6	9.7	13.8	15.0
inhabitant)	1978	2.3	3.3	4.8	5.6

Source: UNO

McGregor Commission's Report was that 'for some purposes, the press must be regarded as an industry like any other although, from the point of view of its contribution to the maintenance of democracy, it has been seen as an industry like none other' (1977, pp. 159–60).

This kind of approach emphasizes the unresolved ambiguity at the heart of capitalist societies with liberal democratic regimes (see the introduction to this book). The divorce that exists in this field today between political theory and socio-economic praxis lies in the fact that on the one hand the media are the most important source of information and interpretation of social and political processes, and on the other they are managed as entertainment for profit (Zolo, 1992). And this cannot but have important repercussions on the functioning of the political system and hence of the relations between state and civil society in Western Europe. For simplicity, the discussion will be limited to the two politically most important sectors of the media: press and radio/television.

Political economy of the media

The primary consequence of economic logic on the development of the West European media since World War II is the concentration of newspaper proprietorship. The principal causes are ever-increasing production costs and competition from television, above all in securing advertising which, besides sales, is the principal source of press income. Its most dramatic impact has been on the one hand the reduction in the number of papers (table 4.6), and on the other the increase in oligo-

Table 4.6 Different types of media

		Britain	France	Germany	Italy
Dailies					
(no. of papers)	1956	114	130	225	107
	1965	110	121	175	92
	1977	90	96	121	72
Television					
(no. of national	1958	2	1	1	1
channels)	1965	3	2	2	2
	1979	3	3	3	7
Cinema					
(no. of halls)	1958	3,913	5,732	7,565	7,414
	1978	1,519	4,513	2,272	10,041

Source: UNO

polistic control. This tendency is perhaps most advanced in Britain which remains, nonetheless, an exemplary case. At the end of the 1970s the four most important groups controlled 85 per cent of the circulation of the national dailies and a similar percentage of the national Sunday papers. The local press in Britain is not very different because four – though not always the same – groups control half of the local dailies and a fifth of the local weeklies. This concentration is not only one-dimensional in the simple sense of the fusion of dailies, but multidimensional giving rise to giant, often transnational, publishing corporations like Murdoch's News International Corporation. There has been, moreover, a diversification of interests which has taken various forms: press groups that have moved into other media fields (television, publishing) as well as other economic fields of activity (insurance, tourism); and the entry into the media field of other giant corporations, like Reed International (wood, paper, ceramics) and Trafalgar House (property) (Curran and Seaton, 1988, pp. 87–8).

The same tendency exists in the other countries. The names of Springer and Bertelsmann in Germany, Hachette and Hersant in France, Berlusconi (Fininvest) and Rizzoli in Italy readily come to mind (table 4.7). Becker (1980) wrote of the Springer group:

> With a turnover of over a billion German marks, this group is the leading proprietor of national dailies; it controls almost all the dailies in Hamburg and Berlin and 90 per cent of Sunday weeklies, and is the most important magazine publisher. Its control of over 40 per cent of the production of all daily and Sunday papers gives it an economic and journalistic power that is out of all proportion to that of its competitors. … The Springer *Konzern* owns: four newspaper groups, various magazine and book publishers, two press agencies, a distribution company, several printing works

Table 4.7 Principal multimedia groups in Europe, 1990

Groups	Average turnover ($ billion)	TV (% ownership)	Dailies (% readership)	Periodicals (% readership)
News International Corporation (Murdoch: Britain)	4.4	48% BSkyB (<1% TV advert)	30% dailies (*Times, Sun, Today*) 31% Sundays (*Sunday Times News of the World*)	2% non-spec. weeklies 3% women's monthlies 4% non-spec. monthlies
Hachette (Filipacchi 35%: France)	3.6	25% Canal 5 (16% TV advert)	10% dailies	7% women's weeklies 23% non-spec. weeklies 9% women's monthlies 9% non-spec. monthlies
Havas (France)	3.7	25% Canal + (2% TV advert)		
Bertelsmann (Germany)	7.5	39% RTL + (26% TV advert) 50% Kanal + (<1% TV advert)	1% dailies 10% Sundays 11% publicity	8% women's weeklies 5% other weeklies 13% women's monthlies 12% other monthlies
Fininvest (Berlusconi: Italy)	4.9	100% Canale 5 100% Rete 4 (58% TV advert) 100% Italia 1 25% La Cinq (France) 25% Telecinco (Spain)	3% dailies (*Il Giornale*)	35% weeklies 13% monthlies
CLT (17% Havas, 27.6% Bertelsmann: Luxemburg)	0.6	46% RTL (Germany) + (26% TV advert) 25% Tele 5 (Germany) (2% TV advert) 100% RTL (France) (<1% TV advert) 25% M6 (France) (8% TV advert) 66% RTL-TV (Belgium)		12% weeklies (*Telestar*)

Source: La Repubblica, 4 March 1992, p. 4, data elaborated from 'Media Moguls in Europe'

and ... shares in a Swiss holding company in paper production.
(p. 39)

Despite this, the press is less centralized on the continent than in Britain,
and the local press – regional in Germany and Italy, provincial in France
– plays a more important role. The *Bild Zeitung* (with more than 5 million readers) is, in fact, the only popular national daily in Germany, while
all the large Italian dailies have a largely regional circulation. This does
not mean that there are no independent and influential daily papers –
the names of *The Guardian* and *The Independent*, *Die Welt*, *Le Monde*
and *Libération*, *La Repubblica* come to mind[9] – but only that they are a
minority voice, addressed to an educated public. However, given the
general tendency, an observation of Golding (1980) seems to apply to all
Western European countries, and this is that 'the tangle of interests that
today link the entertainment and leisure tycoons is such that it is impossible to discuss the problems of the printed word separately. But oddly
this is what we continue to do' (p. 31).

The second consequence of economic logic for the mass media is the
progressive commercialization of radio/TV. In all European countries,
radio/TV was originally conceived and organized as a public service. The
reasons for the change are complex, but two stand out. The first is that
television was seen as an extension of radio: hence it seemed natural to
apply to it the regime created for radio. The second is that there was a
coincidence between private commercial and state interests at the time
of the birth of radio/TV. Industrialists were interested in manufacturing
radio sets – which became an important industrial sector in the 1930s –
while governments were concerned with regulating radio broadcasting
for military (frequencies), political and social reasons. Hence arose the
public control of broadcasting, through a renewable concession to a public corporation (BBC in Britain, EIAR in Italy). It was no accident that
fascist regimes quickly became aware of the possibilities of radio as a
political instrument for direct control of the population and exploited
them accordingly: for instance, the compulsory listening to Mussolini's
radio speeches or Goebbels' Nazi street-listening groups. However, a different solution prevailed in the USA: private business and commercial
interests were too strong to be controlled by the federal government and
hence were successful in creating a private regime of competitive broadcasting.

If the public service monopoly under state control was confirmed for
radio/TV in all European countries in the post-war period, it has
nonetheless found itself in economic difficulty because of either rising
production costs or advertising pressure. Britain was the first European
country to break the public service monopoly with the introduction of a
commercial channel in 1956, even though it remained under the control
of a public authority (IBA): the BBC felt the commercial pressure from
the 'audience ratings war'. In the 1960s advertising progressively became

a part of public service broadcasting in Italy, France and Germany, and in the 1970s commercial local radio stations were legalized after an intensive campaign of pirate broadcasts by clandestine stations (Radio Caroline). In Italy, RAI's public service monopoly was broken as a result of a series of mid 1970s constitutional court judgements that stimulated the blossoming of private stations and the creation of a number of national commercial channels (Retequattro, Canale 5, Italia 1, rapidly united under the control of Berlusconi's Fininvest). On the other hand, in France it was the socialist government that put an end to the public service monopoly in 1984 by authorizing a pay channel (Canal Plus). Today Federal Germany remains the only one of the four principal European countries with a public service television monopoly. It is no coincidence perhaps that it is the only one which does not have a national service but has regional (*Länder*) services. In this situation, then, if Italy in the 1990s was the only one to have experienced an American-style commercialization of its media system, the development of new communications systems – satellite and cable TV – threatens them all with 'Americanization' sooner rather than later.[10] There is little doubt, in fact, that the powerful attack on the concept of public service television in Europe is part of a common plan of the transnational media corporations. It could mean, if successful, the end of an independent European information and cultural space.

The third consequence of economic logic on the mass media, also linked to the concentration of the press and the commercialization of television, is the reduction in access and expression. The problem of media access is very complex: it is not just a question of the ordinary individual being able to express himself publicly on the media, although it is also this. More generally, it is a question of the plurality of opinions expressed as well as the quality of the information broadcast. In this situation, it is worth repeating that the mass media are a one-way instrument of communication, that is the flow is from editorial offices to general public – readers and viewers – and not vice versa. Thus the old thesis, that if an individual does not find the opinions in which he believes published or broadcast, all he has to do is to launch his own paper or set up his own television channel, no longer carries any conviction. Firstly, the media are expensive, and, secondly, they require professionalism that only comes from specialized training lasting several years. Moreover, in all big businesses – and television is now big business – economies of scale count, and, with the vertical rise in cultural production costs in the last few years, the obstacles to the entry of new producers have become even more prohibitive. Hence, 'the freedom of information, today as yesterday,' Marletti (1980, p. 73) has noted, 'is inevitably reduced to the freedom of him who owns or controls the installations, technology and capital necessary to propagate news in the era of planetary communication.' An institutional reason that has also contributed to limit television access should be mentioned too: the concept of the unitary control of a television channel, by either the state or the government or one of the parties. The idea of a television network as a system of expression in which the editorial control is separate from the technical management of broadcasting has never been seriously considered.

Whatever the reason, it is because of the costs that the media have become the tributary of advertising (table 4.8). In the last twenty years, advertising has moved into television in a big way. Television sets, in fact, reached saturation point in the principal European countries around 1970 (table 4.5). Moreover, it has been calculated that television viewing takes up between 30 and 40 per cent of the leisure time of the average European; it constitutes his principal source of information and amusement (table 4.1) and absorbs 25 per cent of domestic expenditure devoted to leisure activities. Finally, we should note that the new communications networks, as they appear, tend to superpose themselves on the existing networks, linked to them but not rendering them obsolete. This is because once a critical threshold has been reached, bigness, on which the mass media operate, unconsciously revitalizes smallness, the basis, on the contrary, of close communication which is founded more on understanding than on information.

Advertising has encouraged two structural tendencies of the mass media, conditioning quality in both information and cultural content. Advertisers are always looking for the largest audience possible or, where this is limited, to specialized (that is affluent) groups. Mass audiences prefer variety and entertainment (soap operas, quizzes, chat shows, sport) – which for television are the cheapest programmes to produce – as opposed to serious programmes (drama, music, documentaries); with regard to the quality of information, mass audiences encourage banality and fragmentation instead of contextualization and synthetic analysis. At the same time, programmes are depoliticized, and unpopular opinions that might cause offence or upset the viewers are expunged to reassure them because the object of the exercise is to ensure a 'guaranteed audience'.

The popular press adopts the technique of the 'human interest story',

Table 4.8 Share of advertising expenditure between different kinds of media, 1984 (per cent)

	Press	Radio	TV	Posters	Cinema	Total expenditure (million French francs)
Britain	63	2	31	4	–	47,139
France	59	9	16	14	2	20,420
Germany	75	7	18	–	–	46,005
Italy	46	5	42	6	1	13,186

Source: *Le Débat*, 1986, p. 27

that is news presentation in a personalized form. A good example is the treatment of information which has been defined as 'a celebration of the status quo'. In view of the importance of images for television, everything is focused on visible politics – ministers' speeches, head of state's travels, parliament[11] – to the exclusion of invisible politics such as administrative praxis, committee meetings, finance. Political problems are discussed with the official representatives of the major institutions. Not surprisingly, elections play a major role in this television view of politics: they are entertainment thanks to the element of uncertainty that encourages dramatization. The search for the largest number of viewers has led to the creation of the myth of the homogeneous public which justifies programme homogeneity. The larger the audience, the easier it is to find sponsors and the greater the possibility of selling programmes to other channels – for instance, the industrially produced American serials, formula 'Dallas'. Finally, the search for an ever-larger viewing public furnishes a useful justification to television programmers for this type of management, namely numbers are such that they can be presented as a demonstration of democracy: 'We give the people what they want to see.'

On the other hand, the search for specialized groups within mass audiences leads to the creation of a dual market: 'tabloids' on the one side, and 'quality' papers on the other. It has been estimated that two-thirds of the tabloids' income in Britain comes from sales as against a quarter for quality papers. This means that the latter have to find advertising revenue to cover three-quarters of their costs as against only a third for the former. This explains, for instance, why the *Financial Times* can prosper with readers who number only 200,000 but are of elite socio-economic status – businessmen and the like - while the *News Chronicle* was forced to close in 1961 in spite of a circulation of over a million copies read by a public of modest social condition – workers and white-collars – who were of much less interest to advertisers. The experience of party papers, above all left-wing, in the post-war period confirms this orientation. The situation of television scheduling is similar: documentary and serious programmes are screened outside peak viewing times, for instance late at night. The search for a more affluent 'quality' audience with more distinctive tastes and needs has substantially influenced the organizational formula of Britain's Channel 4.

We have already referred to two tendencies of the media resulting from commercial pressures. The use of the word 'tendency' is particularly significant in the case of television because it points to the fact that certain processes have not been pushed to their logical conclusion. If commercial pressures were the only ones influencing television scheduling in Europe, 'variety and entertainment' programmes would be more frequent and intrusive than they have in fact been. National programmes, moreover, would have been screened less and those of American origin even more. If this has not happened, it is because television commercialization has been tempered by public service criteria –

and this because of the historical framework within which television developed in Europe. Thus, despite commercial pressures, the public service framework has succeeded, at least for the present, in defending a more open cultural space. For instance, it has obliged programme schedulers to take account of needs other than the highest audience rating, so that serious cultural programmes – opera, drama, historical and political documentaries, classical music and jazz – are also screened at peak viewing times. Television in the 1990s has ensured European viewers, as American commentators have enviously acknowledged, a plurality of cultural experiences that market forces alone would not have secured.

Media and political communication

Relations between television and the government vary from state to state, and not just today. It has gone from the control of information in Gaullist France under the label of the 'ORTF Voice of France' and the twenty-year Christian Democrat use of the RAI as an instrument of party propaganda to the BBC's much publicized 'sense of responsibility' based on political impartiality. The politicians' sensitivity is understandable, particularly since the potential audience coincides with the national electorate. This is even more the case in a public service monopoly regime where the ultimate control resides with the government or the parliamentary parties. We need only recall the confession of the BBC's most famous director general, Lord Reith (1949), that 'it is a powerful and efficient instrument which is apparently independent ... but which [the government] can control at will.'[12] However, the crucial question in this field is: who decides who shall appear on the screen and when? The decisions depend on tacit agreements between channel executives and politicians: they are the result of either informal negotiations or precedent. In these circumstances, a reasonable assessment suggests that if there certainly are cases of distortion and flagrant censorship in political communication by the television authorities in the various European countries, it remains nevertheless true that programmes are – and are believed to be (Table 4.9) – a credible source of information and comment. The latter naturally lies within the limits of 'mainstream opinion', namely that current opinion which matters to dominant groups. It is not that anti-conformist or minority opinions are not broadcast, but that they are rare and their 'subversive' nature is heavily underlined.

There is a second aspect of the mass media's role in political communication, that of their impact on political life, which needs to be mentioned. It is a vast and complex subject which is difficult to treat adequately in a few lines. However, it is possible to consider a number of theses developed in research in this field. Traditionally research on the political effects of mass media breaks down into three periods. In the first – from the 1880s to the 1930s – the media were believed, particularly in America, to have enormous power in influencing public opinion and determining individual political behaviour. Between the wars, it went as far as imputing to the media the power to impose a political system against the people's will, as in the case of the Nazi-fascist regimes. In Europe, the Frankfurt school, although starting from very different premises, came to similar conclusions about the mass media: they were an omnipotent instrument for the manipulation of mass consensus and integration. In a second period which runs from 1940 to 1960 and which was dominated by American empirical research, the media's direct influence on individual opinions and behaviour was rejected. This research, employing survey techniques, was predicated on a very primitive communications model, that of stimulation and effect, that is the mechanical relation between the media message (stimulus) and individual behaviour (effect). Fieldwork was usually carried out during electoral campaigns, and it seemed to show that the media had very little influence on electoral behaviour and other factors rather more so. The results of this research were systematized by Katz and Lazarsfeld (1955) in the famous 'two-step communication flow' model, according to which the impact of the media message is not direct and immediate, from the media to the masses, but indirect and mediated by opinion leaders – neighbours, friends, drinking companions – within different social groups and circles. In other words, opinion leaders intervene to explain – or neutralize – to the group or circle the meaning of the message broadcast by the media.

At the same time, another approach was developed that employed the methods of experimental psychology and arrived at entirely the opposite conclusions. It displaced the focus of analysis from the direct effects of the media to the reception of the message (and information) to point up two significant facts: (1) the individual is more likely to believe in the truth of information, or judgements and opinions, in fields in which he has no direct experience or other sources of information; and (2) the individual's willingness to believe what he is told relates precisely to the degree of trust he has in the message's source. Now, since few people in Western Europe have first-hand experience of politics outside voting, and since radio and television were considered – at least until recently – as especially authoritative sources of political communication, the conclusion was self-evident: the media's effects on West European public opinion were likely to be particularly strong. As soon as the notion of the media's limited political impact began to be propagated, it was immediately contested. In fact, Katz and Lazarsfeld's model was defective in at least two respects: on the one hand it did not take sufficient account of the differences in communication flow between political and commercial messages, and on the other it did not acknowledge the specificity of the television message. In Europe, on the other hand, media analysis remained linked for a long time to the theoretical framework developed by the Frankfurt school.

However, in 1960 a third period began, in which an attempt has been made to reformulate media analysis on an entirely new basis. Earlier research findings were re-examined and it was concluded that, far from showing that the media had no effect, they showed only that people did not necessarily change their minds because of direct media exposure, which is very different from having no effect at all. They showed, in fact, what would be confirmed subsequently, namely that the media raised interest, fixed opinions and, crucially, informed the electorate. Indeed, from the end of the 1970s, television was the principal source of political information for over 70 per cent of the electorate of European countries. Furthermore, the new media analysis widened the area of discussion to include not only the media's effects on the public – namely, what people know and what they think is important – but also the political context, to wit their impact on other institutions. The political framework of the new media analysis was outlined by Seymour-Ure (1974); he focuses no longer specifically on individual perception but on the kinds of relations that the media can develop with the different political actors. Thus the first kind of relationship is that between the population and the political system. The media contribute to the population's information and that, over time, affects the level of its identification with the political system. On the other hand, a press campaign can change the population's perception of a particular problem (he quotes the case of Enoch Powell and immigration in Britain in 1968). The second kind concerns the role of different institutions in the political system. In this case he quotes the British monarchy whose popularity in the 1960s and 1970s is seen as the result of the large and favourable attention that the media gratified it with in those years; and we can add that its present unpopularity corresponds to the adverse publicity that the new generation of 'royals' have attracted in the tabloid press.

The third kind of relationship is that between the different institutions competing with each other, like the various parties, the government and the opposition, the executive and the legislature. The fourth kind regards the relations between politicians and political institutions: the example quoted is that between leaders, militants and electors in the various parties. Finally, the fifth kind is the relationship between the principal political leaders at decisive moments in political life, like a party leadership struggle, or the fight for electoral victory (for instance, the Giscard–Mitterrand debates of 1974 and 1981). The framework, thus outlined, is useful in that it helps identify both the modes in which the new media affect politics and the areas of major influence without which the analysis tends to become dissipated in a meaningless behaviourism (for the credibility of different types of media, see table 4.9).

However, there are three aspects which we need to bear in mind when assessing the media's role in the relations between the state and civil society in Western Europe. The first is the new media's, and particularly television's, definition of social reality. The importance of the conception

Table 4.9 Credibility of the different types of media and the government, 1994

	Fully believe %	Quite a lot %	Not much %	Not at all %	Don't know %
Television news					
Britain	34	51	12	2	1
France	18	56	22	3	1
Germany	31	59	8	0	2
Italy	17	50	26	6	1
Daily papers					
Britain	12	41	33	8	6
France	17	51	16	3	13
Germany	33	51	12	2	2
Italy	18	45	22	6	9
Radio news					
Britain	27	44	9	3	17
France	18	54	18	4	6
Germany	32	54	10	1	3
Italy	13	34	18	5	30
News magazines					
Britain	12	22	9	3	54
France	6	36	30	10	18
Germany	18	41	29	5	7
Italy	11	39	32	6	12
The government					
Britain	1	13	42	41	3
France	5	29	49	14	3
Germany	3	31	46	18	2
Italy	9	13	25	52	1

Source: Libération, 1 April 1994, p. 14

of entertainment in the new media has already been noted. Now, soap operas, comedy, variety and even 'pop' *may not* be intended to have any effect on the social and political views of their audiences. However, there is hardly a joke or a lyric that does not reflect a social attitude, and one with political consequences. We need only recall the sexism implicit in the song 'A Hymn to Him'[13] from the American musical comedy *My Fair Lady*, or the social roles played by women and black people on European television until very recently. Eco (1964) has drawn attention to the fact 'that should appear incredible', namely that the subordinate classes avidly consume bourgeois cultural models believing them to be their own independent expression: 'from screen star models to the heroes and heroines of romances, right up to women's television programmes, mass culture represents and offers human situations that have no connection at all with the consumers' situation and which become, nonetheless, model situations for them' (p. 20). It is an aspect that George Orwell (1968, vol. III) had noted a generation earlier in a well-known essay on 'Boys' Weeklies' and which had induced him to deepen his reflection:

> To what extent people draw their ideas from fiction is disputable. Personally, I believe that most people are influenced far more than they would care to admit by novels, serial stories, films and so forth, and from this point of view the worst books are often the most important because they are usually the ones that are read earliest in life. It is probable that many people who could consider themselves extremely sophisticated and 'advanced' are actually carrying through life an imaginative background which they acquired in childhood ... If this is so, the boys' twopenny weeklies are of the deepest importance. Here is the stuff that is read somewhere between the ages of twelve and eighteen by a very large proportion, perhaps an actual majority, of English boys, including many who will never read anything else except newspapers; and along with it they are absorbing a set of beliefs which would be regarded as hopelessly out of date in the Central Office of the Conservative Party. All the better because it is done indirectly, there is being pumped into them the conviction that the major problems of our time do not exist. (p. 528)

This argument leads to the conclusion that the media contribute – through their definition of social reality – to the creation of that climate which, in Meynaud's (1964) view, is one of the best weapons of contemporary capitalism: 'they give, without seeming to, an entirely false picture of our world' (p. 192). Eco prefers, nevertheless, a more open reading of the television situation, drawing attention to the possibility that the interpretation of the message can occur according to a code which is not that of the communicator:

> A quantitative growth of information, no matter how muddled and oppressive it appears, can produce unforeseen results, according to the law that there is no reformist neutralization in the circulation of ideas. Rather every cultural development – no matter what ideological project is behind it – produces results which in dialectic relation to given circumstances outstrip the forecasts made by the strategists and students of communication [...]. In different places and times the same kind of communication bombardment can produce either habituation or revolt (1964, p. 55).

If the media are able to create a diffuse vision of the world for large strata of the population, they are also capable of creating specific situations. This capacity to provoke a collective response is the second aspect that needs to be kept in mind. Following an indication of Hans Magnus Enzenberger (1982), the notion of manipulation can be used to summarize this capacity, given that the media are always subject to manipulation in the assertions that they make. This manipulation can take a variety of forms. One form is that of 'agenda setting', that is the capacity to determine priorities, as, for instance, in the emergence of issues in an electoral campaign. The media usually follow the issues raised in the political arena by the various political actors – politicians, government, parties – but we should note that in certain circumstances they are capable of imposing a certain issue against the wishes of the great majority of political actors. A major illustration of this capacity in Britain was the case of Enoch Powell and Asian and Afro-Caribbean immigration, referred to by Seymour-Ure (1974). The media coverage given to a speech on immigration by Powell to a small audience in a church hall was such that it was familiar to 86 per cent of the population two days later. Moreover, before the speech only 6 per cent thought immigration was an issue of national importance as against 27 per cent afterwards, while, as a consequence, 70 per cent believed that the government would have to take 'a harder line'. The political result was that Powell had won himself a national audience from one day to the next, and not just for the problem of immigration. Seymour-Ure notes quite correctly that neither Powell nor the media created the race issue in Britain, but, as he argues, the publicity surrounding his speech at a crucial moment – during a parliamentary debate on race relations – pushed immigration to the top of the British political agenda where it has remained ever since.

Moreover, what the media do nationally, global television (CNN) can now do internationally in constructing a 'world opinion'. Jay Blumler has recently observed:

> The news media are not only a selectively focusing and agenda setting force in international affairs. They are also a world opinion defining agency. For at present, they virtually have a monopoly over the construction of world opinion, its agenda of prime concerns, and its main targets of praise and blame. At present, at least, what they tell us about what world opinion apparently holds on a certain matter can rarely be double-checked by international opinion poll results. (quoted by Gurevitch, 1991, p. 186)

In the absence of any international controls, world opinion is inevitably a product of media practices. The latter were memorably described by Gaye Tuchman (1972) as 'the sacred knowledge, the secret ability of the newsman which differentiates him from other people', but which they are singularly unable to identify or define convincingly (p. 672).[14]

We should perhaps add, in this connection, that research has identified a significant difference between the impact of the press and that of television: press effects are delayed (from three to six months) while television impact is almost immediate. Finally, the issue priorities imposed by the media (it is rare that there is a disagreement among the media over priorities) carry, as might be expected, more weight with people who lack strong convictions than those who have them. However, if we also bear in mind that television has extended the political debate to sectors of the population excluded because of lack of interest, we can readily understand why it is claimed that agenda setting is becoming more important for a growing part of the electorate.

If the media are able to change public opinion, they are just as capable of determining what people think is important. Conscious of this power, it is no accident that the media practise a second form of manipulation: the so-called 'media event'. In this form, many items of news are not events at all but are produced by the media, usually according to the logic of what Eco has dubbed 'the production of news by means of news'. They can also be the product of the imagination of an army of specialists created by the development of the communications industry. The most famous media event was American: Orson Welles's 'war of the worlds' in 1938. He simulated a series of radio news bulletins which announced the invasion of earth by the Martians. Today, it is claimed that the collective panic that the programme was supposed to have caused was much exaggerated by the American sociologist Hadley Cantril. Another less fanciful example was the public debate over mugging in England in the 1970s. The media succeeded in creating a climate of collective anguish through the mechanism of giving a new, more hateful, name to an old offence. This, in turn, precipitated a new aggressive sentencing policy which the media saw as the necessary response to an earlier mistaken 'soft' policy. But, as Hall and others (1978) showed in a well-documented study, not only had the rate of increase in violent crimes actually been in sharp decline before the emergence of the press 'mugging' campaign, but also, far from becoming lenient, sentences had steadily become longer. At the international level, moreover, there is little doubt that the so-called 'telediplomacy' of CNN during the Gulf War significantly influenced perceptions of the conflict.[15]

The most obvious political kind of media event is the so-called *ballon d'essai*, that is a political decision announced anonymously by a politician to test public opinion. If the reaction is positive, the decision is officially confirmed; if instead it is negative, it is claimed that the report was an unfounded rumour. Under the heading of *ballon d'essai* can be found all the communications manipulations that make up European politics today: the indiscretion, the off-the-record briefing (informal explanations not for publication or attribution), the calculated suppression or distortion of information through the technique of the press leak, and the game of denial and counter-denial. All are part of the contemporary politician's standard kit, and that of his spokespersons, in the struggle to use and disarm the media which is part and parcel of the political process today. Politicians are not alone in resorting to media events: social movements have recently used them with success to present their demands before the public and so influence the political agenda. Rositi (1984) has suggested that this was the consequence of a certain complicity between the media and the movements resulting from 'a tacit agreement based on a common distrust of every bureaucratic system, including the political system' (pp. 6–7). The result, nonetheless, was to introduce new subjects into political discourse that succeeded in stimulating change and innovation.

In conclusion, in case we have given the impression that the media are omnipotent in the field of political communication, it is worth recalling that Deutsch (1963) warned long ago against overrating media communication and underestimating the incomparable importance of face-to-face contact between people. Indeed, if the former dominates the *dissemination* of information today, the latter remains essential for *understanding* it. Moreover, despite their importance, the media are not the only means of communication in West European political systems. A plurality of other institutions, to be analysed in the coming chapters, contribute at different levels to that network of political communications which links in a double sense – from governed to governors and vice versa – civil society to the state: a network which is the hallmark of the actual democratic regimes of Western Europe. Because, as Habermas has observed: 'the life of political institutions does not come from force but from recognition ... Legitimate power arises only among those who share a common belief in free and spontaneous communication.'

Conclusion

The key to our study of the political context is the structuration of civil society. In the two previous chapters, we have discussed the structural and historical factors determining that structuration. In this chapter, we have discussed the political phenomena that promote change and defend persistence. They are all, one way or another, forms of political participation and it is from this concept that our discussion started. We followed Pizzorno's indication: participation is historically linked to popular sovereignty and, hence, only becomes a political problem with the extension of political rights in the last century. More importantly, in Pizzorno's view, it poses a double problematic. On the one side, it is a vehicle that enables the underprivileged, through collective action, to exploit group-based resources (above all number) in order to correct by political means their misfortune; this was the fundamental purpose of the labour movement and its various institutions. On the other, it is also the weapon of the privileged, as individuals, to reinforce their advantages. Indeed, the very resources that they possess (money, education, access) stand them in very good stead to ensure that their voice is heard. Pizzorno demonstrates that there are four forms of political participation: two individual – civic participation and the political profession – and two collective – social movements and political subcultures.

The democratic ideal presupposes a high level of civic participation by the citizenry. Reality in West Europe is very different: the majority of the population is indifferent to politics, with the notable exception of voting in elections, and only a very tiny minority is 'completely' active in a myriad of political activities. There is considerable dispute over the consequences of this situation for the political system: some contend that mass apathy is a necessary ingredient of actual democracy, others that it renders the system vulnerable. There is less doubt, however, as to who benefits from this situation: the privileged and the wealthy – those whom Galbraith (1992) has recently called the comfortable and the contented – at the expense of the subordinate and underprivileged, and this despite the organization of the labour movement.

Social movements are collective attempts to advance or defend common goals through collective action – usually mass mobilization – outside the established institutions. They arise out of the spontaneous action and enthusiasm of small groups who believe a new kind of life and society is possible. To achieve the utopia to which they aspire they are forced to give themselves an organized structure and, in so doing, they either achieve social change, or are absorbed by the existing institutional structure, or disappear defeated. The crucial point is that they can create public spaces for thinking new ideas, motivating new social actors and generating new formations. Hence, they are a vital factor in changing the cultural structuration of civil society.

Study of social movements is dominated at present by two major paradigms: resource mobilization theory (RMT) and identity-oriented theory (IOT). The former focuses on the instrumentality of movement strategy – the mechanisms by which they recruit and mobilize individual social actors – while the latter highlights how movements produce new identity for society, that is the ways in which macro-structural processes are transformed into social movements. RMT treats collective action as rational actor oriented, which means that it is directed towards the constraints on individual action and, hence, on individual incentives. It believes that men are self-interested as well as rational, so is almost indifferent to the context and content of social movements. It believes that unless the movement can provide individual rewards for its members it will not be able to mobilize its supporters. Thus it views collective action as unstable, problematic and occasional, and concludes that leaders are under pressure to institutionalize movements and pursue low-risk strategies. The result is a tendency to discount the idea that action can be its own reward and disregard the cultural role that movements play.

IOT, by contrast, exalts the cultural role of movements and particularly how they produce new identities for society. They are conceived as historical actors with their own projects. Touraine, the major theorist, believes that the new social movements of the past 30 years are the harbingers of a new society, post-industrial society, and the conflicts that they provoke are responsible for cultural innovation. Hence, a major problem for IOT theorists is identifying the new social movements from the old historical movements because they are predicated as capable of transforming advanced industrial society. This assumption appears to be misplaced, both theoretically and empirically. Indeed, research suggests that new and old movements share many common features both in their socio-political role and organizationally. This would seem to be borne out by analyses of the major social movements – labour movement, Catholic movement, fascism and environmental movement. Hence both paradigms, RMT and IOT, though pitched at different analytical levels, illuminate different aspects of the complex phenomenon that social movements represent.

Political subcultures have been defined as institutionalized social movements in the sense that they do not seek to change society according to a new system of values but rather defend a different system of values to the dominant one by shutting themselves away in distinct social islands. They therefore contribute to the persistence of minority values, usually not in a radical form, but in a negotiated version of the dominant value system. The dominant values are not so much rejected or opposed, as subverted by being given a different sense by the subcultural community as a result of its circumstances. Their persistence and political relevance is all the stronger if they are sustained by an institutionalized associational network. For this reason, it is no coincidence that the major examples in Western Europe are the organized labour and Catholic movements in those countries where these social movements were institutionalized. They explain why ideologies and cultures are able to survive long after the original factors that gave rise to them have disappeared.

Finally, the media are the major mode of political communication in Western Europe today. They constitute a one-way communications system that mediates between a small, relatively specialized group of cultural producers and a mass of cultural consumers. It is important to note that all sectors of the media – publishing, press, cinema, radio and TV, cassettes and CD, and video – are now organized according to industrial criteria and behave according to a market logic. The result is a concentration of press ownership and the commercialization of television with the formation of a limited number of transnational media conglomerates. This means that there is a divorce between the basic liberal democratic requirement of a free flow of information and the economic need to make a profit that has political consequences: differential access to and reduced possibilities of expression for many groups.

The impact of the media on political life is much disputed, and assessment of their significance has changed over the years. Initially the media were thought to be all-powerful and governments sought more or less direct control of them. Today, their impact is judged less pervasive and more indirect. They contribute to the population's information: a specific press campaign can change its perception of a problem overnight. However, the media cannot change basic attitudes: they can mobilize existing beliefs and prejudices, but there is always the possibility of reinterpretation of the communicator's original code. In other words, although the media are a powerful instrument in constructing and defining social and political reality and furnishing political information, face-to-face contacts remain essential for political understanding.

Further reading

J. Curran and M. Gurevitch (eds) (1991), *Mass Media and Society* (London: Arnold).

R. Eyerman and A. Jamison (1991), *Social Movements: A Cognitive Approach* (Cambridge: Polity).

C. Lodziak (1986), *The Power of Television: A Critical Appraisal* (London: Pinter).

D. McQuail (1984), *Communications* (London: Longman, 2nd edn).

C. Parry, G. Moyser, N Day (1992), *Political Participation and Democracy in Britain* (Cambridge: CUP).

C. Pateman (1970), *Participation and Democracy* (Cambridge, CUP).

A. Pizzorno (1970), 'An Introduction to the Theory of Political Participation', in *Social Science Information*, 9, 29–61.

G. Roth (1963), *The Social Democrats in Imperial Germany: A Study in Working Class Isolation and National Integration* (Totowa, NJ: Bedminster Press).

A. Scott (1990), *Ideology and the New Social Movements* (London: Unwin Hyman).

A. Smith (ed.) (1979), *Television and Political Life. Studies in Six Countries* (London: Macmillan).

R. Williams (1971), *The Long Revolution* (Harmondsworth: Penguin, 2nd edn).

R. Williams (1974), *Television: Technology and Cultural Form* (London: Fontana).

J. Yinger (1960), 'Contraculture and Subculture', in *American Sociological Review*, 5, 625–35.

M. Zald and J. McCarthy (1987), *Social Movements in an Organizational Society: Collected Essays* (New Brunswick: Transactions).

5 Parties and Party Systems

Introduction

So far we have discussed the various contextual components which act to structure civil society. Now we must turn to the major political actors – parties and pressure groups – which have historically constituted the principal linkage between civil society and the state, as well as the principal civil society institutions directly active – for many, the propulsive forces – in the constitutional political process (see the introduction to this book). Our schema posits a relationship between civil society and the state and indicates the instruments available for canalizing political demands in civil society – citizens' economic, social and political claims – and presenting them to the state. However, this relationship is a two-way process, permitting at the same time state policies to penetrate civil society and gain legitimacy.

We need to distinguish, at least in very general terms, between these two principal political actors: political parties and pressure groups. This is usually done on the grounds of how they participate in political life. The distinction was theorized in the 1950s by reference to specific differences of role: articulation of political demands in the case of pressure groups; their aggregation in that of political parties. Within this framework, parties seek to capture control of elective institutions in their own name – exclusively if possible or, failing that, in coalition with other parties – and through them the machinery of government, with the object of putting their political programmes into effect. This means that they fight elections to win public office: parliament, government or presidency. On the other hand, pressure groups do not seek to win power and hence do not fight elections, but rather they seek to influence public policy. They endeavour to promote their members' interests, employing all the means available to them, except taking power. Thus, if the identification of parties is relatively simple, that of pressure groups is not. In a certain sense, the latter form a residual category which embraces all those social organizations involved in the political process, even irregularly, which are not parties. This means that it includes not only organized political lobbies, but any social organization that finds itself, for whatever reason and however momentarily, in contact with the political system.

The boundaries between parties and groups are very unstable. Thus religious and social organizations, like the Catholic Church and the trade unions, have 'sponsored' their own parties (for instance, the German Zentrum and the Italian Christian Democrats in the first case, and the British Labour Party in the second). In addition, pressure groups have masqueraded as parties, like Pierre Poujade's Union de Défense des Artisans et Commerçants which presented its own lists at the 1956 French elections and elected over 50 MPs. Finally, the boundary between parties and groups was further blurred in the 1970s as a result of the activity of social movements. Are the German *Grünen* a social movement, a political party or a pressure group, or all three together?

Party types

If the phenomenon of 'party', at least in the guise of faction (*faktion*), is ancient – the Roman *factio* of the Gracchi, or again the Guelphs and Ghibellines of the Italian communal era – the modern concept is recent.[1] Political parties, in fact, only appeared on the political scene in the seventeenth century and in their present form barely 100 years ago. One of the reasons is that the birth and development of modern parties was linked to political participation which became a political problem in Europe only after the recognition of popular sovereignty (chapter 4). Thus, with the progressive affirmation of the representative liberal state in the nineteenth century, there was a general movement for the extension of the suffrage which finally became universal in Western Europe in the mid twentieth century.

The notables' party

The first modern parties emerged in the struggle for the extension of the suffrage: 'the general mechanism of this genesis', Duverger (1951) has observed, 'is simple. First there is the creation of parliamentary groups, then the appearance of electoral committees, and finally the establishment of a permanent connection between these two elements' (p. xxiv). Hence, the birth of that type of party which Weber (1922) called the 'party of notables', constituted essentially of local committees promoted by parliamentary candidates. These committees assembled a limited number of people who met in local pubs or cafés and were active almost exclusively during electoral campaigns. They were led by local notables (hence the name of the party type) of largely aristocratic or bourgeois origin who selected the candidate and funded the electoral campaigns. Moreover, there was often no link, at least initially, between these local committees or any national party. Party identity as such was essentially parliamentary, which explains the famous Burkean definition of party.

The leaders, chosen from among the MPs, decided the political issues and prepared the electoral programmes that were publicized by means of political rallies and the nascent popular press. Indeed, the development of parties in the nineteenth century was linked to the development of the popular press as Gladstone had foreseen in Britain in the 1860s. Support of the sitting MP was the committee's sole *raison d'être*, but MPs had no responsibility to their committee. Political activity, in consequence, was almost exclusively confined to parliament and electoral campaigns. As the suffrage was extended so the parliamentary groups gave themselves an extra-parliamentary organization that linked together the various electoral committees to form a party. Classic examples of this type of party were the British Conservative and Liberal Parties, the French Radical Party and the constitutional liberal and democratic parties in Germany and Italy.

The mass party

The situation began to change in the later nineteenth century, first under the pressure of clerical and nationalist movements, but above all under that of the labour movement, which started to mobilize the working masses. The latter originally found expression in spontaneous riots and mass protest (Chartism), which were slowly transformed into a series of mutual aid organizations (clubs, friendly societies, cooperatives, trade unions: chapter 4) and finally resulted in the founding of socialist parties (SPD in Germany in 1875, PSI in Italy in 1892, Labour Party in Britain in 1900 and SFIO in France in 1905). The socialist parties formed a new type of party; Cerroni (1979) claims, in fact, that they were the first proper parties since the committees of notables belonged to the pre-history of parties. Its distinctive characteristic lay, in his view, in the formula 'an organized machine plus an articulated and structured political programme' (p. 13). This consisted of four principal elements: a mass membership; a national and stable party organization; a body of paid full-time party officials to organize its political activity; and a systematic political programme. It was the first element which supplied the name 'mass party'.

Since the mass party originated in a historical social movement, it conceived its task as one of permanent political activity at all levels of society and not just within the constitutional state institutions. This permanent political activity of education and formation required a stable and articulated political structure, capable of engaging in all kinds of political action in order to involve a growing membership. In addition, because the mass party lacked financiers, it was obliged to fund itself from membership levies. The result was the establishment of a pyramidal organization modelled on that of the state itself (party statute corresponding to constitution; conference to general election; national executive committee to parliament; secretariat to government: Pombeni, 1985, pp. 140–1), but with more democracy than contemporaneous political institutions. The mass party's organization was articulated in local sections (usually on a territorial basis), regional intermediary organizations and national leadership (national executive committee: NEC); the whole was under the authority of a national conference which was held periodically and to which locally elected delegates were mandated. The national conference was the highest party organ which debated and decided party policy, and elected the leadership (NEC, secretariat). Between conferences the party was run by the NEC and the secretariat. All posts of responsibility were elective, while the task of local bodies was to select candidates for local and national elections as well as mandate delegates to the national conference. Finally, candidates, once elected, were required to observe the party programme and discipline in their local council and parliamentary activity.

However, the socialist parties were not the only ones to organize themselves as mass parties, even if they constituted the prototype. In fact, the Catholic movement was organized at the same time in Germany and Italy, first in social and religious associations and then in a party (Zentrum (1870) in Germany; Opera dei Congressi (1874) and Partito Popolare (1919) in Italy). The nationalist movement followed suit in France (Action Française in 1898) with press and parallel organizations.

Duverger suggests a useful distinction between parliamentary and extra-parliamentary parties – between parties born in the political system and those founded in society – which coincides with the distinction between notables' party and mass party. Extra-parliamentary parties, in fact, had no other choice but to organize in civil society since they were excluded from constitutional politics by the restricted suffrage. The so-called 'parliamentary' parties were organized in parliament to support 'their' government. Originally, there were no parties in civil society and the individual parliamentary candidates exploited their social position as notables to be elected. With the extension of the suffrage, a party presence became necessary for the notable to secure sufficient electoral support, but without substantially changing his conception of the party. The strength of this type of party came from its relations with the state; hence power remained in the hands of the parliamentary leaders.

The so-called extra-parliamentary parties, founded to defend and promote the interest of the mass of the population, existed initially in society. Elections and parliamentary seats (when they could contest them), although seen by socialist parties as an instrument of the political struggle, certainly did not, in fact, constitute for many years their principal objective. Indeed, parliament was usually viewed by militant socialists with suspicion, and the socialist parliamentary group was subjected to considerable supervision in view of the element of political compromise which characterized parliamentary life. The major part of the activity of the mass party took place in civil society, because it was part of a larger – class or confessional – movement articulated in a dense network of social organizations. This network acted not only as an instrument of defence of the movement's material interests but also as an institution of social integration. Furthermore, this social movement dimension strengthened the political identity and values of the party in civil society, often ending up by constituting a political subculture of its own (chapter 4).

Other types of party

Two new types of party – the Leninist and the fascist – were important in the first half of the century. The Leninist 'vanguard' party is historically important not only because it led the Bolshevik Revolution, but also because in 1920 its organizational structure was imposed on all working class parties loyal to the Comintern. The vanguard party was theorized by Lenin on the following bases: (1) a vanguard of revolutionary cadres; (2) the workplace cell; and (3) the principle of 'democratic centralism'. The first element refers to the need for maximum political efficiency in a revolutionary party usually operating in clandestine conditions. The cadres, therefore, had to be dedicated to the cause and few in number – the *pochi, ma duri* (few, but tough) of Bordiga, first PCI secretary – that is professional revolutionaries. The second regards the need to secure maximum social penetration with the smallest number of militants controlled by the central leadership. The factory cellule was, in fact, the organizational element *par excellence* of the Leninist party; because it is small, it is the best instrument for permanent agitation, political education and conspiratorial activity, as opposed to electoral struggle, owing to the constant contact between its members. Finally, the third element represents a method for controlling internal debate which secures maximum grass-roots obedience to leadership decisions. The European communist parties came out of the anti-fascist resistance legitimated by the sacrifices made, but, just as importantly, having abandoned the Leninist organizational structure. Togliatti's Partito Nuovo[2] in Italy, like Thorez's in France, was conceived as a mass party open to all who accepted its programme.

The hallmark of fascism as a party type is the militia or vigilante squad (*squadra di combattimento* in Italian, *Scharen* or *Stosstruppen* in German), conceived in military terms. Members are subject, like soldiers, to a paramilitary discipline and training, they wear uniforms and badges, and, grouped in squads with banners and bands at their head, they can be used for demonstrations, but they are also ready to use violence against their adversaries. As Vajda (1976) has noted, in fact, with fascism the tactics take precedence over a programme since the fascist movement never had a political programme. The real objective was the taking of power by force, and hence the only thing that it could do with power was to defend it at all costs: 'if tactics prevail,' Vajda has observed, 'armed organization is the only winning formula.' At bottom, organized fascism is a privately controlled fighting force whose principal political weapon is violence, as the Ulster paramilitaries confirm.

The catch-all people's party

This type of party[3] was theorized by Kirchheimer (1966): he identified a transformation in the big post-war European parties (and particularly the German CDU and SPD), whose major characteristic was electoral mobilization and not party militancy. This electoralization of party activity, that is to say making electoral goals the major party preoccupation, was responsible for a series of changes which in Kirchheimer's view justified the specification of a new type of party. He believed that these changes involved: (1) drastic reduction of the party's ideological baggage, that is an attenuation of ideological appeal in favour of short-term issues and tactics; (2) further strengthening of top leadership groups that put the national interest before partisan advantage; (3) downgrading of the role of the individual party member, with grass-roots militancy increasingly considered a historic relic obscuring the new catch-all party image; (4) de-emphasis of the *classe gardée* (specific social class or confessional clientele) in favour of recruiting voters from the population at large; and (5) securing access to a variety of pressure groups for financial reasons, but also to secure electoral support via interest group intercession. These changes meant a fall in democratic tension within the party, at least in relation to how it was previously experienced, and a centralization of decisions in the hands of the party's top leadership. Paradoxically, they implied an ever weakening party–electorate bond – reduced to election day – which resulted also from the decline in subcultural support.

The reasons for these changes lay, according to Kirchheimer, in the socio-economic, political and cultural developments of the post-war period.[4] The economic boom, with the progressive social settlement that followed in its wake, was responsible for the attenuation of class polarization and a change in the population's basic orientations towards more secular and private individualistic attitudes. This showed itself in the drop in post-war mass party membership and militancy. In the mass consumer society of the boom years, parties were forced to compete increasingly on the electoral terrain. Moreover, since access to power in actual democratic regimes is defined almost exclusively in electoral terms, this naturally became progressively the main focus of party activity. It is no accident, in fact, that Kirchheimer claimed that the nomination of candidates for popular legitimation as office-holders was the main function of the present-day party.

Although it is a suggestive theorization, Kirchheimer was cautious about the possibility of generalizing his model. Despite the fact that he presented the development of catch-all parties as a European development, his model applied particularly to the German Federal Republic, the state which acted as his model. In general, subsequent European developments have not followed Kirchheimer's hypotheses, namely towards a simplification of West European party systems with one or two catch-all parties in every state. And this is in spite of some rise in electoral mobility on the one hand and a decline in ideological polarization on the other, as he had predicted. Nonetheless, his theorization has accurately captured certain processes that have contributed to the generalization of the new party type that we see as a synthesis of the two previous party types – the notables' party and the mass party – around an apparatus, the political machine. The resulting contradictory characteristics have been captured by Baldassarre (1983):

> although not always conservative, it respects the systemic compatibilities of the existing regime; although it has a certain ideological standpoint, it is essentially a party of mediation; although it is engaged in continuous and varied activity, its party organization is weak and is, moreover, in the hands of militants and activists locally; although its leadership is nationally centralized, its ruling group is often formed of leaders who also have a local power base; although it has leaders who have made a career as party officials, it is also made up of a good number of notables ...; although it recognizes the rank-and-file members' right to have a say in the choice of leaders, however, it combines 'internal' and 'external' selection criteria with informal procedures; although not without centralized decision-making procedures, it boasts a very autonomous parliamentary group; although its organization is unitary and not federal, it is internally organized in factions or organized groups; although self-financing (from membership dues), it resorts more often to external sources of funding.
> (pp. xxiv–xxv)

However, not all European parties have adopted a single organizational form, even if the majority have many similar organizational elements which are a reflection on the ubiquity of the political machine and professional politics in parliamentary regimes. Indeed, this development confirms the critique of the early years of the century – that the strategy

of participation in representative regimes would have certain consequences for the mass party. Firstly, involvement in the logic of electoral
competition implies, in the short run, 'ideological deradicalization'
because the party is obliged to adapt itself to the political market: the
SPD's ideological revision at Bad Godesberg in 1959 was only the most
publicized[5] of the European socialist parties' ideological revisions in this
century. Maximizing votes means reducing the antagonistic programmatic elements to a minimum. This tendency was reinforced, for socialist
parties, by participation in government coalitions with centre parties, as
the experiences of the Italian PSI (abandonment of the centre-left programme in the July 1964 crisis) and the German SPD in the 1970s (abandonment of domestic reforms under Brandt in the name of the
Ostpolitik) and the British Labour Party in the 1980s (acceptance of pri-
vatizations and limited taxes) so vividly illustrate.

Secondly, a predominantly electoral orientation rewards the party
apparatus because it promotes a division of labour between professional
politicians (MPs and party officials) on the one side, and militants and
activists who tend to forsake all forms of mobilization on the other. This
is the logic of Michel's 'iron law of oligarchy'. The professional politicians become the rank and file's representatives, that is to say the mediators of party alliances,[6] provoking by the same token grass-roots
demobilization.

Thirdly, the logic of electoral competition extinguishes internal party
democracy because of the need to provide a favourable image to the outside world to attract the 'floating voter' who is the key to a future election victory. The favourable image would be destroyed by a lively and
animated debate. In consequence, the party is presented more as a commodity than as a political project. Fourthly, the 'interclassism' (or class
collaboration) deriving from this strategy undermines the sense of collective identity which was the propulsive force of the mass party at the
beginning of the century. The communist and socialist parties lose that
special quality of being the organized expression of the working class
which was the basis of their appeal to that class. They are not, therefore,
qualitatively different from the other parties: a fact recognized by the
PCI leadership when it dissolved the party and refounded it as the
Democratic Party of the Left (PDS) in 1991.

Finally, a new element has intervened alongside that privileged link
between civil society and the state which was the party: the media, which
allow direct contact, one-way and manipulatory, between leader and
electorate (chapter 4). Thus parties have progressively lost their central
role as a channel of political mobilization. The party apparatus has no
longer any need, in fact, of an army of activists for electoral propaganda
as it did 30–40 years ago; it needs, instead, media specialists and polling
experts.[7] Hence, it is no accident that the popular party type is less and
less an instrument for the political participation of the population. The
people look increasingly to other institutions (pressure groups and social

movements), with a consequent fall in party militancy and a decline in active party membership (table 5.1).

Party finance

Funding is the last, and today the most controversial, organizational problem facing parties. The list of political financial scandals grows ever longer – Flick group in Germany, *fausses factures* in France, Polly Peck and other undisclosed funds in Britain and, above all, *tangentopoli* in Italy in the last decade – and is undermining not only the credibility of the old established parties but also politics and politicians in general. There are three methods of funding: (1) internal financing; (2) donations

Table 5.1   Membership[a] of the principal parties (thousands)

	Communists	Socialists	Centre	Right	
Britain		*Labour Party[b]*		*Conservative Party*	
1945		487 (3038)		nd	
1955		842 (6483)		2800	
1965		816 (6432)		2225	
1975		674 (6486)		1400	
1985		330 (6950)		1100	
France	*PCF*	*PS*	*P. Rep.*	*RPR (Gaullists)*	
1945	381	115			
1955	545	335			
1965	290	70	285		
1975	491	150	95	600	
1985	600	375	190	750	
Germany		*SPD*		*CDU-CSU*	
1945		701		400	90
1955		585		230	35
1965		710		285	100
1975		820		590	133
1985		926		736	184
Italy	*PCI*	*PSI*	*DC*		
1945	1371	700	537		
1955	2090	770	1189		
1965	1615	437	1613		
1975	1730	539	1732		
1985	1595	516	1444		

nd: no data.
[a] Party membership figures vary widely and are often exaggerated; therefore the figures are only to be taken as a rough guide.
[b] Trade union members have dual membership of the Labour Party: they are included in the numbers in parentheses.

from private sources (individuals, companies and pressure groups); and (3) state funding.

Membership dues have almost certainly never covered the expenditure of the major established parties, not even those of the left (communists and socialists) which have always clung to the concept. They have been supplemented with other internal sources – deductions from state salaries, income from property investment and commercial activity or events (*festa dell'unità*) organized by the party. Both PCF and PCI received external funding from the former USSR during the Cold War (as did the DC from the USA, via the CIA). On the other hand, donations from external sources are the major item in most established, and not only right-wing, parties' incomes. Indeed, many left-wing parties rely on funding from labour organizations: British trade unions contribute over 50 per cent of Labour Party funds from the political levy.[8] In addition, 40 per cent of British Labour MPs are trade union sponsored and funded.

On the right and centre, the situation is more murky. Donations often come from individual donors, sometimes in substantial secret sums, like the £2 million given to the British Conservative Party by Greek shipowner John Latsis, or the various millions proffered by Hong Kong businessmen after a private dinner with John Major, all in 1991. However, increasingly they come from private companies, like the donations by the Flick group to Count Lansdorf (FDP) and Kohl (CDU) in 1981 in exchange for reductions in its tax bill, or those by numerous British companies (British Airways, Hansons and the fraudulent bankrupt Polly Peck) to the Conservative Party. The problem with secret donations is that nobody – least of all the electorate – knows what the party has conceded in return for the money.[9]

Perhaps the most significant external source is what must be called 'corrupt funding'. We refer to the 'kick-backs' (*tangenti*) for services rendered: donations to party funds for facilitating administrative procedures (like planning permission for urban projects); and contributions to party funds as a fixed percentage on public contracts. These were the bases of the *fausses factures*[10] and *tangentopoli* scandals that brought the PS in France and the DC and PSI in Italy to their knees in the recent elections (tables 5.7 and 5.9). What they demonstrate is quite simply that party funding was organized as a systematic 'political racket'. The consequences, particularly in Italy, were far-reaching: the fall of the First Republic and the dissolution of the DC in 1994.

The third method – state funding of parties – was introduced in Germany (from 1959), Italy (1974–93) and France (from 1988), but not in Britain. This does not mean, however, that British parties receive no state aid. Indeed, despite the considerable resistance to state subsidies in Britain, grants have been made to the opposition parties since 1975; all parties, moreover, enjoy a form of indirect state aid in the form of specified free time on all national TV channels. Further, the prime motive for introducing state funding of parties in Italy and France was to offset the political scandals provoked by occult financing (*Unione petrolifera*, Montedison's 'black funds' – Sassoon, 1975; and *Carrefour du développement* in France – Mény, 1992a), but it has proved unsuccessful, largely because it never met the parties' expenditure needs. The regulations covering state financing of parties vary from state to state, but generally it takes the form of funds for party running costs and election campaign expenditure, usually on a pro rata basis of votes won at the last election, and now accounts for the major part of many parties' income (20–35 per cent in Germany; 30–90 per cent in Italy in 1990). Despite what appeared in the 1980s as a trend towards state funding of parties in Europe, there are, as von Beyme (1982) has noted, weighty arguments against it. These include: greater state supervision: a decline in party membership and so a growth in political apathy; weakening the opposition within the political system; strengthening the central party apparatus at the expense of ordinary members and local units; and shoring up the system by protecting existing parties from new parties breaking in. Last but not least, it does not solve the parties' financial problems in the longer term, as the Italian and French experience confirms: private donations still remain necessary.

Such arguments more than justify public suspicion of state funding. Indeed, in Italy they reached such proportions – particularly after the revelations of the *mani pulite* inquiry into the *tangentopoli* scandal[11] – that they provoked, amongst other more constitutional developments, including eight popular referendums of 18 April 1993, a referendum on the issue which abrogated the law on public funding of parties by a massive majority. That Italy was a special case can be deduced from the fact that, despite public funding, party debts were piling up: for instance, about 300 billion lire (£120 million) in Italy in 1990 against about £20 million[12] in Britain in 1992. At all events, the scandal has at the very least placed the survival of the former Italian government parties (DC/PPI, PSI) in jeopardy (table 5.9). In spite of this, it remains to mention the positive effects claimed for state funding of parties: these include reducing parties' dependence on pressure from influential donors and hence increasing equality of political access, or again ensuring that party activity is continuous and not just limited to electioneering, which means that they can play a more substantial role in grass-roots political participation.

Be that as it may, it is worth, in concluding this discussion, recapitulating on party power structures and action. We described three parliamentary party types which correspond to three kinds of relations between leaders (or 'notables'), militants and electors. As Charlot (1971) noted: 'all parties are a mix of parties of notables, of militants and of voters; the important thing is to know what they stress and why' (p. 218). The notables' party emphasizes state institutions and parliamentary activity, while the mass party (or better perhaps the militants' party) stresses societal activity and political militancy, and the catch-all party (or better perhaps the voters' party) gives priority to electioneering. Party leaders are usually able to control their parties, but to do so they must take account of the privileged groups in their type of party, because the different party types legitimate different means with which the various privileged groups can disavow their leaders, and which they use from time to time.

With the electoralization of the party struggle in the post-war period has come the domination of the voters' party in the West. The power of party leaders is increasingly based on electoral success (the recent crises of the PCF and PCI, both militants' parties, are particularly significant in this connection); political tactics and the choice of candidates are increasingly dictated by anticipated voter reaction as perceived by polling and other instruments of electoral analysis. Party control, therefore, is increasingly subject to electoral manipulation, that is to say party leaders orchestrate and personalize their appeal to the voters – who on the whole are less politicized – rather than to the militants. The domination of voters' parties means a conservative and personalized politics and a disengagement of party militants, who increasingly seek other institutions to express their commitment to political activity. Finally, the decline in the vote of the old established parties in the major West European states since the 1970s (tables 5.6–5.9) has prompted talk – albeit premature – of the demise of parties (Lawson and Merkyl, 1988; see chapter 11 in this book).

Party systems

'No party exists in a vacuum', Blondel (1978) has observed, which means that parties operate in a specific context. In Western Europe, this context is the competitive struggle between opposing parties sanctioned periodically by universal suffrage. There is an abundant literature on the factors which determine party systems. On the other hand, since parties fit into the political system as the privileged link between civil society and the state, it seems logical that the importance of the different factors should vary according to the viewpoint adopted, namely whether one gives precedence to the influence of civil society or that of the state. Duverger's (1951) study of the relationship between party systems and electoral regimes privileges institutional influence; whereas Rokkan's (1970) emphasizes societal influence and socio-political cleavages. However, the party system in a certain country at a certain moment is the result of a combination of factors, of which it is often difficult to assess the relative weight. To resolve this dilemma, we can distinguish the way in which party competition originated historically from the way it is structured today. This is all the more reasonable since it follows Rokkan and Lipset's (1967) well-known observation that 'the party systems of the 1960s reflect, with few but significant exceptions, the cleavage structures of the 1920s: the party alternatives, and in remarkably many cases, the party organizations, are older than the majorities of the national electorates' (p. 50). In this way, they emphasize not only the significance of the historical dimension – party images were formed and consolidated over time – but also the fact that party systems were structured in a particular historical period, the late nineteenth century, which coincided with the extension of the suffrage – the moment of the institutionalization of mass politics. Finally, this formulation is naturally an extension of Rokkan's models of socio-political cleavages (chapter 3).

The Rokkan-Lipset cleavage model

Party systems are not the simple translation of socio-economic conflicts into political conflict, even if socio-economic conflicts played an important role. In fact, religious, ethno-cultural and other cleavages have often converged in the party system for reasons of reciprocal overlapping and have retained influence right down to the present. The development of the European party system has felt above all the effects of two successive, ideologically loaded, class conflicts: that between landed aristocracy and industrial bourgeoisie, represented by conservative (country) and liberal (town) parties respectively; and that between the bourgeoisie and the nascent proletariat, expressed in party terms in the conflict between liberal and socialist parties. These two conflicts gave rise to three partisan tendencies, but the second, in particular, faced the liberals with a dilemma: conservatives or socialists? The result was that the liberals practised a series of alliances (now with the conservatives, now with the socialists, according to the strength of the parties in the different states). In the end, however, the conflict led to the liberal parties splitting: the right wing joined the conservative parties – Chamberlain's National Liberals at the end of the nineteenth century in Britain – and the left wing chose to collaborate with the socialists, as the French radicals did in the Third Republic.

The conservative, liberal and socialist tendencies thus represented the constitutive components of the European party systems. The socialist area was widened in the aftermath of the 1917 Bolshevik Revolution when the communist factions abandoned the socialist parties to join the Comintern in most European countries. Hence developed the competition between socialist and communist parties which has been an essential ingredient, in different ways, of West European party systems in the post-war period. Although these often overlapping conflicts have formed the basis of European party systems, they have not been the only ones; there were two other major cleavages, religious (clerical versus anti-clerical) and ethno-cultural (centre versus periphery) (table 5.2). These have usually led to the constitution of parties within bourgeois positions: the

Table 5.2 Parties and socio-political cleavages

	Capital/labour		Centre/periphery		Church/state		Town/country
	Bourgeois parties	Working class parties	Centralist parties	Regionalist parties	Catholic parties	Anti-clerical parties	
Britain	Con. Lib.	Lab.		SNP PC UU			Green
France	UDF	PCF PS	Gau. FN	SDLP	MRP	Rad.	Ecolos
Germany	CDU FDP	SPD	Repub.		CSU		Grünen
Italy	PLI FI	PCI/PDS/RC PSI PSDI Ext. left	MSI/AN	SVP PSdAz Leghe	DC/PPI	PRI PR	Verdi

Britain

Con.	Conservative party
Lab.	Labour Party
Lib.	Liberal Party
PC	Plaid Cymru
SDLP	Social Democratic and Labour Party
SNP	Scottish National Party
UU	Ulster Unionists
Green	Green Party

France

FN	Front National
Gau.	Gaullist
MRP	Mouvement Républicain pour le Progrès
PCF	Parti Communiste Française
PS	Parti Socialiste
Rad.	Radicaux
UDF	Union pour la Démocratie Française
Ecolos	Greens

Germany

CDU	Christlich Demokratische Union
CSU	Christlich Soziale Union
FDP	Freie Demokratische Partei
SPD	Sozialdemokratische Partei Deutschland
Repub.	Republikaner
Grünen	Green Party

Italy

DC/PPI	Democrazia Cristiana/Partito Popolare Italiano
Ext. left	Extreme left
FI	Forza Italia
MSI/AN	Movimento Sociale Italiano/Alleanza Nazionale
PCI/PDS	Partito Comunista Italiano/Partito Democratico della Sinistra
PLI	Partito Liberale Italiano
PR	Partito Radicale
PRI	Partito Repubblicano Italiano
PSdAz	Partito Sardo d'Azione
PSDI	Partito Social Democratico Italiano
PSI	Partito Socialista Italiano
RC	Rifondazione Comunista
SVP	Sudtiröler Volkspartei
Verdi	Greens

Source: adapted from Seiler, 1980, pp. 128–9

most important one, without doubt, was the religious conflict. For instance, in Catholic countries, where the church was allied with the *ancien régime*, the bourgeoisie's struggle for control of the state provoked an anti-clerical versus clerical cleavage because the church felt it necessary to organize its own party to defend its interests. This, however, did not happen in France because the church always maintained close ties with the conservatives (the MRP was only a brief interlude since it failed to implant itself in French society). In Italy, the Catholic party (Opera dei Congressi 1874–1904; Partito Popolare 1919–26; and DC 1944–94) succeeded in organizing the subordinate class (the peasantry) and protecting it from the influence of other social forces. It formed a stable subculture thanks to the creation of a vast associational network. The socio-political isolation of the Catholic world, as a result of its rigidly hierarchical organizations and its links with the Vatican, was maintained until World War I and to a large extent throughout the fascist period.

In the continental countries subject to the Catholic versus Protestant cleavage, an important Catholic minority was faced with a liberal elite drawn from a Protestant majority. In Germany this minority created its own party (Zentrum 1870–1933) but in difficult circumstances, namely violent repression of its culture and organizations: Bismarck's *Kulturkampf* 1871–9, but also the Nazi *Gleichschaltung* 1933–45. Finally, in the nordic countries, like Britain, where the Reformation triumphed and the national church collaborated closely with the state, there was no significant religious cleavage which led to the constitution of overlapping religious parties. It was not that there were no religious cleavages between the various Protestant sects, only that they were expressed within the confines of the class parties.

The ethno-cultural conflicts, deriving from the resistance of areas with a clearly defined territorial culture which was poorly integrated into the nation, were responsible for the formation of a number of regional parties: for instance, the Bavarian Christlich Soziale Union in Germany; the Partito Sardo d'Azione and Sudtiröler Volkspartei, and very recently the Northern Leagues, in Italy; Plaid Cymru and the Scottish National Party in Britain. The town versus country cleavage has a particular resonance in Scandinavia with the formation of agrarian parties. However, in the four principal Western European countries, this cleavage did not lead to the creation of peasant parties; it was, in fact, integrated in the existing partisan structure – British Conservatives and Italian Christian Democrats (country), British Labour and Italian and German Socialists (town) – making it perhaps more acute. The green parties have recently been assimilated in the rural dimension of the town–country cleavage (Seiler, 1993).

In conclusion, Rokkan's thesis is simply that the West European party systems were formed in parallel to the extension of the suffrage as the expression of the socio-economic, religious and cultural conflicts of the period. Since the European societies of the time (1820–1920) were wrought by a set of conflicts that took different forms in the different states, their political traditions contained common elements as well as significant differences. Moreover, once the party system was institutionalized, the various political tendencies organized in parties have demonstrated a remarkable capacity for survival thanks to the 'law of first comers'. Indeed, the general shape of each party system has survived great changes: two world wars, transformation of the social and political structures, even fascist and Nazi regimes. This does not mean that certain parties have not disappeared or new ones have not appeared, or that others have not radically changed (see the section on political families in this chapter). But only in the last twenty years, that is since 1968,[13] does traditional party stability appear to have declined, with a growth in electoral mobility and with party realignments, first in Britain and France, and now in Germany and Italy (Dalton, Flanagan and Beck, 1984).[14]

As regards the way in which party competition is structured today, that is its dynamics, the best-known typologies are those of Duverger (1951) and Sartori (1976). If Duverger's is based on a macro-sociological approach in which socio-economic, ideological and above all institutional factors are taken into account, Sartori's is more essential, privileging almost exclusively political factors or competition strategies. It is not that Sartori denies the influence of other factors, but only that he considers them irrelevant to political science analysis.

Duverger's typology

Duverger (1951) attempts to systematize the classic distinction between competitive (open) and non-competitive (closed) party systems and, within the former, between two-partyism and multipartyism on the basis of the number of parties (one, two or many). Competitive party system dynamics are essentially pendular with a centripetal motion, derived from a 'natural political dualism' – 'political choice usually takes the form of a choice between two alternatives' (p. 215) – which is strengthened or weakened by the electoral system. He theorized the effects of the electoral regimes on party systems in the form of 'sociological laws': '(1) proportional representation tends to a system of multiple, rigid and independent parties ...; (2) the majority second-ballot system tends to a system of multiple, flexible and dependent parties; (3) the majority [simple plurality] single-ballot system tends to party dualism [two-partyism] with the alternation of power between major independent parties' (p. 205). Duverger's typology raises three questions: the classification of party systems and its significance; the type of system dynamics and the notion of the 'centre'; and the well-known 'sociological laws'.

Classification of party systems

Duverger admits that it is not easy to distinguish between the two-party and the multiparty systems, despite the apparently simple criterion employed, to wit the number of parties. The reason lies in the fact that 'there exists alongside the major parties a number of small groups' (p. 207). Thus he is obliged to accept a second criterion: party size. This poses the question of how to count parties, but, as Sartori has observed, it is one which Duverger did not succeed in solving satisfactorily.

The classification of party systems raises, however, a more fundamental question: why distinguish between two-party and multiparty systems at all? The reason lies in the consequences: the alternation of parties in power in two-party systems; and the lack of alternation in the case of multipartyism. As Duverger argues, its importance was disregarded in the Cold War because it was overshadowed by the contrast between competitive (open) and non-competitive (closed) party systems, seen as the political criterion distinguishing the two worlds of West and East. 'However,' he claims, 'it is undeniably a fundamental distinction' (p. 206).

Party system dynamics

Competitive party system dynamics, according to Duverger, are pendular on a centripetal basis. This resulted from his assumption that all political alternatives are intrinsically dualistic: a contrast between two contradictory viewpoints. In this way, Duverger denies the existence of centre opinions, centre tendencies or centre doctrines separate in kind from the doctrines of left and right: 'there may well be a centre party but there is no centre tendency, no centre doctrine' (p. 215). Centre opinions are either moderate views of basically oppositional viewpoints or cross-cutting cleavages. It follows that competitive party system dynamics derive either from internal dualisms – party splits between extremists and moderates – or from change in the basic political cleavage. Duverger's dualist conception of the competitive party struggle – castigated by Wildavsky (1959) as 'mystical error' and by Sartori as 'dualistic blinders' (blinkers) – has diverse but parallel origins. First of all, it comes from the idea that parliamentary parties are either in power or in opposition. This serves to connect party system dynamics to the problem of alternation. Secondly, it comes from an interpretative tradition of French post-revolutionary[15] politics in terms of a basic conflict between two major forces: republicans (progress, *mouvement*, left) and monarchists (tradition, *ordre*, right). We need only link this tradition with a similar British one, arising out of the English Revolution – Roundheads and Cavaliers, Whigs and Tories, Liberals (or Labour) and Conservatives – to become convinced that one is dealing with a 'natural political dualism'.[16] Finally, a certain class influence allowed Duverger to ground the party system in society by means of social conflict (class, but also political, religious and ideological). An instance is his well-known schema of cross-cutting cleavages in France in the 1940s and 1950s: 'the multiparty system in France is the result of the non-coincidence of the main cleavages of opinion' (pp. 231–2) (figure 5.1).

Recapitulating: since the centre does not exist as an independent political force, the political centre is thus the result of overlapping cleavages, or a combination of the left–right dimension and the moderate–extremist one. In this view, multipartyism is an arrangement (*le marais* or *le juste milieu*) in which the moderates of both left and right ally to keep the extremists of both wings out of power. The result is a permanent centrism of immobile and paralysing coalitions which, in the case of the French Third and Fourth Republics, Duverger (1967) called 'peopleless democracy' (*la démocratie sans le peuple*).

Sociological laws

Discussion of the consequences of electoral regimes for politics began with the extension of the suffrage and was particularly intense in the second half of the nineteenth century. We need only recall J.S. Mill's (1861) discussion of Hare's single transferable vote system. Thus the fact that electoral regimes are manipulative instruments *par excellence* was well known long before Duverger's formulation of his sociological laws. What Duverger did was to formulate propositions with a certain precision and collect considerable historical evidence to back them. They have, as was inevitable, been the subject of criticism by all those who have studied the problem since, but paradoxically no one has come up with a better formulation, suggesting that the political effects of electoral regimes are not amenable to a more precise formulation.

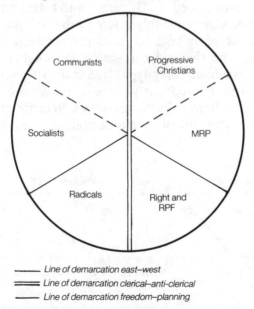

——— Line of demarcation east–west
═══ Line of demarcation clerical–anti-clerical
——— Line of demarcation freedom–planning

Figure 5.1 Overlapping of cleavages in France
Source: Duverger, 1951, p. 232

One of the reasons lies in the fact that Duverger did not define the difference between two-party and multiparty systems in such a way as to allow unequivocal verification. However, despite his severe criticism – laws 'faulty in many respects' – Sartori is obliged to admit that they subsist as 'tendency laws', which he reformulates thus: 'Tendency law 1: plurality formulas facilitate (are facilitating conditions of) a two-party format and, conversely, obstruct (are an obstructive condition of) multipartyism. Tendency law 2: PR formulas facilitate multipartyism and are, conversely, hardly conducive to two-partyism' (1986, p. 64). The plural is important because PR systems are many and have different consequences. In fact, Sartori analyses the manipulative efficiency of electoral regimes not only in terms of the differences between the systems globally, but also in terms of constituency size, a factor neglected by Duverger (figure 5.2). As we can see, the deforming influence of the electoral regime diminishes with the increase in constituency size (as measured by the number of seats): 'The smaller the constituency,' Sartori (1968) has written, 'the greater the "waste" of votes, and hence the greater the impurity; the greater the constituency, the less impurity' (p. 279). One example suffices, that of the British government elected in 1983: with just 42 per cent of the vote, the Conservative Party won 60 per cent or more of the seats in the House of Commons; moreover, losing 1.3 per cent of the vote in 1983, it saw its parliamentary majority triple (from 44 to 144 seats in a House whose membership was increased from 635 to 650). Not surprisingly, Rose (1974) has defined the one-ballot single-member majority system as 'a device for disproportional representation' (p. 112) (table 5.3).

A second factor, overlooked by Duverger and taken up by Sartori, is the structuring of party systems: this refers to the nationalization of the party system when the party vote replaced the personal vote, and coincided, more or less, with the replacement of the notables' party by the mass party as the dominant party type. In Sartori's view, the 'tendency laws' only apply to structured party systems because before that the political situation is too fluid to be characterized in terms of party.

To conclude the discussion of electoral regimes, we should mention

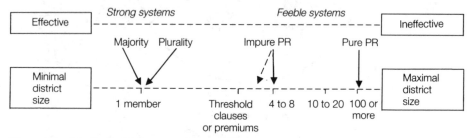

Figure 5.2 Manipulative impact of electoral systems
Source: Sartori, 1968, p. 280; 1984

Table 5.3   Properties of electoral systems

	Electoral formula	Electoral district size (proportion)	Proportionality index %
Britain	Simple majority	1.0	85
France	Majority two ballots (PR 1945–56 and 1986)	1.0	79
Germany	Plurality and PR: d'Hondt	2.0	98
Italy	PR: imperial quota (largest remainder)[a]	20.3	95

[a] Before 1993 when Italy adopted a mixed 75% majority, 25% proportional system
Source: Lane, McKay and Newton, 1991, p. 109

two further points often ignored in discussion. The first concerns the significance of the values given prominence in different democratic traditions. Schematizing to the maximum, we can distinguish between the
Anglo-Saxon tradition which emphasizes the value of 'efficiency', that is
the 'governability' of the system, and the continental tradition which
places the accent on the values of 'constitutionalism' and of 'democratic
representativeness'. In the former the electors vote to choose a government which governs in their name, while in the latter they vote to
express a political opinion that will be represented in parliament.[17] The
choice of electoral regimes reflects the traditions' values: the former
associates efficiency and governability with majority systems and hence
self-justifies them; the latter similarly associates constitutional guarantees and democratic representativeness with forms of PR.[18]

The second point touches a very banal fact that results from the
deforming element of the electoral regime. Briefly, the majority system is
a dynamic system because of the very distortions that it provokes, while
the proportional system is usually static because of the close relationship
between votes cast and seats won. In the former, a small displacement of
votes is often enough to change the parliamentary majority; in the latter,
an electoral earthquake is required. But, since the latter are rare in structured party systems, party systems employing majority electoral regimes
have shown themselves, in practice, to be more dynamic than proportional ones. Moreover, the larger number of parties (facilitated by PR
systems) allows a greater number of mutual compensations between
vote displacements and so reduces overall electoral mobility.

Sartori's typology

Sartori's typology is more complex than Duverger's, but it also recognizes as fundamental the traditional distinction between competitive and non-competitive systems. Given our Western European perspective, the discussion is limited to competitive systems. Sartori's (1976) primary purpose is to identify the remunerative tactics of electoral competition in the various party systems on the basis of Downs's (1957)[19] economic model of democracy and to elaborate a new classification and general typology of party systems that overcame the weakness of Duverger's dualist typology. Like Duverger, in fact, Sartori considers the number of parties important, but, unlike him, insufficient. The problem was that Duverger did not know how to count the parties because he lacked a criterion of 'relevant parties'. Sartori's criteria for counting – parties are relevant which have (a) *coalition potential* or (b) *blackmail potential* – allow him to propose a classification of party systems based on party fragmentation: with less than five parties, there is low fragmentation; with more than five parties, high fragmentation. From this he derives a taxonomy of competitive party systems in four classes: (1) simple pluralism, (2) limited pluralism, (3) extreme pluralism and (4) atomization; the last is a residual case to indicate the point at which the number of parties becomes irrelevant.

However, the number of parties is insufficient to constitute a typology; a second criterion is required which Sartori identifies in the parties' ideological dimension. He defines this in terms of the ideological distance between the parties in the system and this denotes at the same time the ideological intensity of the system. The greater the overall ideological distance between the parties, the more the system is polarized, and vice versa. The number of relevant parties is evidence of polarization, but not *proof*, that is to say the system's polarization needs to be verified without reference to the number of parties. In other words, Sartori starts from the assumption of a relationship between party fragmentation and ideological polarization that is not wholly convincing. In fact, Sartori realized this, when faced with Lijphart's criticism that party systems could be fragmented without necessarily being polarized – as in the case of Holland – and introduced the notion of 'segmentation'. Whatever the case, the two criteria (number of parties or fragmentation, and ideological distance) led him to propose the typology in figure 5.3.

Classifications and typologies are useful only in so far as they assist in understanding how a system functions, that is its mechanics (or dynamics). Sartori's thesis is that there is a relationship between the number of parties (class) and the party system's mechanics (type). Sartori's great contribution, in fact, regards the identification of two types of multiparty system dynamics, moderate pluralism and polarized pluralism: his name is linked to the definition of the latter's properties and mechanics. In detail, limited pluralism as a class defines systems with three to five par-

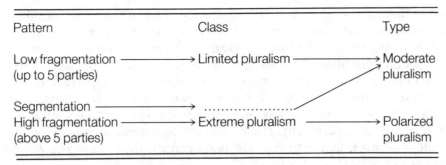

Pattern	Class	Type
Low fragmentation (up to 5 parties)	→ Limited pluralism	→ Moderate pluralism
Segmentation	→	
High fragmentation (above 5 parties)	→ Extreme pluralism	→ Polarized pluralism

Figure 5.3   Sartori's typology of competitive party systems
Source: Sartori, 1976, p. 127

ties. The competitive mechanism is bipolar, like two-party systems, and the competitive strategy is the same, namely the fight for the centre votes, and so centripetal, characterized by 'moderate pluralism': hence the name. The political formula of moderate pluralist systems is the coalition because no party is usually able to form a government by itself; thus what one has is not party alternation, but 'coalition alternation'. The only difference between moderate pluralism and two-party systems, since the system dynamics are the same, is that in the former one party governs alone while the opposition party is sufficiently strong to represent a political alternative which can hope to win the next election to become itself the new government; whereas in the latter no one party is sufficiently strong. For Sartori, the two-party system is defined by government alternation.

On the other hand, extreme pluralism is characterized by a format of more than five parties while the system dynamics of polarized pluralism is multipolar and the competitive strategy is centrifugal, that is the fight for extremes. The characteristics of polarized pluralism, according to Sartori, are: (1) the presence of relevant *anti-system parties* which would change the regime or system of government rather than just the government *tout court*; (2) the existence of *bilateral oppositions* that are mutually exclusive and cancel one another out; (3) the *occupation of the metrical centre* of the system – it is a centre-based system – which implies that the centre is out of competition, hence the centrifugal dynamics; (4) *high polarization* because the ideological distance between the parties is very wide, which means that consensus is low and cleavages are very deep and so naturally system legitimacy is low; (5) the prevalence of *centrifugal drives* which weaken the centre electorally because of the persistent loss of votes to the extremes; (6) congenital *ideological patterning* understood as a *forma mentis*, that is a perception of politics that reflects the mentality of rationalism as opposed to the empirical and pragmatic mentality; (7) the presence of *irresponsible oppositions* because they are not destined to govern and hence to 'respond' to what they promise; and, finally, (8) the display by the polity of an electoral *politics of overbidding* that tends to undermine fair competition, which, according to Sartori, means that 'excessive promises' become the rules of the game and these dangerously undermine the basis of the party system. As we can see, the system dynamics of polarized pluralism are radically different from that of moderate pluralism. Instead of alternative coalitions in which all parties can participate, there is a permanent coalition with a *peripheral participation*, limited to the centre parties – centre-left and/or centre-right parties only – because anti-system parties are systematically excluded from access to government. Hence the political system operates at the ideological level, that is to say 'for' and 'against' the system and *not* on the basis of policy choice.

In short, polarized pluralism is predicated on three essential properties: multipolarity, centrifugal competition and extreme politics. Hence polarized pluralist systems are fundamentally unstable, very fragile and subject to crises. The significance of Sartori's model lies not only in the fact that traditional multipartyism confuses two very different situations (which Duverger's analysis was unable to identify or comprehend), but also that three of the states discussed here (Weimar Germany, French Third and Fourth Republics and republican Italy) have experienced it in this century. Nonetheless, Sartori's typology raises a number of problems: the importance of the numerical criterion in the classification of party systems; the anti-system party concept; the role of alternation; and electoral competition space and system dynamics.

Numerical criterion

Sartori's discussion starts from the numerical criterion, but his initial assumption that there is a more or less linear relationship between party fragmentation and ideological polarization turned out to be not really true. Thus, when forced to state which was the more important in defining the type of system, Sartori quite correctly opted for ideological polarization at the expense of the numerical criterion. In fact, he now claims that the choice of the numerical criterion was necessary in the 1960s because there were no data for measuring the ideological polarity of party systems. Today, these data exist (they come from a series of 1970s European surveys) and have permitted him to construct with Sani (Sani and Sartori, 1982) a 'polarization index' that measures the ideological polarity between parties (figure 5.4).

The index confirms Sartori's expectations; hence he claims that the methodological objections raised against its construction are groundless. However, we can ask in what sense the cross-national data are indeed comparable between themselves.[20] Nonetheless, the data do show a 'natural' difference between moderate and polarized pluralist systems, although *none* between moderate pluralist and two-party ones.

Anti-system parties

The concept of anti-system party was introduced by Sartori to define the polarized pluralist model, because, thanks to the rejection of the political

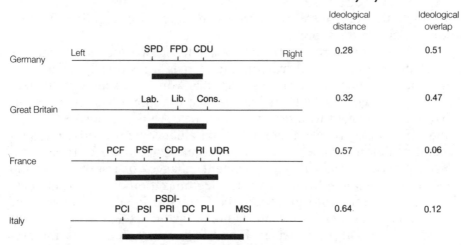

	Ideological distance	Ideological overlap
Germany	0.28	0.51
Great Britain	0.32	0.47
France	0.57	0.06
Italy	0.64	0.12

The ideological distance is a measure of left–right spread; the ideological overlap is a measure of shared convictions (see Sani and Sartori, 1982 for details)

Figure 5.4 Ideological distance and overlap of party supporters in the 1970s. *Source*: Sartori, 1982, p. 261

system by this kind of party, the pro-system parties are forced to act according to the logic of the defence of the system and existing institutions. There has been a lively polemic about the nature and definition of the anti-system party. The criterion generally employed is the acceptance, or not, of the rules of the political system. But an agreement over the definition does not solve the problems of the operationalization of the concept, as Sartori himself has recognized. Recently, he has claimed that the concept merely serves to infer the existence of ideological distance and hence a certain level of polarization. Since the latter can now be tapped by other means – the index of polarization, for instance – the concept's definition has lost its importance for him.

However, the concept retains its importance, if only because of what lies behind it. The fact that the attempt was made to elaborate such a concept is evidence of a certain relation of forces between parties which has a history. The political systems against which the so-called anti-system parties fought were not natural constructions; they were the constructions of those who had the power to decree that the wish to change them radically was illegitimate. The criteria by which a certain party is defined as anti-system, but has mass support, relate to the cultural dimension of the structuration of civil society. This is not as abstract a finding as it might first appear. Party systems are not born ready-made; they developed in the course of the nineteenth century struggles for the extension of the suffrage. Certain social groups and their parties found themselves inside the political system; the others – the majority at the time – were excluded. By definition, therefore, the parties representing the excluded social groups were formed outside the political system – they were extra-parliamentary parties – and in opposition to it. It follows, then, that they were perceived by the forces representing the state system as anti-system forces.

The anti-system forces' struggle took one of two routes: change the system or enter it. As regards the latter, it is a historical fact that no party founded outside the state system has won an absolute parliamentary majority without first passing through an apprenticeship phase of government alliances with pro-system parties. An example is the British Labour Party experience: Liberal–Labour alliance before 1914; Labour–Liberal coalition between the wars; absolute Labour majority in 1945. This sequence suggests that government alliances of this kind are the *condicio sine qua non* for the historical legitimization of anti-system parties. Finally, in the post-war period, the Cold War ideological division of the continent has meant that international factors have determined that certain parties – in particular, PCF and PCI – were defined as anti-system parties and, in consequence, denied all governing legitimacy: for instance, the US veto was exercised by president Carter in January 1978 against PCI participation in the Italian government.

Alternation

In view of the importance of the anti-system concept and above all the ideological polarization that lies behind it in Sartori's analysis, and the role that the Schumpeterian perspective of elite competition has always had in Sartori's (1957; 1987) discussion of democratic theory, we would have expected the mechanism of alternation to loom large in his typology. Not at all; indeed, Sartori has said that although he considers alternation desirable, it is not a crucial variable. He argues that it does not explain what his critics claim that it does. Alternation depends on the structure of the system, *not* the structure of the system on it. Hence to force alternation in certain circumstances is, according to him, a recipe for disaster: it could precipitate a regime crisis, political violence, even civil war (chapter 7). For Sartori, the important variable which explains the working of party systems is the prevalent type of electoral competition.

Space and dynamics

The key to Sartori's typology is the distinction between centripetal and centrifugal competition because the type of competition is determined by opposite kinds of system dynamics. It is based on the notion of spatial electoral competition: its characteristic appears to be unidimensional. Sartori claims, in fact, that the multidimensionality of party conflicts can be summarized by the major dimension; and which empirically, in Western Europe, is left–right. Parties incapable of defining themselves on this dimension are automatically excluded from meaningful electoral competition: they may be able to defend a stronghold, but have no possibility of electoral expansion. It is on the basis of the unidimensionality of electoral space that Sartori derives the emergence of the centre as the strategic area of polarized pluralist party systems.

This poses two problems: (1) whether the left–right dimension effectively summarizes the other political dimensions in polarized pluralist systems; and (2) if so, whether the occupation of the centre means that the system dynamics are centrifugal. As for (1) it is not necessarily the case; it is probable that the relevance of different political cleavages changes over time, through the introduction of new issues. All parties try to maximize the dimensions that are favourable to them. With regard to (2), it is difficult to follow the logic that requires polarized pluralist party systems to be always necessarily centrifugal. What prevents a party near one pole of the left–right dimension – like the PCI in Italy in the 1970s – from seeking votes in the centre? Moreover, if there is a strong centre party – like the DC again in Italy until the 1990s – there is nothing to prevent it too from attracting votes to the centre on the basis of its programme. Indeed, if the centre is considered the refuge of pro-system voters where there are anti-system parties at both poles, we could hypothesize that one of the reasons for the survival of the Italian First Republic for so long,[21] at least in comparison with Weimar Germany and Fourth Republic France, lay in the strength of the DC in relation to the German and French centre parties.

An alternative schema

On the basis of the discussion so far, a number of points have emerged which merit further consideration. First of all, despite the differences of approach between Duverger and Sartori and the latter's critique, the dichotomous nature of party systems maintains a certain validity. Secondly, the numerical criterion, despite Sartori's corrections and although useful initially, is no longer strictly relevant for analysing party systems. Thirdly, Sartori's two great intuitions which have helped advance party system analysis are: (1) the fundamental importance of the ideological dimension, underrated by Duverger; and (2) its consequences for party competition, in the sense of introducing a second and opposing dynamic. On this basis, the real difference between competitive systems is not between the two-party and multiparty systems, as Duverger claimed, but within multipartyism: between moderate (bipolar) pluralism and polarized (multipolar) pluralism. Government alternation – because of its consequences for the political system (for the *modus operandi* of the state institutions: chapter 7) – is more important than Sartori allows. In our view it is, in fact, the other (hidden) face of the ideological dimension. Our alternative schema (figure 5.5) is based on the political dimension, defined in Gramscian rather than Sartorian terms, that is the continuum coercion–consensus. In this schema, as for Duverger and Sartori, the one-party regime poses no problems: it is based on coercion for the simple reason that the opposition is not legalized, and hence it is 'non-competitive' and not really a party system at all.[22]

CLOSED SYSTEM	OPEN SYSTEM	
Non-competitive systems *no game*	Limited competitive systems *positive-sum game*	Fully competitive systems *zero-sum game*
←		→
Coercion		*Consensus*
One-party regime (opposition is illegal)	Non-alternating systems – permanent coalitions or one-party domination (existence of relevant anti-system parties)	Alternating government systems: single parties or coalitions (anti-system parties irrelevant)

Figure 5.5 An alternative schema of party systems

However, problems arise with regard to the open party systems: the discriminating element between 'fully competitive' systems (zero-sum game) and 'limited competitive' systems (positive-sum game) is, in fact, the level of competition, and this is a function of the existence or not of relevant anti-system parties. The fact that an alternative party majority to the present government majority cannot be found without the signifi-cant participation of anti-system parties – in terms of parliamentary votes, government participation (key ministries) – prevents, or rather damages, proper systemic competition. The question posed is thus: when do these conditions exist? In this context, D'Alimonte's (1978) critique of Sartori is more convincing than Sartori's original argument: that fully competitive systems are those where political space is homogeneous, while the existence of anti-system parties by their vary nature, introduces a disturbing or heterogeneous element, which means that political space is multidimensional and *cannot* be summarized in unidimensional terms, as Sartori claims. Where there is a sufficient level of political homogene-ity, parties respond to shifts in public opinion between government and opposition on the basis of the government's action. Competition is cen-tripetal – as Sartori has shown – because electoral competition obliges parties to compose political conflicts on median positions for electoral advantage. Thus the more a democracy is competitive, the more 'eccen-tric' (that is extreme) behaviour is penalized. This raises the question not only of how behaviour is defined, but also of how it is perceived. The answer lies in the course of political struggles, but we must not overlook the fact that each party's resources are not the same. At all events, the tendency to move towards the centre of the political spectrum in com-petitive democracies is usually a result of the fact that the government parties are obliged to respond to the population's electoral humours in order not to lose the coming election.

On the other hand, the limited competitive party systems are such because the electoral space is multidimensional: there is at least a second dimension which is more important than the one along which traditional party battles are fought, and with which it cannot be swapped under any circumstances. This second dimension is that of the anti-system parties (that is those proposing radical change of society or regime) or those that are perceived as such. In this case, the normal competition on the first dimension is overridden by this second dimension. The reason is simple: a certain proportion of voters, who would have voted for an anti-system party on the basis of its programme on the first dimension, refuse or hesitate to do so in the name of the defence of the institutions, because of fears of the consequences for the regime or for society of an electoral victory of the anti-system party. Thus the defence of the institutions becomes an absolute duty for the government parties, justified under various headings ('la difesa della libertà' or 'la scelta di civiltà' in Italy; or 'le choix de société' in France). From this come many of the ills – corruption, scandals, *sottogoverno*, regime profiteering, arrogance of power and government inefficiency as well as violent protest and political alienation – associated with limited competitive party systems: they lack, in fact, clear party responsibility for government action which, not surprisingly, is an incentive for government irresponsibility.

This schema based on the coercion–consensus dimension in terms of the rotation of parties in power, or its absence, has a certain number of consequences. The first regards the state's role in determining the parameters of consensus. A party which does not accept these parameters is defined as anti-system. This means that the parties historically defined as anti-system – like the representatives of the classes excluded in the nineteenth century – were obliged to accept not only the rules of the parliamentary game, but also a certain form of societal organization: market capitalism. In fact, the difference between fully competitive and limited competitive systems can be summarized thus: in the former, there is alternation because the opposition does not represent a real alternative, so it can participate in the zero-sum game; in the latter, there is no alternation just because the opposition does represent a real alternative, and hence the zero-sum game is too dangerous and becomes converted into a positive-sum game. This is the other – hidden – face of electoral competition outlined above, that is to say the restricted ideological parameters of political consensus in actual democracies which place precise limits on the alternative policies of so-called socialist governments: for instance, the Mitterrand government's forced change of policies in 1983. Hence the adage: 'The socialist parties are only guests in power.' Finally, there is the tendency of pro-government parties to theorize their monopoly of power. We need only recall the French Radical Party as the personification of the Third Republic; or again prime minister Moro's concept of Italy as a 'special kind of democracy' in which the DC was condemned to remain always in power in spite of itself, and the PCI always in opposition. This justified a game in which both played their appointed role during the Cold War.

The second consequence is that fully competitive party systems, far from operating on the basis of a natural dualist alternation, as Duverger claimed, have similar tendencies to some limited competitive systems, that is periods of one-party domination. This has been Britain's case for long periods of its history. The alternation operating between 1945 and

1981 was, in fact, more an exception than the rule. Germany and France (since 1958) have known periods of one-party domination: CDU 1949–69; Gaullists 1958–74. This is less surprising than it might appear: it is the reflection, at the representational level, of an ideological consensus thanks to which a certain party or political alliance, at a certain moment, succeeds in mediating the interests of the various groups better than all the other parties.

The third consequence is that historically the anti-system parties were constituted as representatives of the classes excluded from the political system in the nineteenth century. Thus, for instance, the working class parties were defined as 'illegitimate' – that is, founded outside the political system – as were the confessional parties. The communist parties added to this original sin by joining the Comintern first and the Cominform later and supporting actual socialist regimes. In this situation, the only way they could hope to legitimize themselves as constitutional parties was, in addition to abandoning their original goals, to form an alliance with pro-system (usually bourgeois) parties because, in so doing, they gave a pledge of good conduct. This was the rule, as noted: Liberal–Labour in Britain; SPD under Weimar and, after Bad Godesberg, in the Grosse Koalition in 1966 in Germany; the SFIO with the Radicals in France between the wars and in the 1950s; and the PCF, having renounced the dictatorship of the proletariat, in a subordinate position to the PS 1981–4, again in France; PSI with DC in the centre-left in the 1960s in Italy. In this perspective, then, the PCI's proposal of the 'historic compromise' in the 1970s was the only plausible parliamentary strategy, although it did not succeed. Finally, this perspective illuminates not only the routes to constitutional legitimation of historical anti-system parties, but also attempts at 'delegitimizing' opponents practised by some, but not all, pro-system parties. The crude attempt of Thatcher Conservatives, supported by the tabloids, to define the Labour Party as 'Trotskyist' in the 1980s was, in this regard, exemplary.

In conclusion, it is worth observing that although electoral competition is held to be one of the bases of actual democracy, few party systems are, and have been, continuously fully competitive. Germany and Italy experienced periods of non-competition between the wars and, with France, periods of limited competition in the post-war period; Britain, which had experienced a period of full competition between 1945 and 1981, found itself in the 1980s in a period of limited competition, following the 1981 Social Democrat split in the Labour Party.

Political families

It is clear from the discussion that the presentation of Western European parties presupposes a classification, at least in terms of political families.

This can be done on the basis of different factors: ideologies, party types, historical cleavages, social classes represented. All need to be taken into account, but for ease of presentation the parties will be examined according to historical cleavages, the basis of the major political families (table 5.4).

Communists

Communist parties have existed in all four states, but only in two, Italy (PCI) and France (PCF), have they constituted significant components of their respective party systems in the post-war period. In Britain, the electoral strength of the party (CPGB) has been insignificant (the only recent Communist parliamentarian was a peer in the House of Lords!), while in Germany the KPD was declared illegal in 1956 (under a different name in 1979, it has not succeeded since in winning significant electoral support).

The European communist parties were founded as a result of an enduring conflict-ridden split in the labour movement promoted by the Comintern (and provoked by the Bolshevik Revolution and the creation of the first socialist state), which imposed the Leninist organizational model, an iron discipline and a subordinate position to the Soviet Party in the international communist movement. In the 1920s, the KPD was the most important European section of the Comintern, with about 15 per cent of the vote in German elections. However, destroyed by Nazism, it quickly lost all influence with the post-war West German electorate as a result above all of the communists' conquest of power in East Germany, followed by the Cold War and its being made illegal.

In the post-war period, after the dissolution of the Comintern, only the PCF and PCI succeeded in extending their organizational and electoral bases, thanks to their role in the anti-fascist resistance. However,

Table 5.4 Political families represented in parliament

	Britain	France	Germany	Italy
Communists		B → M	S	B → M S
Socialists	B	M → B	B	M → S S S
Catholics		(M)	⌐(B)	B → M
Liberals	M	M S	S	S S
Conservatives	B	B → M	└→ B	M
Neo-fascists		S		S → M
Regionalists	S S S S		S	S → M S S
Greens			S	S

B big (over 25 per cent), M = medium (10 per cent–25 per cent), S small (less than 10 per cent).
( ): parties which have disappeared.
Arrows: parties which have changed size or family.

the PCF has had a different electoral history from the PCI: starting as the largest French party in 1945 with roughly a quarter of the votes, it conserved this position throughout the Fourth Republic, but it suffered its first reversal with the creation of the Fifth Republic in 1958, when its support fell to 20 per cent; it maintained this position until the left came to power in 1981 when its vote suffered a more serious decline, falling to around 10 per cent. The PCI, instead, followed a different parabola, seeing its electoral support rise in all the elections from 1946 (19 per cent) to 1976 (34 per cent); in 1979 it suffered its first reversal, but its support in the 1980s seemed to stabilize around 30 per cent, before it suffered a second and greater decline at the end of the decade (25 per cent). With the party's decision to change its name to Partito Democratico della Sinistra (PDS) and abandon the hammer and sickle, it split, with its successor party taking 16 per cent of the vote in 1992 and the newly constituted Rifondazione Comunista taking 5.6 per cent (20.4 and 6.0 per cent respectively in 1994).

Communist parties developed in those countries where the process of industrialization started relatively late, and hence the political emancipation of the masses coincided with the struggle between socialists and communists for the conquest of the newly enfranchised masses inside the left. On the other hand, communist parties remained weaker in the countries of early industrialization like Britain, where the Labour Party had already succeeded in conquering the proletariat and hence was in a position to defend itself against Communist Party competition. The question posed by the recent decline of the PCF and PCI is whether, as seems likely, it marks the definitive decline of communism in favour of social democracy in Western Europe.

The electoral support of the PCF and PCI was constituted only in part by workers: alongside them was a conspicuous proportion from the middle classes, above all of self-employed workers (table 5.5). In the PCI, there was a larger presence of peasant farmers and traditional petty bourgeoisie (small industrialists and shopkeepers) in the red regions of Emilia-Romagna and Tuscany. However, the workers were the largest single group among the membership and their presence among the leadership groups was larger than in other parties. They remained, nonetheless, a minority in relation to leaders recruited from the middle classes, who also supplied the majority of paid party officials. Finally, the workers and older members were the strongest defenders of the traditional party line, while the reformist strategy was supported by the younger, better educated and more middle class generations. The latter were particularly numerous among those holding elective office at all levels (from MPs to local councillors). The communist parties have always seen themselves as militants' parties.

The major influence of the communist parties in civil society was felt in the trade union and cooperative movements (the latter particularly in Italy). In France and Italy where the unions are strongly politicized, the

Table 5.5 Social profile[a] of electors (E) and members (M) of the principal parties, 1970s (per cent)

	Bourgeoisie	Middle classes	(White-collars)	(Petty bourgeoisie)	Working class	Not active
Communists						
PCF: E	1	28	(22	6)	31	40
M	—	61	(55	6)	28	11
PCI: E	1	23	(11	12)	38	38
M	—	55	(47	8)	32	13
Socialists						
PS: E	1	41	(28	13)	20	38
M	1	62	(52	10)	17	20
Lab.: E	2	28	(23	5)	40	30
M	—	—	—	—	—	—
PSI: E	3	37	(22	15)	21	39
M	1	49	(33	16)	22	28
SPD: E	1	30	(23	9)	41	28
M	1	46	(41	5)	28	25
Catholics						
DC: E	2	29	(9	20)	18	51
M	2	42	(21	21)	16	40
CSU: E	—	—	—	—	—	—
M	2	69	(44	25)	10	19
Conservatives						
Gaul.: E	3	36	(20	16)	12	49
M	—	—	—	—	—	—
Con.: E	3	38	(32	6)	29	30
M	—	—	—	—	—	—
CDU: E	2	49	(28	21)	28	21
M	11	52	(37	15)	11	26

[a] given the variety of sources and categories, the figures are purely indicative.
Sources: various

Communist Party line was decisive in the strategies of the CGT and CGIL which recruited workers from other parties (Socialist, Radical). The CPGB had an influence in the trade union movement which greatly surpassed its very limited electoral influence. During the 1970s, the continental parties came close to power. In 1975, as a result of a series of bilateral meetings, the PCI and PCF (with the Spanish CP) announced their 'Eurocommunist' strategy which was little more than the formalization of the *de facto* post-war parliamentary strategy. Its basis was the theorization of the pacific transition to socialism, by means of a parliamentary majority and a policy of so-called 'structural' reforms. This strategy meant, at the international level, a policy of unrestricted autonomy and a decisive rejection of the Soviet Communist Party's leading role. In 1983 the PCI leader, Enrico Berlinguer, announced that the Bolshevik Revolution had exhausted its 'progressive contribution' to world history. The 'historic compromise' – the Italian version of Eurocommunism – led the PCI, after its 1976 electoral success, to support (but without government responsibilities) the Andreotti government of 'national solidarity' in 1978–9, but for the 1979 elections the PCI withdrew into opposition where it has remained, despite declining electoral support. Following the 1987 electoral defeat, factional rivalries came out into the open leading to the abandonment of democratic centralism at the 1988 party congress. It was the fall of the Berlin Wall in 1989 that precipitated the final transition: the historic decision to change the party's name and to place its political hopes in its future as an ordinary democratic party of the left, finally gained at special congresses in spring 1991.

The PCF, on the other hand, was part of the majority that elected Mitterrand to the presidency in 1981; it joined the 1981–4 Mauroy governments (with four ministers) but went back into opposition in 1984, denouncing the Fabius government's economic policy of austerity, where it has remained ever since, despite electoral alliances with the PS in 1988 and 1993 (table 5.7). The result was the party's political marginalization and a continued, if slower, erosion of its electorate. However, a change of leadership[23] and the abandonment of 'democratic centralism' at its 28th congress (January 1994) suggests that it will belatedly follow the Italian PDS.

Socialists and social democrats

Labour and socialists constitute at present the largest political grouping in the EP. Paradoxically, despite a certain common history – extra-parliamentary origin, similar programmes and ideology, membership of the Socialist International – these parties do not today have either a specific ideology or a particular organizational structure. The only thing that they share is the support of a programme of economic and social reforms in the interests of the working and middle classes within a framework of civil rights and parliamentary democracy. A distinction is usually made between the British Labour Party and the continental socialist parties. The former, founded and sponsored by the trade unions, did not develop a cohesive centralized organization or adopt Marxism as its political ideology, and so was different from the latter, and particularly the German SPD – the model of European socialist parties before 1914 – which was centrally organized and Marxist. The socialist parties were weak and radical in the countries where the communist parties were strong, and vice versa. This was explained in terms of the early or late industrialization of the country: Labour Party and SPD strong and moderate in Britain and Germany; SFIO and PSI weak and radical in France and Italy. But, even if this was true,[24] the situation has changed: the SPD started with 30 per cent of the vote in 1949 and consolidated its strength around 40 per cent in the 1970s after a take-off in the 1960s, only to fall back in the 1980s (table 5.8); while the Labour Party, which was the strongest European social democrat party in the 1940s and 1950s with 45–50 per cent of the British vote, has progressively lost support, finding itself after the 1981 split reduced to 28 per cent in the 1983 elections and, despite a revival at the end of the decade, still losing its fourth successive election in 1992 (table 5.6). In the first all-German elections of 1990, the SPD polled its lowest vote for over 25 years (33.5 per cent).

The SFIO and PSI lost support in the 1950s (the PSI as a result of the 1947 social democrat and 1964 leftist splits; the SFIO due to communist competition); thus the SFIO's share of the vote was 10 per cent at the end of the 1960s, and the PSI had a similar percentage in 1976. The creation of the PS in 1970 changed the course of French politics in the 1970s. It first overtook the PCF, and later secured Mitterrand's election as president of the republic in 1981 with a large parliamentary majority: its vote stabilized around 30–35 per cent in the 1986 and 1988 elections (table 5.7). Craxi, leader of the PSI since 1976, and prime minister from 1983 to 1987, attempted to operate a similar change in his party's electoral fortunes in a governmental alliance with the DC, but failed (table 5.9). Indeed, both parties were in deep trouble in the early 1990s as a result of a series of financial scandals – *fausses factures* in France, *tangentopoli* in Italy – and their votes reduced (PS 18 per cent in 1993 and PSI 2.2 per cent in 1994).

The socialist parties' electoral support comes largely from the lower classes: it is calculated that 90 per cent are salary- or wage-earning, half working class and half middle class (table 5.5). The proportion of workers varies nationally according to whether or not there is a competing communist party or popular-based Catholic party (as in Italy). In contrast to communist parties, socialist parties usually mobilize workers with higher skills and income. Moreover, of the two left-wing parties, socialist support among the middle classes is larger; it makes up a third to two-fifths of their electorates. Finally, they attract the support of a certain percentage of bourgeois electors: liberal professions, higher civil servants and intellectuals. Thus if socialist electoral support is made up of the lower classes, this is not true of party members and much less of party leaders. Indeed, the social composition of socialist party leaders is very different from that of its electorate: politicians of working class origin no longer win top leadership posts, while white-collars and government officials are overrepresented. The socialist leadership personnel is recruited above all from the public sector (civil servants and teachers) and professional politicians (party and trade union officials). From an educational point of view, this personnel is characterized by a degree or professional qualification. This has allowed the formation of a very flexible group of professional politicians, capable of adapting tactically to the most diverse situations, either on the left or on the right, but always within a moderate reformism which emphasizes the 'sense of state'. Not surprisingly, the extreme left has denounced it as 'opportunistic'.

The socialist parties also have a close relationship with the trade union movement. Indeed, it is these relations that define the different types of socialist parties. On the one hand, for instance, there is the British Labour Party which has a federative structure and is dependent on the unions for both its programme and its funding (circa 55 per cent of its income comes from this source). Moreover, some 75 per cent of its members are constituted by the collective union membership, a form of indirect membership: all union members are automatically considered party members unless they refuse personally. All labour organizations (trade unions, constituency sections, cooperative movement, Fabian and socialist societies) are represented at the annual Labour Party conference and on the NEC (party ruling body). However, since the decisions of national bodies are by majority, the trade unions – and above all the big unions like the TGWU, GMB, AEUW, NALGO – have, through the 'block vote', the greater weight both at the conference and on the NEC, while ordinary members and constituency party sections have less weight.[25]

On the other hand there is the German SPD; here the trade unions (DGB) claim to have no party links – and this despite the fact that the majority of party members and party leaders are also union members. This is due to the conception, traditional in Germany, of a division of labour between unions and party according to which the former defend the workers' economic interests and the latter their political interests. In spite of common interests between them, the German trade unions do not enjoy the same institutional influence on the SPD as their British counterparts do on the Labour Party. Moreover, thanks to public funding of parties, the SPD does not depend financially on the unions for electoral campaign funds to the extent that Labour does. However, the SPD does depend on the unions for electoral mobilization.

Finally, mutual independence of socialist parties and trade unions is greater in France and Italy, where the unions are politically oriented towards the left. The reason is simple: in view of the unions' low level of ideological homogeneity, competition between communists and socialists takes place inside the unions. This situation prevents the unions from instituting the same links with the socialist parties as in Britain, and it gives greater space for the development of union-supported left-wing factions inside the socialist parties; this situation is usually avoided in Britain and Germany, thanks to the union leadership's weight in favour of economic collaboration with the government in both countries.

The socialist parties, although founded as militant parties, have been transformed into electors' parties in the post-war period.[26] If reformism has characterized the European socialist parties since the 1920s, it has always had two faces: one 'social liberal' which accepts the existing relations of production and aims at social reforms – economic democracy, welfare state – within the existing constitutional structures; and the other 'radical reformist', linked to the Marxist tradition of changing capitalist relations of production in a socialist direction and prepared to defend a politics of mass mobilization, but always within the framework of constitutional democracy. The history of these parties is a sequence of traumatic oscillations between these two positions, punctuated by periodic splits even after the Comintern fission of 1920–1 (the Labour Party in 1931; the PSI in 1947; the French PSU in 1958; the Italian PSIUP in 1964; the PSI-PDSI reunification and resplit 1966–9; the English SDP in 1981),[27] and with an internal party life characterized by vigorous factional conflict (Tribune, Bevanites, Militant tendency in the Labour Party; *carristi* in the PSI; CERES in the PS; *Jusos* in the SPD).

The parties' social-liberal face has usually prevailed when in office, either alone or in coalition with bourgeois parties (centre-left in Italy in the 1960s; Labour Party in Britain 1964–70 and 1974–9; SPD-FDP in Germany, 1969–82) and the radical-reformist face when in opposition (Labour Party 1979–85, which led to the SDP split in 1981; SPD after 1983), but with a clear reduction in the objectives of social transformation in the longer period, usually justified by the socio-economic conditions of the moment. However, the French PS under Mitterrand was the promoter not only of an alliance with the PCF in the 1970s, but also of a radical-reformist programme which carried its leader to the presidency in 1981. The Socialist-Communist government attempted to implement this programme, but was obliged to reverse it, as the Labour Party had before it, when faced with an economic crisis – which saw it also abandoned by the PCF in 1984 – and return to a more moderate stance. Faced with the historic compromise in Italy, the PSI under Craxi opted for the social-liberal face and the role of privileged ally of the DC in government; in addition, it promoted the image of a better manager of existing society, in the name of 'governability', than its coalition partners until fatally undermined by the *tangentopoli* scandal in 1992–3.

In conclusion, we may note that the socialist parties were in power in the north (Britain and Germany) in the 1970s and in opposition in the 1980s, but in opposition in the south (France and Italy) in the 1970s and in power in the 1980s. Further, if, despite their recent revival, their return to power in the north in the 1990s is still problematic, their loss of power in the south, as a result of recent funding scandals, has been consummate (1993 elections in France; 1994 in Italy).

Christian democrats

Christian democracy has been the major party in two states: Germany (CDU-CSU) and Italy (DC) where the Catholic movements have a long history. Catholic parties (Zentrum in 1870; Opera dei Congressi in 1874) were founded, in fact, to defend the interests of Catholics in the bitter struggle between the church and the secular state in the nineteenth century. The instigator was the church and the arena of struggle was civil society since the state was hostile; this explains the greater weight that it attributed to the Catholic social movements than to the political party. This was also the reason that, despite a certain politico-electoral influence in Germany and Italy after World War I, Christian democrat parties only succeeded in 1945 in extending their support to become the main party in these two states and, for a brief period, in France too with the MRP. At all events, the Cold War was the period of their greatest political fortunes because they benefited from the image of Christianity as the main ideological bulwark against communism as well as economic growth as the fruit of post-war reconstruction. The destinies of the Christian democrat parties were very different. The French MRP, after a leading role in the Fourth Republic, was unable to resist the pressure of Gaullism and was dissolved in 1966; a part of its support was absorbed by the Gaullists, another part linked up with the liberals (Lecanuet's Centre Démocratique) and a final part joined the PS. This fate can be explained in terms of the lack of a tradition of organized Catholicism in France: French Catholics traditionally allied themselves with the conservative and right-wing parties. The German CDU, which was founded as an alliance between Catholics and Protestants, abandoned fairly rapidly the defence of specifically religious interests in favour of economic liberalism (Erhard's Soziale Marktwirtschaft) and conservative social values. In point of fact, the progressive wing abandoned the party in 1952 and joined the SPD in the 1960s, while the CDU took over its various conservative allies. Finally, the Italian DC resisted these threats and temptations, seeking to mediate between social reformist and liberal conservative positions, although the latter usually prevailed. However, implication in the *tangentopoli* scandals and the electoral reform that it has brought in its wake will finally oblige its successor party to choose or face electoral marginalization.

The characteristics of Christian democrat parties can be summed up thus. Firstly, they demonstrate 'interclassism', that is the social composition of their electorate reflects the social structure of Catholism and confirms that their link with the electorate is predominantly confessional, yet they succeed in attracting several groups – particularly among the traditional middle classes and employers (table 5.5) – which are indifferent to religion. The link in this case is clearly conservative: the defence of the status quo. Secondly, the party type is clearly that of the electors' party, even though initially Catholic parties were organized as militants' parties: the militants were the leaders and were members of the various Catholic organizations, including the clergy. The parties' expansion in the post-war period was responsible for the change in party type because they became the refuge for groups of notables: liberals, but also Catholics. Thirdly, they had privileged links with major interests: institutionalized relations with collateral organizations, the principal source of political personnel; but also direct relations with labour (unions) and the peasantry (leagues); and relations of mutual interest with bourgeois interest groups (employers and farmers, both sources of party funding). The links with collateral organizations weakened during the 1970s, but remained more important in Italy than in Federal Germany. Fourthly, political heterogeneity and hence the need for mediation were essential elements, like pragmatism and grass-roots political practice. This derived from interclassism or class collaboration, which provoked conflicts between socio-economic interests, and from the conjunctural historical moment that made Christianity the ideological bulwark of anti-communism. The confessional constraint, that united persons of very different political dispositions, explains the Christian democrat parties' centre or 'pivotal' position in the political spectrum which allowed them to make government alliances with both the moderate left and the moderate right indifferently. Finally, the parties did not have their own political project but support the church's, which – centred on the defence of its material interests (charity, schools) and its values (life, family) – may be synthesized as 'solidarity'.

In the 1960s and 1970s, Christian democracy faced something of a crisis, characterized by internal conflict and loss of votes. There were three main causes: (1) secularization and consequent loss of faith by large sectors of the population and the liberalization of the church following Vatican II; (2) the political thaw between East and West which attenuated its anti-communist appeal, subsequently rendered obsolete in 1989 by the collapse of Soviet communism; and (3) the economic crisis and that of the welfare state which threatened the material basis of Christian democrat class collaboration. The question posed for the DC in the 1990s, in the light of the MRP's and CDU's fate, is: suffer fatal decline or become a secularized conservative party? Or, as some neo-clerical groups (like Comunione e Liberazione in Italy) argue, engage in regeneration? The rise of the *leghe*, followed by the *tangentopoli* scandal, suggest that it may be the former. Moreover, its vote reached a post-war low in 1992 (29.5 per cent) before the full extent of the party's involvement in *tangentopoli* was known. Indeed the effect of the scandal was so traumatic that the party was dissolved and refounded under its pre-fascist name – Italian Popular Party (Partito Popolare Italiano) – in January 1994 in a desperate attempt to stave off total electoral collapse. In March 1994 it polled 11 per cent only of the vote and its representation in the Chamber fell from 206 seats to 29.

Liberals

The liberal parties are minor parties in all states. Indeed, one of the paradoxes of post-war Western Europe is that the major ideological doctrine of the nineteenth century should be represented only by small parties today. This is due on the one hand to the widespread success of liberal ideology which permeated the other political families; and on the other to the particular history of the various European liberal parties, which have practised oscillating alliances (now with the conservatives, now with the social democrats). Today, in fact, the liberal parties are situated at different points on the political spectrum in the different states: on the left, like the French Mouvement Radical de Gauche (MRG) or the Italian Radical Party; in the centre like the British Liberal Party (Liberal Democrats), the German Frei Demokratische Partei (FDP) and the Italian Republican Party (PRI); or on the right as the Italian Liberal Party (PLI) or the loose federation of parties (Républicains Indépendants, Parti Radical, CDS) that make up the Giscardian Union pour la Démocratie Française (UDF) in France. All are essentially of the notables' party type.

This different political collocation between left and right, in addition to a certain political mobility – for instance, the FDP's movement from the right in the 1950s and 1960s to centre-left in 1969, to an alliance with the SPD in the 1970s, and back to the right in alliance with Kohl's CDU/CSU in the1980s – has given the parties a political influence out of all proportion to their size. Indeed, it is only in Britain that, thanks to the majority electoral regime, the Liberal Party has remained almost permanently in opposition since 1945, despite greater electoral support than its continental sister parties. In Italy, Germany and France, liberal party support has been indispensable for the formation of many government coalition majorities. It emphasizes individual freedom and equality, where freedom is understood to mean economic freedom. Anti-clericalism, which was a traditional connotation in the nineteenth century, is now largely forgotten because it would have damaged not only government alliances with the Catholic parties, but also liberal electoral fortunes, above all in the post-war period in the Counter-Reformation countries.

Conservatives

Conservative parties exist only in Britain and France, in so far as the Christian democrat parties are considered more religious than class parties: this is somewhat problematic in the German case, less so in the Italian.[28] Moreover, the French situation is rather special in the sense that if there has always been a large conservative political area, it has only been organized in a coherent manner by de Gaulle, who was able to use nationalist fervour and his own charisma to create a *sui generis* populist force. However, after his departure, the party gradually evolved under Chirac's leadership, being equipped with an efficient apparatus and assuming more conservative features on the British model. In this situation, the British party represents this political family's prototype: as defenders of tradition in all its forms. Its success has been due without doubt to its extraordinary adaptive capacity and its political pragmatism – the acceptance of innovations which it did not want, the better to preserve what is left[29] – which allow it to present itself as the 'natural party of government' and to secure widespread electoral support. Even if it has been in decline in the last twenty years, this has not prevented it from winning four electoral victories in succession (thanks, it is true, to the electoral regime and a split opposition: table 5.6).

The conservative and Gaullist parties share with Christian democracy (and now Forza Italia) solid electoral support among the subordinate classes (workers and petty bourgeois: table 5.5), owing more to traditional and instrumental motivations than religious ones. In addition, they can count on bourgeois and rural support as well as that of the state apparatus (higher civil servants and military). They have established themselves as electors' parties which, although not directly linked to the various bourgeois interest groups (employers, bankers, farmers), are closely connected to them on material grounds (they are the principal financiers of conservative parties), on ideological grounds, and finally for reasons of personal relations: a certain number of businessmen, like Dassault and Hersant in France, Osborne, Black and Du Cann in Britain, have been MPs. In 1994, Silvio Berlusconi's associates and managers had themselves elected to the Italian parliament.

If the conservatives were identified with nationalism and imperialism in the past, they have succeeded in dissociating themselves in the public eye from these ideologies, thanks to their pragmatism. Today, they define themselves ideologically in relation to the welfare state and democracy, which they interpret reductively. In effect, the progress realized in these fields has always been considered more as concessions than as inalienable rights. Hence they are reversible in moments of crisis. In this sense, Thatcher's (but also Chirac–Balladur's and Berlusconi's) neo-liberal programme of strengthening the market economy by dismantling the welfare state, and privatizing state industry and public service, is coherent with traditional conservative premises, which have always regarded the masses – represented by the socialist parties – with suspicion. The other distinctive feature of contemporary conservatism is a programmatic vagueness whose cardinal points are a generic anti-socialism, denounced as destructive collectivism, the recognition of private property and freedom, and a tough attitude on 'law and order'.

Neo-fascists and extreme right

There are the following forces today: Movimento Sociale Italiano (MSI) in Italy, Front National in France, National Front in Britain, and now Republikaner in Germany). Only the first two have succeeded in electing MPs since the war. The MSI have always polled around 5 per cent of the Italian vote since 1948, while the extreme right represents some 10 per cent of the French electorate. However, the latter exploded with the Poujadist phenomenon in 1956 (14 per cent of vote and 52 seats) and again in the 1984 European elections with Le Pen's Front National. From 1958 to 1986, the extreme right was not represented in the French Assembly, owing principally to the two-ballot majority electoral regime, but it triumphantly won 35 seats with the introduction of a PR system in 1986, and succeeded in retaining one seat in the 1988 elections in spite of the return of the old two-ballot regime.

Indeed, it is also the electoral regime which has denied the extreme right parliamentary representation in West Germany and Britain. In 1969, the German NPD only just failed to overcome the 5 per cent threshold to win seats in the Bundestag. In Britain, the electoral threshold of the single-member, single-ballot simple majority system, although purely informal, is even higher. The simple majority electoral regime, in fact, obliges National Front sympathizers to support the Conservative Party, as is confirmed by the selection and election of Conservative candidates who have been National Front members.

These parties are essentially militants' parties with a certain clandestine vigilante-style organization behind them, which find support among groups of young middle class and poor whites in urban areas on the basis of their nationalistic, and ever more anti-immigrant and racist, appeals and their calls for a strong and authoritarian state. They are highly centralized and authoritarian anti-parliamentary forces. All attempts to legitimize the Front National and the MSI as part of the political system failed before 1994. However, it was Berlusconi's political masterpiece to include the MSI (which had hurriedly changed its name to Alleanza Nazionale) in his right-wing Freedom Pole to forge a credible electoral cartel to win a majority at the 1994 elections (13.5% of the vote). The MSI's legitimation was sealed with the appointment of five former MSI members to ministerial office.

Regionalists

The creation of the great West European nation-states, as noted in chapter 3, was also a process of 'nation destroying' for smaller ethnic and cultural units. It is no surprise that, despite suppression, non-state nationalist and regional parties are active in all countries. Thus, for example, the Bavarian CSU is an autonomous party, but its alliance with the CDU, and the fact that its long-time leader Joseph Strauss was CDU candidate chancellor for the 1980 elections, reveal it rather as the regional Catholic wing of the CDU. The same can be said of the Sudtiröler Volkspartei, the German-language party which represents the majority of Italy's south Tyrol population. In Britain, we need to distinguish between the Ulster Unionists, which represent the majority

Protestant population of Northern Ireland – and defend the link with Britain against threat of union with the Catholic Irish Republic – and the Scottish (SNP) and Welsh (PC) nationalists. The latter represent a protest in support of national autonomy against the centralizing power of London in a period of long-term economic and political decline.

The recent economic and political crises in Italy have seen a renaissance of regional parties of which three (Partito Sardo d'Azione, Union Valdotaîne, and Lega Nord[30]) have elected MPs, helped by the PR electoral system in force in Italy until 1994. The last has successfully mounted a protest against the inefficiency and corruption of the traditional established parties and politicians in Rome, and became something of a mass phenomenon in the north. It won almost 9 per cent of the vote and 55 seats in the 1992 parliamentary elections, and 116 seats with a similar vote in 1994. Its constituency was the lower middle classes and small businessmen, but, as it spread, it broadened its social appeal to include public sector workers and some manual workers (Diamanti, 1993). None of the French separatist and autonomist regional movements (Bretons, Basques, Corsicans) have succeeded, as yet, in becoming a significant political force and electing MPs.

Greens

Ecology movements were active everywhere in Western Europe during the 1970s (chapter 4) and have subsequently transformed themselves into parties in the 1980s to contest local and national elections, although they have sought not to conform to any traditional party type. The strongest was the German Grünen which obtained 5.6 per cent of the votes in the 1983 elections, thus overcoming the 5 per cent threshold and winning some twenty seats in the Bundestag. In 1987 it increased both its vote and its seats, but by 1990 it was in something of a crisis – internal divisions as to its role as a party – and its parliamentary representation was only saved by the special electoral regime introduced in the former East Germany. The only other green party to win parliamentary representation in 1987 was the Italian *verdi* (2.5 per cent of the vote and 13 MPs) (table 5.9). However, it was in the 1989 European elections that the greens took off electorally, reaching 10 per cent in the major countries (and 15 per cent of the valid vote in the United Kingdom, although on a very low poll). In the 1993 election the French *verts* also hoped to made a breakthrough, thanks above all to the unpopularity of the PS, but failed: they won a disappointing 7.6 per cent of the vote and no seats. On the other hand the Italian *verdi* formed part of the Progressive Pole, winning eleven seats (2.7 per cent of the vote).

Von Beyme (1982) claims that the ecology movement has two features that mark off its start from those of new parties of the past. The first is that the movement does not have a unified class basis: it is premature to call the new middle class the 'social pillar of the new movement' (p. 131), as many observers have done. The second is that it does not fit into the dominant left–right political cleavage pattern, which means a certain volatility in electoral support because it cuts across existing political divisions. It is a modernist rural dimension of the town–country cleavage.

National party systems

Britain

The British party system has become something of a myth because it is presented as the historical prototype of the ideal model: the perfect two-party system, that is to say with regular alternation. However, this is neither a realistic nor an adequate description. Indeed, historically it has been characterized by both periods of one-party domination and periods of coalition. Both have been more frequent than is generally believed. Indeed, the functioning of the British system in a two-party manner in this century has only lasted some 30 years (1945–80: table 5.6). A fairer description is that of an alternating party, fully competitive system – as moderate pluralism in Sartori's definition – because there are no electorally relevant anti-system parties.

The system is structured around a dominant socio-economic cleavage, the result of early industrialization, which explains the predominance of class parties (Conservative and Labour) and of the ideological component of class conflict. The identification between the two major parties and the two principal organized economic interests (capital and labour) is, in fact, stronger than in other European countries, as is demonstrated by the fact that the Labour Party is largely funded by the trade unions (TUC) and the Conservative Party by the business community (big companies and the City). Finally, in the last twenty years – in parallel with the country's economic and political decline – there has been a revival of regional nationalism (Scottish, Welsh and Irish republicanism) which has reopened the centre–periphery cleavage.

The key to the operation of the British party system lies in the electoral regime, which is the single-member, single-ballot plurality system: 'first past the post'. Such a system not only favours the big parties against the small, but also – thanks to the deformation of the relation of votes to seats, that is winner takes all – increases the mobility of parliamentary representation in so far as it turns small vote displacements into larger seat movements. Thus British parliamentary parties are usually coalitions of political tendencies: 'broad churches'. The rewards for party unity explain some peculiarities and a number of polemics about the British system. One of the more significant of these is the system of 'whips' which secures the discipline of the parliamentary parties on the

Table 5.6 Results of parliamentary elections in Great Britain: votes (per cent) and seats

	1945	1950	1951	1955	1959	1964	1966	1970	Feb. 1974	Oct. 1974	1979	1983	1987	1992
Votes														
Conservative Party	39.8	43.5	48.0	49.7	49.4	43.4	41.9	46.4	37.9	35.8	43.9	42.4	42.3	41.9
Labour Party	48.3	46.1	48.8	46.4	43.8	44.1	47.9	43.0	37.1	39.2	37.0	27.6	30.8	34.4
Liberal Party	9.1	9.1	2.5	2.7	5.9	11.2	8.5	7.5	19.3	18.6	13.8	—	—	—
Liberal-SDP Alliance	—	—	—	—	—	—	—	—	—	—	—	25.4	22.6	17.8
Communist Party (CPGB)	0.4	0.3	0.1	0.1	0.1	0.2	0.2	0.1	0.1	0.1	0.1	—	—	—
Scottish National Party (SNP)	0.1	—	—	—	0.1	0.2	0.5	1.1	2.0	2.9	1.6	1.1	1.3	2.3
Plaid Cymru	0.1	0.1	—	0.2	0.3	0.3	0.2	0.6	0.5	0.6	0.4	0.4	0.4	0.5
Others (including Ulster Unionists)	2.1	0.9	0.5	0.8	0.4	0.6	0.7	1.3	3.1	2.8	3.2	3.1	2.6	3.7
Turnout	73.3	84.0	82.5	76.8	78.7	77.1	75.8	72.0	78.1	72.8	76.0	72.7	75.4	77.7
Seats														
Conservative Party	213	299	321	345	365	304	253	330	297	277	339	397	376	336
Labour Party	393	315	295	277	258	317	363	287	301	319	269	209	229	271
Liberal Party	12	9	6	6	6	9	12	6	14	13	11	—	—	—
Liberal-SDP Alliance	—	—	—	—	—	—	—	—	—	—	—	23	22	20
Scottish National Party	—	—	—	—	—	—	—	1	7	11	2	2	3	3
Plaid Cymru	—	—	—	—	—	—	—	—	2	3	2	2	3	4
Ulster Unionists[a]	—	—	—	—	—	—	—	—	12	12	12	15	13	13
Others	22	2	3	2	1	—	2	6	2	—	—	2	4	4
Total	640	625	625	630	630	630	630	630	635	635	635	650	650	651

[a] Before 1974 the Ulster Unionists were part of the Conservative Party parliamentary group.

basis of party loyalty. A party split is the surest way to ensure an electoral defeat, as has recently been confirmed at the Labour Party's expense. It was the 1981 SDP split that was responsible for the Conservative Party victories of 1983 and 1987 and its role as the dominant party in the last decade. Indeed, party splits mark important turning points in British political history because they usually give rise to a period of one-party domination: 1885, Liberal split and Conservative domination until 1906; 1916, Liberal split and Conservative domination until 1929; 1931 Labour split, Conservative domination until 1945.

In such a situation, the British two-party system is a bipartyism imposed by the electoral regime, although other factors, like the prevalence of the socio-economic cleavage and the relative insignificance of the religious cleavage, have played their part. Even today, the electoral regime holds it together, despite the more or less continuous erosion of support for the two main parties. It is worth noting, for instance, that no party has won 50 per cent of the valid votes in any of the twelve post-war elections, yet only in one (February 1974) did no party win an overall majority of seats in the House of Commons. Indeed, the two main parties, which gained over 90 per cent of the valid votes in the 1950s, won barely 70 per cent in 1974 (table 5.6).

The traditional view of the British party system has always identified bipartisan consensus in many areas of national politics as its hallmark. It was the result of the combination of a largely non-conflictual, or tolerant, culture and the pressure of the electoral regime which obliged parties to resemble each other as much as possible if they aspired to victory at the polls. Thus the government's role – creation of the welfare state, for instance, begun by Churchill during World War II and completed by Labour in the immediate post-war years – is accepted by virtually all parties. Only the fascists and the extreme left criticized the party system because it reduced party politics to 'shadow boxing'.

In the 1970s appreciation of the system dramatically changed and the almost unanimous positive view of the 1950s was replaced by a largely negative one. Indeed, faced with Britain's evident economic and political decline, large sections of public opinion identified the cause in the political system, and particularly in the working of the party system. Finer (1975a) pointed to what he called 'adversary politics', that is the notion that a system in which there were two parties with antagonistic ideological goals and with similar possibilities of power encouraged a style and praxis of extreme and unstable parliamentary politics that was inimical to a stable and efficient economic policy. The political logic outlined by Finer is that of Sartori's polarized pluralism! The hypothesized consequences are the same: lack of governability because the kind of party struggle undermines the electorate's confidence in the existence of common national interests and values. In spite of this interpretation, the majority of political observers today are still struck by the continuity, and not the discontinuity, of British party politics in the post-war period.

Nevertheless, the adversary politics polemic helps to throw light on the limits of the British party system. It is because of its destructive polarization potential (zero-sum game) that there is a consensus in favour of a political stalemate called 'responsible politics'. It is, in fact, the sole condition in which the system is able to operate: if there were no consensus between the parties over the major political problems, the system would cease to operate because the post-war parliamentary majorities are electoral minorities. Moreover, necessary agreement over major problems often encourages violent clashes over minor questions. Gamble (in Gamble and Wakeland, 1984) has argued that the Conservatives promoted Labour's conquest of power in 1923 in order to contain the socialist impulse in the labour movement, supporting the emergence of a moderate and responsible leadership. This objective was pursued in the second post-war period for the same reasons. If the Thatcherite Conservatives have abandoned it, it was because they judged that the moment was right for a frontal attack on the political and institutional strength of Labour as an integral part of their strategy to put an end to Britain's economic decline. The restructuring pursued by the Thatcher governments was not only economic, but political: forge a new free market political agenda and impose in the longer term a new consensus. The results are mixed: the 'economic miracle' of the 1980s turned into a mirage in the 1990s recession, but four straight electoral victories appear to confirm the political success in the sense of consolidating the Conservative Party's position as the dominant party. Certainly, the party system presently operates in the limited competitive mode, manufacturing ever more artificial majorities; hence Conservative Party domination is less secure than it appears. A measure of cooperation between Labour and Liberal Democrats could lead to the eviction of the Conservatives at the next election and probable electoral reform to some form of PR. In the meantime, an air of political stalemate pervades British politics, but how long it will last only time will tell.

France

The French party system suffers from a similar, but contrasting, myth to that of the British, that is to say that it is the historical prototype of the multiparty system. Churchill used to say that 'France has as many parties as types of cheese: over 200!' In one sense, the comparison with Britain is helpful: if developments in the British party system point towards party fragmentation, the French has moved towards some simplification (four main political parties in two large electoral blocs) in the last 30 years.

The problem posed in discussing this transformation is how to explain it. However, first we must reassert the inadequacy of the category of multipartyism, and not only for analysing the French case. The French

Table 5.7 Results of parliamentary elections in France:[a] votes (per cent) and seats

Votes	1945	Oct. 1946	Nov. 1946	1951	1956	1958	1962	1967	1968	1973	1978	1981	1986	1988[b]	1993
Communists (PCF)	26.1	26.2	28.6	25.9	25.9	18.9	21.8	22.5	20.0	21.4	20.6	16.1	9.7	11.3	9.2
Left Socialists/PSU	—	—	—	—	—	—	2.3	2.2	3.9	3.3	3.3	1.3	1.5	0.4	—
Socialists (SFIO-PS)	23.8	21.1	17.9	14.5	15.0	15.4	12.5	18.8	16.5	20.7	22.8	37.8 }	31.6 }	37.6 }	17.6
Left Radicals (MRG)	—	—	—	—	—	1.7	—	—	0.6	1.1	2.1		0.3		0.9
Radicals and allies	11.1	11.5	14.0	10.0	13.5	11.5	7.8	—	—	12.8	2.8	—	0.9	—	—
Popular Republicans (MRP)	24.9	28.1	26.3	12.5	11.1	11.6	9.1	12.8	10.3	3.7	2.3	—	—	—	—
Independent Republicans (RI/UDF)	—	—	—	—	—	—	5.9	37.8 }	43.6 }	6.9	21.4	19.2 }	42.0 }	18.5	19.2
Gaullists	—	—	—	21.7	4.3	17.6	31.9			23.9	22.5	20.9 }		19.2	20.3
Independents/Conservatives	13.3	12.8	12.8	14.0	14.6	20.0	7.7	5.0	4.1	3.3	—	2.7	2.7	2.9	4.6
Extreme right (Poujadists/FN)	—	—	—	—	13.9	3.3	0.9	0.9	0.1	2.8	—	0.4	9.8	9.7	12.5
Ecologists	—	—	—	—	—	—	—	—	—	—	2.2	1.1	1.2	0.4	7.7
Others	—	—	—	—	—	—	—	—	—	—	—	—	—	—	5.8
Turnout	79.9	81.9	78.1	80.2	82.8	77.1	68.7	80.9	80.0	81.2	83.3	70.3	78.5	66.2	69.2

Seats

Communists (PCF)	148	146	166	97	145	10	41	72	33	73	86	43	32	27	23
Socialists (SF10-PS) and allies (MRG)	134	115	90	94	88	41	64	121	57	102	112	279	207	276	58
Radicals and allies	35	39	60	77	71	36	38	—	—	32	—	—	—	—	—
Popular Republicans (MRP)	141	160	158	82	71	55	51	40	31	28	—	—	—	—	—
Independent Republicans (RI/UDF)	—	—	—	—	—	—	33	40	60	54	119	60	119	130	202
Gaullists	—	—	—	107	16	198	229	190	282	173	145	83	153	128	233
Independents/Conservatives	62	62	70	87	94	116	—	—	—	—	—	—	—	13	34
Extreme right (Poujadists/FN)	—	—	—	—	52	—	—	—	—	—	—	—	35	1	0
Others	2	—	—	—	7	9	9	7	7	11	12	9	9	2	0
Overseas territories	66	66	74	83	52[c]	87	17	17	17	17	17	17	22	—	22
Total	586	586	618	627	596	552	482	487	487	490	491	491	577	577	577

[a] Figures refer exclusively to metropolitan France.

[b] Including overseas territories (DOM-TOM).

[c] The Algerian War prevented elections in the Algerian overseas department.

NB: The electoral regimes and the regulations of the French National Assembly are responsible for a distribution of seats by parliamentary party group which does not necessarily coincide with the distribution of seats by party list (see *Journal Officiel, Débats parlementaires* and Mény (1987, pp. 208–10: cf. French edition). Finally, all observers agree on the difficulty of having accurate electoral statistics: difficulties arise from the diversity of lists and alliances which lead to simplifications. The figures published by the Ministry of the Interior are not always the most meaningful or useful.

party system has, in effect, been for most of this century an example of a limited competitive system, that is without party alternation in government, because of the existence of relevant anti-system parties (table 5.7). In the 1980s, it passed into the category of a fully competitive party system because the anti-system parties became largely irrelevant. In Sartori's terminology, it passed from polarized pluralism to moderate pluralism. To explain this change, which is a fundamental aspect of the transformation of the French party system, we need to specify the anti-system forces. During the Third Republic they were the clerico-conservatives, who refused to accept the republic, and the revolutionary socialists (communists after 1920); under the Fourth Republic, they were the RPF (Gaullists), which refused its constitutional arrangements (assembly regime), the PCF (excluded as a result of the Cold War) and the Poujadists in the regime's last two years. The fact that de Gaulle was called on to save the republic in 1958 meant not only a fundamental reorganization of the political system, but the legitimation of a very significant anti-system force. Twenty-three years later, with the left's victory in May 1981, the PCF was able to enter the government in a subordinate position to the PS.

The French party system is structured around a fundamental ideological cleavage issuing from the French Revolution (republic versus *ancien régime*) which the other cleavages (lay versus clerical; capital versus labour; town versus country) both cross-cut and intersect. In the last twenty years the socio-economic fracture has been gradually replacing, although not entirely, the ideological, religion-based one, leading to party simplification: a simple left–right dimension. For historical reasons – slow industrialization, political prohibition of associations in the nineteenth century – French parties remained groupings of notables without national organizations for longer than parties in neighbouring countries. Membership numbers for all French parties (PCF included) are, in fact, lower than in the other comparable countries (table 5.1). During the Third Republic, the notables' local strength was reinforced by the majority two-ballot electoral system because the existence of single-member constituencies allowed them to activate local ties (which were usually clientelist). For this reason, the political forces from the resistance adopted the list system of PR, but unfortunately with departmental constituencies, thus allowing the notables to maintain their local ties and still dominate parliamentary representation because the local organization of the French state was structured at the departmental level.

The great transformation of the French party system under the Fifth Republic results from a series of factors, not all devoid of ambiguity. They are: (1) the reduction of party numbers and, as a consequence, the simplification of the party system; (2) the nationalization of parties, that is the formation and consolidation of national parties at the expense of local ones (RPR, PS, UDF) to replace the notables' party; (3) the formation of coherent and disciplined coalitions in parliament, allowing coherent government and opposition; (4) the PCF's integration in national politics with its abandoning of Leninism and its adhesion to the 'common programme' that made it an integral part of the left alliance in the early 1980s, and so less of an anti-system party; and (5) a general increase in political participation.

The explanation of these changes is largely political. In other words, it is a case of changes in the terms of political competition. We can identify three elements. Probably the most important was the 1962 constitutional amendment which created a new political prize: the election of the president of the republic (the key office) by universal suffrage. The parties were forced to transform themselves into national organizations to secure the electoral support necessary for their candidate's success. As a result, political alliances were formed in support of and against the president's action (*majorité présidentielle* and *opposition*) in parliament. In this connection, it is worth recalling the non-communist left's reorganization in the 1960s which paved the way for the PS and alternation in 1981, and that of the non-Gaullist right which carried Giscard d'Estaing to the presidency in 1974 and the formation of the UDF.

The second change was the reintroduction of the two-ballot majority electoral regime in 1958 which led to the exclusion from the second ballot of all those candidates who did not poll 12.5 per cent of the votes. This offered the opportunity of creating coherent parliamentary majorities. However, too much importance should not be attached to this factor, in the sense that it would not have been enough by itself since it was the Third Republic's preferred electoral system and that regime was characterized by a multiplicity of parties. This time, its effect was combined with the other two factors: the presidential election, already mentioned, and a third, the emergence of a centre-right majority party, the Gaullist Party, owing to the charismatic appeal of de Gaulle. It was not his intention to create his own party – he always considered himself above, when not against, parties – but the institutionalization of support for his action in parliament led to the organization of the party. Its consolidation as a strong electors' party with the ability to impose parliamentary discipline obliged the opposition to act likewise. The result was the 1972 common programme and the PS-PCF-MRG alliance which carried Mitterrand to the presidency in May 1981, after 23 years of right-wing, but Gaullist-based, government domination.

The sense of the French party system's transformation has been interpreted as a change in favour of government alternation between coalitions of right and left (zero-sum game) at the expense of the centre-based coalitions (positive-sum game) which had characterized the Third and Fourth Republics. Many observers are convinced that this change is not fundamental or permanent, and this despite coherent majorities at each successive election (right in 1986; left after Mitterrand's re-election in 1988; and right again in 1993). Certainly, the Mitterrand era (1981–95) saw many electoral changes: PR for the regional elections and parliamentary elections of 1986 (but a return to two ballots for 1988 and 1993); the prominence of the new parties Front National and *verts* in the 1980s. Perhaps the most important watershed was the left's change of tack from a radical to a pragmatic programme in 1983 which led to the PCF's exit from the government in 1984. Nonetheless, Mitterrand's attempt, after his re-election in 1988, to open to the centre under prime minister Rocard failed. The impression is that the institutional coherence of the system is maintained by essentially institutional factors: the so-called *contrainte majoritaire* of the two-ballot presidential elections forces the parties into a two-party strait-jacket, despite growing electoral mobility and fragmentation. Hence the traditional left or right alliances are increasingly electoral formulas lacking significant political content, manipulable to some extent by presidents. The future of the French party system much depends on the outcome of the 1995 presidential election in which, as a result of its 1993 electoral victory, but more so as a result of the crushing defeat of its principal opponent, the PS, the right under Balladur or Chirac, is best placed to prevail.

Germany

The West German party system has experienced a similar transformation to that of the French, only it preceded it. Indeed, the German system's transformation – reduction of party numbers, dominance of two big electors' parties (*Volkspartei*), government stability – has been considered a model of the post-war European trend: the result of the social and ideological changes of the period. More recently this assessment has been reviewed, in the sense both that the model owed too much to specific German conditions and that, as in the case of France, political factors played a more important role than socio-economic ones. Moreover, there is some doubt as to whether, compared with Weimar – the only previous German democratic experience, characterized by a limited competitive party system without government alternation and a multiplicity of parties (including left-wing (KPD) and right-wing (Nazi) anti-system parties) – the present system is totally different, being only marginally more competitive, with partial alternation and with four parties, two big (CDU and SPD) and two small (FDP and Grünen) in parliament.[31]

At all events, crucial for the transformation was the immediate post-war period: the Nazi collapse and the total defeat of 1945 meant a new start in a situation in which German sovereignty was exercised by the Allies. This determined not only the new form of Germany (divided into two states) but also the basic elements of the new West German party system. The latter was more or less fashioned by the time the West

Germans recovered their full national sovereignty in 1955. The Allies authorized only four anti-fascist parties (KPD, SPD, FDP and CDU) before 1948; this meant that they were the only ones able to present themselves nationally at the first parliamentary elections of 1949. It gave them an advantage over their competitors – an advantage which they were able to exploit, with the exception of the KPD. In effect, the latter's consolidation in the west was damaged by Soviet action in the eastern zone, where they created a hegemonic political force (the SED) on the basis of a forced fusion of KPD and SPD, a *fait accompli* which was never accepted by the SPD in the west.

The really original and significant development was the creation of the CDU: a non-confessional Christian (Protestant-Catholic) party which was able to attract conservative-clerical groups because the Allies were hostile, at the time, to openly right-wing parties. Thus the party succeeded in healing one of Weimar's running sores, Protestant–Catholic rivalry. This was also possible because of the division of Germany into two states. In effect the Catholics, who were a minority – a third against two-thirds of Protestants – in the old Reich, found themselves almost equal in numbers with the Protestants in the new Federal Republic. Finally, the parties were already divided into two blocs, one socialist (KPD and SPD) and the other bourgeois (CDU/CSU, FDP and other parties) under Adenauer's leadership: he already controlled the unelected political majority in the institutions created by the Allies during the occupation period. Hence the party system format and operation were already defined before the 1949 elections, but, as mentioned, also confirmed and consolidated before West Germany regained sovereignty (table 5.8).

Despite this, seven parties won seats in the 1949 elections and some observers thought that this would lead to a return to the Weimar system. But this possibility was more illusory than real: the domination of the two big parties and the formation of the two blocs were already operative. A series of political factors further reinforced the new situation. First of all, there were certain adjustments to the electoral law: the electoral regime adopted was a mixture (half and half) of PR and single-member constituencies, but it effectively operated as a proportional system, because the final distribution of seats was made on a proportional basis. In the first elections, the threshold for benefiting from the final distribution of seats was 5 per cent of the vote in a *Land* or the election of one constituency MP. In 1953 this was changed to 5 per cent of the federal vote or one constituency MP, and finally in 1957 to 5 per cent of the federal vote or three constituency MPs. This led to the elimination of all the minor parties except the FDP. The only new party, in fact, that has overcome the 5 per cent threshold has been the Grünen in 1983 and 1987, but not in 1990.[32] The neo-Nazi NPD, which experienced an electoral boom at the end of the 1960s, did not succeed in 1969 and quickly fell apart afterwards.

Table 5.8 Results of parliamentary elections in Germany: votes (per cent) and seats

	1949	1953	1957	1961	1965	1969	1972	1976	1980	1983	1987	1990[a]	1994[a]
Votes													
Christian Democrat Union/ Social Christian Union (CDU/CSU)	31.0	45.2	50.2	45.3	47.6	46.1	44.9	48.6	44.5	48.8	44.3	43.8	41.5
Social Democrat Party (SPD)	29.2	28.8	31.8	36.2	39.3	42.7	45.8	42.6	42.9	38.2	37.0	33.5	36.4
Free Democrat Party (FDP)	11.9	9.5	7.7	12.8	9.5	5.8	8.4	7.9	10.6	7.0	9.1	11.0	6.9
Communist Party (KPD/DKP/PDS)	5.7	2.2	–	–	–	–	0.2	0.3	0.2	0.2	0.6	2.4	4.4
Bavarian Party (BP)	4.2	1.7	0.5	–	–	0.2	–	–	–	–	0.1	–	–
German Party (DP)	4.0	3.3	3.4	–	–	–	–	–	–	–	–	–	–
Centre Party (Z)	3.1	0.8	–	–	–	–	–	–	–	–	–	–	–
Union for Economic Reconstruction (WAV)	2.9	–	–	–	–	–	–	–	–	–	–	–	–
German Conservative Party/German Right Party/German Party of Reich (DRP) 1953–61; National Democratic Party (NPD) since 1965	1.8	1.1	1.0	0.8	2.0	4.3	0.6	0.3	0.2	0.2	0.6	0.3	–
Pan German Bloc/Refugee Bloc (GB/BHE); Republican since 1990	–	5.9	4.6	2.8	–	–	–	–	–	–	–	2.1	1.9
German Union for Peace (DFU); Democratic Action Programme (ADF) 1969	–	–	–	1.9	1.3	0.6	–	–	–	–	–	–	–
Greens (Grünen)	–	–	–	–	–	–	–	–	1.5	5.6	8.3	3.9	7.3
Alliance 90/Greens	–	–	–	–	–	–	–	–	–	–	–	1.2	
Turnout	78.5	85.8	87.8	87.7	86.8	86.7	91.1	90.7	88.6	89.1	84.3	77.8	79.1

Seats

Christian Democrat Union/ Social Christian Union (CDU/CSU)	139	243	270	242	245	242	225	243	226	244	223	319	294
Social Democrat Party (SPD)	131	151	169	190	202	224	230	214	218	193	186	239	252
Free Democrat Party (FDP)	52	48	41	67	49	30	41	39	53	34	46	79	47
Communist Party (KPD/DKP/PDS)	15	–	–	–	–	–	–	–	–	–	–	17	30
Bavarian Party	17	–	–	–	–	–	–	–	–	–	–	–	–
German Party (DP)	17	15	17	–	–	–	–	–	–	–	–	–	–
German Conservative Party/ German Right Party/German Party of Reich (DRP); National Democratic Party (NPD)	5	–	–	–	–	–	–	–	–	–	–	–	–
Pan German Bloc/Refugee Bloc	–	27	–	–	–	–	–	–	–	–	–	–	–
Greens (Grünen)	–	–	–	–	–	–	–	–	–	27	42	–	49
Others	26	3	–	–	–	–	–	–	–	–	–	8	–
Total	402	487	497	499	496	496	496	496	497	498	497	662	672

a All-German elections.

A second factor was the use of article 21 of the basic law by the Federal Constitutional Court to prohibit, for unconstitutionality, both the neo-Nazi SRP in 1952 and the KPD in 1956. It is true that electoral support for the two parties was small at the time (table 5.8). Moreover, attempts to rebuild support for these parties under other names (NPD and DKP) have failed so far: these episodes confirm the small electoral support and hence the irrelevance of these parties in the West German party system in the post-war period down to the present. Whether the new upsurge of right-wing extremism following German reunification will lead to the Republikaner (2.1 per cent of the vote in 1990) winning representation in the Bundestag, only the future can tell.

The third factor was surely Adenauer's success both as chancellor and as CDU party leader. On the one side the Cold War aided his pro-Western and anti-Soviet policy, and on the other Erhard's 'economic miracle' sanctioned the image of his government's efficiency: both these elements legitimated the bourgeois bloc's leader and his party. This helped the assimilation of all the disorganized right-wing groups by the CDU, which thus made itself – thanks to Adenauer's political acumen – the Federal Republic's dominant party with an absolute majority of the vote at the end of the 1950s.

A fourth factor was the SPD's reaction to its own political situation in the 1950s, apparently condemned to the political impotence of permanent opposition, despite the support of a third of the electorate. Hence came the abandonment of Marxism as the party ideology at the 1959 Bad Godesberg congress and the presentation of the party, no longer as a class party, but as a reformist *Volkspartei* open to the middle classes. The 1960s saw the SPD constantly move towards power, both politically thanks to an ever softer opposition, and electorally as a result of more personalized campaigns which were rewarded with significant vote gains. The turning point came in 1966 with the Erhard government crisis, provoked by the FDP's withdrawal from the coalition, and the formation of the Grosse Koalition with the CDU and Kissinger as chancellor. This gave the SPD the opportunity to become legitimated as a government party and in 1969 its leader Willy Brandt succeeded to the chancellorship at the head of an SPD-FDP coalition on a 40 per cent vote.

With this first party alternation in government after twenty years of elections, the two main parties found themselves more or less equal in terms of electoral support; in 1972 the SPD for the first, and only, time outvoted the CDU. However, the government coalition formula was a choice made by the third party, the FDP, and not the electorate, and moreover it was effected in two movements (1966 and 1969). The FDP in 1969 could have chosen a coalition with the CDU – the majority was there – but they chose, instead, the SPD for thirteen years (1969–82), before swapping back, just as suddenly, to the CDU again, this time with Helmut Kohl as chancellor. The second alternation, like the first, was a party decision, taken without consulting the electorate. Kohl did hold elections within six months which confirmed the new coalition, but the old coalition was still mathematically possible. Thus, if alternation exists in Germany, it occurs in a particular way, that is not in an institutionalized way as the result of elections, but in a mediated way as the result of a party decision. This explains, almost certainly, its rarity – only twice in 40 years – as well as the limited change it brings. In this sense it is an example, like Britain in the 1980s, of a limited competitive party system; and the technical reason is surely the PR electoral regime. All the indications are, however, that it is the system the majority of Germans prefer.

The formation, and in monopoly form, of two party blocs (bourgeois and social democrat) confirms the centrality of the socio-economic cleavage in class terms, the more so since the creation of the CDU marked the surmounting of the Protestant versus Catholic confessional conflict. However, the religious cleavage in Germany today is between clericals and lay persons, whether Protestant or Catholic. Moreover, electoral data confirm that socio-economic and religious cleavages tend to overlap, forming the left–right dimension. The Catholic base secured the CDU a cohesion, as did the working class the SPD, which explains to a large extent the solidity of the two parties' electoral support until recently. However, as in other European countries, these cleavages are exhausting themselves – there is even talk of 'the lack of living cleavages' – and new cleavages (often generically defined as 'post-materialist', of which the Grünen would be the carriers, if not the representatives) are emerging and developing; hence there has been increasing electoral volatility and dealignment to which unification has added further uncertainty.

Although the German party system's development is exemplary – indeed, it is often presented as a model – problems were posed by extraparliamentary radicalization during the Grosse Koalition and by the 1970s social movements which gave rise to the Grünen on the one hand, or RAF terrorism on the other, or again by the new rise of the extreme right. The real problem is less the system's legitimacy, as is often thought, and more the parties' political capacity to respond to the changes in German civil society. Moreover, the exceptional nature of the first all-German election of 1990 was such that it is not possible to draw conclusions from its results, other than that it pointed up the substantial differences between the old east and the old west that the subsequent collapse of the eastern economy has surely exacerbated. At all events, the difficult process of internal unification, on which the future political stability of Germany rests, has only just begun.

Italy

The Italian party system differs somewhat from the other three. It is the system which appears to have changed least in terms of format and operation until the 1990s. It is also the system in which anti-system parties have played the most substantial role. In this situation, it is the only European party system in which the two principal parties have been 'sectarian': the DC and PCI were churches rather than parties. In effect, the Italian system replaced, after the disappearance of the Fourth Republic, the French system as the living prototype of classic multipartyism. The system is characterized by excessive fragmentation – fifteen national parties and several regional parties are represented in parliament in 1994, and some, like the Partito Popolare (ex-DC) and PSI, are riven by organized factions – and government instability (table 5.9). It has operated as a limited competitive system – that is to say a positive-sum game – without party alternation in government because of the existence of relevant anti-system parties (PCI and MSI). It is no accident that it was used by Sartori as the model of his polarized pluralism.

The reason for the difference of the Italian party system from the other great European systems lies in the special mixture of political factors which determined the conditions of party competition. Firstly, fascism did not provoke the same break with traditional society that Nazism did in Germany; moreover, it did not end in total defeat. On the contrary, it ended with Mussolini's removal from office, the armistice with the Allies and the armed resistance against the Nazi German occupation. There were thus elements of continuity, above all in the activity of the state, between fascism and the post-war period which did not exist in Germany. Finally, the Catholic Church's integration in national life during the fascist period placed Catholics in a position of strength at the end of the war.

Secondly, the anti-fascist parties, which had reorganized in clandestinity and had led the resistance struggle, also determined the conditions of political competition: the only constraints were that of the international situation and a rather weak civil society. Not surprisingly, being led by pre-fascist leaders, they reconstructed a competitive and constitutional system not dissimilar to that of the pre-fascist period. Thirdly, the party system was strongly conditioned by what Pasquino has called 'international bipolarism', namely the division of Europe into two blocs, all the more so since one of the principal parties (PCI) was strongly identified with the former USSR and the other (DC), as a counterweight, defined itself as the 'American party'. Hence developed the Italian party system's rigidity: the DC as the permanent government party; the PCI as the permanent opposition party; and the small parties in the middle, sometimes in government, sometimes in opposition.

That the parties determined the conditions of party competition can be seen from the attempts to change the electoral law in 1953, when it was decided to give a majority premium of seats to the alliance of lists – the government parties in the circumstances – which won 50 per cent plus one of the votes. The proposal provoked a violent battle in parliament and in the country, in the course of which it was denounced as the *legge truffa* (swindle law) because of its similarity with the Acerbo law which permitted Mussolini to win a parliamentary majority on a minority vote in 1924 and consolidate his power. Despite being approved by parliament, it unleashed a bitter electoral campaign at the end of which the government lists were 50,000 votes short of winning the premium. It demonstrated that a reform of such importance needed the support of the major political parties. Further proof comes from the fact that, after this, talk of electoral reform was banished from political debate for over 30 years. As regards the electoral regime itself – PR list system, employing the corrected d'Hondt method with a limited number of constituencies, that is 32 for the Chamber and 20 for the Senate – it had a very low threshold of access to parliament. It was sufficient for a party to win 50,000 votes in the Rome or Milan constituencies to elect an MP. This explains the survival of certain historical parties (PLI and PRI) with very small percentages of the national vote, but also the entry of new small parties, like DP and PR in the 1970s and the regional parties (Liga veneta and Lega lombarda) in the 1980s. However, as a result of one of the popular referendums held on 18 April 1993, removing the PR element from the Senate electoral law, the government introduced an electoral reform bill for the Chamber which it forced though parliament in July 1993. In future, both houses will be elected on the basis of a complicated combination[33] of one-ballot single-member constituencies (75 per cent of the seats) and nation-wide PR (25 per cent of the seats).

The structuration of political cleavages in Italy is complex: the various dimensions – religious, socio-economic and cultural – cross-cut and overlap. The peculiarities in the Italian case are two. Firstly, the parties' role in the post-war period has been one of social integration, capillary penetration and political implantation. Indeed, the two main parties, PCI and DC, were based on two strong subcultures – Catholic and socialist (chapter 4) – formed at the end of the last century. Secondly, the natural polarization between them was reinforced by the Cold War's 'international bipolarism', which acted on the one hand to delegitimize the PCI as a government force, and on the other to make it the heart of the opposition. The result was a series of coalitions, characterized by government instability (53 governments in the 49 years from 1945 to 1994), that hinged on the pivotal role of the DC, sometimes centrist (in the 1950s), sometimes centre-left (in the 1960s and 1970s).

In this situation, the question of the significant changes in the 1970s is posed: whether the 'historic compromise' and the governments of 'national solidarity' represented something qualitatively new. The question can be considered at two levels: the social and the political. Socially, it referred to the process of cleavage simplification. In the Italian case it meant, firstly, the lessening of the intensity of polarization between DC and PCI. Some observers hypothesized the DC's evolution in a secular-conservative direction and the PCI's in a social democratic one. It was to be the prelude to the DC's displacement towards the centre-right and

Table 5.9 Results of parliamentary elections in Italy: votes (per cent) and seats

	1946	1948	1953	1958	1963	1968	1972	1976	1979	1983	1987	1992	1994[a]
Votes													
Communist Party (PCI/PDS)	18.9	31.0	22.6	22.7	25.3	26.9	27.1	34.4	30.4	29.9	26.6	16.1	20.4
Socialist Party (PSI)	20.7	}	12.7	14.2	13.8	14.5	9.6	9.6	9.8	11.4	14.3	13.6	2.2
United Socialist Party (PSU)	–	–	–	–	–	}	–	–	–	–	–	–	–
Social Democrat Party (PSDI)	–	7.1	4.5	4.6	6.1	}	5.1	3.4	3.8	4.1	2.9	2.7	–
Socialist Party of Proletarian Unity (PSIUP)	–	–	–	–	–	4.4	1.9	–	–	–	–	–	–
Rete	–	–	–	–	–	–	–	–	–	–	–	1.9	1.9
Manifesto/Proletarian Democracy (DP)/ Communist Refoundation	–	–	–	–	–	–	0.7	1.5	1.4	1.5	1.7	5.6	6.0
Christian Democracy (DC/PP)	35.2	48.5	40.1	42.3	38.3	39.1	38.7	38.7	38.3	32.9	34.3	29.7	11.1
Action Party (Pd'A)	1.5	–	–	–	–	–	–	–	–	–	–	–	–
Democratic Alliance	–	–	–	–	–	–	–	–	–	–	–	–	1.2
Forza Italia	–	–	–	–	–	–	–	–	–	–	–	–	21.0
Everyman's Party (UQ)	5.3	–	–	–	–	–	–	–	–	–	–	–	–
Italian Social Movement (MSI/AN)	–	2.0	5.8	4.8	5.1	4.5	8.7	6.1	5.3	6.8	5.9	5.3	13.5
Liberal Party (PLI)	6.8	3.8	3.0	3.5	7.0	5.8	3.9	1.3	1.9	2.9	2.1	2.8	–
Monarchist Party	2.8	2.8	6.9	4.8	1.7	1.3	–	–	–	–	–	–	–
Italy Pact	–	–	–	–	–	–	–	–	–	–	–	–	4.6
Republican Party (PRI)	4.4	2.5	1.6	1.4	1.4	2.0	2.9	3.1	3.0	5.1	3.7	4.4	–
Sardinian Action Party (PSd'A)	0.3	0.2	0.1	–	–	0.1	–	–	0.1	0.3	0.4	0.3	–
South Tyrolean People's Party (SVP)	–	0.5	0.5	0.5	0.4	0.5	0.5	0.5	0.5	0.5	0.5	0.5	–
Northern Leagues	–	–	–	–	–	–	–	–	–	0.4	0.5	8.7	8.4
Radical Party (PR)/Panella	–	–	–	–	–	–	–	1.1	3.5	2.2	2.6	1.2	3.5
Greens	–	–	–	–	–	–	–	–	–	–	2.5	1.9	2.7
Others	4.1	1.6	2.2	1.2	0.9	0.9	0.9	0.3	2.0	2.0	2.0	3.0	3.5
Turnout	89.1	92.2	93.8	93.8	92.9	92.8	93.2	93.4	90.6	89.0	88.7	87.2	86.0

Seats

Seats													
Communist Party (PCI/PDS)	104	183	143	140	166	177	179	227	201	198	177	107	102
Socialist Party (PSI)	115	⎱	75	84	87	–	61	57	62	73	94	92	11
United Socialist Party (PSU)	–	–	–	–	–	91	–	–	–	–	–	–	–
Indep. Progressists	–	–	–	–	–	–	–	–	–	–	–	–	34
Social Democrat Party (PSDI)	–	33	19	22	33	–	29	15	20	23	17	16	–
Socialist Party of Proletarian Unity (PSIUP)	–	–	–	–	–	23	–	–	–	–	–	–	–
Rete	–	–	–	–	–	–	–	–	–	–	–	12	5
Manifesto/Proletarian Democracy (DP)/Communist Refoundation	–	–	–	–	–	–	–	6	6	7	8	35	40
Christian Democracy (DC/PPI)	207	305	263	273	260	266	266	263	262	225	234	206	29
Democratic Alliance	–	–	–	–	–	–	–	–	–	–	–	–	11
Action Party (Pd'A)	–	–	–	–	–	–	–	–	–	–	–	–	–
Liberal Party (PLI)	41	19	13	17	39	31	20	5	9	16	11	17	–
Italy Pact	–	–	–	–	–	–	–	–	–	–	–	–	17
Monarchist Party	16	14	40	25	8	6	–	–	–	–	–	–	–
Republican Party (PRI)	23	9	5	6	6	9	15	14	16	29	21	27	–
Sardinian Action Party (PSd'A)	2	1	–	–	–	–	–	–	–	1	2	1	–
Everyman's Party/Italian Social Movement (UQ/MSI/AN)	30	6	29	24	27	24	56	35	30	42	35	34	110
Forza Italia	–	–	–	–	–	–	–	–	–	–	–	–	135[b]
South Tyrolean People's Party (SVP)	–	3	3	3	3	3	3	3	4	3	3	3	3
Northern Leagues	–	–	–	–	–	–	–	–	–	–	1	56	116
Radical Party (PR)/Panella	–	–	–	–	–	–	–	4	18	11	13	7	6
Greens	–	–	–	–	–	–	–	–	–	–	13	16	11
Others	18	1	–	2	1	–	1	1	2	2	1	1	–
Total	556	574	590	596	630	630	630	630	630	630	630	630	630

[a] Under new mixed majority + proportional system: the Pole of Liberty (right) won 365 seats, the Pact for Italy (centre) 46 seats, and the Progressive Pole (left) 214 seats.

[b] Including 18 Christian Democratic Centre and 4 others elected in the Pole of Liberty's majority list.

the PCI's towards the centre-left and, in consequence, would open up the possibility of two coalitions based on DC and PCI, respectively, on the basis of the attenuation of the confession and the class cleavages. However, the electoral successes of certain regional movements in the 1990s suggest that the territorial cleavage has returned with a vengeance in Italy, as it has in Britain. In Italy, then, there is still no clear trend towards cleavage simplification, as many reformers hoped and confidently predicted.

As regards the political level specifically, if a certain number of changes have occurred – electoral earthquake of the mid 1970s, PCI in a position to overtake DC, DC-PCI government collaboration – they were not sufficiently traumatic to provoke a significant transformation in the working of the party system. The proof is that Italy is the only West European country where normal party alternation in government has not taken place in the post-war period. Indeed, a cast-iron alliance between DC and PSI, based on a division of the spoils between the parties (CAF[34]) and in which the PSI replaced the DC as the hub of the party system, saw Italy through the 1980s. However, it was the collapse of communism in 1989, followed by the deterioration in public finances[35] due to accumulated political corruption and inefficiency, that finally undermined this limited competitive party regime (*partitocrazia*). The *tangentopoli* scandal that broke at the start of the 1992 electoral campaign was simply the last straw for many. For almost the first time, voters abandoned the established national parties (DC, PSI and even PDS) for the new regional (*leghe*) and reforming (*rete, verdi*) lists in substantial numbers, dramatically accelerating political fragmentation. Fourteen different parties were represented in the Italian parliament elected in 1992: a post-war record for Western Europe! Not surprisingly, constitutional reform found itself at the top of the new parliament's political agenda. However, it took a popularly called referendum (chapter 7) in April 1993 to secure the passage of a majority-oriented electoral law and the promise of new elections in spring 1994.[36]

The outcome of the elections, under the new electoral law, was a victory for the right-wing Freedom Pole rather than a parliament dominated by the three poles – right, centrist (Pact for Italy) and left (Progressist) – which most commentators expected. However, the Freedom Pole is itself an electoral cartel of three major forces – Forza Italia, Lega Nord and Alleanza Nazionale – to which must be added the Catholic CCD and Panella. Hence, Sartori's jest that one *pentapartito* has merely been replaced by another. Given the inherently contradictory nature of Berlusconi's new government coalition (the ideology and political interests of the Lega Nord and southern Alleanza Nazionale are violently opposed), the question remains whether the right's electoral victory is indeed the necessary prelude to stable and effective government.

European Union

Despite elections by universal suffrage to the EP since 1979, the EU has not yet seen the development of a functioning European party system. This is because significant transnational European parties have not yet emerged. Loosely organized transnational federations grouped around general principles were created in the mid 1970s in anticipation of the first direct elections to the EP by the three main political groups – socialist (CSP), Christian democrat (EPP) and liberal (LDP). However, they have not developed into parties providing leadership at the European level, principally because they were not involved in daily political activity in an institutional setting and hence have not yet been able to create attachments and loyalties.[37] Furthermore, they have limited resources, having to depend on the EP political groups for support.

Membership of the EP political groups – of which there are ten at present – is by national delegations of MEPs and, although alliances have been forged between national parties for European elections, voting has remained along national lines and so not surprisingly the political groups have difficulty in imposing political discipline on members. This is particularly the case where – as often happens – one or two national delegations decide not to follow the line of their political group. The reasons for lack of transnational political cohesiveness are many. Firstly, since there is no government to sustain, or attack, in the EP, there is no parliamentary division between government and opposition. Secondly, the heterogeneous and multicultural nature of the EP means that all shades of European, as opposed to merely national, opinion are represented: national, regional, sectoral as well as ideological. MEPs, moreover, are often closely associated with the numerous interest groups which make incompatible demands on their support. Thirdly, the range of political beliefs within each group is invariably very wide and the groups thus find it difficult to compose them and come to a common decision on a particular issue. Further, MEPs' future political careers are tied to their national parties at home. Fourthly, the political situation in which the EP finds itself in relation to other EC institutions often requires a common front to defend its institutional prerogatives, particularly against the Council of Ministers. In addition, given that no political group approaches the absolute majority, cooperation between the two main groups (CSP and EPP) is necessary to secure the passage of the budget and other major business. On present form, the development of a genuine European party system is going to be a slow and painful process.

Conclusion

Parties, together with groups, constitute the principal linkage between civil society and the state and thus the motor of the constitutional political process. They fight elections to gain public office and through it control of the government to put their programmes into effect. They are distinguished from pressure groups which merely seek to influence public policies without the responsibilities of office. Despite the definitions, the boundaries between the two are imprecise and some organizations act as both parties and pressure groups.

There are numerous types of party. Following Duverger, we have identified four – the notables' (elite) party, the mass (militants') party, the Leninist (vanguard) party, the fascist (militia) party – to which we have added Kirchheimer's people's catch-all (electors') party. They all have distinguishing organizational features, but only the first two and the last are relevant to parliamentary politics. The elite party focuses on state institutional activity and power lies with the parliamentary leaders. The militants' party is organized centrally to mobilize and proselytize and so depends on the quality and activity of its militants. The electors' party is in some ways a synthesis of the previous two types: its organizational form is the political machine and it develops the division of labour between professional politics (leaders) and supporters (voters). The success of the former is measured in the attraction of the latter.

Parties do not exist in a vacuum in parliamentary democracies; they are in competition with other parties for power through elections, and relations between parties in different countries determine national party systems. There are various analyses, but our discussion is limited to the three major ones. Rokkan and Lipset focus on the historical cleavages which structured the European party systems in their formative period in the nineteenth century, the legacy of which conditions contemporary interparty competition. They identify three main political tendencies – conservative, liberal and socialist – as the constitutive components of national systems. These are complicated in individual cases by further cleavages – religious, ethno-cultural, territorial – which often overlapped and so created the diversity between national systems. Rokkan and Lipset conclude that once institutionalized, the structure of the various national party systems demonstrated a remarkable capacity for survival.

Duverger and Sartori developed the best-known typologies of contemporary party competition. Duverger's is based on the number of parties and distinguishes between two-partyism and multipartyism which give rise to different consequences: alternation of parties in government and lack of alternation respectively. Party competition is pendular on a centripetal basis since political alternatives are intrinsically dualistic. The major factor determining the operation of party systems is the electoral regime, for which Duverger formulated his well-known sociological laws relating two-partyism to majority systems and multipartyism to PR. The laws have been much criticized, but even Sartori's reformulation of them as tendency laws leaves the substance unchanged.

Sartori's typology is more complex than Duverger's because it includes a further dimension in addition to number: the ideological distance between parties. On this basis, Sartori proposes a threefold typology: two-partyism, moderate pluralism and polarized pluralism. The significance of Sartori's typology lies in his insistence on the importance of ideological polarization as well as the distinction between moderate and polarized pluralism on the basis of different kinds of spatial competition: centripetal and centrifugal respectively. Indeed, his name is linked to the polarized pluralist model and its properties.

We propose an alternative schema which attempts a synthesis of the salient aspects of Duverger's and Sartori's typologies. This is based on a political continuum of coercion–consensus which permits the definition of three party system types: non-competitive (closed) system; limited competitive (positive-sum game) system; and fully competitive (zero-sum game) system. The discriminating element is the existence of anti-system parties, and the consequences are alternation (in fully competitive systems) and lack of alternation (in limited competitive systems). Thus the schema permits not only the determination of party competition and strategy but also changes between them, that is to say the movement of a party system from one category to another. Few party systems remain in the same category over a long period.

Most West European parties belong to one of the major ideological political families based on the four underlying societal cleavages. These families are: communist, socialist, Christian, conservative, extreme right (neo-fascist), regionalist and ecological. Parties in each family can be, and were, classified by party type. Moreover, some political families have declined generally speaking (Christian, liberal, communist) whereas others have advanced (socialist and conservative). Another unexpected phenomenon has been the revitalization of regionalist parties.

National party systems are discussed in terms of the principal cleavages and party system types. Thus the British system is structured around a dominant socio-economic cleavage which explains the predominance of class conflict. However, the decline of class conflict has seen the system move from a fully competitive phase to a limited competitive one as a result of the SDP split from the Labour Party in 1981 and the categorizing of Labour in anti-system terms, thus underwriting Conservative Party domination. The French party system, on the other hand, is structured around a fundamental ideological cleavage (progress versus status quo) with which other cleavages overlap. It was, moreover, characterized by a substantial anti-system party component under the Fourth Republic and so knew only limited competition. Changes under the Fifth Republic with the decline of the anti-system element led to alternation and a fully competitive phase in the 1980s.

The German and Italian party systems are structured by multiple cleavages. Competition in the German system was simplified by the electoral law and the virtual disappearance of anti-system elements. However, it has remained in a limited competitive phase, principally because only partial alternation has been possible. PR and major anti-system parties have ensured that the Italian party system has known only limited competition and permanent coalitions around a dominant party since the war. The collapse of communism in 1989 and the end of the Cold War have undermined its basis: the result is the present crisis in which the corruption scandals are merely the most obvious symptom. However, reform of the electoral law in a simple majority direction (despite remaining mixed) has been adopted as the premise to party aggregation and government stability.

Finally, the failure to create significant transnational parties means that the EU has, as yet, no meaningful party system. Such a system seems unlikely until the EP is given significant powers to make and unmake an EU executive.

Further reading

S. Bartolini and P. Mair (eds) (1984), *Party Politics in Contemporary Western Europe* (London: Cass).

J. Blondel (1978), *Political Parties: A Genuine Case for Discontent?* (London: Wildwood House).

M.J. Bull and P. Heywood (eds) (1994), *European Communist Parties after the Revolutions of 1989* (Basingstoke: Macmillan).

M. Calise (1993), 'Remaking the Italian Party System: How Lijphart Got it Wrong by Saying it Right' in *West European Politics*, 16, 4, 545–60.

H. Daalder and P. Mair (eds) (1984), *Western European Party Systems: Continuity and Change* (Aldershot: Dartmouth).

M. Duverger (1959), *Political Parties* (London: Methuen, 2nd edn).

D. Hanley (ed.) (1994), *Christian Democracy in Europe: A Comparative Perspective* (London: Pinter).

O. Kirchheimer (1966), 'The Transformation of Western Party Systems', in J. LaPalombara and M. Weiner (eds), *Political Parties and Political Development* (Princeton, NJ: Princeton UP).

K. Lawson and P. H. Merkyl (eds) (1988), *When Parties Fail: Emerging Alternative Organizations* (Princeton, NJ: Princeton UP).

Z. Layton-Henry (ed.) (1982), *Conservative Politics in Western Europe* (London: Macmillan).

S. M. Lipset and S. Rokkan (eds) (1967), *Party Systems and Voter Alignments* (New York: Free Press).

P. Mair (ed.) (1990), *The Western European Party System* (Oxford: OUP).

P. Mair and G. Smith (eds) (1990), *Understanding Party System Change in Western Europe* (London: Cass).

R. Morgan and S. Silvestri (eds) (1982), *Moderates and Conservatives in Western Europe* (London: PSI/Heinemann).

S. Padgett (ed.) (1993), *Parties and Party Systems in the New Germany* (Aldershot: Dartmouth).

A. Panebianco (1984), *Political Parties: Organization and Power* (Cambridge: CUP).

W. Paterson and A. Thomas (eds) (1986), *The Future of Social Democracy: Problems and Prospects of Social Democrat Parties in Western Europe* (Oxford: Clarendon).

G. Sartori (1976), *Parties and Party Systems* (Cambridge: CUP).

S. Wolinetz (1988), *Parties and Party Systems in Liberal Democracies* (London: Routledge).

S. Wolinetz (1993), 'Party System Change: The Catch-All Thesis Revisited', in *West European Politics*, 16, 1, 113–28.

6 Groups and Interest Intermediation

Introduction

At the beginning of the previous chapter, we outlined the role of parties and pressure groups. They are not only actors of the political struggle in civil society; they also act as privileged channels of communication between society and the state. A distinction was made between groups and parties, on the basis of different roles – articulation and aggregation of social demands, functional and territorial representation – but it did not prove very fruitful. The claim to distinguish between group roles and party roles does not make much sense either, if only because they can, and do, change. In other words, certain roles performed by parties in the past, for instance political mass mobilization, have today become the favourite activity of certain pressure groups, while defending sectional interests has become the concern of many parties. Indeed, the appearance of new problems and methods in the political arena has reopened the apparently stable division of labour between political institutions.

For these reasons, the division of roles between parties and groups is not a stable one: the same organization can operate both as a party and as a pressure group. Finally, the latter constitutes a residual institutional category in the sense that it covers all those social organizations involved in the political process which are *not* parties. In fact, there are no definitive or comprehensive definitions. In this situation, we shall look at three areas: the framework of group analysis; modes of intermediation; and the major groups active in Western Europe.

Problems of group analysis

The traditional analysis of pressure groups poses a set of problems, among which definitions and modes of action are prominent. However, the genesis and establishment of groups in Europe were linked, like those of parties, to the development of political participation. The political rise of groups is usually described as passing through three phases: an initial phase of estate representation in which interests coincided with the social system (*ancien régime*); a nineteenth century liberal phase in which representation was organized on an individual basis and association was entirely voluntary, and hence was fragmentary and unstable, and which phase – the transformation of regimes of representation – saw the birth and propagation of the notables' party; and, finally, a third phase from the end of the last century, characterized by mass parties and stable organized interest groups with multiple goals, professional leaders and bureaucracies. The groups gained a substantial political voice in the policy-making process. The dividing line, at least in Europe, was World War I because the belligerents deemed it necessary to solicit the mass mobilization capacity of interest groups to encourage production, planned resource allocation and price control, and to maintain social peace. Schmitter (1983a) has observed:

> The pre-existing associations of capitalists and workers were officially recognized as intermediaries and very large, semi-public tasks were entrusted to them, they were encouraged (if not obliged) to widen their recruitment and were given financial incentives and material facilities. Where there was no organization in a certain sector of production or strategic profession, the state often intervened to assist in their creation.... The range of interest associations never returned to the status quo *ante bellum*. (pp. 37–8)

In short certain groups were viewed hereafter as legitimate interlocutors of the state in the policy process of European countries, the more so since, in succeeding years, the state continued to increase and widen its activity and interest in the economy and society at large. This public intervention in society was considered a necessary premise for the growth of political demand, and hence sanctioned the relevance of the interest group phenomenon in European political life. In fact, the change in policy output, determined by state intervention in the economy, acted on political input; and the widespread and specialist aggregation of demand by interest groups not only coexisted with the presence of parties – which thereby lost the monopoly of the transmission of political demand – but often led to the marginalization of parties in relation to groups.

With regard to definitions of groups, we have noted that they were something of a residual category, which means that it is virtually impossible to give a clear and comprehensive definition. In fact, they are quite simply organizations seeking to influence public policy. More important than the definition is the implication: that all associations in civil society which refuse to assume responsibility for power can be defined as interest or pressure groups. This is the case, theoretically; however, we can eliminate all those groups and organizations that are not politically active. But this still leaves open the delicate question of certain corps of state personnel. Our analytical framework places pressure groups firmly in civil society, and this is despite the fact that some political scientists (Ball and Millard, 1986, for example) include the public administration and armed forces among pressure groups. We argue that however similar to pressure groups the methods they employ, their power, like their resources, derives from their privileged position as instruments of state power. Hence they should not be so regarded. This said, we make a distinction for higher civil servant unions (like First Division in Britain or DISTAT in Italy) which clearly are pressure groups in our conception.

The elaboration of a useful group typology has always been a problematic undertaking. Numerous attempts have been made, employing the most varied criteria (interests defended, goals pursued, decision centres influenced, methods used, and so on), but they have not really proved analytically fruitful. Firstly, the criteria selected are neither clear nor unambiguous: certain groups enter several categories, so it is impossible to situate them objectively. Secondly, and more seriously, a typology is useful for what it helps us to understand about the group and its probable activity. None of the typologies is able to do this for us. And this is for the simple reason that no group, whatever its influence, voluntarily abandons an instrument of pressure, not even the most banal or conjunctural, without a *quid pro quo*. The only value of the various typologies is to make us aware of the diversity of groups, activities and methods.

One distinction which pervades the literature is worth pursuing because of its repercussions on the modes of interest intermediation. It is the distinction between economic (or 'functional'/'sectional') groups and ideological (or 'promotional'/'cause') groups, which can be reformulated as that between 'interest groups' on the one side and 'pressure groups' in the narrow sense on the other. Interest groups represent the specific interests of their members which are, by definition, the interests of a sector of society and hence are sectional interests, that is restricted to that sector. On the other hand, pressure groups represent some belief or principle which they promote for the good of all; hence their appeal is universal, that is not restricted to a particular social group. Of course, some interest groups may promote or defend causes – as, for instance, the European trade unions do when they campaign for peace, divorce and abortion – but such philanthropy is never a predominant concern of theirs. Interest groups organize the most important social groups in West European societies: they include employers, entrepreneurs, liberal professions (doctors, lawyers, engineers, architects), workers, clerks and peasants. Pressure groups are more numerous and include religious associations (churches and their collateral organizations), civil rights associations, consumer organizations, prisoners' groups, environmental groups, civic groups, peace movements, and movements against racism.

Finally, this distinction between interest groups (sectional) and pressure groups (cause) enables us to isolate a number of current trends: (1) the number of active pressure groups has multiplied and their activity is diversifying; (2) the existing interest groups, and particularly the major economic ones, have become increasingly politically involved because their interests are of such importance that the state cannot ignore them; (3) the groups have increasingly developed their contacts with the state and, consequently, downgraded those with civil society; (4) there has been a formalization of the contacts between interest groups and state institutions; and (5) the new cause groups have begun to use parties as a means of influencing state policy as well as a means of mobilizing civil society.

Channels of pressure

The modes of group action are largely determined by the channels of access to the political system. Naturally, these are the principal national decision-making centres, although they are not necessarily the only ones.[1] Indeed, with the Single European Act, the EU institutions are clearly becoming increasingly significant. At all events, it is possible to identify very schematically four major targets: two are part of the state, that is parliament and the public administration; and two are in civil society, namely parties and the mass media (figure 6.1). Each has its own resources and its own problematic. Thus, for instance, groups can seek representation or a spokesperson in parliament or on a parliamentary

		Constitutional apparatuses	Functional apparatuses
STATE	Target	*Parliament*	*Public administration*
	Resources	spokesperson parliamentary groups	information collaboration
CIVIL SOCIETY	Target	*Parties*	*Mass media*
	Resources	funding candidatures	public opinion direct action

Figure 6.1 Targets and resources of groups in Western European political systems

standing committee. They can provide information and their point of view on particular policies as well as offer collaboration to the public administration in the execution of those policies. They can propose candidates and funds to parties which support their interests. Finally, there are a whole series of techniques available to them to influence public opinion through the mass media, either by direct action (strikes, occupations, sit-ins, demonstrations) or by messages (congresses, polls, press conferences, publicity campaigns).

It is worth looking in greater detail at these four access targets and the resources required to enable groups to play a significant role in the political process of West European states, not only because this illustrates their particular features but also because it provides a means of assessing the various groups' influence. To repeat, the four targets are: parties, parliament, public administration and mass media.

Parties

The classic resource of groups in relation to parties is obviously finance because 'democratic' politics is a costly business. The list of groups funding parties and their electoral campaigns is endless: it begins with private companies and public agencies (but also includes TNCs) which usually fund government and conservative parties – for instance, the Flick (Germany), Montedison, Lockheed, Feruzzi (Italy), Polly Peck (Britain) and SAE-SORMAE (France) finance scandals as regards the occult funding of politicians and parties in recent years – and ends with the trade unions who usually fund labour and socialist parties (today, for example, about 55 per cent of the British Labour Party's funds are contributed by the unions), and passes through every type of group including churches and farmers' organizations.

At the same time, groups do not neglect opportunities for promoting the candidature of their leaders and members. Thus the Coldiretti farmers' association claimed to have a group of 100 MPs in the Italian parliament for every post-war Italian legislature up to the later 1970s as well as some 20,000 local councillors. In Britain, the various unions (NUM, TGWU, GMB, AEUW, MSF) sponsor their own candidates in the Labour Party.[2] In fact, the number of group representatives who have risen to ministerial office is significant: John Davies, director general of the British CBI until April 1970, was elected Conservative MP in June and immediately appointed minister of industry by prime minister Heath; similarly François Guillaume, president of the French FNSEA until 1986, was elected Gaullist MP in March 1986 and appointed minister of agriculture in the Chirac government formed after the elections.

The ease with which the leaders of certain groups become parliamentary and local candidates demonstrates the importance and mutuality of the party–group relationship. The parties seek funds as well as the electoral support of certain sections of the population that the groups are able to mobilize and influence, while the latter seek political pay-offs from their financial and electoral support. It is the very political support of certain groups that gives them an often decisive weight in the appointments to certain ministerial posts: it is claimed, for instance, that the choice of the minister of agriculture in West European states is conditioned by the principal agricultural interest groups.

This often close relationship between interest groups and parties raises necessarily the question of defining the type and kind of interpenetration between the two. It is not easy in some cases to distinguish between the two kinds of organization, particularly because historically they developed in parallel. Three types of relationship are identifiable. In the first, the interest group sponsors the party, that is it not only funds party activity but is responsible in large measure for both leadership recruitment and the kinds of policy pursued. The most obvious example is that of sponsor institutions and sponsored parties, like the unions and the Labour Party in Britain, and the Catholic Church and the DC, before Vatican II, in Italy. In this case, it is obvious that the group can significantly handicap the party's capacity to mediate their particular interests within programmes intended to appeal for nation-wide support. In the second, the group is the emanation of the party and is dependent on the latter. This was the case of the CGT and CGIL unions and the French and Italian communist parties respectively before 1968. In this situation, party control prevents the group from expressing the autonomous demands of the workers, and finishes by imposing an ideological straitjacket on the group's activity. In the third, there is an identity of interest between certain groups and certain parties on important problems, but not on all the relevant ones, so that the party's political programme is never reducible to these groups' interests. This is the most widespread relationship in Western Europe today.

Parliament

Some groups are actively interested in sponsoring parliamentary candidatures and securing the election of their leaders: the reasons are simple. Not only does the parliamentary majority have its word to say on the government's legislative programme, but an MP's prestige is such that it often allows him to intervene personally in official procedures (ministries, agencies, parliamentary committees) to secure a particular decision. The parliamentary committees, particularly in Germany, France and Italy, are endowed with substantive powers. The post of *rapporteur* of a bill often confers the power to speed up or delay debate and so ensure its eventual success or failure. Thus it is easy to understand the influence of the 'amici della Coldiretti' in the Italian parliament (above all in the agriculture committee) or of other groups (business and civil servants, for instance) in other committees (finance and home affairs, for example).

It is well known, in fact, that in the House of Commons many MPs have close ties with professional organizations or represent them directly (as the rules allow) or establish interparty groups (Conservative, Liberal and Labour MPs) with a view to coordinating the defence of their common interests. In this regard, the case of the British Medical Association (BMA), whose interests were represented in the 1950s by an interparty committee of twenty MPs, is often quoted. Among the groups that played an important role in the French Assembly under the Fourth Republic were L'Amicale Parlementaire Agricole, L'Association Parlementaire pour la Défense de l'Enseignement Libre and Le Groupe d'Études sur les Problèmes des Bouilleurs de Cru. In Germany, a 1972 law established a procedure for all groups wishing to enter into relations with the Bundestag, namely that they must register with the president stating their social purpose, membership and representatives. Over 1000 groups have availed themselves of this facility which allows them to make the necessary contacts, exchange information and be called to give evidence to standing committees.

Finally, some interest and pressure groups prefer to select an MP as an official spokesperson for their interests in parliament. In Britain, for instance, it is permissible for a group to keep an MP on a retainer as long as the relationship is registered with the speaker of the House of Commons.[3] Thus, James Callaghan (later Labour prime minister) was the Police Federation's parliamentary spokesperson in the 1950s; similarly, the Confederazione Italiana dei Dirigenti d'Azienda used the services of its leader, DC senator and minister Giuseppe Togni, in this capacity; and the list could be continued at length. Some politicians take this role very seriously and refuse ministerial promotion to remain the group's parliamentary spokesperson: it is said, for example, that the former Labour MP Brian Walden, the bookies' parliamentary spokesperson, refused the ministerial post offered to him in 1974 because the official salary was lower than his retainer from the bookies.

Public administration

As the site of executive power in European states, the public administration is usually regarded as the centre of institutionalized relations between groups and the political system.[4] This is a direct consequence of the state's growing intervention in economic and social life during this century; it means that because of the increase in public subsidies and investment on the one side, and the multiplication of regulations on economic and social activity on the other, the administration's support is often indispensable for the promotion and defence of interests of all kinds. On the other hand, the public administration requires both information and collaboration; the former can often be supplied only by interest groups, and the latter too is usually indispensable for effective intervention in economic and social questions. Thus the groups have a great incentive to become part of the policy process, the more so since the administration has been given the power of regulation in many areas of society. At the same time, more and more new agencies, with powers of consultation and control, are being created and this naturally increases the administration's autonomous power. It is not surprising, then, that groups act so as to be represented on these new bodies and dominate them where they can.

Some writers distinguish between the government and the public administration, that is between the executive in the narrow sense (ministers) and the executive in the wider sense (ministers plus civil servants). The former is important in so-called 'tripartite' relations (much in fashion in the 1970s) between government, employers' associations and trade unions, which formulated economic policy as a result of consultation and negotiation. However, the problem posed by this type of relationship concerns the strength of the groups and the autonomous power of the state, and results from an ensemble of factors, both structural and contingent: the state's constitutional structure; the strength of the economy; the international competitive position; the politico-economic conjuncture; and the notion of national interest.

The latter – that is, the executive in the wider sense of administration – concerns the civil service's permeability to interest groups. There are two theses. The first asserts the civil service's neutrality – in other words, its impermeability to group pressure in the name of the higher interests of the state. Meynaud (1958) advanced two arguments to support this thesis: (1) the stability and independence of the civil service career structure protects them from group favours: and (2) the developed sense of 'public service' leads civil servants to resist the groups' siren voices. It is perhaps no accident that these arguments were advanced in France, even if we may doubt their basic soundness.

The second thesis implies close and active relations between the administration and groups resulting in mutual influence based on the groups' power. If it naturally presupposes a policy of regular consultation and collaboration between them, it raises, nonetheless, the thorny question of the selection of the groups: those recognized by the public administration as the legitimate representatives of the interests with which to collaborate, and those rejected as unrepresentative or illegitimate. There is thus a margin of appreciation left to the civil service which it can use to its advantage. It is worth recalling, for instance, that the French and Italian ministries of labour recognized only the Catholic and social democratic unions as the legitimate representatives of the workers in the 1950s, and refused this status to the communist unions (CGT and CGIL). However, the effective power of the communist unions was such that the ministries in both countries were obliged to recognize them when they wished to coordinate economic development in the 1960s. Similarly, the Gaullist governments refused to enter into dialogue with the minority unions of French agricultural workers. In 1981, the Socialist government reversed this ruling but still had to take account of the powerful FNSEA. These examples illustrate Offe's (1972) axiom according to which the civil service in capitalist countries practises widespread selectivity of interests and so determines differential group access. The factors involved are: the group's capacity to destabilize the social and political order, on the one hand; and its 'social utility' as defined by the state apparatus in terms of the costs of the social reproduction of the system, on the other. Hence the favoured groups, in Offe's view, are central and homogeneous groups ('policy-makers': industrialists, executives, key workers, farmers) because of their economic and political blackmail power; and the disadvantaged are marginal and fragmentary groups ('policy-takers': women, young persons, students, pensioners, the unemployed and the disabled) just because they lack blackmail power. The formers' demands – wages, investments, subsidies, tax levels – are favourably entertained because they are specific and can be costed, whereas the latters' – housing, health, welfare – are general and have open-ended costs. If this axiom is correct, the violence of certain marginal groups becomes comprehensible.

If Offe has indicated a general framework of group–state relations in capitalist societies, LaPalombara (1964) outlined two types of situation which determine specific relations between groups and the public administration. He defined the first as the *clientela* : it is a situation in which the administration recognizes a group (or several) as the legitimate representative of interests in a certain sector and so establishes privileged relations with it (or them). The relations between the finance ministries and the principal employers' associations are an obvious case in point, but there are many others: ministries of education and teachers' organizations; public works and developers; health and doctors; and so on. He defined the second situation as the *parentela*: this represents a situation where a group (or several) succeeds in establishing a privileged relationship with a ministry or a dominant party (if there is one) in such a way as to influence civil service appointments and promotions, and even the post of minister. LaPalombara quotes the case of Catholic Action (AC) and the Italian higher civil service in the 1950s, thanks to the organic relationship between AC and the DC (the permanent government party in post-war Italy). Others have suggested the case of certain industrialists close to Adenauer's CDU in the same period. At all events, it is a situation linked in many ways to the stable domination of a government party, that is for a decade or more.

In LaPalombara's analysis, the *clientela* relationship is superior to the *parentela*, because it is founded on 'position'. In short, it is based on an interest group's strategic position in its sector and the importance of that sector for the government which cannot afford to ignore it, hence making collaboration more or less indispensable. *Parentela* relations depend, instead, on personal ties or ideological affinity which have to be continually reactivated. Without denying the existence of common cultural, social and intellectual interests between higher civil servants and some groups – industrialists, bankers and others – which encourage *parentela* relations, LaPalombara's emphasis on the structural nature of the *clientela* relationship largely confirms Offe's general framework, but from a different standpoint.

There is, moreover, a third type of relationship, not mentioned by LaPalombara, that of 'colonization': a situation where a group combines position and habit to impose its policy choices in its area. Examples include the principal agricultural organizations in Britain (NFU), France (FNSEA), Germany (DBV) and Italy (Coldiretti) and their respective ministries of agriculture.

Finally, the more the public administration becomes sectorially specialized, the more it ignores general and poorly organized groups. Indeed, a division of labour has developed inside the West European state institutions between the well-organized groups linked to ministerial departments, and the ill-organized groups trying to get their voices heard in parliament or, more generally, in civil society.

Media

The media are a residual target because they act indirectly. They are the focus of a whole set of activities which attempt to mould that ambiguous concept which is 'public opinion'. As was noted in chapter 4, the media are not a natural form of communication, but an instrument managed according to a specific economico-industrial logic. This means that the giant groups have a power of control – being often the proprietors of the principal media (newspapers, TV channels) – that other groups have to take into account. In this way, the structure of the media determines, or at least conditions, the activities of smaller and non-media groups. In fact, it is possible to identify, *grosso modo*, two types of action to influence public opinion: (1) that which attempts to form public opinion in the sense of developing a coherent argument; and (2) that which attempts to create a situation by dramatizing, for instance, an event to catch public attention. In (1) enter all those activities that can be called 'civic commitments', that is debates, lectures, press conferences, poster campaigns, polls, delegations, pamphlets; and under (2) enter all those activities called 'direct actions', namely demonstrations, strikes, lockouts, sit-ins, walks, marches, including real and symbolic violence (kidnappings, bombings, civil disobedience). Actions in class (1) are undertaken by all sorts of groups, while actions in class (2) tend to be the monopoly of marginalized groups.

Italy is the Western European country that has experienced the largest variety of direct action in the post-war period, from the Confindustria's investment strike of the early 1960s to the public service 'self-imposed tariff reductions' practised by the various marginal groups in the late 1970s; from the P2 violence to that of the Red Brigades (the Moro affair of 1978 was only the most spectacular of a long series of violent actions). As regards France, on the other hand, we can mention the activity of certain groups, particularly in agriculture, that have a long history of direct action and have been responsible for kidnapping ministers, blocking motorways and railway lines with tractors, blocking the prefectures with unsold agricultural produce and setting local tax offices on fire. And similar, if less dramatic, examples are forthcoming in Britain and Germany. As noted, direct action is usually the weapon of marginal groups which are forced so to act because of lack of other means: above all, lack of access to state decision centres. However, this is only partially true because no group, not even the most powerful and influential, voluntarily renounces any means of pressure available to it. Even major organized groups, like employers' associations and trade unions, resort to direct action if necessary: investment strike, lock-out, wildcat strike, factory occupation, sit-in. On the other hand, the distinction between the two types of action is a bit forced in the sense that many groups regularly employ them. For instance, the association Laissez les Vivre, which has over 70,000 members and which promoted an anti-abortion campaign in France in the 1970s, was engaged in the following activities: information meetings, conferences, publication of newspapers and pamphlets, posters, official delegations, signing petitions as well as street demonstrations and processions and commando raids on abortion clinics.

Finally, some political scientists regard the judiciary also as a target for pressure group activity. This might appear strange in view of the notion of the independence of the judiciary in the European political tradition. For this reason, the judiciary should, at least theoretically, be immune from pressure group activity, and probably is. However, pressure group activity might be relevant in two cases. First, court judgements are passed in a certain politico-social context, and hence are influenced, even unconsciously, by the climate of public opinion at the time. Thus public opinion can, and does, have an impact on court judgements. Secondly, some judgements can, of their very nature, interest certain groups because they can limit their activity or radically change relations between organizations operating in the same field of interest. At all events, the judiciary is not a significant target for pressure group activity in Western Europe, as it is in the USA. That the politicians use the judiciary to resolve certain political problems is not in doubt; however, the judiciary is not an institution that normally interests group activity in Western Europe.

Interest intermediation

Pressure group analysis was linked for many years to the group approach to politics; to the idea first mooted at the beginning of the century by Bentley (1908), and relaunched 40 years later by Truman (1951), that groups are the central element in analysis of political life. Bentley is best remembered today for his contention that: 'the great task in any form of social life is the analysis of groups. It is much more than a classification as the term is ordinarily used. When groups are adequately stated, everything is stated. When I say everything I mean everything' (pp. 208–9). Truman's objectives were more modest: 'examining interest groups and their role in the formal institutions of government to provide an adequate basis for evaluating their significance in the American political process' (p. 505).

At all events, intentional or not, the claim of group theory to provide the key to understanding political life has meant that its failure to furnish a global explanation of politics undermined not only the credibility of group theory as an analytical framework, but also the significance of groups themselves in the eyes of political scientists. Despite this, groups did not disappear from the political scene: and it is no surprise that they reappeared in the concerns of political scientists in a new guise. The growth of sectional groups with substantial economic and social power, like the trade unions and TNCs, that forced the state to share some of its exclusive powers with them, gave rise to a literature which stressed the emergence of a corporate or corporatist society in the West, and in Western Europe in particular. In short there is, some argue, a privileged relation between the state and certain groups – usually employers' associations and trade unions – that has replaced, to some extent, the relation between the citizen and parliament as the basis of the Western political system. It is in this perspective that we will discuss the two basic modes of interest intermediation: the pluralist and the corporatist.

The pluralist mode

Despite the affinity of assumptions between the principal exponents of pluralist theory, it is not easy to reduce their propositions to a coherent and comprehensive paradigm. Simplifying, Schmitter (1974) has defined pluralism as:

> a system of interest representation in which the constituent units are organized into an unspecified number of multiple, voluntary, competitive, non-hierarchically ordered and self-determined (as to type or scope of interest) categories which are not specifically licensed, recognized, subsidized, created or otherwise controlled

in leadership selection or interest articulation by the state and which do not exercise a monopoly of representational activity within their respective categories. (p. 96)

The basic elements are, thus, the existence of a large number of groups in which the leadership is responsive to the opinions and claims of its membership: namely, groups that compete with one another for the allocation of scarce resources. The paradigm attributes a minimal, largely passive, role to the government – pluralists shy away from using the word 'state' – in authoritatively allocating scarce resources: its decisions merely reflect the balance of forces between groups in civil society at a given time. In Bentley's phrase: 'the balance of groups *is* the existing state of society' (pp. 258–9). Thus if groups continue to press their claims, even in institutionalized form, on the government, the latter will always remain independent of, and opposed to, too close a relationship with the groups.

To clarify the implications of the pluralist mode it is helpful to summarize the principal assumptions numerically: (1) civil society is characterized by a plurality of autonomous groups, that is it is an 'associational' rather than an 'institutionalized' civil society; (2) both material and ideological interests are, or can easily be, organized in groups, that is there are no special obstacles; (3) the majority of group members are members of more than one group, and 'multiple membership' moderates commitment to a single interest at the expense of the others; (4) there is competition among groups to influence the government; (5) group competition occurs within a basic consensus about the 'rules of the game', namely through bargaining arbitrated by public opinion, with the renunciation of political violence; (6) the overwhelming majority of groups, including the most important ones, accept the legitimacy of the political process and its outcomes; and finally, (7) the government is not identified with any particular interest, but acts as a neutral and independent arbiter or referee between the interests, and takes into account the groups' representations *and* the 'national interest'. The consequence of these assumptions is a situation, if not of a perfect political market, at least of a free and loyal one: the competition between groups prevents the domination of one group and preserves the balance between groups (or interests).

Outlined in this way, it is not surprising that the pluralist mode has been vigorously criticized, both factually and methodologically, as being rather simplistic. There are three arguments as regards the factual situation. Firstly, critics of the mode accuse it of exaggerating the equality between groups. When it is pointed out that some groups are more powerful than others, and that this reduces the notion of competition and so of natural balance between groups, the pluralists have been obliged to reply that the inequalities are nevertheless non-cumulative. In other words, pluralists recognize the inequality of political resources, but argue that advantages do not accrue exclusively to one group. Pluralists deny, in fact, that any one group can enjoy a monopoly of political resources in a liberal democratic political system. They maintain that all groups possess certain resources (money, status, information, technical expertise, sanctions, votes) that can influence the political process in their favour, if effectively used. At the end of the day, pluralists are prepared to recognize power differences between groups, but claim that they are contingent, that is ever changing and non-permanent.

It is generally recognized today that organized groups are very unequal between themselves: some enjoy lots of resources, others have virtually none. It is also recognized that these inequalities can be structurally based. For instance, Lindblom (1977), a leading pluralist, now claims that in the civil society of industrialized countries there are potentially only a limited number of groups which enjoy a privileged position in relation to government; and one in particular, business, enjoys a unique position essentially because of its structural situation in the economy. The decisions which businessmen take about employment and investment critically shape economic performance and, thus, strongly influence the government's electoral fortunes. This means, according to Lindblom, that business, unlike other groups, has two means of influencing the government: one directly through interest groups; the other indirectly through its structural situation in the economy.[5] Finer (1973) also defended a similar thesis, but less convincingly, with regard to trade unions, which he claimed had become 'the dominant veto-group' in Britain in the 1970s, thanks to their power of social disruption: strikes or the threat of them. However, the experience of the 1980s demonstrated the fragility of Finer's argument in a market economy.

Secondly, critics argue that pluralists underestimate the difficulties of group organization. Because civil society, defined as 'associational', is formed, in the pluralists' view, of latent groups, the fact that a potential group does not organize, or remains politically inactive, means that the group is happy with the status quo. Since all groups are free to organize, the fact that a latent group is not organized can only have this meaning because otherwise it would have become politically organized. However, the problem is more complex. The basic pluralist assumption is the liberal adage: 'everybody is the best judge of his own interests'. But this is in manifest contradiction with the social and political facts, at least in Europe: political obstacles, both formal and informal, including discriminatory legislation and police harassment, have been used in the past, and still are today in certain circumstances, to prevent certain groups from organizing politically, such as by holding meetings and acting as a group. In other words, if the inactivity of a latent group can be an expression of its satisfaction with the status quo, it can also be an indication of its lack of power: any attempt to try and change the system is pointless because the system has nothing to offer it. How else can we explain the tardiness of women, gays and other minority or discriminated groups in organizing themselves? In the same way, it is not difficult to imagine that there are other groups today in a similar position which have not yet overcome their structural weakness, as much ideological as material, to recognize themselves as a group and to start to organize. This does not mean that, despite the enormous work accomplished by women and gays to organize themselves, they, as groups, are today as powerful as more conventional groups. At all events, for pluralists the organization of civil society is considered a fact of life which it is not proper – or, indeed, legitimate – to change.

Thirdly, the pluralists' vision of the state as a neutral or passive mediator of competing interests has also been criticized for its lack of a developed conception of the 'state', as though they considered any superior normative structure as completely superfluous. However, pluralists were obliged to abandon the notion of government – their preferred word – as a passive arbiter because they realized that it implies that governments can have no policy mind of their own, which is, of course, an absurdity. For this reason, pluralists have preferred to embrace the idea that the government is a group actor (or an ensemble of group actors: politicians, civil servants, military) like other groups in the policy process, and whose interests are defined in terms of reproduction: their own re-election in the case of politicians; perpetuation of their power and resources in the case of civil servants; perpetuation of their prestige and resources in the case of the military. If this explains the tendency of the state to favour the status quo, it does not really explain a more significant problem, that is why groups, including the most powerful, bother to intervene with the state at all. The fact that they do is proof that the state has a status and a power which is qualitatively different from that of other groups. Finally, it is only in so far as the state is conceived as playing an active role in composing opposing interests that the pluralist mode can be considered a theory of interest intermediation at all. Otherwise, it is more properly only a bargaining theory between autonomous, usually competing, groups.

The pluralist mode has clear methodological implications (see the introduction to the book) which go beyond mere group analysis. Here, it is enough to mention that aspect of the critique of pluralism that is relevant for group activity: an aspect which explains some of the empirical incongruities. Focusing the analysis of the political system on groups as the determining element of its functioning means, in fact, analysing the system in terms of process, and specifically of the policy-making process. It means, moreover, examining 'how' groups influence the process rather than 'why'. The analysis concentrates on who participates in a decision and *not* what difference the participation makes to the outcome. In other words, the discussion concentrates on one aspect of power and not necessarily the most important. Pluralists analyse 'issues', activities and decisions which make up the first face of power, neglecting 'agenda setting' (non-decisions) which forms the second face of power, that is the structural aspect of power that enables a group to prevent a policy option from appearing on the political agenda and so being considered

(Bachrach and Baratz, 1962; 1963). Finally, according to Lukes (1974), there is a third face of power, the cultural aspect, that of ideological hegemony. In this case, if the dominant ideological climate legitimizes a particular group's interests as the 'national or public interest', then the group's interests are likely to be served regardless of any representations it makes to government. Thus the capacity of a group to control the ideological climate is a relevant aspect that pluralists do not usually take into due account. In this regard, we only need to think of the opposite situation, namely the negative consequences, in terms of trade union power, of the change in the ideological climate in Western Europe in the 1980s resulting from the 1970s economic crises and their interpretation by the media. They furnish a clue to the limits of trade union power in industrial societies.

It is difficult to establish which of the three faces of power is the most prominent. However, the pluralists are almost exclusively interested in the first which is also the most visible. This does not mean that their analyses are false; only that they tend to be limited and partial. That the pluralist paradigm has a certain verisimilitude in explaining group activity can be inferred from its dissemination as democratic theory. It is significant that the neo-Marxist Miliband (1969) should have felt obliged to observe that:

> pluralist theory could not have gained that degree of ascendancy which it enjoys in advanced capitalist societies if it had not at least been based on one plainly accurate observation about them, namely that they permit and even encourage a multitude of groups and associations to organize openly and freely to compete with each other for the advancement of such purposes as their members may wish. (p. 146)

What he contested is not the fact of competition in itself, but 'its claim (very often its implicit assumption) that the major organized "interests" in these societies, and notably capital and labour, compete on more or less equal terms, and that none of them is therefore able to achieve a decisive and permanent advantage in the process of competition' (p. 146).

Finally, every paradigm has its own normative assumptions, that is to say its vision of the world as it ought to be and not necessarily is. Pluralism is no exception. A part of its fascination as a model of analysis of groups and their role in the political process derives, in fact, from this ideological aspect. For instance, it furnished a moral justification to the West during the Cold War: the vision of an open, plural and consensual political system to oppose to another ('actual socialism') presented as closed, monolithic and repressive.

The corporatist mode

In an attempt to overcome the limits of the pluralist mode – its 'descriptive inadequacy' of transformations in the world of interests – a new paradigm was formulated in the 1970s, that claimed to be closer to the facts: neo-corporatism. It recognized the existence of coordinated relations between certain groups and the state where pluralism postulated competition. The origin of corporatism as a modern social theory was Leo XIII's celebrated encyclical of 1891, *Rerum novarum*, in which the pope envisaged a form of 'bargained corporatism' between employers' and workers' organizations in place of class conflict. However, the adoption of a state-controlled and totalitarian corporatism by Mussolini as the social basis of the fascist state was responsible for the elimination of the term from the political vocabulary in post-war Europe, despite the English Fabians' and the German social democrats' interest in the concept in a democratic and progressive form in the 1920s.

The concept was reintroduced into post-war political science in a modified form as a mode of interest intermediation by Schmitter (1974), who defined it as:

> a system of representation in which the constituent elements are organized into a limited number of singular, compulsory, non-competitive hierarchically ordered and functionally differentiated categories, recognized or licensed (if not created) by the state and granted a deliberate representation monopoly within their respective categories in exchange for observing certain controls on the selection of leaders and articulation of demands and supports. (pp. 93–4)

The points of divergence with the pluralist mode are: (1) a limited number of groups represent the major interests, which can be present in any field, but are usually in the economic field, and in particular are the big interest groups representing capital and labour; (2) interest groups are hierarchically structured, which means that they can negotiate in the name of their members because they can ensure the membership's respect of the agreement negotiated; (3) there are close links between these groups and the state, founded on a fundamental agreement on the way the political and economic systems should operate, and which is mutually reinforcing; (4) the state is conceived as having an active, if not clearly specified, role in the mediation of interests; (5) it promotes coordination between groups and the state, while pluralism fosters competition. In other words, it is a mode of interest intermediation in which structural elements – rigidity, order, inequality of access and hierarchy – are stressed in relation to the pluralist mode, in which the opposite characteristics have priority – spontaneity, competition, equality of access and democracy (table 6.1).

Table 6.1 Properties distinguishing pure pluralist and pure corporatist modes of intermediation

	Pluralist	Corporatist
Representation (input)		
Resources:		
in relation to members	Multiple units Overlapping claims Autonomous interaction Voluntary adherence	Monopolistic units Differentiated domains Hierarchical coordination Involuntary contribution
in relation to interlocutors	Mutual tolerance Opportunistic access Consultative access Shifting alliances (log-rolling)	Explicit recognition Structured incorporation Negotiative role Stable compromises (package dealing)
Control (output)		
Role of organization:		
in relation to members	Persuasive conviction Institutional (or leader) prestige Discriminative treatment Selective goods	Interest indoctrination Organizational authority Coercive sanctions Monopolistic goods
in relation to interlocutors	Provision of information Non-responsibility for decisions Autonomous monitoring Mobilization of pressure (protest or disruption)	Organization of compliance Co-responsibility for decisions Devolved implementation Withdrawal from concentration (secession)

Source: Schmitter, 1983b, p. 900

If it is relatively easy to outline the sense of the corporatist mode – that is the need to take account of organic relations between certain interests and the state – it is less easy to be clear in paradigmatic terms, for the simple reason that there is no agreement on the general nature of the phenomenon. Indeed, there are, as with pluralism, a variety of types of corporatism. For some (Winkler, 1976) it is a new economic system (distinct from both capitalism and socialism); for others (Jessop, 1978; Lehmbruch, 1984) it is a new form of capitalist society, different from the parliamentary form, in which corporatist negotiation between big groups and the state replaces party and parliamentary policy-making; for the majority (including Schmitter) it is a mode of interest intermediation. But, as a mode of interest intermediation, it is necessary to distinguish state or authoritarian corporatism from societal or liberal corporatism. The former is theoretically that practised by the European fascist regimes, in which the corporations, according to Schmitter (1974), (p. 102), 'were created by and kept as auxiliary and dependent organizations of the state', that is to say they were managed in a repressive manner. Societal corporatism, to which Schmitter (1983b) gave the name of 'neo-corporatism' to distinguish it from state corporatism, is characterized, as noted above, by the existence of singular, non-competitive, hierarchically ordered, representative organizations which are autonomous in their origins – that is founded in civil society and consensually ruled – and which have developed a symbiotic relationship with the state, in part willed by the groups themselves and in part by the state, to coordinate policy above all in the economic field.

However, there are also divergences regarding the distinctive features of corporatism. Thus, for instance, Grant (1986) writes of 'a process of interest intermediation which involves the negotiation of policy between state agencies and interest groups arising from the division of labour in society, where the policy agreements are implemented through the collaboration of interest organizations and their willingness and ability to secure the compliance of their members' (pp. 3–4). Nevertheless, he insists on the elements of 'negotiation' and 'implementation' as essential aspects of neo-corporatism, adding that, as far as he is concerned, neither the arbitrary imposition of state policies through interest organizations without prior negotiation, nor the negotiation of understandings with no obligation on the part of the interest organizations to secure the compliance of their members, constitutes corporatist arrangements. Or again, for Offe (1981), on the other hand, it is the attribution of 'public status' to organized interest groups that is the hallmark of neo-corporatism. Finally, Schmitter's (1983a) position is different again: initially, he pointed to the monopoly of representation in a sector as the discriminating feature in relation to pluralism; later, he added certain functions undertaken by 'incorporated' groups in policy formulation and implementation.

In this situation, it is not surprising that most political scientists prefer to speak of 'corporatist arrangements' rather than neo-corporatism as a system – the more so, in fact, because there is no agreement as to which countries are neo-corporatist. Some suggest the Scandinavian countries and Austria, Holland and Switzerland as fully neo-corporatist, while others have identified 'neo-corporatist arrangements' in West Germany, Belgium, France and even Britain. Yet others, instead, deny their existence in Britain on the grounds of the persistence of individualist values in civil society and the long-standing liberal tradition. In addition, the arrangements can vary by economic sector and change over time. Thus in France, for instance, the labour sector was considered to be more pluralist than the business sector and the agricultural sector was the most corporatist of all. Again, while France became more corporatist in the 1980s, West Germany became less so. Indeed, most political scientists accept Almond's (1983) invitation to conceive of pluralism and corporatism as two poles of a continuum of interest intermediation rather than as an absolute classification. One schema contains the following fivefold range of possibilities: strong pluralism, structured pluralism, weak corporatism, moderate corporatism and strong corporatism (Zeigler, 1988). This study regards Britain as a case of structured pluralism, France and Italy as cases of weak corporatism and Germany as a case of moderate corporatism (it places the USA at the pluralist pole and Austria, Switzerland and Japan at the corporatist pole). We must bear in mind, however, that the real situation in any country is likely to be very diverse, with elements of both pluralist and neo-corporatist representation and intermediation present.

Corporatist arrangements are concentrated, for all practical purposes, in the economic and industrial policy fields – wages or incomes policies, international trade balance, deficits and so on – and hence concern above all interest (as opposed to pressure) groups. Indeed, they are usually limited to the peak associations representing business, workers and farmers. The objective, as noted, is to coordinate public policy that results from negotiation between the government and these few powerful groups with whom the government chooses, or feels obliged, to deal. The advantages from the government's point of view are that it is dealing with groups which can deliver the compliance of its members to any agreements reached. Hence the groups have an important role to play in implementation. In addition, by removing policy-making from the partisan sphere of parties and parliament and transferring it to specialists in the executive and public administration, it can hope to insulate policy from external pressures, and so ensure coherence and continuity. The advantages for the groups are not only a voice in policy and implementation – business and unions can extract concessions from government – but also the conferring of public status both on themselves and on the agreements they reach. As regards the latter, this means that they are usually binding in law on all the parties.

The main criticism of corporatist arrangements is their essentially oligarchic and anti-democratic nature. They are agreements negotiated, more or less unilaterally, by a handful of individuals in the interests of a small number of very powerful groups, so that they lack democratic legitimacy. Indeed, neo-corporatism is viewed as positively harmful by the neo-liberal right because it favours excessive state intervention and too great a reliance on the state. Finally, we may note that the enthusiasm of political scientists in the 1970s for the development of corporatist policy-making as an essential element reconciling economic prosperity with Keynesian welfarism has waned under the pressure of the 1980s recessions. It was the economic recession of 1980–1, as much as the Thatcher government's trade union legislation, that destroyed centralized wage bargaining in Britain, as the highly skilled labour in the prosperous industries and services took what they could get and Mrs Thatcher could afford to ignore the trade unions. Finally, even in those countries where corporatist arrangements have prospered, they have always been liable to denunciation by the excluded groups, as the violent protests of the ecology movements against their respective governments' industrial, energy and environmental policies in Germany and France show.

A partial synthesis

At the close of this discussion, it is useful to consider the two paradigms in terms of a schema of intermediation along the same political dimension – coercion–consensus – used to differentiate party systems. This permits the outlining of a type of politics for each mode (figure 6.2). The first mode – state corporatism – does not pose problems: in this case groups (corporations) are created and controlled by the state. However, we can ask whether this type can really exist as a mode of interest intermediation, in the sense that by definition the corporations are deprived of all autonomy. In consequence they have no *raison d'être*, as historical experience confirms: for instance, in fascist Italy where the corporations were only a façade without political substance. Thus the fact that the fascist regime defined itself as 'corporatist' had no consequence on political practice which was totalitarian centralism; the corporations appeared as simple 'ideological emblems' that exercised a certain fascination on some sectors of Catholic and international public opinion.

A number of problems are posed, nevertheless, by the other two modes: pluralism and corporatism. As we have seen, they are the modes of intermediation practised in Western democracies. Crouch (1986) has usefully identified the key to them in two different group strategies. The pluralist strategy is necessarily a zero-sum game because in every conflict what one group wins in its sector, its rival group loses. There are always winners and losers. Some interest groups always win, others always lose, and yet others win some battles and lose others: it is the group's structural situation which is decisive. Groups accept this situation – always attempting to improve their position by appealing to parties, parliament or the public administration – either because they find it advantageous, that is they always win because they are powerful; or because they are forced to suffer it, that is they lose because they are powerless to change the situation. In this situation, the only thing that an interest group can

CLOSED SYSTEM	OPEN SYSTEM	
State corporatism *no game*	Neocorporatism *positive-sum game*	Pluralism *zero-sum game*
Coercion		*Consensus*
Authoritarian or totalitarian politics	Corporative politics	Competitive politics

Figure 6.2 Schema of modes of interest intermediation

do in order not always to lose is to develop conflict-reducing mechanisms, such as forms of consultation. In this perspective, a group's success then depends principally on its organizational capacity, its mobilization of resources and the support it succeeds in securing. A group's potential electoral strength is an additional positive factor.

The corporatist strategy is a positive-sum game which, by definition, involves material interests only; 'ideological' interests are, by nature, dialectical – you are either right or you are wrong – and usually non-negotiable, and hence are necessarily excluded. In addition, it is a high-risk strategy (the groups can get their sums wrong over the costs – one group can gain too much and the other lose too much) and so can only be practised in certain conditions, usually in special situations: wartime or military defeat or the loss of hegemony by a traditionally dominant group. Dominant groups in certain sectors are obliged, in such circumstances, to practise this strategy because the zero-sum game is likely to prove too costly. The groups in the sector need direct relations between themselves to avoid miscalculations and mutual mistrust in order to secure an effective interest in cooperation; these are all elements that cannot be improvised. The interests involved in the sector must, moreover, be considered very important by the state – economy, education, health – because, given the potential risks, the groups seek the state's endorsement to give the agreements reached an official character; the state, for its part, is prepared to concede the relevant powers of public regulation for the agreement's implementation. The groups conserve their autonomy because they can always withdraw from the negotiation and denounce the agreement. This is a fundamental aspect which differentiates this mode of interest intermediation from state corporatism and makes it potentially unstable. But, without the element of potential conflict, this mode would lose its *raison d'être*.

What is, then, the current situation in Western Europe? In practice, the differences between the policy of 'permanent consultation' typical of structural pluralism and that of weak corporatism dissolve. Moreover, the conflict level in the corporatist modes is similar to that in the pluralist since potential conflict is a necessary condition of the former.

At all events, if we bear in mind that the corporatist mode is defined by a consolidated practice of positive-sum strategy, two indications are helpful. Firstly, the 'dual-politics thesis' advanced by Cawson (1986) and Saunders (1986) suggests that there is a tendency for political activity concerning issues of production to become focused on central state agencies, to foster corporatist forms of interest intermediation, and to be informed principally by values which emphasize the rights of private property and the importance of sustaining private sector competitivity. Conversely, there is a tendency for questions of consumption to be relegated to provincial or local state agencies where a plurality of interests become involved in political competition to achieve their objectives and where the participants' actions are often informed by values stressing the rights of citizenship and the importance of meeting different social needs. Based on the differences between types of group – interest (sectional) and pressure (promotional), discussed above – this thesis is a useful starting point for distinguishing the various modes of interest intermediation in West European political systems which are essentially mixed. Secondly, as noted, states can be defined in terms of the various proportions of pluralism and corporatism, in accordance with the extension and intensity of pluralist and corporatist arrangements respectively. In this assessment, Germany, France and Italy can be considered more corporatist; Britain, more pluralist (figure 6.2). Of course, this evaluation leaves out of account, the practice in individual sectors or at different territorial sublevels, which can vary very widely.

Interest groups and pressure groups

The exposition undertaken so far requires, to be complete, discussion of the principal interest and pressure groups active in West European states and an assessment, however summary, of their power.

Business associations

The organization of capital is very complex, as is its representation as an interest. It is organized by level – individual company, trade association and national or 'peak' organization – and by sector, that is industry, finance, retailing, services. Thus there are the giant TNCs, like ICI in Britain, IG Farben in Germany, Thompson-CSF in France and Fiat in Italy, which are large enough and powerful enough in terms of their impact on the national economy as a whole to deal directly with the government. One example suffices: Fiat's decision to manufacture the 600 car in 1953 was responsible for a volume of investment equal to 20 per cent of all Italian investments at the time; so a logical consequence was the motorway construction programme (to allow the cars to circulate) which absorbed 10 per cent of Italian public spending for a decade. So it was no wonder that Scalfari (1969) exclaimed some years later: 'Who claims that Italy is not a planned economy? Only it is planning contracted out. It is not done by the ministry of the budget, but by Fiat' (p. 61).

At the second level are the trade associations, like the Society of Motor Manufacturers in Britain, the Verein der Deutschen Elsen und Stahl Produtzen in Germany, the Chambre Syndicale de la Sidérurgie Française and the Fédération Nationale du Bâtiment in France, and the Federazione Sindacale dell'Industria Meccanica in Italy, which are often represented on ministerial consultative committees. Then there are the various territorial organizations – local chambers of commerce, and regional associations like the Assolombarda in Italy – which have different roles and powers in the various countries. Finally, at the apex, there are the so-called 'peak' associations (or *Spitzenverbände*): the Confederation of British Industry (CBI), the Bundesverbande der Deutschen Industrie (BDI), the Conseil National du Patronat Français (CNPF), and the Confindustria. These organizations represent, often through trade associations, as in France, about 70 per cent of their countries' firms. But they have been unable so far to assemble either all the leading manufacturing companies – GEC and Rolls-Royce, for instance, have remained outside the CBI in Britain – or all the important trade sectors. The CBI has never been able to represent the City (finance) which has never wished to organize itself formally,[6] preferring to rely on the governor of the Bank of England to defend its interests with government. Another limitation of the peak associations is their tendency to represent big capital, leaving small business concerns, above all in France and Italy, to organize their own association (Confédération Nationale des Petites et Moyennes Entreprises (PME), Petites et Moyennes Industries (PMI) and Confederazione Nazionale della Piccola Industria (CONFAPI). Only in Germany is the tension between big and small firms not a source of organizational division.

It is generally recognized today that business enjoys numerous advantages in its relation to the political system. Firstly, capital plays a key role in the economy. Despite public intervention in the economy, private enterprise remains the main source of economic activity and, hence, investment decisions rest in its hands. However, we must keep in mind the role that private capital plays in determining economic prosperity to realize capital's potential power and the politicians' susceptibility to it. Secondly, access to government is facilitated by the recruitment of the upper echelons of businessmen, politicians and civil servants from the same social classes and so by their tendency to share a similar background. This is reinforced by the similar educational and cultural formation of the various elites: Oxbridge, *grandes écoles*, Bocconi. In addition, there is considerable movement between the higher echelons of the civil service and business (of the French *pantouflage* kind). Thirdly, the dominant culture of Western Europe is particularly favourable to capital: in Aron's words: 'it goes without saying that in a regime founded on the private property of the means of production, the measures taken by legislators and ministers will never be fundamentally opposed to the interests of property.' Liberal culture legitimizes private capital for which, according to a popular saying, 'money talks'. It is obvious in this situation that business groups support and fund conservative and liberal parties – the parties that defend the social order that secures their privileges. Of course, these groups never lack resources to defend their interests.

In view of the favourable circumstances, there are numerous examples of business's success in imposing its interests, or frustrating those of its opponents. For instance, the British Labour government of 1974–9 failed to implement the Bullock Report on industrial democracy, eased price controls and reduced corporation tax, all at the CBI's behest; in West Germany, business secured the defeat and substantial weakening of the anti-*Kartel* law in the 1950s; in France, the Mauroy government was obliged to reverse its economic policy in 1983 when faced with lack of business confidence; in Italy, the fall of the first centre-left government and the abandonment of plans for economic reform in 1964 were provoked by a similar crisis in business confidence. On the other side, it is possible to find examples, much less numerous, where the state has prevailed over business opposition. Thus the CBI and Aims of Industry did not succeed in preventing the renationalization of the British steel industry by the Wilson government in 1966; nor were their Italian counterparts, despite an investment strike announced by Confindustria, any more successful in stopping the nationalization of the electrical supply industry by the Fanfani government in 1962; nor, finally, was the CNPF able to impede the nationalization of certain big French industrial and finance corporations in 1981–2. This shows that the power of business, although substantial, is not absolute. On the other hand, these organizations had no difficulty in persuading subsequent right-wing governments to denationalize many of the companies, as in France 1986–8.

A notable weakness of business lies, in fact, in the division between its components: big business and small, industrial and finance capital. This division is particularly important in Britain where industrial interests have always been sacrificed on the altar of finance capital, represented by the City: for instance, the priority accorded to the defence of sterling. In Germany, France and Italy, the interpenetration of the two types of capital is much more developed, which reduces significantly the tension between the two. However, if there are such tensions and conflicts – and there are – we must stress that they are less severe than those of other interests. Capital is not an ideological monolith which speaks with one voice; it is organized into a variety of interest groups, but the internal divisions and conflicts have never prevented a fundamental ideological consensus around the defence of the social order.

In conclusion, it is difficult to assess accurately the real power of business because it usually acts indirectly. Business is considered the most powerful interest in advanced industrial society. Aron, for instance, believes that this assessment is so obvious as to be devoid of interest. Perhaps it should be, but since it still is not, we can extend Marsh and Locksley's (1983) conclusion for Britain to Western Europe as a whole: 'Capital is not the first among equals: its power is qualitatively as well as quantitatively different' (p. 50).

Trade unions

One of the post-war myths in Western Europe was the power of the unions, regarded by some as the dominant force (Finer, 1973). But the level of unionization of the workforce varied in the 1980s between 20 per cent and 50 per cent (table 6.2). These figures are to be compared with 17 per cent in the USA and over 80 per cent in Sweden. At all events, they are much lower percentages that those of the firms organized by the business associations. Further, there has been a downward trend in unionization in the 1980s, after a rise in the 1960s and 1970s due to the expansion of the public white-collar sectors.

The structure of the labour movement is complex and varies from state to state. There are category unions for all the important groups of workers – metal workers, textile workers, railwaymen, miners – but in Italy there are also significant territorial organizations (Camera del Lavoro, Unione Sindacale) while in Britain various unions (craft and general) endeavour to organize and recruit the same workers: these are factors which introduce elements of conflict and tension at the grass roots. Nevertheless, trade unions are usually organized in the workplace – shop stewards, *delegati* – through category unions in peak organizations.

In Britain about 90 per cent of the unions are affiliated to the Trades Union Congress (TUC), the umbrella organization of the labour movement, which is dominated by a number of big category unions: those of the transport and general workers (T&GW), engineers (AUEW) and municipal workers (GMB), to which must be added the three white-collar unions for local government officers (NALGO), public employees (NUPE) and technicians (MSF). The TUC benefits from the lack of a rival organization and privileged relations with the Labour Party, but is weakened by the autonomy and decentralized structure of member unions which deprive it of both authority and adequate financial resources, and so undermine its position in negotiations with employers' associations and the government – the latter because it is not in a position to ensure that its members honour any eventual agreement. In

Table 6.2 Unionization of workforce (per cent of active population)

	1950	1960	1970	1980	1990	Public sector 1980	Private sector 1980
Britain	44	44	47	54	43	75	40
France	32	22	23	22	17	35	16
Germany	33	33	32	41	31	58	29
Italy	34	32	41	50	45	42	35

Sources: Lane, McKay and Newton, 1991, pp. 25–6 and Labour Research Department *Fact Sheet* 53.31, 1991, for annual rates; Rose, 1985[a], p. 40 for public and private sectors

Germany, there are three peak organizations: the Deutscher Gewerkschaftsbund (DGB), Deutsche Angestelltengewerkschaft (DAG) (employees) and Deutsche Beamtenbund (DBB) (civil servants), among which the first is clearly dominant, and to which sixteen unions that organize 80 per cent of union members are affiliated. The most powerful among the category unions is the giant IG Metall (metal workers) which furnishes the DGB with more than a third of its membership. The other two peak associations are small and do not count in front of the DGB. The latter is defined as non-political, but it has close ties, above all of personnel, with the SPD and a control over its own members that the TUC would envy, although it is not immune to rifts from individual unions; nonetheless, it is able to negotiate more effective agreements than its British counterpart. This constitutes one of the bases of the corporatist tendencies noted in Germany.

In France and Italy there are not only four peak organizations, but they are ideologically divided: in France, Confédération Générale du Travail (CGT, communist, 40 per cent of union membership), Confédération Française Démocratique du Travail (CFDT, socialist, 30 per cent membership), Force Ouvrière (FO, moderate, 24 per cent membership) and Confédération Française des Travailleurs Chrétiens (CFTC, Catholic, 6 per cent membership); and in Italy, Confederazione Generale Italiana del Lavoro (CGIL, communist-socialist, 45 per cent of union membership), Confederazione Italiana dei Sindacati Liberi (CISL, Catholic, 35 per cent membership), Unione Italiana del Lavoro (UIL, social democrat and republican, 12 per cent membership) and Confederazione Italiana dei Sindacati Nazionali dei Lavoratori (CIS-NAL, neo-fascist, 5 per cent membership). Each peak organization has its category unions and this further weakens the workers. The consciousness of this weakness led, at least in Italy, to a policy of trade union unity in the 1970s, which developed furthest in the engineering sector with the creation of a metal workers' federation (FLM) on the basis of equal representation between the three peak confederations (CGIL, CISL and UIL). However, union unity suffered tensions in the 1980s recession, resulting in a conflict opposing the CGIL to the CISL and UIL over the indexing of wages (*scala mobile*) in 1984: the CGIL's and PCI's opposition was defeated in the 1985 referendum. In these circumstances, it is no surprise that attempts at neo-corporatist arrangements in Italy have not gone beyond periodic consultations and wage restraint.

One of the problems in assessing the power of the trade unions is that they are multifunctional organizations which pursue their members' interests in numerous fields which go from the defence of jobs and wages – 'collective bargaining', except in France – to supplying a whole range of services. Political relations, moreover, are never static and change over time. From this viewpoint, two aspects are particularly relevant in assessment of union power at any given moment: (1) the economic situation, itself changeable; and (2) the government's political orientation, which can also change. In the first case, the category unions have more power in a situation of full employment and economic growth than in one of economic recession and high unemployment. The examples are many: from the French May 1968 to the Italian Hot Autumn of 1969 (favourable situation for the unions) to the German engineering workers' defeat in 1964 and 1982 and the British miners' defeat in 1984–5 (unfavourable situation). In the second case, it is natural that the British Labour and German Social Democrat Parties should consider the unions' demands more favourably than the right-wing parties do, since they claim to be the representatives of their respective labour movements. However, if left-wing parties have often implemented policies shared by the unions, this has not prevented them from pursuing policies hostile to them as well, as the experiences of Callaghan's Labour government in the 'winter of discontent' of 1979 and Mitterrand's Socialist governments and the radical change of 1983–4 testify.

The power of the unions as interest groups results more prosaically from two factors. The first is their involvement in a whole series of commissions and technical committees (health, conditions of work, professional training), for instance the Manpower Services Commission, the Health and Safety Committee and the National Economic Development Council (NEDC) (1962–91) in Britain. The summit meetings between ministers, employers and union leaders to discuss national economic policy are the most visible form of this type of consultation. Examples are the tripartite policy to define the 'social contract' pursued by the British Labour government between 1974 and 1979; and that institutionalized (neo-corporative) *konzierte Aktion* by the German SPD between 1967 and 1977. The limitations of this factor, in terms of power, were revealed by the ease with which the subsequent conservative governments (Thatcher in Britain after 1979 and Kohl in Germany after 1982) succeeded in dismantling this form of cooperation. At all events, it is a strategy to which neither the French nor the Italian governments committed themselves.

The second factor is the unions' fundamental weapon, the basis of their power: the strike or the threat of strike action. Finer (1973) claims that the possibility of creating socio-economic disruption by strike action gives them more potential power than any other group in capitalist societies. However, the strike is a delicate weapon. Firstly, it is essentially defensive. Secondly, its success depends in large part on the particular circumstances in which it is used: the economic conjuncture, the level of worker solidarity, socio-political climate and so on. Thirdly, it depends on the unions' financial resources: for this reason French and Italian unions, which are relatively poor, prefer strikes of limited duration (from 2 to 24 hours). Finally, the legal restrictions on striking are much greater than is generally recognized: only in France and Italy is the right to strike a constitutional right; in Britain the right is not recognized, and only the much weaker 'freedom to strike' exists;[7] and in Germany there are

·d legal restrictions ('political' and sympathy strikes are banned).
ﬨining the power of the unions, we inevitably touch on the weak-
ɔf labour as an organized interest group. These can be summa-
ιus: (1) low membership levels in relation to potential
ﬨ￬ɩpership; (2) interunion divisions (between higher- and lower-paid
workers; between full-time unionized men and part-time non-unionized
women) and the ideologico-political divisions that are much more
important than for capital; (3) financial resources which cannot hope to
compete with those of business; (4) political and ideological climate,
which is usually favourable to business and hostile to labour (confirmed
by polls in Britain and Germany); (5) competition from the new social
movements, for instance the ecological, peace and civil rights movements
which are often in conflict with the unions, further undermining workers'
solidarity.

In conclusion, labour does not have the same weight as business: not
only have the unions not transformed the nature of society in Western
countries, but often they are unable to defend their members' most
immediate interests, such as their purchasing power and their jobs, above
all in the 1980s and 1990s recessions with the return of mass unemployment. In a certain sense, in fact, the power of labour is a function of that
of business and vice versa, and this changes over time. Ball and Millard
have written that:

> When governments are determined and sufficiently cohesive,
> when they appear to have electoral support and when the eco-
> nomic climate is inimical to union strength, the power of the
> unions appears illusory ... if governments are prepared to pay an
> economic price, they can reap political rewards in successful bat-
> tles with trade unions, whether over issues of wages, conditions,
> job security or wider issues of economic strategy. (p. 120)

All this does not mean that labour is without influence; after all it is an
important organized force in advanced industrial countries. It means
only that union successes, which are more incisive in certain fields than
in general, are also more likely in favourable economic conjunctures and
with the support of governments well disposed towards them than in
unfavourable conditions and with hostile governments.

Farmers' organizations

The structure of the farming sector is characterized by a kind of paradox:
on the one hand, the principal national organizations are considered
among the strongest and most efficient interest groups; and, on the
other, it is the sector most dependent on state subsidies. Naturally, this
raises the question: where does the farmers' power come from? The

major national farmers' organizations have a dominant position: the National Farmers' Union (NFU) in Britain and the Deutscher Bauernverband (DBV) in Germany occupy near monopoly positions. The NFU has succeeded in enrolling about 80 per cent of its potential membership and the DBV about 90 per cent; both have a hierarchical structure that favours the dominance of wealthy farmers, despite the federal structure of the DBV and the division of the NFU into separate organizations for Scotland, Wales and Northern Ireland. In consequence, the attempts of other groups, like the smaller part-time farmers in Germany or the country landowners in England, to form their own organizations (the DBLN and CLA respectively) to challenge the supremacy of the DBV and NFU have not been successful and so they remain politically insignificant.

In France and Italy, where there is also a plurality of organizations, one is predominant, respectively the Fédération Nationale des Syndicats et des Exploitants Agricoles (FNSEA) and the Confederazione Nazionale dei Coltivatori Diretti (Coldiretti). The FNSEA attracts about 50 per cent of French farmers and has attempted to incorporate most farming interests to win the support of large and small farmers alike, but this strategy, despite state support, has provoked a series of splits. Thus, in addition to the Mouvement de Défense des Exploitants Familiaux (MODEF), which organizes some 20 per cent of farmers, the Comité de Gueret (1953), the Paysans-Travailleurs in the Fédération Française des Agriculteurs (FFA) (1969), the Groupe Nationale pour la Défense des Exploitants Agricoles (GEA, 1973) and the Mouvement Nationale de l'Agriculture et des Exploitants Ruraux (1975) were created successively. They were all ignored by the French government until 1981 when the socialist government recognized them, giving them access to the policy process for the first time. The Coldiretti, the Catholic small peasant farmers' association, which organizes the overwhelming majority of Italian farmers, dominates the sector in spite of the existence of the lay Confragricoltura (large farmers) and the communist Confederazione Italiana Coltivatori (Confcoltivatori; small farmers).

In Britain and Germany, the farmers' organizations claim to be non-partisan, but although very concerned about maintaining good relations with the government whatever its political complexion, they tend to have closer ties with the right-wing parties: the NFU with the Conservative Party – its members who become MPs are always Conservative, for instance Lord Plumb, former president of the EP and Conservative MEP – and the DBV with the CDU/CSU and, more recently, with the FDP – the German minister of agriculture was always a liberal during the SPD-FDP coalition of 1969–82. In France and Italy, the farmers' organizations are openly partisan: the FNSEA has always had close ties with the right and, above all, with the Gaullists under the Fifth Republic. It was this relationship that Chirac wished to consolidate on his return to power in 1986 by appointing the former president of the FNSEA, François

Guillaume, minister of agriculture. The MODEF, on the other hand, is linked to the PCF, the Paysans-Travailleurs to the PS, while the FFA and GEA have ties with the right. The Coldiretti was, as mentioned, one of the principal and most powerful components of the former DC, in whose lists it elected numerous members as MPs. The Confragricoltura has links with the PLI and the Confcoltivatori with the PCI (now PDS). The latter, in fact, was set up by the PCI in the 1950s to contest the DC's hegemony over the peasantry but without great success.

Since agriculture is in decline and the farming sector has lost a large part of its electoral strength, this is no longer the basis of the farmers' organizations' power. It now comes more from privileged relations with the state, of the kind pluralists have defined as 'colonization'.

The principal farmers' organizations have an 'exclusive' relation with the ministry of agriculture and its various technical committees. The most important meeting is the annual price review between government and farmers' organizations to define agricultural policy. Today, the development of the Common Agricultural Policy (CAP) of the EU means that this annual review now takes place in Brussels. The EU recognizes the Committee of Professional Farmers' Organizations (COPA) on which all the principal national farmers' organizations are represented. However, the national farmers' organizations do not hesitate to press their governments to defend specific national farming interests, especially if agreement cannot be reached in the COPA: for instance, the French government's veto of the GATT negotiations in 1992–3.

Since farmers' organizations lack serious economic sanctions in relation to the national state and the EU, we can ask how corporatist arrangements – that presuppose the existence of contractual power by the group – have developed and, above all, survived in this sector. The answer lies in the non-market conditions created for agriculture in the various countries by their respective governments, of which the CAP was a natural continuation at the European level, namely the post-war decision to support agriculture as a priority sector to avoid the negative consequences of the pre-war agricultural depression and to secure political stability. In other words, the farmers' organizations are not powerful in themselves: it was a political decision taken in a particular conjuncture, including a favourable politico-ideological climate, that led to their being privileged. In consequence, they have received more financial aid than any other economic sector and with fewer financial controls and no loss of autonomy.

However, whatever the explanation, it is clear that the privileges accorded by the state to the principal farmers' organizations to manage directly the various subsidies and aid has given them a decisive power, not only in relation to the other farmers' organizations but also in relation to the individual farmer. In fact, the violence of some groups, particularly in France, when the principal farmers' organizations have decided not to defend particular interests, is proof of the farmers' impotence as an economic interest group. As a declining social group, the principal farmers' organizations have preferred to cooperate with the state in managing the decline in exchange for the distribution of lavish state benefits. This privileged position is under severe strain from the economic recession and, when the break occurs, it will publicly reveal the political weakness of the farmers' organizations.

Professional associations

The various professional activities that constitute the 'middle class' occupations are organized in a series of interest groups. A distinction is generally made between the different professional associations, such as the Law Society, Ordine degli Avvocati, Institution of Civil Engineers, British Medical Association (BMA), Ordre des Médecins, Deutsche Artzeverband, Deutsche Juristenverband, Ordine dei Medici and Federazione Nazionale della Stampa Italiana, and the organizations that assemble certain economic categories, such as the Confédération Générale des Cadres (CGC), Federazione dei Quadri (Federquadri), UDAC, Comité d'Information et Défense and Union Nationale des Artisans et Travailleurs (CID-UNATI). The former are organized like medieval corporations in the sense that they are concerned with entry into the profession (qualifications, training) and professional ethics as well as certain services (pensions, welfare). The state usually accords them official public status to regulate independently the profession and, hence, it creates real areas of privilege for members; moreover, it only intervenes in professional activity if obliged by improper conduct. It is true, for instance, that the British state obliged GPs to work in the National Health Service in 1948, but the deal included giving them a decisive role in its operation. The state in Western European countries is prepared to tolerate privileges by delegating its power in these areas. They are often described as corporative arrangements, but in fact the associations' power is secured by the state itself. Thus the state can oblige the professions to behave in a certain way, as the example of the British doctors illustrates, but it usually prefers not to intervene. It is obvious that such a position is dictated by the predominant cultural orientation, from which the professional associations derive their power.

The second group, on the contrary, is organized along union lines. Many of the 'new middle class' organizations – teachers, lower civil servants – are, in fact, members of trade union peak associations (like the National Union of Teachers in Britain, Fédération de l'Éducation Nationale in France or CGIL and CISL Scuola in Italy); others instead, among which are the French CGC, the German DBB or the Italian Federquadri, which regroup junior managers, public servants and supervisors, prefer to pursue a policy of independence because they believe that the trade unions are too 'workerist' in orientation. For instance, the

Italian Federquadri began to have organizational and political weight only after the 'march of the 40,000' in Turin in October 1980 against the Fiat strike. The most unruly of the organizations of the self-employed has been Poujade's UDCA in France in the 1950s, which organized a series of violent protests culminating in the 1956 election in which it succeeded in electing 50 MPs; and Nicoud's CID-UNATI which was set up as a reaction against the chambers of commerce (accused of neglecting small business) and which followed a similar policy of assaults, burning tax offices, and even political sequestrations in the 1960s and 1970s. This policy, if it was unsuccessful in preventing the decline of the small family business, nevertheless had some successes, for instance the Royer law of 1973, which limited supermarkets, as well as gaining important fiscal concessions. On the other hand, the Italian Confcommercio threatened a campaign of protestation against the Visentini bill of 1984 which subjected the self-employed to a tax regime for the first time, similar to that borne by dependent workers; however, it yielded in the face of the government's firmness. These organizations' influence depends a lot on the government's appreciation of their electoral strength.

The churches

It is no surprise, in view of the importance of religion in European history, that the churches still play an important political role today, even if it is somewhat different from that in the past. In Germany and Italy, the Catholic Church was the sponsor of one of the principal parties (CDU-CSU and DC respectively[8]), while in Britain, the Anglican Church has historically been one of the components of the Conservative Party: in Disraeli's famous remark, 'the Church of England is the Tory Party at prayer.' However, if their role as a political actor has declined in the post-war period – for instance, the direct intervention of the Catholic clergy in electoral campaigns has virtually disappeared since Vatican II – the churches still have interests to defend. It is no longer, in fact, a question of freedom of worship, but rather those of the role of religious instruction in schools – the great question which already divided church and state in the nineteenth century – and the moral organization of the family in the context of divorce and, above all, abortion. Nevertheless, there is a problem in considering the churches, and particularly the Catholic Church, as pressure groups because they do not usually act directly, but rather indirectly through collateral lay groups. The most important are undoubtedly the networks of associations, structures and initiatives (the branches of AC in Germany and Italy) that the Catholic Church promoted in the late nineteenth and early twentieth centuries. More recently, we can mention the Association des Parents de l'École Libre (APEL) in France and the various groups founded to support the

anti-abortion campaign: the Society for the Protection of the Unborn
Child (SPUC) in Britain, Movimento per la Vita in Italy and so on.

To appreciate the significance of the churches as pressure groups, we
must briefly outline their positions. The Catholic Church is the most
powerful: hierarchically organized under the centralized leadership of
the pope and the College of Cardinals in the Vatican (sovereign state
without an army) on the basis of a world-wide organization and a membership divided territorially into dioceses and parishes and ruled respectively by bishops and parish priests. Catholicism is, as mentioned above,
the dominant religion in France and Italy; it is a minority religion in
Britain and now once again in Germany (see table 6.3). The dominant
church in Britain is the Church of England ('the established church')
with an organization not dissimilar to the Catholic Church: an ecclesiastical hierarchy headed by the monarch, the archbishop of Canterbury
and the General Synod. There are national churches in Scotland and
Wales and various other Protestant creeds (Methodists, Baptists,
Congregationalists) as well as the Catholic Church. In Germany, the
Protestant churches are grouped in the Deutsche Evangelische Kirche
which is a confederation of 27 territorially organized *Landeskirche*.

Organization and principles are one thing and real influence something else. The latter is usually judged in terms of church attendance
since church-goers are those who are have the churches' goals most at
heart. Thus, if over 90 per cent of Italians are baptized Catholics, only a
third attend Sunday mass; this figure is to be compared with 20 per cent
in Germany, 10 per cent in France and 15 per cent in Britain. Moreover,
the figures show a notable decline in the post-war period (table 6.4), thus
confirming the 'secularization' of European societies. However, we

Table 6.3 Religious denominations, mid 1970s (per cent)

	Protestants	Catholics	Other religions	No creed	Fragmentation index
Britain	74	14	3	9	0.42
France	2	80	4	14	0.34
Germany	48	46	2	4	0.56
Italy	0	87	0	13	0.23

Source: Lane, McKay and Newton, 1991, p. 21

Table 6.4 Church attendance (per cent)

	1960	1970	1980	1990
Britain	15	13	15	13
France	23	21	12	10
Germany	36	28	21	19
Italy	55	45	36	40

Sources: various

should note two corrections: (1) although the percentages are low, above all in Britain and France, few, if any, other movements or organizations can count on such a large regular following; (2) most church-goers are also members of other organizations (parties, unions, voluntary associations) and thus are not always prepared to support their church on every issue. This obviously affects the churches' attempts to mobilize support at any given moment.

In general, there is little doubt that the churches have, at least theoretically, the numbers to count politically. Further, the most important have a recognized position in various national societies and this confers on some an official position in the state. Thus, for instance, the Church of England, as the established church, has 26 bishops with seats as 'lords spiritual' in the British House of Lords, and other creeds are represented by life peers such as Lord Soper (Methodist) Lord Jakobovits (former chief rabbi); while in the German *Land* of Bavaria, church leaders are appointed to sit in the upper house. Moreover, although Catholic priests are constitutionally prohibited from standing for parliament in Italy, and the election of priests in France is rare (the *chanoine* Kir, *député-maire* of Dijon in the 1950s, was the exception that proves the rule), the episcopal conferences are authoritative bodies and are, therefore, consulted on many issues, and their opinions are accorded serious consideration by government. This influence of the churches on political structures should not lead us to overrate their power. They are influential, or at least the principal ones are, like the Catholic Church in all four countries, the Church of England in Britain and the Evangelical Church in Germany, but they are not always able to impose their views. For instance, internal changes in the Church of England constitutionally require parliamentary consent which can be refused, as was the case in 1984 when the House of Commons rejected the Anglican Church's request for an alteration in the method of appointing bishops.

The churches' power can be assessed by discussing briefly two important issues: education and abortion. The former was one of the principal areas of conflict between church and state in the nineteenth century, the consequence of the development by the state of a secular educational system at the expense of church-controlled schools. In general, the two parties came to some sort of *modus vivendi* before World War II. Nevertheless, religious education has remained an issue even in the post-war period. Thus, in West Germany, Protestant *Land* governments abolished separate Catholic schools in their areas. However, in the 1960s when the Catholic hierarchy attempted to reverse the decision, a fierce controversy broke out and the Catholic leadership suffered a severe defeat because Catholic parents deserted the church. In France, where the Gaullists had negotiated a compromise whereby confessional schools received more funding in return for increased secular control, a major conflict flared up in 1984 at the announcement of the Socialist government's reform of the educational system which the Catholic hierarchy interpreted as an attack on church schools. The Socialist government wished to create a 'unified and secular' public educational system. This time, unlike in West Germany in the 1960s, the response to the church's call, which had the support of the opposition parties, was massive. Faced with this opposition, which culminated in a huge demonstration of over 1 million people in the streets of Paris, the Socialist government withdrew its proposals for reform. These examples and others, above all in Italy, demonstrate that the educational issue can still foster conflicts between church and state; but other than purely religious factors are usually required to secure mass mobilization today.

The liberalization of the abortion laws under pressure from the feminist movement in the 1970s led the churches, Protestant and Catholic alike, to unite in a common opposition. It also saw the mushrooming of groups (SPUC, Movimento per la Vita, LIFE), usually church-inspired, devoted to the repeal of the abortion laws. These pressure groups employed all the usual methods: huge demonstrations, intense lobbying, statements by clergy, propaganda directed at the media, picketing of clinics. However, despite the support of the clergy, they have not been successful so far. Three bills to repeal the British Abortion Act of 1967 presented by Tory MPs have failed. Perhaps the most sensational defeat was that of the Catholic-initiated referendum to repeal the abortion law (194/1978) in Italy in June 1981. The defeat suffered was even greater than that eight years earlier over divorce because not only did the pope intervene personally, which he refrained from doing in 1974, but the votes in favour of repeal fell from 39 per cent to 32 per cent.

This brief discussion confirms the hypothesis that the churches are influential pressure groups, but lack decisive political power. They enjoy financial resources, legitimacy, a certain mass following but must take account of an increasingly secular culture. Moreover, they rarely find themselves united, as they were over abortion: doctrinal differences are reflected in differences of political judgement on different questions, including universal peace.

Ecological groups

The social movements of the 1970s largely formed, mobilized and clashed in the name of the environment. For many people, in fact, the latter is considered as a new non-industrial conception of life which valorizes the unity of man and nature, the rights of future generations and the ecosphere, the quality of life and the community. Despite strong interest in environmental issues in the last twenty years, love of nature has a long history: the romantic movement had already inspired in the nineteenth century the formation of groups like the National Trust (NT), the British Commons Preservation Society and the Town and Country Planning Association in Britain. Hence environmental politics is represented today by two kinds of groups: the older pressure groups (NT, TCPA, Civic Trust, Italia Nostra) and the new 'movement groups' (Greenpeace, Friends of the Earth, CLEAR, German BBU, French Comité Locale pour l'Information Nucléaire (CLIN), *Grünen*, *verts*, greens, *verdi*).

The difference between the two kinds is both structural and in type of activity. The former tend to be promotional while the latter are single issue. As regards the type of organizational structure, the older pressure groups are more centralized and elitist, discourage democratic membership participation and, in consequence, curb all forms of mobilization and popular demonstrations. On the other hand, the newer movement groups usually have a more informal and decentralized organization which appeals directly to the person in the street, and particularly the young, often not requiring formal membership (table 6.5). In fact, the umbrella organizations, like the British CND, the French CLIN or the European Environmental Bureau at the continental level, often have little direct influence over the constituent groups that form their membership; and the latter have no commitment to support the umbrella organization. For this reason, such groups claim to be movements rather than pressure groups (chapter 4).

The older groups take advantage of the institutionalized channels of pressure – contact with the state institutions – and stress expertise and recognized specialist opinion. On the other hand, the newer groups are prepared to exploit all available means and organize every kind of activity. Since they are not usually recognized as representative or bearers of legitimate interests by the competent state authorities, as the older groups are, the newer groups undertake deliberate strategies of direct action and civil disobedience to obstruct, delay or prevent certain officially scheduled activities from taking place. Their problem has been to impose new areas of interest, like the environment, on the political agenda. The fact that ecological issues are now a staple part of all political debates and figure on all party programmes is a measure of their success in sensibilizing political opinion. When we seek to assess the influence of the various pressure groups on concrete decisions, the analysis becomes much more problematic, the more so because their victories are rarely, if ever, total, and short-term gains can be vitiated by long-term developments. For instance, the anti-nuclear groups in France and Germany did not succeed in stopping the nuclear programme in their

Table 6.5 Membership of environmental and allied groups, 1980s (per cent)

	Britain	France	Germany	Italy
Environmental groups	0.3	0.3	0.5	0.9
Anti-nuclear groups	0.3	0.3	0.5	0.9
Anti-war groups	2.0	0.3	1.6	1.2

Source: Eurobaromètre, 1988

respective countries, but only delayed them. Again, Greenpeace has not eradicated whaling, but has only been instrumental in pressing for serious and genuine reductions: in 1984 the International Whaling Commission cut the quota to 10,000 whales a year, but this is threatened with repudiation in the 1990s. Hence, the success of ecological groups should not be overrated, if only because the obstacles to their programmes are considerable. Their opponents are very powerful and often act in unison: producers are opposed to any legislative limits to their activities; and the state authorities are always looking at the cost that environmental protection inevitably involves, despite regular disasters like Chernobyl.

Other pressure groups

These are generally 'cause' groups. Some are very old, like the Abolition of Slavery Society founded by Wilberforce and Clarkson in Britain in 1787 or the Société des Noirs in France the following year. Today, they are very numerous, covering all fields of human concern and endeavour: from the world of animals (Royal Society for the Protection of Animals, League against Cruel Sports, Field Sports Society in Britain, Lega per la Protezione degli Uccelli in Italy) to human rights (Ligue des Droits de l'Homme, SOS-Racisme in France, Howard Society for Penal Reform, Shelter, Oxfam in Britain, Lega per il Divorzio (LID) in Italy, Amnesty International in all countries), to specific projects (Anti-Stansted Airport). Since they are interested in a single cause, they are often successful. For instance, the Italian LID succeeded in getting a divorce law approved and successfully defended it from repeal by referendum; similarly the Lega XIII Maggio, founded on the morrow of the 1974 divorce referendum, was able to get a bill passed legalizing abortion and to defend it in another referendum, and all this in seven years. Finally, the Anti-Apartheid Campaign, started in 1969 to oblige Barclays Bank to forsake its commercial activity in South Africa, eventually produced its desired effect in November 1986; it was calculated that the bank had lost £7 billion in accounts transferred to other British banks in the six years 1980–6. In 1990, the South African government formally abandoned apartheid and liberated Nelson Mandela as the first step towards negotiating a new political constitution.

National systems of interest intermediation

Britain

With a unitary system of government dominated by the executive and a series of non-ideologically divided interest groups, interest intermediation in Britain is dominated both by the major interest groups and by the relations between groups and public administration. This does not mean, however, that there are not other types of groups. Indeed, for reasons of historical tradition – development of voluntary associations, legitimacy of interest representation – Britain has the largest number of groups of any West European country. Moreover, because of the institutionalization of group activity in civil society, the government and the administration not only prefer to involve the relevant groups in their policy programmes, but often leave groups to implement the policies in their stead. Take, for instance, road safety: in the UK the various campaigns are largely in the hands of the AA, RAC and ROSPA, whereas in France, where there is no such tradition, a special governmental body (Comité Interministériel pour la Sécurité Routière) was specifically created to undertake them. Finally, in Britain there are close ties between business associations (CBI) and trade unions on the one hand, and the two main parties on the other, in terms of both funding and parliamentary representation.

The number of interest groups appears to be declining while the number of pressure groups is on the increase. On the other hand, the emergencies of World War II were such as to lead to the formalization of relations between the government and the major interest groups, that is business, unions and farmers, which were further reinforced in the 1960s with the emergence of consultative committees like the NEDC, which replaced informal contacts with ministers. The Wilson Labour government, for its part, promoted the formation of the CBI (a merger between the Federation of British Industry and smaller organizations[9] in a peak organization) in order to develop 'tripartite' negotiations (CBI–TUC–government) to coordinate incomes with general economic policy objectives. This development was defined as a 'corporatist arrangement'. It was a general trend encouraged by the 1970s Labour governments and culminated in Callaghan's 'social contract', which eventually came to grief, after several years of reasonable results, in the famous 'winter of discontent' of 1979. Parallel to this corporatist trend concerning the major interest groups, there was an opposite trend regarding pressure groups that developed new forms of direct action, including violence, more to mobilize the media and the grass roots (CND, national abortion campaign) than to involve the parties and parliament.

The 1980s saw an inversion of both these trends. The Thatcher Conservative governments interrupted the tripartite negotiations and consultations, introducing a monetarist economic policy supported by anti-union legislation. Economic policy is no longer discussed with industrialists and union leaders, but with bankers and financiers. At the same time, 'cause' pressure groups (ecological, women, anti-nuclear, anti-abortion) re-emerged and began a dialogue with the parties. Without abandoning direct action, they persuaded the parties to accept some of their demands and so have them inscribed in the political programmes; even Mrs Thatcher made 'green' speeches in the late 1980s. Interest group activity in Britain is essentially pluralist.

France

The organization and activity of French interest and pressure groups are usually antithetical to the British: their ideological and political fragmentation, a certain lack of legitimacy and a resort to violence in the defence of their interests have been contrasted with the sectorial unity, representational legitimacy and acceptance of the 'rules of the game' of British groups. However, many minor interest groups were active in the Assembly under the Fourth Republic because of its lack of coherent parliamentary majorities, particularly since it was not difficult for a pressure group MP to force weak governments to make concessions: for instance, the activity of the *bouilleurs de cru* in the 1950s.

On the other hand, the introduction of a new planning mechanism – Commissariat du Plan – in the immediate post-war period encouraged a new form of interest group participation, *concertation*, which can be seen as a neo-corporatist tendency. This kind of interest-group/state relationship was reinforced by the Fifth Republic's constitutional changes. The result was a privileged relationship between key interest groups and the state in areas determined by state priorities, and the exclusion of those groups judged hostile to, or irrelevant to, this policy. The consequence of these developments is a mode of intermediation at two levels: a privileged relationship of certain groups – usually business (CNPF) and farmers (FNSEA) – that were consulted, supported and aided; and the non-consultation of other groups that resorted to direct action and ritual violence from time to time to get the state to take account of their interests. The French May 1968, with student dissension provoking a national strike, was only the most sensational example of this strategy in the post-war period. There were numerous episodes of violence provoked by farmers, small shopkeepers (CID-UNATI), Algerian white settlers (OAS), workers, lorry drivers, students. Ritual violence assumed a variety of forms, both real and symbolic, from burning down tax offices and blocking railway lines and motorways, to the occupation of factories, schools and universities and street demonstrations.

The real situation, according to V. Wright (1978), is one of notable dispersion and hence does not easily fall into any of the schemata discussed, because of the coexistence of an infinite number of particular situations; the overall picture, moreover, is complicated by group fragmentation of even the major interest groups. Indeed, Wright claims that one can find not only situations of *clientela*, *parentela* and colonization, but also corporatist arrangements. For this reason, he maintains that it is better to consider each situation individually, that is to say the relations between each decision centre and interest or pressure group. The diversity of relations between groups and the state goes from the group's domination to its subordination, from collusion and complicity between the two to partial recognition and open hostility. And there are situations where there are no relations at all. Despite this, the activities of French interest groups and their relations with the state fall into the schemata outlined above, and can be characterized as a combination of pluralism and corporatism, with a slight bias towards the latter. Under the Fifth Republic, moreover, there has been a trend towards the institutionalization of interest-group/state relations and tripartite negotiations and, hence, some movement towards weak corporatist arrangements.

Germany

Under Weimar, the German interest groups resembled the traditional French interests: they were ideologically fragmented, lacked legitimacy and often resorted to violence. However, one of the consequences of the Nazi *Gleichschaltung* was the suppression of all intermediary social institutions, thus creating a sort of organizational *tabula rasa* in the immediate post-war period. The reconstitution of groups, like the parties, was carried out under Allied supervision which ensured a more coherent organizational structure with the major sectorial interest groups united in a national peak organization (*Spitzenverband*). Moreover, neither the social democrat nor the Catholic movements attempted to rebuild their particular subcultures. The result was, at least for the major interest groups, a tendentially new corporatist mode of interest intermediation, but which operated at two levels, the federal (*Bund*) and the regional (*Land*). The nature of the relations established and institutionalized between the principal groups and the state was formalized in the famous 1967 *Stabilitätsgesetz* (stability law) in the name of *konzierte Aktion*. It is a principle in which economic policy is defined as a joint responsibility of all participants: federal government, *Land* governments and the principal interest groups of business, unions and farmers. In its legal form it is both a recognition of the need for the partners' consent and a commitment by them to implement it.

In this perspective, the mode of interest intermediation is regarded as corporatist, an intermediary model between Swedish-style strong corporatism and British-style structural pluralism. Furthermore, the business and labour organizations are less centralized than the Swedish ones – feeling the effects of the German federal institutional structure which provides for regional negotiations – but the peak organizations have a capacity to control their own members, whether businessmen or unionists, which is lacking in Britain. However, there is little doubt that the German model has hitherto secured an accommodation of interests and a policy coherence unknown in Britain, where more authoritarian means have had to be used. It is difficult to specify accurately to what extent either the old German corporative tradition or the success of the postwar German economy have contributed. It is certain, nevertheless, that the ability of successive federal governments to exorcize the various economic problems without resorting to draconian measures – price control, obligatory incomes policy – has a large place. However, the economic consequences of German unification will test that ability to the full in the 1990s.

If the form of corporatism, which is the *konzierte Aktion*, successfully regulated the relations between the principal interest groups, above all in containing wage drift, it was neither the only mode of interest intermediation, nor accepted by all. Indeed, it has tended to decline in the 1980s and, as noted, it is under severe strain since reunification. In addition, the emergence and successes of the *Bürgerinitiativen* groups in the 1970s are testimony to a dissonance that traditional pressure groups and methods were incapable of representing. The so-called 'marginal' groups – youth, women, foreign workers, consumers – have invented new forms of participation and protest and have created the new politics that has placed a set of new issues – environment, gender, quality of life – at the heart of the political debate in a very few years. The *Grünen*'s passage between movement, party and pressure group is testimony to the difficult problems posed by the new politics.

Italy

The point of comparison for the Italian interest group system is with the French one, since it is also marked by ideological fragmentation and a certain tendency to resort to violence, but it has, on the whole, enjoyed more political legitimacy since the war. Indeed, the specific aspect that characterized interest intermediation in Italy, particularly in the first twenty post-war years, is 'collateralism', that is the close links between the principal interest and pressure groups and the two main parties; in the same way as has the absence of 'cause' or single-issue groups. In contrast to Germany, fascist policy was never as ruthless as the Nazi *Gleichschaltung*. Firstly, Mussolini was obliged, in order to resolve the Roman question, to accept the autonomy of Catholic Action (AC) under the guidance of the ecclesiastical hierarchy; and secondly, the PCI succeeded in maintaining a clandestine presence in the country throughout the fascist period. Thus there was too, in contrast to Germany, greater institutional continuity with the pre-fascist situation. Finally, as a consequence, the Catholic and labour movements were successful in rebuilding their own subcultures (chapter 3) on the basis of a dense associational network which was the basis of their political strength in the pre-fascist period.

Collateralism meant above all the predominance of the type of relationship that LaPalombara (1964) has called *parentela*. In Italy, it was the Catholic Church (through AC) and business (through Confindustria) that established, thanks to the Cold War, this type of relationship with the DC. The collateralism of the Catholic groups lasted until Vatican II, which undermined it; that of Confindustria was cut short in the mid 1950s when the DC preferred to develop the public sector because it was easier to control politically. At this point, Confindustria changed its strategy and accentuated its structural position, that is the *clientela* relationship. The collateral groups linked to the PCI found themselves excluded from *parentela* relationships, except in the regions where the PCI controlled local government ('red zones'), and were obliged to build *clientela* relations based on their sectorial and contractual power instead.

In the 1970s, the situation was radically transformed by Vatican II and the post 1968 social struggles. The consequences were the collapse of collateralism and an unsuccessful attempt to create consociative arrangements – tripartite discussion between government, business and unions in 1977–9. However, in the 1980s there were significant tripartite agreements in parallel with the approval of the budget. The principal content of these agreements was a trade-off between union wage restraint, government tax concessions and public sector price rises. This Italian version of corporatist arrangements was marked by a very low level of institutionalization of state/union relations: limited to the management of certain fields of economic and social policy.

In addition, there has been, as in Germany, a multiplication of new, usually single-issue, pressure groups in the wake of the 1970s social movements which represented the 'marginals'. In contrast with Germany, these have shown themselves readier to act both within the state institutional system – even though from positions of contestation – in founding new parties (DP, PR, *verdi*), and outside it in inventing new forms of participation. Finally, more political groups (Brigate Rosse, Prima Linea, Autonomia Operaia on the left; neo-fascist groups and P2 on the right) have resorted to violence than in Germany (only the RAF). Another sign of change is the decline in the church's influence, traditionally considered the most powerful institution in Italy. An indication of this decline was the crushing defeat which the Catholic cause suffered in the 1974 divorce and 1981 abortion referendums. At present, interest intermediation in Italy combines a measure of corporatism with a large area of pluralism.

European union

In contrast to the situation for parties, the EC quickly became an important arena for interest group activity. Indeed, the Treaty of Rome acted as an immediate stimulus to the formation of European peak associations – Europe-wide interest federations – especially in the industrial, commercial, and agricultural sectors: Union of Industries in the European Community (UNICE), 1958; Committee of Professional Agricultural Organizations (COPA), 1958; Banking Federation of the European Community (BFEC), 1960; etc. Thus by 1970 more than 300 Euro-groups existed. However, workers' and consumers' groups were much slower to organize transnationally: both the European Trade Union Confederation (ETUC) and the European Bureau of Consumers' Associations (BEUC) were established only in 1973; SEPLIS, representing liberal, intellectual and social professions, dates from 1975. By 1985, the number of interest associations recognized by the Commission had reached 659, and it has mushroomed subsequently with the adoption of the SEA. Indeed, although there are no exact figures for 1992 detailing the total number of lobbyists, a figure of 3000 to 10,000 has been given, depending on how lobbyists are defined (Andersen and Eliassen, 1993, p. 39).

In consequence, the variety and volume of interests represented in Brussels are now very extensive. They include, in addition to the Euro-groups mentioned, national associations, like the British CBI and NFU, which have set up their own offices as 'listening posts' and service centres for association members on visits; TNCs, like BP, ICI and Ford; regional and local authorities, such as German *Länder* and French regions; and, finally, non-EU groups, like the American Chamber of Commerce, representing 80 US organizations including TNCs like Colgate Palmolive, General Electric and General Motors, all of which have subsidiaries in EU countries. Perhaps the most striking recent development has been the parallel explosion in the number of professional lobbyists, financial consultants and law firms locating in Brussels, estimated at 3000 in 1990 – a threefold increase in three years. They represent groups that cannot afford an office in Brussels. Nevertheless, given the fields of the EU's primary competence – agricultural, trade, environmental, competition and transport policies – industrial trade associations predominate with about 40 per cent, followed by agriculture and food with about 30 per cent, and the remainder are made up of a variety of commercial, service, labour, consumer and environmental groups.

The Commission has always adopted a receptive approach to interest groups, particularly if they are organized on a Europe-wide basis. Indeed, on occasion it has played a major role in the foundation of Euro-groups, as in the case of COPA – thanks to agricultural commissioner

Sicco Mansholt – or in the more extreme case of EUROFER which was directly sponsored by the EC. It established a procedure of recognition of their special European status, as well as a privileged access to its deliberations. This was initially intended to promote European integration by creating a European process and, for this reason, the Commission attempted to confine lobbying to certified European associations. However, it was subsequently forced to relax this policy and allow an increasing volume of direct contacts with national interest representatives, including non-EU groups.

This openness was as inevitable as it was essential, because the Commission – relatively small and lacking technical expertise – is heavily dependent on consultation with interest representatives, national governments and their officials, and national experts[10] for the detailed information on the conditions – technical standards, legislation and organizational structures – in the various EU states, necessary for formulating policies and drafting directives. One of the consequences is the unpredictability of the European policy agenda. European draft proposals, unlike national policy proposals, are invariably revised several times following representations from different interests and member states. Not surprisingly, keeping track of EU policy initiatives is a major undertaking, made worse by the complex nature of EU decision-making divided as it is between Commission, Council of Ministers and latterly the EP.

Euro-groups have suffered from similar drawbacks to those of Europe-wide party federations. An obvious aspect is the difficulty of reconciling the different national interests of the member associations, with the result that Euro-groups often produce 'lowest common denominator' policies which are so generic in their wording as to make no impact on EU policy. For this reason, national associations, like national parties, have been reticent in providing resources or delegating authority to their European peak associations. A second aspect that hinders, if not undermines, the effectiveness of Euro-groups arises from the fact that all EU decisions are taken by the Council of Ministers, which is organized on an intergovernmental basis. Hence, an interest group whose views on an issue diverge from those of its European counterparts may decide that the best course of action is to persuade its national government to defend its position in the Council of Ministers. This means making use of its contacts at the national level. It may not be difficult to win the national government to its point of view, particularly if it can be presented as a distinctive national interest.

There is a risk, however, that the government will bargain away its position as part of the complex deals that are often the only way of making progress in EU decision-making. As Butt-Philip (1985) has noted: 'The national pressure groups will be very much in the hands of the government officials once the Council of Ministers' negotiations begin' (p. 57). Thus national channels of access are often used in combination with European channels, either through Euro-groups or by direct representations to the Commission. Moreover, the institutional reforms in the SEA have significantly reduced the policy-making influence of national governments in key policy areas, thereby increasing the incentive for interest group coalition building at the EU level. For instance, the adoption of qualified majority voting in the Council of Ministers means that a single national government can no longer block a proposal as in the past.

We may conclude that the fact that there has been a proliferation of Euro-groups does not necessarily mean that they are successful. The European Federation of Chemical Industries (EFCI) is often cited as a successful model, but it is suggested that it may be unusual as it is dominated by a few large TNCs able to formulate a coherent policy on most issues. The situation is more problematic in other policy areas, for instance financial services where an effective Euro-group has failed to emerge because of the lack of equivalent national groups as a result of organizational differences. One thing, which some feared and others hoped for, has not happened: the development of corporatist structures between the so-called social partners (business organizations, trade unions). Indeed, the EU system is characterized as being 'less corporatist and more lobby-oriented than in national European systems' (Andersen and Eliassen, 1993, p. 43).

Streeck and Schmitter (1991) argue that this is due to two factors. The first is the complete absence of significant business factions with an active interest in centralized negotiations with labour. European business quite simply refused to contribute to the transfer of social policy matters from national arenas to Brussels, which they did by not delegating authority to their European peak associations. The result was that all discussions had a strictly non-binding, consultative status. The second factor is that the intergovernmentalism of the Council of Ministers and the one-government veto were sufficient to prevent the emergence of a centralized social policy. Indeed, the EU was never permitted to develop the organizational capacities necessary to reshape powerful interest organizations rooted in national civil societies. Major organized interests were constrained, even if they were otherwise inclined, to cultivate national channels of influence. The EU interest system is a form of 'disjointed pluralism' in which 'interest associations ... compete for attention with national states, subnational regions, large firms, and specialized lobbyists, leaving their constituents with a wide range of choices among different paths of access to the EC's political centre and enabling them to use threats of exit to coerce their representatives into a pluralist responsiveness' (p. 159). Despite limitations and a certain ineffectiveness at present, there is little doubt that the European dimension of interest intermediation will be of increasing importance in the future in all EU member states.

Conclusion

The development of the major interests paralleled that of parties, becoming organized with professional leaders, bureaucracies and mass memberships from the end of the last century. Their contribution to the World War I effort led to them being viewed thereafter as legitimate interlocutors of the state in the policy processes of West European democracies. Their role grew in importance as the state widened its intervention in all spheres of society after World War I. Definitions of groups tend to be extensive, as the notion is something of a residual category referring to all groups that are involved, even momentarily, with the political process. One distinction which is useful is that between economic (sectional) groups and ideological (cause groups) which can be subsumed under that between interest groups and pressure groups in the narrow sense: the former defend the sectional interests of their members, whereas the latter promote some principle for the general good of society.

The modalities of group action are determined by the channels of access to the political system. Four targets for pressure are usually identified: two form part of the state (parliament and public administration); and two are in civil society (parties and the media). Each requires different resources and has a different problematic. Groups can, for instance, seek representation or a spokesperson in parliament; they can furnish information and their views on particular policies as well as their offer of collaboration to the public administration; they can propose candidates and funds to parties in support of their interests; and, finally, they can attempt to influence public opinion through the media by creating the news, either by direct action or through debate.

Interest intermediation has been dominated by two paradigms: the pluralist mode and the corporatist mode. The pluralist mode is part of the group theory of politics which sees politics in terms of the interaction between organized groups. It holds that power in liberal democratic society is necessarily fragmented and dispersed and that a large number of groups, whose leadership is responsive to their memberships, compete with each other for the allocation of scarce resources. Government decisions reflect the balance between groups in civil society at a given moment. Pluralists believe that power is non-cumulative in the sense that those powerful in one area are not necessarily powerful in another. Finally, the pluralist mode assumes that the entry barrier into the political system is low.

The pluralist mode has been criticized both factually and theoretically as being rather simplistic. Factually, critics have accused it of exaggerating the equality between groups as well as the ease of potential organization. The pluralist argument that all groups have access to certain resources that can influence the government in their favour, if correctly used, has been recognized as inaccurate. Indeed, it is now accepted, even by most pluralists, that some groups have a privileged position in a market society based on their structural position in society (business). Further, it is now recognized that lack of organization does not necessarily mean satisfaction with the status quo. It can also mean that the latent group is marginal because it lacks resources and power: an awareness by the members that the political system has nothing to offer them.

The theoretical critique of pluralism argues that, by focusing on the groups as the determining element of the political system, it analyses the system in terms of the participants and the processes: pluralists analyse issues, activity and decisions at the expense of agenda setting (non-decisions) and the ideological context. The result is a partial, rather than a false, analysis. Nonetheless, the very variety of pluralist theory has given the approach a certain resilience: group competition occurs, but rarely in the terms that pluralist theory postulates.

The corporatist mode was expressly developed to overcome the perceived descriptive inadequacy of pluralism, namely the state coordinated negotiations between major interest groups to define policy options in a (usually the economic) field. The key elements were the active role of the state and the requirement that the groups deliver the consent of their members to the outcome in return for a share in policy-making. The paradigm postulated a society in which a small number of hierarchically organized and disciplined interest groups determined and implemented policy in the field. Some theorists argued that it represented a stage towards a new politico-economic system, but the majority saw it merely as an alternative form of interest intermediation to pluralism. It was severely criticized by pluralists, like Almond, as simply a subtype of pluralism and much less an alternative mode of intermediation. In other words, the paradigm was the polar opposite on a pluralist–corporatist continuum. Further, pluralists were not slow to point to the difficulty that corporatist theorists had in specifying empirical examples, both national and sectorial, of corporatism. Indeed, corporatist theorists quickly took refuge in the amorphous notion of neo-corporatist arrangements.

A partial synthesis along the same political dimension as that used to differentiate party systems – coercion–consensus – permits the outlining of the politics of each mode of interest intermediation. The state corporatist mode does not pose problems because it is the façade of a totalitarian state and the corporations lack any autonomy. Pluralism and (neo-)corporatism are the modes of intermediation practised in Western democracies and, moreover, they are based on two different group strategies. The pluralist strategy is necessarily a zero-sum game because in every conflict there are winners and losers. Groups either accept this situation because they find it advantageous (they are winners) or suffer it because they are powerless to change it (they are losers). The corporatist strategy is a positive-sum game which concerns material interests only and is limited to sectors that the state regards as fundamental. An interest group is prepared to negotiate and implement a policy so long as the state endorses it. It is a high-risk strategy because leaders can be disavowed by their members; hence it requires a strong, disciplined and well-organized group to practise. Interest groups, however, conserve their autonomy – a fundamental aspect that differentiates this mode of interest intermediation from state corporatism – which means that they can denounce agreements and withdraw from negotiations.

The principal interest groups organize the major socio-economic groups – businessmen, labourers, farmers and the professions – whereas pressure groups include the churches and the various ecological groups as well as a host of single-issue organizations. Differences between organized groups in different countries derive from national socio-political cleavages and political traditions. Further, most national systems of interest intermediation in Western Europe are mixed: some are more corporatist in some sectors and more pluralist in others, such as in Germany, France and Italy; others are more pluralist in all sectors, such as in Britain. The EU interest system is pluralist because none of the would-be 'social partners' has the international organization capable of making corporatist agreements stick. In addition, business has refused to collaborate in the transfer of social policy from the national arena to the EU, preferring to enjoy the advantages of the national status quo.

Further reading

P. Allum (1980), 'Les Groupes de pression en Italie', in *Revue française de science politique*, 30, 148–72.

A.R. Ball and F. Millard (1986), *Pressure Politics in Industrial Society* (London: Macmillan).

S. Berger (ed.) (1981), *Organizing Interests in Western Europe: Pluralism, Corporatism and the Transformation of Politics* (Cambridge: CUP).

A. Cawson (1986), *Corporation and Political Theory* (Oxford: Blackwell).

A. Ferner and R. Hyman (eds) (1992), *Industrial Relations in the New Europe* (Oxford: Blackwell).

D. Garson (1978), *Group Theories of Politics* (London: Sage).

W. Grant (ed.) (1986), *The Political Economy of Corporatism* (London: Macmillan).

W. Grant (1989), *Pressure Groups, Politics and Democracy in Britain* (London: Allen).

M.D. Hancock (1989), *West Germany: The Politics of Democratic Corporatism* (Chatham, NJ: Chatham House).

A.G. Jordan and J.J. Richardson (1987), *Government and Pressure Groups in Britain* (Oxford: OUP).

G. Lehmbruch and P.C. Schmitter (eds) (1982), *Patterns in Corporatist Intermediation* (London: Sage).

S.P. Mazey and J.J. Richardson (eds) (1993), *Lobbying the European Community* (Oxford: OUP).

C. Miller (1987), *Lobbying Government and Influencing the Corridors of Power* (Oxford: Clarendon).

M. Olson (1982), *The Rise and Decline of Empires* (New Haven, Conn.: Yale UP).

P.C. Schmitter (1974), 'Still the Century of Corporatism', in *Review of Politics*, 85, 85–131.

J.H. Whyte (1981), *Catholics in Western Democracies* (Dublin: Gill & Macmillan).

F.L. Wilson (1987), *Interest Groups in France* (Cambridge: CUP).

G.K. Wilson (1985), *Business and Politics* (London: Macmillan).

G.K. Wilson (1990), *Interest Groups* (Oxford: Blackwell).

PART III

The State

7 Government and Executive Power

Introduction

In the introduction to this book, we outlined a theoretical model of the Western European political system and the relations between civil society and the state that it entailed. In the chapters on civil society we have discussed in some detail the social, cultural and political contexts in which the four major Western European states operate. We saw that they were what one might call structured pluralist societies. In other words, although they were characterized by a plurality of social groups and political traditions, their civil societies were structured by similar socio-economic activities and a largely common historical experience. Now we must turn our attention to the state.

However, before beginning the discussion, we need to be more explicit about what is meant by 'the state'. It is a concept which refers to a historical phenomenon, namely an ensemble of institutions which interact in a more or less coordinated manner within defined territorial boundaries. Thus Tilly (1975) concludes a volume devoted to the formation of the nation-state in Western Europe with the statement that: 'The state ... [is] an organization, controlling the principal means of coercion within a given territory, which is differentiated from other organizations operating in the same territory, autonomous, centralized and formally coordinated' (p. 638). Skocpol (1979) is even more explicit:

> The state properly conceived is no mere arena in which socio-economic struggles are fought out. It is, rather, a set of administrative, policing, and military organizations headed, and more or less well coordinated, by an executive authority. Any state first and fundamentally extracts resources from society and deploys these to create and support coercive and administrative organizations.

Of course, these basic state organizations are built up and must operate within the context of class-divided socio-economic relations, as well as within the context of national and international economic dynamics. Moreover, coercive and administrative organizations are only parts of overall political systems. These systems may also contain institutions through which social interests are represented in state policy-making as well as institutions through which non-state actors are mobilized to participate in policy implementation. Nevertheless, the administrative and coercive organizations are the basis of state power as such. (p. 29)

If these definitions stress the state's coercive aspect, that is to say not only the right to give orders but above all the force to impose obedience, they raise the question of which institutions constitute the contemporary state and why they are organized in the way they are today. An answer requires identifying the nature of the relations between the state and civil society internally, between the state and other states externally, and not just those between the state and the mode of production, as most abstract Marxist theories do.

The state in Europe is part and parcel of an international system of states as well as a specific society, which means that it is conditioned, if not determined, not only by the structuration of its civil society, but also by its position in the world.[1] Thus the state has to operate within the compass of the often contradictory and conflictual relations of both its own civil society and the international community of states. Furthermore, European states are no longer omnipotent – if they ever were – but are now constrained by the international system of economic relations which they no longer dominate as they once did; nor are they simply reactive, although, of course, they do react to political, economic and social events affecting their environment. They are actors: 'The state models society', as Rosanvallon (1990, p. 14) has recently argued, 'no less than it is modelled by the image that society has of the state.'

As a political actor, the state is a subject of socio-economic and political processes as much as an object: this means that it can also create a new social stratum or institute new international relations. It can, for instance, act to establish, encourage and consolidate a new constellation of national and international social forces. Despite this, however, a national or international social bloc constructed in this way is always vulnerable to the action, or reaction, of opposing forces, both in civil society and in the international community of states. Further, this can also happen unwittingly as a result of the instability of the dominant social bloc: state policies adopted can in fact be ill-adapted to the social bloc's consolidation. History is full of examples of state policy in European countries that was not, as many Marxists maintain it always is, functional for capitalist development.

This said, however, even if the state form is obviously not itself derived from the mode of production, the latter still conditions to some extent its general nature. The reason is simple: the state in an industrial society has to secure the minimum conditions for capitalist accumulation. Otherwise Western Europe would not be capitalist and its states would not be 'sovereign' states, in the sense of enjoying a large measure of internal and external autonomy. In brief, without the minimum conditions of capital accumulation, industrial societies cannot survive, that is to say ensure their own reproduction. It is in this very limited sense that the state in Western Europe can be defined as a capitalist state, namely that it depends on the surplus value of the economy to secure its material resources. It retains, however, a notable level of autonomy which means that it can, for instance, undermine capitalism as a form of economic organization, either intentionally or through sheer incompetence, as the Soviet state did with actual socialism in 1989–91. The state is, in effect, caught up in a contradictory situation between the relations of production, the structuration of civil society, and international relations.

From the discussion of civil society it emerged that although social praxis is structured, it is far from unified, and every sector of civil life has different relations both with the state and with the economic system. The nature of the state is determined by the often contradictory relations with these diverse elements, or more concretely with the persons that embody them, because the state, despite its abstract and impersonal conceptualization, is composed of historically conditioned men and women. Thus the state is materially formed of an ensemble of institutions and apparatuses, founded on the centralization of the instruments of violence, formally coordinated in a given territory within which it establishes the laws and secures their observance, while administering bureaucratically the citizens' interests.

Whatever the limits of this view of the state, it is adequate on two conditions. Firstly, the use of violence or coercion is directed as much externally as internally because the capitalist system is an international system of rival nation-states. The international dimension is, as we shall see, a crucial dimension for the formation of the state in Europe. Secondly, the distinction between state and civil society is necessary to secure the state's unity in the face of the contradictory forces active in civil society. In other words, the unitary nature of state action justifies its claim to regulate civil society because it acts in the name of a higher purpose: civil cohabitation. This can be achieved only on the basis of the separation of state and civil society. But, if this is so, the unity of the state apparatuses – their speaking with one voice – is always problematic and has to be constructed politically, which is often difficult. The state consists of those institutions or apparatuses which are directly or indirectly based on the centralization of physical coercion, that is capable of proclaiming rules – laws, decrees, orders – and securing their observance. In saying this, we are aware that certain groups have access to the means of physical coercion and use them, for instance the Mafia and political terrorists; nevertheless there is an organized and coordinated concentration of physical coercion in the state, devolved today to specialized bodies like the armed forces and the police.

In this chapter, we discuss government and executive power; in the next, the administration and policy-making; in the following, subcentral government and centre–local relations; and in the penultimate, the 'dual state' or the special agencies and invisible power.

State forms

It is helpful, as a start, to distinguish between 'state' and 'government' because there is often some confusion. The Anglo-American tradition tends to consider the one as synonymous with the other. However, the continental tradition makes a useful distinction between the 'state' as the general and abstract term referring to the 'public' political institutions, and the 'government' as one of its components, namely the executive branch, alongside others: legislative, administrative, judicial and military branches. If we adopt this distinction, despite the fact that 'the line of demarcation is not clear', as Bobbio (1985) reminds us, it is because it is substantive:

> In a typology of forms of government more attention is paid to the structure of power and to the relations between the different organs which according to the constitution exercise power; in a typology of types of state more attention is paid to the relations of class, to the relations between the power system and society, to ideologies and goals, and to historical and sociological character-istics. (pp. 100–1)

Thus we follow the continental tradition, but with the caution that executive power is examined with legislative power for the simple reason that the two powers are virtually inseparable in Western European states today.

There is, however, no accepted definition of the contemporary state form in Western Europe. Indeed, if there is a more or less acceptable ter-minology for previous forms – feudal state, *Ständestaat*, absolute state – there is none for the contemporary form: there is talk of the liberal democratic state, the representative state, the welfare state, the party state (*Parteienstaat*). We prefer the expression 'Keynesian welfare state' (see the introduction to the book). At all events, the Western state has two fundamental features today: representation, which implies the search for consensus between rulers and ruled, and which has given rise to specific institutions; and administrative power – what Giddens (1986) calls 'self-reflexive monitoring' – and the creation of specialized surveillance apparatuses of all kinds. It is helpful, for an understanding of the contemporary state form, to outline certain aspects of its socio-genesis, the more so since it was a specifically European phenomenon. What follows is not a historical reconstruction, but merely a number of points to emphasize certain significant aspects.

The formation of the European state

The socio-genesis of the state has its origins in the dissolution of medieval society. Norbert Elias (1939) finds it, for example, in the inherent tensions in the feudal system, that is to say between the various feudal lords, each obliged to strengthen himself at the expense of his rivals, with ultimate victory going to the strongest. The end of this process was a limited number of territories in which a ruler exercised a monopoly of coercive power. The key to the ruler's success was control of financial resources which opened the way to greater military potential. The end of the Middle Ages was marked by the gradual monetization of the economy as well as the transformation of military techniques – for instance, the replacement of the knight on horseback armed with a sword by a mass of common foot-soldiers armed with pikes – which rewarded the controller of the new financial opportunities. In this way, military supremacy went hand in glove with financial superiority: the power of taxation. The result was the gradual establishment of a central power (the prince) in a limited number of territories – from around 500 more or less independent political units in Europe in 1500, according to Tilly, to about 25 in 1900 – and the formation of two of the fundamental institutions of the modern state: the public administration and the armed forces.

Moreover, once the monopoly organization of coercive power was firmly established in a given territory, social conflicts tended to change their nature: they were no longer concerned with destroying monopoly rule, but only with the question of who was to control it, and how the benefits and burdens of the monopoly were to be distributed. However, the rise of the absolute power of the central authority has always depended on the existence of tensions between the most important classes, and in particular between the landed nobility and the new urban bourgeoisie. Where the balance between classes was lost, as in seventeenth century England, the supremacy of the central power was seriously threatened. At all events, it was only with the emergence of this central power, and its specialized apparatus for ruling, that it took on the character of the 'state' in the modern sense of 'a government whose decisions are actually implemented': that is an effective government.

However, where the territory became larger and the central power stronger, as in Louis XIV's France, the greater became the number of officials required to administer it and the greater the division of labour among them. The state apparatus originated, in fact, in the court and the administration of the crown estates. The state's administrative institutions resulted from the diversification of the court and the establishment of permanent offices in the provinces. At a certain point in time, there was a separation between the court – composed of the favourite nobles and courtiers who formed a sort of political realm – and the royal household, composed of administrators, which became the basis of the state administration, responsible directly to the crown as sovereign. In France, for instance, Colbert actively pursued the consolidation of a hierarchical system of administration, coordinating central and provincial officialdom to a greater degree than hitherto. In this situation, the crown's servants, recruited increasingly on the basis of competence and not of rank, became ministers, ambassadors, judges and generals. From 'crown officials' they became public servants, trained in legal argument elevated to *raison d'état*.

Otto Hintze (1906) also emphasized the role of military factors in the formation of the European states, putting the accent on the relation between state consolidation and military organization. Conflict between states was, in fact, far more important than the class struggle in determining the state form. He argued, for example, that war and preparation for war explain administrative centralization and the reorganization of the tax system, two fundamental features of the absolute state. This diagnosis was confirmed by Bean (1973) in a well-documented study: 'changes in the art of war practically guaranteed the weakening of the feudal nobility, the concentration of power within each state, and the reduction of the number of states' (p. 221). In this way, the European state was as much determined by, as the creator of, a unique situation: the European system of states. This was the result, on the one hand, of the failure of the two principal medieval powers, the church and the empire, to achieve under their own aegis (*sacerdotium* and *imperium*) the dream of all, the *res publica Christiana*; and, on the other, of the church's emancipation from the temporal power to create its own spiritual power.

The rivalry between church and empire which lasted throughout the Middle Ages encouraged the emergence of a plurality of rival political units,[2] but with a common identity: Christianity. The basis of the system, codified at the Congress of Westphalia (1648) and successive European congresses, was 'the balance of power', namely the coexistence of a certain number of states which were rivals, but which recognized each other's right of sovereignty. It remained, nevertheless, a highly unstable system in spite of the diplomatic codification of the 'balance of power' principle: all states pursued their own interests exclusively. This kind of politics created enormous tensions, whose explosions, as in the Napoleonic wars in the nineteenth century, but above all in the two world wars of the twentieth, placed civilized life in Europe in jeopardy.

The instruments of this kind of politics are diplomacy – institutionalized, not by accident, as a specialized activity in the seventeenth century with the setting up of permanent embassies – and war. Hence Clausewitz's (1832–4) famous remark that 'war is merely the continuation of policy by other means', and the addition: 'It is clear, consequently, that war is not a mere act of policy, but a true political instrument, a continuation of political activity, by other means' (book I, chapter 1, 24).

With regard specifically to military organization, Hintze argued that it was technological changes in weaponry that dictated changes in state forms. He outlined a relationship between military formats – types of weaponry and army – and political forms in the ancient, medieval and modern worlds. In the modern era, which he defined as 'the epoch of militarism', he distinguished three significant periods. The first, the fifteenth to seventeenth centuries, was characterized by an army of mercenaries, armed with pikes and fixed artillery pieces, not integrated in the political order and with a *Ständestaat* state form. The second, the seventeenth and eighteenth centuries, saw the integration of a standing army, armed with muskets and mobile artillery, in the political order and with a centralized and absolute state form, on the European continent; and in England, a small militia and a growing fleet with a parliamentary and decentralized state form. The third, the nineteenth century, witnessed the creation of the 'nation in arms' and the concept of 'total war' – a mass regular standing army, recruited on the basis of conscription – with a constitutional and representative state form: England only had a mass standing army from World War I, although the representative state form dates from much earlier. Hintze also comments on the inherent relation between the *levée en masse* and universal male suffrage, summed up in the Swedish expression: 'one soldier, one rifle, one vote'.

The military format in the second period is very important, not only because it dictated the absolute state form but also because it furnished the model for other developments in the organization of the state apparatus. It was a 'militarist' era; indeed, in the seventeenth century, according to the historian, G. N. Clark (1927): 'war ... may be said to have been as much a normal state of European life as peace, and the history of armies was one of the hinges on which the fate of Europe turned' (p. 98). At all events, the feature of the period was the establishment of the mass standing army, founded on fidelity to the crown and so to the state. It was, moreover, characterized by the professionalization of the art of war; indeed, it was the period which saw the founding of military academies, like Woolwich (1741) and Sandhurst (1802) in England, the École Polytechnique (1794) and St Cyr (1808) in France, the Berlin Kriegsakademie (1810) in Prussia (of which Clausewitz was commandant), and Modena (1756) in Italy. Within the armed forces themselves, the division of labour between officers, who were progressively trained to become public servants, and men, who were increasingly reduced to the rank of disciplined executants of simple and repetitive operations, was enhanced. Permanent troop training was introduced for the first time in the nineteenth century so that the ordinary soldier was able to execute orders automatically. What is relevant is that these developments influenced the organization of the other state apparatuses.

The growth of the armed forces – under Louis XIV the French army became larger than the imperial Roman army at its zenith – and the increase in costs required the expansion and centralization of the administration in general, and tax collection in particular. Initially, princes were obliged to turn to bankers for war credits: hence bankers (and *condottieri*) made and unmade princes. But, faced with the enormous costs of war as an industry, the state was forced to intervene directly in the economy to control the currency and to organize a national system of credit and debit. To this end, the innovations of military organization were adopted by the state, namely the division of labour between experts and executants. Van Doorn (1975) claims that Maurice of Nassau (1567–1625), the great Dutch military leader, invented the techniques of 'Taylorism' in the military sphere three centuries before the American engineer introduced them into industrial production.

The institutionalization of the mass standing army had two other consequences for the state. The first was a differentiation between the armed forces and the other state apparatuses, with an organization functional to the defence of the country from outside attack. Thus, for the first time, the army was no longer the principal instrument of internal security, which was entrusted to other specialized apparatuses with the establishment of regular police forces in the nineteenth century. The second was the promotion of the 'nation' component of the nation-state couple through, on the one hand, the identification of the state with a given territory and fixed boundaries; and, on the other, national service (conscription), which helped to propagate notions of patriotism and citizenship as well as a common language and a national culture. Giddens (1986) has noted that in the nation-state concepts like sovereignty, citizenship and nation are linked and are intimately associated with the notion of territoriality, conceived as the home of a political community created by the state in certain conditions, namely with a certain level of administrative coordination covering the whole country. In conclusion, we can do no better than adopt Tilly's aphorism: 'war made the state, and the state made war' (1975, p. 42).

If we have emphasized the coercive aspects of the formation of the European state, it is because they really are fundamental. Not for nothing did Hobbes (1651) write in a celebrated passage that 'covenants, without swords, are but words, and of no strength to secure a man at all' (chapter XVII). In consequence, the repressive administrative apparatuses – public bureaucracy, armed forces, judiciary, police, special and secret agencies – remain the material bases of contemporary state power. But they are not the only bases: there is another face to the West European state, the formation of representative institutions which have acted, as Bobbio has noted, to counterbalance the power of the crown. He refers to the *Stände*, which were assemblies – parliaments, *états généraux*, diets – that defended the interests of some corporations, above all the towns which were beginning to expand, against the prince. It was the prince who initially set up these assemblies in his search for economic resources to finance his military enterprises. When the prince found ways of securing taxes without having recourse to the *Stände*, as in Prussia and France (where the *états généraux* were not convened between 1614 and 1789), he dispensed with their support and ignored their opposition to his policy. In England, on the contrary, the Stuarts were unsuccessful in doing this, so that when Charles I adjourned the summoning of the Long Parliament in 1641, he precipitated the Civil War; it was the first step towards the recognition of 'parliamentary sovereignty'.

The significance of the *Stände* experience lies in the gradual institutionalization of countervailing powers that limited – because of the potential for conflict that they expressed – royal power. It offered, in fact, a form of government by association between two relatively autonomous forces. Poggi (1978) has argued that the *Stände* contributed to 'civilizing' the political process in Europe:

> much political business now involved the taking and giving of advice prior to giving and enforcing commands; consulting interested parties, official documents and qualified authorities; and reaching decisions or voicing objections to or reservations about decisions on stated grounds. In these largely novel modalities of the political process (often brutally interrupted by straightforward aggression, usurpation, or repression) we can see prefigured the predominantly discursive business-like temper of the internal political processes of the modern state. (p. 57)

In spite of this, the overwhelming majority of the population remained outside and unaffected by these processes: they were mere 'objects of government'. At all events, the importance of the *Stände* was greater in England, where the estates were reinforced from the fourteenth century onwards and were able to defeat the Stuarts' 'absolutist' tendencies in the seventeenth; in consequence, the centralization of the English state was carried out by parliament. In France, on the contrary, the Bourbon monarchy succeeded progressively in centralizing its power and weakening the estates so as to create the 'ideal type' of absolute state. In Germany and Italy, on the other hand, the division of the territory into small kingdoms and principalities was such that the centralization of power remained modest, with the exceptions of Prussia, Sardinia-Piedmont and the Two Sicilies, which were successful in creating strong state structures.

Features of the contemporary state form

Two features characterize the contemporary state form: representation and the capacity to intervene. Both contain elements of continuity and discontinuity. The concept of representation marks a fundamental break in state form – Bobbio calls it 'a genuine Copernican revolution in the evolution of the relationship between rulers and ruled' (1985, p. 115) – because it postulates a new principle of legitimacy, that of popular consent. The nature of the break can be appreciated, at least in terms of political theory, from the fact that the basis of the state's political authority was stood on its head; it no longer came from above (the prince or God), but from below (the people). The premise of the change was the discovery and affirmation of the natural rights of the individual because, if they are, as the seventeenth century jurisconsults claimed, the rights that every individual has by nature and cannot be lost, they imply the natural equality of individuals. Moreover, once natural rights are proclaimed in universalistic terms, it become logically difficult to fix limits to political participation, the more so when state legitimacy is founded on popular sovereignty, understood as the citizens' consent for the purpose of defending their natural rights.

The achievement of the new principle of legitimation – 'the credo of the new era', according to Michelet – displayed elements of continuity. Firstly, the adoption of parliamentary institutions without interruption – despite the Civil War and the restoration of the monarchy as in England, or the establishment of national assemblies as in France, Germany and Italy – was the result of compromises with the existing state power, as were the restricted suffrage and a second chamber with privileged representation (English House of Lords and continental senates). Secondly, it triggered off two converging and contrasting processes of political participation, namely the struggle for the broadening of the suffrage by the subordinate classes and the search for popular consensus by the new rulers (chapter 3).

The consequence of these two developments was the formation of organized political parties, which, as Bobbio (1985) has observed, profoundly altered the structure of the representative state: 'to the point of bringing about a fundamental change in the system of representation itself (which is no longer representation by single individuals but is filtered through powerful associations that organize elections and receive a blank proxy from the electorate)' (p. 115). The result is paradoxically a situation similar to that of the *Ständestaat* – a further element of continuity – in which the political actors are no longer individuals but organized groups (as once were the estates), above all parties but also interest groups. In fact, it is the parties that determine materially, and make themselves the guarantors of, the relations between the state and civil society, depriving parliament of a substantive role and reducing it, according to Laski (1933), 'to the status of a voting machine', which ratifies, more or less passively, 'decisions reached in other places' (p. 77). It is a fact that no typology of the forms of government can afford to ignore the party system. It is the party system which defines the modalities of the exercise of power in contemporary democratic states. For this reason, this state form has been defined by some as a *Parteienstaat*.

To conclude, the existence of parliament, as a political institution, gives substance to an intuition of Schmitt, developed by Habermas (1962), that of a connection between the principle of representation and the publicity of power; in other words, open government. The establishment of parliament, in fact, institutionalizes the idea of the public control of state power and, thus, of the visibility of political acts that is an essential element of democracy: the free formation of public opinion (*Öffentlichkeit*) in a position to assess and judge the government's actions. Without this, it is obvious that elections are meaningless.

The second feature of the contemporary state form in Europe – generically defined as 'capacity to intervene' – is certainly more significant, even though more difficult to state in detail, than representation. It refers to the state machine and the parallel processes of concentration and centralization of power. It is not only the backbone of the state, but also a constant presence that justifies on the one hand Tocqueville's (1856) observation that it is 'the principal element of continuity' of the modern state, and on the other the appellation 'administrative state'. The question which was posed in relation to the absolute state was its capacity to intervene and to control society. There is no doubt about its claim to be 'absolute' – hence the definition – as was made clear in the sixteenth-century debate on sovereignty by Bodin and others. The state was defined as 'sovereign' by virtue of the fact that it was the supreme authority in a given territory, with the power to dictate valid laws applicable to everybody, use force at home and abroad, impose taxes, administer justice, and so on.

However, if the state does not consist of a single apparatus, but an ensemble of apparatuses, the concept of sovereignty still requires a single hierarchy of power with an institution defined as sovereign, to which all the others are subordinate. In the absolute state, the prince was considered, in law and in fact, the sovereign as the incarnation of the state (Louis XIV's 'L'État, c'est moi'). The prince – and through his person, the state – was committed to giving substance to his claim to control associational life in a given territory with the formation of a state apparatus capable of meeting the needs of his subjects, both positively and negatively: prosperity, and not just law and order. To do this, the prince had to recruit and train a body of specialized public servants as well as to develop efficient instruments for understanding and intervening in society: for instance, the Enlightenment and the work of the Physiocrats, in particular; and as instruments, official statistics and the national census established in that period.

If the prince's intention was self-evident, there still remains the question of the absolute state's real capacity to intervene in, and control, society. The omnipotence of the administration should not be exaggerated, as Bobbio (1985) has warned: 'no monarchy became so absolute ... as to suppress every form of intermediate power (the absolute state is not a totalitarian state)' (p. 112). It was in the Enlightenment era, in fact, that Locke (1690) and Montesquieu (1748) proposed the separation of powers – executive, legislative and judicial – as a rational means of limiting the exercise of power. At all events, the absolute state lacked contemporary information technology, population surveillance and control techniques. Indeed, the eighteenth century was the century when civil society became emancipated from the state, and this despite the state's presumption to control the economy through the mercantilist system.

The development of a civil society independent of the state resulted from two main factors, whose importance varied from state to state. The first was the emergence of a capitalist economy, founded on private property and the free market. This and above all the bourgeois groups which were its advocates were sufficiently strong to oblige the state, in countries like Britain, to accept a *laissez-faire* economy. The second factor is a significant element of Wallerstein's (1974) theory of the 'world economy' that highlights the contrast between an economic system already organized on a world scale and the European states ('core states'), which were organized in limited territorial units and in competition with each other: the European states' system. In consequence, none of the European states was able to control the world market completely. Furthermore, the state profits from a prosperous economy: its apparatuses need the financial resources furnished by the economic and business activity in civil society. It was this common interest of state personnel (politicians and civil servants) and bourgeoisie in economic prosperity that explains the relations between the two groups in Western European states. Stuart Hall (1984) argues that:

> the boundaries between 'state' and 'civil society' are never fixed, but are constantly changing. Public and private are not natural divisions, but socially and historically constructed divisions. One of the ways in which the state extends its own sphere of action is to redraw the boundaries between public and private, and to reconstruct the definition of the private, so as to legitimate the state's intervention in areas which were previously considered inviolable. (pp. 21–22)

If we have insisted on the absolute state's capacity of intervention (or rather its limits), it is because it highlights a paradox which underlies the form of Keynesian welfare state. The absolute state's claims were absolute in the sense that the ruler had the right to do anything in the name of the doctrine of *raison d'état*, but the capacity of intervention and social control of the state machine – although qualitatively superior to its historical predecessors – was, in the final analysis, fairly limited in the sense that many areas of civil society remained outside state control. Today the claims of the Keynesian welfare state are more modest, in the sense that state powers are constitutionally defined and subject to periodic electoral control, but the capacity of social intervention and the control of the state apparatuses has grown out of all proportion, because few areas escape inspection. It is not only a question of the apparatuses' multiplication and extension or of the diversification of their functions and competences – agriculture, industry, commerce, public transport, education, health, social security – but above all a problem of the use of special surveillance and control techniques, based on the new sophisticated information systems. Bobbio has commented:

> If it is true that in a democratic state power is more open to public scrutiny than in an autocratic state, it is also true that the use of computers (which are being used more and more to store the personal files of citizens) allows the holders to know more about the public than was possible in past states. The new prince can get to know far more about his subjects than most absolute monarchs of the past. Which goes to show that, notwithstanding the profound transformation of relations between rulers and ruled brought about by the development of democracy, the process of the publicization of power ... is anything but linear. (1985, p. 21)

The two characteristic features of the Keynesian welfare state raise, nonetheless, a fundamental question, the contradiction between constitutional power and discretionary power, between *Rechtstaat* and *Machtstaat* (constitutional state and state power), visible power and invisible power, publicity and secrecy (*arcana imperii*). The problem was posed historically with the transformation of the absolute state – where the dominant principle was that the prince's power was more effective, the more that it was concealed from the people's indiscreet gaze – into the constitutional state characterized by public control of power through the free formation of public opinion, theorized initially by Kant. However, there is no state, whether democratic or autocratic, that has abandoned invisible power to date. Hence the problem today is the limits of the two faces of state power, the one guaranteed by law and the other exposed to the exercise of pure power. In this connection, two notations by Bobbio are helpful: firstly, if all states resort to invisible power, 'there is still a difference between autocracy and democracy in that for the former the state secrecy is a rule, whereas for the latter it is an exception regulated by laws which do not permit it to be extended unduly' (1984, p. 92); secondly, the victory of visible power over invisible is never final, for 'invisible power resists the advance of the visible and is always inventing new ways of hiding itself and of seeing without being seen' (1985, p. 20). We must, therefore, take account not only of the visible aspects of the state form, but also of the invisible ones. If the state form is defined in terms of constitutional criteria, its mode of operation – and this is what interests us – is determined as much by informal elements, which can also be invisible, whether extra-constitutional or secret or not.

The forms of government

The traditional distinction in the forms of government in Europe was Machiavelli's (1513–19) between monarchy or the government of one, and republic or the government of the many, usually an assembly. The great modern territorial states developed, in fact, in the monarchical form, above all in the absolute state era. On the other hand, the republican form remained linked to the government of tiny states, like the Italian city-states or the Hanseatic League. This was the basis of Machiavelli's distinction. However, thanks to one of those ironies of which history is full, the first great republic of the contemporary era, the USA, chose a form of government that resembled more the monarchical – with a popularly elected president as head of the executive, even if in competition with representative assemblies – than the republican form. Moreover, the progressive replacement of royal with parliamentary power in the surviving European monarchies in the course of the nineteenth century meant that the traditional distinction between monarchy and republic lost its meaning. It is no surprise, therefore, that current forms are based on totally different criteria. A first element was formulated by Bagehot (1867), when he stressed the different relations between executive power and legislative power in two types of regime: 'the independence of the legislative and executive powers is the specific quality of presidential government, just as their fusion and combination is the precise principle of cabinet government' (p. 69). In consequence, the two ideal types – the presidential form of government or separation of powers and the parliamentary form of government or the fusion of powers – highlight a distinction that concerns the dynamics of their institutional relations, whether in modes of election, the basis of legitimacy or the balance of their respective constitutional prerogatives.

Constitutional forms

The distinction between the two powers in the two forms can be illustrated, at least as regards the bases of their authority, by means of diagrams (figure 7.1). In the presidential form (model USA) there is a clear-cut separation between executive and legislature, based on the

a) Presidential government (USA)

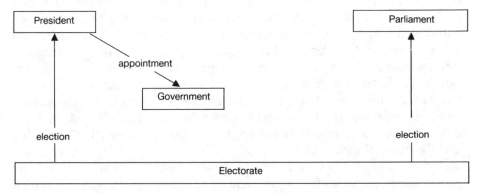

b) Semi-presidential government (Fifth Republic France)

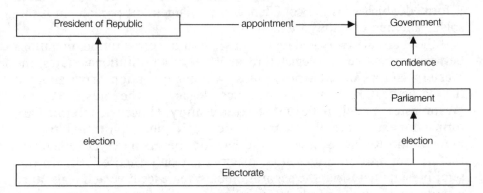

c) Parliamentary government (Great Britain, Italy and FRG)

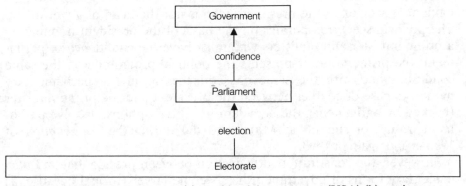

Figure 7.1 Forms of government: (a) presidential government (USA) (b) semi-presidential government (Fifth Republic France) (c) parliamentary government (UK, Italy and FRG)

direct election of the president of the republic – who is head of state *and* head of the executive – and that of parliament, and on the responsibility of the government to the president and *not* to parliament. This model operates on the basis of the following political scenario: the president presents his legislative programme to parliament which examines it and approves it or rejects it, the latter without undermining the president's mandate, or that of the government. In the parliamentary form (model Britain, but also Germany and Italy), there is, on the contrary, a fusion of powers, based on the direct election of parliament and the indirect election of the head of state by parliament – except in Britain which is still a monarchy – and on the responsibility of the government to parliament, which is expressed in the vote of confidence or censure; and, furthermore, on the distinction between the head of state (largely a figurehead) and the head of government/executive (prime minister). This model naturally operates on the basis of a very different political scenario: the prime minister presents his political programme to parliament which examines it and may approve it; if it rejects it there is a government crisis in which the government is forced to resign and either a new government is formed which wins the confidence of parliament, or parliament is dissolved and new elections are held.

If these are the two ideal types that govern the constitutional relations between executive and legislature in Western constitutional states, the Western European countries, almost without exception, have adopted the parliamentary form – a historical legacy of the prestige of the Westminster model in the nineteenth century. However, intermediary forms do exist, like the semi-presidential regime illustrated by the French Fifth Republic, in which the relations between executive and legislature can also be represented diagrammatically (figure 7.1b). In this semi-presidential form, the separation between executive and legislature is more apparent than real; it, too, is based on the direct elections of both the president of the republic and parliament, but, in contrast to the pure presidential model, also on the responsibility of the government to parliament as well as to the president, who is not the head of government. The political scenario operates on the basis of the president nominating a prime minister and ministers who must have the confidence of parliament; the prime minister presents the political programme in the same conditions and with the same consequences as in the parliamentary model. In case of conflict between the president and the prime minister (backed by parliament), the president has three options: dissolve parliament, resign or submit, as Mitterrand did during the *cohabitation* of 1986–8 and again in 1993.

However, the constitutional distinction between presidential and parliamentary forms of government has become largely formal because, as Bobbio has again pointed out, it is 'constructed on mechanisms with which the system of constitutional powers should function rather than on their effective functioning' (1985, p. 105). Today the actual form of government in Western Europe is 'party government'.

The executive and its prerogatives

The word 'government' is ambiguous as to what it covers. The same is true of the expression 'executive power' since it comprises two institutional realities and two types of personnel which, for heuristic reasons, it is useful to distinguish: ministers, who form the political executive (cabinet[3]); and civil servants, who man the public administration. It is the latter who carry out much of that political activity in the wider sense, that is the executive's politics, or politics *tout court*. In this chapter we are interested in the former – that is to say the political executive in the narrower sense – because the latter work under the constitutional responsibility, and according to the political direction, of the former. The public administration and the policy process, including relations between politicians and civil servants, are the object of chapter 8.

The cabinet seems to have had a dual origin – king's council, but also parliamentary committee – which has allowed it to compose two opposing needs: the royal desire to govern (in contemporary language, leadership) and the subjects'/citizens' will to have a voice (today, political communication). This dual aspect of the cabinet – executive and legislative – must be stressed because it explains its effective functioning and limits, and the conditions of such limits. Bagehot shrewdly defined it as 'a combining committee – a *hyphen* which joins, a *buckle* which fastens the legislative part of the state to the executive part of the state. In its origin it belongs to the one, in its function it belongs to the other' (p. 68). Thus if it is the centre of policy formulation, at least constitutionally, it also has a parliamentary management role, for the simple reason that every government that wants to stay in power must necessarily be able to control legislative decisions.

In this situation, what are the constitutional prerogatives of the executive? As a premise, however, we need to note that Britain lacks a written constitution:[4] its constitutional law is composed of statutes and conventions which have no different status from other laws. This means that they can be modified by a simple parliamentary majority. France, Germany and Italy, on the other hand, have 'rigid constitutions', which means not only that constitutional law takes precedence over all other forms of law (administrative, civil, penal[5]) as a source of principles proclaimed and interpreted by a constitutional court (Conseil Constitutionnel, Bundesverfassungsgericht, Corte Costituzionale), but also that the individual articles can only be modified as a result of special procedures, usually qualified majorities (three-fifths or two-thirds) in both houses, and sometimes referendum. A fundamental feature of West European constitutions is their 'normative' quality, namely they have an ensemble of procedural dispositions that limit the exercise of government power to prevent arbitrary acts justified in the name of the will of the people.

The constitutional prerogatives directly attributed to the government, or prime minister, in parliamentary regimes are usually rather limited and generic: suffice it to look at the relative dispositions of the West European constitutions (articles 54–61 of the German basic law, section II of the French Fifth Republic constitution of 1958, and articles 92–6 of the Italian republican constitution of 1948). The British prime minister Sir Anthony Eden succinctly specified the British ones: 'the right to choose one's colleagues and request the dissolution of parliament and, if a Conservative, to nominate the party chairman'. In fact, these dispositions more or less establish, national details apart, that the prime minister determines general policy and is responsible for it. The reason is very simple and depends historically on the fact that the struggle for establishing a parliamentary regime ended with the transfer of national sovereignty to parliament, with the sovereign (the queen in Britain, presidents of the republic in Fourth Republic France, in Germany and in Italy) as a symbolic figurehead. Thus it is no accident that the constitutional prerogatives are attributed both to the head of state and to parliament.

In the first case, with the exception of France because of the dual executive of the semi-presidential form, the prerogatives of the head of state cannot be exercised personally, but require the counter-signature of the prime minister and competent ministers. Instances of the head of state's prerogatives in parliamentary regimes are those of the president of the Italian republic which include, *inter alia*, commanding the armed forces, ratifying international treaties, presiding over the higher council of the judiciary, convoking and dissolving parliament, promulgating the laws, sending messages to parliament, granting pardons, and appointing five constitutional judges and five life senators. Those of the German president appear more restricted: the command of the armed forces, for example, is in the hands of the minister of defence in peacetime and in those of the federal chancellor in wartime. In Fifth Republic France, in addition to the traditional prerogatives of a figurehead head of state which the president can, in numerous cases, exercise personally and without ministerial counter-signatures, he has the right (article 16) to declare a state of emergency which he can personally supervise, as de Gaulle did in 1961 during the Algerian crisis. The political consequence is that the constitutional prerogatives of the head of state, a representative personality in a parliamentary regime, are exercised, in fact, by the government and prime minister. In France, because of the difference of regime, in normal times – that is when the president of the republic is the recognized leader of the parliamentary majority – he exercises both his own and the government's prerogatives.

In the second case, the attribution of political sovereignty to parliament means the ability to 'make and unmake' the laws. Moreover, the fact that governments must have the confidence of parliament means hypothetically that parliament can choose the government. Indeed, according to Bagehot, in the middle of the last century what he calls the 'elective function' was parliament's main task: 'the main function of the House of Commons is one which we know quite well, though our common constitutional speech does not recognize it. The House of Commons is an electoral chamber; it is the assembly which chooses our President [the prime minister]' (p. 150). Finally, parliament is provided with a set of mechanisms for controlling the government (questions, committees of inquiry, motions of censure). However, the development of the party system has turned upside-down the relations between government and parliament – executive and legislature – theorized by Bagehot: instead of parliament controlling government activity, it is the prime minister and cabinet who control parliamentary activity. In the case of Britain, for instance, Eden concluded that the few prerogatives of the prime minister specified earlier 'amounted to a formidable total of power'. The result in the actual democracies of today is a situation in which the executive and its leader, the prime minister, exercise in fact the sum of the constitutional prerogatives (i.e. the formal powers) of the executive *and* the legislature.

The role of parliament

Parliament has been defined as an assembly or system of assemblies based on a 'representative principle' that determines the criteria of their composition. Up to now, we have spoken of parliaments as though they were the direct expression of universal suffrage. But this is not the case, since the four parliaments are bicameral and in each only one house, the lower – House of Commons in Britain, Assemblée Nationale in France, Bundestag in Germany and Camera dei Deputati in Italy – is effectively elected by universal suffrage. The other, the upper house, is formed in various ways: the Italian Senato della Repubblica is the only one elected by universal suffrage, but by electors who are 25 years of age and over; the French Sénat is elected by indirect suffrage of the *grands électeurs* (*députés, conseilleurs généraux* and delegates from communal councils); the German Bundesrat is made up of members of the *Länder* governments (three to six members per *Land* according to population[6]); and the British House of Lords is composed of hereditary and life peers. The second house is usually less important and does not have the right to bring the government down, except in Italy: its different composition is justified by the need to represent the nation in a different form. Thus the Bundesrat represents the federal element in Germany (it has a form that resembles the House of Princes of the Second Reich), the Italian Senate represents the regions and the French Senate represents the 'local communities' (*collectivités locales*). The British House of Lords is a pre-democratic and feudal house that is without representative justification: however, the nomination of politicians and other public men and women to life peerages in the last 30 years was intended to give it the role of a house of sages. In case of conflict between the two houses, the regulations establish diverse solutions: either the supremacy of one house (in the British case the House of Commons prevails) or a committee of mediation of both houses (*navette* in the French case; *Vermittlungsausschuss* in the German).

A second aspect that deserves attention is the internal organization of parliament. An element common to all the European houses is the presidency (the speaker in Britain), which is the principal organ of internal regulation and procedure. In general, the assemblies have the right to control their own agenda and their own work, but in France, according to the 1958 constitution, this passed into the government's hands. In Britain in the second half of the last century, the government introduced various restrictive procedures (including the guillotine or closure debate) as a remedy to the filibustering of the Irish nationalists. In Germany and Italy, the agenda is fixed by agreement between parliamentary party groups. Perhaps more important is the organization of parliamentary standing committees, made necessary by the number of MPs and the ever growing amount of work. The organizational criteria vary from state to state: the committees are particularly important in Italy because they have the power (article 75) – with certain guarantees for the minority[7] – to legislate (it is worth bearing in mind that 75 per cent of Italian legislation is passed in committee); and much less important in Britain where, until recently (before 1979[8]), *ad hoc* committees were formed for legislation, and where most bills are still debated and approved on the floor of the house. The more stable the membership of a committee – as is usually the case with standing committees – the greater is its political cohesion and, in consequence, its political weight. Italian practice suggests that the decisional process tends to differ between committee and the floor of the house: negotiation and bargaining in committee (90 per cent of the laws approved in committee are unanimous), majority vote on the floor (as the English and French examples confirm) (table 7.1).

In his analysis, Bagehot indicated five functions of parliament: elective, expressive, teaching, informing and legislative. What is interesting is the significance that he attributed to the sociological functions: expression, teaching and informing. Indeed, institutional analysis has always given an almost exclusive importance to the constitutional and procedural aspects of parliamentary activity, namely the confidence – Bagehot's elective – function, in the first place, but also the classic parliamentary function, the legislative, 'of which of course', Bagehot also wrote, 'it would be preposterous to deny the great importance, and which I only deny to be *as* important as the executive management of the whole state, or the political education given by parliament to the whole nation' (p. 153). However, for both these functions the situation has radically changed as a result of the development of the party system: the stronger the executive and the greater its control of the parliamentary majority, the smaller and more organic the legislative output – Britain, France and Germany in relation to Italy[9] – and the more private member legislation

Table 7.1 Annual average legislative output as bills presented and acts passed, 1960s and 1980s

	Britain			France			Germany			Italy		
	Bills	Acts	Acts/bills (%)	Bills	Acts	Acts/bills (%)	Bills	Acts	Acts/bills (%)	Bills	Acts	Acts/bills (%)
1960s												
Government bills	69	64	93	70	49	70	104	92	88	332	266[a]	80
Private members' bills	80	11	14	248	10	4	62	21	34	882	154	17
Total	149	75	50	318	59	19	166	113	68	1215	420[a]	35
Govt bills and acts as % of total	46	85		22	80		63	81		26	62	
1980s												
Government bills	46	45	98	107	98	91	36	26	72	439	248[a]	56
Private members' bills	111	16	14	444	15	3	24	8	33	1163	55	5
Total	156	61	39	551	113	21	60	34	13	1602	303[a]	19
Govt bills and acts as % of total	29	74		19	87		60	77		22	72	

[a] Includes decree laws
Source: various parliamentary publications

becomes marginal. Indeed, the major part of the bills approved is government legislation (table 7.1). The most important reforms of parliament introduced in Western Europe in the post-war period have, in fact, had as their goal either the protection of government against erosion of parliamentary majority – for instance, the German constructive vote of no confidence (article 67 of the basic law), limitations on votes of censure by only counting opposition votes in France (article 49 of 1958 constitution) and abolition of secret votes on third readings of bills in Italy (in 1988) – or the reduction of legislation in favour of executive regulation as in Germany (article 34), or again the use of the *vote bloqué* or 'package vote' in France (article 44) and decree laws in Italy (article 77).[10]

On the other hand, the sociological functions indicated by Bagehot are those which are most prized today by the supporters of parliamentarianism. The expressive function – that is representation – is the very essence of democracy: the support of parliament elected by universal suffrage is the basis of Western European governments' legitimation; and we can add that parliamentary representation legitimates the opposition parties too. This remains true even though the qualifications for being a political majority (in terms of valid votes won in general elections) are, in many cases, anything but convincing (chapter 5). The teaching and informing functions operate today as the principal forms of parliamentary control on the government; questions and select committee reports are used, in fact, by the opposition as instruments of publicity and denunciation of the government's action or inaction. But, to operate successfully, they require the amplifier that is the media to secure the necessary widespread public propagation of information and criticisms, although the press is often an inadequate instrument for this task. When the government and ministers are forced to justify a certain policy, thanks to parliamentary questions and reports, they reveal information that otherwise would not be published. And without information there can be no political debate.

The teaching function fulfils two needs: on the one hand, criticism of government policy and the proposal of an alternative policy by the opposition parties demonstrate the limits of the former and remind the government that its mandate can be reversed at the next election; on the other, the confrontation between government and opposition, in parliamentary debates during the legislature, gives continuity to political life which would otherwise be reduced to sporadic electoral campaigns. Parliament supplies, in fact, a permanent channel of expression for party competition: the very heart of representative democracy. It permits the coexistence 'under the same roof' of a plurality of political forces and allows that 'reciprocity of behaviour, communication and collaboration' which helps to create a fundamental cohesion between political forces which can be a precious element in moments of grave national crisis. But often, as an Italian MP has observed: 'the house is empty. It fills up only on the great occasions, when there is the firework spectacle of the clash between party leaders, but, even in this case, the decisions are already taken, the debate only registers party positions without anyone daring to change opinion at its conclusion' (Radi, 1973, p. 126). This merely serves to confirm Alfred Grosser's (1964) widely quoted verdict: 'Everywhere the legislative initiative has passed into the hands of the administrations. The legislatures sometimes amend, rarely reject, usually ratify. Their members continue, indeed, to call themselves collectively "the legislative power" in the law books, but in most cases they merely participate in the procedure of registration' (p. 161).

Party government: the majority factor

Bagehot was the first person to appreciate the significance of the majority factor as the key to the executive's power in parliamentary regimes. It was subsequently theorized by Dicey (1885) and, much later, systematized by Duverger (1951; 1955). Since the British party that won the general election had an absolute majority in the House of Commons that was prepared to support its leader as prime minister, and his cabinet composed of party parliamentary colleagues, Dicey theorized that the cabinet was in effect chosen by the electorate and directly responsible to it. In place of parliament as the elector of the prime minister and cabinet in Bagehot's liberal version, Dicey, in a more 'democratic' version, emphasized the axis between the government (prime minister) and the people (electorate). Thus, transposing a celebrated aphorism, we can say: 'it is the people who reign, but do not rule.' It was the difference in the working of parliamentary government in Britain and on the continent – Third and Fourth Republic France, Weimar Germany and liberal and republican Italy – that induced Duverger to formulate and refine two models of parliamentary government: (1) 'majority government' or *la république des citoyens*; and (2) 'non-majority government' or *la république des députés*. They were founded on two opposing logics: (1) zero-sum game and (2) positive-sum game. He noted (1982), moreover, that this distinction between them could be extended to semi-presidential regimes of the French type, as was confirmed by the *cohabitation* experience of 1986–8, and we see no reason why it cannot be extended to pure presidential regimes like the USA.

The characteristic features of each of the models can be summarized in a set of specific points.

Majority government (zero-sum competition)

Firstly, two parties (or alliances of parties) can hope to win parliamentary majorities and have sufficient party discipline to ensure their cohesion because the winner takes all and the loser is completely marginalized until the next election. The winning party (or alliance) is able to form a homogeneous government and apply its political programme. Secondly, the government can expect to last a whole parliament, and so is stable. The only likelihood of crisis is internal and, in view of the political consequences for the government party (that is, loss of power), crises are rare. Thirdly, the government is powerful because the prime minister exercises, as head of government, executive prerogatives *and*, as head of the majority party, parliamentary powers. The opposition is reduced to engaging in the teaching and informing functions, with a view to making the electorate aware of the stakes at the next election, because the separation between government and opposition is politically rigid. Fourthly, the citizens, as electors, choose at the election, through the vote for a party, the government and its leader. Electoral propaganda in this situation is naturally concentrated on party leaders, as would-be prime ministers, and their programmes, and so has a presidential aspect. The result, according to Duverger, is that this model can be defined as a form of 'direct democracy' in the modern, and not the classical, sense of the term, that is to say a system in which the government and its leaders are directly elected by the citizenry. Moreover, since the government has the means of governing during its mandate, the government is judged at the subsequent election on its record for which it is responsible and hence cannot escape responsibility. Finally, in moments of grave political conflict between government and opposition, the government can always appeal to the electorate to resolve it by an early dissolution, as prime minister Heath did in February 1974, even if with rather disconcerting results!

Non-majority government (positive-sum competition)

Firstly, no party (or coherent alliance) can normally hope to win a parliamentary majority and, hence, no party is completely marginalized. The government is formed necessarily on the basis of heterogeneous and fragile coalitions. In consequence, the partner parties have difficulty in agreeing to a government programme of action which is, therefore, usually generic and limited. Secondly, the government is usually unstable because it is at the mercy of a coalition member withdrawing for tactical reasons. The fear of the political success of one of the coalition partners leads to the other parties preventing the government's common action. Thirdly, the prime minister is deprived of the means of acting effectively, because he is not only not the recognized leader of the parliamentary majority, but often not even that of his own party, and so he is obliged to bargain continuously with the party leaders of his coalition partners over the government programme. He can also be obliged to seek and negotiate the support of the opposition parties to secure approval of certain government measures. In consequence, the separation between government and opposition is often politically confused. The opposition parties, in tactical alliances with dissatisfied groups of government coalition backbenchers, can bring the government down, or even get some of their policies adopted. Thus the opposition often plays, as the Italian example shows, an active role in the legislative programme. Fourthly, at the election, the citizens as electors do not choose the government as such. The prime minister and government are chosen by the party leaders on the basis of parliamentary seats won and lost. Since a variety of coalition combinations is possible, party leaders are free to act as they judge fit and can change the coalition formula during a parliamentary session without recourse to elections. This stimulates the rulers' irresponsibility because of the lack of a clear responsibility for government actions. The result, according to Duverger, is what he calls a 'mediated democracy' because party leaders act as 'mediators', organizing different coalition combinations in line with their interpretation of the immediate political situation, and without the electors being able to intervene in this process. The government parties usually cannot be punished by the electors because of the lack of a credible alternative majority. There are, in fact, several oppositions and *not* one opposition able to become a parliamentary majority.

These models of Duverger are extreme ideal types, in the sense that they specify polar situations. Concrete reality is always more complex; there are many mixed situations. However, Duverger (1951) argues that there are two further elements that we must bear in mind in understanding their working. One is the nature of the party system and the other is political, or more correctly governmental, alternation. For him, the two are intimately linked and take us back to the discussion on party systems (chapter 5): political alternation is the discriminating factor that determines the two opposing logics – zero-sum game and positive-sum game – which differentiate the two models of party government.

Government alternation

The necessary condition for alternation is the absence of sizeable parliamentary 'anti-system' parties. However, Hamon (1977) specified three further conditions. (1) Alternation must guarantee, to the political forces that leave office and go into opposition, the legal possibility of winning power back. In other words, the new rulers must be prepared to give up power, if defeated at subsequent elections. (2) Alternation requires a minimum of consensus on fundamental national values, such as respect for basic human rights and the political institutions. (3) Alternation presupposes that the new majority does not violently disturb existing social structures. In other words, it can introduce reforms, but only in so far as they are spelt out in their electoral programme. Hamon argues that if these conditions are not respected, then the door is open for civil war.

In this perspective, Duverger (1964), for instance, has defended the thesis that the reign of the so-called *marais* – that is the French centrism of the Third and Fourth Republics – was the only way in which parliamentary democracy could be implanted in France. The socio-political conflicts were too deep after the traumas of 1789, 1848 and 1870 for a progressive party and a reactionary party to be able to face each other electorally without the risk of civil war. Mutual legitimation was, in fact, missing. Thus there was no alternative to a weak and immobile 'centrism': multiparty non-majority government made compromise possible between apparently irreconcilable opposites. Only with the Fifth Republic was the necessary mutual recognition forthcoming, but it still took 25 years for the first alternation (1981) to occur. The same logic was implicit in the theorization of Christian Democrat leaders, for whom Italy was a 'special type' of democracy, namely a 'besieged democracy', which, as much for external as for internal reasons, could not afford the luxury of government alternation with the Communist opposition. It would have created an untenable political crisis. Hence were created the permanent multiparty coalitions promoted by the DC. The argument today is that with the end of the Cold War, what was possible in France is now possible in Italy: 'the story of constitutional reform', Fusaro (1991) has noted, 'is the effort to build a democracy that is no longer crippled and which is able to function better, not because it has failed; on the contrary: it is just because it has given such good results over the years and because, also thanks to it, Italy has changed enormously. Above all, its citizens and their expectations have changed' (p. 28). Lack of alternation, it is claimed, is the 'crippling' aspect of Italian democracy. Hence it is no coincidence that the first fruits of constitutional reform in Italy, even if under duress – *tangentopoli* and the fiscal crisis – took the form of a mixed-majority electoral regime, forced through parliament in summer 1993 in the wake of the popular referendum of 1993 (Allum, 1993; see chapter 5 in this book).

Be this as it may, alternation is never a simple matter. The lack of a credible alternative – namely, an opposition capable of becoming the majority – is too convenient a position for a government party or coalition, which effectively has the means of defining the opposition 'anti-system', to abandon readily. It is not just a case of artificially dramatizing what is at stake; it is also one of the government's own identification with the right to office. Grosser (1985), for instance, wrote of the 'alternation' in Bonn in 1969:

> the CDU ... not only demonstrated disappointment and rancour. It was offended as though the exercise of power was a natural right for it, as if the Christian Democrat chancellor had a legitimacy superior to that of a Socialist. In 1981, similar reactions occurred in France, when alternation took place after the same majority had been in power for twenty-two years. (p. 157)

In the 1980s, there was a systematic attempt by the Thatcherite Conservatives to impede alternation in Britain by accusing the Labour

Party of Trotskyism in order to delegitimize it as a credible political alternative to a Conservative government.[11]

Now, if we examine the way alternation operates in practice, we will see that it is a much more complex phenomenon than its theorization would lead us to suppose. In fact, there is not just one type of alternation. Quermonne (1986) distinguishes three types: absolute alternation; relative alternation; and mediated alternation. Absolute alternation occurs where there is a transfer of government from one party majority to another, with all the parties in power going into opposition and vice versa. The obvious example is Britain in the first 35 post-war years when Conservatives and Labour both alternated in office three times, roughly for an equal period. However, since the SDP–Labour split of 1981, the Conservatives have remained in office, winning three further elections: the Conservatives have had 31 years in power since 1945, Labour only 17. The other example is Fifth Republic France in 1981, when president Mitterrand won the presidential elections in May, immediately dissolved the National Assembly and led the left to victory and an absolute parliamentary majority in June. In the following parliamentary elections in March 1986, the right alliance triumphed with an absolute majority; yet Mitterrand remained in the Elysée palace to complete his seven-year term, appointed Chirac, leader of the right, as prime minister, and accepted the *cohabitation*. This, according to Quermonne, was not an absolute alternation, but only what he calls a relative alternation. However, semi-presidential regimes with differential mandates for the presidency and for parliament raise a special problem when compared with parliamentary regimes. We prefer, nevertheless, to consider the 1986 and 1993 alternations, like the 1988 one (which saw the return of the left), as absolute because, despite his special prerogatives as head of state, president Mitterrand was no longer leader of the parliamentary majority during the *cohabitation* periods and became something of a figurehead. At all events, in the 35 years of the Fifth Republic, the right have been in power for 25 years and the left for 10.

The third type of alternation for Quermonne is mediated alternation: a situation in which the major party of the government coalition goes into opposition and is replaced by the major opposition party, but a third minor party remains in power, changing political alliances. Germany furnishes the obvious concrete illustrations: in 1969 the CDU was forced into opposition and an SPD-FDP coalition was formed; and in 1982 the SPD was forced into opposition and a CDU-FDP coalition was formed. Since this type of alternation is partial – at the political level of the parliamentary majority and not that of the people through elections – we prefer to ignore Quermonne's second type and define the third type as relative rather than mediated alternation. Finally we can note for completeness that, in the 44 years of the Federal Republic, the CDU has been in power for 32 years, the SPD for 16 years, but the small FDP for 39. On the other hand, in Italy, as noted above, there has been no alternation, whether absolute or relative: the DC is the only party which has remained continuously in power for almost 50 years before it was dissolved and its successor evicted from office.[12]

This said, it is worth insisting on the distinction between the two types of alternation because they are part of two different political scenarios. Absolute alternation occurs as a result of an election – it is determined by the electors – while relative alternation occurs as a result of a reversal of party alliances in parliament, and hence is organized by the party leaders independently of the results of an election, as the German example demonstrates. Thus absolute alternation is linked to majority government and lack of alternation to non-majority government. Relative alternation is in the middle between the two because the power of the government is that of the majority system but the electoral dynamics are those of the non-majority system. At all events, in the first case there is a symbiotic and direct relationship between citizens, elections, government competition and policy (zero-sum competition): this is the situation of Britain and France today. In the second case, the relation is mediated and indirect (positive-sum competition): this is the situation of Italy today,[13] and was that of Third and Fourth Republic France as well as Weimar Germany. Germany today finds itself, as it were, in limbo, in the sense that it does not readily fit into Duverger's schema.

The limits to executive power

A majority government concentrates in its hands the powers of both executive *and* legislature. In other words, as long as the government can count on its parliamentary majority – this is also true in non-majority systems – the limits to the executive's power are meagre. Comforted by their majorities, in fact, a British prime minister and a French president can do almost anything without meeting significant constitutional limits. There are conventionally three types of counterweights: the opposition parties, local autonomy, and the constitutional courts, which can exercise a certain control over the government, but the effective action of each is limited. There is a fourth, often overlooked but perhaps the most important today: the European Union.

The opposition parties, which theoretically represent the classic constitutional countervailing power in the majority system, are powerless by definition, being a minority. Their task is criticism because the only power they have comes from the teaching and informing functions of parliament with a view to winning the next election. However, there is evidence to support the thesis that the opposition parties, like parliament itself, constitute more of a formal than a real limit to the power of the executive. In majority systems, in fact, two factors influence the government and its leader. The first is the government's own backbenchers. The government's power is unchallengeable as long as it can be sure of its majority, and hence the government's principal problem is to 'humour' the backbenchers: for example, the whip system in Britain to ensure party discipline. The government also has a whole arsenal of weapons to secure, in normal times, their continued support: appeals to party loyalty (the fall of the government only serves the opposition); promises of patronage (office and honours); and expulsion (the possibility of losing one's seat). The second factor is public opinion polls. As long as they are favourable to the government, the prime minister is strong; but if they become unfavourable, particularly with an election in the offing, the government, but above all the prime minister or president, are all vulnerable. The approach of an election and the possibility of electoral defeat test the loyalty of MPs, who are seeking re-election, to the prime minister. This explains, for instance, the replacement of Macmillan by Lord Home in 1963 and Mrs Thatcher by Major in 1990. Party leaders are also particularly vulnerable after an electoral defeat, as the examples of Lord Home in 1965 and Heath in 1975 (former Conservative prime ministers) in Britain illustrate, not to mention those of Joachim Rausch and Oscar Lafontaine (SPD) in Germany in the 1980s.

Local autonomy refers to the powers that opposition parties exercise in subcentral governments which can be used to curb the central government's enthusiasms. It is clear that this is more important in federal states like Germany than in centralized unitary states like Britain. Indeed, in Germany, with its executive–administrative relations that involve the *Länder* directly and allow them, through the Bundesrat, to effectively limit the power of the federal government, a premium is placed on harmony and cooperation that often makes purposive, coherent national policy impossible to achieve. In Britain, on the other hand, the central government can override local authorities at will. For example, with a simple act of parliament it can abolish local authorities, as the Conservative government did in 1986 with the metropolitan councils and the GLC, all Labour controlled. In fact, the much-vaunted British local autonomy has been greatly reduced by the centralizing trends of the Thatcher government, which has not only reduced local powers but even claimed the right to fix taxing and spending levels. In Italy, and France after the 1986 regionalization, there is now a more substantial level of autonomy than in Britain. Despite all this, local autonomy does not, except in the case of Germany, often constitute a significant countervailing power to a majority government.

The final national institutional counterweight is represented by the constitutional court which exists in France, Germany and Italy, but not in Britain. This is because they have written constitutions in which constitutional law is the supreme law and supraordinate to all other legal norms and regulations. In Britain instead, as noted, parliamentary sovereignty prevails, which means a much narrower concept of judicial review – limited to the 'natural construction of statute'. The result is that recourse to the law is rarely a realistic remedy for challenging administrative actions. In Britain, in fact, the only formal limits on parliament are those represented by the obligations assumed on entry into the EC in 1973 and by the ratification in 1951 of the European Convention on Human Rights; in consequence of which British governments have regarded as binding most decisions made by the European Court of Human Rights in cases brought by British citizens. To enjoy these rights British citizens have to bring cases to the European Court in Strasbourg, which is a long and costly procedure.[14] As regards the other countries, we need not spell out the details: individual citizen and public authority access in Germany; only public authority access in France and Italy. The important point is that the constitutional courts represent a counterweight of a different kind, namely they are a formal constraint in the sense of a judicial review of the conformity of the legislation (both in content and form) with the constitution, which all parties are obliged to respect as a guarantee of constitutional democratic government.

The EU, as a constraint on national executive power, introduces a different dimension, real but imprecise. It is not simply a case of accepting EU regulations, directives and decisions, although they can be important,[15] but that national governments find themselves in something of a subcentral government situation. The EU was promoted because Western European states became increasingly aware that they were no longer capable of determining their own economic futures alone. The fundamental dynamic of the EU means that states must adopt more constrained policies to remain active and effective members: presence is more important than winning or losing any single decision. A member state that bargains too hard becomes a pariah within the EU and is isolated, as Mrs Thatcher found to her cost in 1990. With 'qualified majority voting' in the Council of Ministers, as a result of the Maastricht Treaty, cooperation, compromise and coalition building are going to be more than ever the name of the game in the EU that even large states will ignore at their peril.

It is no accident, therefore, that in a situation of majority government Duverger should have recognized that the formal limits on national executive power have shrunk considerably: 'in law, the British prime minister could suppress the minority parties and elections', he wrote in 1982 (pp. 194–5), 'and decree dictatorship, but his/her conscience forbids it', and went on to proclaim his conviction that 'democracy is based above all on the beliefs planted in men's hearts.' We can doubt whether these beliefs alone will always be sufficient, particularly in moments of grave crisis. It is likely that an overt authoritarian coup by a government, like suppressing elections or dissolving the principal opposition parties, would provoke such a reaction in civil society as to force the government to back down. Incidentally, membership of the EU, in which a democratic political regime is now one of the solemnly proclaimed principles, makes it less likely, as no West European state today could afford to be ostracized. However, this does not prevent governments from initiating small, and not so small, steps in that direction, namely 'creeping authoritarianism'. There are numerous instances, such as the *Berufsverbot* of 1972 in Germany. In Britain there was the duty of trade unions to ascertain by vote every ten years whether a majority of their members want to subscribe to the political fund which, *inter alia*, funds the Labour Party. The Thatcher government's proposal did not attain its objective in 1986, otherwise it would have deprived the Labour Party of 70 per cent of its funding at the time and so the material possibility of fulfilling its role as the principal opposition party. In these conditions, the limits of executive power in a majority system derive less from the play of the state's representative institutions than from other state apparatuses – leaking of secret documents provoking scandals in Britain, the investigation of illicit government party funding by investigating magistrates in France (*fausses factures*) and Italy (*tangentopoli*) – or from civil society *tout court* or, finally, from international obligations (EU membership).

Non-majority governments are by definition coalition governments, which are considered, following Lord Bryce's (1921) opinion, to be necessarily weak, unstable and inefficient. But, as often happens in such cases, reality is more complex. Firstly, coalition government, abhorred in Anglo-Saxon countries, is preferred on the European continent in the sense that it is the rule while single–party governments are the exception. Secondly, the average duration of coalition governments is not, according to Blondel's (1985, pp. 114–15) data, significantly different from that of single-party governments. It is only when the components of the coalition exceed five, in fact, that government stability declines dramatically: from 2.4 years to less than one year. This general trend is confirmed in the data for the four countries (table 7.2). Thirdly, the data suggest that the discriminating element is whether there is, or is not, a coherent parliamentary majority: where there is, even with coalition governments as in Germany and the Fifth Republic, government stability rivals that of Britain (single-party government); but where there is not, as in Italy, government instability has prevailed. However, in the states where the government is sure of its parliamentary majority, the formal

Table 7.2 Number and duration of governments and heads of government to end of 1990

| | Government | | Heads of governments | |
	Number	Duration	Number	Duration
Britain (from 1945)	17	2 y 7 m	9	5 y
France (from 1958)	17	1 y 11m	11	2 y 11 m
			4[a]	8 y
Germany (from 1949)	16	2 y 6 m	6	6 y 10 m
Italy (from 1945)	49	11 m	19	2 y 4 m

[a] President of the republic

limits to executive power are meagre. The question this poses is whether the situation is different in states, like Italy, with non-majority party systems and unstable governments.

The hypothesis is that in this situation parliament counts for more just because there is no coherent majority. The answer in the case of Italy appears to be affirmative: parliament counts, but not for the reasons hypothesized. In fact, governments fell not because they had no parliamentary majority, but because they lacked internal cohesion. The reason – Di Palma (1977) noted – was simple: they were not governing coalitions but *legitimizing* coalitions. The Italian Constituent Assembly, in having to choose between two basic goals – constitutionalism (representation) and efficiency (governability) – after the twenty years of Mussolini's totalitarian fascist regime, chose, not surprisingly, the former. Hence, the larger the coalitions were for reasons of democratic legitimacy, the less politically cohesive they were, which explains their instability. The centrist formula destroys electoral competition because it denies the possibility of an alternative; this promotes the luxury of instability, party disagreements and immobilism. The government operated on the basis of the widest possible consensus. Thus, despite the government majority, the opposition had its say in the legislative programme, not formally, but in informal negotiations which took place, according to Sartori (1964), in 'a series of multiple bargains' in parliament. It was for this reason that parliament counted, that is not as a centre of formal control of legislation, but as 'a powerful and effective negotiating centre' (p. 301). It was not the MPs as MPs who decided, but the party leaders who were also MPs, because government activity was tightly controlled by the parties, to such an extent, in fact, as to deserve the name of *partitocrazia* (partyocracy). In such a situation, we suggest, as a final paradox, that the influence of the Italian opposition parties (PCI/PDS, above all) has been similar to that of the British governing party backbenchers. Not surprisingly, the major part of Italian legislation was approved unanimously or almost. It is a method of governing, common to all centrist government, in dribs and drabs: the big problems are eluded. The centrist formula allowed free institutions to function and take root in Italy during the Cold War, but, as hinted above, the costs – the public debt and public expenditure deficit – now far outweigh the benefits. Hence results the present crisis of the Italian political system and the first faltering steps of constitutional reform: the introduction of a mixed-majority electoral regime and the victory of a right-wing electoral cartel.

Methods of direct democracy

Prior to the 1970s, the use of referendums was rare. In Italy, a referendum was held in 1946 to decide the fate of the monarchy, which was rejected by the narrowest of margins. However, its use was common in

France, where it had a long and vexed history: indeed, democrats saw it as an instrument used by dictators, like Napoleon III, to manipulate public opinion. Finally, de Gaulle institutionalized it in article 11 of the 1958 constitution; and used it in his struggle against the parties as the instrument of his 'dialogue with the nation'. But, after his successes at the beginning of the 1960s to seek approval of his Algerian policy and the election of the president by universal suffrage, defeat in the referendum on regional reform in 1969 led to his resignation. Since then it has been little used by successive French presidents: Pompidou used it for the entry of Britain into the EC, and won but with a very low turnout; and Mitterrand for approval of his New Caledonia policy in 1990 and approval of the Maastricht Treaty in 1992 – won by a whisker at 51 to 49 per cent!

The state where the referendum has had the most interesting developments in the 1970s and 1980s is Italy. Although article 75 of the 1948 constitution provided for a referendum to repeal specific laws, the legislation for its use was only passed in 1970 after the enactment of the divorce law to meet the Catholic lay organizations' protests against it. The Catholic attempt to repeal the divorce law failed, but under pressure from the Radical Party and other groups, 26 other laws have been subjected to referendum by popular initiative (that is by petition of 500,000 signatures collected in six months): the first nine failed, but sixteen of the next seventeen were successful. The significant thing, however, was the decline in turnout: from over 85 per cent in the 1970s to less than 50 per cent in 1990 (the positive result was nullified because the quorum of 50 per cent of the electorate was not met). However, in the 1990s the referendum has become the chosen, if inadequate, instrument of constitutional reform by triggering modification of the Italian electoral system. The 1991 referendum on reducing preference votes in elections demonstrated the strength of opinion in favour of electoral reform,[16] while the eight referendums – and, specifically, the amendment of the Senate electoral law in a majority sense, which won over 90 per cent of the votes cast in April 1993 – made it imperative. Indeed, the Ciampi government formed in its wake placed the introduction of a mixed-majority electoral regime at the top of its political agenda, and, as noted, succeeded in forcing it through parliament by the summer recess (chapter 5).

In Germany and Britain, the political tradition is opposed to the use of the referendum. In Germany, Hitler's use of the plebiscite was such that it was considered an anti-democratic instrument, and today it is limited to the *Land* level for territorial reorganization (article 29 of the basic law). In Britain, it has only been used twice, both in the 1970s, and not as a democratic instrument – its use is in contradiction to the concept of national sovereignty vested in parliament – but to resolve a party dilemma. The first, in 1975 to sanction the renegotiation of Britain's conditions of entry into the EC, was intended to prevent a Labour Party split. The second in 1979 was to approve devolution for Wales and

Scotland, but its negative outcome led to the fall of the Callaghan government through a vote of censure in the House of Commons followed by defeat at the polls.

In conclusion, despite the existence of a political climate favourable to greater direct participation by the people in major political decisions in the 1970s – but against this there was the opposition of the parties which saw the referendum as a rival instrument to the representative parliamentary system of which they were the major exponents – the results of the referendary experience were rather disappointing. This has been particularly true in Italy, where it has only an abrogative, and not a propositive, function, although its role has been fundamental in the 1990s as a catalyst for promoting constitutional change. The referendum is a cumbersome instrument to be used with caution because of the risks of excessive simplification that it involves. The European democratic tradition is essentially parliamentarian, that is to say founded, with all its limits, on the representative principle.

The national political elite

In addition to the functions already mentioned, parliament is responsible for a further task: the recruitment of the government's political personnel; in other words, the pre-selection of ministers. In three of the four states, in fact, ministers are MPs: the exception is Fifth Republic France, where there is incompatibility between ministerial office and a parliamentary mandate. In the early years of the Fifth Republic, de Gaulle appointed many ministers from outside parliament, but subsequently even he recognized the legitimizing power of election, obliging his ministers to stand for parliament in order to resign immediately after election. Thus the majority of French ministers have a parliamentary connection, even in the Fifth Republic.

More generally, the concept of representation has a plurality of meanings that go from representation as the 'mirror' of the population represented (representativeness) to representation as a trustee relationship of an abstract and Rousseauian 'general will' usually defined as the national interest. The latter had its most famous formulation in Burke's celebrated 'Speech to the Electors of Bristol' (1774) in which he said:

> Your representative owes you, not his industry only, but his judgement; and he betrays, instead of serving you, if he sacrifices it to your opinion ... Parliament is not a *congress* of ambassadors from different and hostile interests ... but parliament is a *deliberative* assembly of *one* nation, with *one* interest, that of the whole; where, not local purposes and prejudices, ought to guide, but the general good, resulting from the general reason of the whole. You chose a member indeed; but when you have chosen him, he is not

the member for Bristol, but he is a member of *parliament*.
(Burke, 1987, pp. 109–10)

However, representation in the first sense refers to a correspondence
between the social composition of MPs and that of the electorate. And
this for the reasons specified by another British politician, Nye Bevan
(1952):

> A representative person is one who will act in much the same way
> as those he represents would act in that situation. In short, he
> must be of their kind ... Election is only one part of representa-
> tion. It becomes full representation only if the elected person
> speaks with the authentic accents of those who have elected him.
> That does not mean that he need be provincial nor that he speaks
> in the local vernacular. It does mean that he should share their
> values, that is, be in touch with their realities. (pp. 14–15)

Members of parliament: a collective profile

If, as Cotta (1976) has noted, the class dimension is the only one given
serious consideration in terms of sociological representativeness, it
involves others, such as the gender, territorial, ethnic, linguistic and religious dimensions. Of these, often the only one thought to be relevant is
the territorial. At all events, even the most summary look at MPs' social
composition suggests that one should be talking of '*un*representativeness' and *not* representativeness. MPs are overwhelmingly male and middle-aged, predominantly middle class and in the professions, and usually
university educated. This merely confirms a well-known fact that politics
is a middle class occupation because political skills are middle class skills
(table 7.3). An Italian MP has claimed that: 'the person who does not
understand the inside machinations, the thousand little tricks that win
votes, will never be elected an MP. Support is always the fruit of diligent
preparation and meticulous organization. Spontaneous support does not
guarantee success' (Radi, 1973, p. 43).

However, the middle class's position is not completely uniform, as the
data might suggest. First of all, there has been a substantial change in the
social origin of MPs in the 100 years from the middle of the last century
to the end of World War II. In this period, the nobility and the grand
bourgeoisie (the notables) which dominated European parliaments in
the first half of the nineteenth century were reduced to a small minority.
On the other hand, the workers, who were excluded by restricted suffrage until the late nineteenth century, represented a similar minority.
Secondly, the difference of social origin has a party basis: MPs of working class origin were elected almost exclusively in left-wing party lists
(labour, socialist and communist); similarly, MPs of noble and upper

Table 7.3 Selected characteristics of MPs, 1950s and 1980s (per cent)

	Britain		France		Germany		Italy	
	1950s	1980s	1950s	1980s	1950s	1980s	1950s	1980s
Gender								
Men	96	94	98	94	91	85	96	87
Women	4	6	2	6	9	15	4	13
Occupation								
Lawyers	22	16	16	6	8	6	21	12
Other professions (doctors/engineers)	4	3	18	19	6	2	6	10
Civil servants	3	4	11	17	21	17	5	7
Army	6	2	1	1	–	–	1	1
Business/management	22	28	22	17	20	15	10	11
Teachers (inc. univ)	7	14	10	26	5	13	19	20
White collar	1	4	2	3	3	4	2	3
Manual workers	14	11	1	3	2	1	1	3
Farmers	7	3	12	3	11	5	2	2
Journalists	8	7	5	3	7	2	4	2
Party or trade union	3	5	–	1	16	32	28	8
Other	3	3	2	3	–	3	1	23
Age on election								
Under 40 years	14	19	34	–	13	51	32	22
40–50 years	31	38	34	–	30	38	32	39
Over 50 years	55	43	32	–	58	11	36	39
Education								
University graduates	55	63	64	78	52	68	71	84
MPs (number)	630	650	552	577	499	497	596	630

Source: various parliamentary publications

bourgeois origins were elected in centre and right-wing party lists. Thirdly, if lawyers are a privileged profession among MPs of all nations – 'the natural aspirants to political careers' for the reasons Weber (1922, p. 875) noted – civil servants also have a prominent place in the French and German assemblies, as do businessmen and teachers in the British and Italian houses respectively (Mastropaolo, 1993). Finally, women remain very seriously underrepresented, which has led to discussions to improve female representation ('elect 300 women MPs' in Britain,[17] *la parité* movement in France).

There is, nonetheless, another party-based difference: the middle class MPs in the right-wing parties are associated with money and tend to have links with the world of finance and commerce, whereas those in the left-wing parties are 'intellectuals' and tend to be linked with the world of ideas. This said, there are elements of progressive uniformization of parliamentary personnel, above all in terms of meritocratic recruitment and progressive professionalization. The latter holds in two senses: 'in the sense that they have a life-long commitment to a specialist career in politics, and in the sense that they are drawn from the professional middle classes' (Burch and Moran, 1985, p. 3). Unfortunately it is difficult to estimate, on the basis of the available data, the number of professional politicians, but they now appear to represent over two-thirds of all MPs in Western Europe.[18]

The centre of interest today has moved from social origins to parties because research suggests that social origin is less important than career and present occupation in determining MPs' attitudes. This confirms Robert de Jouvenel's well-known adage that two MPs, one of whom is a revolutionary, have more things in common than two revolutionaries, one of whom is an MP. The party career is, in fact, the key to MPs' recruitment and hence to representation. However, sociological representativeness is not the most important element in the representative principle (and *pour cause*, since it is largely a case of 'social unrepresentativeness'). Representation in the Western world is now conceived as the representation of interests rather than of persons and as such it is secured by institutional mechanisms. It is for this reason that real representation is partisan (or party) and is secured by the electoral system: better in Italy[19] and Germany with PR than in Britain and France with plurality systems.

Members of parliament: patterns of recruitment

Parliamentary personnel are the result of party careers on one side and the parties' public image on the other, with the recruitment process constituting the central element. Political careers obviously vary in the various West European states, but Panebianco (1982) has proposed two models which help clarify the situation. One is a 'centripetal' model which implies recruitment by cooption of the organizational centre, as occurs in the strongly institutionalized parties (mass parties), equipped with a centralized organization capable of controlling candidatures; hence those wishing to make a political career must adapt to the centre's requirements. The other is a 'centrifugal' model which implies a horizontal type of recruitment because it is possible to convert social resources into political resources. This is the typical situation of weakly institutionalized parties (notables and catch-all people's parties) in which the leadership is usually composed of a plurality of groups in various alliances or conflicts and so incapable of controlling candidatures. In the former, the vertical integration of the leadership group is secured by the fact that the power centre is located with the party leadership, as a result of which party careers are strongly structured with entry at the bottom and a slow climb up. In the latter, instead, such a possibility is usually excluded because the power centre is located in the parliamentary group, to which it is possible to accede directly. Indeed, parliamentary candidacies are often solicited from outside personalities for the contribution in terms of the votes, funds or technical competence that they can bring to the party.

Such a situation encourages, in the big organized parties, the candidature of militants and explains the presence, in certain parties, of MPs coming from certain underrepresented social groups, like the working class and the petty bourgeoisie. This is particularly true of left-wing parties which pursue a policy which encourages the recruitment of working class and trade union candidates to strengthen their links with the class which they claim to represent historically. It is also true that the same parties have made a similar effort to support and elect women candidates, but with much less success so far. However, the problem is not so much that the quota of MPs of modest origins is higher than in the other (bourgeois) parties, but that they remain such a minority in these parties too. This is explained by the strength of social mechanisms that benefit professional politics and handicap the lower classes, and that have not been overcome by the political bias in favour of the latter. The proof lies in the fact that MPs of working class origin are no longer workers when elected: they are professional politicians who have made a career as full-time party or union officials before standing for parliament. Hence, when elected, they effectively have a middle class occupation which confirms that a political parliamentary career can no longer be improvised. The alternative to a professional political career is a career with similar experience, as in an interest group or in a public administration, central or local, that is able to provide specific technical competence.

Examples of this situation are found in the political careers of MPs in all West European states. Thus Loewenberg (1967) concluded his study of German parliamentary life by observing that, in addition to party activists, the selection process 'seems to favour candidates enjoying the support of locally prominent interest groups, including those local government officials having an influential local political clientele' (p. 83). He added that 'it might also leave room for the candidacy of men and women not previously active in politics, if they have the support of an interest group with strong political influence in the party for which they seek nomination.' In fact, the 1960s Bundestag was made up of four types of MP: professional politicians (25 per cent), interest group representatives (30 per cent), part-time professionals (30 per cent) and civil servants (10 per cent). Herzog (1971) stressed that subcentral government positions (particularly in the *Länder*) were essential to win and keep a parliamentary seat in Germany. Italian research suggests a similar situation: Guadagnini (1983) speaks of

> the progressive standardization of career patterns for entry into parliament, a political career structure as a series of relatively well-defined stages: some, like party or local government office and in part in the unions, have increasingly tended to become over time ... a necessary step to a parliamentary career. (pp. 284–5)

This was particularly true for the two major parties (DC/PPI and PCI/PDS) until the 1990s, but party control was increasingly problematic in the other parties. It was hindered by the use of the preference vote in the choice of successful candidates which often escaped party control.

However, there was a major change in 1994 as a result of the new mixed-majority electoral system and the political disqualification of so many former MPs owing to judicial investigation. Not only were two-thirds of new MPs in their first election, but 40 per cent claimed that they were without political experience. They had been recruited from civil society by new political forces (Forza Italia, Lega Nord, Alleanza Nazionale etc.) to replace the discredited former party politicians.

In Britain, according to Blondel (1963), it is the composition of local constituency parties that determines the selection of parliamentary candidates. Conservative associations, which are predominantly middle class, tend to choose candidates with solid middle or upper class backgrounds who are politically active. For Labour, it depends on the constituency: in those constituencies dominated by a specific economic activity such as mining, railways and shipyards, the category union – miners, railwaymen, engineering workers – usually controls the local Labour Party and has one of its own union members selected; in the others, the constituency Labour Party is run by the intellectual petty bourgeoisie which usually chooses party activists. In both parties a local government career can help as evidence of political experience, but candidates usually present themselves directly for election without any local political experience, a situation particularly widespread among Conservative MPs until recently.

On the other hand, the fact that local office was a traditional requirement of the *cursus* of French MPs for all parties, except the PCF, is an indication of their organizational weakness. And if there are instances of direct candidature in parliamentary elections without local office (*parachutage*) – indeed, in the Fifth Republic they have been on the increase – these successful MPs immediately attempt to consolidate their local electoral position with local office. The example of Philippe Seguin, member of prime minister Raymond Barre's *cabinet*, suffices: he was 'parachuted' into the Epinay constituency by the Gaullists in 1978 and, after his successful election to the Assembly, he stood as leader of a centre-right alliance to become mayor of the town in 1979. There is no doubt, however, that the French parties prefer to present as candidates persons with strong local positions; but the membership of a ministerial *cabinet* is also a factor that helps election to parliament, as Jacques Chirac demonstrated in the 1960s. Finally, to be the mayor of a big city or president of a departmental general council gives the prestige, the resources and the opportunities to become a national political figure: Gaston Deferre (Marseilles), Jacques Chaban-Delmas (Bordeaux), Pierre Mouroy (Lille), Michel Noir (Lyons), all owed their national roles to their prestige as big-city mayors. But the French MPs, in the Fifth Republic, tend now to be local personalities with local influence.

The parliamentary career has been discussed as though it was just another professional career, but the situation is, of course, more complex. Firstly, the turnover of MPs is not large; the new members at each election are normally around 20 per cent. Thus there is a continuity that justifies the notion of 'political class', although it should be noted that at critical moments, like the end of a war or following a change of regime, the proportion of new members rises to 50 per cent (British House of Commons in 1945), 55 per cent (Italian Camera in 1948), 61 per cent (French Assembly in 1958), 70 per cent (Italian Camera in 1994), and even 96 per cent (German Bundestag in 1949). Secondly, this does not necessarily mean a long parliamentary career for the majority of MPs. Dogan (1967) has calculated that about 45 per cent of the Third Republic's MPs and 40 per cent of the Fourth Republic's were elected only once; figures for Britain suggest that in the period 1918–39, 60 per cent of MPs sat in the Commons for less than ten years. The length of a European MP's career is between ten and fifteen years (two or three legislatures) at most. The figures are, nonetheless, deformed by several very long parliamentary careers which raise the national averages, for instance Churchill (over 50 years), Macmillan, Butler, Callaghan and Heath (over 40 years) in Britain; Clemenceau (over 50 years), Herriot and Chaban-Delmas (over 40 years) in France; Andreotti, Fanfani and Iotti (over 45 years) in Italy. Thus Blondel's suggestion that the parliamentary career in Britain is mainly 'a career to become an MP' applies more generally. It means that the career of the majority of MPs is consumed in getting into parliament, so that when they finally get there, they remain 'extras' on the political stage.

This kind of situation has two consequences: (1) the election to parliament, for the majority of MPs, is more important for their own personal careers than for national politics; (2) this facilitates party supremacy and the control of parliament by party leadership; it is both their cause and their effect. Indeed, 25 per cent of MPs never take part in parliamentary debates and another 25 per cent take part very rarely. On the other hand, parliamentary activity is dominated by the interventions of that 10 per cent of MPs who represent the government and party leaderships.

Ministers: a collective profile

Having seen who are MPs, we must now turn our attention to the small minority who constitute the rulers, in the proper sense, ministers: the consecration of all successful political careers. Whom we should consider as a minister is not a simple matter because there is now a hierarchy of offices in the executive sphere between cabinet minister and minister of state and junior minister in Britain, *ministre d'état* and *secrétaire d'état* in France, *Minister, Staatminister* and *Parlamentarischer Staatssekretär* in Germany, *ministro* and *sottosegretario* in Italy. This situation is due to the growth in government personnel. As regards the sociological representativeness, the situation does not greatly change if one considers the larger group, or only the smaller one: the cabinet. The data are clear: these groups are recruited from an even more limited social area than MPs, that is they come almost exclusively from the upper middle classes (table 7.4).

They confirm, in fact, the social *un*representativeness of the ruling personnel. Ministers are chosen on rigorously territorial bases in France, Germany and Italy, and much less in Britain, except for the Scottish and Welsh Offices and not always then.

The political personnel present, therefore, an ever more restricted and privileged social composition as one ascends the hierarchy of power: from electors to militants, to MPs and to ministers. The sociographic features of ministers are threefold. There is an absence of women: the careers of Mrs Thatcher and Madame Cresson are the exceptions that prove the rule, for female representation in ministerial office is largely symbolic, both in numbers and offices (social affairs, women's condition) ministers are of mature middle age, usually in their fifties and early sixties. Finally, they have a professional background such as lawyer, teacher, higher civil servant or army officer. Blue-collars and white-collars are not the only ones to be strongly *under*represented; so are farmers and businessmen to a lesser extent. The explanation is simple and lies in the recruitment patterns. Blondel (1985) has identified a number of recruitment profiles, two of which are particularly important in Western Europe. The first is usually considered the normal one in parliamentary regimes: the party-cum-parliamentary route. It is the product of a

Table 7.4 Characteristics of ministers, 1945–1981 (per cent)

	Britain	France	Germany	Italy
Gender				
Men	96	96	93	99
Women	4	4	7	1
Occupation				
Army	5	3	–	1
Lawyers	17	19	26	30
Civil servants	9	25	6	4
Business/management	17	13	18	15
Engineers	2	7	3	1
Teachers	11	16	6	29
White collar	3	2	–	1
Manual workers	8	3	6	1
Farmers	2	3	3	–
Party or trade union	6	–	10	4
Other	19	9	21	14
Age on coming to office				
Less than 45 years	18	28	25	14
Between 45 and 65 years	75	69	68	75
More than 65 years	7	3	6	11
Education				
University graduates	72	82	71	95
Duration in office				
Average (years)	(4.6)	(3.4)	(5.6)	(3.9)
Less than 1 year	12	40	11	36
2–5 years	57	44	47	41
5–10 years	24	11	30	14
Over 10 years	8	5	13	9
Specialist or generalists				
Specialists	13	26	43	15
Generalists	77	66	45	64
no data	10	8	12	21
Held office				
Held one office	54	50	70	54
Held several offices	46	50	30	46
Ministers (number)	219	236	103	214

Source: Blondel, 1985, p. 277; Blondel and Thiebault, 1991, pp. 25–7

specific evolution that occurred in European parliamentary systems in the nineteenth century, namely the will of parliament to impose on the monarch those ministers who were acceptable to it in place of civil servants and officials, who were believed to be too pliant to him. In this way, the principle that ministers should be drawn from parliament was established. The second profile is the civil service route, Dogan's (1979) 'mandarin ascent': this, given the origins of the modern public administration (chapter 8), is the oldest route and, in some sense, the most natural, the more so since civil servants are usually the best informed on government affairs and procedures. Other routes include non-parliamentary political careers – either party or union or interest group – and military careers or business, but the latter are rare in Western Europe.

Ministers: patterns of recruitment

The party-cum-parliamentary route certainly predominates in the recruitment of ministers, but not exclusively so. Once again, the reason is simple: the party-cum-parliamentary route is the only one, among those indicated by Blondel, that is representative in the liberal democratic sense. The others are essentially instrumental, either in their reference to a specific group or in their appeal to competence. In parliamentary regimes, the key to executive power lies in support, in terms of both parliamentary solidarity and political representation. There are exceptions even in Britain, where the party-cum-parliamentary route is virtually obligatory in the selection of ministers, but where there is also the practice of appointing as ministers (one or two per cabinet) eminent persons in the worlds of business, trade unions or administration, usually giving them a seat in the House of Lords: for instance, Lord Mills (minister of power in the 1950s), the trade unionist Frank Cousins (minister of technology in 1964), the ex-director of the CBI, John Davies (minister of industry in the 1970s) and Lord Young (minister of industry in the 1980s). This suggests that instrumental factors, and usually specific competences, carry some weight, even in Britain.[20]

It is no accident that the mandarin ascent is practised in France and, to a much lesser extent, in Germany, given the administrative tradition going back to the absolute state, which stresses (technical) competence. Back in favour with de Gaulle in 1958, the mandarinate now represents, in its various forms – direct appointment of higher civil servants, cooption of high-flyers in ministerial *cabinets* – the route of almost 40 per cent of the Fifth Republic's ministers. Paradoxically the most brilliant recruit of this route, president Pompidou, was the French president who least used this channel in the selection of ministers of his various governments. German ministers are recruited from a variety of backgrounds and experiences, including party officials, prominent members of Bundestag committees, members of *Land* governments and members of the higher civil service. Von Beyme (1979) comments: 'careers tend to be long and cumbersome. Access to higher executive offices needs an average of two legislatures. Some quick take-offs in the early 1970s (the so-called *Senkrechtisstarter*) remained unsuccessful exceptions' (p. 112). In Italy, on the other hand, the emphasis has always remained on representativeness as the criterion of selection. This has meant that routes other than party-cum-parliament have been rare,[21] but also that there was an extremely rigid link (particularly in the period 1948–76) between preference votes and ministerial appointment in the First Republic (Calise and Mannheimer, 1982).

Interest in recruitment routes of ministers is not limited to the explanation, certainly partial, of the lack of social representativeness of the top people in the executive. It serves also to understand the qualities that ministers bring to their office. A long parliamentary apprenticeship – between ten and fifteen years is the West European average – leads to the development of certain skills, above all in oral communication and public relations. It is said in England that 'the House of Commons is a school for ministers', because it is in demonstrating his parliamentary talents that the MP is recognized as a 'politician with a future'.[22] But the office of minister requires other skills which can be defined as 'managerial', namely the capacity to deal with mountains of paperwork and get straight to the nub of the problem, and the ability to delegate tasks to civil servants and subordinates.

Parliamentary activity clearly does not prepare the MP for his future tasks in ministerial office. This explains, perhaps, the role played by the ministerial hierarchy (which exists in all states, although not in as sophisticated a form, on various levels, as in Britain) that offers a clear progression of experiences and responsibilities in the executive. Such experience, according to Rose (1974), 'makes [it] possible and probable for cabinet ministers to undergo intensive role socialization for years prior to reaching cabinet, first as an MP, then progressing from the status of PPS to junior minister, then to ministerial office outside the cabinet before becoming a cabinet minister at the top of a government department' (p. 365), even though these posts were not conceived as a training ground for cabinet office, and the time spent in them does not necessarily impart the skills to be used in it. Calise and Mannheimer (1986) noted a similar phenomenon in First Republic Italy:

> Apprenticeship as under-secretary has become, increasingly, a necessary step, and, not less important, anything but casual. The length and continuity in the office of under-secretary is, in fact, one of the requirements for the most brilliant ministerial careers. (p. 473)

In France and Germany, the phenomenon is less significant because of the role of mandarin ascent; in fact, many of the *secrétaires d'état* are appointed from among civil servants because of their specialist competences, without as a result of this becoming full ministers later on. This has allowed Birnbaum (1977) to claim that there is a division of labour between government and parliament in France; the former is responsible for the direction of national policy and the latter the administration of local life. In Germany, on the other hand, parliament is only part of a wider training for political leadership, which is shared with leadership positions in other walks of life: civil service, *Land* government, party or interest group leadership.

If ministers' tasks are multiple (departmental policy leadership, departmental management, defence of departmental proposals in cabinet, parliament and party, public relations, negotiation with groups and in the EU[23]) and the party-cum-parliament career pattern does not offer a specific training to deal with them, it is instructive to see the priorities that ministers themselves attribute to their various tasks. The only study of this problem is British and was carried out by Heady (1974). It shows that British ministers consider that their principal task is that of representing their department and presenting its legislative programme in parliament as well as in party discussions and pressure group consultation. On the other hand, they place departmental policy leadership and management in second place. Perhaps rather significantly, in view of the traditional image of ministers as policy initiators, is the low priority generally accorded to this task. The conclusion is that ministers invest their energies where their skills can best be deployed. In this situation, the ministerial recruitment model produces a group which finds it more remunerative to give priority to the task of departmental representation simply because it uses its parliamentary experience of presentation and public relations. The task for which they are least prepared is that of policy initiation – the ability to identify important problems before they appear on the political agenda and to suggest adequate and practicable solutions – and most ministers, according to the British data, prefer to elude it.

There is in all this, however, something of a paradox: if a proposal needs three years (Heady's estimate) to be implemented, British and French ministers (average duration in office 2.5 years) as well as Italian (average duration 1.7 years) do not remain long enough in the same department to develop a proposal and carry it through to its conclusion. Only German ministers (average duration in the same office 4.5 years) regularly have the time to carry through a policy that they initiated. We must recognize, nonetheless, that the profile of ministerial careers is complex. Firstly, the average period in office in Western Europe between 1945 and 1981 was relatively long – Germany 5.6 years, Britain 4.6, Italy 3.9, France 3.4 – but the proportion of ministers who remained in office for more than five years was a minority in all states, and those who were in office for less than one year reached 36 per cent in Italy and 40 per cent in France. Secondly, there was the practice of 'reshuffles' which was widespread in Britain and less so in France, Germany and Italy. It was relatively rare, in fact, that a government, except in Germany, remained unchanged for two years. The norm is for some ministerial changes to be made almost every year. It is part of the executive's rejuvenation process on the one hand, and that of rotation from post to post, on the other – processes which have led Blondel to speak of all governments' permanent 'restlessness'. Thirdly, despite these constant trends for change, a small minority of long-serving ministers change post only from time to time. In France, Britain and Italy, this minority did not exceed 10 per cent of ministers; in Germany it accounted for 13 per cent. Although Germany is the country where ministers' duration in office is the longest, it is also the country in which the proportion of one-post ministers is the highest at over 70 per cent; in Britain, France and Italy where the period in office does not exceed 2.5 years, this percentage falls to around 50 per cent.

From all this, it emerges that there is a small nucleus of long-serving ministers in key departments. Sometimes this is the same department: Couve de Murville, French minister of foreign affairs for ten years under de Gaulle; Ludwig Erhard, German minister of finance for almost fifteen years under Adenauer; Hans-Dietrich Genscher, German foreign minister for eighteen years in the 1970s and 1980s; and Emilio Colombo, Italian treasury minister for ten years in the 1960s. More often they serve in different departments: Macmillan, Butler, Callaghan and Healey in Great Britain, Fanfani and Andreotti in Italy, Messmer and Chirac in France. These long-serving ministers form an inner circle of the political elite capable of ensuring the continuity of executive power, above all in regimes like First Republic Italy or Fourth Republic France (that is countries with non-majority systems), where government instability leads one to fear the worst. In this situation, in fact, majority government systems run the greater risk of a traumatic break, above all if party alternation in power becomes infrequent: a party may return to power with a leadership lacking experience of ministerial office, as was largely the case of British Labour in 1964 and the French left in 1981.

The problem implicit in this analysis of ministers is whether the two aspects – apparently contradictory – of the minister's role, the representative and the policy-making, are both essential. Posed in these terms, it is virtually impossible to give a firm and unambiguous answer. The European democratic tradition of the last two centuries tends to favour the former, but without ever rejecting the latter. Moreover, there have been periods – fascism and Nazism in Italy and Germany, not to mention World War II – in which the latter has been extolled. The paradox is that, on the one hand, a purely 'political' government with merely symbolic legitimation functions has never existed; on the other, it is not clear whether ministerial policy skills are absolutely necessary for adequate government coordination. At all events, in the 1970s crises the supremacy of the logic of representation was severely criticized and the need for policy skills was invoked in its stead; hence, for instance, the call for a 'government of technicians' in Italy. However, there is little doubt that in the 1980s the trend has been towards strengthening decision-making at the expense of representation under pressure from international and domestic economic and political events, although there have been legitimate doubts about any increase in technical effectiveness. What is clear from the Italian case, for example, is that the parties exploited crises to reinforce, by means of 'majority summits' (Criscitiello, 1993), their direct control over the executive. In the end, however, this development probably precipitated the terminal crisis of the First Republic; and reformers turned to majority electoral reform as a solution to the reinforcement of the executive. A similar trend towards partisan control of government, although less marked institutionally, can be discerned in the other countries, like the authoritarian style of the Thatcher governments in Britain.

The power of the executive

Outlining the national specificities of executive power is not easy because, as an Italian politician remarked, pure power is like the phoenix (*l'araba fenice*), or in Matastasio's celebrated verses, 'Cosa sia ognuno lo dice, / dove sia nessuno lo sa' ('Everybody says what it is, / but nobody knows where it is') (Radi, 1973, p 97).

Britain

The key to executive power in Britain is the majority mechanism: the party leader of the parliamentary majority is prime minister from the very fact of being the leader of the majority party and remains so as long as he is able to keep this position. The result is that the central institution – the keystone of the British government system – is the cabinet, and not because of its location at the top of the state structure. The cabinet is a collegial institution, chosen and presided over by the prime minister: its decisions are those of the government and not a specific ministerial department. Hence its basic functions are coordination and mediation, that is resolving the possible conflicts between ministers, so that they are the expression of a single voice (collective responsibility). The prime minister's principal task is party management, namely ensuring party solidarity, or at the very least the confidence of the parliamentary majority; this is the *condicio sine qua non* of the office.

The prime minister certainly does not lack resources to carry out this task; indeed, the resources are so great that many contemporary observers speak of prime ministerial government and no longer of cabinet government. The first resource that the prime minister can count on is party loyalty: MPs of the majority party want the success of their government. Of course, if they judge that the continuation of the present policies will lead to electoral defeat, the prime minister can be removed, as happened to Macmillan in 1963 and Thatcher in 1990. The second resource, and perhaps the most important, is patronage: the prime minister's right to choose the government personnel – cabinet ministers, ministers of state, junior ministers and parliamentary private secretaries (PPSs) – which today represent a third of the majority party's MPs. In addition, the prime minister has a whole series of other incentives available to reward loyal support of the government – titles, appointments to committees and state agencies – to which MPs as ambitious professional politicians cannot but be susceptible. On the other hand, despite having the right, the prime minister is not always free in his choices, given the heterogeneous nature of British parties and the need to satisfy the different party tendencies. For instance, in the choice of ministers, a prime minister has to bear in mind that a rival might be more dangerous outside the cabinet (where he may organize a party revolt) than inside (where he is obliged to accept 'collective responsibility').[24]

The prime minister's national power has increased in the post-war period also as a result of the growth and complexity of government activity, which has led to the creation of a series of small cabinet committees appointed and coordinated by the prime minister. Since the prime minister controls the cabinet's composition, organization and agenda, there is evidence to suggest – such as the Westland affair of 1985–6 – that he/she is in a strong position to organize and manipulate decisions to his/her advantage. If we add the power to dissolve the House of Commons – a weapon, it is claimed, to discipline rebel MPs – and the mass media's 'personalization' of politics (which identifies the party with its leaders), we quickly arrive at Lord Hailsham's (1978) 'elective dictatorship' thesis.

Without wishing to disregard the force of these arguments, we can, however, find examples and episodes that contradict it. If the prime minister tries to push his colleagues too far down a road that the majority do not wish to go, he can be obliged to abandon the attempt, as Wilson was forced to do over trade union reform in 1969; or to resign, as Eden was over Suez in 1956–7. On the other hand, the cabinet committees give the major departmental ministers as much power as the prime minister. And while it is true that the prime minister decides the dissolution of the Commons, if he makes a mistake and loses the election he is likely to lose not only power but the party leadership too (Heath 1975, Callaghan 1980). Finally, as regards the personalization of politics operated by the media, the position of individual politicians depends a lot on the 'TV image': TV can politically destroy a politician as it did the Labour leader Michael Foot in 1983, but the Conservatives Heath, Thatcher and Major won the elections of 1970, 1979 and 1992, respectively, despite a rather negative image.

This discussion is likely to be inconclusive, largely because it is based on a false premise, namely the notion that the prime minister and his ministers must necessarily be in conflict. The fact is that the prime minister is bound to his cabinet as much as its members are to the prime minister, but also that certain ministers count more than others. In this sense, the relative power of the prime minister and the cabinet changes over time. A prime minister is usually stronger than his party immediately after an electoral victory, above all if it is unexpected, as with Heath in 1970; and weaker when electoral fortunes decline, as with Macmillan in 1962–3 after he had sacked half the cabinet. Mrs Thatcher was much stronger after the Falklands 'victory' than before, or in the late 1980s. Thus, whether the power is personal or collegial, a prime minister's success depends on his/her ability to interpret his/her party's 'gut feeling'. In this sense, the best policy is one everyone (ministers and MPs) shares. Electoral success is the criterion by which MPs (whether in government or opposition) judge their leaders' policies.

There is no doubt that the British executive's power is enormous and, as long as its leaders are in agreement and do not lose the support of their parliamentary majority, formal controls are almost non-existent. Paradoxically, the biggest limits to its power come from forces outside the control of the British government, above all from those linked to the international situation. We only have to think of the consequences for British political life of Suez in 1956 and the Falklands in 1983, or participation in NATO and the EU (Maastricht, 1992–3), or the different economic crises which have marked the post-war period (devaluation of the pound in 1949 and 1966, IMF loan in 1976, exit from the ERM in 1992). One of the most serious British problems in the post-war period has been, in fact, the refusal of its political leaders to understand the real meaning of its changed position in the world into a power of the second rank and to draw the necessary consequences.

France

The Fifth Republic has seen the emergence and consolidation of the presidency of the republic as the central institution of the French political system. It is well known that de Gaulle, as the creator of the new regime, was determined to strengthen the executive's power at the expense of parliament and the parties: the 1958 constitution, in fact, secured executive supremacy through a reduction of the legislature's power, but created, at the same time, a diarchy (president and prime minister) at the head of the executive. As a result there has been a significant change in the president's powers according to the political situation. The president, elected by universal suffrage since 1962, has important prerogatives as head of state and to act in states of emergency (article 16) or in situations of political confusion (article 5). But it is the prime minister, supported by a parliamentary majority, who governs.

One of the paradoxes of the Fifth Republic's development is that the system of parties, which de Gaulle wished to liquidate definitively, has adapted itself and played a major role. It has supplied those coherent and disciplined parliamentary majorities which the Fourth Republic's executive lacked. In effect, the introduction of the election of the president of the republic by universal suffrage acted as a catalyst for a change in the party system, obliging the parties to organize coherent and stable alliances to take their leader to the Elysée palace and secure the necessary support for the president's 'government' to implement his programme. Thus the president, in spite of himself, has become the recognized leader of the parliamentary majority, with the same interests in parliamentary management as the British prime minister. According to Duverger (1986):

> [The president's] great power owes nothing to the constitution. Its basis was very simple: the existence of a solid and coherent majority in the National Assembly, loyally obeying the head of state. Supported by it, Charles de Gaulle, Georges Pompidou, Valéry Giscard d'Estaing and François Mitterrand have dominated, for 24 years, the legislature, the government, the administration, the judiciary, the army and foreign affairs. In this way, a new Jacobin monarchy, absolute but republican, has been established, founded on universal suffrage which elected the president and a majority subject to his orders. The variations in the Elysée's authority ran parallel to the oscillations in the Palais Bourbon's docility to it. (p. 8)

If things were certainly more complex under de Gaulle, Pompidou and Mitterrand (1981–6) than Duverger's description suggests, the situation was rather different under Giscard and Mitterrand during the *cohabitation*. President Giscard d'Estaing did not control the alliance that elected him, because he was the leader of a smaller and subordinate party that failed to change the relations of forces in its favour at the 1978 election. This meant the abandoning of projects, like the capital gains tax in 1976, which the Gaullists, the majority party in the alliance, disapproved of, and the eventual resignation of prime minister Chirac. It led, finally, to disguised guerrilla warfare in parliament between 1979 and 1981, which was a factor, among others, in Giscard's defeat in the 1981 presidential elections. President Mitterrand, on the other hand, had to face a hostile parliamentary majority in 1986; he decided to finish his seven-year mandate – appointing the leader of the right-wing majority, Chirac, as prime minister – and not to resign. But, in this way, he saw his powers much reduced. *Cohabitation* does not mean that the president has no powers. However, the powers he still has are very limited; they are those deriving from article 5 of the constitution – that is, they ensure respect for the constitution and the working of the institutions – which allow him some resort to a procedural veto, namely refusing to sign some decrees and sending them back to the Assembly. In any event, the use which Mitterrand made of them enabled him to win the 1988 presidential election and, with the left's victory in the parliamentary election, to regain his full powers. However, the Socialists' débâcle at the polls in the 1993 parliamentary election left the president faced with a second period of *cohabitation*, but this time faced by an overwhelming right majority. His behaviour was as in 1986, but much more cautious since he would not be standing again in 1995.

In conclusion, beyond the constitutional differences, there is a certain similarity between the French president's situation and the British prime minister's when they enjoy their full powers, namely when they enjoy the support of a coherent and solid parliamentary majority. Both, in fact, derive their power from their position as the political leader of the parliamentary majority. They both have an interest in maintaining and developing it: it is thus that public opinion polls play an important role in the politics of both countries. In this view, the French executive's power is similar to the British – even if derived from a non-collegiate tradition – but it is further strengthened by the centralization of the state administration. In addition, the president has the weapon of the referendum, but this too is double-edged, as its lack of use in the last twenty years indicates. Finally, differences in the length of presidential and parliamentary mandates mean the increased possibility that the president and prime minister are of opposing political convictions, an outcome that can oblige them to engage in a forced *cohabitation*; it is a risk which the British prime minister does not run. The limits on executive power in France are of the same kind as in Britain, namely deriving from forces outside its control, linked above all to the development of the international situation, of which the wars in Indo-China and Algeria in the 1950s, or more recently the oil crises, were major examples. The French government realized, earlier than the British, the changed circumstances, which explains why it took a leading role in promoting the EU (chapter 10).

Germany

The chancellor is the keystone of the German executive, and not the *Kabinett*, and this despite the fact that the Federal Republic is a parliamentary regime. The domination of the executive by the first chancellor, Konrad Adenauer, in the 1950s was such that the German political system was defined in those years a *Kanzlerdemokratie*. It is generally considered today that the factors that contributed towards Adenauer's supremacy were mainly contingent and declined subsequently; in consequence, the executive power in Germany now reflects the classical arrangements of majority government, but in a federal context.

What were the factors that determined the chancellor's supremacy? They were of a constitutional nature and were willed by the authors of the basic law to prevent the paralysis of the executive, as in Weimar, which was considered directly responsible for Hitler's rise. Firstly, article

65 lays down that the *Kabinett* depends directly on the chancellor, in the sense that he is personally responsible for it to the Bundestag that elected him (article 64). Secondly, article 67 strengthens the chancellor's personal position in relation to the Bundestag, thanks to the 'constructive vote of no confidence' (*konstruktives Misstrauensvotum*) which obliges him to resign only if the Bundestag, at the same time as voting a motion of no confidence, elects a successor with an absolute majority. The procedure has only been used twice: the first unsuccessfully against Brandt in 1972; and the second successfully against Schmidt, replaced by Kohl and with a change of government alliance – CDU/FDP in place of SPD/FDP – ten years later. Thirdly, article 65 also reaffirms the *Kanzlerprinzip* – adopted initially in 1871 – with the *Richtlinienkompetenz*, that is the power to determine the government's general policy, in order to strengthen the chancellor's position in relation to the *Kabinett* and the ministers. Indeed, the dominant relationship in policy-making is between the chancellor and the individual departmental minister and not the *Kabinett* as a group. Germany, like France, has a non-collegiate tradition of government.

The power of the executive and its leader are to be judged, however, in relation to its parliamentary majority. At this point the classic factors of party government – the chancellor's support by the majority parties, above all by his parliamentary party group (*Fraktion*), and his electoral popularity – come into play. It follows, then, that if the chancellor has the constitutional right to designate the ministers, he is not totally free to do so. He must, of course, take account of his *Fraktion*'s political situation. The position of a German chancellor is usually more complex than that of a British prime minister because German parliamentary majorities are almost exclusively the coalition of two parties out of three (four in the 1980s). This means that an alternative alliance is usually possible; hence the chancellor must take account of the political requests of his coalition partner, above all in terms of posts and persons. In this sense, Adenauer enjoyed a privileged position in relation to his successors: the CDU was not yet institutionalized as a party and Adenauer was thus able to dominate it thanks to his electoral successes, attracting into its orbit the small ephemeral parties founded in the immediate post-war period, and so win overwhelming electoral victories (1957) – aided and abetted in this by the 'economic miracle' and the international situation (Cold War), factors which were to decline subsequently.

From this it is clear that the chancellor's main task, like that of the British prime minister and to a lesser extent that of the French president, is party management, or in the German context, coalition management. The crucial area is the relations between the chancellor, his own party's president, the leader of the parliamentary group (*Fraktionführer*) and the coalition party leaders. Hence, it was no accident that Adenauer combined the roles of chancellor and president of the CDU as did Brandt in the SPD. As a result, the political problems leading to Erhard's

(Adenauer's successor) resignation are explained by the fact that he was not a party man and never controlled the CDU. During the Grosse Koalition period, a series of informal committees were set up to mediate conflicts between the CDU and the SPD. Occasionally, negotiations between the coalition partners for the formation of the government were sealed in a formal agreement. In this situation (Kiesinger 1966–9, Kohl from 1982) the chancellor plays the role of team captain, which suits the political needs of coalition government better. Moreover, if Brandt and Schmidt played a more active and incisive role as chancellor, they were also more constrained by their party's democratic tradition, which acted as a break on their domination. However, we need only note the changes of government alliances that occurred outside electoral periods (1966 Grosse Koalition; 1982 from SPD/FDP to CDU/FDP) to convey the importance of this task (and of the *Fraktion*'s role). This said, the chancellor's power *vis-à-vis* ministers is limited, despite the *Richtlinienkompetenz*, by each department's ministerial autonomy. This autonomy is founded on the German tradition of the minister as specialist in his field. In fact, German ministers tend to remain in the same department for relatively long periods – up to seventeen years (1949–66) in the case of transport minister Hans-Christian Seebohm of the CDU[25] – and do not experience the rotation common in other states. Moreover, dismissals and resignations are rare and this means that policy decisions, in this field as in others, are more the result of negotiations between coalition leaders and *Land* governments than personally imposed by the chancellor. Indeed, the parties consider the ministerial departments in their hands as so many party fiefs to be exploited and defended.

In this situation, and making the appropriate national distinctions, the German executive's position is not too unlike that of the British executive. Both depend on the support of a stable parliamentary majority. But stability has been greater in Germany than in Britain: three relative alternations against five absolute alternations. However, once in office with a secure parliamentary majority, the British executive has greater power at home than the German, and not only because its majority is one party and not a coalition, even if this is significant. The chancellor's patronage is much more limited than the British prime minister's. It is true, nonetheless, that the chancellor enjoys, like his British counterpart, the advantages that accrue from the personalization of politics, and thus both major German parties designate their leaders as 'candidate chancellors' for the elections. But, if this helps attract votes, the possible coalition majorities remain firmly in the hands of the party leaders, chancellor included. Finally, the power of dissolution of the Bundestag can only be decreed by the president of the republic and only in certain specific conditions: a vote of censure followed by the non-election of a successor within 21 days. It is no accident that it has happened only twice as a result of a political manoeuvre by the successful chancellor to legitimate his victory in the Bundestag with popular approval (1972 and 1983 elections).

The greatest limit to executive power in Germany derives from the fact that it, unlike Great Britain and France, is a federal state. German federalism is founded on a division of labour, in which legislation is largely federal and policy implementation is a *Länder* responsibility. This means that the federal government has to take account of the *Länder* governments' orientations, the more so since the *Länder* are directly represented in the upper house (Bundesrat) of the federal parliament. The latter's approval is necessary not only for constitutional amendments, but also for all legislative proposals that directly concern the *Länder*. If, as was the case in the 1970s and again in the late 1980s and the 1990s, the Bundesrat has an opposition majority it is capable of causing the government serious problems, as, for instance, those caused by the CDU-led opposition in the Bundesrat to the ratification of Brandt's *Ostpolitik* treaty in 1972. It was to overcome this type of conflict that the notion of 'cooperative federalism' (chapter 9) was developed in the 1970s with its premium on consensus. The result has been a policy process that tends to resist reform initiatives and defies sustained attempts to manage policy developments (Katzenstein, 1987).[26] Finally, as regards the international situation, the German government is subject to the same constraints as the British and French, to which was added, at least in the past, its position as a defeated nation in World War II in search of international rehabilitation – hence its role in the promotion of the EU – and placed on the borders of the Iron Curtain, with all that this implied. German unification at the end of 1990 has clearly introduced a major shift in its international position, opening a completely new phase in which its leaders can be expected to play a greater role both in Europe and on the international stage.

Italy

Since the Italian state has had a very different form of government – non-majority system – to the other three, its executive has had significantly different characteristics. The main feature of the Italian executive since the war has been government instability: 53 governments in 49 years. But there is paradoxically a second, less well-known feature: the executive personnel is among the most stable in Europe (the prime minister in 1992, Giulio Andreotti, entered the government 46 years earlier). This is the result of the fact that ministers began their governmental careers with an apprenticeship as under-secretary. Moreover, the DC was the only party in Western Europe that remained uninterruptedly in power from the end of the war until 1994 and held the prime ministership from 1945 to 1981 and again from 1987 to 1992. This paradox is explained by the fact that the members of the Constituent Assembly wanted to establish a pluralist democracy in the place of the collapsed dictatorship; hence the constitution combined the rules of a classic parliamentary government with a PR electoral regime. The result was permanent coalitions in which the executive was more or less controlled by the Christian Democrat political elite.

The Italian executive's power is very variable and has usually been exercised in a very informal and non-collegiate manner. The cabinet (*Consiglio dei ministri*) very rapidly became a purely formal centre; the interministerial committees, introduced in the post-war period to coordinate government activity, quickly lost their initial role. The hub of executive power is the Prime Minister's Office (Presidenza del Consiglio) through a network of formal and informal relations with the key state institutions – Ministries of Finance and Interior, Council of State – and with the party secretariats of the government coalition partners. It did not matter, according to Cassese (1980), that the prime ministership changed hands so long as it remained in the same party, as it effectively did until 1981, and the key politico-administrative elite personnel was stable. Significantly, the prime ministers who have held the post longest – De Gasperi, Fanfani, Moro, Rumor (DC) and Craxi (PSI) – were all party secretaries, the exception being Andreotti (DC). This was despite the DC tradition that required the party secretary to resign his party post on assuming executive office – a tradition that developed because the DC leaders feared, in the 1950s, a possible authoritarian perversion by a leader who united in his hands, as Mussolini had done,[27] both party power and state power. This demonstrated, nonetheless, that in Italy too the prime minister's power was linked to power over the party, even though no party enjoyed a stable parliamentary majority and all governments were the result of interparty negotiation, in which the prime minister designate was usually not the most important player.

In short, the problem of executive power in Italy has derived from the spreading of power between a plurality of centres – formal and informal, state and party, central and provincial – as a result of political compromises between the coalitions and socio-administrative developments, quite simply because the government was unable to rely on the stable support of its parliamentary majority. Thus the head of government faced an almost impossible task of coordination and mediation. It was no surprise, in such conditions, that every so often a partner party would withdraw from the ruling coalition, provoking a government crisis. But the political elite's stability and the informal mechanisms operated to secure the minimum necessary continuity for all to be reconstructed as before with one or two concessions or compromises. Cassese (1980) has suggested that 'flexibility' was the system's principal resource. But the price to be paid for such a system has been that the executive's power was necessarily exercised by continuous resort to conflict mediation between factions, groups and parties: this excluded, almost by definition, coherent political leadership.

In an attempt to overcome these deficiencies in the 1980s, the parties accentuated their control over the executive, endeavouring to become themselves a 'government institution' by means of a directorate (or majority summit) of the *pentapartito*[28] party secretaries. This mechanism succeeded in ensuring a certain stability during the Craxi government (1983–7), but it did not contribute to a greater policy coherence in government action, as is clear, for instance, from the inability to control public expenditure and reduce the public debt. Finally, Italy is the most exposed of the four states to external constraints (chapter 10), as its post-war history amply demonstrates. Hence the collapse of communism and the end of the Cold War had significant internal effects. Indeed, together with the need to meet the fiscal crisis and the simultaneous outbreak of the *tangentopoli* scandal, it was instrumental in precipitating an institutional crisis which brought the First Republic to its knees. Constitutional reform, which had been on the political agenda throughout the 1980s but not acted on, became irresistible after the popular referendum of April 1993: the first fruit was a mixed-majoritarian electoral system approved in summer 1993 (chapter 5), and although it enabled a heterogeneous right-wing electoral cartel to win a majority in the 1994 elections, it is far from clear whether it will ensure greater executive stability. Hence it will not be the last reform, as other measures will be required to secure a strong and responsible executive. There is talk of the direct election of the head of the executive (prime minister).

Conclusion

The state consists of an ensemble of public institutions and apparatuses, founded on the centralization of the instruments of violence, and formally coordinated in a given territory on which it establishes laws and secures their observance while administering the interests of its citizens. In Western Europe, however, it forms part of an international system of states (UNO, NATO, EU), which means that it is conditioned as much by international relations as by those of its own civil society. In addition, the state is a political actor in its own right, that is to say it is the subject of the socio-economic and political processes of which it forms the framework. It can act as well as react. This means that it seeks to determine its situation as well as to be determined by it.

The socio-genesis of the Western European state goes back to the dissolution of medieval society. The rivalry between feudal lords obliged each to strengthen himself at the expense of his rivals, with victory going to the strongest. The key to success was control of financial resources which opened the door to greater military potential. Military supremacy went hand in glove with financial superiority. It was only with the emergence of a central power and its specialized apparatus for ruling that, around the seventeenth century, it took on the character of the state in the modern sense of a government whose decisions are implemented, that is an effective government.

Hintze has stressed the role of military organization in European state formation and the relation between military technology and state form: mercenaries and *Ständestaat*; standing army and absolute state; national mass army and constitutional and representative state: one soldier, one rifle, one vote. History confirms that coercion was a fundamental element in European state formation and explains why the repressive administrative apparatuses – public bureaucracies, military, police, judiciary, secret agencies – are still today the material bases of contemporary state power.

Two features characterize the contemporary state form: representation and the capacity to intervene in society. The concept of representation marks a fundamental break in state form because it postulated a new principle of legitimacy, that of popular sovereignty. However, it also displayed elements of continuity in the development of parliamentary institutions. Moreover, it triggered two converging and contrasting processes of political participation: the broadening of the suffrage and the search for popular consensus by the rulers. The consequence was the formation of organized parties which profoundly altered the structure of the representative state: individual representation was replaced by group representation. The party system is an integral part of the form of government today.

The capacity to intervene is even more significant. It refers to the state machine and the parallel processes of the concentration and centralization of power that is only tempered by constitutional principles. Thus, if the absolute state's claims were absolute in the sense that the ruler could do anything in the name of *raison d'état*, its capacity of intervention and social control were limited in the sense that many of the areas of social life remained outside state control. Today, the claims of the Keynesian welfare state are more modest in the sense that the state's powers are constitutionally defined and subject to periodic electoral control, but the capacity of state apparatuses' social intervention and control has grown out of all proportion because few areas escape its supervision. This poses the vexed question of the state's invisible power and its extent.

There are essentially two constitutional forms of actual democratic government, presidential and parliamentary, which are distinguished on the basis of executive–legislative relations. Presidentialism is constitutionally defined by their separation and parliamentarianism by their fusion. However, a third intermediary constitutional form of government can be distinguished: semi-presidentialism, which has a dual-headed executive of president and prime minister and in which the latter's power comes from parliament. Hence in this form the separation of executive and legislature, the distinguishing element of presidentialism, is more apparent than real. Most West European states have adopted the parliamentary form; indeed, only France, Austria and Portugal have semi-presidential regimes.

However, the constitutional distinction between presidential and parliamentary regimes has become largely formal because it is constructed on mechanisms by which the system of constitutional power should operate rather than their effective functioning. This is determined by the working of the party system. The basis of the Western European executive is the cabinet (a committee of ministers) which, owing to its dual origin (in parliament and outside), has a dual function: the managing of the government majority in parliament and supreme government decision-maker. The power of the executive and the prime minister derive from the parliamentary management role. The extent to which the leader of the executive can control his majority in parliament is the extent to which he can exercise the constitutional powers of both the executive *and* the legislature.

Western European parliaments are bicameral: the lower house is elected by universal suffrage, and the upper house (elected or not) represents the nation in some other form, whether regional (Italy and Germany), the provinces (France) or social privilege (UK). Only the elected Italian Senate has the power to dismiss the government. Bagehot indicated five functions of parliament: elective, expressive, teaching, informing and legislative. He gave pride of place to the sociological functions – expressive, teaching and informing – and they are the most prized today. The expressive function (representation) is the very essence of democracy; it is the basis of the government's legitimacy and, indeed, that of the opposition parties too. On the other hand, the teaching and informing functions operate today as the principal forms of parliamentary control of the government, although they require the amplifier of the media to secure the widespread public propagation necessary for success.

Nonetheless, the decisive element in the forms of government is, as indicated, the party system, what we call 'the majority factor'. Duverger formulated two models of party government: (1) majority government and (2) non-majority government, respectively founded on the two opposing logics of (1) a zero-sum game and (2) a positive-sum game. Each has its own characteristics in which the logic of the former reinforces cohesion and aggregation while the logic of the latter accentuates particularity and fragmentation. The difference is between a government designated by the electorate and that mediated by the politicians. Duverger believes that the majority/non-majority distinction can be applied to the semi-presidential form of the French type, and we see no reason why it cannot be applied to the pure presidential US type as well.

The discriminating element between the two models of party government is party alternation in government. The necessary condition for alternation is the absence of sizeable anti-system parties. Alternation, moreover, requires three further conditions: (1) it must guarantee the political forces that leave office the legal possibility of winning power back; (2) it assumes a minimum consensus on national values; and (3) it presupposes that the new majority will not disturb existing structures. However, alternation is not that simple; indeed, there is not just one type. Quermonne has distinguished three types: absolute, relative and mediated. Absolute alternation occurs where there is a transfer of power from one party (or alliance of parties) to another. Relative alternation is limited to semi-presidentialism and takes place when the presidency changes politically but not the parliamentary majority (or vice versa). Finally, mediated alternation occurs when the major party of a government coalition goes into opposition and is replaced by the major opposition party, but in alliance with a third, minor party that remains in power, changing alliances. Absolute alternation corresponds to majority government while mediated alternation is the only political change possible in non-majority government. In the post-war period, Britain and France have experienced absolute alternation, Germany mediated alternation, and Italy, as yet, no alternation at all.

A majority government holds in its hands the powers of both executive and legislature: as long as it can count on its parliamentary majority, the limits on executive power are meagre. Conventionally, there are three kinds of countervailing power: opposition parties, subcentral autonomy and the constitutional court can all exercise some constraint on the use of governmental power, but the effective action of each is limited. There is a fourth countervailing power, often overlooked but perhaps more significant today: the EU. Non-majority governments are, by definition, coalition governments; they are usually considered to be weak, unstable and inefficient. Reality, however, is more complex. Coalition governments of less than five parties are as stable as single-party government: France and Germany in comparison with Italy. Parliament is believed to count for more in countries where government majorities are unstable and incoherent. In fact, however, it is not parliament as an institution that counts for more but the parties that use their representation in parliament to extract the best partisan deal.

The referendum as an instrument of direct democracy is not widely used, principally because the European democratic tradition is essentially parliamentarian. Further, the historical experience of its plebiscitary use by dictators did not recommend it to liberal democrats. Nonetheless, its use has been institutionalized in the French and Italian constitutions. De Gaulle used it in the 1960s in his struggle with the parties but, following his defeat in the 1969 referendum on regional reform, it has fallen into disuse in France. Mitterrand used it to ratify the Maastricht Treaty on European Union in September 1992 and won by a margin of less than 2 per cent of the vote. In Italy, its political role has been considerable, despite the fact that the popular referendums can only be held to abrogate (and not propose) legislation. Some 25 referendums have been held since 1974. But it is the referendums of the 1990s that have had the most significant effect because they have acted as a catalyst for constitutional change of Italy's moribund First Republic.

In Britain and Germany, the political tradition is even more opposed to the referendum. Thus it has only been used twice in Britain: in 1975 to ratify the country's renegotiated entry into the EEC; and in 1979 to approve devolution in Scotland and Wales (which it failed to do). In Germany, its use is restricted to the *Land* level and then only to approve territorial reorganization. The parties have always opposed the referendum as a democratic institution because they see it as a potential rival. Certainly, it is a cumbersome instrument to be wielded with caution owing to the risks of the excessive simplifications that it usually involves.

Parliament fulfils a further task: the recruitment of the governing personnel, that is the pre-selection of ministers. In Britain, Germany and Italy, ministers are selected from MPs, and, although in France there is a formal incompatibility between a parliamentary seat and ministerial office, most ministers have a parliamentary connection. MPs are elected as political representatives of the people, but their composition is sociologically unrepresentative of the electorate. They are male, middle-aged, predominantly middle class and usually higher educated. This selection confirms that political skills are middle class skills. Nonetheless, there is some difference based on party: middle class MPs in right-wing parties tend to be associated with money, those in left-wing parties with ideas. In spite of this, the trend is towards a progressive uniformization of parliamentary personnel in terms of meritocratic recruitment and professionalization: politics as a career. Professional politicians probably represent some two-thirds of all MPs in Western Europe.

There are basically two models of parliamentary recruitment: (1) the centripetal model that implies recruitment by cooption by the organizational centre which occurs in mass, centrally organized parties; and (2) the centrifugal model that implies a horizontal type of recruitment which enables would-be politicians to convert social resources (money, notoriety) into political capital, and which occurs in weakly institutionalized catch-all parties in which the leadership is composed of a plurality of factions. In the former, the power lies in the central party machine; in the latter in the parliamentary group. It explains the presence of certain social groups in mass party representation (workers as Labour/Socialist MPs) and of certain interest group representatives in catch-all party parliamentary groups. Standardized *cursus* – local government or party office – have tended to become the form in all parties. Finally, there is a distinction among MPs between those destined for a long career and the majority who have a relatively short career in one or two legislatures. Thus the political career of most MPs is a career to become an MP and, when they at last succeed in winning a seat, they are 'extras' with mere walk-on parts.

Ministerial recruitment, not surprisingly, is even more unrepresentative than that of MPs: it is male, mature middle-aged and political professional. Two significant recruitment patterns are identifiable: (1) the party-cum-parliamentary route which is the traditional pattern of parliamentary regimes; and (2) the mandarinate route, particularly relevant in France, which is based on expertise of governmental affairs. The parliamentary route gives the minister legitimacy but does not prepare him for the tasks of office. This explains the ministerial hierarchy – PPS, junior minister or under-secretary, minister of state, cabinet minister – which is intended to socialize ministers into their new roles. However, despite all the tasks that a minister is expected to perform, those with a parliamentary background invariably place the role of representation and consultation ahead of policy initiation and departmental management in their preferences. This suggests that they accord least priority to what they are least prepared for – policy initiation – and what the outside world considers to be their primary task. Finally, if a policy proposal needs three years to be implemented, only German ministers remain in office long enough to develop a proposal and carry it through to completion. Government reshuffles and instability usually impede this in Britain, France and Italy. In addition, there are two kinds of ministerial personnel: an inner circle of long-serving ministers in key departments, and a majority of short-term ministers in less important posts. The inner circle ministers are particularly important in non-majority governments because they ensure continuity in a situation where government instability leads one to fear the worst.

The basis of executive power in Britain, France and Germany is, in their different ways, party management. The leader of the parliamentary majority remains head of government so long as he is able to keep the majority together. The modalities vary between countries. In Britain, the prime minister must keep his backbenchers happy. In Germany, the chancellor must secure the continued support of his coalition allies. In France, the situation is more complex as it depends on whether the president is head of the parliamentary majority, in which case the prime minister is his lieutenant and owes his position to him; or not (*cohabitation*), when the prime minister is his own man. Party management is to some extent less central in France and Germany than in Britain, in view of the constitutional protection of the government's parliamentary majority.

Italy, with a non-majority government system, has had a very different experience. The power of the executive, in so far as it has been ensured, has been secured by the stability of the executive personnel and its informal institutional networks. Its basis was mediation which proved increasingly difficult and costly in the 1980s. In the 1990s, it collapsed under the pressure of events – end of Cold War, fiscal crisis, *tangentopoli* – leading to pressure for significant constitutional reform, starting with a mixed-majority electoral regime, adopted in summer 1993 and enabling a new but heterogeneous right-wing coalition to win an electoral majority in March 1994. Time will tell whether it can secure executive stability.

Further reading

J. Blondel (1982), *The Organization of Government* (London: Sage).
J. Blondel and F. Müller-Rommel (eds) (1988), *Cabinets in Western Europe* (Basingstoke: Macmillan).
J. Blondel and J.-L. Thiebault (eds) (1991), *The Profession of Government Minister in Western Europe* (Basingstoke: Macmillan).
N. Bobbio (1989), *Democracy and Dictatorship* (Cambridge: Polity).
V. Bogdanor (ed.) (1985), *Representatives of the People? Parliamentarians and Constituents in Western Democracies* (Aldershot: Gower).
D. Butler and A. Ramney (eds) (1978), *Referendums: A Comparative Study of Practice and Theory* (Washington, DC: AEI).
M. Duverger (1959), *Droit constitutionnel et institutions politiques. I: Théorie générale* (Paris: PUF).
K. Dyson (1977), *The State Tradition in Western Europe* (Oxford: Robertson).
A. Giddens (1986), *The Nation-State and Violence* (Cambridge: Polity).
A. Grosser (1964), 'The Evolution of European Parliaments', in M. Dogan and R. Rose (eds) (1971), *European Politics – A Reader* (London: Macmillan, 445–58).
O. Hintze (1975), *The Historical Essays of Otto Hintze* (ed. M. Gilbert) (Oxford, OUP).
G.W. Jones (ed.) (1990), *West European Prime Ministers* (London: Cass).
M. Laver and N. Schonfield (eds) (1990), *Multiparty Government: The Politics of Coalition Party Government* (Oxford: OUP).
A. Lijphart (1984), *Democracies: Patterns of Majoritarian and Consensus Government in Twenty-One Countries* (New Haven, Conn.: Yale UP).
T.T. Mackie and B.W. Hogwood (eds) (1985), *Unlocking the Cabinet: Cabinet Structures in Comparative Perspective* (London: Sage).
P. Norton (ed.) (1990), *Parliaments in Western Europe* (London: Cass).
G.-F. Poggi (1978), *The Development of the State* (London: Hutchinson).
J.-L. Quermonne (1988), *L'Alternance au pouvoir* (Paris: PUF).
R. Rose and E. Sulieman (eds) (1980), *Presidents and Prime Ministers* (Washington, DC: AEI).
E. Sulieman (ed.) (1986), *Parliaments and Parliamentarians in Democratic Politics* (New York: Holmes & Meier).

8 Public Administration and the Policy Process

Introduction

Discussion of the government and executive power in relation to other political institutions – parliament, parties, groups – has proceeded up to now as though ministers alone made policy decisions. Liberal democratic constitutional theory certainly encourages this view: the government defines policy (decision-making) with the help of parliament and the public administration executes and administers it (implementation). It was developed from Max Weber's (1921) classic distinction between politics and administration. Weber believed that the election of the politician endowed him with legitimation and induced a sense of responsibility in him because he was accountable to the electorate for his actions, while the appointment of the civil servant conferred no such legitimacy because it required no accountability for his actions. 'According to his proper vocation,' Weber argued, 'the genuine official … will not engage in politics. Rather, he should engage in impartial "administration" … Hence, he shall not do precisely what the politicians … must always and necessarily do, namely, *fight*' (p. 95).

   Yet, nobody believes any more in a clear distinction between political and administrative activities: policy and execution. Nonetheless, the theoretical presumption of such a distinction is the cause of much ambiguity because it forces people to think in terms of 'decision' and 'execution', when decisions are usually a mixture of both. The result is that political scientists end up by discussing the relative influence of politicians and civil servants in the policy process, instead of scrutinizing the origin of the policy initiatives that determine government policy and the way in which they are brought to bear on the policy process, and examining the bureaucracy's specific functions – those which give civil servants their influence and power.

The central state administration was created by the monarch as an extension of the royal household to provide him with an instrument of government. Hence, it was entrusted with specific functions which give it political resources, the principal of which is a monopoly of official information. No state apparatus operates in a vacuum: the relations between executive and public administration depend on the latter's social and ideological cohesion and its links with civil society. In this situation, discussion of the role of the public administration requires some consideration of the following: the concept of bureaucracy; its organization and the composition of its personnel; and the various aspects of the policy process, both paradigmatically and empirically.

The concept of bureaucracy

Weber (1922), the first person to define the concept systematically, was obsessed by bureaucratic domination in modern political life. 'In the modern state', he claimed, 'the actual ruler is necessarily and unavoidably the bureaucracy, since power is exercised neither through parliamentary speeches nor monarchical enunciations, but through the routines of administration' (p. 1393). Thus it is no accident that he located the concept at the very heart of his organizational theory of the state. As a result, bureaucracy has become one of the key terms of contemporary social science. It is generally agreed that the term has several meanings. Originally it meant the 'bureau (office) system' of government, namely a state apparatus staffed by appointed officials, organized hierarchically and dependent on a sovereign authority. Its extension to the political and economic fields gave rise to a second meaning, that is bureaucracy as a structure that applies to all organizations characterized by a 'routinization' of tasks and procedures, and the impersonalization of authority and hierarchy. Finally, the word has acquired a pejorative connotation in everyday speech: namely, as 'red tape' that evokes delay and repetition, needless complication, inflexibility and so on.

Weber's model of bureaucracy forms part of his discussion of power (*Macht*), which has to be distinguished from authority (*Herrschaft*). Power implies force and coercion, while authority implies legitimacy and inner justification. Weber (1922, p. 215) identified three kinds of authority: (1) traditional authority resting on custom; (2) charismatic authority founded on the personal prestige of a leader; and (3) legal authority based on appropriately enacted rules. Hence, for him, bureaucracy is the most developed form of rationally created legal authority: 'the most rational known means of exercising authority over human beings' (p. 223). It is characterized by a set of specific features.

Firstly, the powers and tasks have a non-patrimonial character: the official is the holder and *not* the proprietor of his office. Thus he cannot pass it on to his heirs and is obliged to vacate it at the end of his period of service. This marks a fundamental break with family-type traditional authority (patrimonialism) where power and appropriation are intimately linked.

Secondly, the powers and tasks are impersonal: they do not depend on the office-holder's personal prestige and so any form of charisma is lacking. The head of a service is obeyed because the competent authority has made him responsible for that service. Bureaucratic organization tries to reinforce this sense of the impersonal and the predictable as much as possible: posts, names, uniforms, official duties are all finalized towards this end. Thus the tasks and powers of each office are clearly specified to prevent mutual interference; and no one has the right to act outside his powers. The intended result is that bureaucratic activity and its consequences are perfectly predictable.

Thirdly, the offices and their powers are hierarchically organized: every official must obey his superior and can direct his inferiors. In principle, no one can act outside his hierarchical position; thus power is divided all the way up the hierarchy. The offices, moreover, are defined not only in terms of authority, but also in terms of technical specialization. This means that each task requires a trained person to carry it out. Hence the official climbs the hierarchy within his own speciality, according to a specific *cursus* (or career pattern).

Fourthly, the bureaucracy is formed of professional civil servants with a specific career structure. Appointment, training, promotion, discipline, privileges and pension rights are all regulated in a precise and detailed manner. Entry examinations are competitive, with specified educational requirements or other qualifications. In addition, seniority is the chief criterion of promotion towards the summit of the administrative hierarchy. Finally, security of employment is greater than in other forms of employment because bureaucratic organizations operate according to administrative regulations and not commercial practice. These define not only the internal relations between civil servants, but also those between civil servants and external users.

Although the development of industrial society in the first half of the century confirmed Weber's sociological analyses, in the sense that it saw 'the relentless advance of bureaucratization', the Weberian model of bureaucracy was questioned by American functionalists (Merton, Selznick and Gouldner) in the 1930s for being too optimistic and overstating its efficiency. The focus of their critique was that Weber had neglected the 'human factor' and the universe of informal relations that develop inside complex organizations, thus presenting a mechanical view of human behaviour which provoked, in fact, a series of dysfunctions. These informal elements, according to Ferraresi (1980):

> conflicting with the standardized behavioural rigidity required by bureaucratic organization, cause reactions that lead the official to lose sight of the *end* for which the rules and procedures were

established and to stick to behavioural details imposed by the letter of the regulations (*ritualism*). The result is inflexibility, incapacity to adapt rapidly to changing situations and lack of resources to deal with unexpected circumstances. Parallelly, inflexibility determines a corporate spirit which isolates officials from the public and makes the bureaucracy less effective in fulfilling its institutional duties. (p. 34)

This causes, in fact, conflicts between superiors and clerical staff, clerical staff and public, which involve a great loss of energy and resources since the organization has to waste time solving these disputes – those between expertise and authority – instead of pursuing its goals. Many believe such bureaucratic defects are endemic because attempts to overcome them end up by further strengthening the organization's bureaucratic character.

The functionalists, who raised doubts about bureaucratic efficiency in the Weberian model, did so, however, without rejecting Weber's approach. This was left, instead, to the 1950s neo-rationalists – Simon, Lindblom, Crozier – who recognized the free and active nature of those in an organized structure. They criticized the principle of the 'one best way' – the notion that once the goal was fixed there was one way to achieve it evident to all – and replaced it with the notion of 'bounded rationality': the fact that man is not capable of absolute rationality, limited as he is by practical and cognitive problems like time and cost. Every decision, therefore, is necessarily made within a pre-established value framework. In this view, monocratic hierarchical organization no longer appears as the very incarnation of rationality, but is a more or less useful instrument according to the circumstances.

Crozier (1963) developed this approach to propose a new theory of bureaucratic forms. The power of a person in an organization depends on his capacity to control the sources of uncertainty – that result from internal conflicts – which are decisive for the proper running of the organization. The power struggle dominates the play of human relations in an organization. The organization can respond to this problem in one of two ways: either by fixing power relations in rigid structures; or by providing the minimum necessary coherence. The former response corresponds to forms of bureaucratic organization that act basically as a protective structure for civil servants in the sense that it provides them with the minimum security for collaboration with colleagues – stable career structure, minimum rights against arbitrary action – but prevents, at the same time, correction of error. In other words, it promotes Veblen's (1899) 'trained incapacity'. The latter response corresponds to forms of non-bureaucratic organization like private firms – where the imperative is to win and retain a clientele – cooperatives and even decentralized services in which more open modalities prevail, for instance the possibility of personal initiative and widespread consultation. Crozier's contribution is to have focused attention on the cultural dimension of bureaucracy. His studies have highlighted particularities of French administrative practice and are influenced by his home model as much as was Weber by nineteenth century Prussian bureaucracy.

At this point, the concept of bureaucracy can be linked to the concept of 'technocracy', that is the rule of 'specialists'. This does not really exist, as such, in any state in the world at present. However, the word covers another aspect: the fact that in the public administration, as in other big organizations, the specialists generally control the information necessary to make many decisions and, for this reason, are very influential. Further, the word 'technocracy', like bureaucracy before it, has also taken on a pejorative connotation: 'technocrats', Alfred Sauvy used to say, 'are the technicians we dislike.' Nonetheless, Galbraith (1967) formulated the specific concept of 'technostructure' to define the role of technicians who, in big business corporations, tended to combine together. Duverger (1972) extended the notion to political organization in Western capitalist countries, which he defined as 'technodemocracies'. For Galbraith, the giant corporations can only be directed collectively because of the very sophistication of the information required to make decisions, that no one individual can control or be expert in. Thus the technostructure consists of a group of specialists, each of whom controls an aspect of the information, or expertise, required to make the decision. The confrontation of the various aspects within the group is the only way to assess the value and relevance of each to the decision in hand.

While Galbraith does not consider the applicability of the concept to the world outside the giant corporation, Duverger, as noted, does and suggests its relevance to large financial and administrative complexes, of which the most notorious is the 'military-industrial complex' referred to by president Eisenhower in his 1960 valedictory address. In the European context, however, Duverger pointed particularly to those complexes which link the treasury, the central bank, credit institutions, the state and para-state agencies. It is a way of saying that the policy-making groups in Western European states comprise key ministers, higher civil servants, party, interest group and business leaders and recognized experts.

The administrative structures

If the absolute state era saw the birth of the modern public administration, the nineteenth century was the crucial era in its development. The administration, in fact, despite important advances in the absolute era, remained nonetheless very rudimentary and non-systemic, such as not really to justify the modern definition of 'bureaucracy'. It is generally agreed that Napoleon was responsible for establishing the first real public administration in Europe, and not only in France but also in the conquered states of his empire. The elements were the reorganization of both the central administration of ministerial departments and the territorial administration on a coherent basis, with the introduction of annual budgets, accurate accounting for each administrative unit, the rationalization of tax collection and the reorganization of the judicial apparatus in an articulated and logical manner – the Code Napoléon of 1807 – as well as the reform of the educational system and the reorganization of the armed forces.[1]

In so far as the Napoleonic administrative system depended personally on the emperor, in the sense that it was his personal emanation, it fell with him. However, despite this, because it was a much superior and more efficient organizational schema than its predecessors, France and the states that had been under Napoleonic rule, like Prussia and Sardinia-Piedmont, were able to lay the foundations of a modern administration. Britain did not participate in this movement and had to wait until the famous Northcote-Trevelyan Report of 1854 to create a modern administration.

In general terms, the actual division of executive and administrative power between a complex set of ministerial departments and territorial administrations respects the principles of the Napoleonic reorganization. At that time, government activity was despatched by five fundamental ministerial departments: finance, foreign affairs, war, justice and home affairs. The first four covered well-defined fields of government; the fifth had the residual powers, like civil status, police, church affairs, public works, local government and so on. Under the pressure of growing industrialization, urbanization and social change, the public administration was extended and assumed responsibility for a whole host of new activities and functions (table 8.1). Already by the end of the nineteenth century the number of ministries had more than doubled with responsibility for things like roads, canals, bridges, harbours, railways, housing regulations, water supply, health, education and culture. At the same time, the administration began to become interested in the great social and labour problems: conditions of work and accident insurance, public health and social welfare. During World War I there was a further increase in public activity, which continued between the wars and even accelerated further after World War II.

Table 8.1 Ministerial departments, 1849 and 1982 (number)

	1849[a]	1984
Britain	12	22
France	10	42
Germany	12	17
Italy	11	28

[a]Or on national unification.
Source: Rose, 1984, p. 238

The growth of public activity in Western European states can be measured by a number of indices: (1) the state budget increased from about 10 per cent of GDP at the beginning of the century to 30–5 per cent in the 1950s and to around 45 per cent in the 1980s; (2) the composition of public expenditure changed from one largely given over to defence and maintenance of public order to one dominated by welfare and public economic investment; (3) the proportion of public employees in the active population rose from around 5–10 per 1000 in 1900 to around 25 per 1000 in the 1970s; (4) the composition of civil servants changed as new professional figures – managers, technicians and scientists, doctors and teachers – took their place alongside the traditional white-collar civil servants to the point of becoming a majority in some administrations (tables 8.2, 8.3, 8.4 and 8.5).

We can conclude that if the nineteenth century was crucial for the transformation and development of the public administration – on the heels of the national revolution – the twentieth century saw the great qualitative leap in its expansion and proliferation, creating the Keynesian welfare state. Thus the characteristic feature of the public administration today is its bigness – big government – whether it be in the numbers of administrations, employees, matters dealt with or money spent. Initially, expansion took the form of the creation of new ministries: agriculture, industry and commerce, education, labour. But, as public intervention in society grew, a whole series of new autonomous public agencies ('public body' in English, *öffentliche Anstalt* in German, *établissement public* in French and *ente pubblico* in Italian), with special goals and objectives, developed and proliferated. The result was a very complex administrative-institutional situation defying all classificatory logic.

Attempts to analyse public administrative structures according to organizational principles have not given very convincing results. In fact, the four principles of administrative science (Gulik and Urwich, 1937) – territory, process, clientele and purpose – are often contradictory. For instance, the principle claimed to be dominant in administrative organizations, namely the primary goal for which the administration was originally created, is often ambiguous, either because the goal changes over

Table 8.2 Expenditure and tax revenue, 1950s and 1970s/1980s (per cent GDP at current prices)

| | Public expenditure | | Taxes | |
	1950s	1970s	1950s	1980s
Britain	32.2	44.5	28.6	39.7
France	33.5	41.6	30.9	44.5
Germany	30.2	44.0	31.4	44.6
Italy	28.1	43.1	24.9	41.1

Source: Cassese, 1980, p. 305; OECD, *Economic Outlook*, 49

Table 8.3 Evolution of public expenditure in selected sectors, 1950s and 1980s (per cent GDP)

	Britain	France	Germany	Italy
Education:				
1950s	3.9	3.6	3.6	2.8
1980s	5.4	5.7	5.1	5.5
Difference	+1.5	+2.1	+1.5	+2.7
Health:				
1950s	2.9	2.3	2.5	1.4
1980s	4.7	6.0	6.5	5.9
Difference	+1.8	+3.7	+4.0	+4.5
Income maintenance:				
1950s	6.4	11.2	11.5	10.1
1980s	11.7	17.9	19.0	15.4
Difference	+5.3	+6.7	+7.5	+5.3
Economic infrastructure:				
1950s	1.1	3.1	1.9	–
1980s	3.0	4.0	5.3	4.8
Difference	+1.9	+0.9	+3.4	+4.8
Debt interest:				
1950s	3.9	1.3	0.8	2.2
1980s	4.6	1.5	1.9	6.2
Difference	+0.7	+0.2	+1.1	+4.0
Defence:				
1950s	8.5	6.0	3.8	–
1980s	4.7	3.4	2.9	1.9
Difference	–3.8	–2.6	–0.9	+1.9

Source: Rose, 1984, p. 308

Table 8.4 Public employees as a proportion of the active population, 1910s to 1980s (per cent)

	1910s	1930s	1950s	1980s
Britain	7.1	10.8	26.6	31.7
France	7.1	8.9	17.5	32.6
Germany	10.6	12.9	14.0	25.8
Italy	4.7	7.8	11.4	24.3

Source: Rose, 1985, pp. 9–11

time or because goals multiply. Furthermore, the creation of an organization produces its own goals. Finally, in the organization of the public administration there are contingent political factors which can determine the structure at any given moment: for example, the number of departments, the division of responsibilities between departments. It is not,

Table 8.5 Distribution of public employees in selected sectors, 1950s and 1980s (per cent of total public employees)

	Britain		France		Germany		Italy	
	1950s	1980s	1950s	1980s	1950s	1980s	1950s	1980s
General Administration	9.7	11.5	2.1	2.1	8.6	6.1	3.3	2.3
Finance	1.0	1.3	3.6	3.1	5.4	3.3	3.3	2.1
Defence	19.5	7.3	20.8	10.3	nd	10.7	23.2	8.4
Public order	1.1	3.0	4.4	3.5	3.5	4.6	3.9	2.1
Social security	3.2	7.0	1.9	3.4	8.7	6.8	1.9	2.1
Health	7.8	17.2	10.1	22.8	12.1	17.1	8.3	14.4
Education	9.8	21.2	7.4	16.1	10.0	13.8	12.1	21.4
Total (millions)	6.2	7.6	3.5	6.2	2.9	6.6	2.3	5.1

Source: Rose, 1985, various tables

therefore, that the influence of these principles is denied – every administrative structure has a goal or goals, employs certain processes, has a privileged relation with a certain clientele and is responsible for a certain geographical area – only that it is difficult, if not impossible, to understand and analyse administrative structures according to a single principle or a hierarchy of these principles.

Administrative structures reflect the political needs and preferences of a historical period more than the abstract principles of administrative science. For ease of exposition, it seems helpful to discuss them under three heads: ministerial departments; special public agencies; and institutions of control and coordination. Subcentral government agencies are the subject of the next chapter, even though national and local services often interlock. Some national services require some officials to operate in the provinces, like the *recteurs d'académie* in France or the *provveditori agli studi* in Italy: they are state officials invested with a responsibility, that of education, which is a national responsibility subject to central government control. In Germany, which is a federal state in which the *Länder* officials effectively participate in the formation of national policy, this centre/local distinction has less sense. That is also true, at least historically, for some aspects in Britain: national policy implementation in certain sectors is delegated to local government, such as education, social services and planning.

Ministerial departments

These are still today the core of the central administration in Western Europe. Their number and their tasks vary from state to state, but also over time in the same state. In general, the number of ministerial departments has oscillated between fifteen and twenty. Changes are usually more important in Britain and France than in Germany or Italy. The reasons are mainly political: the wish to entrust certain responsibilities to a particular politician – for instance, the creation of the Ministry of the Budget for the former governor of the Bank of Italy, Luigi Einaudi, in Italy in 1947, or of the Department of Technology for the trade union leader, Frank Cousins, in Britain in 1964[2] – or to signal the government's determination to take on board a particular problem – for example, the setting up of the Ministry of Women's Condition by president Giscard d'Estaing in France in 1974 or the Department of Energy by prime minister Heath in Britain in 1973.

However, in Britain and France there was also a preoccupation in the 1960s and 1970s to create the most administratively efficient organizations for different 'policy areas', and this gave rise to a series of experiments with 'superministries'. Thus three departments (Public Works, Transport and Construction) were united in France to form the Ministère de l'Équipement which was responsible for 'infrastructure', a new policy area. In Britain, the Departments of Foreign and Commonwealth Affairs, Health and Social Security and Industry and Trade were united to create the Foreign and Commonwealth Office (FCO), Department of Health and Social Security (DHSS) and the Department of Trade and Industry (DTI), respectively. But, at the end of the 1970s, misgivings over the benefits of size led to a retreat from this policy: in Britain in 1976, Transport was re-established outside the Department of the Environment, and in 1989 Health and Social Security parted company; in France in 1978, the Ministry of Finance was split into the Budget Ministry and a Ministry of the Economy; whilst the Ministry of Equipment was separated into the Departments of Transport and Environment (Environnement et la Qualité de la Vie). This tends to confirm that departmental structures respect contingent political preferences more than abstract principles.

Each department is directed by a minister politically responsible for its activity, and hierarchically organized in a series of divisions (or directorates) which have a specific sector of responsibility. At the head of each is a senior civil servant who is the highest official in that sector. The divisions are divided into subdivisions run by a higher civil servant subordinate to the divisional head. Similarly, subdivisions are divided into sections on the same pattern. The number of divisions varies between departments and even in the same department over time: in the same way as the departments are divided and amalgamated, divisions can be moved from one department to another. There is, however, some difference in internal departmental organization between Britain and Germany on the one hand, and France and Italy on the other.

In the former states, there is a top civil servant (permanent under-secretary in Britain; *Staatssekretär*[3] in Germany) directly responsible to the minister for the department's action; while in the latter, the heads of the divisions (*directeurs* in France and *direttori generali* in Italy) are responsible to the minister, each for his own sector, with the exception of the Ministry of Foreign Affairs in both states and the Ministry of Posts in France and the Ministry of Defence in Italy, where there is an overlord (*secrétaire-général* and *segretario-generale*) above the divisional heads. This means that coordination between divisions inside departments is treated in Britain and Germany as more of an administrative problem, except that in Germany the *Staatssekretär* in conjunction with the *parlamentarischer Staatssekretär*[4] acts in a more openly political manner than his British counterpart; whereas in France and Italy the problem of coordination is openly recognized as having political connotations and, hence, the minister is more directly involved through his *cabinet ministériel*.[5]

In France and Italy, ministers have a small private staff of their own (*cabinet ministériel* and *gabinetto ministeriale*). It consists of fifteen or so generally young, high-flying, higher civil servants – *grands corps* in

France, *magistrati* and *consiglieri di stato* in Italy – who are on temporary loan to the minister, and whose task it is to provide the minister not only with ideas and advice, but also assistance in running the ministry, particularly in coordinating departmental activity and supervising the minister's pet schemes. In contrast, the personal office and *Ministerbüro* of British and German ministers are much smaller (three to five persons) and their activity is limited to routine administrative tasks and publicity (PR, media). Despite the *cabinet*, one of the paradoxical consequences of the enormous centralization of ministerial power in the French and Italian administrations is to disperse effective power. As a result of the excessive accumulation of dossiers, the top civil servants cannot examine all the matters coming for signature. Thus they often sign documents unaware of the content and the implications, convinced that the matters are not controversial. And not infrequently, lower civil servants do likewise, assuming that the decisions have been vetted higher up. To this must be added the conflicts between divisions and between 'specialists' and 'generalists' as well as, in the case of France, between the *grands corps*. It is no surprise, therefore, that the result of Italian, and to a lesser extent French, departmental organization is often confusion and fragmentation.

However, new horizontal coordination and control structures have been introduced in the four states alongside, if not replacing, the traditional hierarchical structures, thus making the departmental organization much more complex. Finally, all departments have a series of special advisory committees to assist them in their administrative and legislative action. Particularly important are those of certain key ministries, like the finance, defence, education, agriculture and public works departments. For the most part, they are committees with a legal status, like the Health and Safety Committee of the Department of Health in Britain; the *Conseil Supérieur de l'Éducation Nationale* of the Ministry of Education in France; the *Finanzplanungsrat* and the *Konjunkturrat* of the Ministry of Finance, the *Bildungsrat* of the Ministry of Education in Germany; or the *Istituto Superiore della Sanità* of the Ministry of Health in Italy. They vary widely in structure, sphere of action and composition. A common element is the participation of civil servants and consultants from outside, usually acknowledged experts in the field or representatives appointed by the major interest groups active in the area. They fulfil a very significant function in supplying the administration with information and advice on technical problems, above all as regards the preparation of legislation and regulations. Thus it is natural that these committees have become the focus of pressure by interest groups of all kinds.

Special agencies and public enterprises

In the last century, as mentioned, recourse was made to forms of public institution – *öffentliche Anstalt*, non-departmental public bodies (often called QUANGOs[6]), *autorité administrative indépendante* (AAI), *ente pubblico* – other than ministerial departments, to undertake new tasks deriving from the growing public intervention in society and in the development of the welfare state. The reasons were simple. Above all, there was the need for more political autonomy to pursue certain activities than existed under direct ministerial and parliamentary control. These are activities of the type that Luhmann (1971) has called 'goal-oriented programmes' in contrast to 'situation-dependent programmes', that is to say those in which results are given priority over procedures – commercial activity or long-term planning – which need technical know-how that departmental structures make it difficult to secure. A further reason for choosing non-departmental administrative structures is the quest for greater flexibility that makes experimentation with new administrative methods and forms of organization possible.

The development of these structures has reached such a level that they defy all classificatory logic. It is possible, nonetheless, to distinguish a certain number of groups: for instance, executive public bodies engaged in commercial (firms) or quasi-commercial (services) activities. Despite this, it is not easy to classify the commercially active public bodies according to criteria applicable to all four states. Among the commercial/quasi-commercial public bodies in Britain, for example, there are both public corporations (British Railways Board, British Broadcasting Corporation) and public companies of which the state is the sole owner (the former British Leyland, now Rover, before its recent privatization); but companies in which the state had a shareholding (even if a majority one), like BP and ICL, were considered ordinary private companies. The situation in France contrasts somewhat with that in Britain: the commercial public bodies are split fourfold between *régie* (RATP), *agence* (Havas), *établissement public* (Renault, Edf, Gdf) and *société d'économie mixte* (SNCF, Air France, Elf-Erap); the last enjoys, in law, greater autonomy, thanks to private shareholders, in relation to the others, which are directly dependent on the government. The legal differences are in fact misleading, in the sense that the *régies* have enjoyed, in practice, an independence from government intervention in marked contrast to some *établissements publics* that have always been maintained under strict ministerial control, as the history of the former Régie Renault demonstrated. The level of autonomy that an executive public body enjoys depends to a large extent on the political situation. Nonetheless, relations between public bodies and departments are often fraught with tension, because of ministerial attempts to increase control and that of public firms to defend their autonomy.

The Italian situation is different from both the British and the French. In fact, it is possible to identify three broad groups: public undertakings (*azienda*) or autonomous administrations (*amministrazione di stato dei monopoli*) (ANAS, Amministrazione delle Poste e Telegrafi, Azienda di Stato per i Telefoni): the subsidiary public bodies (*ente ausiliario*) that form the so-called 'para-state' sector (INPS, ENIT, ACI, CONI); and the commercial public bodies, among which are the giant state-holding corporations (*ente di gestione*) (IRI and ENI and others, like INA, ENEL and the public banks). The public undertakings operate within the department and, although they are separate from the departmental organization, they do not have legal personality: this differentiates them from the French *régie* with which they are often assimilated. The organizational model of the state-holding corporations – *ente di gestione* – is an interesting alternative form of state intervention in a mixed economy in its own right because, although responsible to the Ministry of State Holdings, the individual firm has a much more indirect relation with the political authority than in the case of the public corporation in Britain or the *établissement public* in France. This is because the system provides for three levels of organization: at the base are the individual firms which are private companies; they are regrouped in a series of financial holding companies which own part, or all, of the shares in the individual companies and form the middle level; and finally the financial holding companies are responsible to the state-holding corporations (IRI in all sectors, ENI in energy and chemicals, EFIM in industry in the south). The state-holding corporations are a sort of buffer between the department and the individual firms. The power of the department is restricted to the overall investment plans of the holding companies and the appointment of the boards of directors, which means that it is limited to consultation and the laying down of the overall objectives while their execution is left to the corporations themselves (Posner and Woolf, 1967).

It is also possible to identify, among the other public bodies, two specific groups. The first comprises public agencies with regulatory or supervisory functions: they are set up to carry out enquiries or collect delicate information, always in place of the minister, so that their conclusions and decisions acquire a certain authoritativeness. One thinks, in the case of Britain, of the Civil Aviation Authority, the Commission for Racial Equality, the Monopolies and Mergers Commission, the IBA; in the case of France, of the Commission des Opérations en Bourse, Commission de la Securité des Consommateurs, Conseil de la Concurrence, Conseil Supérieur de l'Audiovisuel; or, in the case of Germany, of certain *Bundesoberbehörde* (federal administrative agencies), like the Bundeskartelamt (commercial competition and monopolies); and, in the case of Italy, the CONSOB (monitoring stock exchange activities).

The second group is the 'task force', that is agencies created to tackle and solve a specific problem. Here, one thinks of the French *mission* or *délégation*, of which the best known is the Commissariat du Plan set up in 1946, under Jean Monnet's direction, to organize economic reconstruction in post-war France. It was so successful that its consultative procedures and its five-year plans became an integral part of the French governmental system. A second French example is the Délégation à l'Aménagement du Territoire et à l'Action Régionale (DATAR) which was established in 1963 to stimulate industrial decentralization to the poorer regions and which was followed by four *missions interministérielles*.[7] Italian examples of this type of special agency are the Cassa per il Mezzogiorno and the CIPE. The Cassa was created in 1950 to promote the economic development of the south, and its direction was given to an apposite interministerial committee because it was to have had an 'extraordinary' character – that of furnishing extra resources and not merely substitutive of traditional governmental resources. In the 1960s a similar procedure was adopted for economic planning with the establishment of the CNPE, which was set up in 1962 and was transformed into the CIPE in 1967. Since both were multisectorial and coordination was essential, it was thought that an interministerial committee was the organ most suited to direct them. Unfortunately, both the Cassa and the CIPE ended up hamstrung by the traditional procedures of the Italian government machine on which they depended for the execution of their respective projects, and were dissolved in the 1980s.

These two groups do not exhaust all the kinds of existing public bodies, which are exceedingly numerous. There is almost no public activity, in fact, for which there is not a special agency. A few more examples may be given. In Britain there are advisory bodies, composed either of experts or of representatives of interests in a specific sector, which are responsible for the distribution of public funds in that sector; among these are scientific research councils and the Arts Council, the Manpower Services Commission and the University Funding Council (UFC). Similar bodies are found in other countries: Wissenschaftsrat in Germany, CNRS in France and CNR in Italy (scientific research). In Italy, national insurance is, as in Germany, administered by an autonomous public agency (INPS) and not by a ministerial department as in Britain. These public bodies are subject to public law, endowed with legal personality and an independent management. They are also subject to the supervision of the Ministry of Labour which can issue general directives, but not intervene directly in the agencies' activity.

The list of such bodies is endless. If we add that we have only mentioned national examples and that there are also agencies at the subcentral level, almost certainly still more numerous – particularly in a federal state like Germany – then it is clear that the number is enormous. In Britain the number has been estimated at over 5,500 with a budget of £46 billion,[8] whereas in Italy it is somewhere in excess of 40,000. Indeed, when La Malfa, as minister without portfolio, reported on them as early as 1951, he described the whole sector as 'a limitless mass'. His conclusions are worth quoting because recent studies in other countries suggest that they are of more general application:

> Their status, their structure, the forms of control to which they were subject and their place within the machinery of government were utterly incoherent. Some were public bodies, some were private firms, some technically autonomous state institutions. The legal status of some of these enterprises was so obscure that the courts were continually giving widely diverse judgements as to their position. (quoted in Chapman, 1959, pp. 58–9)

There is no doubt that the growth in the number of public bodies and special agencies has meant that 'in no Western country', as Panebianco (1986) has argued, 'is the central ministerial administration any longer the quantitatively dominant component of the administrative system' (p. 406). It has also meant that the agencies have furnished an enormous opportunity for patronage, by appointing, on the boards of directors, government supporters; this is an opportunity of which all governments have taken advantage to the full.

The effects of this development are, according to Panebianco, to increase the complication, and so the fragmentation, of the administrative system, which has lost, little by little, that characteristic of being a relatively compact organized macro-system which it once had. This has led to an increase in 'intrabureaucratic competition', that is conflict between ministries and between ministries and special agencies. Such conflict, which is present in every bureaucratic system, becomes particularly bitter in times of economic recession when budgetary cuts are imposed. In such moments, the various organizations fight one another using all the resources of power and influence that they can command, including the 'pressure capacity' of the interest groups in their sector to tilt the scales in their favour. The problem of the repartition of public expenditure has, in fact, become acute because it is no longer a conjunctural problem; it has become a permanent fact of life for West European states to the extent that public expenditure already absorbs a high level of economic resources, around 45 per cent of GDP. Thus its further increase now makes the repartition of public expenditure a zero-sum game, as British politics in the 1980s demonstrated: for instance, the setting up of the so-called star chamber, cabinet committee Misc 62 to adjudicate on ministerial spending demands.

Institutions of control and administrative coordination

The control of the administration raises problems of legitimacy and conception. As regards the first, the question is the distinction between two types of control: that of legality – the administrative acts must conform to the law – and that of policy – the administration must follow the government's or parliament's declared policy orientation. The former is the task of the courts and the latter of parliament. In practice, however, things are not quite so simple: problems of legitimacy also pose problems of equity and reasonableness; and discretionary powers – invested increasingly in the administration – raise political questions that go far beyond purely legal formulations. In such a situation, neither the ordinary courts nor parliament is usually able to exercise an adequate control. Turning to the second problem, the different conceptions of the state, there is a major difference between the Anglo-Saxon and the continental (or Napoleonic) traditions. The basis of the former is parliamentary sovereignty – the notion of the unlimited power of parliament – while the second is founded on the *Rechtsstaat* (or state based on law) – the idea that the state is the expression of the legal order. The result is a very different institutional structure of administrative control. In Britain, parliament is the core of the system, while in France, Germany and Italy, administrative law and the system of administrative courts are the centre of the system.

In the British system of administrative control, the power of parliament is expressed in the constitutional doctrine of 'ministerial responsibility', namely that ministers are accountable to parliament for both their own actions and those of their departments, even though it is generally accepted that, because of the scale of government, this is no longer possible in practice. Hence, they can be, in extremely serious but also extremely rare cases, the object of a motion of censure. The rarity is because civil servants act in the name and on behalf of ministers, and a motion of censure against the minister for his department's action is tantamount to censuring the government and is likely to affect adversely its standing and that of the governing party in public opinion. The conclusion can only be that control of the British administration is above all political and is subject increasingly to political expediency. Another consequence of this form of political control is the so-called 'ethic of confidentiality' which governs relations between ministers and civil servants and which makes it an offence, codified in the Official Secrets Act of 1911 (redrafted in 1990, but now without a public interest or previous publication defence), for civil servants 'to divulge any information gained by them as a result of any appointment to any unauthorized person either orally or in writing without previous official sanction in writing'. The ethic is a significant barrier to more open government and has led to a growth in the number of anonymous 'leaks' of official documents to the press in the 1980s (Tisdall and Ponting affairs).[9]

The British parliament has endeavoured to create from time to time some new instruments to improve the control of administrative action. One thinks, above all, of the extension of the select committee system and of the ombudsman (parliamentary commissioner for administration). Two select committees have always been particularly important, the Public Accounts Committee and the Expenditure Committee. The former was established in 1861 to consider the reports of the comptroller and auditor general who audit each department's accounts, notify any irregularities and can summon officials to explain. The latter was established in 1971 to monitor forward planning of public expenditure and its consequences for the policies involved (replaced by the Select Committee on the Treasury and Civil Service in 1979). In addition, six other select committees were set up which specialized in various subjects from nationalized industries to race relations. Nobody doubts the usefulness of the work of these committees in opening up the policy process to scrutiny and more informed discussion. For this reason the system was extended in 1979 to cover the major ministerial departments (fourteen in all); however, their impact has been limited, not least because, although they have issued some very critical reports, they have been resisted by civil servants who have shown reluctance to assist their deliberations, and governments with secure parliamentary majorities have preferred to ignore them (chapter 7).

As regards the ombudsman established by parliament in 1967 to investigate cases of alleged maladministration, it was something of a palliative, in the sense that: (1) he can only examine cases referred to him by MPs who act as a 'filter'; and (2) his recommendations are not binding. In addition, the office has a very small staff (90 persons), thus making a real, but limited, impact on departmental action: in the 27 years, 1967–93, out of 21,995 cases submitted, the ombudsman examined 6627 and found elements of maladministration in 2114 or 32 per cent.[10]

To complete this view of the British institutions of administrative control, mention should also be made of the ordinary courts which have the power of judicial review to determine whether departmental action is *ultra vires*, that is whether the action has been authorized by parliament. Traditionally, the British courts have been reluctant to intervene in cases where political judgements are involved, accepting the government's motivation so long as it was not manifestly illegal, but this has changed recently and the judges have become more critical of government. In addition, the courts are supplemented by a system of administrative tribunals which consider disputes between a citizen and a public body. In view of the fact that the system has grown *ad hoc*, there are doubts about the tribunals' independence from the administrative bodies themselves.

The *Rechtsstaat*, as a concept, emerged on the continent of Europe, and above all in Germany, in the nineteenth century as a more appropriate instrument than the politico-parliamentary one – partly owing to the weakness of continental parliaments – to defend citizen rights against an overpowerful government. It is defined in terms of two features: (1) the state is subject to a body of law which also constitutes the basis of all administrative action; and (2) the state establishes an independent power with the task of guaranteeing that administrative acts conform in practice to the law and the principles underlying it. Thus, the *Rechtsstaat* is founded on a constitution that sets out the relative competences of the various state institutions as well as the individual citizens' rights. This system of administrative control in the *Rechtsstaat* is organized in a network of administrative courts separate from, and independent of, the ordinary judicial system, and subject only to its respective national constitutional court, and then only for constitutional questions. In this network of courts, it is possible to distinguish a central administrative court (Bundesverwaltungsgericht in Germany, Conseil d'État in France and Consiglio di Stato in Italy) and local administrative courts,[11] from courts with special jurisdiction in public accounting (Rechnungshof, Cour des Comptes and Corte dei Conti). In Germany, there is also a series of specialized administrative courts (Finanzgericht, Sozialgericht, Arbeitsgericht) established after the war to relieve the Bundesverwaltungsgericht.

The administrative courts in the three states are competent to resolve disputes between private citizens and the administration or between different units of administration. They not only deliver judgements but also investigate the facts of a citizen's complaint against the administration. This means that they can annul a decision either for abuse of power or for procedural defect, as when, for instance, the administration uses its powers for undeclared purposes. The latter point is important because it allows the administrative courts to investigate the motives behind administrative decisions where the correct procedure has been observed. However, the tasks of the administrative courts in the three states are not the same. Thus, for instance, the French Conseil d'État and the Italian Consiglio di Stato have a consultative role – by which bills and administrative decrees must be submitted by the government for a consultative opinion – which the German Bundesverwaltungsgericht does not have. Moreover, the concept of 'administrative act' is defined more restrictively in Germany than in either France or Italy.

On the other hand, the administrative courts responsible for the state accounts (Rechnungshof, Cour des Comptes and Corte dei Conti), in addition to their jurisdiction over the use of public funds – embezzlement and the like – are responsible for supervising departmental audits and preparing an annual report for parliament. There is a trend in recent years for them to investigate not only the accuracy of the accounts but also the efficiency of the administration under examination, and so their reports are not limited to criticizing abuses and inefficiency; they often point to defects in governmental policy and, in the French case, make proposals for reform. The success of the latter depends, however, on the government's reaction, which is usually half-hearted. The main limit to the action of these courts is that they act necessarily *a posteriori*,[12] and in consequence their reports, despite their accuracy, are always delayed, as for instance the 'thousand billion lire' scandal of the Italian Federconsorzi in the 1960s demonstrated.

The control of the administration by the administrative courts system has been attacked in France and Germany as being slow and excessively rigid and formalistic. In consequence, the Office du Médiateur (a weak version of the ombudsman) was established in France in 1972 to investigate minor citizen complaints alleging unfair, rather than illegal, administrative action. Such a development has usually been opposed in Germany, except in the very exceptional case of the armed services, where from 1955 an ombudsman has been able to receive soldiers' complaints; very recently the Rhineland-Palatinate *Land* has introduced such a figure (*Bürgerbeauftragte*) at regional level with unpredictable consequences. It is opposed because it would create a crisis in the *Rechtsstaat*, introducing a new category of administrative act, half-way between legal and illegal acts. Despite the criticism of the control of the administration in relation to the citizen, as much in Britain as in France and Germany, the three states' governments are very reticent about developing the ombudsman's powers. The reason is simple: the more efficient the political control, the greater the administration's bureaucratic formalism. 'If these procedures', Finer (1980) has noted, 'secure the civil servant a certain level of security, they also limit him to that level.' As yet, dissatisfaction with the administration in Italy has not given rise to any reforms in this field, although some regions have been discussing the introduction of a regional ombudsman for some time.

Finally, there remains the problem of political control: control by parliament. The *Rechtsstaat* tradition gives much greater weight to legal as against political procedures for the defence of the fundamental rights of citizens, and so for the control of the administration. This also happens because the separation of powers in countries of this tradition is conceived in terms of the specificity of the roles of the different institutions. Parliament in Britain is not a countervailing power, that is to say a place of opposition to government or government policy. On the contrary, its role is to legitimate the government by supporting its action. It was parliament's weakness – the fact that it was never sovereign – and the absence of homogeneous parliamentary majorities which strengthened the development of the *Rechtsstaat* on the continent of Europe in the late nineteenth and early twentieth centuries. On the other hand, this sceptical view of the possibilities of politico-parliamentary control of the administration was, after the rise of organized parties, more realistic than the British viewpoint. Since the government controls the parliamentary majority, it is difficult to argue that it would allow a vote of censure of the administration which public opinion could interpret as a vote of censure of the government itself.

If this is how things stand, the only control of the administration today is that coming from the coordination of government action in the various fields of activity. The institution carrying out this formal task is the 'government' itself (the cabinet or council of ministers). But, as the supreme organ of government, its activity is limited to largely formal meetings, usually weekly, in which government decisions, almost entirely taken in other places, are confirmed. This is because the number of decisions requiring government approval has grown out of all proportion in the last 100 years. Hence, not surprisingly, a set of institutions and informal mechanisms has developed.

Among these institutions, there is an ensemble of cabinet committees (over 200 in Britain), interministerial committees (as in France and Italy) and permanent committees of federal and *Land* ministers (in Germany), with their numerous subcommittees and working parties, both permanent and *ad hoc*, all more or less with the task of securing the agreement of the interested parties in their sector. Moreover, with the gradual 'Europification' of the context of national policies, special cabinet committees, serviced by specific bodies (European Unit in the Cabinet Office in Britain, Secrétariat Général du Comité Interministériel pour la Coopération Économique Européenne (SGCI) in France, Ufficio per la Coordinazione delle Politiche della Comunità Europea in Italy), were set up in the various countries to coordinate their policies towards the EU and prepare their various negotiating stances in Brussels. Finally, turning to informal mechanisms of coordination, we can mention the networks of personal contacts among groups of higher civil servants such as in the *grands corps* and the Ministry of Finance in France or the Treasury in Britain; or again the more or less regular meetings between higher civil servants in strategic positions who know whom to contact to resolve various problems.

In the four states, however, there are seemingly a number of key institutions: the Cabinet Office and the Treasury[13] in Britain; the Bundeskanzleramt, the Finance Ministry and the Central Bank in Germany; the presidency of the republic, the prime minister's *cabinet*, the *secrétariat du gouvernement* and the Finance Ministry in France; and the Prime Minister's Office and the Treasury Ministry in Italy. In Britain, the Cabinet Office, under the direction of the cabinet secretary – the head of the home civil service – is responsible for the activity of the cabinet and the cabinet committees. There was an attempt in the 1970s to give a more direct impetus to government coordination through the creation of the Central Policy Review Staff in 1971, but it was not judged a great success and it was dissolved in 1983. Since then, the prime minister has used the Cabinet Office and a small group of policy advisers, the prime minister's Policy Unit composed of nine people. The Treasury's coordinating activities derive from its financial responsibilities and, above all, the control of public expenditure. Its agreement is necessary for all expenditure, and its interest in administrative efficiency has led it to sponsor the introduction of a series of management programmes – Public Expenditure Survey Committee (PESC), programme analysis and review (PAR) – that have given it an even greater say in the content of departmental policies. In addition, the majority of permanent under-secretaries are recruited from higher civil servants in the Treasury, witness to the quality of its personnel.

In Germany, the Bundeskanzleramt (Chancellor's Office) has an even more important coordinating role than the British Cabinet Office: it was chancellor Adenauer, and above all his *Staatssekretär* Hans Globke, who used the *Richtlinienkompetenz* principle to organize the office as a centre of government coordination. Furthermore, Globke introduced a system of civil servant rotation between the Chancellor's Office and the ministerial departments in order to have contacts there. Policy initiatives are worked up by one or two departmental ministers in meetings with the chancellor and officials from the Chancellor's Office. Cabinet committees are few, meet infrequently and have little influence; more important are the various *Konferenze der Minister der Länder* in which federal and *Land* ministers coordinate policy. Thus the Chancellor's Office has become the focus of the federal government and this despite federalism and a lively tradition of departmental autonomy. The Finance Ministry's coordination role parallels the British Treasury's and for the same reasons.

In France, government coordination is carried out by cooperation between the presidency, the prime minister's *cabinet* and the secretary-general of the government, who organizes the agenda of the Conseil des Ministres. However, the real policy discussions take place elsewhere, and specifically in (1) informal meetings of the president and a minister, normally but not always, in the presence of the prime minister and the official responsible for the sector in the presidency; (2) *ad hoc* meetings of groups of ministers, chaired by the president; (3) interministerial committees of ministers interested in a particular decision or policy chaired by the president or prime minister. The role of the various *cabinets ministériels* (and above all the higher civil servants with contacts in other *cabinets*) is crucial for coordination. Once again, the Finance Ministry plays a key role as in other countries, not only because of its financial responsibilities, but also because of its 'superior' staff ('it is not so much in criticism as in negotiation that they are "unbeatable"' claims former top Finance Ministry civil servant, François Bloch-Lainé, 1990, p. 10).

In Italy, the problem is not so much the lack of institutions as the lack of will to use them. As in Britain, coordination is officially carried out in various interministerial committees, but the number is excessive and the prime minister often lacked effective power over the other ministers, because of the coalition formula, to ensure respect of the decisions taken. However, attempts were made in the 1980s to extend the prime minister's power. Thus, for instance an inner cabinet (*consiglio di gabinetto*) was created in 1983: it consisted of a small number of the most important ministers (usually seven), including one leader from all the coalition partners. In addition, an economic cabinet on similar lines responsible for macro-economic decisions was set up. In 1988, as a result of the restructuring of the Prime Minister's Office (law 400/88) and reform of public finance, the prime minister's authority was reinforced at the expense of individual ministers. Thus the old formula of 'government by separate ministries' was replaced by a new one: 'government by a limited sovereignty prime minister' (Criscitiello, 1993, p. 585). The limitation was less governmental than political. Hence, as mentioned, the chief method of policy coordination has been by means of the majority summit, an informal arena of extra-governmental party bargaining that became progressively institutionalized in the 1980s. If it contributed to executive decision-making while the *pentapartito* was politically dominant (that is, up to the 1992 election), it was abandoned when the coalition collapsed.

Such administrative policy coordination as there is – judged woefully inadequate by many – is achieved by the Treasury Ministry, usually supported by the Bank of Italy, using monetary rather than fiscal weapons. The Treasury has, in fact, civil servants in all departments through the Central Audit Office which is responsible for departmental accounts, and this ensures it a strong position. However, the Italian higher civil service is essentially executant and not policy oriented. Hence, it is the Council of State that provides a reservoir of advisers for ministers who fill the ministerial cabinets and provide what coordination there is. Nonetheless, this is limited as the Italian administration remains characterized by a series of departmental fiefs, in which everyone defends his own, and hence by a chronic flaw in the circulation of information:[14] the cause and consequence of political hyper-factionalism.

In conclusion, the real contrast remains between the British system of collegiate government and the continental non-collegiate systems. In Britain, despite Mrs Thatcher, collective discussion of policy by groups of ministers is still effective. In Germany, France and Italy, it is not: individual relations between autonomous ministers and the head of government are decisive and explain the significance of some policies and the insignificance of others.

The public service

The public sector employs a large number of people – estimated at between a quarter and a third of the active population of the four countries (table 8.4) – even though all public servants are not civil servants (*Beamte, fonctionnaire, funzionario*). One of the reasons, in fact, for creating new institutions with specific goals, other than experimenting with new forms of administrative organization, is that of recruiting a different kind of person with particular skills without being bound by civil service rules. On the other hand, the definition of civil servant varies widely between the four states. For instance, university professors have civil servant status in France, Germany and Italy, but not in Britain. However, if the analysis is limited to the personnel working in ministerial departments – our primary interest – the numbers are much more modest:

about 250,000, of which the administrative elite of higher civil servants represents at most 5000 with a core of top policy-makers of a few hundred persons.

Civil servants

The civil service is traditionally divided into four classes which have different titles in each state. France has the simplest nomenclature with A, B, C and D; in Germany they are respectively *höherer Dienst, gehobener Dienst, mittlerer Dienst* and *einfacher Dienst*; in Britain, administrative class, executive class, clerical class and messengerial class; and in Italy, *carriera direttiva, carriera di concetto, carriera esecutiva* and *carriera ausiliaria.*[15] This structure is largely due to the common educational pattern in European countries, based on the three cycles of primary, secondary and higher, because the organization of the different civil service careers was linked to various school-leaving ages. Recruitment is habitually by competitive examination and requires, for each class, a minimum educational qualification, which in Britain is: degree for the highest class; A levels for the intermediate; GCSE (or equivalent) for the third; and primary school for the fourth, although people may enter this class late in life as ex-servicemen, rather than straight from school.

The four classes correspond to the tasks performed by modern public administration. In short, 5 per cent of civil servants are in the highest class and are responsible for policy-making and all that entails; 30 per cent are in the second class and are responsible for the detailed management of ordinary administration (i.e. routine tasks) and supervision of subordinate personnel. The third class accounts for 50 per cent and carries out mechanical tasks (typing, accounting, dealing with the public), while the fourth class is made up of messengers, chauffeurs, guards and porters. In addition, there are several groups of professional staff (engineers, economists, scientists) in special grades standing outside the four classes, which in Britain, for example, formed a separate corps, the scientific civil service, until 1971.

This system of classes has been strongly criticized in the post-war period, above all in Britain and Germany. The stress on academic qualifications as a condition for entry into a certain class prevented career mobility; it not only imposed barriers in the way of the able civil servant being promoted as far as his talents justified, but was also a serious obstacle to the administration's overall efficiency. In Britain, career inflexibility was attenuated to some extent by the expansion of higher education, because from the 1970s the graduates among the successful candidates for the executive class have constantly been on the increase. In consequence, the pressure for in-service promotion from the executive to the administrative class was also on the increase, a situation recognized by the Fulton Report at the end of the 1960s. It recommended, among other things, that the class system should be replaced by a unified grading structure covering the whole service – the so-called 'open structure' – which was established in 1971. However, it was only partially implemented so that if there is a unified structure in theory, the old structure of three classes with three points of entry remains in practice.[16] Indeed, the proportion of graduates recruited by open competition at the level of the old administrative class – as administrative trainees or high-flyers – is always a large majority, and in-service promotion (graduates or not) from the old executive class always a small minority (between 10 per cent and 30 per cent annually in 1972–82). Finally, in the 1980s the Thatcher governments initiated a move to reduce numbers by hiving off executive sections of the civil service into independent bodies (the so-called New Steps Agencies, like the Benefits Agency).

In Italy too, the need for greater administrative efficiency was felt and led to the establishment in 1972 of an elite of *dirigenti* which form part of the *carriera direttiva*, but with rank and salary above the old *direttori generali*. The intention of the reform was not to establish a new career class – in fact, the old four-class structure was reduced to a single class divided into eight functional divisions, from doorman to graduate head of section – but rather a new kind of administrative function, namely the specialist in general management, to which members of the *carriera direttiva* would have access as and when they demonstrated such capacity. To this end the reform was accompanied by a reorganization of the process of selection and training of higher civil servants, but so far the reform has not given the expected results. The result, in fact, has been to create a new career class at the top, the more so since seniority rather than merit has been the real criterion of promotion to *dirigente*.

Given the civil service system of classes and the different academic qualifications required for entry, it is no surprise that the social origins of Western European civil servants are what has been called 'a compendium of all the strata of the middle classes'. Indeed, the white-collars represent *grosso modo* the lower middle class, the executive civil servants the middle middle class and the higher civil servants the upper middle class. Moreover, the civil servants in the four states adopt, of necessity, the way of life, appearances and habits characteristic of the position they occupy in the social hierarchy, as many writers – from Balzac and Dickens to Courteline and Brancati – have illustrated to the point of caricature. And this even when their salary is insufficient to meet the needs of their particular station. Finally, public service is no longer the instrument of social promotion that it was in some states, above all France, in the nineteenth century. Today it appears more as one of the many careers open to the middle classes.

In three of the four states – France, Germany and Italy – civil servants' conditions of service are regulated by public law: French *Statut général des fonctionnaires* of 1946 (amended in 1959); German *Bundesbeamtengesetz* of 1953 (amended in 1977); and Italian *Testo unico degli impiegati civili dello Stato* of 1957. These are administered in some cases by a specific public body (Direction de la Fonction Publique in France) and are subject to the jurisdiction of the administrative courts. In Britain, on the contrary, the situation is more complex and ambiguous: the behaviour of civil servants is regulated by an informal code of conduct – recently amended as regards the duties of confidentiality by the cabinet secretary – which is basically non-legal in character. This is because British civil servants are formally 'servants of the crown' and therefore hold office 'at the pleasure of the crown', which means that they have no contractual rights that are enforceable in the courts. In practice, however, their position is not very different from that of the civil servants of other European countries. In general, all civil servants enjoy security of tenure, which means that they can be dismissed only for grave dereliction of duties (treason, corruption, gross incompetence), and only after a long and complex disciplinary procedure. They usually have very favourable pension rights (that is, indexed to the cost of living), trade union rights (the various civil servant unions are powerful in the four states) and, under certain conditions, the right to political activity (joining a party), except in Britain where this is precluded in the name of the political neutrality of the civil service.

On the other hand, duties include principally the obligation to serve the state with loyalty, neutrality and discretion. The situation varies as regards the right to strike, fight elections and, if elected, sit in parliament and defend the constitution. The limits on the right to strike are less in Britain and Italy than in France and Germany. It is obvious that limits to the right to strike are imposed on certain categories responsible for maintaining the security of the state: higher civil servants, armed forces, police, secret services. However, in France the right is subject to the obligation of a week's notice, while in Germany it is not recognized at all; in Italy wildcat strikes are banned, and in Britain there is a tradition of no striking in essential public services.

French, German and Italian civil servants can stand as parliamentary candidates; if successful they go on unpaid leave[17] until the end of their term of office, and have the right to be reintegrated without any loss of seniority. In Britain, civil servant candidates are obliged to resign from the service and have no right to reintegration; in fact, the two careers are incompatible and the choice of a political career means the termination of a career in the civil service. This helps to explain why so many French and German[18] civil servants engage in a political career – indeed, Sulieman (1984) argues that the French regulations positively encourage it, particularly for higher civil servants – while their British counterparts, on the contrary, eschew it. In such a situation, the case of the Italian civil servants represents something of an anomaly: they enjoy the same advantages as their French and German colleagues but, like their British colleagues, the overwhelming majority eschew it. The explanation is political: the distinction between politics and administration was introduced by fascism which needed posts for its partisans, and was continued in the post-war period as a result of the pre-eminence assumed by the parties.

Finally, as regards the defence of the constitution, the differences between the various national civil servants are less of substance than of law. Every civil servant has the obligation to serve the state with loyalty. All civil servants who occupy sensitive posts with access to official secrets are positively vetted by their respective secret services and are liable to dismissal for subversive activity. In Britain, which lacks a written constitution, this obligation is understood both in the wider sense of loyalty to the crown, and in the more narrow sense of undivided loyalty to ministers. Recently, the limits of this loyalty of civil servants to ministers have been questioned, namely whether it should not also include a duty to protect the 'public interest'. So far, no British government has been prepared to recognize such an obligation, preferring to consider itself the unique expression of the public interest, and the judges have usually upheld this view (Ponting case, 1985).

In Germany and Italy, the respective constitutions lay down, for obvious reasons, the requirement of total loyalty of civil servants to the established institutions. Curiously, it was in Germany, and not Italy, that this clause had its most striking consequences: the *Radikalenerlass* (or radicals' decree) of 1972, better known as the *Berufsverbot* (or professional ban). The 1953 law developed the requirement of loyalty to the constitution into the notion that civil servants should be 'active defenders of the democratic order'. When, after the failure to overthrow parliamentary democracy by non-parliamentary means, the German student movement (APO) changed its strategy in 1970 and advocated 'the long march through the institutions' – that is subverting them from within – the federal government took fright, perceiving it as a real threat to the integrity of the public service. Thus the federal minister of the interior, in collaboration with the *Land* ministers, issued a circular, the *Radikalenerlass*, in 1972, reminding public authorities of the democratic order clause in the 1953 law. The result was the investigation of the political background of all candidates for the public service – a very large category in Germany – and the dismissal of so-called subversives, mainly communists but also some social democrats: more than a million people were investigated and a thousand or so were dismissed or not appointed.

In Italy, on the contrary, where terrorism in the 'years of the bullet' (*anni di piombo*) was much more serious than in Germany, constitutional loyalty to the republic was never used as a weapon of discrimination against those whose faith in liberal democracy was considered doubtful. This is even more curious in view of the fact that the communists were the object of great political discrimination during the Cold War years. We can only conclude that, paradoxically, political consensus in the 1970s and 1980s was greater in Italy than Germany, where the population was prey to fears of 'the enemy at the gates'.

The administrative elite

If the mass of civil servants are employed in routine tasks that are intended to ensure the proper functioning of the state machine, they are nonetheless directed by a restricted group of higher civil servants – perhaps a few hundred persons – at the top of the public administration: civil servants who are in permanent contact with ministers and who are co-responsible for the formulation of government policy. This group is generally considered the key group in the functioning of the state, so much so as to deserve the appellation of 'administrative elite', not only because it constitutes a privileged and direct link between public administration and constitutional government, but also because it determines the orientation and output of the administrative machine. Lord William Armstrong, former head of the British civil service, has stated his view that the civil service does, indeed, have a great deal of influence: 'the biggest and most pervasive influence is in setting the framework within which the questions of policy are raised.' It comes from what Weber called *Dienstwissen*, ('knowledge of the service'), namely the way in which the administrative machine operates, as illustrated in the British TV series 'Yes, Minister'.

Some see the administrative elite of certain West European states (Gaullist France, for instance) as a monolithic nucleus and go as far as to identify this core group with the ruling class *tout court* and not simply to see it as one group, more or less powerful, according to the circumstances, among the several which make up a state's ruling class. Certainly, the osmosis between the top politicians and administrators as well as businessmen is greatest in France – the administrative elite is a veritable seedbed for the political class – but it is not the only country. In Britain and Germany, senior civil servants enjoy a somewhat similar position of eminence. In the latter, it is recognized in the fact that those occupying the top administrative posts (*Staatssekretär* and *Ministerialdirektor*) are known as *politische Beamte* (political civil servants) because they are appointed and dismissed at the government's discretion – that is on overtly political criteria – for which they receive substantial statutory and financial guarantees. Indeed, only in Italy is this not the case: Cassese (1984) has persuasively argued that the 'higher civil service is not structurally integrated in the ruling class' (p. 42) and in consequence 'it does not take part in the policy-making process or it plays a secondary role' (p. 44).

At all events, Panebianco (1986, p. 401) has usefully outlined four criteria that help to characterize and distinguish European administrative elites: (1) social origin and status; (2) modalities of recruitment, socialization and career patterns; (3) open or closed character; and (4) relation between generalists and specialists. As regards the first criterion, it is necessary to stress the unrepresentative social origins of the higher civil servants in the four states – an even greater unrepresentativeness than in the case of the parliamentary politicians. Indeed, the social base of the recruitment of high civil servants is extremely limited. For the authors of the Michigan study (Aberbach, Putnam and Rockman, 1981): 'top administrators come from that tiny minority of the population that is male, urban, university educated, upper middle class in origin, and public affairs oriented' (p. 81). In all states, but particularly in France and Germany, there is a high rate – over 50 per cent – of family recruitment: the children of former civil servants. This happens, moreover, despite different methods of recruitment in each state: centralized recruitment in Britain (Civil Service Commission) and France (competitive *grandes écoles*); decentralized in Germany (by authority, *Bund* and *Land*) and in Italy (by ministry). The peculiarities in the origins of higher civil servants result from each country's socio-cultural specificity: overrepresentation of middle class Oxbridge arts graduates in Britain; of Parisian upper middle class *énarques* in France; of middle class law graduates in Germany; and southern lower middle class law graduates in Italy (table 8.6).

However, Panebianco wisely warns not to confuse the social origin of a group with its status and class prestige. There are significant differences between them. French and British civil servants enjoy much more prestige than do Italian, whereas the German are somewhere between the two. Many factors contribute to the prestige of an administrative elite at any time: historical traditions, recruitment methods, forms of socialization and more besides, including comparable remuneration to the private sector. In the case of France, the system of the *grands corps d'état* (*conseil d'état*, *inspection des finances*, *cour des comptes*, that is the specialized bodies of administrators as well as the bodies of technicians grouped into *mines, ponts et chaussées, télécommunications, génie rural*), was created by Napoleon to administer the post-revolutionary state, and each body today has its own rules, norms, privileges and identity. Recruitment is assured by the *grandes écoles* (Polytechnique, Centrale, ENS and, since the war, the École Nationale d'Administration (ENA), via the Parisian Institut d'Études Politiques) which have succeeded in monopolizing the formation of the top personnel of the French administration.

It is generally agreed that it is the training of the *grandes écoles*, and above all of ENA, that inculcates that 'caste' character which many consider to be the distinctive feature of French top civil servants: the so-called *grands commis de l'état* (those who are placed in the top places on leaving ENA). It is true that the French administration is dominated by members of the *grands corps*, who are a minority, even among higher civil servants, but in their action express a strong corporate solidarity and identity with their *corps*. These – as Marceau Long (1980), a former secretary-general of the government, has pointed out – not only are the negative qualities of 'closed little societies', but also 'reinforce without

Table 8.6 Selected characteristics of senior civil servants, 1970s (per cent)

	Britain	France	Germany	Italy
Father's occupational status:				
high management and professional	51	66	46	46
lower management and professional	17	30	21	36
skilled non-manual	16	3	19	15
lower non-manual	5	0	2	0
skilled manual	5	1	11	3
semi- and unskilled manual	8	0	1	0
Civil servant's educational background:				
below university level	14	na	1	0
law	3	na	65	53
humanities	38	na	2	0
social sciences	12	na	17	36
technical, hard sciences	26	na	14	10
university major unknown	7	na	2	1
One or more relatives in politics or the civil service now or in past	54	50	80	75
Father employed in government	20	na	32	41
Spent at least one-quarter of adult life outside their respective national government	12	37	49	2
Served in a national ministry other than present ministry	51	na	32	18
Sample (number)	89	73	91	81

Source: Aberbach, Putnam and Rockman, 1981, tables 3.2, 3.3, 2.7 and 3.8, pp. 52, 55, 71 and 74

any doubt, the level and competence of the sense of public service' (p. 44). In addition, the prestige and charisma of the administrative elite have been fostered and strengthened by concrete achievements, like France's economic development which was perceived as a specific contribution, willed and carried through by the administrative elite. In addition, the great post-war French projects (Caravelle, Concorde, SECAM, TGV, nuclear technology) are all associated with state intervention and, hence, attributed to the *grands commis*.

In Britain, in contrast to France, the administrative elite has suffered from the country's continuous economic decline in the post-war period,[19] for which in the 1960s it was considered largely responsible, for instance in the Fulton Inquiry of 1966–8. This blamed its elite recruitment from Oxbridge arts graduates at the expense of science graduates and graduates from other universities. Moreover, the kind of selection – open competitive examination on graduation, with the accent on the candidate's 'character' and on on-the-job training, practical and *not* theoretical[20] – has been such as to form a social elite of professional administrators with a 'generalist' outlook as opposed to a specific 'specialism' which it judged to be 'narrowing'. At all events, the combination of student life in Oxbridge colleges and adult life in London clubs seems to be responsible for a socialization that fosters a strong group sense, particularly relevant among the higher civil servants in the Treasury.

In Germany, the higher civil service has lost since the war the corporate identity, the *Beamtenethos* of the old Prussian administrators about whom Weber wrote. Unlike their French and British colleagues, German higher civil servants do not receive their academic training in high-prestige schools. If a legal background is no longer required, most in the general administrator category have studied law at one of the many German universities with no recognizable concentration in any one school. Hence, it has become possible to talk, in the case of the top federal civil servants, of the persistence of a *Juristenmonopol*. This has become a subject of heated controversy, given the increasing emphasis on long-range public planning. Aspirants to higher posts extend their training by doing a doctorate in law or related subject. Finally, they can spend six months or a year on a course in administrative techniques at the Administrative Sciences College (Hochschule für Verwaltungswissenschaften) in Speyer. Thus if the German administrative elite lacks the prestige of the British and French, this, according to Mayntz (1984), is due to the lack of homogeneity in social background and the absence of a common educational experience at one or a few elite schools. The departmental recruitment practice, moreover, militates against the development of a corporate identity among the administrative elite. The personal loyalty of the German higher civil servant is to his particular department while that of the French is to his *corps* and the British to his service class as a whole.

In Italy, instead, all the significant elements – lack of an administrative tradition, fragmentary recruitment (by ministry), absence of a specific administrative training, slow promotion, and low pay – converge to confirm the relatively low prestige of the Italian higher civil service, which the great expansion of the Italian economy in the post-war period has not really shaken. Indeed, Italian economic expansion has occurred despite, rather than because of, the Italian administrative elite. It is a fact, however, that the common southern origin and the homogeneous legal background support an administrative culture which stresses values like authority, hierarchy and procedural formalities.[21] It was responsible, according to Cassese (1984), for a *modus vivendi*, or 'pact', between the administrative elite and the political class in which the former traded political influence for predictability and security in their relations with politics. Proof of this comes from the fact that young technical and scientific graduates who choose the public sector look to a career in the special agencies and public enterprises which is where, with the ministerial cabinets, as noted, Italian policy is made.

Finally, there is a general contrast in attitudes and ideology between national politicians and higher civil servants. The Michigan study (Aberbach, Putnam and Rockman, 1981) summarizes this contrast in the distinction between 'governance' on the part of civil servants and 'politics' on that of politicians. Politicians have an ideological and theoretical frame of reference that leads them to judge problems in terms of distribution and redistribution of resources. They are convinced that different solutions will have different consequences for different groups, and this makes them sensitive to the conflicts that certain actions might provoke. In short, they are interested in promoting policy solutions that will benefit, as far as possible, the groups they represent, and this is naturally their primary motivation. Civil servants, on the other hand, have a less general and more detailed view of reality: they are interested in the technical and administrative, but also political, practicability of the different possible solutions. They are more sensitive to problems of collective goods than those of distribution and so tend to underestimate the possible sources of conflict and injustice that a particular policy might cause.

This contrast between the two groups in the policy process respects in general the role differences between politicians and civil servants identified by Weber: the notion that politicians and higher civil servants are both engaged in policy, but bring different competences and interests – representation of social interests by politicians, technical competence by civil servants – which endow each group with a different perspective and so a specific vision of its own role and responsibilities which differs from that of the other actor. This is perhaps a rather too simple way of saying that administrative politics – which is the civil servants' arena – is different (that is, it has different rules) from parliamentary and party politics, which are the politicians' arenas.

It is also no surprise that, according to the Michigan data, there is a similar contrast at the ideological level. Politicians are more polarized and civil servants more moderate or pragmatic. Politicians present problems and issues in terms of broad alternatives; civil servants, instead, in terms of making adjustments at the margins of current policy. Moreover, civil servants preach moderation and resist, as a body, pressures for change. Thus their vision appears 'non-ideological', but the authors of the Michigan study reject this view, arguing to the contrary that: 'the very consistency and coherence of the bureaucrat's centrism suggests that it *is* an ideology' (p. 166). For this reason, they assert that the difference of ideological orientation between politicians and civil servants furnishes a potential for conflict between the two groups of actors in the policy process that makes cooperation difficult, particularly in periods of radical government, whether of left or right, as the examples of the Thatcher and Mauroy governments in Britain and France in the 1980s respectively confirm.

Career patterns in the public service indicate differences in both promotion criteria and levels of institutional mobility. In the case of promotion, there are two separate criteria, seniority and merit, but most European public services operate a system which combines the two. It is clear, for instance, that for the top jobs merit criteria – even if only that of partisan political sympathy – are applied, except in Italy where seniority remains the rule. In general, a career with promotions by seniority applies up to a certain level in the hierarchy, but with a parallel system of rapid promotion, by merit, for 'high-flyers': young higher civil servants destined for the top posts, like the so-called *énarques* (former ENA graduates) in France or the 'fast stream' in Britain. On the other hand, institutional mobility gives higher civil servants wider experience and militates against specialization. It is the rule in Britain but is excluded in Italy, where civil servants remain in one ministry; while in France and Germany secondment to another ministry or agency is reserved for certain privileged groups, namely the *grands corps* and the *Bundeskanzleramt*. The consequence is that interministerial rivalry is intense in Italy, much less in Britain, where service-wide loyalties prevail, and intermediary in France and Germany.

The third criterion used to characterize the administrative elite is whether it is open or closed, that is, whether there is mobility between the administrative and other elites. This can take the form either of 'entry' (recruitment of outsiders to top administrative posts) or of 'exit' (appointment of top civil servants to top posts in outside organizations). Where there is no mobility of this kind, there is a 'closed' administrative elite; and where both types are widely practised, there is an 'open' administrative elite. In Western Europe, in contrast to the USA, all administrative elites are 'semi-closed', in the sense that there is little or no 'lateral entry' into the higher civil service, except the admission very recently of a limited number of 'political advisers'.[22] It is true that in Germany the existence of *politische Beamte* permits the government to appoint to top posts from outside the federal civil service – from industry, trade unions and the *Länder* – as well as outside the ministry. Most of these appointments have been made from the *Land* civil service and have been used by the political executive to fill the top posts with incumbents enjoying its full confidence. In addition, the British and Italian administrative elites can be defined as 'closed' because they do not admit 'lateral exits' either, that is a civil service career is not a springboard in middle age for a career in politics or in the economic sector as in France (*pantouflage* system) and to a lesser extent in Germany. The higher civil service has become a major breeding ground for political careers in Fifth Republic France as a result of the privileges enjoyed by members of the *grands corps*[23] that not only facilitate successful entry into the political arena, but also eliminate the element of risk normally associated with a political career. Finally, a new development in Britain has seen an increasing number of higher civil servants accept well-paid jobs in the City on retirement (obligatory at the relatively early age of 60 years), like former head of the civil service Lord William Armstrong, appointed chairman of Midland Bank in 1975.[24] The greater or lesser permeability of the administrative elite relates to the degree of horizontal integration or separation of the various economic, political and administrative elites in that particular country. Permeability is greatest in France and least in Italy, with Britain and Germany between the two.

The final criterion is the distinction between 'specialist' and 'generalist' administrators. It goes without saying that it is a distinction of the greatest ambiguity, since the term 'generalist' covers two types of civil servant: the general administrator without any specific training (British type) and the general administrator with an administrative training, often legal (French and German type). Hence it is not easy to see, in such a situation, what conclusions can be drawn from the fact that the British system[25] is defined as a system where there are specialists (scientific civil service), but they are subordinate to the generalists; the French system as one where 'administrative' and 'technical' roles are separate and each is responsible in his own sphere of action; and finally the Italian system as one where there are no specialists except in the extraordinary administrations, i.e. the *enti pubblici*. Perhaps this distinction exhibits too many of the elements of the polemic over 'technocracy' and 'technocrats', which in France, as a result of Meynaud's (1964) writings, was symptomatic of a changing of the guard in the administrative elite from the old 'generalist' civil servants to the new 'specialist' technocrats, usually economists.

The policy process

It might seem incorrect to talk of the policy process in the singular, particularly as the enormous development of state activity in recent decades has split policy-making into a series of sectorial processes – agriculture, transport, health, education and so on – each with its own policy community.[26] In this regard we can note a paradox, namely that, despite considerable differences between sectorial processes in the same country, research suggests that a common European pattern[27] is emerging. It can be used to support our intention to treat the policy process in the singular. Indeed, the use of the term 'process' is intended to convey that we are dealing with a set of ongoing 'decisions', while the reference to 'decisions' refers to the exercise of state power. Finally, analysis cannot be limited to decisions, but must also take account of the whole policy process from the emergence of issues to their treatment and outcome. The principal paradigms of the policy process will be discussed first before moving on to look at the policy cycle and the relevance of national policy styles.

The synoptic paradigm

It was Simon (1945) who first attempted to specify precisely what decision-making involved, and formulated what has become known since as the synoptic or 'rational-comprehensive' paradigm.[28] Simon's starting point is the definition of a decision as a choice between alternatives: it follows logically that a rational choice involves selecting alternatives 'which are conducive to the achievement of ... previously selected goals' (p. 5). This is possible only if the organization concerned has defined goals and objectives because it is they that give meaning to administrative behaviour. In short, according to Simon, administrative behaviour is purposive and rational if it is guided by goals. However, because there may be a number of ways of reaching goals, the rational decision-maker, when faced with the choice between alternatives, should choose the alternative most likely to achieve the desired outcome. Theoretically, then, 'rational decision-making involves the selection of the alternative which will maximize the decision-maker's values, the selection being made following a comprehensive analysis of alternatives and their consequences' (Ham and Hill, 1984, p. 77). In practical terms, rational decision-making involves five steps: (1) the listing of all alternative strategies; (2) the determination of all the consequences that follow upon all these strategies; (3) the evaluation of the consequences according to the organization's value system; (4) comparative evaluation of all these sets of consequences; and (5) the selection of the best alternative.

The synoptic paradigm, so simple to outline in theoretical terms, presents serious problems which Simon himself quickly recognized. Firstly, it assumes that organizations are homogeneous as regards values, but this is not always the case. Differences can arise, for example, between administrators and managers. In the public administration these internal differences can translate themselves into conflicts between the politicians' intentions and the civil servants' practical solutions. Secondly, the synoptic paradigm presupposes full and exhaustive information on all the consequences of the alternatives. This is a practical impossibility, which means that knowledge of the consequences is necessarily incomplete and, hence, evaluation involves considerable uncertainty. Thirdly, there is the problem of separating facts and values, means and ends. The paradigm postulates prior specification of ends by administrations and the means for achieving them. But this poses great problems in practice. The synoptic paradigm, in fact, is an idealized view of decision-making, *not* an empirical description of the process. Given the departure of practice from theory, Simon, in his later work, elaborated the notion of 'bounded rationality' to describe decision-making in practice. Bounded rationality involves the decision-maker choosing an alternative that is intended not to maximize his values but to be 'satisfactory or good enough'. The positive consequence of this is that it enables the decision-maker faced with a decision to simplify by not examining all the alternatives. However, the negative consequence is that important options may be ignored, with disastrous results.

The incremental paradigm

Faced with the limits of the synoptic paradigm, but above all convinced that it imposes impossible conditions, Lindblom (1959) was stimulated to produce an alternative paradigm, more descriptive and less prescriptive, called 'incrementalism' or the incremental paradigm (table 8.7). Lindblom's starting point was the opposite of Simon's, that is the decision-makers' actual practice: faced with a set of complex problems, they do not attempt a comprehensive analysis, but develop a series of procedures to simplify the problems and their calculations. This series of problems Lindblom termed 'disjointed incrementalism'; it can be likened to a strategy that supplies a 'succession of limited comparisons of policy alternatives'. It can be described as follows: instead of specifying objectives and then assessing what policies would fulfil these objectives, the decision-maker reaches decisions by comparing specific policies and the extent to which these policies will result in the attainment of the objectives. The incremental paradigm adapts problems to human capacities, reducing the need for information and the costs of analysis. Such a strategy, moreover, helps one to recognize that policy problems are 'very fluid' and that ends are fitted to means and not vice versa as is generally assumed.

The strategy provides for 'successive limited comparisons' capable of continually redefining the problem because, as Wildavsky (1979) has remarked, political problems are not so much solved as superseded. The test of a good policy is no longer that it is the most appropriate means of achieving a desired goal or that it maximizes the decision-makers' values,

Table 8.7 Models of decision-making

Rational-comprehensive paradigm	Successive limited comparisons
Clarification of values or objectives distinct from and usually prerequisite to empirical analysis of alternative policies	Selection of value goals and empirical analysis of the needed action are not distinct from one another but are closely intertwined
Policy formaulation is therefore approached through means–ends analysis: first the ends are isolated, then the means to achieve them are sought	Since means and ends are not distinct, means–ends analysis is often inappropriate or limited
The test of a 'good' policy is that it can be shown to be the most appropriate means to desired ends	The test of a 'good' policy is typically that various analysts find themselves directly agreeing on a policy (without their agreeing that it is the most appropriate means to an agreed objective)
Analysis is comprehensive; every important relevant factor is taken into account	Analysis is drastically limited: Important possible outcomes are neglected Important alternative potential policies are neglected Important affected values are neglected
Theory is often heavily relied upon	A succession of comparisons greatly reduces or eliminates reliance on theory

Source: from Lindblom, 1959, quoted by Ham and Hill, 1984, p. 81

as Simon suggested, but rather that it secures the decision-makers' agreement or that of all the interests involved. The strategy is, indeed, inspired by Lindblom's notion of 'partisan mutual adjustment', which he considered the most widespread governmental coordination mechanism. It is the process by which independent decision-makers coordinate their behaviour, involving either adaptive adjustments – 'in which a decision-maker simply adapts to the decisions around him' – or manipulative adjustments – in which a decision-maker 'seeks to enlist a response desired from the other decision-maker'. Each of these adjustments is further divided into a variety of more specific behaviours, including negotiation and bargaining, lateral exchange and changes over time.

Despite the fact that the paradigms have been presented as polar models of decision-making, in reality, as Lindblom has emphasized, there is considerable similarity between Simon's 'bounded rationality' and Lindblom's 'successive limited comparisons'. Furthermore, Lindblom's disjointed incrementalism is still considered a reasonable description of how decisions are actually made in European public administrations. A comment by former British higher civil servant Sir G. Vickers (1965) suffices: 'Only if nothing "good enough" is found ... are other possibilities seriously considered' (p. 91). However, Lindblom's paradigm itself has not escaped criticism. The most significant critiques have come from Dror (1964) and Etzioni (1967) and touch two themes: (1) the incrementalist paradigm's applicability is more restricted than Lindblom believes; and (2) it is essentially conservative and anti-innovative. The incrementalist strategy, according to Dror, is only acceptable if existing policies are generally satisfactory – for the policy-makers and the major interest groups – and there is a high degree of continuity in the nature of the problems and the means for dealing with them. These are requirements which are not always met in complex societies; indeed, far from it. Furthermore, in the absence of every prescriptive element – present in the synoptic paradigm and acting as a stimulus to the decision-maker – the strategy favours a policy of 'no effort' by decision-makers. Dror's alternative is not a return to the synoptic paradigm, but a 'normative-optimum model' which seeks to combine 'realism and idealism' and focuses on decision-making procedures: the so-called 'meta-policy-making'.

The second criticism is that of Etzioni which is directed at the conservative aspect of incrementalism, but in a more political and partisan sense than Dror. If the heart of a decision is the agreement between decision-makers (and interest groups) and there is differential access to the decision-making process between groups and citizens, it is clear that this favours the powerful and privileged and hinders the weak and marginal. As Etzioni observes, 'consensus and inequality are preferable to dissent and equality' (p. 387). His alternative paradigm, called 'mixed scanning', is based on the distinction between 'contextuality decisions' and 'item decisions'. The former are fundamental because they 'set basic directions' and provide the context for the latter. In the former, the decision-maker undertakes a broad review of the field of decision without engaging in the detailed exploration of options suggested in the synoptic paradigm. This broad review enables long-run alternatives to be examined and leads to contextuality decisions. On the other hand, the item decisions lead up to, and follow on from, contextuality decisions. In this way, according to Etzioni, it should be possible to identify two distinct types of decisional process: one for contextuality (fundamental) decisions and the other for item (incremental) decisions.

Lindblom's (1970) response to his critics was to reassert his belief in the incremental paradigm, but to admit that he had failed to clarify the distinction between incremental policy and incremental analysis: incremental policy involves political change by small steps and may, or may not, result from incremental analysis. The distinction, then, is between the process of decision – incremental analysis – and the scale of change brought about by the decision. The feature of incremental politics is that only small changes result from decisions, even though, as Lindblom stresses quite correctly, there is no reason why large changes cannot result from a succession of small steps. Moreover, Lindblom recognizes also that he failed to distinguish properly between the very different types of incremental analysis: simple, disjointed and strategic. The first involves analysis limited to a consideration of alternatives, which are only incrementally different from the status quo. The second involves analysis limited to a few familiar alternatives, an intertwining of goals and values with concrete aspects of the problem and a greater concern with the problem than the goals sought. The third involves analysis limited to those specific routines selected to simplify complex policy problems. As Premfors has commented: 'incremental analysis is a form of disjointed incrementalism which, in turn, is a form of strategic analysis' (1981, p. 120), demonstrating that Lindblom, in refusing synoptic analysis, has modified his initial formulation substantially. Thus, if the initial formulations of Simon and Lindblom represent two polar positions of the conceptualization of the decision-making process, both in their subsequent reformulations find themselves in the company of Dror, Etzioni and Wildavsky. As regards Lindblom's notion of 'partisan mutual adjustment', it is worth pointing out that he now accepts (1977) that it is inadequate as a concept and that it is active only in ordinary issues of policy; and it is absent from the grand politico-economic issues.

There remains to discuss the budgetary process which forms the very heart of the policy process. It has been studied by Wildavsky (1964) who emphasizes 'its extraordinary complexity', the extremely limited period for preparation and the enormous number of items involved. Not surprisingly, therefore, the procedure adopted is one of successive simplifications. Wildavsky's thesis is that the principal method employed is what he calls the 'incremental method': the basic element used to determine the size and content of this year's budget is last year's. There is no global examination of the budget, but all the attention is focused on a certain number of increases and cuts. According to Wildavsky, the American budget is usually determined by two simple decisions: (1) the public agencies calculate their requests on the basis of a fixed percentage increase; and (2) Congress reaches a final figure on the basis of a fixed percentage cut of the public agencies' requests. Moreover, in their study of the British public expenditure survey (PES) system and programme analysis and review (PAR), Heclo and Wildavsky (1974) came to the conclusion that far from increasing rationality in policy-making, they merely strengthened incrementalism. These examples are not intended to suggest that incrementalism always triumphs, or that important changes in both policy and policy analysis do not occur, only that the general trend favours incrementalism.

As a coda a new paradigm should be mentioned, the 'new institutionalism' which has been developing in North America, even though it is still in a somewhat embryonic state (March and Olsen, 1984). It expresses above all a certain dissatisfaction with the existing paradigms, and specifically the inconsistency between what is observable and the content of contemporary theories. At the same time, it asserts that the organization of political life makes a difference, that is the idea that political and collective action is determined as much by norms and symbols as so-called rational calculation. For instance, some of the paradoxes of the policy process, for March and Olsen, are due to the theoretical presumption that the main point of decision-making is the decision itself: 'for many purposes that presumption may be be misleading. The processes of politics may be more central than their outcomes' (p. 742). This would explain why it is that decisions which deny the logic of the synoptic paradigm cause so little stir. Or again, why present paradigms postulate that one is dealing with problems looking for solutions, but entirely overlook the other possibility, namely that there are also solutions looking for problems. Finally, institutional processes structure policy situations but their implications have hardly been analysed at all so far. The new paradigm is not well developed as yet – March and Olsen call it 'an empirically based prejudice' – but as a search for an alternative idea to simplify the subtleties of empirical wisdom in a theoretically useful way, it appears to have a promising future.

In conclusion, there was constant criticism of Western political science in the 1960s to the effect that it systematically overvalued policy formulation at the expense of policy implementation, input at the expense of outcomes. The reason is simple: according to the traditional academic view, once the decision was taken, implementation followed automatically or mechanically. After Pressman and Wildavsky's (1973) pioneering study, it was realized that this was not the case. On the contrary, a decision is the result of a long series of prior events and sets in motion a further long and complex chain of events. As Françoise Giroud (1977) wrote of her own ministerial experience: 'in practice between policy and implementation, everything is diluted, deformed, reformed, transformed, bogged down and several years later results in – or never results in – measures which bear only a faint resemblance to the original policy' (pp. 97–8). Not surprisingly, the implementation process is full of opportunities for delays,[29] conflicts and unintended consequences which amply justify the statement that 'implementing a policy is participating in decision-making': it is a way of saying that all those who are responsible for policy implementation have power to determine the outcome. This power is all the more important in those areas which, because of the nature of administrative activity, require a large dose of discretionality in the means, content and timing of implementation (for instance, doctors in health programmes, teachers in educational programmes and so on). Pressman and Wildavsky's thesis contends that a public policy has more chance of failing, the greater the number of 'decision points' – that is where every participant has an implied veto power as regards the project's implementation – between formulation and completion. Implementation is not a separate phase from the formulation phase: both are an integral part of the policy process which is a continuous one of identification, elaboration and implementation with reciprocal inter-action and negotiation between the actors – politicians, civil servants, interest groups and even ordinary citizens.

The policy cycle

Describing the policy process without distortion is not easy. The most used metaphor is the cycle which has, at least, the merit of reminding us of the non-resolutive aspect of a large part of the policy process. In fact, it is not only difficult, but arbitrary, to define the beginning and the end of the process. It is no accident if Wildavsky (1979) has talked of 'policy as its own cause'. At all events, any starting point can be justified, as, for instance, Heclo and Wildavsky (1974) do in their study of the British budgetary cycle (figure 8.1). In fact, the liberal democratic constitutional model – according to which it is the parties that formulate the political programmes which, in case of electoral victory, are presented by their member ministers to the civil servants, who prepare the individual pro-jects for cabinet approval and submission as bills to parliament – solves the problem of the policy process in the same way, that is arbitrarily, fol-lowing a constitutional and not a political logic. In this logic, the parties with their deliberations and programmes initiate the process and parlia-ment with its vote of approval terminates it.

However, such a description is both idealized and reductive at one and the same time. As is well known, only a small part of a government's ini-tiatives are formulated in party instances; the overwhelming majority are prepared, instead, in ministerial offices which monitor ongoing situations and prepare measures for submission to the cabinet and thence, if neces-sary, to parliament as a bill for approval. Moreover, as already noted, the policy process does not terminate with the approval of the bill in parlia-ment. A policy has to be implemented and administered day by day; and decisions taken in the implementation stage can be, and often are, more important for their effects on the citizenry than the initial decision. Indeed, the overwhelming majority of decisions taken by the public administration and other state agencies originate in problems raised by the implementation of earlier policies.

As a result of the reductionism and legal formalism implicit in the tra-ditional constitutional model, Lasswell (1956) – the father of the so-called 'policy sciences' – attempted to define the various phases of the policy process. The advantage of the policy cycle approach is to indicate

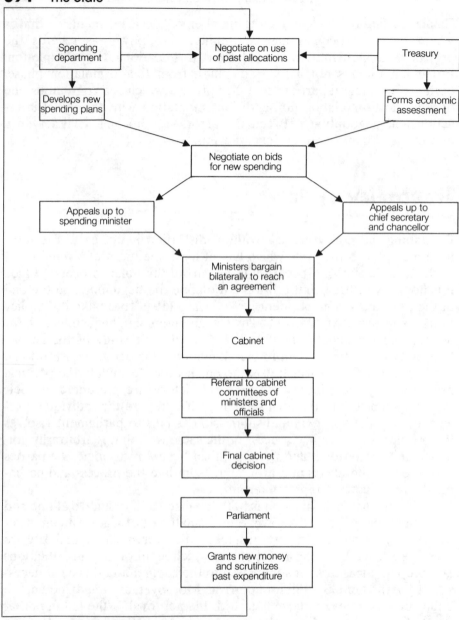

Figure 8.1 The British budgetary cycle
Source: Heclo and Wildavsky, 1974, p. 5

the interaction between political institutions and the socio-economic environment. It stresses, moreover, the dynamic nature of the policy process. Indeed, it does not abstract state activity from the ongoing political situation, nor does it claim that decisions are final. Policies are always in a state of flux, a fact which suggested to Wildavsky the statement quoted above. The policy cycle approach has, nonetheless, been criticized, principally on two grounds: (1) that it implies a chronological linear sequence in the phases of the process, when in reality things are more fluid; and (2) that it underestimates the active and shaping role of the state apparatus and the public agencies, from whom, in modern capitalist societies, action is usually requested.

The phases

One of the most recent models is that of Hogwood (1987), who identifies eight phases (figure 8.2). The model is useful because it renders the problems of the policy process more comprehensible, even at the risk of imposing an excessive simplification on a complex process with changeable and imprecise boundaries. Above all, it does not always happen that the various phases occur in the order outlined; they usually do, but different sequences can, and often do, happen.

In the first phase, the question is: how do the issues emerge? To solve this problem the concept of 'policy agenda' was invented: it is defined as the list of issues that policy-makers choose, or feel obliged, to pay serious attention to. There are, however, no generally agreed lists of what issues are on the policy agenda of a state at any given moment. But the concept

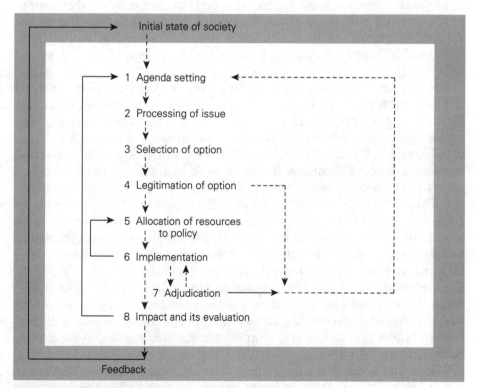

Figure 8.2   The policy process
Source: Hogwood, 1987, p. 12

is useful in helping to understand why certain issues succeed in getting on it and others do not. Hogwood has suggested that it is also helpful to distinguish between *systemic policy agendas* and *institutional agendas*. The former refer to the issues which are specific to a particular 'policy community'[30] as deserving of government attention. The latter refer to the problems inside a specific state body to which civil servants and politicians give attention. A second distinction concerns the difference between *recurring* issues – items that appear regularly on policy agendas, like public expenditure, taxation and social security – and *new* issues that are identified for the first time, such as the environment. The latter either disappear or become recurrent items. Genuinely new issues are becoming rarer all the time for the simple reason that relatively few areas of society remain outside government involvement and so the majority of issues result from the implementation phase of prior policies.

The principal political actors are in at the origin of issues – interest groups, parties, mass media as well as the state institutions, including the judiciary, and today significantly the EU institutions and specifically the Commission. It is obvious that a crisis – like the energy crisis in 1973/4 – can push a relatively secondary problem (oil supplies) to the top of the political agenda in a few hours. Finally, for an issue to be considered seriously, it needs to be legitimated, in the sense of being recognized as an appropriate topic for state action. This depends not only on the content of the demand but also on its source: who is behind it. Issues that do not succeed in getting on to the political agenda correspond to the 'non-decisions' of Bachrach and Baratz's (1962; 1963) 'second face of power' (chapter 6).

The second phase considers the issue from the moment that it gets on the political agenda. Hogwood (p. 48) identifies five types of processing. Firstly, the government can place an issue on the political agenda and impose its project without consultation or public discussion; but, to be able to do this, it must first have a viable project already worked out and the political means to impose it, that is, to be in a position to pay the necessary political price which the opposition may exact. Instances include the Thatcher policy which provoked the year-long miners' strike of 1984–5 and its cost to the British economy; or De Gasperi's decision to modify the Italian electoral law in 1952, forcing through parliament the so-called *legge truffa* (swindle law) against the united opposition. It is a high-risk strategy, as De Gasperi discovered to his cost at the 1953 elections, where the majority clause failed to operate for lack of 50,000 votes. Secondly, an issue can be processed within the ministerial departments without outside consultation. This is usually what happens in the case of foreign affairs and defence. Examples are the decision to construct the British atomic bomb taken by the Attlee government in 1949 (Hennessy, 1986); or that to establish the French *force de frappe* taken by de Gaulle in the 1960s. Occasionally, economic issues are handled in this way, particularly when there is an economic crisis: currency devaluations are usually decided after secret talks between the treasury or finance ministry and the central bank. However, even in these cases, consultation with international bodies (IMF, NATO, EU) and diplomatic allies (European partners, USA) occurs with increasing frequency.

Thirdly, there is consultation with the interested groups: this is the most widespread form of processing of an issue and covers an extremely wide range of practices 'from cosmetic ritual to meaningful bargaining' between government and groups. At all events, it is a two-way process: the public administration, in responding to group pressure, seeks information, consensus and cooperation. Given the state's central role in public regulation – it is the legitimate public authority, by definition – it lays down the rules of consultation. Thus, if the government cannot always establish with whom to consult – certain groups are so powerful that their exclusion would render the consultation meaningless, for instance employers in the case of investment – it does insist that groups observe the rules, above all the idea that the right to consultation implies the duty of accepting that the final decision rests with the government. Fourthly, an issue can emerge from the implementation of an earlier decision or policy, that is it can impose itself on a group – professional group or public servants like those in local government or the para-state sector – and must be handled by it. Fifthly, there are a certain number of issues, usually on questions of principle, which are inappropriate for handling within the public administration because they divide the electorate or the parties, and so they need to be dealt with by a strongly legitimating institution, usually parliament or occasionally referendum. This is the case, for instance, with civil rights issues like abortion, divorce and the death penalty, and with entry into the European Community or Union.

The third and fourth phases concern the handling of the issue by the state institutions. In fact, these two phases are considered by many to be the core of the policy process. In the third phase, the various coordinating committees, both inside the ministerial departments and the cabinet (interministerial committees, cabinet committees, even interparty 'summits') come into play. It is in this phase, then, according to a widespread opinion, that civil servant influence is most widespread and keenly felt. Ministers, so the argument runs, are too busy with official duties to have time for constructive thought and, further, do not usually remain in office for very long; while civil servants enjoy greater stability through lower turnover, know the administrative machine better, have greater access to the relevant information and, in consequence, are better endowed to formulate long-term policy. In truth, however, top civil servants are too busy to think creatively. They depend, in fact, on the papers originating in the departmental sections and outside in much the same way as the ministers depend on the staff of their personal office or *cabinets*. It is this structural blockage, among other things, that enhances the influence of interest groups, particularly when they are in a position to supply well-documented and well-argued advice, as often happens on important issues. This is also the phase when the 'European' dimension comes into play because it is the moment in which negotiation in the EU's Council of Ministers occurs on EU-related matters. Moreover, since the volume of EU business is large and increasing, national government control is correspondingly smaller and decreasing.

In the fourth phase, that of parliamentary approval, the principal problem is the solidity and coherence of the government majority. In states like Britain, France and Germany where there are normally solid majorities, the government has a much greater control of legislative output and a greater capacity to secure the approval of its programme than in states like Italy, where such government majorities have been much weaker. Nevertheless, even in the countries with solid majorities, the government knows that it cannot afford to dismiss the opinions of its backbenchers[31] on certain issues without risking a parliamentary defeat: even British governments have suffered defeats in the House of Commons, as in 1992 over clauses in the Maastricht bill. Moreover, in a federal state, like Germany, the government can face serious problems with the *Länder* representation in the Bundesrat, particularly when, as at the present time, the opposition is in a majority. In spite of this, Grosser's (1964) verdict, quoted in chapter 7 – that 'everywhere the legislative initiative has passed into the hands of the administrations. The legislatures sometimes amend, rarely reject, usually ratify' (p. 161) – remains substantially true. This is also because most legislation today takes the form of 'delegated legislation', that is giving 'executive agencies', usually the public administration, the authority to make rules and issue regulations which have the force of law.

The fifth phase, the financial one, is certainly the most important because most policies imply expenditure (table 8.3). But it is just for this reason that it represents the most widespread administrative activity and that least tied to a time sequence: it occurs at all levels of the administration (and not just at the top) and can affect a project or a policy at any moment. Budgetary decisions determine not only the project's or policy's priority, but also its profile and time-scale. Further, since budgets are annual, financial priorities and commitments can be reviewed without overt changes in government policy or legislation. This helps explain two fundamental facts: (1) the treasury or finance ministry has a central role, for financial requirements 'integrate' state activity, despite its sectorialization as regards particular decisions or policies; and (2) the budget is an indicator of government priorities, for budgetary analysis reveals how government priorities and intentions change. It is true that the long-term nature of many spending projects makes it more difficult to make short-term changes and limits them to marginal adjustments. However, in the long term substantial reorientation can be made, as the Gaullist experience in France in the 1960s or the Thatcher one in Britain in the 1980s demonstrated. However, we must not overlook the relations between the immediate conjuncture and the constraints imposed by the international situation, which the national budget must, of necessity, take into account. Burch and Wood (1983) have commented: 'there is a kind of self-generated momentum in spending policy which belies attempts at direction and control. In such a Kafkaesque world of unforeseen events and unexpected consequences the administrative dispersion and diffusion of policy-making seem appropriate' (p. 161).

The sixth phase is implementation. It is worth noting, by way of premise, that some policy analysts prefer to avoid using the word 'implementation' because it lacks clarity: it confuses, they claim, the various policy-making activities with their consequences. Further, some policies do not need a formal decision (or legislation): they simply emerge from the practices followed by public officials in a certain sector or area. Finally, in the case of other policies, the response of the interest groups involved can substantially modify the impact. For instance, the refusal of the British trade unions to register as required by the Heath government's Industrial Relations Act of 1971 rendered the act inoperative. It is obvious that implementation varies according to the type of policy, namely whether it is a case of observing new regulations (safety regulations at work, for instance) or of supplying a service (health, transport, for instance). Unfortunately there is, as yet, no adequate typology for analysing this field. Nevertheless, the limits to implementation can be of three types: (1) failed implementation; (2) delayed implementation; and (3) unexpected consequences.

To be able to evaluate policy implementation, the objectives need to be clear and well defined, but this is rarely the case. In the majority of cases the policy-makers are only vaguely aware of the consequences of a policy, which are often the opposite to those initially intended. For instance, the legislation introduced in many European countries to protect the interests of tenants and control rents resulted, in fact, in a reduction in the number of rented homes available and a rise in rents thanks to a number of expedients not foreseen by the legislation. 'Effective implementation' requires, according to Sabatier and Mazmanian (1979), the following elements: clear objectives, lack of ambiguity, the skill and capacity of implementers, the support of groups and politicians, and the continuation over time of the priority given to the policy. To these Burch and Wood (1983) add the desirability of minimizing the number of decisional points, adequate financial resources and good monitoring techniques. It goes without saying that it is rare that all these elements are found in the same place at the same time. Finally, the situation is complicated by the fact that, in some cases, the decisions taken – and not taken – and the policies pursued were never intended to solve the issues but only to mislead the people, that is to create diversions or redefine the issues so as to lead people to believe that they had been resolved.

The seventh phase, which is a subphase, concerns disputes and is generally considered more important in continental countries than in Britain, whether in terms of judicial review or the administrative courts' scrutiny, because of the latter's lack of a constitutional court (chapter 7). However, in Britain too, the judiciary can have some influence on policy. At all events, the modalities of judicial intervention in policy-making are essentially two: (1) the definition or interpretation of the law; and (2) the control of ministerial activity and that of the state institutions. Examples of the former are the judicial review (*Normenkontrolle*) of the German Bundesverfassungsgericht and the *interpretative di rigetto* sentences of the Italian Corte Costituzionale, which are often partial annulments that declare a law to be constitutional provided that it is correctly interpreted (that is to say, as rewritten by the court); or again the abstract monitoring of the French Conseil constitutionnel; or finally certain decisions of the British House of Lords. In all these cases the courts have often taken on a policy role, giving 'advice' to the political authorities, as, for example, the German constitutional court did in the university admissions cases of the 1970s when it virtually dictated the conditions of university admission and the final legislation 'conformed closely to the policy directives of the court';[32] or the French constitutional court did when it defined the modalities and fixed the indemnities of the socialist nationalizations of 1982; or the British House of Lords did in outlawing the GLC's 'fair fares' policy in 1982. Judicial interventions of the second kind generally consider abuse of power; examples are the French court's declaration that the 1979 budget was unconstitutional; the German court's famous 'television judgement' of 1961 in which it declared Adenauer's attempt to create a national television network unconstitutional; or the Italian court's 1975 judgement declaring that the RAI's television monopoly was unconstitutional, which opened the way to national private television channels. Thus there is reason to believe that in Germany and Italy the courts have become an important arena for processing political conflicts, whereas in Britain and France, despite some important judicial review cases, they have not.

In addition, there are two European courts – the European Court of Human Rights and the European Court of Justice (ECJ) of the EU – which can review, in specific circumstances, member states' policies to see whether they conform to the European Convention on Human Rights or EU regulations respectively. It is symptomatic, in view of Britain's lack both of a written constitution and a system of administrative courts, that 25 per cent of the 320 cases accepted by the European Commission on Human Rights (up to October 1985) were brought by Britons and that British government policy was condemned in twelve of the eighteen cases brought before the court, and for which subsequent amending legislation was deemed necessary.

The situation in the ECJ is somewhat different. As a parenthesis, we should recall (as noted in the introduction to this book) that the EU is completely dependent on member states for implementation of EU policies because it has neither the mandate to bypass national governments, nor the grass-roots administrative 'executant' capacity (personnel or resources). This explains the largely legal approach to policy in the EU hitherto: creating the appropriate regulatory framework in all member states, and securing its transposition into national legal norms and their observance (non-compliance can be tested by individuals and companies in the ECJ). As regards national non-compliance, Italy is the state which has had the highest number of 'letters of formal notice' of infringements and the highest number of references (159 since 1982) to the court, while Britain has had the lowest number (20). Moreover, Italy is the only state where there is a clearly discernible rising trend of infringement proceedings against it in recent years. Finally, it has the dubious distinction of being the state that has the poorest record in complying with ECJ judgements: 21 outstanding in 1990.

The eighth and final phase, that of policy impact and evaluation, should logically be the most important, in the sense that it is the one in which the results of state action should be apparent. It can be, particularly if the policy provokes a decisive response by organized groups; but often it is not, simply because the state authorities are not aware of their policies' impact. The results of state action or inaction are multifarious. Firstly, the issue can simply subside: for instance, a change of perspective can make a problem appear of no further consequence, as was the case of the mid 1960s European manpower shortage. Secondly, the issue can appear resolved, like Britain's chronic balance of payments problem in the 1980s due to North Sea oil, only to reappear with a vengeance, in that example at the end of the decade with the decline of the oil reserves and recession. Thirdly, state action can result either in satisfaction, or in dissatisfaction and protest, and both, paradoxically, can provoke similar consequences in terms of further state action: in the first case, pressure to continue with the policy; and in the second, pressure to change it for more effective action. In the latter, it may lead to a displacement from the initial issue to the state policy itself which can become the new issue; for instance, in the case of a vaccination programme for a certain disease that, as a result of provoking side-effects, displaces the issue from the prevention of the original disease to that of the vaccinations. In the absence of vigorous reaction by interested social groups, policies are usually accepted and become routine. In fact, not only is evaluation of policy impact difficult in itself, owing to the lack of acceptable evaluation criteria; but European state institutions usually lack the capacity and the will to carry it out. Furthermore, in the rare cases where evaluation has been carried out, it does not often appear to have been taken into account in subsequent policy planning. At most, it has been used to redefine the problem; hence, it has had a much more indirect influence. However, there are, in the changing climate of the 1990s, indications that there is a new understanding in Europe of the need for impact evaluation of state policies. But whether this will have any effect on the quality of future policy-making and implementation remains an open question.

National policy styles or cross-national policy sectors?

The discussion so far has been predicated on the assumption that the same policy process is valid for all policy sectors. But it is clear that this cannot be the case. We only have to think, for instance, of the differences between domestic policies on the one hand, and external policies on the other. The latter are more conditioned by international pressures than by domestic ones, and hence are the direct responsibility of the executive; whereas for the former interest and pressure groups are usually much more directly involved, and therefore often have a much larger say. Thus, if the policy process can vary according to the sector involved, it can also differ in different national political systems and at different historical moments: that is, according to the local political situation.

In this situation, two analytical perspectives are discernible, based on two different relations between politics and policy: the first approach is that of policy styles, where, according to Freeman (1985), 'politics determines policy'; and the second is that of policy sectors where, on the contrary, 'policy determines politics' (p. 469). In the case of the first approach, Richardson (1982) and others have proposed a simple two-dimensional matrix to identify policy styles, defined as 'the preferred operating procedures' (p. 13) of national policy-makers. The two dimensions are: (1) the government's approach to policy-making, namely whether policy-makers favour synoptic or incremental policy-making procedures, in short whether they are more active and propulsive than reactive; and (2) the policy-making relationship between state (government) and civil society (other actors), that is whether the government is accommodating and seeks to reach a consensus with private groups or, on the contrary, seeks to impose its will on them in spite of their opposition. These two dimensions furnish four policy styles or policy-making modalities: concertation, status preservation, activist and regulation (figure 8.3).

Kinds of decision-making		Relations between state and civil society	
		Negotiation/ consensus	Imposition/coercion
	Synoptic (active)	Concertation	Activist
	Incremental (reactive)	Status preservation	Regulation

Figure 8.3 Typology of policy styles
Source: Richardson, 1982, p. 19

The first two styles involve consultation and/or negotiation between the state institutions and private groups. In the first case, 'concertation', it is generally a 'neo-corporatist' negotiation with policy agreed between government leaders (top politicians and civil servants) and major interest groups (employers, trade unions and farmers' leaders) like the German *konzierte Aktion* or British tripartism of the 1970s; while in the second case, 'status preservation', it is one of routine collaboration and consultation of the incrementalist type between public administration and interest/pressure groups in working parties and departmental consultative committees, as in pluri-annual policy implementation. The other two styles, instead, imply imposition, if not coercion. In the case of the 'activist' style, the government feels obliged to act imperatively either because it believes it knows and/or understands the national interest better, or because time is of the essence (so does not permit the luxury of consultation) and delay could have disastrous consequences – for instance, in foreign policy, economic crises. This is the executive style *par excellence*, with the government acting independently, even in an authoritarian manner. Hence, it is rarely found in liberal democracies. The final style, 'regulation', is the traditional so-called 'bureaucratic formalism', in which the attempt is made to resolve social and political, and even economic, problems by legal means without seriously consulting the relevant interest/pressure groups. It is a style which only involves the public administration and parliament: a good example is the Thatcher government's anti-union legislation in the 1980s.

The matrix in figure 8.3 is a fairly useful tool, despite its schematic character, because it helps simplify objectively complex situations. For instance it specifies, with a certain approximation, which are the strategic policy-making arenas in certain situations: between executive and interest groups in the concertation style; between public administration and interest/pressure groups in the status preservation style; the executive alone (or with the government party) in the activist style; and between executive, parliament and public administration in the regulation style. Paradoxically, this matrix furnishes arguments which support the policy sectors approach as much as the policy styles one, for which it was originally formulated. Firstly, there are examples of all four styles in the policy processes of Britain, France, Germany and Italy: for instance, Hayward (1986) has shown that in France an activist style in the nuclear field coexisted with concertation and status preservation styles in other sectors. Secondly, the status preservation style characterizes policy-making in Western democracies, either as used in the matrix or in reality. The matrix, in fact, has been properly criticized because it is insufficiently discriminating for West European states which tend to have similar policy styles. Thirdly, it is not without significance that all governments, when they wish to take a radical stance, adopt, at least publicly, an activist style (Thatcher in Britain, de Gaulle in France, even Craxi in Italy): they resolutely assert a political will, justified by the popular mandate received from the electorate. Fourthly, when conservative governments abandon the status preservation or activist styles, it is for the regulation style, while social democrats and left-wing governments tend towards the concertation style. Thus the SPD-FDP alliance in Germany tended towards the concertation style in the 1970s, while Kohl's CDU-FDP alliance in the 1980s, like the Thatcher government in Britain, opted for the regulation style.

However, there could be a historical explanation: mass mobilization in the post-1968 climate pushed governments towards greater consultation and negotiation in all sectors; in the 1980s the reaction against what was seen as excessive participation – the result of the great growth of groups in the preceding decade – has pushed them in the other direction, towards the regulation style. In this situation, it does not seem helpful to define the British and Italian policy styles as closer to the status preservation style than the French, just because in the British case the 'logic of negotiation' traditionally prevails, in the Italian case the 'party spoils system' and in the French case, finally, 'technocratic decisionism'. Nonetheless, such an approach does seem useful when examining EU policies where common goals are sought, but national implementation is often variable and final results are invariably different. It would help to explain, for instance, the obstinacy of certain governments – the British, but also the Danish – in negotiation. The British and Danish governments apply the rules carefully once adopted, whereas the French and Italian governments are more concerned in making the decision than in implementing it once it has been decided. This means that the latter are more accommodating and flexible in negotiation. Italy, as already noted, has become a specialist in the art of non-implementation of EU directives.

In the second approach, which privileges the policy–politics relationship, that is to say policy sectors, the best-known attempt to develop a causal link between types of policy and policy-making modalities was by Lowi (1964; 1972). He started from the hypothesis that there are only a limited number of policies because their very nature imposes limits on the options open to policy-makers. The result is a pattern of policies which are pretty predictable, in terms of actors, options, procedures and strategic points. He distinguishes somewhat abstractly four policy types – distributive, constitutive, regulative and redistributive – on the basis of a number of theoretically significant characteristics. Despite the suggestivity and logic of Lowi's schema, its empirical operationalization has proved difficult and this has limited its utility to date.

For this reason, the notion of policy sector has been redefined in terms of policy subsystem, which refers in practice to the various state programmes for each sector: economy, education, health, housing, taxation, income maintenance, urban planning – the chapter titles of Heidenheimer, Heclo and Adams (1990). The basic assumption is that every policy sector is organized, more or less informally, in policy communities which group the persons who count in that sector: politicians, civil servants, interest group leaders, academic experts. However, Regonini (1985) has noted that 'the range of significant actors has tended to become considerably larger to include not only the top civil servants and pressure group leaders concerned in one way or another with an issue, but also experts, intermediaries of various kinds and even single person-alities with some recognized individual influence' (p. 338). Some sectors are larger, covering several policy communities (figures 8.4 and 8.5) and many are transnational, having an EU dimension. In this situation, the basic hypothesis of the policy sector approach, according to Freeman, 'predicts *differentiation* within individual countries across sectors and *convergence* across nations within sectors' (p. 486).

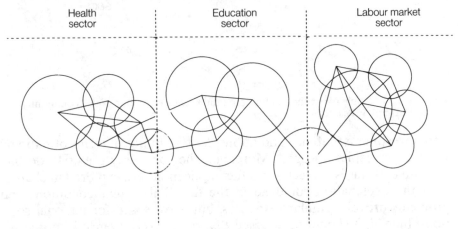

| Health sector | Education sector | Labour market sector |

Figure 8.4   Example of policy sectors and policy communities
Source: Richardson, 1982, p. 89

Unfortunately, there are no studies to confirm or rebut the validity of this hypothesis. Moreover, confirmation poses real problems. It requires identifying goals, means and outcomes, something that is not easy. If, as Heidenheimer, Heclo and Adams argue, there is a wide convergence on economic policy goals in Western countries – full employment, price sta-bility, economic growth – and on the means for measuring them, the same cannot be said for 'good education', 'adequate health care' or 'decent housing'.[33] When we come to consider the means, the situation is further complicated because, in some countries, certain services are fur-nished by the state (National Health Service in Britain), while in others there are mixed public and private systems (Germany and France) and in yet others they are wholly private (USA); the same is true for educa-tion, housing and so on.

With regard to outcomes, Rose (1985) has undertaken an initial explo-ration of the hypotheses of the policy sector approach, finding partial confirmation. He found, for instance, that public employment in six West European countries showed a wide variation as regards the numbers employed in the six programmes considered – pensions, health, educa-

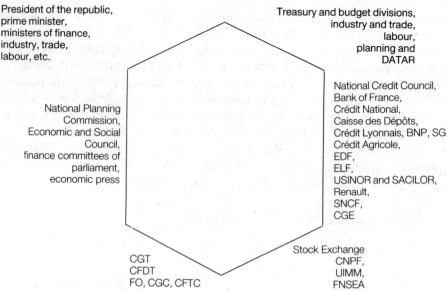

President of the republic, prime minister, ministers of finance, industry, trade, labour, etc.

Treasury and budget divisions, industry and trade, labour, planning and DATAR

National Planning Commission, Economic and Social Council, finance committees of parliament, economic press

National Credit Council, Bank of France, Crédit National, Caisse des Dépôts, Crédit Lyonnais, BNP, SG Crédit Agricole, EDF, ELF, USINOR and SACILOR, Renault, SNCF, CGE

CGT CFDT FO, CGC, CFTC

Stock Exchange CNPF, UIMM, FNSEA

Figure 8.5 Example of a policy community: the French economic policy community
Source: Hayward, 1986, p. 24

tion, investments, defence and public debt – but not in terms of national income per capita engaged. Moreover, the variability seems to decline over time. If this is correct – and the implications are explored in chapter 11 – the explanation could lie in the fact that similar conditions and problems provoke similar responses, but leave space for national solutions. Indeed, it should be stressed that policy convergence is more pronounced in certain sectors (social security, pensions, environment) and less in others (education, health care) where national solutions remain more relevant. Finally, it has been suggested that convergence increases in periods of economic prosperity because it reinforces European collaboration. This convergence has not been fatally compromised as yet by the economic crises and uncertainties since the 1970s, and for that the EU must take much of the credit.

Conclusions

Since Weber, bureaucracy has been a key concept in political science. It has several meanings, but in the contemporary West European state it refers to the routinization of administrative tasks and procedures which are the elected politician's natural support. While Weber considered bureaucracy the most rational means of exercising authority over human beings, American functionalist sociologists pointed to Weber's neglect of the human factor in complex organizations which led to bureaucracy becoming dysfunctional, with means substituting goals as the basis of bureaucratic behaviour. They introduced the problematic of human relations into the sphere of administrative action which Crozier developed with the notion that a person's power in an organization depends on his capacity to control sources of uncertainty arising from internal conflicts.

The origin of contemporary West European administrations is to be sought in the royal households of the European monarchies of the absolute era. However, the crucial period of their development was the nineteenth century where they were expanded to meet the social needs of the industrial revolution and subsequent mass urbanization. The result was the development of a complex set of ministerial departments and territorial administrations. In the twentieth century, as a result of two world wars and the Keynesian welfare state, there was a further increase in state activity and the creation of further administrative structures. In consequence, the major characteristic of the public administration in West European states today is its bigness – big government – whether in terms of the number of administrations, employees, matters dealt with or money spent.

Despite the fact that it is not possible to analyse contemporary administrative-institutional structures according to any classificatory logic, they are usually considered under three heads: ministerial departments, special public agencies and institutions of control and coordination. Ministerial departments are still the core of the central administration of all European countries. The number and tasks vary from state to state, but also over time in the same state. In general, the number oscillates between 15 and 25, but the reasons for the increase or decrease from government to government are political: the need to accommodate a particular politician or signal a government's determination to tackle a new problem.

Internal departmental organizational differences exist between Britain and Germany on the one hand, where a top civil servant is directly responsible to the minister, and France and Italy on the other, where the heads of division are responsible to the minister. This means, among other things, that coordination between divisions inside departments is treated in Britain and Germany as more of an administrative problem than in France and Italy, where it is recognized as having political connotations and hence the minister is more directly involved through his personal *cabinet*. All departments have numerous advisory committees on which sit civil servants and outside advisers, usually representatives of the leading pressure groups active in the field, and academic experts who can feed in information and technical advice.

The field of special agencies and public enterprises is extremely complex and many of them represent attempts by the state to grapple with a specific problem at a particular historical moment, like the creation of the Italian para-state sector in the 1930s. Aside from the various nationalized enterprises, it is possible to identify two specific types of public agency. The first is those with a regulatory or supervisory mission which are often set up to carry out enquiries or collect delicate information in place of the minister, so that the conclusions and corresponding decisions acquire a certain authority. The second is the task force, that is agencies created to tackle and solve specific problems. These two types, moreover, do not exhaust all the special agencies because the list is endless and has furnished, not surprisingly, an enormous opportunity for patronage which governmental parties have not hesitated to exploit. The result has been to increase the fragmentation of the administrative system, which has lost the compactness that it enjoyed in Weber's time, and has led to an increase in intrabureaucratic rivalry.

Control of the administration involves problems of both direction, in that policy must follow the government's declared aims, and legitimacy, in that administration must conform to the law. The former is the responsibility of parliament and the latter that of the courts. This distinction highlights a major difference between the Anglo-Saxon conception of parliamentary sovereignty and the continental concept of *Rechtsstaat*: the idea that the state is the expression of the legal order. The consequence is two different institutional structures of administrative control. In Britain, parliament is the core of the system and its basis is that of ministerial responsibility to parliament, while on the continent control is the responsibility of the system of administrative courts. The significance of the administrative court system is not only that the courts are competent to resolve disputes between private citizens and the administration, but that they can investigate the reasons for a decision and annul it, even when the correct procedure has been observed.

Coordination of government action is the responsibility of the cabinet, but its meetings have become almost entirely formal and serve mainly to furnish information. Coordination today is carried out by cabinet and interministerial committees, while policies are often initiated at informal meetings and discussions between a minister and a small number of top civil servants overseen by the head of government. The key ministry in all European countries is the treasury through its control of expenditure. The major contrast, however, is between the British system of collegiate government and the continental system of non-collegiate government. In Britain, collective discussion of policy by groups of ministers is still real; in France, Germany and Italy it is not because relations between individual ministers and the head of government remain decisive.

The state is the largest single employer in Western European countries: the public service accounts for about 30 per cent of the active population in the four countries. However, not all public employees are civil servants which, despite different definitions from country to country, are a much more restricted category. Finally, the numbers of those working in ministerial departments are even more modest, and of these the administrative elite of higher civil servants represents at most 5000 with a core of a few hundred top policy-makers.

The civil service is traditionally divided into four classes which correspond to the tasks performed: the highest class is responsible for policymaking; the second class deals with the management of ordinary administration; the third class carries out routine tasks; while the fourth comprises messengers, guards and porters. This class structure has been severely criticized and has become a bit more open in the post-war period. In general, conditions of service are regulated by a code or statute giving civil servants security of tenure, favourable pension rights and the right, under certain conditions, to engage in political activity. A major contrast exists between Britain, where civil servants are obliged to resign to stand for parliament, and the continental countries, where they are put on unpaid leave and can reintegrate their service without any loss of seniority or pension rights. Thus in Britain higher civil servants eschew a political career, as they do in Italy (for other reasons); whereas in Germany some turn to politics, as many do in France since the ENA system positively encourages it.

The administrative elite of top civil servants, that is those in permanent contact with ministers, is the key group in the running of the West European state. This is because it constitutes a privileged and direct link between the public administration and the constitutional government at the same time as determining the orientation and output of the administrative machine. Its power and influence result from its knowledge of the administrative machine and the way it operates.

Higher civil servants are recruited from a restricted social area that is male, urban, university educated, upper middle class in origin and public affairs oriented. Family recruitment, moreover, is high, particularly in France and Germany where there are civil servant families. This recruitment occurs despite the use of different methods in the various states: centralized in Britain and France; decentralized in Germany and Italy. Finally, the prestige of the higher civil service varies between states, being very high in France (thanks to the *grands corps*), high in Britain and Germany, but modest in Italy. Promotion by merit and recruitment of high-flyers prevail in Britain, France and Germany, whereas seniority is the rule in Italy.

Administrative elites in Western Europe, in contrast to the USA, are semi-closed in the sense that there is virtually no lateral entry, except that very recently a limited number of political advisers have been admitted, but they usually remain isolated and rarely stay for more than a brief period. The British and Italian administrative elites are also closed in the sense that they do not encourage lateral exit either, whereas in France and Germany the civil service can be a springboard for a career in politics or the private sector. Finally, British and Italian higher civil servants are generalists, that is to say administrators without any specialized training, in contrast to their French and German colleagues, who are specialists as a result of their specialized administrative training at ENA and Speyer respectively. Indeed, French higher civil servants are often considered technocrats just because of their specialized training, but this definition owes as much to polemical writing as to any novel skills.

The policy process in the post-war period has been dominated by two major paradigms: the synoptic and the incremental. The former was developed by Simon in an attempt to formulate a rational approach to decision-making. A decision was defined as a choice between alternatives, and logically a rational choice involves selecting the alternative most likely to achieve the selected goal. It requires knowledge of the alternatives and their consequences: assessment of the consequences in terms of the administrators' value system and the selection of the best alternative. Simon quickly realized that his paradigm imposed insuperable problems, for instance full and exhaustive knowledge of all the consequences of all the alternatives. Most decisions, in fact, are taken with incomplete knowledge and hence evaluation involves considerable uncertainty. For this reason, Simon, in his later work, introduced the notion of bounded rationality, that is the acceptance of a satisfactory alternative in the circumstances which was not necessarily the best. The advantage was that it enabled the decision-maker to simplify the alternatives; the disadvantage was that it might result in important options being ignored with unfortunate consequences.

Awareness of the limits of the synoptic model led Lindblom to produce a more descriptive and less prescriptive alternative paradigm: incrementalism. It was based on the decision-makers' actual practice: faced with a set of complex problems, they do not attempt a comprehensive analysis but develop a series of procedures (rules of thumb) to simplify the problems and their calculations. This Lindblom termed disjointed incrementalism, and it consists of a series of limited comparisons of policy alternatives. It adapts the problems to human capacity, reducing the need for information and the cost of analysis. Policy problems are fluid, with ends being fitted to means rather than means to ends as is generally assumed. The test of a good policy is no longer that it is the most appropriate means of achieving a desired goal but rather that it secures the decision-makers' agreement. It is a case of partisan mutual adjustment, which Lindblom believed is the most widespread governmental coordination mechanism in operation – through continual negotiation and bargaining – and which is best illustrated in the state budgetary process.

The incremental paradigm has been widely criticized. Dror, for example, claims that its application is limited to those situations where existing policies are judged to be satisfactory and there is a high degree of continuity. These requirements are not always met in complex societies. A second criticism is that it is basically conservative, both because it favours a policy of no effort by decision-makers and because, if the heart of a decision is the agreement between decision-makers and groups, and there is differential access to the policy process, it is clear that this will favour the powerful and the privileged against the weak and the marginal.

Finally, there was constant criticism in the 1960s that Western political science systematically overvalued policy formulation at the expense of policy implementation, that is input in place of output. It was believed that once decisions were taken, implementation followed automatically, even mechanically. This is not the case: on the contrary, a decision sets in motion a long and complex chain of events, full of opportunities for delay, conflict and unintended consequences. Indeed, those responsible for implementation have considerable power to determine the success or failure of a programme. Wildavsky asserts that a policy's chance of success is determined by the number of decision points: the greater the number, the greater the likelihood of failure.

The most common metaphor to describe the policy process is the policy cycle, which has the merit of drawing attention to the inconclusiveness of much policy-making. It is difficult, even arbitrary, to define the beginning or end of the process as much policy is its own cause. The disadvantage of the metaphor is that it implies a linear time sequence, namely a series of successive phases, when in reality things are usually much more fluid. However, as a model, it has its utility in pointing up what is involved in policy-making. Hogwood has proposed an eight-phase model as follows: (1) agenda setting; (2) issue treatment; (3) selection of alternatives; (4) institutional legitimation; (5) commitment of resources; (6) implementation; (7) resolution of conflicts; (8) evaluation of policy impact. The last may simply mean redefining the problem to give the impression that it has been resolved, for we must bear in mind that in many cases the policies pursued are never intended to solve the issue but only to show willing, that is to lead people to believe that they were being tackled.

The final problem is whether the same policy process is valid for all policy sectors in the same state or differs cross-nationally for individual policy sectors. It appears that the policy process can vary not only according to the sector involved but also within national systems and at different times. Two perspectives have been developed to analyse this situation. The first is that of policy styles – defined as the preferred operating procedures of national policy-makers or of a policy sector – and a simple two-dimensional matrix has been formulated that identifies four styles or policy-making modalities: concertation, status preservation, activist and regulation. The matrix is useful not only in helping to simplify objectively complex situations, but also in specifying the strategic policy-making arenas in varying situations. It suggests that the status preservation style is the characteristic policy style of Western democracies, but changes to other policy styles occur in different political situations: for instance, would-be radical governments invariably adopt the activist style.

The policy sector approach endeavours to develop a causal link between types of policy and modes of policy-making. Lowi elaborated the most sophisticated model, which identifies four policy types – distributive, constitutive, regulative and redistributive – on the basis of a number of theoretically significant characteristics. Unfortunately, the operationality of Lowi's schema has been limited. For this reason, the notion of policy sector has been redefined in terms of policy subsystems which in practice refer to the various state programmes in each sector: economy, education, transport, health. The basic assumption is that each policy sector is organized more or less informally in policy communities which group the people who count in that sector. Some sectors are larger, covering several policy communities, and many today are transnational, having an EU dimension. The basic hypotheses of the policy sector approach predict differentiation within individual countries and convergence across nations within sectors.

Further reading

J.D. Aberbach, R. Putnam and B. Rockman (eds) (1981), *Bureaucrats and Politicians in Western Democracies* (Cambridge, Mass.: Harvard UP).

J. Armstrong (1973), *The European Administrative Elite* (Princeton, NJ: Princeton UP).

B. Chapman (1959), *The Profession of Government* (London: Allen & Unwin).

M. Dogan (ed.) (1975), *The Mandarins of Western Europe: The Political Role of the Top Civil Service* (New York: Sage).

C. Ham and M. Hill (1992), *The Policy Process in the Modern Capitalist State* (Brighton: Wheatsheaf, 2nd edn).

M. Harrop (ed.) (1992), *Power and Policy in Liberal Democracies* (Cambridge: CUP).

A.J. Heidenheimer, H. Heclo and C.T. Adams (1990), *Comparative Public Policy: The Politics of Social Choice in Europe and America* (London: Macmillan, 3rd edn).

J.E. Kingdom (ed.) (1990), *The Civil Service in Liberal Democracies* (London: Routledge).

E.C. Page (1985), *Political Authority and Bureaucratic Power: A Comparative Analysis* (Brighton: Harvester).

B. Peters (1984), *The Politics of Bureaucracy* (London: Longman, 2nd edn).

J.-L. Quermonne (1991), *L'Appareil administratif de l'état* (Paris: Seuil).

J.J. Richardson (ed.) (1982), *Policy Styles in Western Europe* (London: Allen & Unwin).

F.F. Ridley (ed.) (1979), *Government and Administration in Western Europe* (Oxford: Robertson).

R. Rose (1984), *Understanding Big Government* (London: Sage).

E. Sulieman (ed.) (1984), *Bureaucrats and Policy-Making: A Comparative Overview* (New York: Holmes & Meier).

9 Subcentral Government and Centre–Local Relations

Introduction

So far we have discussed only the central state institutions: national government, parliament, ministerial departments and public agencies. Now the time has come to widen our horizons and explore first the state's territorial organization, that is subcentral government – regions, provinces and communes – and its relations with the national government; and subsequently, in chapter 10, the special services – diplomatic service, armed forces, secret service – that oversee the state's relations with the outside world of other states and international organizations. The state, after all, is the expression not only of a political authority incarnating a social order, but also of a territory. Indeed, without a territory, there is no nation-state.

The existence of subcentral governmental institutions alongside the central state's field agencies raises the question of their specific role, which can be posed in the form of the following alternative: subcentral government or subcentral administration? In other words, is subcentral government conceived as a *partner* of central government in furnishing services to the citizen, as in the first case; or is it, instead, merely the *agent* of central government, as in the second case? Behind this alternative lie two different conceptions of the role of subcentral government which, although not entirely incompatible, are often in conflict.

In the former, it is a case of pluralism, of democracy – that is of 'the commune as the basic cell of democracy' – and of the dangers of the concentration of power in too few hands. This implies, therefore, a margin of political and administrative autonomy on the part of subcentral government to decide policy locally: 'Stadtluft macht frei' ('town air makes man free') runs the German proverb.[1] It is claimed, for instance, in support of this conception that local bodies know local problems and feelings, and so what is suitable, better than the central authorities possibly can. Central authorities, in fact, are obliged, by their very nature, to adopt general policies that are often abstract and inflexible. In the second conception, on the contrary, it is a case of management and efficiency in delivering services and these require the control of central over local authorities. In this conception, subcentral government's margin of autonomy is reduced to the minimum. Indeed, the claim is that local autonomy would have no other effect than that of dispersing and fragmenting the state's political power, so as to seriously compromise governability. Further is added, in keeping with the Jacobin tradition, the notion that general policies are necessary to ensure the equality of treatment of all citizens. Certainly, behind this argument often lurks the central government's fear that subcentral government will, in implementing alternative policies at the local level, undermine its own policies. At all events, territory is inevitably a privileged terrain of social conflict, and all the more so because national representatives, that is MPs but also ministers, are elected on a territorial basis in parliamentary democracies.

Aspects of both conceptions are to be found in the subcentral government arrangements of all West European states. Each has, in homage to representative democracy, a subcentral government system elected by universal suffrage, but also formally subordinate to central government. Moreover, with the development of the welfare state and the enormous expansion of public services provided directly to the citizen, the role of subcentral government has grown enormously, but so has the complexity of the problems with which it has to deal. This explains, perhaps, why reform and reorganization in this field have been so general and so widespread in the last three decades – Germany in the 1960s, Britain and Italy in the 1970s, France in the 1980s and Britain yet again in the 1990s – and also why the form and content have varied so widely.

To understand and appreciate the significance of subcentral government and the place it has in the different states, it is helpful to consider briefly some models, placing them in the context of the formation of the modern state in Europe. Subsequently, we shall discuss subcentral government structures, the local political elites, urban politics and centre–local relations.

Models of subcentral government

The most widely known models of territorial organization of the European state are the classic ones of the constitutional lawyers: the federal state and the unitary state. In the former, to use Wheare's (1951) well-known definition, taken over from Lord Bryce:

the powers of government are divided between a government for the whole country and governments for parts of the country in such a way that each is legally independent within its own sphere. The government for the whole country has its own area of powers and exercises them without any control from the governments of the constituent parts of the country, and these latter in their turn exercise their powers without being controlled by the central government. In particular the legislature of the central government has limited powers, and the legislatures of the states or provinces have limited powers. Neither is subordinate to the other; both are coordinate. (p. 19)

As regards the unitary state, Wheare is just as explicit: 'the legislature of the whole country is the country's supreme law-making body in the country. It may permit other legislatures to exist and to exercise their powers, but it has the right, in law, to overrule them; they are subordinate to it' (p. 19).

However, the classical constitutional view conceives federal and unitary states as two opposed models which can be placed at the two poles of a continuum that runs from integral decentralism to extreme centralism (Friedrich, 1968). If we do this, we must keep in mind that it is a case of the allocation of constitutional powers and *not* of the organization of politico-administrative power, that is they are models of the visible face of power. This does not mean that they are less important, only that they are insufficient to fully apprehend centre–local relations in contemporary West European states. At all events, according to this model, the federal state is characterized by subcentral governments – usually regional – that exercise a set of significant constitutional powers in full autonomy of the central government. Both levels of government have their own legitimacy, founded on elections by universal suffrage, and their own administration, capable of implementing their policies in the areas of their powers. Finally, there is a series of institutions of control, such as a constitutional court, to ensure respect of each's power.

The unitary state is characterized, instead, by a central government and a central administration that exercise power over the whole country. There can be, and usually are, elected subcentral governments – regions, provinces, districts and communes – with their own administrations, but their powers are limited and, further, are exercised at the pleasure of the central government.

Of the four states, one is federal (Germany) and the other three unitary (Britain, France and Italy), but it goes without saying that none can really be described in terms of Wheare's models. For instance, the German concept of federalism is not the classical 'dual-state' concept theorized by Wheare;[2] it does not consist of two separate structures, each equipped, institutionally and administratively, in its own field of competence. Instead, it is a mixed system, characterized above all by the fact that the *Länder* (states) both participate in and administer federal policies under a clearly assigned responsibility of their own. For this reason, it has been defined as an example of 'executive-legislative federalism' or 'administrative federalism'. As regards the unitary states, we may note that British local government has, like the German *Länder*, significant executant powers in spite of increased supervision and the privatization of services in the 1980s. Finally the Italian and French regions have been given a level of political decentralization considered by many to be incompatible with a unitary state. This is not only because Wheare's models are ideal types, but also because constitutional analysis deals only with the visible face of power.

At this point, it is helpful to introduce a second set of models elaborated by policy analysts who start from the premise that the power which counts is the power to deliver services, and hence is centred more on policy implementation mechanisms – the hidden face of power – than the allocation of constitutional powers. Gordon Smith (1972), for example, distinguishes between what he calls 'fused hierarchies' and 'dual hierarchies'. In the former, central administration field services and local government services operate in tandem, usually supervised by a central government official: the prefect in France – the prototype of the fused hierarchies model – and also in Italy. It was for this reason that it used to be said that: 'the prefecture is the focal point of departmental power.' In the latter, local self-administration is quite divorced from the central administration's field services, thus giving a system of detached or dual hierarchies. In this situation – represented by Germany, but also by Britain to a certain extent until the 1980s - it is the central government that is responsible for policy formulation, *but* subcentral government and its administration that implements it.[3] This is because central government has, as noted, a non-executant role in these policy areas: that is, it lacks, in contrast to the fused hierarchies model, field services in these areas. For this reason, the central government has to rely on subcentral government for effective service delivery and this allows the latter to preserve an element of autonomy in the face of central government. In Germany, this autonomy is reinforced by federal practices; in Britain it was 'protected' until the 1980s by central government's disinterest.

One way to understand the problem posed for the state by subcentral government and its consequences for centre–local relations is to insert the two models just outlined in their historical context. The history of the European state is, as we have seen, the history of the establishment of a strong central power, capable of defending the national territory and its population against foreign foes. To do this, it required two instruments: armed forces and a tax-collecting administration or exchequer (chapter 7). In this situation (1600–1850), state activity was very limited: diplomacy, war, justice and finance were all the activities of the central power and all were carried on in the capital; hence its interest in the daily life of the provinces was extremely limited, even non-existent. The state, in fact, lacked the means of intervening in provincial daily life, outside acts of repression and tax gathering, even if it had wanted to; welfare (called 'charity') was left to the church which had the means with its parish structure – organized significantly enough territorially – and its personnel, the clergy. However, as the great national states were formed, significant differences in the relations between the capital and the provinces, the centre and the localities, developed between the continental countries of France, Prussia but also Italy on the one side and England on the other, under the pressure of geopolitical factors and historical events, above all the operation of the European state system.

In France, both because of state building by conquest and dynastic alliance, as well as the state–church conflict, the state pursued a policy of active intervention in the provinces wherever possible. It created a body of administrators organized in a hierarchical manner (*intendant* and *sub-délégué*), directly dependent on the central power (*comptrolleur-général*), to control the provinces with the express intention of undermining and destroying the old local autonomies. Later, the tax-gathering regime was strengthened so that in the eighteenth century the tax burden imposed on the peasantry by the French state grew significantly. At the same time, the central state started to intervene directly in local economic life to organize the so-called 'mercantilist system'. The result was, in Tocqueville's (1856) words, 'under the old order, as nowadays, there was in France no township, borough, village, or hamlet, however small, no hospital, factory, convent or college which had the right to manage its affairs as it thought fit or to administer its possessions without interference. Then, as today, the central power held all Frenchmen in tutelage' (pp. 79–80).

There is no doubt, then, even if Tocqueville exaggerated a little, that an administrative system covered the whole territory; and further, as Tocqueville himself demonstrated, the new post-revolutionary administrative hierarchy – government, prefect, vice-prefect, mayor – created by Napoleon did nothing more than replace the old – king, *intendant*, *sub-délégué* – to control the whole life of the department with the help of a national police force (Gendarmerie Nationale), and ensure public order in the whole country. Not surprisingly, this new body of civil servants was recruited from the new middle bourgeoisie and *not* from the old landed aristocracy. The nobility, in fact, were attracted to the royal court in the capital to engage in 'high politics', as the *Mémoires* of the Duc de Saint-Simon (1788) vividly illustrate.

In England, instead, for mainly geopolitical reasons, things developed differently. National unity was achieved very early (more or less with the Norman conquest of 1066) and this created local loyalty towards the centre which meant an absence of wars of unification.[4] Moreover, its island position protected it from invasion by the major continental powers. The consequence was the absence of a standing army – the navy has always been the senior service in Britain, the main force for the protection of the trade routes – and so a somewhat less severe tax burden than in France.[5] More important was a political division of labour between centre and periphery, resulting from the Glorious Revolution of 1688, that Bulpitt (1983) has called the 'dual polity'. It was founded on the isolation of the central government from the provinces: the former engaged in 'high politics' – war, diplomacy, morality, law – while the latter attended to 'low politics' – local services and welfare.

In a certain sense, the national elite disinterested itself in low politics, leaving them quite happily in the hands of the provincial elite (the famous gentry) with the proviso, clearly understood but never spelt out, that the latter recognized the supremacy of the central power and supported its high politics and was able, at the same time, to guarantee control of the provinces. Parliament, as representative both of national sovereignty and of the provincial forces, became, quite naturally, the focal point of the British political system and the mediator of the dual polity, which probably explains the prestige and exalted status of the centre and the low status of local government to this day. In consequence, the centre did not create, as in France, a body of central administrators until very much later (the second half of the nineteenth century), or an executive capability – that is field service capability – in the provinces until the mid twentieth century, and then in some areas only. In the nineteenth century, the dual polity operated pretty well: initially because local services were very limited; later with the development of welfare, the centre entrusted responsibility for new services to local government – which had become elected in the last decades of the century. Thus, despite its legal subordination to the national government, local government enjoyed high levels of operational autonomy. This was paradoxically the basis of Britain's reputation as the home of 'local self-government'.[6]

Problems began to arise in the aftermath of World War I with the formation of a body of local government officers – local officials with specialized professional training in civil engineering, education, health – who had a professional interest in the local consequences of growing national programmes. After World War II, the relations between central and local government were further complicated by increased state intervention into everyday life and the different solutions adopted by the central government, either entrusting the service delivery to local government or creating new public agencies with independent management, like the regional health authorities. Two elements became the source of conflict between central government and local authorities. The first was public expenditure which, owing to the ever-increasing cost of public services, was never sufficient to meet public demand and so finished up dominating not only the state budget, but also the functioning of the national economy, a matter which the national government could no longer disregard. In other words, the old low politics had become the new high politics, a fundamental shift that was general to Europe (table

9.1). The second was the arrival on local councils of a new local political elite, after the nineteenth century social leaders, the political persons of the 1920–70 period (Lee, 1963), who often did not share the same views as the central elite. The result: local government has been subjected to almost continuous institutional change since the war which contrasts with the central government's centuries of unbroken constitutional continuity.

At this point, turning back to France, we may note that the introduction of elections to the departmental *conseils généraux* in 1871 and to the communes in 1884 helped to change radically the earlier situation of local power, particularly as the mayors of important communes and the departmental presidents were often MPs and even ministers. This meant that the prefect, despite the fact that he was formally invested with executive power in the department as the state's official representative, could not but take account of the interests and wishes of locally elected national representatives. He resorted to indirect tutelage over the implementation of decisions because most communes were obliged to call on the state's technical services. At the same time, local politicians rapidly adapted to this situation. The consequence was a collusion between prefects and local notables, analysed and documented by Worms (1966), in which the prefect consolidated his power locally by distributing state resources and the local politicians increased their political authority by privileged access to the central administration in Paris. Moreover, if tensions arose the local politicians could blame the prefect as all decisions were made under his authority as chief executive officer in the department. This became the 'clientelistic'[7] basis of the local government relations of the Third Republic that have more or less continued down to the present.

In conclusion, if the institutional arrangements between England and France are very different – in France, power seems united and formally organized in a hierarchical, almost military, way; in England, it is organized in two distinct powers with the semblance of great autonomy, that is local self-government – in practice, however, they are not all that dif-

Table 9.1 Shift of central government from high politics to low politics: from central to nationwide programmes (per cent of public expenditure)

	Britain		France		Germany		Italy	
	High	Low	High	Low	High	Low	High	Low
1840s	81	19	91	9	–	–	–	–
1870s	–	–	–	–	69	31	78	22
1890s/1900s	58	42	86	14	55	45	76	24
1930s	39	61	57	43	41	49	66	34
1970s	26	74	36	64	36	64	40	60
Shift	55%		55%		33%		38%	

Source: Rose, 1985b, p. 17

ferent, as recent events have shown. Thus we can sustain an apparent paradox, namely that the French system has been the subject of a genuine, if limited, attempt at political decentralization in the regional reforms of the 1980s, which had its parallel in the Italian regional reform of the 1970s; while the English model has been subject to increasing centralization, above all in the Thatcherite legislation of the 1980s, with rate capping, the abolition of the metropolitan counties (1986), the ill-fated poll tax of 1990 and the subsequent decision to reorganize local government into a single-tier system, reducing the number of councils still further.

Structures of subcentral government

The structure of subcentral government varies widely and hence it is difficult to identify any common logic. We are faced with a complex situation. There are *grosso modo* two kinds of subcentral government statutes: (a) the one, as in Britain, comes from parliament and so subcentral authorities can exercise only those functions specifically delegated to them, which means that they are subject to the doctrine of *ultra vires*; or (b) the other, as in France, Germany and Italy at the present time, derives from the constitution which establishes autonomous subcentral authorities and guarantees their existence and powers. The number of tiers of government, including the central government, is usually four in Germany (*Bund, Land, Kreis* and *Gemeinde*), in France (*état, région, département* and *commune*) and in Italy (*stato, regione, provincia* and *comune*); while in Britain, instead, it is usually three (state, county and district, plus parish in some areas, in England and Wales; state, region and district in Scotland), soon to be reduced to two. The number of government units at the various levels varies even more widely: there are 22 regions, 96 departments and 36,527 communes in France;[8] 20 regions, 95 provinces and 8098 communes in Italy (but the number is destined to change with the coming into force of the new law on local autonomy, 142/1990); 16 *Länder*, 543 districts and 16,128 communes in Germany; but only 47 shire counties, 36 metropolitan districts, 334 non-metropolitan districts plus 32 London boroughs and the City of London in England and Wales, to which must be added 9 regions, 53 districts and 3 island authorities in Scotland, without including Northern Ireland.

The different subcentral government tiers vary in importance from state to state: the weak link in France is the region, in Italy the province, in Germany the district, to which can be added the parish in England.[9] The reasons are largely historical. The French regions are mere aggregations of departments without any historical roots and few resources; while the Italian provinces were originally conceived as geographical units for statistical purposes with few powers, but have survived because the local organization of many social institutions – parties, trade unions, voluntary associations – has used them. In addition, the organization of the different units also varies between states. Indeed, the only thing that they have in common is that they all comprise elected councils, with the single exception of the City of London which survives as an oligarchy of medieval-style corporations. In France and also in Italy – at least, until the application of laws 142/1990 and 81/1993 – the powers and organization are identical for all authorities of the same tier, but this is not the case in Britain and Germany. Finally, even the developmental trends have varied: in France and Italy, there has been a move towards political decentralization with the introduction of a new tier – the region – and a small increase in the number of departments and provinces, but virtually no change in the number of communes; in Britain and Germany, movement has been in the opposite direction, towards reduction in the number of elected authorities and towards political centralization, above all in Britain. For instance, the districts were reduced from 425 in the 1950s to 237 in the 1980s and the communes from 27,836 to 8501 in West Germany before unification; while in Britain the reduction was even greater, from 1841 local authorities before the 1972 reform to just 521 (458 districts and 63 counties and regions) afterwards (table 9.2).

Page (1991) has explained this difference in terms of clientelism and localism which were present in France and Italy and absent in Britain and Germany. In the former 'the importance of local government for the power of national politicians meant that the communes could not be amalgamated and reformed to fit central government conceptions of efficiency' (p. 135). In the latter 'the absence of close ties based upon networks of what may be termed clientelism leaves central government free to shape local government according to its perceived needs ... for a century in Britain, the conception of the role of local government has been as an institution with sufficient financial and legal capacity to deliver major public services' (p. 136). Indeed, the argument is that in view of the interdependence between central and subcentral government there are only two solutions: either to adopt, as the British have increasingly

Table 9.2 Number of local authorities, average population and number of councillors

	Number		Variation	Average	Number of
	1950s	1980s	(%)	population, 1980s	councillors
Britain (district)	1,841	458	−75	125,000	28–120
France (*commune*)	37,983	36,394	−4	1,500	6–49
Germany (*Gemeinde*)[a]	24,386	8,501	−65	7,200	15–80
Italy (*comune*)	7,810	8,098	+4	7,100	15–80

[a] Germany refers to the Federal Republic before unification in 1990.
Sources: Rose, 1984, p. 240; Widdicombe Report, 1986, research vol. IV (Cmnd 9801), pp. 140–1

done, an authoritarian and centralizing policy to ensure that central decisions are implemented satisfactorily; or to institute, as the continentals
have increasingly done, instruments of collaboration to promote consensus and cooperation. In view of their diversity, it is necessary to outline
separately the local government structure of each country.

Britain

The present system of subcentral government in the United Kingdom is
complex. There are different systems in England and Wales, in Scotland
and in Northern Ireland[10] (figure 9.1). However, the organization of the
limited number of different authorities is reasonably similar, even if different from that of the central government. It is founded on the principle
of government by committee, that is 'government by, of and through
committees'.

All local authorities comprise a council elected on the single-member,
one-ballot majority system – either every four years for the counties, or a
third of the members annually, except for the year of the county council
elections, for the districts – and invested with decision-making power.
The committee system involves both local government officers who prepare the decisions, and councillors who take them, in policy determination. The only official positions are those of the chairs[11] of the various
committees which coincide with the different local government services.
The office of mayor, in the district councils which have borough status, is
one of pure representation and is elected annually on the basis of seniority, usually irrespective of party. The most important councillor is, in fact,
the group leader of the majority party on the council, or in the case of a
hung council, the party group leaders.

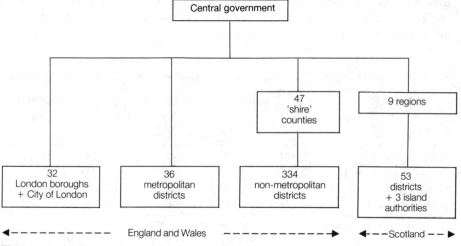

Figure 9.1   Structure of subcentral authorities in Great Britain

On the other hand, just as important hitherto in the organization of local government in Britain is the role of the local government officers. One of the peculiarities of the structure of the British state is that the central administration has a largely non-executant role. In fact, the only ministerial department with its own field service, that is local offices, is the Department of Social Security (DSS). This means that the central government depends on local authorities for the effective execution of a significant part of its policies as well as for technical and specialist knowledge because the professional personnel in the British administration are to be found among the body of local government officers (table 9.3). Since the 1972 reform, the chief officers of the different services – education, health, urban planning, housing, finance – who are all professionally qualified, form a coordination group, the principal officers' management team, under the direction of the chief executive. However, despite the attempt of the reform to push the local administration down the road of corporate management, it seems that a sectorialism based on the long-standing tradition of close relations between committee chairs and chief officers of the relevant department has prevailed. Further, with the growth of party control of local authorities – another consequence of the 1972 reform – the influence of the committees and the full council has declined in those authorities with secure one-party control, while that of the caucus of the majority party has correspondingly increased, as well as the influence of the chief officers' team as a coordinating office of professional advice.

Elected local authorities are, as noted, constitutionally subordinate to parliament and their existence, powers and competence derive exclusively from statute. This means that their operation is subject to a strict interpretation of the legal rule of *ultra vires*: they may only act – with certain limited exceptions – if they can show positive authority for their actions in a specific law. Their subordinate position means, in consequence, that they are conceived, by central government, as simple service agencies, whose powers and functions can be changed by simple parliamentary majority. This means that the centre has power to mandate – that is to require by law that a local authority do something – and it can inspect local services and audit accounts. Such power allows the centre to prevail over recalcitrant local authorities, hostile to its view of appropriate service provisions, with the ultimate threat of suppression. This is a strategy that successive Conservative governments pursued in the 1980s with the object of increasing the centre's capacity to control local government services and, above all, spending.

The 1972 reform created a two-tier structure of subcentral government – counties and districts – in a non-hierarchical relationship with each other, but with distinct functions for the whole country. The distribution of functions between the different subcentral authorities is made more complex by the fact that it varies territorially between England and Wales on the one hand and Scotland on the other (table 9.4). This divi-

Table 9.3 Distribution of personnel, revenue and expenditure of subcentral authorities, 1980s

	Britain		France		Germany		Italy	
Personnel (thousands)								
Central government	1056	(26%)	2833	(66%)	855	(24%)	1882	(74%)
Intermediate authorities	–		–		1713	(48%)	60	(3%)
Local authorities	2970	(74%)	1433	(34%)	1010	(28%)	586	(23%)
Distribution of revenue (%)								
International organizations	2.3		0.6		2.2		0.4	
Central government	71.7		49.3		31.7		63.2	
Intermediate authorities	–		–		23.1		–	
Local authorities	10.6		7.1		8.9		0.7	
Social security	15.3		43.0		34.1		35.7	
Expenditure (%)								
Central government	73.2		78.9		45.5		75.6	
Subcentral authorities	26.8		21.1		54.5		25.4	

Sources: Rose, 1985a, tables 2.6, 3.7, 4.9 and 5.6; Mény, 1987, p. 464

Table 9.4 Allocation of service responsibilities to subcentral authorities, 1984–1985: local (L) and intermediate (R: regional or provincial)

	Britain	France	Germany	Italy
Security police	L	–	R	L
Fire	L	L	L	–
Justice	L	L	–	–
Pre-school, primary and secondary education	L	–	–	–
Vocational, technical and higher education	L	L R	R	L R
Adult education	L	L	–	–
Hospitals and health	R	L R	–	L R
Family welfare	L	L R	L	L R
Housing	L	–	L R	L R
Town planning	L	L	L	L R
Refuse	L	L	L	L
Leisure – arts	L	L R	L	L R
Leisure – parks and sport	L	L	L	L R
Roads and road transport	L	L R	–	L R
Ports	–	R	–	L
Airports	L	R	–	–
Agriculture, forestry, fishing and hunting	–	–	–	L R
Electricity	–	–	L	L
Commerce	–	–	–	L
Tourism	–	L R	L	R
Water	R	–	L	–

Source: Widdicombe Report, 1986, research vol. IV (Cmnd 9801), p. 135

sion of functions effectively created three separate systems of local government (two in England and Wales and one in Scotland) with two kinds of local authority each, instead of six. This was made all the truer by the fact that, without making one kind hierarchically superior in the three systems, the county (region in Scotland) administered the most important services financially, and this ensured that it had a superior status. However, the situation was further complicated in England and Wales in the 1980s as a result of the abolition of the six metropolitan counties and the GLC in 1986, so that today there are two systems side by side: (1) in the big conurbations, a single-tier system, the metropolitan districts and the London boroughs, with their own functions and those of the former metropolitan counties and GLC respectively; and (2) in the other areas, a two-tier system, the shire counties and the non-metropolitan districts, each with its own functions. The differences in the two systems, in fact, coincide *grosso modo* with those between urban and urban-rural zones. This is subject to yet further change as the Major government has recently announced its intention to introduce a single-tier system for the whole of Britain in 1995. As regards finance, subcentral authorities have the right to set a local tax, but the major part of funding comes from central government in the form of grants-in-aid as well as loans (for major investments) (table 9.3). This reliance on central funding has allowed the central government a large measure of control over subcentral government finance which it has endeavoured to strengthen by successive legislation on rate-capping and the replacement of the rates by the disastrous poll tax, rapidly replaced in turn by a new property tax, the council tax, in 1993.

Finally, certain services are administered by special decentralized public bodies. The best known are the regional health authorities, with their subordinate district health authorities, responsible for administering the National Health Service. In view of the central government's constitutional power to modify subcentral government functions by statute, it is hardly surprising that the former has used this faculty to strip the latter of many of its functions, particularly if it opposed central government policy. This was a process that began in the inter-war years – poor relief – and has continued in the post-war period, reaching, as noted, assault proportions in the 1980s. Thus, for instance, local authority gas, water and electricity services were transferred after 1945 to national boards which were floated on the Stock Exchange as privatized companies in the 1980s; and inner-city renewal was handed over to non-accountable urban development corporations, like the London Docklands Development Corporation.

France

French subcentral government has experienced significant change in recent years – 1982–6 reforms[12] – and thus its operation is subject to some uncertainty. Institutionally, it is organized as a three-tiered system (region,[13] department and commune), without one tier being considered superior to the others, even though the regions – established as a unit of subcentral government by ordinary legislation without recourse to constitutional amendment (Le Cacheux and Tourjansky, 1992) – comprise a certain number of departments which, in turn, are divided into a very large number of communes (figure 9.2).

The institutional structure of all three kinds of subcentral authority is very similar. Each comprises a council elected by universal suffrage which elects, in its turn, an executive: a president, or a mayor in the case of the communes. Thus regional councils are elected every six years on a PR system of departmental lists, while the departmental councils are elected on the single-member, two-ballot majority system: half the departmental councillors every three years. The elections for the communal councils take place every six years and the electoral system depends on the size of the commune: in those with less than 3500 inhabi-

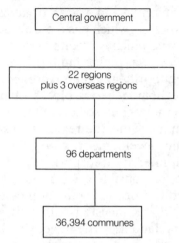

Figure 9.2   Structure of subcentral authorities in France

tants it is the two-ballot majority system and in those with more than 3500 inhabitants a mixed two-ballot majority-proportional system. Finally, in Paris, Marseilles and Lyons the mixed system is applied not at the commune level but at the district (*arrondissement* [14]) level. The system in force under the Fifth Republic prior to 1983, gave all the seats to the winning list, so that the minority lists were not even represented on communal councils, except for Paris, Marseilles and Lyons, where the minority lists might win the majority in some districts.

The executive officer of the three kinds of authority, once elected, is assisted by a committee (*bureau* in the case of regions and departments; *adjoints* in the case of communes), but remains responsible for the political and administrative decisions of the authority, even though he can delegate it in a certain sector to a vice-president or an *adjoint*. His role is to prepare the council's agenda, its budget and its activity in the fields of its competence. Council meetings, even in the regions and departments, are infrequent; hence the president and the mayor are the most important persons in their respective authorities. The activities of the three kinds of authority are no longer subject to the prefect's tutelage as they were before the 1982 reform. Today, the prefect has only an *ex post* power of control, that is he can submit, within two months, any act which he considers illegal to the regional administrative court. In addition, he can withdraw the complaint, if the dialogue between the authority and another body (usually another state agency) allows the act to be modified. However, it should be stressed that however important these changes in this aspect of the prefect's power were legally, they were politically less significant since they merely formalized a long-consolidated political practice. Indeed, the proportion of acts annulled by the prefect before the 1980s reform was exceedingly small: less than 1 per cent. Finally, in the case of the regional authority, there is, in addition to the regional council, also an economic and social council made up of the representatives of economic and social organizations – industrialists, trade unionists and experts – which has a purely advisory role.

The division of powers, which is certainly the most visible aspect of the political decentralization, was defined in terms of the technical capability of the three kinds of authority and their closeness to the population. The idea was to distribute homogeneous blocks of powers to each type of authority: planning to the region; social welfare to the department; town planning to the commune. Thus the region is responsible for vocational training and economic development, while the department was given social services, health, intercity transport, school buses and rural works. Finally, the commune, responsible for certain fundamental services like hospitals and refuse collection, and some non-essential services like public libraries and housing, is invested with new powers in the field of urban development and land use. The novelty is that it is now the mayor, and not the prefect, who is charged with preparing the plans of land occupation, and the latter merely ratifies them as long as they comply with the regulations in force.

The law does not distinguish between the same kind of authority, even though there are enormous differences of size between many of them, above all as a result of the very large number of small communes: the difference, for instance, in terms of population, resources and technical capability between the city of Marseilles (900,000 inhabitants) and the island of Hoedic (150 inhabitants) in the Morbihan means that certain powers can only be used by a limited number of communes (the large ones). Hence the small communes are obliged to call on the state's technical resources to provide certain services, which ensures the continued influence of the latter over local affairs. In some areas, intercommunal cooperation has been widely developed since 1959 through the creation of the SIVOM (*syndicat intercommunal à vocation multiple*). Finally, in other areas which have remained the responsibility of central government, like education and culture, the central government now uses the subcentral authorities' technical resources. For example, the three kinds of authority are associated in planning and siting schools and determining the number of pupils – the regions for grammar schools, the departments for secondary modern schools and the communes for elementary schools – while the state retains its responsibility for the curriculum and for the number and remuneration of teachers.

According to one of the general principles of the 1980s reforms, the transfer of powers was to be accompanied by a corresponding attribution funding by the central state. This new funding took the form of special financial transfers, namely *dotations* indexed to the cost of living. Thus, for instance, the automobile registration tax was transferred to the regions (to fund professional training) and a percentage of the property tax was given to the departments (to finance welfare services). These fiscal transfers were integrated with a *Dotation générale de décentralisation* to the three kinds of authority. On the other hand, the reforms did not modify the complex system of local taxes (*taxe professionnelle*; *taxe d'habitation*; *foncier bati* and *foncier non-bati*) which were so insufficient as to need supplementing with various state subsidies. The latter have been simply replaced by two block grants: *Dotation globale de fonctionnement* in 1979 to cover some of the revenue costs of local government, and *Dotation globale de décentralisation* in 1983 to cover a percentage of the costs of the transfer of functions. Finally, a major new subsidy for capital expenditure, particularly for departments, the *Dotation globale d'équipement* was also introduced in 1986 which progressively replaces specific block grants and gives local authorities greater discretion over their investment and revenue policy. However, given that the grants cover only a part of the costs, the central government has used political decentralization to discharge a number of public expenditure budget items on to subcentral government. At the same time, the former has promoted formal agreements (*contrats*) with subcentral authorities on planned spending programmes for specific purposes. Thus, although the central state has supplied a growing proportion of subcentral government finance, nonetheless the total amount of public expenditure available to them has fallen.

To complete this review we need to consider briefly the prefectoral institution which, before the 1982 reform, was the keystone of French provincial administration. In fact, the departmental (or regional) prefect was simultaneously the state's official representative in the department, the government's representative (responsible for the coordination of public policies), the principal representative of the Ministry of the Interior (responsible for public order, the collection of political and electoral intelligence and the controller of departmental and communal administrations) and, above all, chairman of the departmental (and regional since 1971) executive charged with determining departmental policy. With the 1980s reforms, the prefect has lost his role as departmental executive, which was transferred to the president of the departmental council who now became the central political figure.[15] For the first time, local politicians were forced to become local administrators, instead of merely local representatives. This is a major change in French local government practice.

The prefect remains the state's official representative in the department; however, he depends no longer on the Interior Ministry but on the prime minister's office and has become responsible for coordinating the ministerial field services[16] in the department. He remains responsible, nonetheless, for public order and the collection of political intelligence. If he no longer enjoys today the prestige and formal powers that he once had, he still has a significant influence which derives from his knowledge of the state administrative machine. As noted, in the case of the rural communes – the overwhelming majority – the mayors often ask the prefect to act in their stead, particularly where they lack the necessary resources.

Germany

German federalism makes for a complex system of subcentral government. As noted, it is not one of discrete units existing beside or below one another with clearly defined competences; it was always based on substantial elements of intergovernmentalism, even before the constitutional reforms of 1966–9 – introduction of 'joint tasks' (*Gemeinschaftsaufgauben*: articles 91a and b of the basic law) – which were merely the logical consequence of the practical need for close cooperation between the federal government and the *Länder*. In this connection, we must bear in mind the fact that the *Länder* are guaranteed a voice in federal policies through their representation in the Bundesrat. Indeed, the extensive power of the Bundesrat to scrutinize and reject large areas of federal legislation, particularly in the fields of finance and constitutional reform, means that *Länder* interests are fully represented in the German policy process. In addition, the *Länder's* position is further reinforced by the federal government's reliance on them for policy implementation. Public service provision, with few exceptions (railways, postal services), is in the hands of the *Länder* or local government, acting on behalf, or more commonly as agents, of the federal government but 'under their own responsibility' (*Selbstverwaltung*).

Subcentral government in Germany is also organized on the basis of a three-tiered system (*Land*, district and commune) (figure 9.3). The *Land's* institutional structure is similar to that of the federal government which is not the case of the district and commune. This is because the latter's structures are determined by the individual *Land* constitutions (*Gemeindeverfassung*) and, therefore, feel more than the *Länder* the effects of the diversity of German regional traditions and the great disparity in size between the different *Länder*.[17] The *Land* institutions con-

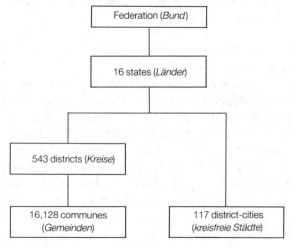

Figure 9.3 Structure of subcentral authorities in Germany

sist of an elected assembly (*Landtag*) – with the exception of Bavaria which has a second assembly (*Senat*) of corporative representation – that elects an executive composed of a *Ministerpräsident* and a *Kabinett*. The three city-*Länder*, Bremen, Hamburg and Berlin, have a different organization because the assembly elects a collegiate executive (*Senat*), presided over by a mayor (*Oberbürgermeister*). *Landtag* elections take place every four to five years using various PR systems. The *Land* executive is usually small (8–10 members), appointed by the *Ministerpräsident* who is responsible for the activity of the *Land*. Since the primary task of the *Land* is administration and *Landtag* sessions are infrequent, the majority parties tend to select figures of proven administrative ability as members of the *Kabinett* of the *Länder*.

The structures of the lower tiers (districts and communes) are more complex. Firstly, the *Länder* are divided into districts and the districts into communes. However, 117 of the largest communes (*Grossstädte*) are authorities in their own right (*kreisfreien Städte*: district-cities) and are independent of district supervision. Secondly, many of the small communes have united to form associations to furnish certain services. Thirdly, the district as a local authority has a dual role: on the one hand, it is an elected authority that carries out certain tasks that the communes are unable to do; and, on the other, it is the lowest level of state administration. Thus its principal administrator (*Landrat*), selected by the district council, acts as a supervisor of the communes in his area. Nevertheless, both types of authority are organized around a council (*Kreisrat, Gemeinderat* and *Stadtrat*), directly elected by PR, every four years, except in Bavaria and Baden-Württemberg, where half the council seats are contested every three years. The form of executive also varies according to the *Land*, but one can identify schematically four types: (1) the collegiate, elected by the council (*Magistrat*: Schleswig-Holstein and Hesse); (2) the mixed personal collegiate, in which the council elects a college (*Senat*) that selects a *Bürgermeister* (Hamburg, Bremen, Berlin[18]); (3) the purely personal, with a *Bürgermeister* or *Oberbürgermeister* directly elected either by the electorate (Bavaria and Baden-Württemberg) or by the council (Rhineland-Palatinate and the East German *Länder* of Brandenburg, (Mecklenberg-West Pomerania) Saxony, Saxony Anhalt and Thuringia); and (4) the English committee system in which the council delegates the power to a *Gemeindedirektor* or *Stadtdirektor* (Lower Saxony, North Rhine-Westphalia[19]) with the object of ensuring a distinct division between political and administrative agents. The period in office of the executive is always longer than the council, from a minimum of six years in the cases of Baden-Württemberg and Hesse to twelve in those of Lower Saxony and Schleswig-Holstein, but the average is eight to ten years. Despite the variety of institutional forms of the executive at the local level, the German tradition limits the council to a deliberative role and power is granted to a strong executive capable of formulating and implementing appropriate policies.

The *Land's* exclusive legislative powers are very limited: education and culture, police and the organization of local authorities (table 9.4). Indeed, the federal government's exclusive powers are also relatively limited: foreign affairs, defence, currency, trade and customs (article 73 of the basic law). The largest area of legislative power covers what is defined as 'concurrent' (article 74), that is the competence of both the federal government and the *Länder*. Nevertheless, the power of policy initiation lies firmly with the federal government, thanks to the principle of the supremacy of federal law over *Land* law. There are also other situations in which the federal government can intervene in areas of exclusive *Land* competence, such as, for instance, in the power to enact 'framework provisions' (*Rahmengesetz)* or 'general rules'; or where the law of one *Land* would damage other *Länder* or the national interest; and finally to protect the country's economic and legal unity. The result is that the amount of original *Land* legislation is relatively small.

A situation of this kind confirms that the *Länder* have limited formal powers. However, as noted above, the real power of the *Länder* in the German federal system comes not from their formal responsibilities but from their administrative functions, that is from the federal government's reliance on the *Länder* for policy implementation and service provision, reinforced by the need for the Bundesrat's approval of legislation. In fact, German 'cooperative federalism' has seen the establishment of a vast network of agencies and committees to provide coordination between the federal government and the *Länder*. *Bund–Länder* relations operate on three levels (*Gesamtstaat*, 'whole state'; *Bundesstaat*, 'federal state'; *Kommune*, 'third level'[20]) with their corresponding groups of coordinative and cooperative institutions – the various conferences of the federal chancellor and *Länder* minister-presidents, of the federal and *Land* ministers (*Ständige Konferenz der Ministerpräsidenten* and *der Minister der Länder*), the permanent advisory council (*Ständiger Beirat*) of the Bundesrat, the plenipotentiaries (*Bevollmächte*) and the permanent legations (*Landesvertretungen*) of the *Länder* to the *Bund* – which enable the federal and *Länder* governments to discuss, negotiate and make agreements on problems of common interest. Often, the accords reached are formalized by state treaties (*Staatsverträge*) and administrative agreements (*Verwaltungsabkommen*) that have the full force of law. These practices were institutionalized in the constitutional reforms of 1966–9, introducing the notion of 'joint tasks', that is concerted *Bund–Land* action in specified sectors, like university development, regional economic policy, agricultural policy and so on. The federal government was, for instance, authorized to intervene and co-finance projects to promote the development and fairer distribution of resources, above all in favour of the poorer *Länder*. Today, in fact, the talk is of *Politikverflechtung* (interlocking policy-making), particularly since unification. Nonetheless, we must bear in mind, as noted, that in the German system of intergovernmental relations 'divergent interests are brought together through a policy process that resists central reform initiatives and defies sustained attempts to steer policy developments' (Katzenstein, 1987, p. 47).

The responsibilities of the lower subcentral units – districts and communes – are of two types: obligatory and voluntary. The former are laid down by law, federal and *Land*, and many are, in fact, carried out by the districts, above all in the case of small communes which lack the necessary resources to undertake them. The latter derive from a doctrine of general competence that allows a commune, but *not* a district, to act in the interests of its area and its inhabitants (article 28 of the basic law). These powers are not unimportant because they enable communal authorities to make specific contributions to local life, like the vast array of recreational and cultural facilities for which German local government is justly reputed. It is self-evident that these services depend directly on the available financial resources: hence, large cities have in principle more opportunities of providing them than small towns and villages.

The federal government has no direct control over subcentral government; indeed, it has traditionally minimized its connections with local government, dealing primarily through the *Länder*. Judicial review of the administration is, nonetheless, well established in Germany and the review mechanism has been reinforced in Rhineland-Palatinate by the introduction of a local ombudsman (*Bürgerbeauftragte*). Control of local government, moreover, is the responsibility of the *Länder* and is exercised in two principal ways. The first is that already mentioned, by the district administrator (*Landrat*) who supervises and coordinates communal activities. He acts as agent for the *Land* ministry of the interior to ensure that the communes work within the law and provide adequate services. The second is that by the *Regierungspräsident*, a sort of 'prefect' appointed by the *Land* and responsible to the ministry of the interior. All the *Länder*, except Bremen, Hamburg and Schleswig-Holstein, are divided into a number of administrative districts (*Regierungsbezirke*) and the district president and his staff are *Land* civil servants who have wide powers of supervision of the districts and communes. In addition to controlling the police and seeing that local governments act within the law, they manage various *Land* projects. Finally, this supervisory administration is considered archaic and anti-democratic by most local politicians, but so far they have not succeeded in getting it abolished.

In the field of subcentral finance too, the German federal system differs not only from classic federal states, but also from unitary states. In other words, it is not based on a system in which two authorities (*Bund* and *Land*) administer concurrent tax powers independently, or on one in which one authority (usually the central state) administers all the taxes on behalf also of subcentral government. In the German system, instead, the two authorities (*Bund* and *Land*) jointly administer the taxes which are distributed (*Gemeinschaftssteuern*) between the three groups of institutions (*Bund, Land* and local authorities) on the basis of revisable percentages (table 9.3). In fact, on the basis of the compromise reached in 1969 on fiscal reform and enshrined in the amendment of article 106 of the basic law – which affirms the principle that the *Bund* and the *Länder* are equally entitled to adequate financial resources for the discharge of their functions – the following distribution of income and corporation tax receipts was agreed: *Bund* 43 per cent, *Länder* 43 per cent, local authorities 14 per cent. In the case of VAT, distribution was left to the Finance Act, subject to the Bundesrat's approval: hence, to the necessary agreement of the *Länder*. Finally, as regards the business tax (*Gewerbesteuer*), the *Bund* receives 20 per cent, the *Länder* another 20 per cent and the local authorities 60 per cent. These are the three most important types of tax because they raise some 70 per cent of German tax receipts. The remainder comes from certain small and exclusive taxes, like customs and registration for the *Bund*, local and property taxes (*Grundsteuer*) and automobile registration for the *Länder*. One of the consequences of the German system of the fixed distribution of tax receipts was the insignificant use of federal grants for specific *Land* or local authority projects and services, which are much used in other European countries. However, given the level of services provided, they could only be sustained with the aid of a network of grants and subsidies from the federal and *Land* authorities. This has increased throughout the 1970s and 1980s and led, in many people's eyes, to a significant loss of autonomy to, and encroachment by, the centre.

A final point as regards the distribution of fiscal receipts between the *Länder* concerns the 'equalization' techniques or *Finanzausgleich*: distribution in favour of the poorer *Land*. These techniques are of two types: (1) vertical equalization, namely a proportion of the jointly collected revenues are earmarked specifically to help bring the tax income of the poorer *Länder* up to the average; and (2) horizontal equalization, under which the richer *Länder* are required to subsidize the poorer. Before unification, four *Länder* were donors and six beneficiaries. Not surprisingly, however, these provisions have been the source of continuous conflict because the wealthier *Länder* have been reluctant to forgo their own resources and the poorer *Länder* have resented their dependence on their more fortunate neighbours. But the authorities that really do have a reason to complain are not the western *Länder*; they are the big cities, which have not seen their resources rise in keeping with their expenses. Although they receive their part of income and business taxes, supplemented by local property tax (*Grundsteuer*) and service charges as well as growing federal and *Länder* subsidies, they are crippled by debt and forced to raise loans on the open market in order to finance programmes of capital investment. In this, however, they find themselves suffering like so many municipalities in the Western world from the so-called 'urban fiscal crisis'. To help shoulder this growing burden, the federal government introduced the Structural Aid Act (*Strukturhilfegesetz*) of 1988. However, this reparative measure was quickly overtaken by unification whose costs have severely disrupted *Länder* finances. The Treaty of Unity originally provided for the integration of the eastern *Länder* in the fiscal equalization mechanism for 1995. Moreover, it also provided for a growing portion of the *Länder* VAT share from 55 per cent in 1992 to 70 per cent in 1994. Neither survived the economic breakdown in the east in 1991. The federal government, which had promised that unification would not necessitate new taxes, pressurized the western *Länder* to accept a greater financial burden. They agreed to give the eastern *Länder* 100 per cent of the *Länder* VAT share until 1994. After much negotiation the *Länder* reached a common front on the future of the financial equalization system at the Solidarity Pact negotiations in Potsdam in March 1993. Broadly speaking the outcome, which will take effect from 1 January 1995, left the existing mechanisms of financial equalization virtually unchanged. It incorporates the aim of ensuring that each *Land*, in east and west, should enjoy 95 per cent of the average financial capacity of the *Länder* community as a whole after equalization, with the major burden (two-thirds) of contribution falling on the *Bund* by means of a redistribution of a large tranche of its VAT revenues to the *Länder* (Jeffery, 1994). Whether this outcome will be acceptable in the longer term is open to question.

Finally, finance is proving one of the greatest problems for the integration of the eastern *Länder*. It has been temporarily eased by aid programmes, but they will require a reconstructed domestic economy if they are to provide services on a par with those in the western part of the country, and that will take time.

Italy

The Italian system of subcentral government is similar to the French (figure 9.4). This is no surprise. Firstly, Italy adopted the Napoleonic model of the centralized state, introduced into Piedmont during the French conquest, and then extended it to the rest of the peninsula after unification in 1860. The Napoleonic model provides for a system of subordinate local authorities, with limited powers, and subject to central control through the state's representative in the provinces, the prefect. Secondly, the French have repaid the compliment by adopting many of the elements of the Italian system of regional government in the 1980s. And it is thanks to the regional reforms of the past two decades that the French and Italian state systems can be defined as regional, rather than unitary, states.

At all events, in its institutional structure, the Italian system of subcentral government is, like the French and German, three-tiered: regions, provinces and communes. However, in contrast to the French, the tiers have a certain hierarchical relationship between them, in the sense that the region is superior to the province and the commune, even though the

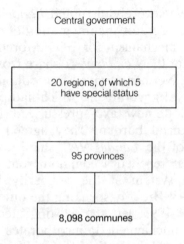

Figure 9.4 Structure of subcentral authorities in Italy

province is not superior to the commune. In fact, the control powers over the province and commune are now exercised by the regional control commission (Comitato Regionale di Controllo). In addition, there are two types of region, special and ordinary: the former are either islands or frontier zones with special problems – socio-economic in the cases of Sicily and Sardinia, linguistic and cultural in the cases of Val d'Aosta, Trentino-Alto Adige and Friuli-Venezia Giulia – and whose allegiance to the state could initially be deemed problematic. Nonetheless, they are similar structurally, but the special regions have more powers than the ordinary regions. Once again, in contrast to France, there has been no attempt in Italy to organize the various powers of the different tiers of subcentral government according to a theoretical scheme of functions. Even here, however, an effort has been made in the last decade to rationalize the powers of subcentral authorities: this was the case of the *Ordinamento delle autonomie locali* (law 142/1990). It is based on seven 'pillars': local autonomy, division of responsibilities between council and *giunta* (executive), role difference between politicians and civil servants, efficient services and administrative action, reform of controls, and specific roles for the region, the province and the metropolitan areas, to which must be added an organizing principle for local finance (Fossati, 1990). The law creates a new authority, the metropolitan area, defined as the zones comprising the listed communes – Turin, Milan, Venice, Genoa, Bologna, Florence, Rome, Bari, Naples and Cagliari – and communes linked to them by ties of close integration. The institutional levels within the metropolitan areas are twofold: the metropolitan city and the commune.[21]

The organization of all subcentral authorities was very similar and more or less reproduced the institutional form of the central government: each had a five-yearly elected council and an executive – the *giunta* under the direction of a president or mayor (*sindaco* in the case of communes) – elected by the council. The electoral regime used for almost all subcentral authorities was the same as for the national parliament, namely the PR list system. However, important changes were introduced for communes and provinces in 1993 (law 81/93). This reduces the number of councillors[22] and the length of the electoral mandate (to four years) as well as limiting the period in office of mayors and provincial presidents (to two terms). But the most important change was the replacement of PR by majority electoral systems in all communes together with the direct election of the mayor on a two-ballot system in communes with more than 15,000 inhabitants. The new system is complex, but the mayor's list or coalition is given two-thirds of the seats on the council of communes with less than 15,000 inhabitants and 60 per cent in those with more than 15,000. The remaining seats are distributed among the minority lists on a proportional basis.

The council was formerly responsible for formulating the main policies of the authority: it enacted legislation, approved the budget and controlled the activity of the junta, a collegiate body of councillors (*assessori*) which acted as an executive organ presided over by the president or mayor. Each *assessore* was responsible for one or more of the authority's service departments, but the junta directed the local administration, prepared the budget and projects and submitted them to the council for approval. However, law 81/1993 has now replaced this collective responsibility of the junta by the direct responsibility of the mayor or provincial president. He personally appoints and dismisses the *assessori,* and directs the activity – policy, budget, projects – of the commune/province. He is not bound by the vote of the council and can only be forced to resign as a result of a formal vote of no confidence in him, but this means the automatic dissolution of the council and new elections.

The control of subcentral authorities in Italy is similar to France, which is not surprising given that the French regional reform of the 1980s adopted the methods introduced in the 1970 Italian reform. It is exercised by a regional control committee – appointed by the central government in the case of the regions, and the region in the case of provinces and communes – and by the government commissioner (*commissario del governo*) for the regions, or the prefect for the provinces and communes. In principle all local government acts should be submitted for verification by the committee within 30 days if laws, and 20 days if administrative regulations, and all those acts not quashed in this period become executive. In cases of conflict, the constitutional court is competent in questions of legality. The role of commissioners and prefects consists above all in overseeing the good working of the regional and local administrations, that is to say to order enquiries where irregularity and abuse of power are suspected and to intervene where the authorities do not fulfil their responsibilities. The difference between the commissioner or prefect and the committee is that the former must limit their opinion to questions of legality of the acts, while the latter may also express a judgement on the validity of the administrative and financial criteria followed; appeal is to the local administrative courts (*tribunali amministrativi regionali*). The power to dissolve a local authority administration belongs to central government, but it is implemented, of course, on the recommendation of commissioner or prefect. Today, it is adopted only when a council refuses to meet or when it is unable to form a stable majority – or is guilty of mismanagement or irregular administration. The role of the prefect and commissioner contrasts today with what happened in the past when the central government dissolved local authorities as much to support its political manoeuvres as for administrative malpractice. Finally, in the very small communes, where the mayor knows little about the law and administration, the communal secretary (*segretario comunale*), and through him the prefect,[23] is often the *deus ex machina* of the situation. Indeed, despite their independent status, small communes are limited in their ability to take effective action by lack of financial and staff resources.

The picture of the division of responsibilities between authorities is particularly complex and, in recent years, has become more complex (table 9.4). Initially, provinces and communes were conceived as simple agents for supplying certain state services to the local population, under the prefect's control. The functions were of two kinds, mandatory and optional, which meant in fact that only the big communes had the resources to provide the latter. Indeed, optional functions enjoyed, as in Germany, the status of residual functions, that is activities in the interest of the local population that were not expressly forbidden by law. However, the creation of the regions in 1970 saw a substantial modification in the division of responsibilities. Firstly, the 1948 constitution had endowed the regions with three kinds of legislative power: (1) exclusive; (2) complementary; and (3) integrative. The first is modest, and is only possessed by the special regions and for certain matters only, like agriculture, public works and urban planning. The second is also limited, covering only those sectors specifically mentioned in article 117 of the constitution, to which all the regions have added a similar power in the field of regional economic planning. The special regions have further complementary powers in fields like public health, insurance and commerce. To act in these areas, the two types of region must comply with the basic principles established by parliament in 'framework laws' (*leggi quadro*) or the general legislation in force in the field. Finally, the third concerns the power of the regions to adapt the single provisions of national legislation to the needs and conditions of the various regions. In comparison with the legislative and administrative powers of the German *Länder*, those of the Italian regions, like their French counterparts, are very modest indeed. An attempt was made, however, in the late 1970s, during the period of the government of 'national solidarity', to extend the regions' political autonomy. A decree of 1977 established that the regions had a role to play in formulating national policies. To this end, as in Germany, a vast network of sectorial advisory and consultative committees was set up, incorporating the voice of the regions in policy-making at the national level. At the summit was the standing committee of the state and regions (Conferenza Permanente Stato-Regioni), a consultative committee of national and regional governments intended as a forum through which the regions had access to the central government on a wide range of policy issues.

Secondly, the modalities of the transfer of powers from the state to the regions in 1977, and above all the principle of 'organically linked sectors', not only modified the responsibilities of the different subcentral authorities, but also extended that of the lower ones: provinces and communes. The organizing principle is that in every area the central government should perform a legislative and general planning role, the regions a legislative and specific planning role and the lower authorities, usually the communes, an administrative role, organically conceived. Moreover, it was thought that, in this way, another problem could be resolved, namely the regions' unwillingness to delegate powers and functions to lower authorities on the pretext that this would undermine their authority. The result of this attitude of the regions was to promote a new direct relationship between the central government and provinces and communes, so as to bypass the regions. Similarly, the most important regions have set up information offices in Brussels in an attempt to institute direct contact with the EU, bypassing Rome.

At all events, the new *Ordinamento* of 1990 adopts a criterion of the distribution of powers that no longer follows the hierarchic importance of the authorities, but is based on the institutional role that each of them, province and commune, is effectively capable of exercising in its respective community and within its own territory. The distribution is determined by function. Thus the commune is the local authority with general purposes restricted to its own territory, representing its own community, attending to its interests and pursuing its own development, principally in matters of the social services, land use and economic development. The province, which is the intermediary authority between commune and region, is responsible for provincial interests in a certain number of fields of an intercommunal nature. Within the metropolitan areas, both the communal and provincial powers will be exercised by the metropolitan city. The remaining communes in the metropolitan areas will have a residual planning role. Finally, as regards the regions, the new law sets a new norm of dubious constitutionality, which obliges them to organize the exercise of administrative powers at the local level through the communes and provinces. Further, it outlines a method of cooperation between central and subcentral tiers in which decisions are made by means of a participative process rather than imposed by a superior level on an inferior one. Given the *Ordinamento*'s novelty and its lack of application, together with the complexity of the subject, it is difficult to be more precise at the present time.

Subcentral government finances have also been the object of numerous – some say 'schizophrenic' – changes in recent years. Paradoxically, the trend has been in the opposite direction to that of responsibilities, that is, towards centralization rather than decentralization. In the 1950s and 1960s, the commune enjoyed substantial financial autonomy, thanks to local taxes and loans that it was able to count on. A first change resulted from the creation of the regions which, despite the fact that article 119 of the constitution guaranteed them financial autonomy, saw them refused their own tax-raising powers. The regions cannot, in fact, collect excise duties or adopt provisions that hinder the circulation of goods from region to region; moreover, regional financial policies must correspond to those of the central government. The regions were conceded revenue from two sources: (1) regional taxes, specifically public land and property; and (2) quotas on regional yields of national taxes which supply a common fund (*fondo comune*) with complex rules for distribution among the regions, with the object of attenuating the existing disparity between them. It is readily apparent, however, that this apportionment was not very generous if we bear in mind that regional taxes, which alone can be considered as the regions' 'own' resources, represent only 10 per cent of the regions' total budget; the rest is provided by the state. In addition, they do have the right to contract loans and issue their own bonds to raise investment capital.

A second and more substantial change resulted from the tax reform of 1973 which suppressed most of the existing local taxes and replaced them with government grants in proportion to their lost tax revenue increased by fixed annual percentages (table 9.3). This naturally robbed subcentral government of its autonomy since its finances now depended almost exclusively on the centre in the form of subsidies. The origin of the centralizing development, which occurred with the full approval of local authorities, was the 1970s inflation and the central government's need to strengthen macro-economic policy instruments as well as to simplify the tax system. The result was reduced communal budgets and the cutting of local services. The subsidies took the form of financial transfers (*fondi di dotazione*) without any conditions over their use, which has left local administrators a fairly free hand. The central government had the powers and means to coordinate local policies, and indeed a new local finance system based on renewed but limited local taxing capacity was expected in 1978. However, law 43/78 merely extended the transitory regime inroduced by the tax reform which is still the operative basis of the system today (Fraschini, 1992). Further constraints on local budgets (on spending, on hiring personnel and on revenue, making compulsory increases in certain taxes and fees) were added in the 1980s in an attempt to keep current budget deficits under control. The problem still awaits a solution in a specific local finance and tax bill provided for in the *Ordinamento* (law 142/1990).

To conclude this review of subcentral government in Italy, two further aspects need to be mentioned. The first concerns the role of the prefect and the government commissioner. As in France – indeed, before in time – there was an important reduction in the prefects' power which was accelerated by the regional reform. They lost their role as controllers of local government, but have conserved certain general functions, like the collection of political intelligence and the right to order inspections in cases of suspected mismanagement or irregular administration of local authorities. In 1981, they were given responsibility for civil defence and public order as well as for the coordination of the activities of provincial and communal public agencies, through a technical and legal advisory service. The prefect is now part of the ministerial field services, but he is not responsible for coordinating them as is his French colleague. The existence of regional, provincial and communal offices in the same locality often leads to duplication and confusion of responsibilities and activities, a characteristic feature of the Italian administration.

The second aspect is the creation of a series of intermediate or *ad hoc* agencies for supplying certain local services on an intercommunal basis. Examples include the consortium (*consorzio*), like the highland community (*comunità montana*), set up in 1971 to deal with the specific problems of mountain communes; the area (*comprensorio*), now dissolved, created by the regions as an intermediary administration for economic planning and development between itself and the communes, but which failed through lack of cooperation; and the local agency (*unità locali*), like the USL (*unità socio-sanitarie locali*, local health authorities) which were established in 1978 to manage the national health service. The USL regroup a certain number of small communes or big-city urban districts and are administered by party nominees appointed by the communes. However, they have faced considerable difficulty in becoming established, above all as a result of the voracious appetite for political patronage and consequent cost spiral which the central government has great difficulty in containing, much less reducing.

The structure of subcentral government and its articulation in Italy are complex: the existence of an extended network of autonomous subcentral authorities suggests a widespread decentralization at all tiers. However, they have had to live with a number of informal elements, like party organization and the nature of the provincial political elite, which have considerably reduced the real autonomy of subcentral government as well as its efficiency. It is the latter that the recent reforms are seeking to redress.

The provincial political elite

The inclusion of subcentral authorities in the representative democratic system poses a number of questions about the provincial political elite:

its features, its representativeness and whether it forms a distinct elite or not, separate from and in competition with the national political elite. A banal aspect, but one not without significance, is the fact that the number of local politicians varies enormously from state to state. This is due to the great disparity of elected subcentral offices in the four states. Thus it is no surprise to discover that communal councillors in France are half a million (509,278), whereas in Britain they are less than 25,000. In Italy and West Germany, they number around 150,000.[24] However, these differences mean that in the countries where the number of councillors is particularly large, some groups are more important than others: the mayors of the small communes in France, for example, in relation to the communal councillors, or the mayors of communes with over 30,000 inhabitants in relation to small commune mayors. In the countries where the number of councillors is not very great – Britain, in the present instance – such differences are obviously less important.

The local politicians: a collective profile

Despite these differences, the sociological profiles of local councillors are, all things considered, remarkably similar, in the sense that they can be described as predominantly male, middle-aged, middle class and usually well educated (table 9.5). In other words, the liberal professions, public and private executives and the tertiary sector are overrepresented, while manual workers, lower white-collars and, to a lesser extent, farmers are underrepresented. They are profiles which, at first sight, recall those of MPs[25] and other elite political actors. It is further proof, if it were necessary, that politics is a middle class activity because political skills are middle class skills.

There are, nevertheless, a number of aspects of the provincial political elite which are worth highlighting. The first concerns the social representativeness in the different countries: the smaller the population of the local authority, the more representative of the population are the councillors. There are no data for the 500,000 French communal councillors, but the profile of the 36,000 mayors, of which 37 per cent are still today peasant farmers, is sufficiently representative. To be convinced, we need only compare these data with the profiles of the 8000 Italian mayors or the 6000 German *Bürgermeister*. The counterfactual is that the greater the authority's population, the greater middle and upper class domination. In this regard, it is sufficient to compare the data for the departmental councillors and those of communes of over 30,000 inhabitants in France or the communal councillors of the provincial capitals in Italy. Moreover, it is no accident that the German *Land* MPs (*Mitglied des Landtages*) resemble the MPs in the Bundestag more than they do the district and communal councillors.

Table 9.5 Selected characteristics of local councillors, 1960s/1970s and 1980s (per cent)

	Britain		France			Germany	Italy		
	County/district councillors		Dept councillors	Mayors			Communal councillors		Mayors
	1960s	1980s	1980s	1970s	1980s		1970s	1980s	1980s
Gender	%	%	%	%	%	%	%	%	%
men	88	81	95	98	96	nd	98	95	97
women	12	19	5	2	4	—	2	5	3
Occupation									
Liberal professions and business	29	28	28	10	7	nd	10	12	17
Salaried middle class	22	18	35	17	19	—	26	44	57
Self-employed	18	5	13	56	34	—	35	17	8
(of which farmers)	(4)	(1)	(11)	(45)	(29)	—	(22)	(6)	(3)
Manual workers	21	8	2	2	4	—	20	12	3
Pensioners	10	25	17	11 ⎤	10	— ⎤	9	6 ⎤	4
Others	0	14	5	3 ⎦		— ⎦		4 ⎦	
Age									
Under 45 yrs	19	26	—	—	23	nd	55	65	53
45–60 yrs	45	38	—	—	45	—	35	28	36
Over 60 yrs	36	36	—	—	32	—	10	7	11
Education									
University graduate	21	22	—	—	8	nd	12	20	30
Secondary school	46	48	—	—	32	—	38	52	58
Councillors (number)	(3.970)[a]	(1.557)[a]	(3.801)	(36.570)	(36.394)	nd	(143.522)	(150.596)	(8.049)

[a] = sample; nd = no data
Sources: various

The second aspect regards the systematic underrepresentation of manual workers and lower white-collars, and this independently of the population of the local authority. It is true that left-wing parties have traditionally striven to promote the representation of the lower classes, systematically presenting workers as candidates. In any case, participation as elected councillors in the activities of their authority is objectively difficult (times of meetings) for full-time workers and clerks, particularly in the private sector. For the same reason, the proportion of pensioners among local councillors in Britain and France is relatively high: they, at least, have the time available, which the workers lack. The left-wing parties' commitment to be represented, if possible, by persons of modest social origin has meant that the lower classes are represented to some extent on local councils, above all in urban areas. In fact, there is a certain difference of partisan representation – more middle and upper class on the right and more middle and lower class on the left – which relates to type of authority. The result is that where the left is strong, usually in urban areas, the authorities tend to be politicized; and where the right is strong, usually rural zones, the authorities tend to be depoliticized.

The third aspect concerns the changes in local representation over time: (1) in the longer period (the last 100 years); and (2) in the shorter period (since the war). In the longer period, there has been a progressive replacement of local notables (often large landowners and local manufacturers) with professional politicians (often of lower middle and working class origin). In the shorter period, there has been a decline in the representation of agriculture (and even industry) and their replacement by the new tertiary professionals (teachers, social workers and public servants). In this connection, we may recall an old English political polemic to justify local government reform on the grounds of the decline in quality of local councillors. It is argued that local government no longer attracts the high-quality candidates of yesteryear,[26] because the big industrialists and other, not well-defined, men of quality are not prepared to stand for local office any more. The remedy proposed is to reduce the number of elected local councils and increase their size and, in consequence, their political importance with the express intention of attracting this kind of candidate. Behind this polemic, however, lies an attack on the democratization of local government and the representation of the lower classes, and through them of the Labour Party. The reform did not, in fact, hit the local representation of the Labour Party too hard, thanks to its implantation in urban areas; the objective was attained instead in 1986 with the suppression, as mentioned, of the six metropolitan counties and the GLC. The 1995 reform proposes to reduce the number of councils further and, in all probability, lower class representation.

The fourth aspect touches the councillors themselves in the sense that it refers to certain distinctions among them. We have already mentioned differences in the representativeness of the provincial political elite in the four states due to differences in the number of councillors. Now we need to turn to another difference, resulting this time from the different political roles of ordinary councillors and leading members: mayors, chairs,[27] group leaders. It is a distinction similar to that between back-benchers and ministers at the national level. Not only are the leading members usually older than the average councillor, with greater administrative and council experience, better educated, from more professional occupations and almost exclusively male, but they also have a rather different conception of their role that derives from a basic division of political labour. Ordinary councillors are motivated by a concern to represent their particular ward and to solve their constituents' problems and, hence, leave major policy initiatives to the leaders. For this reason, they are often apolitical and resent the intrusion of parties into local politics. The leading members, on the other hand, are primarily interested in developing their authority's policies and influencing its future strategy, and much less in individual constituents' problems. Indeed, some conceive their role on the council as a stepping-stone to a career in national politics.

Relations with national political elite

This final point leads quite naturally on to the specifically political aspect of the provincial political elite, namely its relations with the national political elite. We have already noted the strategic role of local office in the *cursus* of MPs in France, Germany and Italy (chapter 7). Indeed, local councils have been called 'recruitment agencies' for the national elite in these states. Mabileau (1985) has proposed three distinct schemata to define the relations between local and national political elites, which contribute to understanding the situation in the various countries: (1) a horizontal schema, characterized by a rigid separation between provincial and national political elites; (2) a pyramidal schema, where the national political elite is recruited from the higher posts in the political hierarchy, whether it be party, groups or business, as well as subcentral government; and (3) a vertical schema, defined by the succession and/or accumulation of local and national elected offices and an ascending political *cursus*.

The first schema – the horizontal – describes the British situation. Britain is the European country where the separation between provincial and national political elites is the most distinct. British MPs, in fact, have rarely been elected local councillors (only 30 per cent) and are usually not interested in local politics, considered to be 'low politics'. Moreover, as Sharpe (1979) has observed, 'it is true that from time to time local leaders do emerge on to the national stage but they are very rare and their ascendancy is entirely due to personal circumstances' (p. 48). The reasons are twofold: (1) in British local authorities there is an absence of an executive office like the mayor or regional/provincial president in France and Italy and, hence, a lack of an institutionalized leadership at local level; and (2) the number of MPs who have held local office is traditionally small and dual office-holding is frowned upon.[28] Indeed, it is claimed that the ties which Herbert Morrison, home secretary in the 1945 Attlee government, maintained with the old London County Council cost him the leadership of the Labour Party because he was accused of being a Tammany Hall style boss. The election to the House of Commons of local politicians like Ken Livingstone, leader of the former GLC 1981–6, and David Blunkett, leader of Sheffield City Council 1980–7, raises the question as to whether they represent a new political elite – the new urban left – for whom local politics is part of 'high politics', or whether they are exceptions that confirm the traditional rule referred to by Sharpe. At all events, the consequence remains the same: 'local government has few friends at the court of Westminster.'

The second schema – the pyramidal – applies, according to Mabileau, to the US, but can also to Germany. If the majority of federal MPs began their political careers in local government, it is above all the mayoralty of a big city or the presidency of a *Land* which opens the door to federal leadership. For instance, three of the last five chancellors (Kiesinger, Brandt and Kohl) had been leaders of their respective *Land* before becoming federal leader. Moreover, Johannes Rau and Oscar Lafontaine (SPD candidate-chancellors at the 1987 and 1990 federal elections) were both *Ministerpräsident* of their respective *Land* on their adoption as leaders of the SPD. In this connection, the ties between federal and *Länder* political elites are sufficiently strong for the two main parties (CDU and SPD) not to hesitate to send a prestigious national politician from Bonn to lead their lists in a *Land* where their power is electorally threatened. Finally, while it is true that members of the Bundestag do not combine local and national office, it is worth remembering, nonetheless, that the members of the Bundesrat are all *Land* ministers.

The third schema – the vertical – represents the French and Italian situations, characterized by close ties between the two political elites. Not only do political careers in both countries begin with local office, but it is an ascending *cursus*, from minor posts to more important ones, so that the 'best' accede by stages to the top. In fact, over 75 per cent of Italian MPs and 90 per cent of French MPs hold, or have held, subcentral office. There are, however, differences between the situations in Italy and France. In Italy, for instance, the key to political career, whether local or national, has lain in the party apparatuses. They decided candidatures and thus whether a person should continue in local office or accede to parliament. For this reason, party office has been just as important in the political *cursus* as subcentral office. Moreover, it was just because of the party control of political careers that the incompatibility between holding certain subcentral offices – big-city mayor or regional councillor – and a seat in parliament was introduced in the 1960s. The intention was to prevent the accumulation of elected offices, which benefited certain ambitious politicians, and so secure a wider distribution of the important political offices.

In France, instead, where parties are less strong, local office is itself the key to a political career and, at least until the law 85-1405, the plurality of local and national elected offices (*cumul des mandats*) was the rule. It has been calculated that the National Assembly elected in May 1988 counted 262 mayors, 63 *adjoints*, 279 departmental councillors and 141 regional councillors (Knapp, 1991, p. 20). If more than 85 per cent of French MPs held at least one office, 52 per cent held two. Moreover, 137 MPs relinquished 142 elected local offices for reasons of incompatibility. A local office has not been an absolutely essential stage in every political *cursus*, in the sense that it has become fashionable for ministers, directly recruited from the higher civil service – a novelty of the Fifth Republic – to be 'parachuted' into provincial constituencies for parliamentary elections; however, if these former civil servants wish to continue a political career and secure control of the parliamentary seat won in this way, they are obliged to build a local power base by seeking subcentral office. Hence, the ties between provincial and national political elites are extremely close.

The implications of the ties between the two political elites has been spelled out by Mabileau in commenting on his three schemata:

> the integration of a part of the local elites in the national elite facilitates communication between centre and periphery. This contributes to the system's stability, ensuring a community of ruling elites. But it also accentuates resistance to change because of the common interest of the two elites in conserving the structures and networks of relations that determine their hold on power. (pp. 581–2)

To conclude this analysis of the provincial political elite, political factors are more important than sociological, if only because they allow a clear distinction to be made between Britain, with its rigid separation between provincial and national political elites, and France, Germany and Italy, with their different levels of interpenetration between the two political elites. In saying this, it is worth noting a trend – just visible in Italy, but not yet in France – towards a greater differentiation in the subcentral political elites. In other words, some Italian big-city mayors and regional councillors – the so-called *partito degli amministratori* – no longer consider local office as a stage in a political career whose goal is to become an MP, but as worthwhile in itself. The Italian parties had hitherto controlled candidatures and decided local alliances, almost always in terms of national strategy. However, the recent changes in the local electoral system, together with the crisis of the traditional parties, are likely to accentuate such a trend. Certainly, this is the interpretation of the outcome of the first local elections held under the new communal electoral regime in summer and autumn 1993.

Subcentral power

It was a widely held view until recently that subcentral authorities had no effective power; and where it was not a pure fiction it was a residual power. The basis of this view was a formal conception of the state in which subcentral government was subordinate to central power; that is to say it consisted of instrumental agencies carrying out the will of the centre. Edmund Dell (former Labour minister) echoed this particularly, but not totally, English sentiment when he declared dismissively that: 'the municipality is simply the administrative office of central government'. However, there were other, more solid, reasons for denying that subcentral government has any autonomous power of its own: (1) the ever-increasing financial dependence on central funds; (2) the 'rhetoric of *apoliticisme*' – to use Kesselman's (1967) felicitous phrase – cultivated by many local politicians; and (3) the citizens' general demand to receive equal treatment over the whole national territory which only the centre is capable of securing.

The first reason is based on too literal an interpretation of the popular adage that 'He who pays the piper calls the tune.' In fact, of course, the central government is often constrained to furnish funds to subcentral authorities over which it has no effective control, either because they are granted unconditionally or because of inadequate instruments of financial control. One of the reasons for decreasing the number of local government units is to facilitate central control.[29] In the case of the rhetoric of *apoliticisme*, instead, political parties have always taken an interest in local elections since local government was democratized in the last century. They reasoned that what was at stake was sufficiently important politically to justify their commitment. Subcentral authorities have always furnished some local services and control of them was always in the hands of local administrators. Since the local authorities were the representative institutions closest to the grass roots, control of them naturally gave rise to an identification: services, policies, politicians, politics. In other words, local government became, just because of its closeness to the ordinary citizen, the site of the formation of political consensus, in the sense that the citizen's perception of the local action of a party contributed to its political standing as a national party. Certainly, this was the reasoning that lay behind the strategies of the socialist parties (municipal socialism of the turn of the century) and the communist parties (PCF's and PCI's post-war municipal communism). At all events, the control of subcentral government has become more important with the development of the Keynesian welfare state since central governments have been obliged to decentralize the administration of many of the new services into its hands – and so the distribution of the benefits – just because it was nearer to the individual citizen. In this connection, *apoliticisme* and its concomitant, the hostility towards the politicization of local government, were often nothing less than the reaction of the dominant classes to the loss of their local power. This is the proof that local power counts, but prefers to remain hidden for that very reason.

Finally, the concept of citizens' equal treatment was an argument in the hands of the centre that could be used to justify direct intervention in local affairs as well as the refusal of greater local autonomy. It is one which the central governments of Western European states have not hesitated to use, as the Thatcher government's decision to fix a uniform business rate throughout Britain in 1988 illustrates. Similar arguments were deployed by the Italian constitutional court in the 1960s to uphold restrictive interpretations of local autonomy.

However, in the 1970s local power came to be recognized as a real, if limited, power. Paradoxically, it was in France that, partly as a result of the massive urbanization (*l'explosion urbaine*) of the 1960s and 1970s, a specific analytical perspective of a structural neo-Marxist orientation was developed under Althusser's influence. This was the 'collective consumption theory of urban politics' elaborated by Castells (1972) and his school, in which urban (and local) politics had a specificity in capitalist society that derived from its function of furnishing social consumption: social services, education, housing. And this was because the spatial articulation of capitalist development occurred in such a way that international and national production was organized in individual firms that were concentrated in urban areas and, hence, these became the key sites of the class struggle. Since private firms were unable to supply the collective services necessary for the reproduction of the labour force, the state was obliged to assume the burden or risk the breakdown of social cohesion. Initially, Castells claimed that state activity in the urban field was functional to the needs of capitalist development and was dictated almost exclusively by economic factors (to wit the rate of profit). Later, he modified his approach, placing more emphasis on the social aspect – the class struggle – in the sense that, in his view, the concentration of production and social consumption in urban areas made them the site of systematic contradictions and so of potential anti-capitalist protest. This was even more the case because the public provision of social services necessarily politicizes them. For Castells, therefore, the study of urban politics comprised two principal sectors: urban planning, that is to say state intervention in the urban system; and urban conflict and protest movements.

In keeping with their structural neo-Marxist inspiration, Castells and his school explained urban politics in terms of the dominant logic of capitalism, that is to say in terms of class domination. However, they were obliged to recognize that urban politics had a certain autonomy of its own that was originally presented as an aspect of Poulantzas's conception of the 'relative autonomy of the state'. Subsequently, they introduced concepts like 'local political apparatuses', 'municipal politics' and 'communal institutions', which comprised the 'local political stage'. The last was defined as the site of 'the expression of class and class fraction interests at the urban level', and created an area of uncertainty where class interests were not immediately determined by the economic system, but were mediated by the central and subcentral state apparatuses. They were 'sites of negotiation' in which decentralized class power was able to assert itself against the economic logic of the central state system.

This analytical perspective has been rightly criticized not only for some of its rather rigid Marxist assumptions – which are not amenable to empirical analysis, like the ill-defined concept of 'monopoly capital' – but also for its own concepts and particularly for the fundamental one of 'collective consumption' which is, amongst other things, exceedingly elastic as to its specific nature and content. Nevertheless, interest in this approach to urban politics is twofold. Firstly, its use of the concept of the 'local', as Mabileau (1985) has observed, has had:

> the indisputable merit of revalorizing economic factors and social processes derived from a general social theory. Local government is not reduced to administrative and political mechanisms; it is analysed in the context of economic strategies and social conflicts. This is a dimension that other kinds of analyses reject on the grounds of the autonomy of the political and the neutrality of the state. (p. 572)

Secondly, it is the origin of the dual-politics thesis – or dual-state thesis formulated by Cawson (1986) and Saunders (1986) (chapter 6) – in which the needs of production are located in political processes at the central (national/international) level, and those of social consumption at the subcentral (local) level. This implies different modes of interest intermediation and the promotion of different value systems: market and private property at the centre; collectivism, citizen rights and social welfare at the periphery. The dual-politics thesis has been helpful in understanding how the efforts of some European governments, and notably the British, to control the financial power of subcentral government are part of a larger, more general, strategy of subordinating social goals to the economic, so as to increase rates of profit. However, this thesis is open to the same criticism as Castells's model of urban politics, namely the problem of an acceptable definition of 'social consumption' and the ambiguity inherent in classifying public expenditure in this regard.

On the basis of this discussion, it is clear that the notion of subcentral politics remains largely problematic. In the first place it is evident, for example, that in uniform institutional frameworks, like those of France and Italy, there are great differences in the power of a mayor of a big city and that of a tiny commune because of the differences of resources –

financial, technical – available to the former and denied to the latter, who are thus often limited in their ability to take effective action. Secondly, there is also a difference that derives from the diversity of institutional frameworks of the various subcentral government units, whether between countries or between authorities in the same country. Thus it is as much an error to undervalue the legal powers regulating subcentral government as to overvalue them as the sole source of power, which the institutional tradition has tended to do.

At all events, there appear to be three elements that help towards defining the nature of subcentral power. The first is what has been called 'peripheral power' and refers to the power or political influence that the provincial political elite can exercise on the basis of its social power and which the national political elite has to take into account. This is, for instance, the so-called 'notable's power', represented by the *député-maire* in France. The second refers to the so-called 'network power', namely that of all the political actors (elected and appointed) who count in subcentral political decisions: for instance, the policy communities and policy networks (chapter 8) which are particularly significant in Britain and Germany. The problem in subcentral politics is also one of access because the complex of policy communities and networks constitutes the core of subcentral as well as central power. The third is electoral mobilization: here different elements enter into play, such as the frequency of local elections, turnout at elections (table 9.6), and so on. Nonetheless, electoral mobilization promoted by local politicians can, if successful, lead to a counter-power. This was the case, to some extent, in the conflict that opposed certain Labour-controlled municipalities (GLC, Liverpool, Sheffield and certain London boroughs) to the Thatcher government in the 1980s. But it was significantly undermined by the traditional low turnout in British local elections, which made it easier for the centre to prevail in the short term, but only at the expense of raising with a vengeance, yet again, a more fundamental problem: the role of subcentral government.

In conclusion, it remains to repeat that the policy process at the subcentral level follows substantially the same sequences as the central policy process and faces many of the same problems. In fact, in many sectors, it is an integral part of the central policy process. The two decisive phases are those of decision and implementation. In the case of

Table 9.6 Turnout in local government elections, 1980s (per cent)

	Min.–max.	Average
Britain (district)	20–60	40
France (*commune*)	65–75	70
Germany (*Kreis, Gemeinde*)	50–90	70
Italy (*comune*)	80–90	85

Source: Widdicombe Report, 1986, research vol. IV (Cmnd 9801), p. 146

decision this is due to the fact that the constraints on political action are numerous and severe: financial, legal, technical. As regards implementation, subcentral authorities are usually considered policy implementing and *not* policy conceiving agencies. This situation is particularly acute in Britain because, as noted, many central departments lack field services for policy implementation and have had to rely on local government. It is also the case of Germany, as noted above, as a result of the state's federal structure, and which the application of the *Politikverflechtung* principle was intended to overcome.

In France and Italy, despite more formally centralized subcentral government systems, practice may not be, after all, that different from Britain, if not Germany. Some evidence for this suggestion has come in the form of a comparative statistical study of urban policy in the four states (Aiken et al., 1987), which showed that only in England and Wales was there a significant correlation between party control and policy output measured in terms of social service expenditure. In the other countries, the correlations were not significant or negative. But Hoggart (1987) has cast methodological doubts on the validity of the significant correlations for the English and Welsh towns. Hence, the conclusions of a comparative study of Birmingham and Lyons, based on a qualititive analysis, bear quoting:

> In each case an overall balance of political power between primarily national and primarily local institutions produced a situation in which, despite the central authorities' ultimate dominance and long-run ability to direct the flow of urban decisions, provincial resistance to external control and sensitivity to local political pressures is never entirely stifled or overwhelmed. French central agencies enjoyed a variety of administrative, financial and political means for making things happen in provincial cities, but Lyonnais authorities extracted considerable autonomy by deflecting, resisting, and subverting those interventions. British ministries supervise local authorities closely to be certain that precisely drawn laws and regulations are respected, but within those legal restrictions Birmingham's officials relied upon their legal judgement and political will to determine the amount, timing and substance of local actions ... The surprising finding is that despite rather high levels of central intervention ... in both countries, substantial policy differences in implementation resulted from the different ways in which intervention occurred. The difference between Britain and France is less some aggregate level of centralization or amount of intervention in the entire system and more the number and variety of political organizations at both levels that take an active part in designing and implementing urban renewal projects. (Webman, 1980, pp. 143–4)

Between centre and periphery

The terms 'centre' and 'periphery' are intended to take account of the relations between central and subcentral, national and local, politics, but they are imprecise conceptions. It is never clear what is intended to be included or excluded in a particular case. Nevertheless, as regards the constitutional relationship between the two, we are dealing with an asymmetrical, even if ambiguous, relationship. The centre in the form of the national government has the constitutional and financial power to determine public policy; in consequence, we are obliged to talk of residual power as regards local or subcentral government. But – and this is the reverse side of the coin – it is by no means certain that the centre can use its undoubted power (or more exactly, its use has often heavy costs and great risks for central government); hence, it is more proper to talk of 'interdependence'. Interdependence, however, is not equality; indeed, it is compatible with a large dose of inequality. It means only the absence of total dependency. In the case of subcentral government in West European states, it means two things: (1) elected subcentral authorities have certain political resources which the centre has to take into account; and, in consequence, (2) the relation is one that can be defined as 'politico-administrative mediation'.

Indeed, terms like 'centre' and 'periphery' suggest a much simpler relationship than actually exists in the four countries. For instance, 'centre' points to a single source of national power with a single national goal, and 'periphery' to a plurality of more or less equal subcentral authorities. However, the state in Western Europe is formed of a multiplicity of central institutions (ministerial departments and public agencies of various kinds) that rarely, if ever, speak with one voice. Often, in fact, what seems at first sight a conflict between centre and periphery turns out, in reality, to be a conflict between two instances of the central state, one of which has succeeded in mobilizing subcentral authorities to its cause. On the other hand, a similar situation can occur at the periphery, as there are, in the four states, a differentiated complex of elected subcentral authorities – regions, provinces, districts, communes – to which must be added a whole series of non-elected local public bodies. All of this is a way of saying that the state at the periphery is very differentiated and so relations with the centre are naturally complex. This is without taking into account the organization of civil society – parties, movements, groups, associations – in the provinces which comprise as many other elements that cannot be ignored. Centre–periphery relations are therefore complex, made up of cooperation, complicity, conflict and – why not? – confusion.

The problem of the relationship, seen from the centre, can be summarized in the question of how to conciliate legitimacy with efficient execution of public policies. And this is because, on the one hand, if legitimacy comes from elections, in representative democracies these are always organized on a territorial basis; and, on the other, the development of the Keynesian welfare state has been accompanied by the substantial transfer of policy implementation, above all in the social services, to local authorities, as closer to the citizenry. The problem of locality is not an abstract problem: citizen perceptions of public policy have always had very concrete socio-political consequences. 'How central governments and their territorial subunits are linked politically', Tarrow (1978, pp. 1–2) has noted, 'is not only a problem of intergovernmental relations, but also one of managing the class and interest conflicts of modern societies.' It is true that the organization of political mass movements around provincial objectives is hazardous – only the Sudtiröler Volkspartei in the south Tyrol, perhaps the CSU in Bavaria, and more recently the Italian *leghe* [30] can be said to have succeeded in the enterprise – but it is just as true that certain functional groups, like the working class or the peasantry, have been organized on a territorial basis. This is a fact, above all in the case of the working class, that right-wing governments have always been very careful to take into account: the abolition of the GLC and the metropolitan counties by the Thatcher government in Britain in 1986, for instance, was due to a wish to deny the Labour Party, and the new strata that it represented (new urban left), this institutionalized channel of political expression.

As regards the transfer of new administrative responsibilities to the periphery, we must bear in mind the general economic context. During the *trente glorieuses*, national governments were quite happy to decentralize social service provision to local authorities and fund their provision. After all, the growth of national wealth increased with the rise in service provision. In the 1970s, however, with the 'inflation explosion', national governments discovered the 'fiscal crisis' and began to worry about the problem of public expenditure, and subcentral government finance in particular. If, as Sharpe (1981) has noted, the problem was provoked almost exclusively by inflation, it was nonetheless worsened by the growth of local public expenditure and the rigidity, in terms of revenue, of local tax structures. At the same time, however, because the expansion of public services was an initiative of the centre, it claimed the right to intervene to fix the level of service provision. In other words, it had maintained control through central funding.

In general, Western European states have preferred to leave service provision in subcentral government hands, and limit the centre's intervention to reducing its financial contribution: thus obliging the local authorities to make the difficult choice of cutting services and supporting the consequences in terms of political unpopularity! Not surprisingly, therefore, this strategy of offloading responsibilities and functions to the periphery has had negative consequences: either an agreement is negotiated,[31] but at the price of often substantial changes in proposed government policies; or the central government imposes its policies unilaterally, provoking a confrontation with subcentral government, a fact which multiplies the unintended consequences of the policies. The latter are the more likely, the more the welfare state has strengthened (where it has not itself created) powerful client groups in this or that sector: doctors, para-medics in health; teachers in education; social workers in welfare.

At all events, it does appear that the links between centre and periphery are conditioned by forms of politico-administrative mediation specific to each country. This is the result of a combination of two factors: political structures, both formal and informal, on the one side; and national traditions on the other. Thus, for instance, in countries like Britain and Germany where the central administration is largely non-executant, policy communities and policy networks become the basic instruments in the hands of the centre for influencing the implementation of national policies in the provinces and at the local level. In consequence, the centre has every incentive to construct them. On the contrary, in the countries with a central implementation capability through their own field services, like France and Italy, policy communities and policy networks are less important. In fact, in contrast to the previous situation, the centre is able to provide the periphery directly with the services desired by it. Moreover, as regards political integration, there is a significant contrast, noted above, between the isolation of national and provincial political elites in Britain and their interpenetration on the continent.

European union

We may also note that the EU has introduced a new element into the centre–periphery equation: the so-called 'triangular relationship' of Europe, state and region. It has taken time to develop and varies in importance across the EU. The European Regional Development Fund (ERDF) was set up in 1975, but national governments kept a tight control over it, applying the 'non-additional' rule under which EC contributions were regarded as reimbursement for national funding on the projects selected. The Commission tried to gain control over it and make it the instrument of a genuine regional policy, and has had the support of regional governments and interest groups in this. However, the complexity of the administrative problems involved and the smallness of the EU bureaucracy made direct administration impossible. Moreover, regional funds are small in relation to the overall EU budget, although they are planned to triple as a consequence of the SEA and the Maastricht Treaty.

Nonetheless, things have recently begun to stir: the EU and the regions have strengthened their power in some states and institutional linkages have begun to emerge. The regional policy directorate of the Commission and subcentral authorities have promoted contacts and exchange to improve their information flow. Thus several regional and local governments have sought direct links with the EU, opening offices in Brussels. Despite the opposition of national governments, the practice has spread and includes all the German *Länder*, six French regions and two departments, various Italian regions and four British local authorities. The main purpose of such offices is to monitor developments in the Commission so as to put pressure on national governments to respond. The EP, in its struggle to expand its influence against national governments and the Commission, has been a natural ally of the regional governments pressing for more recognition in the EU policy process. This has led to the recognition of the formal right to consultation and the establishment in 1988 of the Consultative Council of Regional and Local Authorities: the Maastricht Treaty provides, in fact, for a stronger, but still consultative, council of regions.

Developments, as indicated, vary widely across the EU. In Britain, where there are no autonomous governments for the peripheral nations of Scotland and Wales, the latter are represented by the respective government departments: Scottish and Welsh Offices. This means that although they may, as part of the national administration, be able to influence the British negotiating position on EU matters, there is the suspicion, particularly under Conservative governments, that their interests are seen as bargaining counters to be traded off in negotiation. In France and Italy, as a result of the interpenetration of national and provincial elites, subcentral representatives often find themselves sitting in the EU institutions, thus securing a territorial input to EU policy-making. However, it is in Germany that regional participation in EU policy-making has gone the furthest. The *Länder* not only influence German EU policy through the Bundesrat, but also participate in the German delegation to various EU forums. For instance, a *Land* civil servant (*Länderbeobachter*) can attend the Council of Ministers as a non-speaking member of the German delegation as well as preparatory meetings for the Council held by the Ministry of Economic Affairs. Moreover, following the passage of the SEA, the Bundesrat's role in EU affairs was strengthened. Hence, there is little doubt that the level of German regional input to EU policy-making is quite significant.

Some people (Hill and Rhodes, 1977) see, in the enhancement of EU initiatives on behalf of the regions, the possible erosion of member state autonomy which is likely to be aided and abetted by the expansion of EU legislative competence and by the development of the single market. According to this 'Europe of the regions' scenario, the future lies with the regions which are set to become the dominant unit of government in the EU, eventually replacing the national states. However, we have to say that such an outcome is most unlikely, at least in the foreseeable future. Nonetheless, it is worth pointing out that if the EU were to pursue the federal route to a supranational polity, the most likely model is the German Federal Republic, and this for two reasons: firstly, German federalism is built on the intergovernmentalism of the Bundesrat which could form a role model for a supranational council of ministers; secondly, the Brussels bureaucracy, like that of Bonn, is small and is obliged, again like the German federal administration, to leave policy execution to national or subnational administrations.

Britain

The British subcentral government system is characterized by two structural features: the isolation of provincial political elites and the central role of policy networks. They derive from a political tradition founded on the so-called dual polity and codified in two assumptions. The first is 'leaders know best', which refers to the constitutional convention that attributes to the central government all the powers necessary to carry out its policies, and to its correlative that any action to prevent it from doing so is anti-constitutional. The solution to possible incompatibilities with the autonomy of local government was furnished historically by the dual-polity thesis: this stated that the central government dictated law and policy, and left local government to execute them. It is predicated on the widely held belief that local councillors are 'second-class politicians, arousing indifference or contempt' (Sampson, 1983, p. 223). The second assumption can also be summarized in a lapidary phrase 'best professional practice', which refers to the criteria that guide both policy formulation in the various networks and execution by local authority personnel. By means of this assumption a certain homogeneity of the local implementation of national policy is secured.[32]

However, the dual polity has been undermined in the post-war period by the 'professionalization' of services, resulting from the development of the Keynesian welfare state, and the politicization of local government. The initiative for this development came, as always, from the centre and was elaborated in a segmental way in the policy communities and networks. In the 1970s, with the intensification of economic decline, the central government could no longer ignore the consequences of its social policy. Initially the government pursued a policy of negotiation with the different local government associations (AMA, ACC, ADC), but later, coinciding with the 1970s Labour governments, it attempted to formalize negotiation in a real strategy of incorporation – by reinforcing the associations as its allies at the expense of the policy networks – conceived as a first step towards a greater control of local government expenditure. The return of the Conservatives to power in 1979 opened a third phase, which has been characterized by a veritable assault on local government services and more draconian control over finance, both expenditure and taxes, which led to the poll tax fiasco in 1990 and more reform: the council tax and a proposed further reduction in the number of authorities.

The new Conservative strategy was fuelled by the resurgence of a right-wing ideology that identified public expenditure as the cause of inflation in particular, and of the decline of the British economy in general. This resulted in rate-capping,[33] and the so-called poll tax which brought down Mrs Thatcher in 1990. The consequence of the unilateral imposition of such a strategy has been a bitter confrontation – litigation, disqualification of councillors – with certain Labour councils, which has revealed the dependence of central government on local authorities for execution and service delivery in many fields. Its solution has been to reduce local government services by a whole panoply of devices – deregulation, compulsory competitive tendering and hiving off – not to mention passing the services to private sector bodies or public agencies *not* locally democratically accountable, like the inner-city development corporations, and, finally, the abolition of the Labour-controlled GLC and metropolitan counties.

For the rest, the logical result of confrontation has been a continual flight from reality: the centre has continually given itself greater powers in relation to local government, but these have not shown themselves to be an adequate substitute for a proper strategy aimed at gaining the confidence of subcentral government. On the contrary, it has generated suspicion and uncertainty, not to speak of unintended consequences. Hence, the Major government's final throw: yet another local government reform with the promise this time of the introduction of a single-tier system for the whole country. Not surprisingly, Rhodes (1988), author of the major study of centre–periphery relations in Britain in the 1980s, concluded that 'the phrase "policy mess" encapsulates the period more accurately than "centralization"', as a result of abandoning the 'dual polity operating code, and its associated strategies, for "a command code"' (p. 396), and predicted that the disparity between the political intentions of the centre and its actual achievements can only grow. This has certainly proved to be the case in the early 1990s.

Germany

German subcentral government belongs to a different tradition. Indeed, some claim that it is incorrect to talk of centre–periphery relations in the Federal Republic, if only because its spatial structure is that of a plurality of centres, rather than a centre and a periphery. On the other hand, however, despite the fact that the state has a federal structure, the federal government's leadership is accepted in the policy formulation of subcentral authorities more readily than in most federal states.[34] In this connection there is much talk of 'cooperative federalism', and this points up the interpenetration of all tiers of government. The key word, however, is *Politikverflechtung*, which is founded on two elements: (1) the sharing of political tasks (from initiation to implementation); and (2) a tradition of conflict avoidance. They are the two sides of the same coin, that is to say the search for consensus is made necessary, if not promoted, by the political involvement of the main tiers of government and administration. The veto power that they have at different moments of the policy process has made cooperation between *Bund* and *Länder* obligatory, if serious political crises are to be avoided. Two structural elements combine to facilitate collaboration between the various tiers of government: one is the development of policy networks which provide a way of overcoming conflict by breaking problems down into their constituent parts; and the other is the interpenetration of politico-administrative elites, both federal and territorial.

There appear to have been two critical moments in the relations between the federal and subcentral governments in the post-war period: the late 1960s, and the 1980s and early 1990s. The first was linked to the economic recession of 1966 – the first since World War II – and had important political consequences: the formation of the Grosse Koalition. As regards subcentral government, but not the *Länder*, it hit local government finances very hard because local authorities were dependent on the local business tax for revenue. Further, as in most other West European states, two-thirds of public investments were made by local authorities, and hence they were doubly tied to the national economy. This situation posed intergovernmental coordination in a new light. To try and resolve it, an extended process of vertical coordination between governmental institutions in all tiers was introduced side by side with the lateral coordination that had existed since the establishment of the Federal Republic. These consisted of economic and finance planning councils (*Konjunkturrat und Finanzplanungsrat*) which gave a push to the institutionalization of the policy networks mentioned above. At the same time, a constitutional reform was introduced, creating a new basis for intergovernmental relations with the establishment of the 'joint tasks', noted above. This phase has often been defined and criticized as a centralization phase. But that seems too strong, in the sense that even if it did undoubtedly imply restrictions on subcentral government activity, nonetheless it did not allow the federal government to impose its will. Coordination and consensus remained the basis of intergovernmental relations so that solidarity between the *Länder*, as between the local authorities (districts and communes), prevented the federal government in the first case, and the *Länder* in the second, from imposing their policies unilaterally.

In the 1980s, the situation became much more complex: the high level of consensus necessary to make the *Politikverflechtung* system work was such that it often led to a situation of stasis or political immobility. And this was at a moment of serious economic crisis and social change: the development of metropolitan zones, and new social problems like drugs. The result was a trend, observed elsewhere, for the centre to shift new problems on to the periphery without the resources to discharge them satisfactorily, thus creating violent socio-political tensions – terrorism – which provoked, in their turn, an opposition demanding radical decentralization. Behind this movement, known as 'politics from below' – which affected the national parties, or at least their leaders' speeches – there was a complex mixture, amongst which a critique of the institutions was only one, and perhaps not even the most important, aspect. For example, we need only recall the grass-roots activity of the *Bürgerinitiativen* groups and the *Grünen* in the 1970s in making the Germans aware of social and environmental problems to comprehend the new political agenda.

However, the problem posed in the 1990s, at least from the point of view of the subcentral authorities – and the cities, in particular – is whether they will be able to prevent a further centralization in the management of public services. To succeed, they will have to undertake an aggressive strategy in support of local interests capable of defeating the centre's strategy of shifting the burdens on to subcentral government, even if this is done under the mask of 'decentralization'. Certainly, the questions surrounding the appropriate agencies for service provision and the provision of an adequate financial base still have not been properly sorted out. But there can be doubts as to the political will of local authorities, given the heightened constitutional and financial tensions resulting from unification. Indeed, the evidence is that integration of the former East German *Länder* is proving disruptive: although the treaties of 1990 on German monetary, economic and social union contained detailed provisions for a common policy framework, they did not solve the problem of formulating policy at the centre. The result has been 'divided policy-making' with different policies in the two parts of Germany. For instance, the eastern *Länder* have neglected the traditional *Bund–Länder* bargaining processes as well as ignoring joint decisions of the *Länder* ministers' conference. In addition they, together with Berlin, have started to meet regularly to discuss the demands to make of the *Bund* and the western *Länder*, to which the centre acceded, but not the western *Länder*. The result of this has been increased uncertainty in national policy outcomes.[35] Nonetheless, it is widely recognized that divided policy-making is not a solution, but merely an expression of a lack of national integration. It cannot continue for too long, particularly in the wake of the 1992 single market, without substantial loss of autonomy by the *Länder*.

France and Italy

In both these states, the key to centre–periphery relations lies in the interpenetration of the tiers of government, fostered by that between central and provincial political elites. This similarity with Germany can seem paradoxical at first sight, given that the two states are unitary states, in which case we would have expected to find, as the legal norms suggest, a unilateral penetration of the periphery by the centre. But, as Tarrow (1977) has shown, the interpenetration has a historical origin in both countries in their particular experiences of building a modern state. However, the different political styles of French and Italian political elites, which strongly influence centre–periphery relations in both countries, arise from the fact that these experiences were very different, although they have a common element: 'clientelism'. In France, a strong central administration, represented by the prefecture and by the commune in the provinces, reinforced by the Napoleonic myth of the state personifying the national will, were such that the administrative system became and remained the dominant channel of political communication between centre and periphery, even if mediated by the political elites: *clientèlisme*. In Italy, instead, a weak central administration, represented only partially by the prefecture and the commune in the provinces and weakened by the lack of a national myth, was such that the political communication between centre and periphery was effectuated by extended personal relations (*clientelismo*) and its political concomitant, mediation (*trasformismo*) (chapter 3). In the former there was no space for parties – in any case, weakly organized – to establish a significant political role at the local level; while in the latter the parties, on the fall of fascism, staked out a local political space, taking over the clientelist system institutionalized under fascism.

For these reasons, it was logical that centre–periphery relations are mediated, in France, by relations between elected local politicians (mayors and presidents of departmental councils who are often MPs) and civil servants (prefects and subprefects) and supported by a *dirigiste* ideology; and, in the Italian case, by relations between party officials (locally elected politicians, MPs and faction leaders) and supported in their turn by a 'populist' ideology. All are policy brokers. The French prefect defends the interests of his department in Paris as well as that of the centre in his department. The Italian party faction leader busies himself as much with local issues as with national policy. Although the advantages of this system of centre–periphery relations are well known – a symbiosis and convergence of interests which ensure the system's stability – the disadvantages are less well known. For instance, the French system has shown itself incapable of articulating all the demands of local civil society. Thus, groups like small shopkeepers, who are unable to get their demands heard, have found no alternative to violent protest (Poujadism in the 1950s; UNICATI in the 1960s and 1970s). Further, the complicity between national and provincial, political and administrative, elites was such as to frustrate attempts at reform of the system by the centre, as the Gaullist-Giscardian experience showed.[36] It can be objected that the socialist reforms of the 1980s proves the contrary, but, while introducing a new tier, much of the content merely codified earlier departmental and communal practices.

As regards Italy, centre–periphery relations have paid the price of a generalized clientelist system – that is to say a system in which political consensus and electoral support are traded against political and administrative protection and favouritism – in widespread incoherence: not only are legal norms uncertain but also the choice of political priorities is often confused. All this makes the coordination of public policy extremely problematic, if not impossible. Dente (1985a) claims that the impact of clientelist politics on centre–periphery relations has been to strengthen the trend towards a fragmentary, departmentalized relationship, expressed principally in terms of licences, administrative measures and control, that is to further reinforce the juridical administrative tradition of special links between a specific subcentral government institution and a specific ministerial department. This explains the multiplication of sectorial agencies and unifunctional consortia observed in several regional studies (Riccamboni, 1988). It was to overcome these tendencies and to promote political stability and accountability that new regimes were introduced for communal elections (law 81/1993).

This brings us to the question of whether the regional reforms in the two states – Italy 1970, France 1982–6 – have had significant effects on centre–periphery relations. As regards France, the decentralization reforms have greatly enhanced the functions and resources of the subcentral authorities at the expense of the state field services. It is claimed that their success was due to the fact that they combined real change, but anchored to the solid structure of the provincial politico-administrative system. The key was the strong network of provincial political notables who combine national and local office ('le sacre des notables': Rondin, 1985). Indeed, Mény (1992b) claims that it is a case of 'government of notables, by notables, for notables' (p. 19). France, it should be said, whatever the legal fictions, was never in reality so centralized, or so dominated by Paris, as the stereotype painted in so many textbooks. This said, two particular changes should be mentioned, although their effects appear contradictory. The first is the limitation of the *cumul des mandats* to two important elected offices (law 85-1405), which was aimed at broadening elected political representation. It came into force for the 1988 election, but already seems to confirm an established practice: the tendency to keep elected posts in the family. Where before son succeeded father as mayor or departmental councillor on retirement, now, being obliged to give up certain offices for incompatibility, the politician has a relative elected in his stead, as former prime minister Chirac had his wife in his parliamentary constituency in the Creuse. It is also significant that where powerful politicians have been forced to give up a mandate, they have preferred to abandon the regional one. The second – a consequence of the decentralization reforms and the continuing holding of several offices together (for instance, minister and big-city mayor), despite law 85-1405 – is the increasing resort to *éminences grises*, often recruited from members of the prefectoral corps disenchanted with the loss of executive power.[37] In other words, because of the politicians' inability to devote themselves adequately to two such important posts, and the fear of the consequences, in political career terms, of the loss of the subcentral office, they constitute a personal *cabinet* to manage the latter. In this way, the director (*chef du cabinet*) of certain departmental presidents and big-city mayors becomes the effective manager of these institutions and *not* the elected politician. This is a new phenomenon in France, similar in some ways to the US city manager. Thus to the high number of civil servants elected as MPs and councillors we must now add a growing number of non-elected civil servants carrying out the political and administrative tasks of elected politicians. It is another aspect, noted and stressed by Mény (1987), of that assumption of power by civil servants which has become such a characteristic feature of the Fifth Republic.

The situation in Italy is more complex, but also more problematic. The establishment and the development of the regions has not only increased the number of relevant actors in the policy process, but also created multifaceted relations: between state, regions, provinces and communes as well as between state and communes; socio-economic and political as well as administrative. Indeed, it has created a dislocation of the centre within the political and administrative system. Power remains with the centre, but it lacks the means of imposing its will and, therefore, has to negotiate with the regions. Relations have, in fact, been mediated until recently by the parties which are centrally organized. Decisions are taken at the centre as a result of complex coalition bargaining in which the distribution of resources to the regions and regional (that is to say factional) party leaders has been an important element. Hence, performance necessarily reflected the changing balance of coalition power at the centre and the changing priorities of national government. For this reason, the regions were often used as a testing ground not only for new policy approaches but also for new coalition formulas. Not surprisingly, they are as directly affected as the national arenas are just now by the present crises of the traditional parties. Thus we can adopt Dente's (1985b) conclusion that 'the creation of the regional governments has changed the form more than the substance of the centre–local relationship' (p. 146), but with the proviso that the system is not static and the future depends as much on the outcome of the country's present political crisis as on the regions themselves. 'A trend towards more modernized administrative behaviour is certainly present': the question is 'whether it will be able to supersede the [hitherto] dominant mode of legality and politicization' (p. 146).

A last word. The trend towards decentralization has been one of the characteristics of the institutional development of Western European states in the post-war period: the *Länder* in Germany; the regions, first in Italy and then in France. Only Britain has been out of step after the failure of the Scottish and Welsh devolution referendums of 1979. In 1981, the Council of Europe adopted a charter on local self-government that sought to protect local government autonomy as the 'touchstone of democracy'. The one major European nation which has consistently refused to sign the charter is the United Kingdom. This leaves us with a bitter paradox: whereas the traditional centralized unitary states in Europe seek, in one way or another, to reverse their historic centralizing tendencies, the traditional home of 'local self-government' is well on the way to becoming the most tightly centralized and espousing all that goes with it. Indeed, the question raised on the continent is 'whether the prevailing British conception of local government now diverges too far from the European norm' (Blair, 1991, p. 57).

Conclusion

There are two conceptions of subcentral government in the territorial politics of West European states: acting either as partners or as agents of central government in furnishing services to the citizen. In the former, it is a case of democracy at the grass roots and the dangers of the concentration of power implicit in centralization. In the latter, it is a case of management and efficiency as well as equality of treatment in local service delivery. Aspects of both conceptions are found in subcentral institutional arrangements. In addition, the development of the welfare state and the concomitant expansion of public services have led to subcentral government's role growing accordingly at the same time as the complexity of the problems with which it has to deal. This explains why reform and reorganization have been so general and widespread in all states in the last 30 years.

The best-known models of territorial organization are the classic constitutional ones that oppose the federal state to the unitary state. In the federal state, there are two powers, each autonomous in its own sphere (dual state); while in the unitary state, one (central) authority is supreme, even if subordinate (subcentral) authorities may be set up. Of the four states, one (Germany) is federal and three (Britain, France and Italy) are unitary. However, German federalism does not exemplify the classic dual-state concept, since it does not consist of two separate powers, each exclusively competent in its own sphere, but is rather a mixed system in which substate (*Länder*) authorities both participate in and administer federal policies. Furthermore, France and Italy now have a level of decentralization that many consider to be incompatible with a unitary state.

In addition to the constitutional models, there are also functional models of subcentral government. For example, Smith has distinguished between what he calls fused and dual hierarchies. In the former, the central administration field services and local governmental services work in tandem, supervised by a central government official (prefect), whereas in the latter local administration is divorced from the central administration field services, thus giving rise to a system of detached (or dual) hierarchies. The central government formulates policies and subcentral authorities implement them.

The problems posed by subcentral government and their consequences for centre–local relations can be elucidated by contrasting the French historical experience of the central state penetrating the provinces and imposing its authority over them with the British experience of the development of a dual polity as a result of the central government leaving the provinces in the hands of the provincial elites so long as they recognized its ultimate supremacy. A division of labour developed between high politics, the province of central government, and low politics, the province of local government. It thrived until the institution of the welfare state transformed low politics into high politics and the central government could no longer ignore local government. In France, the introduction of local elections changed the balance of power between the centre and the provinces because most national politicians became local office-holders. The consequence was collusion between prefects and politicians in the course of which the prefect consolidated his power by distributing state resources as the politicians desired; and the politicians increased their political authority through privileged access to the central administration in Paris. It was responsible for a clientelist system that was copied in Italy and has continued more or less down to the present.

The structure of subcentral government and administration varies widely. In France, Germany and Italy it has a constitutional basis; in Britain it has not, being subject to statute and able to be abolished by a simple parliamentary vote. The number of tiers of government varies also: four in France, Germany and Italy; three in Britain, shortly to be reduced to two. Further, the number and size of subcentral units also vary widely, particularly (at the extremes) between Britain (few/large) and France (many/small). Moreover, the British and the German governments have been able to reduce the number and increase the size of local government units because of the absence of clientelist ties which have frustrated such attempts in France and Italy.

The British system of subcentral government works on the basis of government by committee. All local councils are elected and invested with decision-making authority. However, the committee system involves local government officers, who prepare the decisions, as much as local councillors, who are responsible for the decisions, in policy determination. The only official positions are the chairs of the committees which coincide with local government departments. Because the central government lacks field services, it is dependent on local government structures for local service delivery, and hence the role of local government officers – who form the professional personnel of British administration

– is of particular importance. They are the people with the professional and technical knowledge of how to get things done. Attempts at greater central control of subcentral government through constitutional subordination have been the source of serious conflict between central and local government in the 1980s, particularly in the field of local government finance. One solution at cost cutting has been the privatization of local public services leading to yet another reform of local government structure aimed at reducing the number of elected units.

The French subcentral government was reorganized in the 1980s to introduce a third elected tier: the region. All subcentral authorities are elected and in turn the councils elect an executive officer (president/mayor) who is assisted by a bureau to whom he can delegate authority, but he remains accountable. The activity of the executive is subject to approval by the council, but no longer to the tutelage of the prefect. He can only submit decisions he considers illegal to the administrative courts. The division of powers between the three kinds of subcentral government authorities is defined in terms of technical capability: planning to the region; social welfare to the department; and town planning to the commune. The law does not distinguish between the same kind of authority in terms of powers, even though they may differ enormously in size and resources. Thus small communes are obliged to call in the central administration's technical resources to provide some services. Finally, local taxes are insufficient to cover expenses, and hence the transfer of powers to subcentral government has been accompanied by a certain number of special transfers.

Federalism in Germany has made for a peculiarly complex system of subcentral government. This is because it is based on a large dose of intergovernmentalism and the consequent need for close collaboration between the federal government and the *Länder*: policy implementation is almost exclusively in the hands of the *Länder*. They have the same institutional structure as the federal government, but the sub-*Land* authorities vary according to the *Land* (some with the British committee system; others with US-style city manager; yet others with collegiate executives). The federal government, moreover, has no direct control over sub-*Land* authorities, which are in the hands of the respective *Land*. Finally, judicial review of administration is well established.

Relations between the federal government and the *Länder* are resolved by intergovernmental negotiation which has spawned a vast network of agencies and committees to provide the necessary cooperation and coordination. It was institutionalized in the late 1960s, giving rise to the *Politikverflechtung* (interlocking policy-making). In the field of subcentral government finance, the German system also differs from the classical federal model of separate sources of finance. In Germany, the federal government and the *Länder* jointly administer taxes that are distributed between the different types of authority on the basis of constitutionally backed, but revisable, percentages. They are supported by a grants system for certain services and projects and equalization techniques intended to ensure that the poorer *Länder* do not suffer too much from smaller receipts. However, unification and the consequent need for resources of the eastern *Länder* have undermined subcentral finance for the moment, despite a recent compromise (Solidarity Pact, 1993).

The structure of Italian subcentral government was modelled on the French system, although the French paid the Italians the compliment of basing their regional reform on the Italian regional system. One difference is that there is a certain hierarchical difference between the tiers in Italy that does not exist in France. The organization of the subcentral authorities was very similar to, and reproduced more or less, the institutional form of the central government, but this suffered important modifications in 1993. Today the mayor or provincial president is directly elected for a fixed mandate and is personally responsible for the activity of his authority. He can only be forced to resign on a vote of no confidence in him which is followed by immediate dissolution of the council and new elections.

The distribution of powers between subcentral authorities is determined by function: the commune has general purposes limited to its territory; the province those of an intercommunal nature; and the regions a coordinative role. Within the newly designated metropolitan areas, both communal and provincial powers will be exercised by the metropolitan city (when set up). Subcentral government finances have been subjected to numerous changes in recent years and the trend has, paradoxically, been in the opposite direction to powers, namely towards centralization rather than decentralization. This has reflected the fiscal crisis of the state in the 1970s. Today, subcentral government finance depends for over 50 per cent of its expenditure on central government subsidy that takes the form of unconditional financial transfers. The central government has the power and means to coordinate local policies, but has lacked the will to use them. Finally, as in France, the prefect lost his role as controller of local government with the introduction of the regional reform. This was given to the various local administrative courts. The prefect's role is now limited to public order and the coordination of local public agencies.

Despite the difference in the number of councillors in different states, the sociological profile of all provincial political elites resembles that of their national political elites: predominantly male, middle-aged, middle class and usually well educated. It confirms that politics is a largely middle class activity because political skills are middle class skills. As with other elites, there has been a progressive democratization in the recruitment of local representatives in the last 100 years. Thus local notables have given way to party politicians; new urban professionals in the tertiary sector have replaced rural and industrial occupations. The most significant aspect of the provincial elite is its relation to the national political elite. Once again, it highlights a distinction between Britain and the continental states: in the former, there is a clear separation between the two elites, that is local councillors are not MPs and vice versa; whereas in the latter there is interpenetration between the two, that is either local office is an important stage in the *cursus* of the aspiring politician as in Germany and Italy, or the plurality (*cumul*) of elected offices is the rule as in France. The implication is that the integration of a part of the local political elite in the national political elite facilitates communication and understanding between centre and periphery while accentuating resistance to change and vice versa. Certainly, this is one of the explanations for the differences in centre–periphery relations between Britain and her continental neighbours.

It was a widely held view until recently that subcentral authorities had no effective power in West European unitary states. This was based on the formal conception of the state in which subcentral authorities were subordinate to central power. In addition, it was reinforced by substantive arguments, such as local government's dependence on central funds as well as the citizens' general demand for equal treatment over the whole national territory that the central government was alone capable of securing. However, in the 1970s local power came to be recognized as real, if limited. Castells claimed that the urban phenomenon had a specificity in capitalist society as the site of social consumption. This gave urban, and so local, struggles an interest in their own right that could not be understood in terms of national politics alone. The merit of this type of analysis was to show that subcentral politics had dimensions other than those arising out of administrative and institutional mechanisms alone. Further, it led to the formulation of a dual-politics/dual-state thesis: the needs of production are located in national political processes, and those of consumption at the local level. They are distinct and they relate to different modes of interest intermediation: neo-corporatist at the centre; and pluralist at the periphery. Nonetheless, the notion of subcentral power remains largely problematic and seems to depend as much on circumstances as institutional frameworks, namely local situations or conflicts which the national political elite has to take into account.

Discussion of centre–periphery relations is often obscured by the imprecise nature of the two terms, since it is never clear what is included and excluded. At all events, it is constitutionally an asymmetrical relationship: the centre has the institutional and financial means to determine public policy, so subcentral power is residuary. However, it is by no means certain that the centre can use its undoubted power, or more precisely is prepared to pay the price, in terms of political unpopularity, for its use. Hence it is more appropriate to talk of interdependence, and so centre activity is best defined as politico-administrative mediation. The relationship seen from the centre is how to conciliate legitimacy with efficient execution of public policies, and this is not an abstract problem as concrete interests and perceptions are involved: national electors live in localities. In general, West European states have preferred to leave service provision in subcentral government hands, but maintain control through central funding. This has had negative consequences because the offloading of responsibilities without adequate financial provision has led to serious confrontation with local authorities or inadequate policy compromises, that have multiplied the unintended consequences of the policies. Finally, the development of the EU and the doctrine of subsidiarity have introduced a new element in the centre–periphery equation, turning it metaphorically into a triangular relationship: Europe, state and region. Some subcentral authorities have attempted to develop direct relations with the EU. However, despite the Commission's interest in a regional policy, it has made little impact as yet: regional funds have been small and national governments have refused regional representation in national policy negotiating teams.

The characteristics of the national systems point up a number of contrasts. The first is in the institutional framework between federal and unitary states (Germany in relation to Britain, France and Italy). The second is in the relations between national and provincial elites: clear separation between the two in Britain as against interpenetration of the two in France, Germany and Italy. The third is in implementation capability between those states in which the central administration is largely non-executant and lacks such capability and those in which the central administration has its own field services and so has such capability (Britain and Germany in contrast to France and Italy). The fourth is in the general trend towards institutional decentralization (Britain out of step with France, Germany and Italy). Indeed, Britain's refusal to sign the European charter on local self-government, which protects local democracy, raises the question: does the prevailing British conception of local government now diverge too far from the prevailing European norm?

Further reading

D.L. Ashford (1982), *British Dogmatism and French Pragmatism: Central–Local Policy-Making in the Welfare State* (London: Allen & Unwin).

R. Batley and G. Stoker (eds) (1991), *Local Government in Europe: Trends and Developments* (London: Macmillan).

M. Burgess (ed.) (1986), *Federalism and Federation in Western Europe* (London: Croom Helm).

J. Chandler (ed.) (1993), *Local Government in Liberal Democracies* (London: Routledge).

M.J. Goldsmith and E.E. Page (eds) (1987), *Central and Local Government Relations: A Comparative Analysis of West European Unitary States* (London: Sage).

A.B. Gunlicks (ed.) (1981), *Local Government Reform and Reorganization* (Port Washington, NY: Kennikat Press).

C. Jeffery and P. Savigar (eds) (1991), *German Federation Today* (Leicester: Leicester University Press).

Y. Mény and V. Wright (eds) (1985), *Centre–Periphery Relations in Western Europe* (London: Allen & Unwin).

R. Morgan (ed.) (1986), *Regionalism in European Politics* (London: PSI).

E.C. Page (1991), *Localism and Centralism in Europe: The Political and Legal Base of Local Self-Government* (Oxford: OUP).

R.A.W. Rhodes and V. Wright (eds) (1987), *Tensions in the Territorial Politics of Western Europe* (London: Cass).

L.J. Sharpe (ed.) (1979), *Decentralist Trends in Western Democracies* (London: Sage).

L.J. Sharpe (ed.) (1993), *The Rise of Meso Government in Europe* (London: Sage).

10 The State and Invisible Power

Introduction

In the discussion on the forms of the state (chapter 7), we drew attention to the role of military capability. The reason was simple: the state's primary purpose is to ensure its own survival and the security of its people. In a famous lecture Otto Hintze (1906) is clear: 'all state organization was originally military organization, organization for war' (p. 181). The same view is expressed in Weber's (1921) well-known definition of the state with its stress on the monopoly of the legitimate use of physical force within a given territory. These two elements – effective control at home and defence from outside threat – require military organization and capability. European state formation was, as explained, the result of a long, and often violent, process in which military capability and fiscal pressure went hand in hand. The construction of an effective military machine, which was, at the same time, the ruler's principal instrument in defining and controlling the country's frontiers, imposed a heavy tax burden on a generally reluctant population. This not unnaturally provoked fierce and lasting resistance – for instance, in the innumerable tax riots between the fourteenth and eighteenth centuries that were the principal source of conflict between rulers and ruled in this period.[1] But military power provided the ruler, at the same time, with the means to suppress popular revolt, and so close the circle.

However, military capability was relevant to the European state in a second and more fundamental sense: its survival in the international arena. And this has also had important consequences for the internal functioning of the state: justification of *raison d'état* and invisible or covert power. In effect, the European states were established and developed within a system of rival, often hostile, states for which war and peace were seen as natural, indeed structural, elements. It was no accident, therefore, that for Rousseau, as for Kant, the multiplicity of states was the principal cause of war, because for centuries war was the normal, and indeed legitimate, way of settling conflicts. On the other hand, civil wars were as numerous as wars between states. At all events, what is true of war is also true of peace, because if it is true that without states there would be no wars, it is just as true that without the state there would be no civil peace. In so far as the state effectively controls the legitimate use of force in its territory – that is succeeds in pacifying the population and becomes, as a result, a state – it secures civil peace within its frontiers. Besides, despite the abuse of this monopoly that can occur from time to time – Mafia, political terrorism – it is as nothing compared with the consequences of its erosion: the *bellum omnium contra omnes*, amply illustrated by recent events in the Balkans.

War and peace, symbolized by Aron (1962b) in the figures of the soldier and the diplomat, represent the two opposing aspects of international affairs, in which every state retains, at least theoretically, the right to visit justice on another state and be the sole arbiter of going to war or not. It is for just this reason that the international situation poses problems for the leaders of the Western democracies. This is what can be called 'two dimensionality': the fact that domestic politics is subject to constitutional restraints, while international politics, instead, is usually founded on power (*Macht*). The conclusion generally drawn is that foreign affairs are of a different nature to home affairs; and, hence, different logics are applied to the two different types of politics. It is at this point that we again encounter *raison d'état*, the basis of 'invisible power', which is to be contrasted with 'visible power': the two faces of power mentioned earlier. This duality – dual state – was inscribed in the heart of the West European state at the very moment that a legislative assembly legitimated from below was introduced into a bureaucratic state organized on the hierarchical principle, and in which the two, as a result of the international situation, have never been able to integrate into a single organism. Bobbio (1983) comments that:

> the history of the dual state can be interpreted as the resistance of the state based on power to the state based on law: at certain moments the state based on power appears as a survival of the past destined to disappear; at others it reasserts its supremacy and the state based on law is kept within the bounds in which it can still perform a useful function in a very restricted area of social life, like private law. The moments in which the state based on power reasserts its supremacy are moments of serious domestic or international crises. In general ... the state based on power is destined to survive in international affairs even in those countries where, in domestic affairs, the state based on law has already triumphed. (p. xxii)

The reason is that a state's foreign and defence policies are more likely to be successful where its real intentions are concealed. If this is the case, then it poses the student with a problem of documentation that is also a problem of method. The latter is simple: whether or not democratic formulation – that is to say with effective political control – of policy is really possible in West European states in the fields of foreign affairs and security. As regards documentation – a necessary condition for any form of political control – it is usually vitiated by official secrecy. Certain special corps, like the British MI5 and MI6, did not exist officially until the 1990s; hence they were not a proper subject for discussion (Gill, 1994). Further, other corps, like the armed forces and the police, often interpret public discussion of their activity as a hostile act.

In view of our general approach, we start from the general – foreign policy – to arrive at the specific – security – and will discuss successively the following apparatuses: the diplomatic corps, the armed forces and the secret services.

Diplomats and diplomacy

We have already referred to the international context in which the West European states were formed, namely made up of a multitude of rival states in competition among themselves. Rivalry meant conflict – conflict which the rulers attempted to dominate as much as possible by using the various methods available to them: diplomacy, political domination, international organization. The result was the so-called 'European states' system': the framework in which attempts were made to structure, by means of rules, procedures, understandings and other diplomatic expedients, the relations between states and preserve the peace. Hinsley (1963) argues that the European states' system – which still holds the world in its framework – only emerged in its mature form in the eighteenth century: 'the present-day structure of world international relations is a structure between great powers, and it has come down in unbroken descent from the days when such a structure first materialized in Europe' (p. 153). If Hinsley is right, then a brief outline of the nature and evolution of the European system is unavoidable.

The European states' system

From its inception, at the end of the Middle Ages, the European states' system has always been multipolar. Its principal feature, in fact, was the survival of a plurality of states, despite the constant rivalry and intense competition between them. The reason for this was that in the incessant diplomatic manoeuvres and frequent wars, no state, or alliance of states, was able to establish a stable domination and subordinate or eliminate all the other states. It was not that some states – Spain in the sixteenth, Austria in the seventeenth and France in the seventeenth and eighteenth centuries – did not attempt to dominate the continent, inspired by the dream of establishing a modern *res publica Christiana*. But their power was never strong enough to overcome the alliance of hostile states that their ambition inevitably provoked. Around the middle of the seventeenth century, a group of five more or less equal powers emerged which were stronger than the rest, but which realized that they were individually unable to dominate the continent politically and militarily. Hence it was necessary for them to act in concert to secure a semblance of order on the continent. For this reason, they subscribed, in the Treaties of Westphalia (1648), to the formal recognition of separate sovereignties in one society of nations and to the stipulation that the states were equal as well as independent. In this way, they created the basis of a system of public law between states (*jus gentium*), the necessary premise for a regulated form of international relations, and so diplomacy as a professional activity. The constant rivalry between states was moderated also by the recognition of belonging to a common civilization – Christian and in law – but above all by the sheer expediency of maintaining a balance of power between themselves.

The advantages of this system were driven home at the beginning of the nineteenth century by the Napoleonic adventure, which can be considered as the umpteenth attempt – Hitler's being the last to date – to reconstruct the mythical universal *res publica Christiana*, this time under French domination. At all events, there is no doubt that the European powers of the anti-Napoleonic coalition were obsessed in 1815 with re-establishing the balance of power concept; hence they gave it explicit form at the Congress of Vienna of that year. The congress system they established – besides being the first conscious attempt to find an alternative both to the old aim of one-power domination and to the spontaneous eighteenth century balance of power – can be regarded as the first example in European history of the acceptance, by the great powers, of the need to waive their individual interests in pursuit of a stable international order.

The congress system began a period of close collaboration between the great powers that lasted ten years. More significant perhaps is the fact that when the congress system proved unworkable, collaboration between the great powers was not abandoned. Indeed, the congress system was replaced by a looser, less demanding association, the so-called 'concert of Europe', which, instead of presuming to govern the world as its predecessor had, limited itself to dealing with problems as they arose, at least until 1870. Its success is attributable to two sets of reasons: (1) the lack of a preponderant great power on the continent (Britain, generally recognized as the dominant power of the period, was, in the circumstances, an external power with largely world-wide interests outside

Europe); and (2) the fear, common to all states, of encouraging revolution, in the event of military defeat.[2] The concert's objective was simple: avoid war at all costs. Thus its guiding principle was just as simple: no action that would modify the status quo was permitted. However, if the principles were simple, their application was much more difficult, particularly in a world made up of a plurality of different states, as the Crimean War (1854–6), for instance, was to demonstrate.

The international situation was radically altered in the last decades of the nineteenth century and became progressively more unstable in spite of appearances. Firstly, there was a enormous development in weapons technology and military organization – an arms race under the twin thrusts of industrialization and mass mobilization – which placed a heavy burden on the public finances of several states. Secondly, the broadening of the suffrage progressively introduced a new element into domestic politics: public opinion.[3] It was something that rulers had increasingly to take into account in formulating foreign policy. These two elements were responsible for two parallel developments: (1) the absolute growth in state power as a result of the organizational needs of ever greater efficiency; and (2) nationalistic mobilization of public opinion in support of militarism, owing to an identification of economic and political progress with the conquest of national citizenship. In addition, there was a further, more destabilizing factor for the system, namely changes in the economic and military strengths of the great powers: the decline of the Habsburg Empire, shorn of nearly all of its Italian provinces and forced to make large concessions to its Hungarian component; the instability of the Balkans resulting from the decay of the Ottoman Empire; and the birth of two new states, imperial Germany and Italy. Above all, the birth of imperial Germany in 1870[4] undermined the European states' system because it gave rise to a great power capable of imposing its domination on the continent. In 1918, and again in 1940, Germany destroyed the balance of power on which the European states' system was based. Indeed, the two world wars confirmed, with unimagined ferocity, that there was no state or alliance of states in Europe capable of checking German power.

As proof of this, we need only recall the following observations that illustrate the coordinates of the post-war situation. Firstly, only the intervention of the USA, an extra-European power, in 1917, and above all the arrival of American troops in Europe in spring 1918, prevented, *in extremis*, a German victory and ensured the Allied success some months later. Secondly, German domination of the continent was total in 1940 and Britain was incapable of turning the tide by itself. The German defeat in 1945 was secured by not one but two extra–European powers, the USA and the USSR. Thirdly, in this perspective, the treaty of Versailles of 1919, which wanted to re-create 'yesterday's world' – the European states' system as it was before 1914 – was totally artificial because it did not deal with the German problem, that is the disparity between its power and that of the other European states. At all events, the treaty was condemned from the moment that the USA refused to join the League of Nations and a humiliated and mutilated Germany regained its military power at the end of the 1930s.

It was no accident, therefore, that the destruction of the Hitlerian state and German military power by the Americans and Soviets created a new situation in Europe. The latter was no longer master of itself, or of its own destiny; this was in the hands of two superpowers, the USA and the USSR. The organization of Europe in two 'ideological' blocs was the consequence of the conflict between the superpowers in the post-war period: the Cold War. Each institutionalized its presence in its bloc (NATO, OEEC, WEU, Council of Europe, EEC in the West; WTO, Comecon in the East) to establish a system that was to last for over 40 years, that is until 1989. It has been claimed by the Americans (Kissinger, 1979) that the stability of this division of the continent derived, above all, from the partition of Bismarckian Germany, accepted by the Germans for security reasons during the Cold War.

The Atlantic alliance

The return of the Soviet Union as a superpower in 1945 introduced a totally new element into the European balance of power equation. The Soviet Union was not just another state, but the 'first socialist country' in world history – that is to say a 'revolutionary subject' which officially questioned the legitimacy of the capitalist system – as well as the opponent of the West European states that had sought to stifle the 1917 Revolution at birth. This explains why the West European states accepted, during the Cold War, not a traditional alliance but a permanent and 'organic' relation with the other superpower, the USA, a relationship underwritten in the Atlantic charter. As Gambino (1988) has explained:

> right from the start the link with the United States lost, for West Europeans, the character of a decision justified in terms of the balance of power and military security, to acquire a specific emotive content and an 'ideological' connotation. It became a 'choice of civilization'; hence not an essential means, concrete and limited in time, of 'power re-equilibrium', but a metapolitical reality, thus virtually a dogma, of such transcendental significance as to dissuade all close and critical scrutiny of the instruments through which it was achieved and was embodied. (pp. 36–7)[5]

American financial assistance for European reconstruction – the Marshall Plan – secured American capitalism a *droit de regard* (that is, inside knowledge: type and sector of investments) and control of the economic reconstruction of the beneficiary countries. It was, moreover, a *droit de regard* that was not limited to the economic field, but was fatally extended to the political system: secret funding of government parties as well as non-communist trade unions and infiltration of the secret services.

Gambino has defined the Atlantic bloc as an 'imperfect protectorate' because the relations between states were not assimilable to either of the two types of links that states had historically established between themselves: alliances and protectorates. In defending his definition, Gambino emphasized the distinction between the two types. An alliance is established when one or more independent states decide to act together in certain circumstances against one or more other states, because they believe that they have some common interests. The important point is that the commitment undertaken is limited: mutual support only occurs in certain circumstances and not in others. It is never automatic because at the crucial moment every state is free to decide whether, in the specific situation, its 'national interests' are best served by breaking, rather than honouring, the commitment.

In the case of the protectorate, the type of link established is very different, even if legally difficult to define. A state abandons, partially or totally, its sovereignty in favour of another state. The important point, in this case, is that the guarantee of intervention by the stronger state to defend the weaker, in case of attack, is automatic. This is usually achieved by stationing some of the protector state's troops in the protected state. The decision to honour its commitment by the protector state is justified in terms of the will to protect 'something that it considers as already its own, an integral part of its sphere of influence' (p. 45). Gambino added that if this definition is technically clear, it is less so in practice, 'because the entire course of history continuously furnishes examples of "limited sovereignty"'.

Gambino has observed, moreover, that the situation was further complicated in the post-war period by the fact that the dominant position of the USA and USSR in world politics had, for 40 years, placed all the other states, with the exception of the non-aligned states, within the power system of one or other, or both, superpowers. And this was thanks to their nuclear superiority. In any case, the reason why he opted for the definition of 'imperfect protectorate' to characterize the European system was that 'it is one thing to have to take account of certain objective situations, and quite another to refuse to take, in this "context" ... those few independent initiatives that it allowed' (p. 45). Finally, he claimed that the nature of the links in the Western bloc had not changed substantially since the war, even though the economic relations of forces and interests have changed considerably. The US wanted the Europeans to make a substantial contribution to the defence of Western Europe, *but* they were opposed to giving up the dominant position that they have traditionally enjoyed in the NATO decision-making process. The US position was spelled out quite brutally by Henry Kissinger (1982): 'we sought to discourage the Europeans from unilateral initiatives to Moscow; America had the stronger hand. The tactic served its purpose; European pressures for concessions decreased in direct proportion as we developed our option toward Moscow' (p. 136). There are numerous examples of unilateral US intervention, decided without consulting their European allies, like the 1986 bombing of Libya. Indeed, the US has little or no experience of treating allies as equals. All this confirms that NATO had, according to Gambino, 'all the appearances of an alliance relationship, but [was] really a protectorate one' (1988, p. 146), even though rather a peculiar protectorate since, in the case of the European allies, we are talking of some of the most industrialized states in the world. The West Europeans were quite happy to go along with this arrangement because it kept some awkward questions off the European agenda: the German question and Europe's place in the world. They found it more comfortable to accept US leadership than risk confrontation over a distinct European identity or foreign policy. The collapse of the Soviet military threat brought to an end the centrality of the European commitment in US foreign and defence policy. Moreover, it reopened once more all the old problems – the German question, the Balkans – which the Cold War division of Europe had apparently settled, this time within a more multipolar economic and security context than had existed since 1945.

The European Union

This discussion leads on to a definition of what has been called the 'civilian'[6] aspect of the European system, that is to say of the EU. We noted in the introduction to this book that Jacques Delors has described it as an 'unidentified political object'. According to Hoffmann (1983), before the SEA the EC had the configuration of an 'international regime'. By this he meant that it had a set of norms of behaviour and rules of procedure that facilitated cooperation between member states on a broad range of issues. For individual members, the EC offered opportunities while at the same time imposing restraints. Thus, if it limited a state's freedom of unilateral action and imposed financial burdens, like the Community budget, it promoted bargaining with other members on internal affairs, such as regional, social and agricultural policies, and cooperation in external affairs. Hoffmann believed, in fact, that the development of the EC at that time could be explained in terms of a paradox: policies for common goals reinforce the Community while those founded on a strict reciprocity (*do ut des*) reinforce individual national states. Now, it is well known that the latter predominate, thanks to the forming of interest coalitions and the negotiations between them, and they contribute to member states' capacity to act at home and abroad. In this way, interstate cooperation promoted by the EC was of great assistance to member states in overcoming the economico-industrial crisis of the 1970s and 1980s. This did not mean that member states had abandoned national domestic policies and solutions; far from it. It meant quite simply that the overall balance of opportunities and restraints was positive. Thus Hoffmann claimed that the EC, understood as an 'international regime', 'has served not only to preserve the nation-states, but paradoxically to regenerate them and to adapt them to the world of today' (p. 35).

Since then, and particularly since the SEA, Hoffmann has changed his mind, arguing that the EC can no longer be characterized as an international regime because 'it is much more centralized and institutionalized … and receives a much higher level of commitment from its members' (Keohane and Hoffmann, 1991, p. 10). As noted in the introduction to this book, they contend that the EU is an experiment in pooling sovereignty and not in transferring it from states to supranational institutions. Its distinctiveness is that it has executive capacity (the Commission), legal status (ECJ) and financial resources (Community budget), but Keohane and Hoffmann warn against considering it as in any way resembling an emerging state: 'if in comparison with international organizations the Community looks strong,' they contend, 'in comparison with highly institutionalized modern states it appears quite weak' (p. 12). However, the EU has a political system, but it rests, in the final analysis, on the national political systems of member states.

The problem that intrigues Hoffmann is to understand how this transformation beyond the level of an international organization came about – namely, the institutional changes implicit in the SEA – since it was largely unanticipated (particularly by political scientists). As is well known, the original project of the EU, as with the Schuman Plan of 1950 for coal and steel, was that once the original decision was taken to set up supranational institutions in one sector on the basis of the Saint-Simonian dream of the logic of the market and technological imperatives, a 'spill-over effect' would be created to extend the area of integration to other sectors – because modern industrial economies are interdependent – until it covered the main fields of economic and political activity, so as to establish the federal state that the EU founders intended (Haas, 1958). Hoffmann, as a 'realist' theorist, was sceptical of this 'neo-functionalist' argument basically because it went against the grain: he noted in 1965 that it could be successful in the realm of welfare (what he termed 'low politics'), but when integration entered the realm of power ('high politics') it came unstuck because the two realms remained very different, as de Gaulle made clear in the previous year when he made the issue of the EEC budget a question of national sovereignty. Hoffmann's argument was that low politics (welfare and economics) is susceptible to negotiation and compromise, while high politics (national sovereignty and security) is not, and, although the saliency of an issue may change over time in terms of importance, the distinction remains.

The solution to his problem Hoffmann finds in a combination of spill-over (effects of membership enlargement) and realist (European states' waning international competition) theses, since neither alone explains the new-found impetus for EC institutional development in the second half of the 1980s. The crucial component was, nonetheless, the convergence of preferences of the major European governments round 'deregulation' which seemed to require reform of the decision-making system, and hence the SEA, to be effective. 'Its ratification resulted less from a coherent burst of idealism than from a convergence of national interests around a new pattern of economic policy-making ... Reliance on "mutual recognition" rather than harmonization reflected the decision to focus Community attention on the removal of barriers rather than on means of economic intervention' (Keohane and Hoffmann, 1991, pp. 23–4). Here we need to stress two elements: (1) the revival of the 1980s was a case of 'negative integration' (removal of barriers) and not 'positive integration' (action to promote harmony between members); and (2) the existence of EC institutional arrangements promotes common action in that it enables states to calculate incentives when there is a convergence of national interests. However, it is the convergence, or lack of it, that is the predetermining factor in any advance. The significance of this factor was verified in the European crisis of 1992–3 when the lack of policy convergence between Germany and the other member states led first to Italy and Britain exiting from the ERM, and later to the fixed parity between France and Germany being diluted, if not completely abandoned.

Middle-sized powers and TNCs

At this juncture in the discussion, it is helpful to set out a number of points. The first is obvious: the division of Europe into two blocs – each under the hegemony of a superpower – is no longer relevant since 1990, but there is little clarity on the future shape of the continent following the collapse of the Soviet Empire. Political discourse is trapped in a time warp and the only alternative to the bipolarity of the last 40 years is historical: the multipolarity of the pre-war years with all the dangers of regional conflicts that it implies. Certainly, NATO still exists, but the loss of its rationale and so the basis of US leadership in Europe has led to a frantic search for a new political role of cooperative peace building, for which a new forum (NACC) for East European states was set up at the Rome summit in 1991. The second is that in Western Europe, in spite of the moves towards European integration, nation-states still remain the basis of political power in the area. The third is that, owing to the development of multilateral relations – as much at the world level (UNO, IMF, World Bank) as at that of the European continent (NATO, EU,

Council of Europe, WEU, CSCE) – intergovernmental organization (IGO) relations (that is relations organized within an institutional framework) prevail in the foreign relations of West European states at the expense of traditional diplomatic relations (that is bilateral relations between state and state). The fourth is that Britain, France, Germany and Italy are 'middle powers'. This means that they are characterized by large populations, considerable national wealth and substantial armed forces (Berridge, 1987). Moreover, they have interests and influence in one or more regions of the world, comparable with those of the superpowers in the world globally. This is why they are often referred to as 'regional great powers', but perhaps it is also in recognition of the fact that they were great powers in their own right until World War II. The reference in the case of Britain is to its nuclear arms capability and its lingering influence in the Commonwealth; in the case of France to its nuclear *force de frappe* and major influence in the Arab world and sub-Saharan Africa (*la francophonie*); in the case of Germany to its power and prestige as the major economy in Europe; and, finally, in the case of Italy to the Vatican and its residual influence in Latin America.

Reference to these states' power raises delicate questions about their independence as well as their impact on international relations. The answers vary and are largely dictated by the orientations of the different theoretical schools: realism, pluralism and structuralism (Smith, 1994, pp. 3–5). Given that the West European states have depended, since the war, on NATO (and hence the USA) for their security in the event of a now improbable attack from the former USSR, and that Britain and France[7] still have the capability of mounting a military intervention in the Third World in defence of their interests – although with contrasting results, as the various colonial wars from Indo-China to the Falklands have shown - the question becomes more complex when we move to the economic field. It is self-evident that there is no longer any state that is not influenced by events in the global economy. We need only recall, for instance, the two 1970s energy crises. However, the real question concerns the continuous influence – exceptional events aside – of the international economic system on the West European states: what room for manoeuvre have they, if any? The answer is further complicated by the fact that the West European states rarely act alone, independently and coherently.

In this connection, we should mention Wallerstein's (1974) world system theory because of its intellectual influence in recent years. He argues that the international division of labour determines the nature of the state and not vice versa. According to Wallerstein, in fact, the development of capitalism in the sixteenth century resulted from the dialectical interaction of three distinct socio-economic realities: core, semi-periphery and periphery. Each had specific political requirements. Thus each country had to generate the forms of state that corresponded to its place in the system: core economies required strong states and peripheral economies weak ones, while the semi-peripheries needed mixed states. The national economies grew as a result of interaction with each other. In this situation, the only rigorous analysis, according to Wallerstein, must start from the system's global properties because the properties are merely 'parts of a whole reflecting that whole' and it is this whole that is the logical basis of the system. The central feature – the very essence of capitalism – is the differentiation of the properties of the system both economic and political: the operation of the market leads to the accentuation of differences, not to their reduction, as the Princeton developmental school claimed. The states are the derivatives of the world system and not the component units of it; for this reason they cannot – in Wallerstein's view – be conceived of outside it. According to him, the international division of labour controls the variance of political forms allowed to the component units, while the position in the division of labour dictates the specific form: states at the core are strong; states at the periphery are weak.

There is no need to prolong discussion of Wallerstein's system model here (for this see Worsley, 1983; Giddens, 1986). It is enough to note, as Gourevitch (1978) has done, that Wallerstein's reasoning is fundamentally circular: a core position needs a strong state and not vice versa. It is just as, indeed more, plausible to argue instead that the global economy resulted from a multiplicity of decisions, both political (of the various states) and economic (of the transnational corporations).[8] Hoffmann has observed that the West European states 'as usual, are constrained by the effects of their own moves: they are submitted to common forces, often beyond their control; but they are not governed by these forces' (1983, p. 30). What pressures do they create for the state? Firstly, there are those arising from international monetary instability, oil supplies, common commitment to open economies. Secondly, there is economic restructuring, now an absolute priority, whether for growth or international competition. Thirdly, there is the contradiction between welfare expenditure and productive investment. There is little doubt, therefore, that the room for manoeuvre of the Western European states in the global economy is rather limited. Indeed, it is all the smaller, the greater the integration of the national economies in the world market. Since they are not self-sufficient economies, their normal functioning depends on world trade.

At this stage, the forces that today challenge the state most directly in the international field deserve a mention: the transnational corporations (TNCs). The size of their operations – the sales of the seven largest TNCs in the 1980s exceeded the UK's GDP! – and the nature of their relations are such as to justify the definition of 'state indifferent'. A hypothesis popular in the 1960s claimed that they were capable of imposing their will on both their 'home' and their 'host' states: in other words, that the activity and development of the TNCs had reduced the states' ability to control them, and hence the states' capacity to manage their own economies, which meant abdication of an important part of their sovereignty.

Today, it is recognized that this hypothesis exaggerates the TNCs' political power. In truth, not only is it difficult to prove that the TNCs are able to impose their will on even Third World states, without inside protection and support, but there are good theoretical reasons for doubts about their power to control any state. Firstly, home states have a whole armoury of benefits to bargain with TNCs, like tax and anti-trust exemptions, provision of guarantees for foreign direct investment, and diplomatic support in the event, for instance, of moves to expropriate or nationalize the assets in host states. Secondly, host states can offer, or refuse, access to their territory, availability of labour, protected local markets, tax or other financial privileges, and government contracts. Finally, states have a repressive apparatus in the form of military and police forces that TNCs lack.

In voicing this criticism, it is not suggested that TNCs lack influence, even in West European political systems. It is merely to suggest that if states do not oppose certain activities of TNCs as vigorously as they might, this is usually because they do not want to. It is a way of saying that the government policy of that particular state supports TNCs' activities, or that, in the case of abuse, there is complicity between government leaders in that state and the directors of the TNCs, as recent events in Italy have publicly revealed.[9]

Classical diplomacy and new diplomacy

Such is the context in which discussion of diplomatic activity is set. Diplomacy, besides being the means through which states regulate their official relations with other states, is also the principal instrument for the execution of foreign policy. By diplomacy is generally understood 'the management of international relations by negotiation', and hence the making and implementation of foreign policy. For some, however, it only concerns the execution (the conduct of foreign relations) and not the making of foreign policy, because of the latter's political nature. This was the thesis, for instance, of former British ambassador Sir Alfred Duff-Cooper in his defence of the profession in the 1940s: 'the business of diplomacy is the carrying out of policy ... the art of diplomacy is the manner of carrying it out' (in Plischke, 1979, p. xii). In support of the general view, however, is the fact that the diplomatic corps, as foreign office civil servants, has a first-hand role in foreign policy-making, even though, of course, under the direction of the government's political control. And this is all the truer because continuity in interstate relations is the essence of a foreign policy, because international power relations are usually less variable than domestic ones.

We repeat this distinction in our discussion: we shall start from an outline of diplomatic activity and pass on to a consideration of the foreign policy of Britain, France, Germany, Italy and the EU. The principal task of a state's diplomacy is to conduct, as successfully as possible, relations with other states. This means identifying areas of common interest for mutual benefit, and, where necessary, keeping eventual conflicts under control so that they do not lead to war. Thus if negotiation is the chief diplomatic activity it includes a wide range of other modes: exchange of views, arbitration, conciliation, mediation, adjudication and representation – both to uphold the state's dignity and to defend its own nationals on a foreign state's territory – to which promotion of national trade was subsequently added.

Negotiation was not, in fact, the initial reason for establishing the first diplomatic missions in Europe during the Renaissance: it was to monitor events in rival states, and, where necessary, ensure a continuing dialogue with them. Hence the celebrated aphorism of the English diplomat Sir Henry Wotton (1604): 'an ambassador is an honest man sent to lie abroad for the good of his country.' Today the discretion, or better secrecy, of most diplomatic activity is justified as an essential element for the success of interstate negotiation. Former US secretary of state Kissinger (1979) has argued that 'the sequence in which concessions are made becomes crucial, it can be aborted if each move has to be defended individually rather than as part of a mosaic before the reciprocal move is clear' (p. 803). Nevertheless, we should not ignore the significance of the other modes in justifying diplomatic secrecy: for instance, the size of the diplomatic personnel accredited to embassy staff (military, cultural, economic, commercial attachés[10]) and their tasks; or again the numbers of staff expelled from time to time for spying or other 'non-diplomatic' activities!

It is no surprise, therefore, that diplomatic practice includes a complex ensemble of procedures and techniques, both formal (diplomatic notes, *aides-mémoire*, *communiqués*, official visits, treaties) and informal (private conversations, oral exchanges), many of which were codified at the Congress of Vienna in 1815. The purpose is to facilitate communication between states, so as, through elaborate ritual and protocol, to increase 'certainty' in a field where uncertainty is the rule: uncertainty which is due in large part to the fact that a state's military security requires on the one hand the acquisition of maximum intelligence of other states, and on the other the divulgation of minimum intelligence of one's own. This military requirement conflicts with diplomatic practice that demands certainty. It was to meet such demands that diplomatic instruments were formalized to create a finely tuned set of measures, both cooperative (exchange of information, economic and technical assistance, mutual security obligations) and punitive (sanctions, boycotts, expulsions, suspending diplomatic relations).

It remains to add that the recruitment of the European diplomatic corps does not differ greatly from that of other civil servants (chapter 8). As regards the foreign service elite, the general trend in all states was towards a more socially selective – more aristocratic – recruitment than for other higher civil servants, but this is disappearing, as is the tradition that ambassadors should be exclusively male. On the other hand, the appointment of political personalities to certain important embassies (Washington, Moscow and European capitals) still continues (Lord Soames to Paris, Peter Jay to Washington for Britain in the 1970s, Gilles Martinet to Rome for France in the 1980s).

In Europe, there are two further developments that should be mentioned. The first regards the disappearance of traditional or 'classical diplomacy'; the second concerns specifically the EU. Classical diplomacy, in its admirers' eyes, is essentially direct representation and largely bilateral negotiation by professional diplomats. In the European diplomacy of the nineteenth century, it went without saying that every state of note was represented by a trained diplomatic corps 'possessing common standards of professional conduct'. In this connection, the codicil to the Congress of Vienna in 1815 set forth a general outline of proper diplomatic practice – defined by Nicolson (1939) as 'a written rather than a verbal art' – as well as establishing diplomatic titles and protocol. An integral part of this proper practice was the principle of 'diplomatic confidentiality', considered the sole basis for serious negotiation. The practice provided for secret clauses, some of which were important enough to mark the diplomatic history of the early years of the century and were denounced at the Treaty of Versailles.[11] It was no accident, in fact, that the first of president Wilson's fourteen points of January 1918 provided that in future there should be nothing but 'open covenants of peace, openly arrived at'. Even Nicolson (1954) himself, a former diplomat and a great admirer of classical diplomacy, felt obliged to admit that 'confidential negotiations that lead to secret pledges are worse even than the televised diplomacy that we enjoy today' (p. 78).

The 'new diplomacy', as opposed to the classical, is characterized by multilateralism – often called 'diplomacy by conference' – and by a broadening of the range of diplomatic participants: from heads of state and of government at the various summits (G7, European Council) to technical experts and specialists at the numerous intergovernmental conferences. It is unnecessary to outline the reasons for this change. Suffice it to recall the enlargement of the society of states, the shrinkage of world horizons resulting from the technical revolution in the fields of transportation and communication, and the consequent growth in the matters to be dealt with by diplomacy as well as the democratization in the form of the state and the end of the traditional distinction between foreign and home affairs. In arguing that contemporary diplomacy is defined by its diversity of forms, and above all by its multilateralism – negotiations among states (in the plural) and *not* between state and state (in the singular) – we do not mean that this development is a twentieth century novelty. The history of multilateralism, in fact, goes back at least as far as the Congress of Westphalia of 1648. The novelty lies rather in the fact that it forms the framework of contemporary international relations which are relations between intergovernmental organizations (IGOs), of which the UN is only the most ecumenical. For instance, whereas 4800 international treaties were negotiated and registered with the League of Nations in 25 years (1919–45), this grew to almost 9500 under the UN in the next 25 years (1945–70) – 375 treaties a year as against 195 in the earlier period. As discussed above, the most significant IGOs in Western Europe at the present time are NATO and, above all, the EU.

National foreign policies

Now, situating foreign policy-making in a historical perspective – the 'stubborn presence of the centuries' cannot, alas, be ignored – it is clear that neither Britain nor France has fully succeeded in drawing all the implications of the loss of their status as great powers. Since possession of nuclear weapons did not significantly increase the two states' defensive capability,[12] the acquisition and maintenance of a nuclear capability could be justified only in terms of national prestige: as world powers and permanent members of the UN Security Council they felt, of course, obliged to have a nuclear capability. In any case, the possession of nuclear weapons made no difference at all to the division of Europe between the two superpowers in the 1970s and the 1980s. Moreover, despite their membership of the EC, Britain, France, Germany and Italy maintained, and even developed, different foreign policy orientations and priorities.

However, Britain had the greatest difficulty in adapting to the new post-war international situation. Two reasons are generally mentioned: one fundamental and the other more immediate. The former resulted from its geopolitical position – an offshore island – and hence its separate development from continental Europe as an imperial power with global, and not just regional, interests. For three centuries, the principal preoccupation of British foreign policy was the freedom of the seas, trade and peace. In consequence, it saw its relations with Europe in a negative light: avoid at all costs entanglements with continental powers but, at the same time, prevent a single power from dominating the continent. The immediate reason was, instead, psychological: Britain saw itself as one of the war victors in 1945; and victory justified, in its own eyes, its imperial past and so authorized it to go on as though nothing had changed. Thus British attitudes were very different from those of its continental neighbours: the British were largely indifferent to that wave of idealism that furnished the energy for the various attempts at European integration.

Britain

In a famous speech in 1948, Winston Churchill placed Britain at the point of intersection of 'three circles': British Empire, English-speaking world and Europe. They not only defined the axes of British foreign policy, but placed Britain in a unique position in the world with special global responsibilities. In fact, however, the three circles of influence did not have the same weight in policy: the first two took precedence over the third. The first lost credibility immediately, almost without the British being aware of it. The decision to grant India independence in 1947 removed at a stroke the strategic asset of the Indian army which was the basis of British power in the Far East. The result was 'imperial overreach', quite simply that Britain no longer had the means of playing a global political role. But even worse, despite relatively smooth decolonization in the 1950s and 1960s, which was costly in both financial and political terms, British foreign policy refused to recognize the consequences of the loss of empire.[13] So, although no more than a European power, Britain deluded itself that it could continue to play an important role at the head of the Commonwealth as a 'third force' between the two superpowers, and so have a special influence in international affairs.

In order to continue to play this role, but without the means, Britain invented the notion of a 'special relationship' with the USA – the product of the intimate wartime collaboration between Churchill and Roosevelt, reinforced by cultural and sentimental ties – which became the main axis of British foreign policy in the post-war period. The special relationship was not, in fact, a relationship of equals but one of British subordination to America with all the negative consequences that this implied: relations with Europe, with the Middle East, with the Far East. This view of British foreign policy has still not lost its appeal to British leaders, even after Britain's entry into the EC, as statements by two recent prime ministers, Callaghan and Thatcher, demonstrate. The centrality of the special relationship for Britain is justified politically at two levels: (1) fundamentally, as the basis of military security, it embodies the perception that defence of national interests is not possible without US support (as Suez illustrated negatively in 1956, and the Falklands positively in 1982); and (2) by extension, it places Britain in a better position to represent and interpret European interests and concerns to the USA. This claim to act as mediator between Europe and the USA is not, however, without serious difficulties, in view of the refusal of the other European powers to recognize this British role and also the USA's attitude towards Germany's economic role today. Nevertheless, it comforts Britain's desire to continue to play a 'world role' (such as it is).[14]

As regards the third axis, Europe, the British position has always been, and remains, ambivalent.[15] It was only towards the end of the 1950s, despite assertions to the contrary, that the British began to realize that they were no longer a great power and that their future was now linked to Europe. However, the special relationship allowed de Gaulle to present Britain as militarily and economically dependent on the USA, and not an independent European country – that is a sort of American Trojan horse – and thereby to delay British entry into the EEC for over a decade. Indeed, entry in 1973 on the eve of the first big post-war recession meant that Britain did not enjoy the economic benefits that partisans of the EEC had predicted. The result has been the British government's largely 'semi-detached' position: either rejecting proposals for the development of the EU by other members; or defending its own narrowly defined national interests to the bitter end (financial contribution, social charter). Nonetheless, it has played a full role in the European institutions, notably the EPC. All this suggests that Britain's adaptation to its real post-war situation is not yet complete; on the contrary, there still remains a large dose of nostalgia for a role that the country is no longer capable of sustaining. The Falklands War in 1982 illustrated perfectly the limits of British power: victory was only possible thanks to American and EC support; it is a lesson that British leaders seem slow to learn.[16] We can, therefore, agree with Spence's (1984) laconic judgement on Britain's post-war foreign policy that 'too much has been attempted with too few resources' (p. 195).

France

French foreign policy has been the most active and vigorous in Europe, particularly in the period of de Gaulle's presidency. The country came out of World War II, despite four years of occupation, on the side of the victors, thanks to de Gaulle. However, France was forced to rethink its traditional positions, such as its alliances with Eastern Europe. Moreover, the acceptance of the Atlantic alliance in the 1940s was more suffered than embraced, because France still believed itself to be a great power. Indeed, French foreign policy can be understood as an attempt, more or less successful, according to the moment, to regain its lost rank: an attempt which was interpreted most dramatically by de Gaulle with his concept of *grandeur*, but with an essential continuity also by his successors, Pompidou, Giscard d'Estaing and Mitterrand.

The substance of French foreign policy can be defined by three expressions (analogous to those coined by Churchill for Britain) – *grandeur*, Europe and Third World – even if the words are bigger than the substance they are intended to convey. Thus *grandeur* means 'national independence' based on the nuclear *force de frappe*; Europe means a 'special relationship' with Germany; and, finally, Third World means privileged relations with West Africa. Nonetheless, French leaders showed themselves to be more clear-headed than their British colleagues, in the sense that, knowing that a policy was worth only the means, they had fewer illusions about the means. They acted in such a way as to give France the necessary means, first economically and then militarily: nuclear weapons built independently of the US and ready by the end of the 1950s. Moreover, de Gaulle succeeded in ably exploiting France's geopolitical position since NATO's defence of Europe from Soviet attack necessarily included the defence of France. In this way he was able, after the Anglo-American refusal of a three-man directorate with France at the head of NATO, to take the French armed forces out of the integrated military command in 1966 without denouncing the alliance, and thus give substance, at the same time, to his doctrine that 'France defends itself by itself, in the way that it finds most appropriate.' Hence was achieved the credibility of a role of relative autonomy in world affairs, partly by *rapprochements* with the USSR and the Atlantic alliance, and partly by keeping both superpowers at a distance with openings to China and towards Latin America. It is a policy which his successors have, significantly, not wished to abandon: they have confirmed the central role of the strategic nuclear force, but inserted it, since 1976, within the context of the notion of *sancturisation élargie*[17] with the intention of giving it credibility as a symbol of the country's rank and independence.

More important, however, was the second axis of French foreign policy, reconciliation with Germany, because it was not only the *sine qua non* of France's post-war international position, but also the basis of European integration. After rivalry and three wars with Germany in 70 years, the problem for France, in the immediate post-war period, was simple: how to prevent a future conflict between the two nations. We mentioned the wave of idealism that engulfed the continent in those years that induced France to propose from 1950 various types of community as vehicles of European integration. It was a continuation of this wave that led, under de Gaulle and Adenauer, to the Franco-German treaty of friendship and cooperation in 1963 – on the morrow of de Gaulle's veto of British entry into the EEC – that sealed the special relationship between the two nations. In the French policy of friendship with Germany, there was also an interested calculation: since Germany could not exercise a leadership role in Europe in the foreseeable future, France could hope, instead, to exploit the weight of an industrially reconstructed Germany to secure hegemony for itself in Europe and so a political role on the world stage. This possibility was all the greater because Britain, at the crucial moment in the 1950s, boycotted European integration. The French calculation proved to be substantially correct: West Germany became the strongest economic and conventional military power (within NATO) in Europe, without reducing France's interest in the special relationship but, on the contrary, strengthening it for the simple reason that it became even more important for France to prevent a conflict between the two states. This took on a particular significance after German unification in 1990: the development of European political union to anchor

Germany in the Western European coalition proposed jointly with Germany in April 1990 and sealed at the Maastricht summit of December 1991. President Mitterrand reasoned that it was 'better to promote the complex independencies of Europe, built up over the past forty years, than to allow the nationality principle to become triumphant in Germany and Europe' (Story and de Carmoy, 1993, p. 203). This explains French pressure on Germany to commit itself to the creation of a Franco-German army corps, as the embryo of a European defence force answerable to the EU and *not* NATO and so restricting the latter's powers. Unfortunately, Germany's national situation remains delicate and the economic problems of unification are much graver than anticipated. Hence the ensuing German recession has stalled the impetus to political union expected from the Maastricht Treaty.

The third axis of French foreign policy was, like the British, of imperial origin: relations with the former French colonies, principally in West Africa. Decolonization lasting twenty years was a painful experience for the French. The war in Indo-China, ending in defeat at Dien Bien Phu in 1954, was followed by war in Algeria. The latter had serious domestic political repercussions, like bringing down the Fourth Republic and de Gaulle's return to power. A further repercussion was the granting of independence to the West African colonies (twelve in all) by de Gaulle, but in conditions that ensured that all but one became client states, formally independent but under French protection. This protection was reinforced by the fact that French troops remained stationed in their territories: 'Africa is', according to a French foreign minister of the 1970s, 'the only continent where France can, with five hundred soldiers, still change the course of history.' These states were important to France for a number of reasons: (1) cultural, for they give substance to the concept of *francophonie*, and the importance of language should not be underrated in France's 'civilizing mission' abroad; (2) economic, for they secure access to important raw materials, including oil, and the franc monetary area adds weight to Paris as an international financial centre; and (3) political, for French influence in Africa gives substance to its world role in international affairs, and also emphasizes that it is a friend of the Third World.

In general, French foreign policy has been more clear-sighted and coherent than British, even though its goals have been similar. It has attempted to align means and ends, exploiting favourable opportunities to its advantage. However, France also suffers from the same contradiction as Britain in the international field: too restricted an economic base and insufficient resources to sustain the ambitions of a global presence.

Germany

It is no surprise that post-war West German foreign policy was largely conditioned by the Nazi inheritance. In fact, it was forced to adopt a totally new orientation. In this connection, it is appropriate to see West German foreign policy in terms of a strategy to restore its full independence in the international arena given that the Allied occupying powers' diktat had initially conceded it only a limited and conditional sovereignty. Only today, perhaps, with its independence restored and its unity re-established, is Germany seen once more as a nation no different from the others, and more powerful than most.

In this situation, German foreign policy can be defined very simply: make a virtue of necessity. This has meant, until very recently, seeking areas of autonomy within the Western system, on the assumption that autonomy would grow with integration, and hence has required giving up the Bismarckian policy of balancing East against West. It also implied abandoning German unification for an unspecified period. Post-war West German foreign policy was, in fact, based on three fundamental elements: (1) loyalty to the Atlantic alliance; (2) the EC and the special relationship with France; and (3) relations with the GDR and Germany's eastern neighbours (*Ostpolitik*).[18] The basic aspect of the first element was the close alliance with the USA, considered absolutely necessary for the new state's security because it was in the front line of the Cold War as the Iron Curtain between the Eastern and Western blocs ran along its borders. The first chancellor, Adenauer, shared the US position during the Cold War, namely the strategy of Soviet 'containment' which involved the irreversible integration of the Federal Republic into the Western alliance prior to any discussion of German unification. The latter, for Adenauer, was only conceivable on terms dictated by the West – that is the assimilation of the GDR in the FRG – implying nothing less than a total refusal to acknowledge the existence of the GDR, and, perhaps more importantly, the formation of a military capability superior to that of its hostile neighbour. Adenauer accepted the proposal of the EDC so readily because it allowed German rearmament; and, when the EDC foundered in 1954, Germany welcomed its replacement by NATO. The Federal Republic has always furnished the largest conventionally armed military contingent (table 10.1) for the defence of Western Europe under NATO's supreme command. Up to now, however, both the West and the former USSR have refused to allow Germany the possession of nuclear weapons.

Coherent with its option of a security policy under the umbrella of the Atlantic alliance has been the German enthusiasm for European integration, and particularly for reconciliation with France. Adenauer and his successors at the head of the federal government, whether of CDU or SPD persuasion, have always seen in the construction of Europe an

Table 10.1 Armed forces since World War II

	Britain	France	Germany	Italy
Military expenditure				
1950s:				
% GDP	8.5	6.0	3.8	nd
1960–1970s				
Military budget ($)	5.6	6.2	5.2	2.4
Per capita expenditure ($)	100	123	90	44
% GDP	5.1	4.4	3.5	2.1
1980s:				
Military budget ($)	25.4	19.3	18.4	7.1
Per capita expenditure ($)	443	437	371	153
% GDP	5.4	4.1	4.3	2.5
1990s:				
% GDP	4.2	3.5	2.6	2.1
Men under arms (thousands)				
1950s	689	595	–	235
1960s	519	1025	466	531
1970s	370	506	484	413
1980s	327	492	495	370
Reservists:				
1970s	435	540	625	545
1980s	281	457	750	799
Paramilitary forces	–	85[a]	20	81[b]
Military manpower ratio				
1960s	0.808	1.839	0.755	0.755
1970s	0.642	0.969	0.790	0.786
1980s	0.550	0.916	0.808	0.645

[a] Gendarmerie Nationale.
[b] Carabinieri.
Source: *Military Balance*, International Institute of Strategic Studies, London, various years

instrument for German rehabilitation that would permit the FRG to become more like other nations once more, and also to build something new on the continent in place of the former national rivalry. This explains the warm response to all the French initiatives in this direction in the 1950s, which reached their height with the 1963 Franco-German friendship treaty. It sealed the special relationship between the two nations with all the consequences already noted: informal EC directorate; and Europe as Germany's national goal, 'the Federal Republic's *raison d'être*', according to chancellor Kohl's definition at Davos in 1985. The special relationship with France is usually considered, on the German side, the principal positive result of European policy to date. And this is despite the fact that political leadership has voluntarily been left to France, except, of course, discussion of the details (above all the costs[19]). The only great initiative launched by the Germans before reunification, in fact, was the establishment of the ERM proposed by chancellor Schmidt in 1979. At the time, it was believed that it would mark a fundamental political change in the EC, with the Federal Republic openly assuming leadership. It did not, as chancellor Kohl preferred a more discreet political role than his SPD predecessors, at least until the explosion of the 'actual socialist' regimes of Eastern Europe. Indeed, it is only since 1989 and the unification of the two Germanies that he has taken up an active role.

German unification dramatically altered the state's position in the international arena, but at the same time reasserted, somewhat paradoxically, previous orientations. The restoration of full 'sovereignty' swept away at a stroke almost all the previous limiting features of the post-war settlement which, as noted, were designed *inter alia* to contain Germany. However, the environment in which the new Germany has to operate has suddenly become more complex with the collapse of communism and the breakup of the former USSR. Previously, NATO looked after German security and the EC ensured German access to international trade. In addition, there was the expectation that, as the largest and economically most important state on the continent, united Germany would assume a larger profile in international affairs, and this reawakened fears of a new German domination of the continent.

It is in this context that the three fundamental orientations of German foreign policy have been reaffirmed. Thus, to allay fears of German domination and reassure France, Kohl used the special relationship to call for an IGC on European political union with the intention of creating a permanent institutional structure within which the EU could develop a common foreign and security policy in parallel with that already taken to promote economic and monetary union. At Maastricht, the Germans offered to relinquish a large dose of national political authority to the EU in return for a common EU security policy as a guarantee of their genuine European commitment. The opposition of a number of states, principally Britain, meant that they were only partially successful, as the institutional procedures agreed went no further than formalizing the informal arrangements developed to implement the SEA: they remained intergovernmental and *not* supranational. The result is that while the Maastricht Treaty does not bind Germany into a common EU foreign policy and, hence, remove the temptation of a 'strongest alone' policy, at present the German government continues to accord a priority to the relationship with France: for instance, defence of the French franc within the ERM, and public support for the French position on agriculture in GATT negotiations.

As regards the second orientation, the US had taken note, even before unity, of Germany's powerful position with president Bush's 'partners in leadership' offer of spring 1989. The Germans have always been particularly anxious not to compromise a US military presence in Europe, and hence wanted NATO to develop a political role as the guarantor of pan-European security. The latter became more urgent with the appearance of political instability and unrest on its eastern borders. Unfortunately, both partners have been disappointed with the other's reaction. The US was dissatisfied because the challenge of a leadership role in world affairs was one which, as the Gulf crisis of 1990–1 demonstrated, neither German public opinion nor German elites were equipped to meet. Germany's reaction was hesitant, and judged unconvincing, limited as it was to a major financial contribution. This was partly due to the constitutional inhibition (article 87A of the basic law) of participating in out-of-area conflicts and partly due to the lack of public debate on the circumstances in which force might legitimately be used. The German government has moved to revise the constitutional limits on the use of force, but no public debate on the exercise of power or German strategic interests has so far taken place.

German disappointment with the USA concerns the third orientation of post-war German foreign policy: its relations with its Eastern neighbours, and specifically the Western response to the economic and security vacuum left by the collapse of the Soviet Empire as well as the ethnic conflicts that this has released. The central thrust of its *Osteuropolitik* is to assist the transformation of its Eastern neighbours through a policy of cooperation, association and integration within national, European and transatlantic frameworks. Nonetheless, Germany is well aware that alone it lacks the necessary resources, particularly with the unexpectedly greater costs of unification; for this reason it has made successive attempts to promote burden-sharing, with little response from the USA (hence the disappointment) and Japan. Failure could be catastrophic, as Germany has been trying to make other Western countries aware, because breakdown would threaten not only the stability of Germany itself, but the EU as well. The Balkans imbroglio with the spill-over risk of east–west migration is an obvious lesson.

The conclusion is that Germany's new international role for the foreseeable future is likely to be essentially focused on Europe: 'the biggest change', Roger Morgan (1992, p. 115) has observed, 'could perhaps be summarized by saying whereas for forty years the term *Europapolitik* – policy for Europe – has essentially meant policy towards and within the EC, the new Europe will bring a redefinition.' He indicates that the balance of German interests and preferences will remain overwhelmingly in the West, but a new ingredient of purposeful interaction – a 'bridging' (*Brücke*) role – will be added. However, the success of future German foreign policy depends largely on the success of the German economy: will it be able to bear the weight of the demands, both internal and external, that are being placed on it?

Italy

Political indifference to the outside world has led some observers (ambassador Quaroni, for instance) to assert that 'Italy has no foreign policy in the real sense of the word.' Italian foreign policy has been dictated by outside powers and institutions (USA, NATO, EC). There is no doubt that after the Mussolini adventure, Italian leaders decided to adopt a very low profile on the international stage – and this despite ex-chancellor Schmidt's scornful judgement that the lack of Italian policy was due to a lack of government *tout court*. It is possible, nonetheless, to identify two foreign policy orientations: (1) loyalty to the Atlantic alliance; and (2) European integration. NATO membership, pursued by De Gasperi in 1949, despite very strong opposition at home, has underwritten Italy's position in the Atlantic alliance throughout the whole post-war period. The crucial factor in this decision was fear of communist subversion during the Cold War and its domestic consequences.

There is no doubt that the Atlantic alliance has acted as a political guarantor of the country's socio-political status quo. It is also true, moreover, that the US assumed a *droit de regard* over Italian political affairs to the point of giving substance to the conviction that the only thing that interested the US was containing the communists and preventing their entry into the government: something they were prepared to prevent at any price and using any means. Hence, Italian membership of NATO was sought to avoid international isolation and its possible consequences. In this situation, Italy has shown itself to be a loyal supporter of NATO, ready to back all projects and initiatives, whether collective or US, and to fulfil its military commitments to the alliance. Beyond this, however, Italy has not wished to commit itself. Certainly it did not take initiatives of its own,[20] preferring to leave these to the other NATO member states and to US leadership.

Its position in the field of European integration was very similar. From the beginning, Italy has been an enthusiastic supporter of European unity. Like the Federal Republic, it saw in the various French initiatives of the 1950s a way of returning to the international fold after the fascist period. Italian leaders, unlike their British and French colleagues, have not sought a role of their own on the international stage. Moreover, Italian entry into the EEC was seen, above all by certain southern political leaders, as a means of binding Italy to the process of European development and securing for Italy the future as a European, and not a Third World, country. Joining the EC has turned out to be one of the success stories of post-war Italian diplomacy.

Once again, however, Italy did not take the initiative in the construction of Europe, but it responded positively to all the other member states' suggestions. In this sense, Italy has certainly been the EU's most loyal member. Its particular contribution has been as mediator in the various EC conflicts – as, for instance, in the case of the British financial contribution, or again over the enlargement of the EC to Spain and Portugal, resolved after eight years' negotiation during the Italian presidency in 1985. However, there is a certain paradox that, despite the Italian enthusiasm for the EU, there has also been a certain reluctance to translate it into operation and implementation. The gap between policy line (principle) and implementation (practice) has been particularly striking: Rome holds nearly all the records for delays and infringements of EU directives, number of proceedings by the Commission for lack of implementation of directives, the number of ECJ judgements, the number of judgements not executed and the number of second judgements (Merlini, 1993, p. 235), with the consequence of undermining a large part of Italy's European credibility. Moreover, the Berlusconi government formed after the 1994 elections appears much more Euro-sceptic than its predecessors, indicating a cooling of enthusiasm for European integration in Italy, hitherto the most pro-European country.[21]

Finally, we should note a change in the Italian diplomatic presence in the 1980s towards a higher international profile. For instance, Italy took part in a military expedition abroad for the first time since the war when it contributed troops to the UN peace-keeping force in Lebanon in 1984. Moreover, it clashed violently with the USA over the *Achille Lauro* hijacking affair in 1985. In addition, prime ministers Craxi, De Mita and Andreotti and foreign minister De Michelis were all more active, both in the European summits and in visits to Washington and Moscow, than their predecessors.

European Union

Since 1970, when European political cooperation (EPC) was launched, the EC member states have become progressively aware that there are common European interests and that these can best be advanced if Europe speaks with one voice instead of twelve. Despite the obstacles, the habit of consultation and exchange of information led to common and distinctive positions on an array of subjects, from the Arab–Israeli dispute and the Falklands, to Poland, CSCE and arms control negotiations, as well as disagreements on some others (recognition of Croatia). The initial common action was outside the EC treaties, but pressures naturally built up for member states to conduct their foreign policies within the EPC under the aegis of the EC. This was recognized in the SEA where foreign policy was accorded a title of its own. Euro-enthusiasm in the latter 1980s, combined with the upheavals in the East, led to the creation of the common foreign and security policy (CFSP) as the third pillar of the European Union in the Maastricht Treaty.

The provisions are complex, the more so since defence – the vital component of any realistic foreign policy – remains very much the prerogative of NATO (although WEU is given a role). What it is important to stress is that Maastricht does not envisage a single European foreign policy, but merely a 'common' one; hence there is room for disagreements and individual action. Moreover, foreign policy remains very much intergovernmental, even if majority voting is permitted on minor issues. Foreign policy 'guidelines' are established at European councils; and the presidency of the EU represents it in relations with third parties. It must be stressed that the essential basis of the CFSP remains consultation and exchange of information. Indeed, it cannot be more because it lacks both instruments and resources: 'there is no effective system of supranational crisis management,' Lodge (1993, p. 232) writes, 'forward and contingency planning, mobilization of appropriate independent administrative, political, financial or military resources. Rudimentary resources coupled with the continuing dependence on the independently controlled resources and hence goodwill of the member states inhibit the evolution of a genuine, supranational EC capability.' In this situation, it is hardly surprising that its foreign policy action is 'responsive and reactive rather than proactive and defensive'.

Unfortunately for the EU, 'Europhoria' in the later 1980s and the 1990s, resulting principally from its economic success and the transformation of Eastern Europe, has been responsible for excessive expectations, particularly by third parties (US included), of what it could deliver, and so a credibility gap has appeared between expectations and capabilities, highlighted by the Yugoslav tragedy. As Jacques Delors explained in 1991, the EPC only had three weapons to deal with the Yugoslav crisis: public opinion, the threat of withholding diplomatic recognition and economic sanctions (Salmon, 1993, p. 257); it used all three. Thus it can be argued that criticism of the failure of the EU to make an adequate response over Yugoslavia, once civil war had broken out, is somewhat misplaced because it lacked the necessary means: military forces, technical expertise and logistical resources. Moreover, the CFSP is further weakened by the six-month rotating EU presidency, which undermines continuity, despite the troika.[22] Thus the commitment to a common European foreign and security policy is more symbolic than real, because to become viable it requires 'a potent military capability, a working consensus under which the capabilities should be used and a credible willingness to act when agreed conditions exist' (p. 268). At present, these clearly do not exist.

Soldiers and civil–military relations

The central role of the military in the formation of the European nation-state was illustrated in chapter 7. However, interest in the military is not usually directed at its most evident aspect, namely that without military organization the state would not exist – this would be a banality if it had not been ignored for so long by Western political science – but rather at the more subtle and complex aspect of the relations between military organization and form of state. It is a subject that engaged the curiosity of politicians and political philosophers alike, among others Machiavelli, for whom foreign mercenaries and the *condottieri* were the ruin of the Italy of his time, and hence who advised rulers to keep a firm control over the military; 'General' Engels, according to whom it was the technological change in weaponry that dictated the change not only in modes of warfare, but also in the form of state; or again Weber, who saw in military organization the prototype of modern bureaucracy. Moreover, the foreign policy of a European state is meaningful to the extent that it has the military capability to back it up. All in all, this merely confirms Hintze's conclusion to his 1906 lecture: 'in the immediate future, things will remain as they always have in the course of history: the form and spirit of state organization will be determined not only by social and economic relations, but primarily by the needs of defence and attack, that is by the organization of the military and of war' (p. 215).

In this situation, the characteristic feature of the military, as an institution, is that they have a monopoly of the legitimate use of force: in Lasswell's (1935) expressive phrase, they are 'the managers of the instruments of violence'. Hence the question is not 'whether' the military participate in policy but 'how' they participate and at 'what level': 'no military, in short, can be shorn of political influence save through the rare step of total abolition' (Welch, 1976, p. 2). It is necessary, therefore, in order to appraise the political role of the military in West European states, to discuss briefly four areas: (1) military organization; (2) social composition of the officer corps; (3) civil–military relations; and (4) the concept of the 'military–industrial complex'.

Military organization

Three types of military format[23] have been distinguished in the formation of the European nation-state: (1) the mercenary armies of the *Ständestaat* era (1400–1600); (2) the standing army of the absolute state period (1600–1700); and (3) the 'nation in arms' or mass army of the modern representative state (1800–1900). In the post-war period, Janovitz (1975) has shown that there are elements of two formats, which suggest that we are in a transition period: the mass army is in decline, but not yet passed away, and a new format, called the professional army, is emerging. Nuclear weapons have turned the conception of warfare upside down, profoundly transforming military institutions whose purpose has changed from the use of violence to the dissuasion of violence.

At all events, despite the fact that the contrast between the two formats is not easy to specify, we can note a number of features. Firstly, there is the contrast between two fundamental modes of recruitment: conscription against professional (voluntary) engagement. Conscription is based on the concept of 'citizenship': on the one hand the duty of every citizen to defend his country, and on the other the need for manpower to fight a total war. Professional recruitment results from the new military technology – sophisticated weapons systems – which requires a corps of specialists: the emphasis is on professional efficiency with the assistance in terms of manpower, if necessary, of reservists. Secondly, there is a difference of behaviour and mentality in the two formats between the *grandeur* and 'heroism' of the patriotic military tradition on the one side, and the 'servitude' or 'rational and scientific professionalism' of the new military managers on the other. This change, in fact, poses a problem of adaptation to the new situation on the part of the officer corps. Their corporate comments echo the nostalgia of de Vigny's thoughts at the end of the Napoleonic epic: 'Today, as the conquering spirit withers, the only greatness which a noble character can bring into the military profession appears to me to be less in the glory of fighting than in the honour of suffering in silence and of accomplishing with steadfastness duties which are often odious' (*Servitude et grandeur militaires*, 1835).

Thirdly, there is also a certain contrast in the relative insignificance of the distinction between military and civil sectors characteristic of total war on the one hand, and its importance in the corporate identity of the 'new military' in the professional army on the other. It is well known that in the time of total war, the distinction between civil and military loses its meaning because a large part of the population is 'called up' and the rest of the civilian population is subject to similar dangers: air raids and so forth. It is this similarity of the new military functions and those of the civilian population that induces the professional military to differentiate themselves and accentuate certain aspects of the traditional military ethos, like ideological rigidity, conservative orientation and social isolation, to preserve their corporate identity.

Fourthly, if the conscript mass army, through the concept of citizenship and the nation in arms (*Das Volk in Waffen*), has historically developed a certain association with the representative democratic state, we are bound to ask with what sort of state is the new professional army format likely to be associated. It is well known that the political supporters of a conscript army maintain that conscription ensures the armed forces a popular and hence democratic base, which secures a broad social consensus. For them, the introduction of a professional army would mean opening it up to political manipulation, since, in the last analysis, it will do what is best for the military itself and not necessarily what is best for the state. If this reasoning is correct, the association could be with the form of state, defined by Lasswell (1941) as the 'garrison state'. It need not necessarily be a dictatorship, even though it has certain authoritarian elements; it would be a government based on an alliance between civilian and military leaders,[24] in which the military exercised substantial political and administrative power. The military would retain organizational autonomy to the extent that it succeeded in making the appropriate alliances with civilian political factions.

Lasswell outlined two basic conditions for the development of the garrison state: (1) the power elites are sufficiently attached to power to be prepared to use large-scale coercion, if and when they judged repressive action was necessary to maintain their supremacy; and (2) the power elites share the conviction that their remaining in power, in the immediate and medium term, depends on their will to suppress internal and external opposition. From this, it logically follows that power is centralized in the hands of the executive and the military at the expense of the legislature and parties; and that technological, scientific and industrial means are subordinated to security considerations which are paramount. For this reason, he claimed that its development would be favoured by a long period of international tension. Finally, we must repeat that this form of state is not a model that exists, but a hypothesis formulated in order to evaluate certain developments in recent decades (World War II and the Cold War).[25]

It remains to add, finally, that the crisis of military goals in advanced industrialized states – the growing awareness that nuclear weapons render war senseless – led Janovitz to propose a new role for the military of these states as a peace-keeping force through the new concept of the constabulary force. This concept was intended to provide a continuity with past military experiences and traditions while also offering a basis for the radical adaptation of the military profession. 'The military establishment', Janovitz (1960) wrote, 'becomes a constabulary force when it is continuously prepared to act, committed to the minimum use of force, and seeks viable international relations, rather than victory, because it has incorporated a protective military posture' (p. 418). The obvious example of this concept in action is the establishment of United Nations peace-keeping forces, which can be seen as a first step towards the concept of an 'international police force', that would be the heir to the present armed forces. Some military observers believe this experience fundamental for determining a change of perspective and of relations between the military world and civil society, and hence of a positive revalorization of the military profession. And this is because 'these forces are the opposite of the modern politicized totalitarian army: pragmatism as against absolutism, voluntary solidarity and plurality as against enforced cohesion and uniformity and expert assistance as against ideological missionism. The future international army, being a permanent global police force, can only be created by a progressive transformation of the traditional national forces into multinational, supported, integrated and controlled forces' (Van Doorn and Mans, 1968, p. 375). Nonetheless, the limits of the great powers' commitments to such developments are evidence of the enormous difficulties to be overcome to turn Janovitz's dream into reality. In the meantime, NATO's rapid reaction force set up at the Rome summit of 1991 is a further step on the road to the achievement of the constabulary concept.

If such is the problematic posed by the two contemporary military formats, what is the situation of the military establishments in Britain, France, Germany and Italy? The first point concerns the role of the Atlantic alliance which is the reference point for the military activity of all West European states. The armed forces of three states, Britain, Germany and Italy, are, in fact, integrated in NATO's military command, whose supreme commander is always a US general. In other words, if NATO was established on the basis of a political agreement, which requires unanimity of intent, nevertheless it was, as mentioned above, initially conceived as part of the US strategy to stabilize Western Europe politically and economically in an anti-Soviet stance. For this reason, 'NATO strategy has largely been American strategy'; other countries have been consulted, but in the end 'other members have had to fit in as best they can' (Smith, 1980, p. 41). The only state to resist military integration into NATO was France, whose armed forces were taken out of the NATO supreme command by de Gaulle in 1966. However, a decade later, president Giscard d'Estaing found a way of reintegrating them through participation in the Defence Policy Committee (DPC), but France retained an independent command structure.

The significance of military integration in NATO was to restrict severely the independence of the armed forces of the individual member states. It meant quite simply that they could not act militarily without US approval – or, at least, disapproval – as the Suez fiasco of 1956 amply illustrated in the case of Britain and France. Moreover, the German armed forces, as noted, were constitutionally inhibited from being deployed outside the NATO area, which meant that they could only be used to defend NATO territorial integrity, as the German reaction to the Gulf War illustrated. Since 1990, however, European security policy has been in a state of flux and with it NATO strategy. It is no longer faced, as it had been for 40 years, with problems of deterring and defending the West against large-scale Soviet offensive operations with a strategic objective, but now has to contend with the limited use of force either within a state or across borders, such as the fighting in the former Yugoslavia.

This change provoked a debate on NATO's future in which significant national disagreements came out into the open. Nonetheless, an acceptable compromise was worked out at the Rome summit of 1991 that confirmed the continuing utility of the alliance. The previous conditions of collective security were maintained: continued stationing of US troops in Europe; continued adherence to an integrated military command structure; continued adherence to the principle of defending close to NATO borders; and continued adherence to nuclear strategy. At the same time fundamental changes were accepted, namely extensive withdrawals and massive reductions in NATO conventional forces and nuclear weapons[26] by the mid 1990s; and the creation of a rapid reaction force; however, attempts to extend NATO's area of military operations and broaden the conditions under which it can intervene were resisted, despite the Gulf War. NATO's new strategic concept thus states that it can now pursue its original aims more effectively, in a radically changed security situation, through political means.[27]

The second point regards military organization, properly speaking: the fact that Britain has adopted the professional army format while France, Germany and Italy have kept the conscript army format. This arrangement follows the national traditions: in Britain, in fact, there has always been resistance to conscription, introduced for the first time during the great emergencies of this century, the world wars. National defence was traditionally secured by the royal navy, the senior service. It is true that national service was continued until 1961 but, once the empire was liquidated and the decision taken in favour of nuclear weapons, economic pressure was such as to confirm the tradition of a small, voluntary, professional army.

On the continent, instead, the conscript army prevailed – based on the concept of the citizen-soldier, which has never had currency in Britain. France is the nation where the concept was most clearly articulated as a means of civilian control of the military. Conscription was first introduced during the revolution, and was quickly institutionalized and hence widely accepted; indeed, so much so that in the twentieth century it was extended to the notion of national service – that is to say as much civilian (*la coopération*) as military. It is no accident, therefore, that France is the country where the commitment to conscription – despite the choice of nuclear weapons[28] and the end of empire – remains the strongest. In Germany, too, conscription is linked to the concept of citizenship, thanks to the contemporaneous introduction of universal male suffrage by Bismarck in 1871. However, more important for this discussion is the concept of 'citizen in uniform' in the Bundeswehr, as the basis of German rearmament in 1956. Since it was limited to conventional weapons and fully integrated into the NATO command structure, manpower was fundamental and hence the reintroduction of conscription was logical. To secure a content to the concept of citizens in uniform, a specific programme of civic and military training (*innere Führung*) was developed and applied, which stressed the soldier's duty to maintain an awareness of his obligations to society at all times. Finally, in Italy, conscription has remained for both political reasons – to furnish a large popular base – and military reasons: to maintain the personnel at functional levels at an acceptable price.

The third point touches on some recent trends that are difficult to detail owing to the uncertainty of official data (table 10.1). Military expenditure seems to have remained at the same levels, despite inflation, throughout the post-war period: certainly there have not been sudden rises in Europe as in other historical periods. It has been calculated that military expenditure in NATO states rose 2.6 per cent per annum from 1951 to 1981 and represented between 2.9 per cent (Italy) and 5.1 per cent (Britain) of GDP,[29] the average of industrialized states. This figure of 3–5 per cent can seem rather small. However, when calculated as a percentage of public expenditure, military expenditure is three times as large (10–15 per cent), which gives a better idea of the economic cost of the military, even though the general trend over the last twenty years is towards a reduction, to be accelerated in the 1990s thanks to the 'peace dividend' accompanying the end of the Cold War. As regards the men under arms, the trend here too, since the 1960s, is towards a reduction – here again to be accelerated under NATO agreements. The phenomenon was explicable initially on the basis that, even in the conscript army nations, defence depends more and more on increasingly technologically sophisticated and costly weapons systems. Thus the length of national service was reduced and the number of exemptions was increased. It is no surprise, in this context, that the state that was able to make the greatest reduction was Britain, which has a relatively small professional army. The end of the Cold War has opened a new era: the abolition of conscription has found its way on to the political agenda in France, Germany and Italy for the first time!

The regular officer corps

Even more than with the other categories of state personnel, the differences between officers and men is such that the military group that counts is the elite which comprises the regular officer corps, from whom the senior ranks are drawn. There has been a substantial, but gradual, democratization of this corps in the last 100 years, so that recruitment has changed from an exclusively high social status – the aristocracy – to one more representative of society as a whole: prevalently middle class (table 10.2). This process has gone furthest in Germany where, as a result of the defeat of Nazism and the need to rebuild the German armed forces *ex novo* in the 1950s, there has been a dramatic decline in the social status of army officers. As regards their British colleagues, 40 of the 50 highest-ranked officers in 1981 were of higher social origin, having attended one of the prestigious English public schools. The only one of the armed services which has an officer corps of more modest social origin is the air force. Finally, there is also a strong trend in officer recruitment of military families: of sons following in their fathers' professional footsteps.

The political significance of this kind of recruitment is twofold. Firstly, it confirms Mosca's (1895) well-known thesis, according to which civilian control of the military is facilitated by the social links between the mili-

Table 10.2 Social origin of high-ranking officers (per cent)

	Britain	France	Germany	Italy
1870s				
Aristocrats	50	nd	94	nd
Middle class	50	nd	6	nd
Number	(80)	nd	(178)	nd
1890s				
Aristocrats	40	nd	81	nd
Middle class	60	nd	19	nd
Number	(63)	nd	(254)	-
1910s				
Aristocrats	35	nd	67	50
Middle class	65	nd	33	50
Number	(48)	–	(263)	(32)
1920s				
Aristocrats	27	nd	38	20
Middle class	73	nd	62	80
Number	(45)	–	(149)	(25)
1930s				
Aristocrats	22	nd	34	13
Middle class	78	nd	66	87
Number	(45)	–	(177)	(47)
1940s				
Aristocrats	nd	38	18[a]	nd
Middle class	nd	62	82[a]	nd
Number	(36)	nd		nd
1950s				
Aristocrats	25	32	nd	nd
Middle class	75	68	nd	nd
Number	(44)	(nd)	nd	nd

nd: no data.
[a] At the end of the war.
Sources: Pasquino, 1971, p. 600 and sources quoted; *La Nouvelle critique*, 57, 1959, p. 107

tary and the political elites, thanks to common values: usually a political, economic and social stake in the status quo. In the case of the West European states, in the post-war period, a significant proportion of officers have, in fact, come from the same social area as the new political elites: the middle classes. Secondly, the 'gradual' nature of the democratization of the military elite – a process which has lasted more than 100 years – has meant that it did not represent a challenge to traditional military values and, in consequence, did not provoke a sudden status crisis for the military elite. The democratization of recruitment did not lead, as

Janovitz (1975) noted, following in Tocqueville's (1835–40) footsteps, to a similar democratization of its mentality or behaviour. On the contrary, the 'military mind' remained rigid in its adherence to the values of hierarchy, group conformity, discipline and blind obedience – in the dogmatic belief of 'my country, right or wrong'. Moreover, it led, in the absence of correctives, in certain more extreme cases – those of quite a few French and Italian senior officers in the 1950s and 1960s – to reactionary political activism. However, as Wright Mills (1956) observed of the United States, the social origins of the career officer are less important than for any other social type, adding:

> The training of the future generals and admirals starts very early and so is well grounded: the service which [an officer] enters absorbs him to such a point that his life is completely centred on the military world, and as long as this situation remains, it matters little that he is a carpenter's or a millionaire's son. (p. 184)

This postulates that socialization in a military environment (military schools and colleges) counts for more than birth in the formation of the so-called military mind. It is founded on an ethic that Huntington (1957) defines as basically 'pessimistic, collectivistic, oriented towards force, naturalistic, militaristic and instrumentalist ... in brief, realistic and conservative'; in a word, anti-democratic. Against this, however, we must report that an ever-growing specialization – with accompanying intellectual quality and educational standards – has begun to take place in the military elites, so that they have started to move towards a plurality of orientation of their various component corps at the expense of the former corporatist homogeneity. If this is true, it suggests that the relation between the military and political elites, and particularly those of a conservative persuasion, is one of commonality of interests, opinions and advice rather than the simple subordination of the one to the other.

Civil–military relations

The problematic of civil–military relations usually revolves round the involvement of the armed forces in the nation's politics. A certain level of military involvement in government is inevitable from the very existence of the military as a state institution. Hence the problem is above all one of identifying the level because, as Finer (1962) has observed, there is no reason for the commonly held view that civilian control of the military is 'natural'. In fact, the military have certain overwhelming advantages over the other political institutions for intervening directly: superior organization, a monopoly of firepower, to name only the most obvious.

Finer distinguishes four levels of involvement/intervention that correspond to as many modes of action. They can be seen in terms of a continuum of civil–military relations that go from (1) civil supremacy (constitutional influence) to (4) military supremacy (coup, supplanting civilian government), passing by (2) active military participation (obstruction, blackmail) and (3) indirect military control (dictating civilian government policy). There is no need to go into the details here. It is sufficient to note that Finer's analysis is axiomatic: it relates the military's propensity to 'intervene in politics' – defined as 'the armed forces constrained substitution of their own policies and/or persons for those of recognized civil authorities' (p. 20) – to the level of the country's political culture, defined as the 'observed degree of attachment to civil institutions' (p. 18). In other words, military intervention is least likely in states with a high or 'mature' political culture because the legitimacy of military rule is 'unobtainable', and most likely in states where political culture is minimal since legitimacy is 'unimportant'. Further, Finer's analysis is limited to institutional politics and thus excludes whole areas of military involvement (economic, social and cultural affairs: Edmonds, 1988, p. 75).

At all events, West European states fit quite naturally into Finer's level 1 of military involvement in politics. Indeed, Finer's theory would appear to be prompted by Mosca's assertion that the civilian control of the military in the centres of European civilization 'represents a most fortunate exception, if not absolutely without parallel, in human history' (p. 229). However, if this statement is broadly acceptable – the occasional lapses into level 2 military involvement in politics and modes of action (see below) should not be overlooked – we still need to look for the explanation.

The initial framework of civil–military relations was outlined by Huntington (1957). Central to it was the concept of professionalism. He conceived the military career of the regular officer as a fully developed profession, even if of rather a special kind, because it exhibits the three basic features of a profession: expertness, corporate loyalty and social responsibility. However, the military operate in a political context without any consideration for political, ethical or other non-military factors in such a way that their professionalism can be defined as expert technical knowledge in the use of violence, a corporate self-identity and a social responsibility, in the sense that their management of violence is carried out for goals approved by the larger political community: the nation-state, in this instance. Hence, according to Huntington, the professional officer corps is obedient and loyal to the state's political authorities, dedicated to using its professional knowledge and technical expertise to ensuring the security of the state, and politically and morally neutral.

This professionalism, as a service ethic, is the decisive factor in keeping the military out of politics. The reason is that the framework that Huntington elaborated gives priority to the relations between experts and politicians, which, in this field, is the problem of the cleavage between the military and the political spheres: this cleavage is the source of tension between two different spheres of interest, but it also provides the key to civil–military relations. This is because, while the military know that they are technically competent in their field, they equally recognize that they are incompetent outside it. As a result, they lack political competence since it lies outside their field of competence, which is specifically military. It is for this reason, in Huntington's eyes, that the military leave politics to the politicians. Indeed, the military ethic incorporates the obligation not to take action which is inimical to the policies of the state they serve. Thus the tasks and responsibilities of the military are restricted to representing the military's needs – equipment, weaponry, personnel – to the political authorities, furnishing professional advice and finally, when charged, carrying out the relevant decisions.

According to Finer, Huntington's logic is sound, but his premises are false; and this because he defines military professionalism in a certain way and deduces a certain service ethic from it. If the military do not follow the military ethic – as they manifestly do not from time to time – they are defined as not professional! But Finer's critique goes further, arguing that the elements of military professionalism identified by Huntington, far from impeding the military from intervening politically, actually push them in that direction. Thus, for instance, the corporate awareness of being a profession serving the state can, in certain critical circumstances, lead them to oppose government policy, in the name of the superior interest of the state or nation as they conceive it. Or again, their responsibility for national security can give them a view of the state's basic military requirements which can be in conflict with those of the government. These are not abstract arguments, as Khrushchev's (1971) memoirs make plain. He recalls a conversation with president Eisenhower:

> 'It's like this. My military leaders come to me and say, "Mr president, we need such and such a sum for such and such a programme". I say, "sorry, we don't have the funds." They say, "We have reliable information that the Soviet Union has already allocated funds for their own such programme. If we don't get the funds we need, we'll fall behind the Soviet Union." So I give in. That's how they wring money out of me ... Now tell me, how it is with you?'
>
> 'It is just the same. Some people from our military department come and say, "comrade Khrushchev, look at this! The Americans are developing such and such a system. We could develop the same system, but it would cost such and such." I tell them there's no money; it has all been allotted already. So they say, "If we don't get the money we need and if there's a war, then the enemy will have superiority over us." So we discuss it some more and I end up by giving them the money they ask for.'
>
> 'Yes,' he said, 'that's what I thought.' (pp. 519–20).

For Finer, the only way to ensure adequate political control over the military is that they *explicitly* believe in the principle of civilian supremacy; but this cannot be reduced to a problem of professionalism as such. It is, as Finer remarks, part and parcel of a larger problem, namely the military's acceptance of constitutional arrangements, for which we need to look elsewhere. Before we do so, we ought perhaps to point out that acceptance of constitutional arrangements does not necessarily mean belief in democracy; it helps, of course, but, as suggested, democracy and the military mind remain largely antithetical.

What then are the sources of the belief in the principle of civilian supremacy, that Mosca claimed to be unique to Europe? One source would be the lucid justification of the political direction of military affairs, formulated by Clausewitz (1832–4), according to which 'subordinating the political point of view to the military would be absurd, for it is policy that creates war. Policy is the guiding intelligence and war only the instrument, not vice versa. No other possibility exists, then, than to subordinate the military point of view to the political' (p. 607). But, despite the profound influence of Clausewitz on modern strategic thought, it is rare that coherent reasoning determines the collective behaviour of men or institutions. A second source would be the constitutional arrangements which explicitly state that political power is conferred by popular sovereignty, and hence that the government's legitimate authority derives from free elections; and, further, that the armed forces are explicitly subordinate to political power. This is the case of the French, German and Italian constitutions. They specify certain modes of constitutional control of the military: (1) investing the supreme command of the armed forces in the head of state: (2) putting the armed forces under the control of a special institution, like the French Conseil Supérieur de la Défense Nationale, or the Italian Consiglio Supremo di Difesa (in which key politicians and military leaders are members); (3) the need for parliamentary consent for declarations of war, as in the German basic law (article 80A). But, as in the case of strategic thought and professional military ethic, constitutional arrangements are as likely to confuse shadow with substance, for the reason that Hobbes spelled out long ago: 'covenants, without swords, are but words, and of no strength to secure a man at all.' In other words, it is not the existence of the arrangements in themselves that guarantees their respect, as many historical examples attest. They have to be institutionalized. However, the existence of constitutional rules, like a professional ethic, has a certain advantage, that of defining the legal situation, a fact which can only strengthen the political authorities' legitimacy in case of an eventual conflict with military leaders.

A third source would be Mosca's well-known thesis on the integration of the military leaders into the ruling class. In fact, Mosca maintained that an officer corps of aristocratic origin was the most appropriate for the limited democracy of his time, in so far as only an officer class which had effective social links with other members of the elite – mostly aristo-

crats themselves – could supply the necessary guarantees of social equilibrium. Thanks to its sense of honour the government could count on
the military's loyalty, although it remained outside the partisan political
struggle. Mosca reasoned that in virtue of the common values and the
economic and social privileges – 'birth, culture and wealth' – that both
the officer corps and the political elite enjoyed, there should not be any
real conflicts between the two. A fourth source, more political than
social, would be the so-called 'citizen in uniform'. The thesis in this case
is the opposite of the previous one and was made explicit by Tocqueville
(1835–40) 150 years ago: 'in democracies it is the private soldiers who
remain most like civilians; and it is on them that national habits have the
firmest hold and public opinion the strongest influence. It is especially
through the soldiers that one may well hope to inspire a democratic
army with the same love of liberty and respect for law as has been
infused into the nation itself' (p. 846). The reasoning is that in an army
with broad popular recruitment, the officer corps is obliged to take
account of the soldiers' orientation; and this is even more so when the
concept of the 'army, school of the nation' is integrated with conscription
and so ensures – at least in theory – a common experience for conscripts
and regulars. In the eyes of left-wing politicians, this is the surest way of
securing civilian control of the military and preventing political manipulation by military leaders.

All these aspects contribute to strengthening civilian control, but none
is sufficient by itself. The important thing, to recall Finer, is that the military really do believe in the principle of civilian supremacy. However,
beliefs are not formed in a day; they take time. Moreover, they are
formed in the course of a country's history; and in a precise geopolitical
context and in a specific institutional framework. The importance of
these historical experiences was already understood by Mosca when he
noted that: 'as a matter of fact, it has been possible to subordinate the
standing army to the civil authority, only through an intense and widespread development of the sentiments on which juridical defence is
based, and especially through an exceptionally favourable sequence of
historical circumstances' (p. 229).

This is not the place to analyse the historical and geopolitical factors
that were responsible for the diverse roles of the military in Europe.
Suffice it to note the contrast between the British and the continental
countries' experiences. In the case of Britain – an island – a standing
army was the exception, thanks to its lack of a land frontier, and hence
its defence until 1945 was entrusted to the navy: these were factors that
facilitated political control of the military. In the case of the continental
countries with long land frontiers, on the other hand, the army became,
in Raymond Aron's phrase, 'the nation's protector', and hence it was
much more difficult to institutionalize political control of the military.
Thus despite a long experience of subordination, at least formally, of the
armed forces to the civilian power – summed up in the case of the French

army in the nickname *la grande muette* – generals like Weygand could justify their autonomy with the thesis that 'the army is nothing but ... the nation'; other examples can be cited, like that of general von Seeky, who claimed in 1921 that 'the army should become a state within the state through military service; in fact, it should become the purest image of the state.'

From all this we can deduce that if Europe's 'unique' history supports the notion of civilian political supremacy, there have nonetheless been various attempts by the military to give themselves an active political role as and when the opportunity occurred. But these attempts have been rare, all things considered, and all have been unsuccessful in the last 100 years. And this is true, if we take the Curragh mutiny in 1914 (Britain); the Kapp putsch of 1920 or the generals' plot against Hitler[30] in 1944 (Germany); the two serious coups in Algeria in 1958 and 1962 (France); or the various attempted plots in Italy, such as De Lorenzo in 1964 and Borghese in 1970.

Analysis of the various British, German and French (but not Italian) episodes suggests that they were encouraged by a period of tension and conflict in the relations between the armed forces and the civilian government, in which the state's authority was weakened, and that the principal factor in the failure of the military manoeuvres was the reaction of public opinion, that is to say the more or less resolute opposition of the civilian population to their plans. This was particularly evident in the Kapp putsch when, having installed Kapp in the chancellery and having forced the legitimate government to flee to Dresden, the army found itself ignored by the whole civilian population. In effect, after the proclamation of the general strike, followed by five days' isolation in the chancellery, Kapp fled to Sweden. The similar attempts of the French officers in Algeria confirmed this thesis: in 1958 the military intervention showed that they could bring down the government and even a regime, but not impose a new one. De Gaulle came to power thanks to a favourable movement of opinion and resolved the country's political and constitutional crisis. In 1961, de Gaulle's resolute opposition and the civilian population's lack of support for the generals' cause ensured the failure of the rebellion within five days. In short, the conclusion for these three states would seem to lie, not with Hobbes, but with Rousseau (1762): 'let us then admit that force does not create right, and that one is obliged to obey only legitimate powers' (book I, chapter III).

The Italian case appears more problematic to the extent that the political interventions of the military were not the result of a confrontation between armed forces and political power, but the involvement of certain sectors of the armed forces, intelligence services, terrorist groups and even the Mafia in strategies of political destabilization: in other words, in attempts to prevent any effective movement of the political axis to the left.[31] Hence arises the difficulty and ambiguity in comprehending the series of tragic events – attempted plots, strategy of tension, terrorist bombings – which have continued right down to the present (bomb explosions in Rome, Milan and Florence 1992–3).

Thus, if the form of civilian control has been more or less maintained throughout the post-war period in Western Europe, it has been above all at the cost of the substantive democratic process. We have already noted the antithesis between military mind and democracy, so it comes as no surprise to conclude that current military policies impose severe limits on the constitutional democratic process. Military issues in general and fateful matters in particular, like war and nuclear strategy, are decided by a very small policy elite *without* public debate. Indeed, in a recent study Bruce Russett (1990) claims that decisions on national security in Western democracies are 'insulated from popular control and knowledge' (p. 148). Thus, at the secret meetings where military decisions are taken, it is usually unnecessary for the military leadership to challenge the civilian power's authority: the mere threat of a diffuse sanction suffices, for instance that of lord Montgomery, chief of the British imperial general staff, in 1949 during the Korean War, to resign along with the whole of the army council, if the Labour government reduced conscription to less than eighteen months.

Furthermore, experience shows that most politicians, and above all those on the left, show little interest in military matters and prefer to leave what they consider to be a specialized and technical field to the military. Dr David Owen (Labour navy minister in the 1960s) observed that:

> working within a defence ministry one becomes increasingly aware that the military are reluctant to accept guidance in the detailed process of policy-making. Yet this is the very area which should be the major concern of a politician ... The insidious process of military indoctrination, a heady mixture of pomp and secrecy to which most politicians involved in defence are susceptible, tends to blunt one's normal sensitivity. One can easily become part of the very military machine that one is supposed to control. (1972, p. 14)

It is probable that a similar situation of psychological subordination to the military[32] – even in fields like foreign policy and public order, through official secrecy and security – exists in the other West European states. At all events, defence policy in Western Europe is the result of a complex set of formal and informal relations between a very restricted group of politicians, higher civil servants, arms manufacturers and military leaders in the context defined by NATO in which the military defend their priorities as they understand them. The Italian situation was described by D'Orsi (1971) some years ago:

> In the last analysis, we can explain the extra-constitutional relations between politicians (in or out of government, but in the area

of the centre and right-wing parties), generals and arms manufacturers as follows: the armaments industry strongly conditions the
operation of the armed forces; the politicians act as go-betweens
and seek advantages in terms of power, both from the armaments
industry, or rather from the economic spheres that underpin it,
and from the military elite; the latter, split into hostile groups,
seek to build a personal type of power based on precarious
alliances with politicians and a modest cut, even indirect, of the
armaments industry's profits. (pp. 154–5)

The military-industrial complex

The fourth and final area to discuss is the concept of the military-industrial complex. It was coined to take account of an American phenomenon and, moreover, is not very precise. In fact, there are two versions.
One is that of Wright Mills (1956), according to which there is integration between the principal political, economic and military institutional
spheres in the US. In this version, the USA is ruled by an economico-
military elite which is subject to no countervailing powers – neither from
the political elite nor from the population whose vote has a purely formal value. Several years later, Galbraith (1967) assimilated the concept
of a symbiotic relationship between armed forces, government and
industry into his analysis of the 'technostructure' (chapter 8) to explain
the absolute domination of technocracy and the giant corporations in
society. In his version, the nature of the decision-making process of the
giant corporations is such that it requires a structure in which the technical and political aspects are coordinated.

In the second version, which was of neo-Marxist orientation (Baran
and Sweezy, 1966; Mandel, 1972), it is claimed that arms production is to
be explained in terms of the needs of capitalism in peacetime: stimulating economic growth, promoting prosperity at home, expanding economic and political interests abroad, and providing a rationale for the
dominant political and economic oligarchy. The military-industrial complex is thus nothing more than the social form of such imperatives. There
is, however, some agreement on the facts that gave rise to the concept in
the US: (1) increased participation of the military in government; (2)
organized intervention (public relations) of the arms lobby in all areas of
society; (3) the large number of workers that depend on the arms industry; and (4) the proliferation of former officers employed in firms working on military contracts.

Neither of the two versions, however, really stands up to rigorous
scrutiny in Western Europe. For them to do so, we would have to show,
firstly, the specific links of interdependence between the arms industry
and the other industrial sectors; and, secondly, that the economies of
these states were so dependent on these links that the politicians were

obliged to accept the dictates of the arms industry as a productive necessity. It is true that the arms industry is one of the most important sectors in Western Europe, but this does not mean that these states are dependent on it alone for their prosperity. If this is so, then we can conclude that the military-industrial complex does not dictate to West European states to the extent that it does in the USA. Such a conclusion, moreover, is intended to suggest not that military leaders and arms lobbies are not influential in Western Europe – often, they manifestly are[33] – but rather that they do not constitute an overwhelmingly cohesive group, despite coalitions of interest in the major West European states, and their interests are not necessarily the same as those of the government. As Giddens (1986) has observed, the only validity that the concept of the military-industrial complex can have relates to the US and derives from the element of coordinated planning made necessary by superpower rivalry, which was part of the arms race that Gorbachev first, and the breakup of the former USSR subsequently, have succeeded in slowing down, if not halting as yet.

Special agencies and *arcana imperii*

Arcana imperii – secret activity by the guardians of the state, according to a classical definition – has a long history,[34] but in the modern world its contribution to diplomatic history, if not political and military history more generally, is claimed to be the 'missing dimension'. The reason is simple: it contradicts democratic principles and disavows the claim of the Western democracies, proclaimed continuously throughout the post-war period, to be open societies with 'visible governments' and 'power without masks'. For this reason, as Bobbio (1984) noted with his usual shrewdness, the topic of 'invisible power' has been neglected by contemporary Western political science.[35] It has not always been so: the Machiavellian tradition which included the sixteenth and seventeenth century French school of political writings discussed it at length. The subject of the 'dual state' recalls Bagehot's (1867) analysis, in which he distinguished between the 'dignified' or visible parts, and the 'efficient', or invisible parts, of the English constitution (see the introduction to this book). The logical basis of *arcana imperii*, at least for its backers, is also relatively simple: without the state, there would be neither civil peace nor visible government; therefore every act, moral or immoral, which fosters the good of the state is legitimate. The conception of the dual state has acquired dramatic relevance for public opinion in Western Europe with the explosion of terrorism in the 1970s and 1980s.

An essential element for governing has always been the need for intelligence about one's own country as well as about one's enemies' countries. In fact, the objective of the opening of the first diplomatic missions in Renaissance Europe was to exercise a form of scrutiny of the activity of rival states. Today, emphasis is placed on the fact that the principal task of the intelligence service is to obtain and analyse information about foreign states that policy-makers need, and that this cannot always be acquired by conventional methods. In other words, it is a case of monitoring the activity, military above all, but also economic and political, of other states. In general, some 80 per cent of intelligence is collected overtly through the channels that generically inform public opinion: press agencies, mass media, publications. What they lack, however, is what is called in professional jargon 'strategic intelligence', namely the future military plans and capabilities of enemy, or potentially enemy, states. For this, recourse is had to a variety of covert methods and techniques: secret agents, informers, telephone bugging, breakins, blackmail, bribes and threats. All this is undertaken so that the government is able to formulate effective policies in the fields of foreign affairs, defence and even political economy.

If detailed intelligence and correct appraisal have always been important, they are even more so today in a world still dominated by the risk of a nuclear holocaust: one mistake and it could be Armageddon. Nevertheless, the list of errors of appraisal of the military intentions of potential enemies is embarrassingly long. For instance, the surprise Nazi German attack against the USSR in 1941; or the Japanese attack on the US fleet in Pearl Harbor in the same year; or the installation of Soviet missiles on Cuba in 1962; or again the Tet offensive in Vietnam in spring 1968 which caught the USA on the hop. And one could continue: the Israeli surprise at the Arab attack in the Yom Kippur War of 1973; the British surprise at the Argentinian invasion of the Falklands in 1982; or that of the West at the Iraqi occupation of Kuwait in 1990. The causes were various: disinformation, distorted views of the enemy from prejudice, unfounded expectations.[36] All of which confirms that failures in this field are inevitable. The question posed, to which we can give no proper reply, owing to 'official secrecy', is whether this is just the tip of the iceberg.

The intelligence and security services

Whatever the truth, if intelligence collection is the principal task of the secret services, it is evident that they have to protect themselves against similar initiatives from enemies or potential enemies. This second task, better known as counter-espionage or counter-intelligence, has two specific aspects: (1) the protection of official secrets and classified information, often economic in addition to military and political; (2) the protection of the state's own intelligence structure from penetration by the secret agents of a hostile foreign state, like the infiltration of East

German agent Günther Guillaume into chancellor Brandt's personal office; his unmasking in 1974 led to Brandt's resignation.[37] However, counter-intelligence activity is directed not only against foreign nationals, but also against the state's own nationals suspected of sympathies for a foreign state or political regime. It is here that political abuses can occur: the surveillance of groups and individuals, on the pretext of subversive activity, can easily be extended to government's domestic political adversaries, as illustrated, for example, by the affair of the secret service files in Italy in the 1960s through to the 1980s (Ferraresi, 1992), or the bugging of the editorial offices of the satirical newspaper *Le Canard enchaîné* by the DST in France in 1972.[38]

Finally, secret services can be entrusted with two further tasks. The first is 'disinformation', that is disseminating entirely or partially false information with the object of neutralizing enemy agents or provoking situations of discontent, disorientation and demoralization in an enemy state in order to induce its leaders to take certain decisions rather than others. One thinks, for instance, of the false documents spread by the Allies during the war to mislead the Germans about the Normandy landings in 1944, or the activity of the Soviet agent P.-C. Pathé with his bulletin *Synthèses* distributed in France from 1955 to 1974. The second task is 'covert action', which includes a wide variety of actions. One is *subverting* the enemy, by supporting terrorists, assassins, resistance movements and insurgents: for instance, US support for the Contras in Nicaragua, or that of the French SDECE for Hissène Habré against Goukouni Oueddei and the Libyans in Chad in the 1980s. Another is *terrorizing* the enemy through paramilitary activity to weaken the state's power structure, such as the American air raid on Tripoli in 1986 against Gaddafi, or to discredit a group, for example the sinking of Greenpeace's ship *Rainbow Warrior* by the French SDECE in Auckland (NZ) harbour in 1985 to prevent it protesting against the resumption of French nuclear testing in the Pacific. A third is *special operations*: covert military assistance, assassination, scandals, blackmail. Examples include the numerous British and French clandestine operations in their colonies or former colonies, one of the most recent being the 'elimination' by the British SAS of three alleged IRA terrorists in Gibraltar in 1988.

Secret services are generally classified into four types: (1) intelligence service; (2) secret intelligence service; (3) secret service; and (4) security service. The first type of organization's task is the collection, evaluation, dissemination and exploitation of intelligence. It becomes the second type if all, or part, of this activity is carried on covertly. But it can also perform tasks other than intelligence, in which case it becomes the third type. Finally, if its tasks include the protection of an individual or an institution, it can be considered the fourth type. In actual fact, however, the various organizations operating in this area in Britain, France, Germany and Italy cannot be defined in terms of these four types of service. The situation is more complex and, moreover, varies from state to state. Two distinctions have, nonetheless, a certain value. The first is between foreign and domestic intelligence. In Britain, a distinction is made between the secret intelligence service DI6, formerly MI6 (foreign intelligence and counter-espionage), and the security service DI5, formerly MI5 (domestic intelligence and counter-espionage); in France between the Direction Générale de la Sécurité Extérieure (DGSE), formerly SDECE (foreign intelligence and counter-espionage), and the Direction de la Surveillance du Territoire (DST) (domestic intelligence and counter-espionage); and in Germany between the Bundesnachrichtendienst (BND) (foreign intelligence) and the Bundesamt für Verfassungsschutz (BFV) (domestic intelligence and counter-espionage). The second distinction is between military and civil services, like the Servizio per le Informazioni e la Sicurezza Militare (SISMI), formerly SIFAR, and the Servizio per le Informazioni e la Sicurezza Domestica (SISDE), in Italy.[39]

In all European states, there are special agents active in the field of secret intelligence and security. The reason, it is claimed, is to avoid having to depend on one service only. Thus the British (Defence Intelligence Service), French (Deuxième Bureau), German (Militärischer Abschirmdienst) and Italian (Servizio Informazioni Operative e Situazione) military have their own intelligence units, usually coordinated at the level of the defence ministry. Moreover, there are also special police corps, like the Special Branch in Britain, the Renseignements Généraux and the Sûreté Nationale in France, and the Arma dei Carabinieri and the Corpo di Pubblica Sicurezza in Italy, charged with national security problems. The armed forces and police in every country have their special intervention groups: the SAS (Special Air Service: military) and the SPG (Special Patrol Group: police) in Britain; the GIGN (Groupe d'Intervention de la Gendarmerie Nationale) in France; and the Corpo Speciale dell'Antiterrorismo dei Carabinieri in Italy. Finally, there are also organizations like the British Government Communications Headquarters (GCHQ) and the French Groupement de Communications Radioélectriques (GCR), which are responsible for intercepting and decoding radio communications.

Invisible power and political control

This imposing complex of organizations and special corps poses a number of problems for a discussion of invisible power. The first problem is quite simply that it is becoming increasingly clear today that this list is far from complete, above all as regards secret and clandestine agencies and groups responsible for 'dirty' operations. For instance, revelations in 1990 of the variously code-named secret network (Operation Stay Behind, Gladio in Italy, Glaive in France, Schwert in West Germany), created under NATO auspices, confirm the existence of networks parallel to the individual member states' institutional ones, no different from those of which the Warsaw Pact was formerly accused. The second problem is relatively simple and regards the recruitment and socialization of the members of these special corps. We have already noted the class origin of the upper echelons of the diplomatic corps and the armed forces: the secret services are no different. It is no accident that the public schools supplied agents like Philby and Maclean, as well as the directors of MI5, Dick Goldsmith-White, Roger Hollis, Martin Furnival-Jones, Michael Hanley and Howard Smith,[40] or that the ranks of the aristocracy provided the heads of the French secret services, like the comte de Marenches, director of the SDECE, and his deputy, colonel A.G. de Marolles. However, as regards instead the police chiefs, the data suggest a different social origin to the other elites, namely a lower middle class extraction, particularly in the case of Britain. In general, few had been to the university and most officers had started on the beat. In the continental states, the average educational level of the police hierarchy is superior to that in Britain.[41]

However, the attitudes of the various special corps appear more homogeneous: for instance, the police tend to recruit persons of conservative orientation, with authoritarian personalities, who are socialized into what has been called 'cop culture'.[42] It is a rather closed world and the police officer usually feels isolated in relation to the rest of society; hence there is a certain machismo. In this situation, a particular perspective of the divisions within society and distinctive stereotypes as to who and what is a criminal are formed. Exemplary in this connection was the reply of the chief constable of Manchester to a question on the greatest threat to the preservation of law and order in Britain in 1979:

> basic crime as such, theft, burglary, even violent crime, will not be the predominant police feature ... The threat to 'law and order' today comes from 'seditionists', 'political factions whose designed end is the overthrow of democracy as we know it' – persons at work 'in the field of public order', in industrial relations and politics, whose aim is to 'subvert the authority of the state and ... involve themselves in acts of sedition'. (quoted by Thompson, 1980, p. 210)[43]

The third problem concerns the political control of the population. However, it is obvious that there is substantial diversity between the police forces of Britain, France, Germany and Italy in organization and methods as a result of different formative experiences and national structures and practice. These are usefully summarized in table 10.3. The main contrast is between the decentralized (bottom-up) forces with some local accountability in Britain and Germany, and the centralized (top-down) forces accountable to national political institutions in France and Italy. Despite this diversity, there are signs of convergence in European police systems, particularly in relation to those features involving task performance, like training and specialization, where standards of efficiency can be applied.

As regards political surveillance, it is well known that no political meeting takes place in any country without the presence of an informer and that all movements are infiltrated. The history of the European labour movements, in fact, has been written thanks to police reports (Special Branch, Renseignements Généraux, Carabinieri), according to the techniques perfected by Joseph Fouché, Napoleon's minister of police. There are three aspects worthy of note. Firstly, there are no limits to the number of people who can be placed under surveillance, if it is true, as the British Labour home secretary Merlyn Rees publicly stated in 1977, that 'the Special Branch collects information on those whom I think can cause the state problems.' There is talk of 3 million personal files in Britain,[44] and as many, if not more, in other countries. With the development of computerization, encouraged amongst other things by the fight against terrorism, all this information can be handled by a central police computer system (the police national computer in Britain). Minority groups, above all foreign immigrants and non-whites, are particularly at risk. Secondly, this surveillance can take all forms imaginable, from phone tapping to opening mail, to photographing and videoing all political demonstrations. Telephone tapping requires the authorization of the Home Office or the judicial authorities, but the published figures of authorizations are not very credible (about 500 a year, and mainly for crime and drug trafficking). Thirdly, candidates for public employment, above all at a senior, but also today at an executive, level are positively vetted, which means an investigation into their private and social life, as well as their political opinions and activity. Those who have social relations considered to be subversive (during the Cold War, it was sufficient to be leftish,[45] and not only communist) are excluded from a career in the public service. Today in Britain, it is not just a case of information classified as 'assistance to the enemy', but simply any information politically embarrassing for the government of the day (for instance, the Ponting affair of 1985).

People rightly protested in other European countries against the *Berufsverbot*, the radical decree that permits the German authorities, both federal and *Land*, to sack any public servant who holds views that are judged to be opposed to the basic law,[46] but they overlooked the fact that similar things happened, often bureaucratically and without suscitating similar protests, in their own countries. As regards the criteria used in these cases, often nothing is known officially; in the British case the government refuses to answer questions in the House of Commons on the grounds of national security and official secrecy, as in the case of the GCHQ staff's loss of union rights in 1984. We do not wish to suggest that the situation is that described by the hero of George Orwell's novel, *Nineteen Eighty-Four*, Winston Smith, tracked down also by the 'thought

Table 10.3 Structure of national police systems

	Britain	France	Germany	Italy
Tasks				
Formal	Narrow	Extensive	Extensive	Extensive
Informal	Extensive	Some	Few	None
Political	Very modest	Modest, extensive intelligence	Modest	Extensive
National structure				
Nature of authority aggregation	Decentralized	Centralized	Decentralized	Centralized
Number of distinct forces	Singular	Plural	Singular	Plural
Nature of control				
Political	Local, representative	Central, bureaucratic	Local, bureaucratic	Central, bureaucratic
Legal	Subject to unified legal code	Subject to administrative court system	Subject to administrative court system	Subject to administrative court system
Internal organization				
Rank Organization	Singular	Bifurcated	Bifurcated	Bifurcated
Training	Civilian	Civilian	Military	Military
Functional specialization	Considerable	Considerable	Considerable	Considerable
Role behaviour and image				
Perceived character	Trustworthy, approachable, respected	Distrusted, unapproachable, efficient	Authoritarian, unapproachable, honest	Feared, corrupt, quixotic
Mode of intervention	Individual, informal	Formal	Formal, in groups	Punitive, in groups
Armament	None	Armed	Armed	Armed

Source: Bayley, 1975, p. 341

police', but some Italians could certainly be forgiven for thinking so. Undoubtedly steps, if only minor ones, have been taken in that direction in all West European states.

The last problem touches the political power of the special corps. It is virtually impossible to appraise accurately given the element of official secrecy. Without adequate information, there is no real possibility of effective control. The one thing that we can say is that the ideas and movements that support positions defined as subversive by the ortho-doxies of the special corps have great difficulty in finding expression because of the surveillance and harassment to which they are subjected. This does not mean that the positions considered orthodox by the special corps are not shared by the majority of the population, but the resort, in increasingly heavy-handed ways with increasingly sophisticated tech-niques, to *arcana imperii* can only deprive the so-called 'civil rights' of their content. Minority groups quickly become aware that 'spying, bru-tality, arbitrary use of power and preparedness to take the law into their own hands is an integral part of the nature of any police system' (Chapman, 1970, p. 81).

Finally, a much more specific point concerns the collection of informa-tion: any one who expresses dissent quickly realizes that any information about him is an instrument of power, as the inquisitor O'Brien brought home to Winston Smith in *Nineteen Eighty-Four*. Obvious examples of secret service blackmail are the SIFAR files and the various dirty tricks in Italy from the De Lorenzo affair in the 1960s to the P2 scandal in the 1980s. As regards the former, the Beolchini enquiry confirmed that all sorts of information were collected:

> items that had no conceivable relation with state security, but concerned the most intimate and reserved details of private life; when as a result of the very nature of the material collected, one had every reason to fear that the documentary information could be used to damage the person, in the pursuance of unclear goals and unconnected with the public interest. (quoted in Martinelli, 1968, p. 225)

All the evidence is that this judgement can be extended to the latter. Ferraresi (1992) has recently noted that the relations between Italian politicians and the secret services are traditionally governed by exchanges of favours, but: 'in this instance, the exchange centres around secret files held by Intelligence and used rather routinely for the purpose of blackmail, which makes Italy's political scene unique compared with other advanced countries' (p. 42).

Another instance, which suggests that Ferraresi's judgement of Italy is a little harsh, is journalist Chapman Pincher's (1978) reconstruction of MI5 hostility to the Wilson Labour governments, which also found an echo in the English spy Peter Wright's best-seller *Spycatcher* (1988).[47]

According to Pincher, 'the undermining activities which Wilson complained of were not only genuine, but far more menacing than he revealed. Certain officers inside MI5, assisted by others who had retired from the service, were actually trying to bring the Labour government down and, in my opinion, they could at one point have succeeded' (pp. 16–17). More recently, the revelations over the Italian Gladio illustrate an even more serious situation: groups of civilians, trained in unconventional warfare to organize, under NATO auspices, a form of armed resistance in case of Soviet invasion of the country, were used for covert, unconstitutional and violent actions (provocations and massacres) against left-wing parties and political groups (De Lutiis, 1991). As Ferraresi has pointed out: 'it is not a large step to move from these revelations to the conclusion that Gladio was a private army of the parties of the centre-right' (p. 37). This explains perhaps the reluctance of governments to discipline the special corps, from the French affair *des généraux* of 1949 to the British Stalker affair in 1986. These incidents merely confirm the general relevance of the conclusions of the Beolchini enquiry: 'it turns out that it acted outside any control and so was able to develop its action in an anomalous way, outside proper and legitimate limits without any responsible directive' (in Martinelli, 1968, p. 260).

Discussion on invisible power would be incomplete without a reference to the terrorist phenomenon in Western Europe in the 1970s and 1980s, all the more so since links have emerged with secret agents. In view of the phenomenon's complexity, discussion is limited to a few rapid notations on the various national situations. The British case is particular, in that it involves mainly a limited area, Ulster, and in this sense has some analogies with Corsica, even though the problem has a longer history. In Germany and France terrorism has been limited to a certain number of sensational actions, like the abduction and assassination of the German industrialists' leader Schleyer in 1977, or the assassination of the Renault boss Best in 1986, because it was the activity of small groups who lacked any consistent support in the rest of society. Only in Italy, in certain specific cities (Turin, Milan, Padua, Rome and Naples) and in certain limited periods (1973–4 and 1977–9) did the terrorists succeed in enjoying some popular support. In all states terrorism has been tackled as a problem of public order, that is as a non-political problem, and treated as criminal activity. The political authorities' problem has been to demonstrate the credibility of the fight against terrorism without playing the terrorists' game of introducing repressive measures contrary to liberal democratic values.

For this reason, the response was articulated at two levels: (1) a centralization of repressive resources – special anti-terrorist squads, new security procedures, use of information technology – usually implemented by administrative means; and (2) international cooperation, and in particular within the EU, to define a European legal area and to update extradition procedures. We can conclude by observing that terrorism had less dramatic consequences than was feared, above all when seen in the light of the European history of the first part of the century, in the sense that it was possible to avoid a creeping authoritarianism. This was due in Germany to the limited nature of the movement; and in Italy, paradoxically, to political immobilism that protected the country from a leap in the dark, that is from embarking on repressive political action.

In this situation we would do well, as Bobbio (1984) repeatedly reminds us, not to underrate the consequences for democracy of invisible power. It flagrantly contradicts the democratic principle that requires the exercise of power to be visible. However, the solution lies not in dismantling the secret services or the special corps – because, as Bobbio himself has pointed out, 'there never has been a state, whether autocratic or democratic, which has done without them' (p. 92) – but in placing them under effective democratic control. A first step would be to define their tasks and prerogatives by legal rules that would permit their victims (simple citizens) to defend themselves against abuse without being accused of lack of patriotism. This is already the case in France (decree of 1982), Italy (law 801/1977) and Germany. It is obvious that legal rules have their limits and an effective democratic control requires much more. A second step should be parliamentary control exercised by a standing committee. This exists only in Italy, where law 801/1977, as a result of numerous scandals, established an appropriate committee, the Comitato Parlamentare di Controllo sui Servizi, made up of four deputies and four senators, bound by official secrecy, but with the right of appeal to both chambers.[48]

In contrast, there is nothing of the kind in Britain: the government strenuously refused to define publicly the tasks of the secret services, reaffirmed by the Official Secrets Act of 1990, and to subject them to effective democratic control before 1992. Until now they have operated under the responsibility of the prime minister and could not be discussed, even in parliament,[49] just because they were secret. The official doctrine remains that announced in 1924 by the then foreign secretary, Sir Austen Chamberlain: 'it is of the essence of a secret service that it must be secret, and if you once begin disclosure it is perfectly obvious … that there is no longer any secret service and that you must do without it' (quoted in Andrew and Dilks, 1984, p. 15). This seems to have been the official view that has prevailed in Italy, despite law 801/1977, if it is true that Gladio continued its clandestine activities in conjunction with the secret services unbeknown to parliament until 1990.

'One should remember' – wrote Thomas Jefferson almost 200 years ago – 'that any autonomous power, in any government, is an absolute power.'

Conclusion

Military capability has always played a role in West European politics. State formation resulted from a long, and often violent, struggle both to assert control over national territory and to ensure its survival in the international arena. Peace and war symbolised in the twin figures of diplomats and soldiers represent the two opposing aspects of the state's interest in international affairs which justified *raison d'état*, invisible power and the so-called secret state (the occult activities of the intelligence and security agencies). It is often claimed that not only are the rules of international politics different from those of domestic politics, but also a state's foreign and defence politics are more likely to be successful if its real intentions are not publicized.

The international context in which West European states have historically operated was one of conflict among a plurality of rival states that their rulers attempted to dominate using the instruments available to them: war, diplomacy, alliances, international organization. The result was the European states' system: a framework of rules, procedures and diplomatic expedients that endeavoured to regulate, from the seventeenth century, the relations between states and preserve peace. It was organized round five great powers which were stronger than the rest, but which realized that they were individually unable to dominate the continent militarily and politically. Thus they developed the notion of the balance of power, that is fluctuating alliances between a number of states to offset the power of hostile alliances and establish an international structure (system of public law). It did not prevent, however, individual great powers (Spain, Austria, France) from attempting to dominate the continent at different moments.

After the Napoleonic adventure, the Congress of Vienna attempted to found a more stable system of collaboration, the concert of Europe. It succeeded in preserving the peace on the continent for almost 100 years. However, it became progressively more unstable as the nineteenth century advanced and eventually broke down under the strains of industrialization and democratization, and the resulting nationalistic mobilization of public opinions. The dislocation of the Habsburg Empire and above all the unification of Germany destroyed the balance of power by creating a great power capable of dominating the continent for the first time since the collapse of the Holy Roman Empire. Two world wars confirmed that there was no European state, or alliance of European states, capable of checking German power.

European liberation by extra-European powers (USA and USSR) in 1945 created a totally new situation on the continent. Europe was no longer master of its own destiny; it was in the hands of two superpowers whose ideological conflict divided the continent in the Cold War and led to the institutionalization of their power in two monolithic blocs that were to last for 40 years. The Western Bloc, organized round NATO, quickly created what Gambino has called an imperfect protectorate because Western Europe was dependent on the presence of US troops and nuclear weapons for its security: America called the tunes both militarily and politically.

The civilian face of Europe saw the development of supranational cooperation in the economic field, leading to the establishment of the EC. This originally had the configuration of an international regime, that is a set of norms and procedures facilitating cooperation between member states on a broad range of issues. As a result of the SEA and the Maastricht Treaty, it developed into something more: what has been called an experiment in pooling sovereignty. It was stronger than an international organization because it had executive capacity and (limited) financial resources, but weaker than a supranational state.

Hoffmann explains the unexpected impetus for institutional development in the 1980s as a combination of functional spill-over – the effects of membership enlargement – and political realism, due to waning European competitiveness consequent upon a convergence of policy preferences of the major EC member states around deregulation which required, to be effective, reform of EC decision-making and hence the SEA. In other words, it resulted less from a coherent burst of idealism and more from a convergence of national economic interests. The revival, moreover, was an example of negative integration (removal of barriers) and not positive integration (active intervention promoting harmony between members).

The collapse of communism rendered the division of Europe into two ideological blocs no longer relevant: multipolarity has once again replaced bipolarity, but there is little clarity as to the future of Europe. NATO still exists, despite the loss of its original rationale, and the nation-state remains the basis of political power. However, as a result of the development of multilateralism, IGO relations prevail in the foreign relations of West European states. Indeed, the latter are now caught up in the global economy where they are challenged by TNCs whose relations with individual states are often ambiguous.

This is the context in which diplomatic activity – the principal instrument for the execution of a state's foreign policy – presently occurs in Western Europe. Negotiation is the major diplomatic activity but includes a wide range of modalities: exchange of views, arbitration, conciliation, adjudication, representation, now trade promotion. It was not the original reason for establishing diplomatic missions: this was to gain intelligence of rival states' activity and facilitate communication between states. In general, European diplomatic corps were socially selective in their recruitment, but this has largely disappeared, as has the tradition that diplomats should be exclusively male. At the same time, classical bilateral diplomacy has given way to the new diplomacy, the so-called multilateral diplomacy by conference with a broadening range of participants from summits of heads of state (G7, European Council) to technical experts and specialists at numerous IGCs. The number of international treaties doubled from about 200 per year in the inter-war years to about 400 per year in the post-war period.

European states' foreign policy orientations are powerfully influenced by their countries' historical traditions. Thus British foreign policy has revolved round three axes: Empire/Commonwealth as a third force between the superpowers; Atlanticism or special relationship with the USA as guarantor of its world role; and Europe, to which it has remained in a semi-detached position, despite entry into the EU. Britain has endeavoured to ignore its decline into a middle-rank European power and this has cost it dear economically. In contrast, French foreign policy has been the most active in post-war Europe, particularly during de Gaulle's presidency. It too has revolved round three axes: *grandeur*, Europe and Third World. *Grandeur* meant the nuclear *force de frappe*, symbol of France's world power status. Europe meant reconciliation and hence a special relationship with Germany. Third World meant privileged relations with former French West Africa and the Arab world. French leaders, moreover, were more clear-headed than their British colleagues and gave themselves the means of their foreign policy: for example, de Gaulle's exploitation of France's geopolitical position to withdraw from NATO and play an autonomous role between the superpowers. Nonetheless, the relationship with Germany has been at the heart of France's post-war international position and the basis of European integration. It was a matter not only of preventing future conflict between the two states, but of enabling France to use Germany's economic power to play a role on the world stage as the leader of the EU (a leadership recently undermined by German unification). France's interest in the supranational development of the EU has been to tie in Germany.

German and Italian foreign policies have largely been conditioned by the outcome of the war and the need for international rehabilitation. This explains their enthusiastic adhesion to all international initiatives seeking their participation: the Atlantic alliance as guarantor of European security, and European economic integration as guarantor of the continent's prosperity. German reconciliation with the French was the motor of European integration as sealed in the 1963 treaty of friendship. Germany had a further problem because of the division of the country: its relations with the GDR and its eastern neighbours. This problem has engaged German foreign policy since unification; it has tried to interest its partners in how to prevent chaos in Eastern Europe spilling over into Germany and by extension Western Europe. At the same time, it has sought to allay fears that it will use its new weight as the largest and most powerful state in Europe to dominate the continent by offering to merge its power in a more supranational European union, but it has only been partially successful in this, largely owing to British opposition.

Since 1970, member states have become aware that there are common European interests and that these can be best advanced by speaking with one voice. Hence they have developed, within the EPC, the habit of consultation and exchange of information. This led to common positions on many subjects. This was recognized in the SEA, which institutionalized EPC. In the Europhoria of the late 1980s, there arose an exaggerated belief in the capacity of the EC to develop a common foreign policy, and hence it figured as the third pillar of the EU in the Maastricht Treaty. Excessive expectations were disabused by the Yugoslav tragedy, which revealed that the EU did not have the means for an interventionist foreign policy, dependent as it was on the independent resources of its members. Thus commitment to a European common foreign and defence policy at present is more symbolic than real.

The characteristic feature of the military as an institution is its monopoly of the legitimate use of force. Hence the question is not whether the military are involved in politics, but how and to what extent. This depends on three factors: military organization, officer corps and civil–military relations. Military organization has changed over the centuries and a number of formats have been identified: mercenary armies; standing armies; mass armies; and professional armies. Janovitz has suggested that advanced industrial states are in a transition period between the mass army (based on conscription, patriotism, total war, citizenship) and the professional army (based on regulars, managerialism, sophisticated arms systems). It has been argued that the mass army corresponds to the liberal state, while Lasswell hypothesized that the professional army might relate to what he called the garrison state (a state in which security considerations are paramount).

British, German and Italian armed forces are integrated into the NATO military command: this means that Europe has militarily been subordinate to the USA, which has not only guaranteed European security but determined defence strategy. Britain and France have been able to act militarily only with US approval, as the Suez fiasco amply illustrated. In addition, Britain is the only West European state that has adopted a professional army format; France, Germany and Italy still have mass armies based on conscription. However, the new military situation in Europe resulting from the collapse of the former Soviet Empire combined with costs has placed the question of conscription on these states' political agendas for the first time. Indeed, military expenditure is likely to decline as all states take advantage of the so-called peace dividend under NATO troop reduction accords.

Officer corps recruitment has become more democratic over the past century, changing from exclusively aristocratic to prevalently middle class. This process has been gradual and has gone furthest in Germany (because of Nazism). Moreover, there is a strong tradition of sons following in their fathers' military footsteps in all states. The significance of officer recruitment from a similar social area to other elites is to facilitate political control through common values. Moreover, the fact that democratization occurred gradually over 100 years avoided provoking a sudden status crisis among military elites. On the other hand, it did not lead to a democratization of values, but rather to an authoritarian conservative orientation. Finally, it is argued that socialization in military institutions is more important than social origin in determining the mentality (military mind) of the officer corps.

The problematic of civil–military relations concerns the level of involvement of the military in government. A certain degree is inevitable from the very existence of the armed forces as a state institution. Finer distinguishes four levels of involvement/intervention: (1) civil supremacy; (2) active military participation; (3) indirect military control; and (4) military supremacy. These correspond to different levels of political culture: direct military intervention is less likely in countries with high or mature political culture and vice versa. His theory is axiomatic and contrasts with that of Huntington for whom military professionalism was the key to civilian supremacy of the military. This was because the more the military were professionals, the more they realized their competence was military, the more likely they were to leave policy to the politicians as outside their sphere. Moreover, the professional military ethic incorporated the notion of obedience to the political authorities on the basis that the military serve the nation-state whose policy is determined by the political authorities. Finer criticized Huntington's thesis on the grounds that the military's very professionalism, far from impeding the political intervention of the military, could in fact provoke it in the name of the state's superior interests if they judged the politicians were betraying it. He claimed that the only way to secure the non-intervention of the military is for the latter really to believe in the principle of civilian supremacy, and this cannot be reduced to a question of military professionalism.

There are various sources for the belief in the principle of civilian supremacy. One is Clausewitz's notion that war is a mere instrument that must be policy led: hence military supremacy over the political is absurd. A second is institutionalized constitutional arrangements which, although they may confuse shadow with substance, have the merit of legitimizing the political authorities and so rallying popular support in any conflict with military leaders. A third is Mosca's thesis that the integration of the military leaders into the ruling class through recruitment from similar social background reduces their disposition to intervene. A fourth source is the conscription thesis mooted by Tocqueville: an army with a large popular rank and file obliges its leaders to take a much larger view of national interests than those of the leadership for fear of civil war. All contribute to strengthening civilian control, but no one is sufficient by itself. This said, one must not overlook instances of military involvement in politics which have verged on outright intervention: the 1958 and 1961 military risings in French Algeria; or the De Lorenzo and

Borghese plots in Italy. Hence civil supremacy has never been as clear-cut as constitutional arrangements would lead one to believe.

The military-industrial complex refers to a symbiotic relationship between the armed forces, government and industry in advanced industrial states. The concept has various versions: Wright-Mills and Galbraith focused on the institutional links that benefited each party; whereas neo-Marxists, like Baran and Sweezy, explained the relationship in terms of the social imperatives of capitalism. However, despite the truth of many of the facts alleged to support the concept, the presumptions made were too many to be convincing. Thus, although it is undoubtedly true that military leaders and arms manufacturers are influential, the cohesiveness between the three groups presumes a conspiracy theory that remains largely unproven, particularly since the end of the Cold War.

The activity of the secret intelligence and security services is claimed to be the missing dimension of politics. Moreover, it is generally a neglected topic of Western political science. The existence of invisible power undermines the principles of liberal democracy. Nonetheless, all West European states have both civilian and military intelligence and security services which are responsible for intelligence and counter-intelligence (espionage and counter-espionage) and which are not limited today to military matters but include, perhaps more importantly, commercial and industrial affairs. These services are also entrusted with covert action that covers a wide variety of activities (subversion, paramilitary activity and special operations). The existence of these services poses serious problems of accountability in a democratic state since little is publicly known about them: governments take the line that they are basic elements of state security and that the essence of a secret service is that it is secret. Hence they usually deny actions attributed to them and issue censored reports when obliged to set up enquiries. Nonetheless, the post-war period is replete with examples of their abuse of power. Political subversives, who are often broadly defined and have included the personnel of some left-wing governments, have been subject to surveillance, disinformation and harassment. The Cold War justification of much of such activity has largely evaporated and has led some states, despite terrorist activity (or perhaps because of it), to introduce a measure of legal control, but it is very limited as yet.

Further reading

C. Andrew and D. Dilks (eds) (1984), *The Missing Dimension: Governments and Intelligence Communities in the Twentieth Century* (London: Croom Helm).

G.R. Berridge (1987), *International Relations: States, Power and Conflict since 1945* (Brighton: Wheatsheaf).

R.K. Betts (1978), 'Analysis, War and Decision-Making: Why Planning Failures are Inevitable' in *World Politics*, 31.

S. Bok (1986), *Secrets: On the Ethics of Concealment and Revelation* (Oxford: OUP).

W. Carlsnaes and S. Smith (eds) (1994), *European Foreign Policy: The EC and Changing Perspectives in Europe* (London: Sage).

A.W. DePorte (1986), *Europe between the Superpowers: The Enduring Balance* (New Haven, Conn.: Yale UP).

M. Edmonds (1988), *Armed Services and Society* (Leicester: Leicester UP).

F. Ferraresi (1992), 'The Secret Structure Code-Named Gladio', in *Italian Politics: A Review*, 7, 29–48.

S.E. Finer (1976), *Man on Horseback: The Role of the Military in Politics* (Harmondsworth: Penguin).

G. Harries-Jenkins and C.C. Moskos (eds) (1981), 'Armed Forces and Society', special issue of *Current Sociology*, 29, 3.

D. Hooper (1987), *Official Secrets: The Use and Abuse of the Act* (London: Secker & Warburg).

A. Horne (1984), *The French Army and Politics, 1870–1970* (London: Macmillan).

M. Janovitz (1960), *The Professional Soldier* (New York: Free Press).

M. Janovitz (1975), *Military Conflicts: Essays in the Institutional Analysis of War and Peace* (Beverly Hills, Calif.: Sage).

R.O. Keohane and S. Hoffmann (eds) (1991), *The New European Community: Decision-Making and Institutional Change* (Boulder, Col.: Westview).

E. Pliscke (ed.) (1979), *Modern Diplomacy: The Art and the Artisans* (Washington, DC: AEI).

M. Story (ed.) (1993), *The New Europe: Politics, Government and Economics since 1945* (Oxford: Blackwell).

W. Wallace (1990), *The Transformation of Western Europe* (London: Pinter/RIIA).

W. Wallace (ed.) (1990), *The Dynamics of European Integration* (London: Pinter/RIIA).

11 Actual Democracy in Western Europe since the War

La numerazione dei 'voti' è la manifestazione terminale di un lungo processo in cui l'influsso massimo appartiene proprio a quelli che 'dedicano allo stato e alla nazione le loro migliore forze' (quando sono tali).

A. Gramsci, Quaderni del carcere.[1]

Introduction

Our long journey through the political institutions and processes of the four major Western European states has revealed the complexity of the mechanisms of power in actual democratic regimes: the multiplicity, but also the inequality, of groups and organizations, not to mention the plurality of actors and activities involved in civil society; the plethora of policy decisions as well as the perverseness of many of the outcomes of state action. The discussion was necessarily segmental given that the thematic approach adopted privileged the disaggregation of the political system and focused attention on selected components of civil society and the state.

At the same time, it disclosed a number of common features: middle class societies (chapter 2); political families (chapter 5); organized interests (chapter 6); the state structures of administration (chapter 8) and the armed services (chapter 10). It also revealed patterns of political interaction: the correspondence between party systems, political stability and governmental authority (chapters 5 and 7); and the nature of the policy process (chapter 8). At this stage, it seems helpful to step back and take a global view of the post-war politics of the West European states in an attempt to appraise its 'democratic' qualities. One way of doing this is by discussing what was at stake in the light of the major paradigms of actual democratic politics in the post-war period. After all, the conflict between capitalism and democracy runs like Ariadne's thread through the politics of post-war Western Europe, even if the circumstances have radically changed in this half-century.

The post-war period is usually divided into two: (1) a relatively long period of political stability and economic prosperity (*les trente glorieuses* – chapter 1); interrupted by (2) an almost equally long period of politico-economic crisis that has lasted for almost twenty years and from which the West European states had not yet emerged when the international context was dramatically and fundamentally transformed. It is as well to recall here that the Keynesian welfare state – the dominant state form in Western Europe in the post-war period – was founded on an inherently unstable compromise between capital and labour, in which organized labour accepted the logic of profit and the market, and capital recognized the political rights of the subordinate classes as well as their entitlement to a satisfactory standard of living (introduction to the book). It is important to stress that the economy developed according to a 'capitalist' logic while politics, instead, officially accepted a 'democratic' logic.

This said, what struck the political scientists, liberal pluralists and neo-Marxists alike was the political stability of the boom years. Certainly, it is worth emphasizing the historical achievement of the welfare state because it has been rather denigrated in the 1980s as the source of all Western Europe's ills. Indeed, the Swedish economist Gunnar Myrdal (1960), one of the protagonists of the Keynesian compromise, was not exaggerating when he noted that:

> the welfare state had such a powerful influence in releasing the potential productivity of the people that, in the dynamic process of its gradual achievement, an improvement in the working and living conditions of the poor could be carried out in an economically progressive situation, without depressing the conditions of most of those who were initially better off and who, in the first instance, had to pay for the reforms. (p. 121)

However, this political stability was only relative in the boom years: we need only recall the violence and uncertainty of many of the Cold War and decolonization confrontations – NATO in 1949 for Italy, Suez in 1956 for Britain, Algeria in 1958–62 for France – to realize its limits. Indeed, the judgement actually illustrates that the political scientists were convinced that the major conflict of the age (capital against labour) had been finally vanquished; hence their disregard of the other, just as significant, sources of political instability that characterized those years. Nonetheless, despite their judgement, about 1970 the tension between the needs of capital and the demands of democracy exploded and the Keynesian compromise started to unwind, opening a new period of political instability that the political scientists quickly dubbed 'the crisis of democracy'.

In this situation, to clarify what was at stake and the light it throws on actual democratic politics in Western Europe, we must review not only the two theses on political stability – the one liberal, the 'end of ideology' (Shils, 1955) or the 'democratic class struggle' (Lipset, 1959), and the other neo-Marxist, the 'one-dimensional man' of Marcuse (1964) – but also the way in which the Keynesian welfare state effectively operated, namely by means of the electoral business cycle. Successively, we will discuss the crisis and the crisis paradigms elaborated by both the liberal pluralists and the neo-Marxists. This will permit us, finally, to appraise the key to actual democratic practice, namely 'the impact of parties' (Castles, 1982) and to confirm whether it is true, as Sartori (1987, vol. 1, p. 148) claims, that 'a democratic system is largely, in actual operation, a party system.' Because, if votes do not count and it makes no difference which party is in power, then this raises the question, which is in no way rhetorical: how genuine is European democracy in the last decade of the twentieth century?

Political stability and the electoral business cycle

In the 1950s, in the middle of the Cold War and at the start of the economic boom, but as part of the ideological war between intellectuals, Shils (1955) and Bell (1960) declared the 'end of ideology'[2] and the demise of Marxism-Leninism, while Lipset (1959) announced the 'democratic class struggle'.[3] For the latter, in fact, Western democracies were, in a famous phrase, nothing less than 'the good society itself in operation' (p. 403), in the sense that they had resolved the fundamental political problems of industrial society. So it was claimed that neither Marxism-Leninism nor the violent class struggle had any longer a *raison d'être*; hence the demise of ideology and so conflict. Actual democracy had attained genuine consensus: 'The ideological differences dividing right and left had been reduced to a little more or a little less government ownership and economic planning', so that 'no one seemed to believe that it really made much difference which political party controlled the domestic politics of individual nations' (pp. 404–5). And this was thanks to the triumph of the social revolution: 'the workers have achieved', Lipset went on, 'industrial and political citizenship; the conservatives have accepted the welfare state; and the democratic left has recognized that an increase in overall state power carries with it more dangers to freedom than solutions for economic problems' (p. 406).[4] There were, he was prepared to recognize, a number of social cleavages that gave rise to political conflicts, but, far from becoming ever more violent and explosive, they had been domesticated by the institutions through which they found disciplined and constitutional expression: principally parties and unions. Thus Lipset could assert that 'in every modern democracy conflict among different groups is expressed through political parties which basically represent a "democratic translation of the class struggle"' (p. 220). In consequence, parties, elections and parliament guaranteed conflict without revolution, the more so since economic growth and widespread affluence were constantly eroding the very bases of conflict itself.

For Marcuse (1964) – the guru of the 1968 student movement – the problem, in contrast to the liberal pluralists, was how to explain the apparent socio-political harmony of those years which should, from his neo-Marxist perspective, have been conflictual. He found the explanation in certain developments of advanced industrial societies that created a general state, what he calls 'repressive desublimation',[5] instead of a revolutionary subject:

> the enchained possibilities of advanced industrial societies are: development of productive forces on an enlarged scale, extension of the conquest of nature, growing satisfaction of needs for a growing number of people, creation of new needs and faculties. But these possibilities are gradually being realized through means and institutions which cancel their liberating potential, and this process affects not only the means but also the ends. The instruments of productivity and progress, organized into a totalitarian system, determine not only the actual but also the possible utilizations. (p. 255)

In short, science and technology had become not only fundamental forces of production but also new forms of ideology that legitimized enslavement to the logic of production and eliminated all forms of conflict and dissent assimilating them. Or in Merquior's (1986, p. 159) colourful phrase, 'humanity [is] repressed in a technological cage': the 'welfare-warfare society'.

At all events, the result was the triumph of 'instrumental reason' and the consequent 'depoliticization' of political life in which the media had a primary role in perpetuating a vicious circle with no way out: 'If the established society manages all normal communication,' Marcuse asserted, 'validating or invalidating it in accordance with social requirements, then the values alien to these requirements may perhaps have no other medium of communication than the abnormal one of fiction' (p. 247). The media, in other words, under the double pressure of the advertising industry and the relentless drive to increase consumption, created a 'false consciousness' that people did not recognize as such. In fact, Marcuse went as far as to suggest that the only way that the system could be undermined, and so a way out found, was the non-functioning of television and allied media: this, he added, 'might thus begin to achieve what the inherent contradictions of capitalism did not achieve – the disintegration of the system' (p. 246). There was just a chance that 'the historical extremes [might] meet again: the most advanced consciousness of humanity and its most exploited force' (p. 257), in a revolutionary protest. However, he did not really seem to believe in it – at least in 1964 – repeating straight away that 'it is nothing but a chance'. 'False consciousness' was too strong.

Despite the theoretical differences between the two analyses, several commentators (Macintyre, 1970; Held, 1987) have stressed the similarity of the conclusions, as regards both the high degree of integration achieved in this period and the strengthening of political stability that was claimed to result. However, because of the tensions between politics and economics inherent in this type of political system, even at moments of the greatest political stability, we need to look at the way in which the Keynesian welfare state actually operated in the post-war period. This can be usefully done using the notion of the 'political business cycle'. The starting point is a brief article by Kalecki (1943) in which he argues that it is impossible to maintain full employment by means of public expenditure – the basis of the Keynesian welfare state – in a democratic capitalist system. And this is for the simple reason that the capitalists would not tolerate it since it would undermine their power in relation both to the state and to labour. Full employment would, in fact, neutralize the labour market as the essential instrument of social control in capitalist systems. Hence arose the notion of a political business cycle which, in Kalecki's view, would result from government action subject to the political pressure of the capitalists in favour of recessive measures on the one hand, and that of the masses in favour of expansive measures on the other. The political business cycle for Kalecki, then, was merely the translation, in terms of economic activity, of the relation of forces between classes in capitalist society. Finally, he postulated only two situations in which a capitalist economy could be managed without tension in conditions of full employment: (1) fascism; and (2) a non-authoritarian regime in conditions of a not well-defined 'fundamental reform'.

Things, as we know, did not go in the post-war period as Kalecki had predicted: the Keynesian welfare state functioned reasonably efficiently and Western Europe experienced 30 years of virtual full employment, even though with limited and relatively brief economic cycles. Nevertheless, it is worth noting that, besides the schematic nature of Kalecki's analysis, it advances more weighty arguments than those needed to explain the politico-economic oscillations that punctuated the post-war boom years. For this reason Salvati (1981) has suggested that Kalecki's analysis is a tool of long-term analysis, like Kondratieff's and Kusnet's 'long cycles'.[6] It is, therefore, more relevant to the crisis decades of the 1970s and 1980s than the boom decades of the 1950s and 1960s:

nonetheless, the reasoning that he outlined in the 1940s was prophetic in the sense that it anticipated by 30 years the arguments used by business and the new right to attack the Keynesian welfare state.

In the meantime, however, the notion of the political business cycle was reformulated within a totally different theoretical context, that of the neo-utilitarian theories of democracy of the 'public choice' school (Buchanan and Tullock, 1962). They derived originally from the works of Schumpeter, and above all of Downs (1957). It was an economic approach to democracy based on the competitive market model, in which elections are conceived as a political market, where public goods obtained from government programmes are exchanged, with the politicians in the role of entrepreneurs who deal in public goods and the citizen-electors in the role of consumers of public goods, using votes as currency and power as profit. The model's basic assumption is that all actors mechanically adopt the same behaviour: they maximize their own interest, which for the citizen-electors means their own well-being, and for politicians (and so for parties) means their own electoral popularity. Once it is ascertained and assumed that government popularity (*popularity or vote function*) depends, above all, on economic factors – usually, disposable income, unemployment and inflation – and that a government, or rather the government parties, wish to be re-elected, it naturally follows that the government will use the instruments of economic policy to maximize its popularity in the approach to elections; and this will have effects on the economy (*reaction function*). The interaction of these two functions determines a cyclical movement of economic activity, which the public choice school has called the 'electoral business cycle'. In contrast to Kalecki's political cycle, it is elections, and *not* social classes, that are the motor of the cyclical movement identified by the model.

In spite of the ambiguity of the results of the vast research literature (Whiteley, 1986), the position can be summarized in the following terms. Firstly, the electors are aware of the economic situation in the sense that it is possible to establish a certain correlation between government electoral support and certain economic variables: inflation, unemployment. It was not for nothing, therefore, that Giorgio Galli declared that 'politics, today, is the organization of the economy.'[7] Secondly, parties endeavour to manipulate, within certain limits, economic policy so as to increase their popularity in the run-up to elections. It should be said that if Finer (1980) claimed that this was, at least as far as Britain was concerned, 'a question of proven fact', the statistical evidence is less clear. Thirdly, such manipulations explain better than Kalecki's political cycle the brief and limited movements that characterized the economies of the principal Western states in the post-war boom years. The fact that the parties can manipulate economic policies for electoral reasons (*pace* Finer) does not mean that they always do, or that this is always successful. And this is for a variety of reasons: the government gets the timing and/or the state of the economy wrong, and/or the international constraints (balance of payments) prevent it. Otherwise, the victory of the opposition parties in Britain and France would be inexplicable. In conclusion, we can agree with Salvati (1981) when he notes that if the focus is on interaction between politics and economics in the short term in 'normal' economic conditions, then it is towards the electoral cycle model that we should turn. Finally, this model, at least in its initial formulation, implied no destabilizing effects on the functioning of the economy, as was the case, instead, in Kalecki's political cycle. It is for this reason that the model can furnish a useful instrument for reading the economic cycles in normal years, like those of the post-war boom.[8]

Another version of this approach inserted the electoral cycle in a wider context, that of the 1970s crisis. It is no accident, in fact, that Brittan (1977) called his version *The Economic Consequences of Democracy*. In short, he argues that economic destabilization is inevitable brought about by four assumed constituent elements of the electoral cycle: (1) rational and self-interested behaviour by politicians seeking to maximize votes; (2) a political menu limited to a trade-off between unemployment and inflation; (3) a time lag between the effects of expansive measures on employment and their inflationary consequences; and (4) electors with short memories and imperfect foresight, so that they do not give full weight to the likely post-electoral consequences of the measures. The explanation, according to Brittan, lies in the role of the trade unions which, thanks both to the 'excessive expectations' generated by the logic of democratic capitalism and to the use of their market position, leads to a deterioration in the trade-off between inflation and unemployment so that each economic cycle starts from the inflation level reached in the previous one. The result is that the cyclic manipulation of the economy associated with electoral campaigns, far from limiting itself to brief and limited oscillations, transforms itself, in Brittan's scenario, into an inflationary spiral.

This scenario explains not only the 1970s economic crisis but also Brittan's pessimism, perceptible in his view that 'liberal representative democracy suffers from internal contradictions, which are likely to increase in time, and that, on present indications, the system is likely to pass away within the lifetime of people now adult' (p. 247). Politico-economic stability, in his view, has lasted as long as it has only as a result of particular and unrepeatable circumstances, among which were the survival of traditional and pre-capitalist behaviour, and above all a limited and irregular political manipulation. This is another way of saying that the Keynesian compromise, founded on a particular division of labour between the democratic aspect (full employment) and the capitalist aspect (high level of effective demand), was an inherently unstable compromise. However, we need to ask how realistic is Brittan's scenario. It is quite clear on the basis of the assumptions outlined above that it is excessively simplified and deterministic, and does not stand up to more realistic hypotheses. In fact, Bordogna and Provasi (1984) observe in conclusion to their critical analysis that 'the inherently destabilizing consequences of the relations between economics and politics depend critically on the very specific hypotheses regarding the function of government benefits and the behaviour of electors postulated by the scenario, rather than on the functioning of the democratic regime as such' (p. 86).

Crises and crisis paradigms

Paradoxically, or perhaps logically, the same group – Bell, Lipset, Huntington – which had declared the demise of class conflict in the 1950s, proposed some fifteen years later the 'overload' thesis and the ungovernability of democracies. Its manifesto was the notorious trilateral commission report, *The Crisis of Democracy* (Crozier, Huntington and Watanuki, 1975). The paradox, moreover, did not concern the authors only, but also the very notion of ungovernability; and this for a number of reasons. Firstly, it was the thesis of the 1968 student movement that 'things cannot go on like this' because of an imminent crisis. The students' thesis was based, according to Offe (1984), on the conviction that 'class contradictions, in however modified a form, and the ensuing struggles must result in the dissolution of the basic structure of capitalism, together with its corresponding political constitution and cultural-ideological system' (p. 65). Secondly, the US pluralists, after having vehemently denied, even in 1968, the political relevance of the class struggle because it had been definitively resolved by the Keynesian compromise, completely changed their position, proposing and propagating from the mid 1970s a crisis paradigm that depended directly or indirectly on it and its insufficient institutionalization. Naturally, it was not presented in these terms; they spoke, on the contrary, of the limits, indeed the failure, of 'the institutional mechanisms of the Keynesian welfare state'. Huntington argued, in fact, in the trilateral report that 'what the Marxists mistakenly attribute to capitalist economics, however, is, in fact, a product of democratic politics' (p. 73). Hence in the 1970s and 1980s, it was the liberal pluralists and those intellectually close to them, including the new right public choice theorists, rather than the leftists (Marxist or not), who claimed that 'things cannot go on like this.'

The basis of the so-called ungovernability thesis was extremely simple: it lay in the observable disproportion between the escalation of demands (or expectations) on the one hand, and the lack of politico-administrative efficacy on the other, which was dysfunctional for the efficient regulation of social and economic affairs. As Crozier pithily noted in the trilateral report: 'the more decisions the modern state has to handle, the more helpless it becomes' (p. 13). The thesis has an undeniable descriptive efficacy because it is based on a logical mechanism, even though it poses theoretical problems. The mechanism operates according to the following logic (Held, 1987, pp. 230–3). 'Increased expectations' generated by parties and groups representing diverse and competing interests, fuelled by the mass media, lead to an overload on the state apparatuses. The latter, constrained by fiscal policy, are rendered incapable of satisfying such expectations. This leads to a decline in governmental authority, authority which is necessary to resist the proliferation of demands; this, in turn, leads to a growing citizens' lack of trust in the state that undermines the bases of economic growth. A vicious circle is set in motion which is self-replenishing, with all the crisis potential implied by the non-functioning of the political and economic systems. The practical problem, for the mechanism's supporters, is to break the vicious circle at all costs; this means dissociating the economic from the political, in order to reduce the overload on government and hence the expectations. It was at this point that the contradiction at the heart of the Keynesian compromise was revealed, as the trilateral report recognized:

> The heart of the problem lies in the inherent contradictions involved in the very phrase 'governability of democracy'. For, in some measure, governability and democracy are warring concepts. An excess of democracy means a deficit in governability; easy governability suggests faulty democracy. At times in the history of democratic government the pendulum has swung too far in one direction or the other. At the present time, it appears that the balance has tilted too far against governments in Western Europe and the United States. (p. 173)

The expansion of democracy was responsible for the overload on government, and consequently for the crisis of governability. Once again, faced by the incompatibility between capitalism (governability) and democracy (general expectations), the trilateral commission, like so many before it, pressed for an authoritarian solution. Hence its message: a market economy and the strengthening of the state's authority. Moreover, we can note the significant use, but in a contrasting perspective, by the trilateral commission of the same phrase to describe the incompatibility between governability and democracy as Marshall (1950) had used 25 years earlier to express that between citizen rights and capitalist class system, that is to say, 'at war' (see the introduction to this book). At all events, what the trilateral commission had in mind as being excessive were citizenship rights. Hence, its hidden agenda[9] was the dismantling of the Keynesian welfare state, which for the neo-conservatives 'is the enemy of liberty', with the end of full employment and the reintroduction of labour market discipline to control subordinate class expectations and above all trade union claims.

At this point is posed the theoretical question of ungovernability – to wit the origin of the disproportion between citizen expectations and state response capability. Contrary to what Huntington and others claim, all the explicative hypotheses of the phenomenon – new needs, party and group competition, social complexity – even though valid individually in functional terms, can be collectively related to a single fact, which he decisively rejects, namely social conflict: not only class, but gender, race, generation. In this situation, there is no solution because the gap between expectations and responses is inherent in the organization of capitalist society. This explains the contradictory nature of the various remedies proposed by liberal pluralists and neo-conservatives, in which pragmatism predominates. Thus if neo-conservative therapies are certainly capable of suffocating social conflict, restoring governability in the short term, nevertheless the conflict remains to revive, perhaps in a different form, at a later date.

The second paradigm, the neo-Marxist 'legitimation crisis', usually associated with the names of Habermas and Offe, shares some of the elements – for instance, the modern state's need of consensus, the erosion of state power – of the previous paradigm, even though it obviously starts from very different assumptions. In the neo-Marxist perspective, most state intervention in society is seen as a set of strategies for avoiding more serious crises deriving from class conflict (see the introduction to this book). These crises are the result of the contradictions in which the state is enmeshed in advanced capitalism: on the one side, the need to sustain the accumulation process – from which it draws its own resources – and the private appropriation of resources; and on the other, the need to maintain mass citizen loyalty or support by presenting itself as the impartial arbiter of class interests, so as to legitimate its own power. Class antagonisms can, according to Habermas (1973), occur in all the three subsystems – economic, political-administrative and socio-cultural – in which the social system is articulated, with various 'crisis tendencies'. He identifies four of them. Two are system crises: the economic crisis, by which the economic system does not produce the requisite quantity of consumable values; and the rationality crisis, by which the administrative system does not produce the requisite quantity of rational decisions. A further two are identity crises: the legitimation crisis, by which the legitimation system does not provide the requisite quantity of generalized motivations; and the motivation crisis, by which the socio-cultural system does not generate the requisite quantity of action-motivating meaning (p. 49). In contrast to orthodox Marxists, Habermas does not believe that an economic crisis is 'logically necessary'; he claims, instead, that it can be contained, so long as the consequences are displaced to other subsystems. However, such 'strategies of displacement' have a price: they set other crisis tendencies in motion. Thus an economic crisis displaced towards the political sphere can provoke a rationality crisis (that is, the inability of the state to produce sufficiently effective decisions); a rationality crisis displaced towards the socio-cultural sphere can trigger a motivation crisis; and finally a motivation crisis can, in its turn, lead, once more in the political sphere, to a legitimation crisis: in other words, the withdrawal of the state's mass support.

The possibility of a legitimation crisis – a rare event, in any case – depends on whether capitalism's system of values is more or less in line with the state's needs, or whether, on the contrary, it is too rigid:

> Only a rigid socio-cultural system, incapable of being randomly functionalized for the needs of the administrative system, could explain a sharpening of legitimation difficulties into a legitimation crisis ... A legitimation crisis, then, must be based on a motivation crisis – that is, a discrepancy between the need for motives declared by the state, the educational system and the occupational system on the one hand, and the motivation supplied by the socio-cultural system on the other. (Habermas, 1973, pp. 74–5)

In simple terms, a legitimation crisis would result from a misfit between the requirements of the functional integration of accumulation (*systemic* integration) on the one side, and those of *social* integration (social identity) on the other, so as to secure the necessary base of consensus. It is in this sense that Habermas can claim that 'in the final analysis, *this class structure* is the source of the legitimation deficit' (p. 73).

At all events, the state is normally able to manage the tensions between the economic structure (capitalism) and the political-administrative institutions (actual democracy) in advanced capitalist societies, but, beyond a certain limit, the situation can get out of hand because they become too severe and everything enters into a state of crisis. At this point, which he is unable to predict, Habermas foresees two solutions: either the establishment of an authoritarian state, as in Europe in the 1920s and 1930s; or, instead, a fundamental transformation, with the progressive development of a socialist alternative; the latter would be the conclusion of a slow socio-economic evolutionary process rather than the result of a revolution, in which Habermas does not believe.

Habermas's analysis is both very complex and very schematic and, hence, lacks clarity in places. For instance, as Held and others have noted, the distinction between legitimation and motivation crises is rather obscure: at some moments they are considered distinct, at others a single set of events. However, the principal political criticism that can be made of Habermas (as of the Parsons school of US functionalists too) is of his insistence on the state's need of legitimacy in advanced capitalism, both to operate efficiently and to secure adequate socio-political stability. But social integration in the sense of an acceptance, shared by the mass of the citizenry, of the norms of the dominant culture, not only does not seem necessary in Western States, but also does not appear to have historically ever really existed (chapter 3). Research in the area in fact, confirms Gramsci's intuition, known as 'contradictory consciousness', namely that the mass of the population have two normative levels of reference: an abstract level in which they express an often substantial agreement with the dominant norms; and a second level in which they often demonstrate total indifference to the same norms, when they do not express open dissent. Moreover, to secure the subjection of the subordinate classes, there is, in addition to the state's repressive instruments, Marx's 'dull compulsion of economic relations' that Habermas surprisingly discounts as contrary to the ethos of the Keynesian welfare state. At all events, what seems to count is the consensus of the ruling groups – among whom the political and administrative elites are necessary, if for no other reason than that they are responsible for the efficient operation of the state's repressive apparatuses – for the dominant values. In fact, as Gramsci was one of the first to point out, normative dominant conceptions help more to maintain the cohesion of the ruling groups than to organize the consensus of the subordinate classes.

The question arises as to the extent to which these two paradigms further an understanding of the politics of the West European states at the present time. While the overload and ungovernability thesis has been widely discussed in the media – and hence has enjoyed a certain credibility in ruling circles – the legitimacy crisis thesis has remained more or less restricted to the academic world. This has meant that the former has had some influence on the policies pursued in the various states, in contrast to the latter. Nonetheless, the rather catastrophic predictions of the ones – the suicide of democracy – and of the other – authoritarian regime or the promise of a socialist alternative – have proved incorrect so far. There has not been (or rather it has been greatly exaggerated) that decline in the state's authority – and hence of its apparatuses' ability to act (chapters 7–10) – which, for both theses, was the crux of the crisis. Thus the thesis that 'things cannot go on like this' appears mistaken because things have, in fact, continued to go on more or less like this.

The social discontent in the various countries was not, in fact, a particularly new phenomenon; nor was it directed against the state as such or against its democratic organization, but rather against specific governments and parties.[10] Social conflict has always been an integral part of politics in capitalist countries. Moreover, there has not been in the 1970s and 1980s a credible alternative, in terms of either new institutions or new strategies, capable of constituting a reference point for dissident groups, usually marginalized and divided among themselves. As regards the state apparatuses' capacity to act, there suffice the examples of the defeat of terrorism in Germany and Italy in the 1970s (chapter 10) and of the anti-inflationary policies in Britain and France in the 1980s. In the case of the latter, in fact, widespread use was made of what Offe has called 'strategies of displacement', through the application of the principle of the selectivity of interests. In other words, the anti-inflationary policies implemented by the various governments displaced the negative effects on to the marginal sectors of the population – subordinate groups, women, young people, pensioners, black people – sparing the strongest groups that were able to defend themselves: Thatcherism, but not exclusively; also Kohl's policies in Germany; and even Mitterrand's in France.

Since there would appear to have been no dramatic decline in the state's position, we are obliged to ask the reasons for the ruling and intellectual groups' alarmist reactions to the 1970s crisis. There are at least two possible answers. First of all the crisis followed the *trente glorieuses*, the real post-war miracle. Moreover, the very economic success gave, thanks to the Keynesian techniques, such prestige to the social sciences, principally economics, that people really did believe that it was possible not only to manage society rationally, but also to practise forms of social engineering: 'technocracy' (chapter 8). The inability of the social sciences to keep their promises in face of the 1968 social and student struggles, naturally meant, for the ruling and intellectual groups, a profound disenchantment. This explains, in part, the alarmism. A second answer can be sought in the international sphere which acted as an amplifier of the crisis. Certain events – suspension of the convertibility of the dollar in 1971, and the Yom Kippur War in 1973 – effectively destroyed the post-war international monetary order (that of Bretton Woods), *condicio sine qua non* of the *trente glorieuses*. The effects were just as dramatic because that monetary order had protected Western Europe from external disturbing influences. It seemed to many, above all among the ruling groups in the early 1970s, that everything was collapsing and that the world was returning, as Dahrendorf (1988) has suggested, to Hobbesian anarchy: 'power rather than the law determines what happens between nations' (p. 121), but, we can add, also at home. The titles of some of the books published in those years give the flavour: *The Collapse of Democracy, La Crise de l'état providence, Crisi di governabilità e mondi vitali, Ist die Demokratie noch regierbar?, The New Despotism, Les Démocraties sont-elles gouvernables?, Can Government go Bankrupt?, The New Totalitarianism.* This should come as no surprise, because in every era even the wisest men have been gravely mistaken about the possibilities of their century. Thus it seems that Keynes himself wrote in a letter to the French minister of finance in 1926 that he considered it impossible 'from a political point of view' that public expenditure could ever exceed 25 per cent of national income, a figure which has been exceeded in all Western European states throughout the whole post-war period, arriving at around 40 per cent in the 1980s. 'But contemporaries always have a tendency', Dahrendorf has observed, 'to claim secular significance for the ephemeral; the frisson of living in important times is hard to resist for intellectuals' (p. 125).

The fact that the two paradigms have greatly underestimated the state's capacity for survival and recuperation does not mean, however, that they are without interest. Many of the developments noted – growth in political participation, decline of party systems and overload on government on the one hand, or certain crisis tendencies like those of administrative rationality and socio-cultural motivations on the other – have actually occurred in Western Europe, above all in civil society, even though they have not yet provoked the predicted consequences for the state. To have an idea of the changes that have occurred, it is enough to recall the decomposition of the class structure (chapter 2); the action of new social movements and the new forms of political participation (chapter 4); the decline of the traditional parties, reduced to electoral machines with ebbing support, and the establishment of new green and national-regional parties (chapter 5); the activity of the new pressure groups, single-issue groups (chapter 6); not to speak of the expanding international literature (for all, see Inglehart, 1977; 1990).[11] In effect, the 'new politics' has developed out of the experiences of 1968, placing topics like 'quality of life', the environment, peace, gender on the political agenda. Inglehart, for instance, speaks of a new ideological cleavage between materialist (quantitative) and post-materialist (qualitative) values. The new politics accentuates the importance of access to political means and resources: free speech for minorities; access to the state's decision-making processes; capacity for political participation; the possibility of organizing, if necessary, demonstrations and other forms of behaviour that challenge political elites. All this means that the citizen is less dependent on the traditional oligarchically organized institutions (parties, trade unions, churches) and relies increasingly on new forms of participation (citizen movements) and alternative channels of information, with the consequent disorganization and fragmentation of interest representation. Inglehart (1990) concludes:

> The impact of this process tends to be concealed by the fact that it is occurring with falling rates of political party loyalty ... While electorates are becoming more politicized, their behaviour is becoming less constrained by established organizations. Thus, the rising *individual-level* potential for political activism is partially offset by a decline in the organizations that have traditionally provided external mobilization. The iron law of oligarchy has been weakened, and the old political elites are gradually losing control. This ... has been conducive to the emergence of new political movements and political parties. The rise of the West German Greens ... reflects ... the emergence of a postmaterialist constituency whose outlook is not captured by the existing political parties; and the emergence of a growing pool of voters who are politicized but do not feel tied to established parties ... This points to a growing potential for elite-directing political behaviour, aimed at achieving specific policy changes, rather than simply providing support for one set of elites instead of another. Politics in western societies is gradually becoming less institutionalized and less predictable, but is being brought under increasingly close public scrutiny. (pp. 369–70)

Whatever the potential of such new behaviour, the important thing for the moment is that, despite the obvious tensions, the old politics survives, and with it the traditional institutional arrangements, elites and methods – in short, actual democracy or the party system.

Votes count, but resources decide

If we have insisted so much, in the preceding pages, on the compromise between capital and labour as the basis of the Keynesian welfare state, it was to show that reformism was the context in which the political struggle took place in Western Europe in the post-war period. It is true that the compromise has collapsed to some extent in the last twenty years, but it is also true that there has not been, as yet, a return to the pre-war situation; the latter is testimony to the institutionalization of certain relations. The essential element of the Keynesian compromise was the fact that the economic has remained under private control and the political has developed according to a 'democratic' logic, understood as party competition periodically sanctioned by universal suffrage. The result is the displacement of social conflict from the economic field to the political. This was the origin of Lipset's (1959) 'democratic class struggle' and the real significance of the citizenship rights theorized by Marshall (1950). In this Schumpeterian vision of democracy, the subordinate classes express their political demands in the party struggle and it is through their party's success that they influence public decisions.

Do parties make a difference?

Since political decisions are usually constrained – so much so that policies formulated with certain goals in mind are often thwarted by other groups or result in unintended and pernicious consequences – we can no longer avoid the question raised in the introduction to the book: do parties make a difference? Even though the Keynesian compromise effectively permitted results of great historical significance – the workers gained previously unknown standards of living and the employers secured political stability and unprecedented profit levels – its basis was, nonetheless, extremely fragile. It depended on uninterrupted economic growth while control of the economy remained in private hands. This raises a second question: is there space for a reformist politics in a period of economic stagnation?

In the case of parties, we need to remember that they are the principal actors of the European political system, and this for two reasons. Firstly, they are, with interest groups, the privileged channels of access between civil society and the state, a channel, however, which operates in both directions (chapters 5 and 6). But since parties exist above all to propose and realize political programmes, we can agree with Sartori (1976) that they 'are *the* central intermediate and intermediary structure between society and government' (p. ix) – that is, theoretically superior to interest groups in representative democratic regimes – because they are constitutionally empowered 'to determine national policy' (article 49 of the 1948 Italian constitution, but similar norms are found in the German 1949 basic law and the French 1958 constitution). They are, in fact, entrusted with the task of aggregating interests, selecting demands and reconciling them within the constraints of the political system. Secondly, our analysis places parties and the nature of the party system at the centre of the real organization of executive power (chapter 7). In consequence, the form of government in Western Europe is 'party government', and this means that government stability depends on the working of the party system. It is clear then the importance that the impact of parties acquires in this situation.[12]

The Schumpeterian model of democracy assumes that parties present themselves to the electorate on the basis of programmes that offer the voters a real alternative, and that the winners of the election form the government and implement their programme. This was certainly the rhetoric, if not the political reality, of actual democracy of the 1940s to 1960s in Western Europe. However, in the 1960s and 1970s doubts and a certain scepticism about the importance of parties – Kirchheimer's (1957) well-known 'waning of opposition in parliamentary regimes' – were expressed that led to the question: do parties count? We should remember that there has always been some scepticism about the real nature of actual democracy, above all on the part of elitists and the less fortunate. The latter's sentiment was vividly expressed by Philpotts, one of the characters of Robert Tressell's *The Ragged Trousered Philanthropists* (1914):

> 'Wot I always say is this 'ere ... there ain't no use in the likes of us trubblin' our 'eds or quarrelling about politics. It don't make a dam bit of difference who you vote for or who gets in. They're hall the same: workin' the horickle for their own benefit. You can talk till you're black in the face, but you won't never be able to alter it.' (p. 14)

It was reproposed a few years ago in the title of a book by British left-wing Labour MP Ken Livingstone: *If Voting Changed Anything, They'd Abolish It* (1988). One consequence of this distrust has recently been voiced by Galbraith (1992): 'what is new in so-called capitalist countries – and this is a vital point – is that the controlling contentment and resultant belief is now that of the many, not just the few. It operates under the compelling cover of democracy, albeit a democracy not of all citizens but of those who, in defence of their social advantage, actually go to the polls. The result is government that is accommodated not to reality or common need but to the beliefs of the contented, who are now a majority of those who vote' (p. 10). He certainly had Reagan's America in his sights, but it is also clear that he believed that the general argument was relevant to Europe, like Thatcherism in Britain.

Nonetheless, the scepticism to which we refer is different: it is that of mainstream political science (Lipset, 1959; Cutright, 1965). The arguments are various. Firstly, electoral programmes and manifestos are nothing more than public relations, that is to say rhetorical documents – full of electoral promises – that party leaders, if victorious at the polls, have no intention of keeping. Thus, for instance, Blondel (1978) has observed that 'in the majority of cases programmes are unclear, often limited in scope, and not closely connected to the goals which the party proclaims', to conclude that 'it is because the programmes which parties propose are not in fact programmes in the full sense that so much is left to governments and to bureaucracy in daily decision-making' (pp. 122, 132).

Secondly, party programmes do not offer a real choice, or offer only an extremely limited one. To appreciate this criticism, we would need to find clear and unambiguous criteria, which is not easy. We can, however, take note of two elements: (1) the fact that arguments of the 'choice of society/civilization' kind have been at the centre of relatively recent electoral campaigns (Italy 1976, France 1978, Britain 1983) supports the thesis that the choice was real; but (2) research into party programmes (Thomas, 1980) indicates a reduction in the ideological distance of the various issue positions, and so the lack of a real choice. Finer (1975b) makes no bones about the situation, claiming that 'these shopping-list type manifestos simultaneously do too much and too little. When a government sets out to be "faithful", it is frequently unwise; and when it has learned to be wise, it is frequently "unfaithful". "[Their] honour rooted in dishonour stood, / And faith unfaithful kept [them] falsely true"' (p. 380).

Thirdly, to propose a programme offering a real choice is one thing; to implement it, once in government, is something else. There are many examples of governments that have made U-turns once they have won power. We need only recall the British examples of Wilson in 1967, Heath in 1972–3, Callaghan in 1976, and even the Conservatives in 1990, or the French example of the Mauroy government in 1983–4. Blondel (1978) concludes that 'the effectiveness of parties in translating these programmes into policies is no greater. Even in states where parties have played a sizeable part in electoral and parliamentary life over a long period, their real influence in the realm of policy-making seems to be rather weak' (pp. 129–30). Winning power means the opportunity of political action, implementing a specific policy, but also finding oneself constrained by many limitations: socio-economic conditions, interest group demands, the climate of public opinion and, perhaps most important of all, the international situation, with its economic, as much as political, conditioning. Not surprisingly, the former minister Denis Healey had reason to warn of these limits on government action at the 1982 Labour Party conference: 'So, comrades, there's a problem here. General elections don't change the laws of mathematics.'

One of the factors that have disoriented the discussion on the parties' impact on politics in West European states comes from confusion about what is meant by political change. As we have seen, neither the elitists nor the Marxists believe in actual democracy. The extremists on both sides, whether neo-conservatives or real socialists, are largely responsible for this confusion, at least in the sense that for the former only the establishment of a market society with a minimal state and for the latter only a socialist society without a market would be a real political change. All the rest – more or less taxes, more or less services – is too banal to be considered. But, as Polanyi (1944) has shown in the case of self-regulating market societies and as the actual socialist regimes have demonstrated in those of societies without markets, neither the one nor the other can exist. Or more accurately, they cannot exist with representative democratic regimes. In Western Europe, we are talking of capitalist societies with Keynesian welfare states, in which a mixture of market norms and state regulations rules. In consequence, the 'banal' changes of regulations, now pro-market, now pro-state, far from being irrelevant, are the very stuff of politics.

The thesis that parties 'make a difference' has, nonetheless, found convincing, even though contested,[13] empirical support in this area of studies in the last fifteen years. These studies confirm that party choices are relevant for the working of West European political systems; and that the electorate is usually aware of them and votes accordingly, rewarding and penalizing the parties on the basis of the implementation of their previous programmes or the credibility of their present ones. There remain, however, as is natural, areas of uncertainty as regards the specific modalities and the intensity of party influence in different sectors in the various states. It appears, for instance, that such influence is greater in the social field and less in the economic field; greater in the field of pensions policy than those of educational and health.

What emerges from this research,[14] despite all its methodological limitations, is that in the states where socialist and social democrat parties have been in power for a sufficient period to implement their programmes – thus without the constraints deriving from coalition arrangements – public expenditure has increased, as has its redistributive character. On the other hand, in the states where power has been in the hands of moderate or conservative parties, social expenditure, and particularly the income maintenance sector, has remained significantly more restricted. Fabbrini (1988) has written, in conclusion to a review of this research, that:

> On the substantive level, there appears to be little doubt about
> the centrality which political factors have had in generally influ-
> encing the post-war dynamic of public expenditure ... The model
> of the representative process is much more than a linkage model,
> that is a model in which the elector-citizens clearly transmit their
> policy preferences to the government, which then implements it.
> In reality, the parties have never functioned as simple lines of
> communication between the public's demands and government
> policies, and that both because the electorate does not always
> send clear messages on specific points of policy to the government
> and because the government, in the case that such messages were
> sent but did not meet the government's wishes, has sufficient
> authority not to consider them, or to do so only formally or in a
> limited way. Thus the representative process in a democracy
> appears very complex: it is the principal actors of policy-making
> (and in particular the parties) that frequently structure social
> demands and re-elaborate them in the form of policy options.
> (pp. 161–2)

Parties count, then, but not by themselves; they are part of an ensemble
of organizations which are rivals, such as interest groups, powerful
administrations and institutions, like the central banks and constitutional
courts. All intervene with their resources or are involved, directly or
indirectly, in the policy process. In the final analysis, the parties' weight
depends on a plurality of factors, among which the most important are
the relations that they have with certain interest groups, their ability to
mobilize certain key social groups, the level of institutionalization of
neo-corporative structures as well as the homogeneity and coordination
of the various state apparatuses: all factors which vary as between states.

If parties count in Western Europe, this gives a backing to the myth
which is the basis of actual democracy, namely that the concept of citizenship is meaningful, if only because voting offers a choice, limited perhaps, but real; it leaves open, however, the question of how much the
parties count. In the pluralist perspective discussed in the introduction to
this book, we illustrated the constitutional logic according to which the
government parties formulate the policies that are implemented by the
state apparatuses, but we also noted a second logic, called 'efficient',
which turns the former on its head, in the sense that it is interest groups
and certain state apparatuses that are able to impose their policies on the
government, parliament and parties. According to this second efficient
logic, the latter merely offer a façade of legitimacy to what is a not really
very democratic political process. However, how justified such a logic
really is in Western Europe remains, in present circumstances, a very
open question.

Finally, in view of talk of the decline of the role of parties, above all in
relation to the new politics – illustrated by the dramatic fall in political
militancy, the growing public frustration with parties, the rising rate of

electoral abstentionism, the number of party funding scandals – we must repeat that party government in Western Europe survives. If it survives, however, it is for want of better: no real alternatives have yet appeared, in terms of either representation or decision-making; there are no proposals around that would get rid of parties altogether. It may perhaps be that parties are on the wane, as some claim: Touraine in *Le Monde* (16 September 1989) spoke of the 'autumn of political parties'. But, as Calise (1989) has pointed out, 'the decline is, in reality, always a little slower than predicted' (p. 213). In the meantime, we can do no better than paraphrase Churchill's well-known aphorism on democracy to the effect that 'party government is the worst form of government ever devised by the minds of men – except all the others'.

Is reformism viable in Western Europe today?

As regards the second question – is there space for a reformist politics in a period of economic stagnation? – the answer can only be conjectural. The left's traditional answer is well known. It was formulated, for instance, by Laski (1935) during the Great Depression, when he asserted that capitalists would suppress, if necessary, democratic institutions, rather than see their interests subordinated to that of the majority of electors: 'capitalism in distress could not afford the luxury of a liberal policy' (p. 273). It was essential, therefore, that a reformist party respect constitutional rules, otherwise it risked becoming a conspiratorial sect. However, there comes a point when the crisis exceeds a critical threshold: then, the choice is between surrender and social war. 'So far, on the evidence of history,' Laski argued, 'any social class which has sought to redefine its position in the state in any fundamental way, has always had to achieve its end by violent revolution' (p. 326). And this is for the simple reason that pacific methods are not sufficient: they have not succeeded in any state in securing the transferral of wealth and power from one class to another. The paradox is, however, that if some violent revolutions have secured such a transferral, none has done so by establishing new political and civil rights, or, indeed, merely conserving those existing previously. It was just this situation that Orwell (1968) denounced at the end of World War II (in a review of Hayek and Zilliacus), when he wrote:

> these books together summarise our present predicament. Capitalism leads to dole queues, the scramble for markets, and war. Collectivism leads to concentration camps, leader worship and war. There is no way out of this unless a planned economy can somehow be combined with freedom of the intellect; but this can happen only if the concept of right and wrong is restored to politics. Both these authors are more or less aware of this, but

given that they are not able to indicate a concrete way to put it into practice, the combined effect of their books is discouraging. (vol. 3, p. 119)

We can ask what, in these 50 years, has changed for a reformist politics. From a certain point of view, very little; from another, a great deal. In theoretical terms, very little; but in practice, a great deal.

One change has been that, if in the period of the *trente glorieuses* the capitalists accepted willy-nilly the conversion of the zero-sum game (class conflict) into a positive-sum game (some social rights and economic growth), in the years of crisis, when Keynesian mechanisms were no longer able to ensure economic development, they did not hesitate to denounce the social rights and press the state for a return to the zero-sum game to avoid, in their view, the very bankruptcy of the state itself. Bourgeois logic remains unchanged: there is an economic crisis, hence there are no funds to finance social rights. In this situation, there is no other alternative: social rights must be suppressed to reduce public expenditure so that the national economy can return to equilibrium. According to this logic, it is a simple technical operation rendered necessary by the objective conditions: 'there is no other way.' This bourgeois logic, however, has to be disavowed: it is not true that the funds are lacking, because social rights can always be funded by raising the fiscal charge. In consequence, according to a reformist logic, the problem is political, not technical, that is to say the distribution of the fiscal burden between classes. In fact, the dismantling of the Keynesian welfare state by the neo-conservative governments has had to face the strong support which social rights enjoyed among the population at large. In this situation, neo-conservatives preferred to change strategy: instead of abolishing social rights *sic et sempliciter*, they claimed that they are prepared to recognize them as necessary services, while refusing the concept of social right. Because the state is, in their view, an inefficient furnisher of services, the necessary ones should be provided by the market, which is always the best mechanism of resource allocation. There is a certain irony, in addition to selective memory, in this reasoning: it wilfully forgets that it was just the inefficiency of the market in the 1930s – namely the fact that the natural equilibrium of the market economy was stabilized at a level so much below the full utilization of all resources, demonstrated by Keynes (1936) – that justified state intervention in the first place. Moreover, the state furnished many services either because the private sector was not prepared to provide them in the first place or because it could not do so profitably.

The implications are at least threefold. Firstly, the criticisms of the two sides, against market inefficiency as well as state bureaucratic inefficiency, suggest that extreme solutions are untenable in advanced industrial societies; and that the only viable solution is a mixed market–state economy. In other words, there are consumer goods that can be most efficiently supplied by the market; and services (education, health) that can be better secured collectively by the state. Naturally, the proportions of public and private are open to discussion and are likely to vary from state to state. Secondly, the post-war period divides into two phases, and in each the pendulum has oscillated between public and private. In the first phase, 1945 to 1970–5, there was an attempt to tame the market through democracy; in the second, still in progress, the opposite strategy was tried, that of taming democracy by means of market 'imperatives'. In the first period, political criteria had priority; in the second economic criteria – reinforced by the restructuring imposed on national economies by the international monetary and commercial systems – are in the ascendancy. Whatever the case, it is important to stress the cyclical character of these oscillations and the fact that they did not exceed certain limits: in the first phase considerable space was left to the market; and in the second considerable, if less, space is left to the state. Hence, despite the apparent triumph of the economic, the political remains as always relevant. As Fabbrini (1990) has, in fact, recently observed: 'political competition in the democracies ... seems to open new possibilities for the action of reformist-oriented parties and coalitions today' (p. 12). Thirdly, the replacement of the state by the market, in supplying the fundamental services, changes the meaning of social rights – 'entitlements' become mere 'provisions' in Dahrendorf's (1988) terms – because access (redefined 'choice') is determined by the ability to pay. The citizen is reduced to the status of client, which means losing both the right to criticize the level of services – in a market situation, the only remedy open to the client is not to use the service – and the entitlement to benefit, if poor.

A second set of changes arises because the ruling groups attempt, in periods of economic recession, not only to reduce social rights, but also to strengthen the repressive state apparatuses. It is no surprise, then, that the 1970s and 1980s, have seen the use of repressive measures, such as the establishment of various special police corps (British SAS, French GIS, Italian Antiterrorismo); the erosion of civil and union rights (German *Berufsverbot*, British anti-union laws); and the use of 'invisible' power in the West European states. Despite several worrying developments, the post-war crisis period has not yet known anything comparable to the 1920s and 1930s, namely the suppression of democratic institutions hypothesized by Laski on the basis of pre-war experience. The post-war European experience, in fact, far from seeing a repeat of the pre-war situation, has seen the extension of actual democracy, first in Southern Europe (Spain, Portugal and Greece) in the 1970s and now in Eastern Europe in the 1990s. This development suggests two conclusions as regards Western Europe. One is that the socio-political climate has dramatically changed in the post-war period with the taking root of representative institutions in countries where they were not very institutionalized before the war, namely Germany and Italy.[15] Another is that the 'citizenship' concept has become, despite all its limitations, a significant aspect of this climate. It is no accident that the concept has become fashionable in reformist circles (Charter '88 in Britain; Italian left: Veca, 1990). An important aspect in this development is not only the reaction to defend the *droits acquis* of the Keynesian welfare state, but initiatives to extend them in crucial areas. Two of them deserve particular mention: information and economy. For the former, certain considerations of Bobbio (1984) on the 'paradoxes of democracy', and above all the reassertion that the essence of democracy is 'open government' by 'visible power', are pertinent. The central idea is that the citizens can express their political will only if they have all the relevant information, something which is far from being the case in Western Europe. And this is because, in addition to the attempts of the economic forces themselves to control the information processes and the media, the state apparatuses too seek to keep from public view, where possible, many aspects of power, through a complex set of mechanisms and processes, from official secrets and 'crypto-government' to *sottogoverno* and clientelism. Information is an area which, with the end of the Cold War, can be considerably extended without any serious security risks for West European states. Thus European legislation along the lines of the American Freedom of Information Act would be a first step in this direction. The problem of the extension of democracy to industrial firms is obviously more controversial. The fact that it is being discussed (Dahl, 1985; Macpherson, 1985) shows that, as with information, it is a field where there is space for reformist policies.

A third change for reformist politics arises because, although defining and extending citizen rights is certainly useful, it is not sufficient; it helps people know their entitlements, but if the concept of citizenship is to be meaningful, it must be rooted as much in civil society as in the state, not in only one country but in the whole continent. After all, a contingent majority can always change the laws in one country and so reduce citizenship; on the other hand, if it was rooted in the various national societies, it would be lived as, and be, an integral part of the European citizen's life and hence it would be more secure. Keane (1988) has recently argued for the need to increase the density of civil society in Europe, that is to develop both the non-state and the non-market spheres. It is well known that in all West European countries (chapter 4), civil society has been enriched by a variety of new forms of sociability (from different types of autonomous civil associations to 'invisible' networks of small groups), as a result of the social movements active in the 1970s and 1980s. This suggests a further area where there is space for a reformist politics: developing the rights of everyday life, having as a point of reference what might loosely be called a Gramscian strategy. Elements of such a strategy have been outlined by Crick (1987). He warns that the road to a possible socialist society can only be long and difficult, particularly in states with long-established representative institutions, and hence it requires a long-term strategy. This must necessarily carry enfranchised public opinion with it for each step it takes in order to counterbalance the weight of its adversaries' resources; otherwise the risk is, as in Britain in the 1980s, of going backwards. At all events, the strategy is articulated at three different levels: (1) short-term tactical reforms (the life of a parliament) within the system to build a basis of popular confidence in advance; (2) middle-term strategies to change the system; and (3) long-term persuasion to work a new system in a new spirit (p. 111). What is required is to make the citizen's everyday experience compatible with socialist values (liberty, equality and fraternity), while the programmatic elaboration, at the strategic-political level, should be capable of demonstrating convincingly that the 'ethically desirable is sociologically possible'. It is a strategy of small steps which combines two Machiavellian notions: the traditional one of 'politics as the art of the possible' with the more ambitious one of 'politics as the science of enlarging the area of the possible'.

At this point, however, we face a very serious problem that could thwart any kind of reformist strategy in European countries: it is the problem of north–south relations. The West European states belong to the wealthy and privileged north, while the rest of the world represents the enormous poverty-stricken south. Dahrendorf (1988) has recently observed that 'a civil society in one country is strictly not possible' (p. 46), meaning by civil society 'a society of citizens in the full sense of the word' (p. 24).[16] Citizenship implies universal rights, that is to say guaranteed for everyone, as well as duties. The belief that capitalism is able to secure the well-being of everyone, as its apologists claim, has been refuted by the fact that the economic development of the north has been, and is, a development 'paid for' by the south. In other words, the north has discharged on to the south the social and environmental costs of the economic processes that were the basis of its development. The paradox of the idea of citizenship in a capitalist society finds a confirmation in 'racism', that is in the wish to keep away, and hence exclude from citizenship rights in Europe, immigrants from the Third World who, in ever growing numbers, seek in the north those conditions of life that capitalist development has so far only offered to Western peoples. 'More and more people (it appears)', Dahrendorf has noted of Europeans 'do not want to live in a multiracial or even a multicultural society ... They demand their own niche, if not their own region or country' (p. 156). In this perspective, the limits of a reformist politics are connate with the experience of the nation-state. The widespread conviction was that world integration would result from the universal expansion of the market which would lead both to a general and spontaneous redefinition of the international political world picture and to widespread social homogenization. This does not appear to be the case, nor do the Europeans want it. European integration, then, risks becoming increasingly the construction of a 'European fortress', a living absurdity: the negation of its whole history.

Conclusion

The aim of this study has been to discuss the working of democracy in the major West European states. The approach was thematic and so the discussion of necessity segmental. It revealed, nonetheless, both functions and malfunctions, complexity and commonality. One common feature that dictated much of the discussion was the state form – the Keynesian welfare state – which was based on an inherently unstable compromise between capital and labour. Indeed, the conflict between the needs of capital and those of democracy, as set out in the introduction to the book, was the underlying leitmotif informing politics in the West European states since the war.

The post-war years are usually divided into two phases of similar duration: (1) a period of economic prosperity (*les trente glorieuses*) and very relative political stability (1950s and 1960s); and (2) a similar period of economic crises and political turbulence (1970s and 1980s) from which the West European states have yet to emerge. However, the context in which those states operate has been dramatically and fundamentally altered by the great transformation in world politics of the early 1990s.

The first phase was dominated by a debate over the post-war democratic political consensus which, it was believed by both liberal pluralists and neo-Marxists, the Keynesian welfare state had definitively achieved. The pluralists argued that it had enabled the workers to achieve industrial and political citizenship without unduly disarming the capitalists who had broadly welcomed this development. In consequence, parties, elections and parliament guaranteed the democratic resolution of political conflict without revolution.

The problem for neo-Marxists was how to explain the working class's relative lack of combativeness and its acceptance of the social and political order in those years. It was found in the scientific and technological revolution that had transformed the forces of production into a form of ideology which legitimized enslavement to the logic of production. The result was the triumph of instrumental reason and the depoliticization of political life in which the media played a primary role.

The actual functioning of the West European democracies was claimed to revolve round the so-called electoral business cycle. This operated on the assumption that all actors maximized their own short-term interests: it meant for electors their own well-being, and for politicians their own popularity. Once it was ascertained that government popularity depended on economic factors, it was assumed that the government would use its control of economic policy to maximize its popularity in the run-up to elections and that this would affect economic activity. The interaction of politics and economics would thus determine a cycle whose motor was elections. Empirical research to identify and verify the existence of electoral business cycles in West European countries has nourished a vast literature, but provided only ambiguous results. Thus, while some political scientists are convinced that the manipulation of the economy by politicians is a proven fact, it must be objected that the fact that manipulation is possible does not mean that it is always attempted or that it always works: the politicians can get the timing wrong or international constraints may prevent it. Otherwise, the victory of opposition parties would be inexplicable.

A more sophisticated version of the same basic thesis linked the electoral business cycle to the economic crises of the 1970s, suggesting that the continued manipulation of the economy for electoral purposes effectively destroyed the trade-off between inflation and unemployment that was the basis of the Keynesian compromise. The thesis was excessively deterministic, predicting the collapse of democracy within a generation.

The second phase generated a debate over the economic and political crises of the 1970s and 1980s. Once again there was a confrontation between liberal pluralists and neo-Marxists. The former advanced an ungovernability or overload thesis, based on the disproportion between the escalation in political demands and the governments' lack of politico-administrative efficacy in meeting them. As a result, the Keynesian welfare state was taking on more tasks than it was capable of fulfilling. This led to a decline in government authority that weakened its capacity to resist the continued proliferation of political demands, the whole setting in motion a vicious circle that undermined economic growth and provoked an economic crisis. Hence the practical problem for governments was to break the vicious circle at all costs; this meant dissociating the economic and the political and so reducing popular expectations and the overload on government. The mechanism for achieving this was a return to the market and privatization of public economic activities and services. Liberal pluralists claimed that the problem was not too little democracy (as the May 1968 students alleged) but too much democracy.

The neo-Marxist legitimation crisis paradigm shared some of the elements of the overload thesis, but started from different premises. Most state interventions in society were seen as strategies for avoiding more serious crises deriving from class conflict. These crises were the result of contradictions in which the state was necessarily involved: on the one hand, its need to sustain accumulation and private appropriation of resources; on the other, its need to secure mass loyalty (its basis of legitimacy) by appearing to be the impartial arbiter of class interests. Class antagonisms pervaded all the subsystems in which the social system is articulated and created crises tendencies in all of them. They intercommunicated and most strategies tended to displace the crisis from one subsystem to the next, setting further crisis tendencies in motion: the result was a potential breakdown in loyalty and hence a full-scale legitimacy crisis. The state was normally able to manage the tensions between the economic structures and the politico-administrative institutions, but only up to a certain point, beyond which they were likely to get out of control.

How accurate were these paradigms for understanding the functioning of West European democracy in these years? Certainly, the rather catastrophic predictions of both were misplaced in the sense of underestimating the state's capacity to act: the crux of the crisis for both paradigms. Things have, in fact, gone on as before, despite the confident prediction of both paradigms that they could not. The social discontent of the 1970s was not a new phenomenon and state action in the 1980s was sufficient to bring critical situations (economic and terrorist) under control, using the very displacement mechanisms denounced by the neo-Marxists: in short, 'divide and rule' triumphed. Given the state's capacity to deal with the crises, the question arises: why were the politicians and intellectuals so alarmed in the 1970s? Two answers have been suggested: (1) in view of the success of Keynesian techniques in the 1950s and 1960s, politicians and social scientists (economists) really did believe in their ability to manage society rationally; (2) certain world events undermined the international structures (Bretton Woods) that had protected West European economies from disturbing influences up to then, so that it did actually seem to these elites that everything was collapsing into anarchy.

However, despite the paradigms' poor appraisal of the state's capacity to survive and act, they nonetheless throw light on many of the developments that were occurring then: growth in political participation; decline in the party system; government overload; not to mention crisis tendencies like administrative irrationality and socio-cultural motivational change. They engaged the new politics issuing from 1968, even if they did not find answers for it. Nonetheless, the old political structures – parties, elections, elites – remained in place.

The questions raised by actual democracy in West Europe are many, but two in particular warrant discussion. (1) Do parties matter? (2) Is there space for a reformist politics in a period of stagnation or recession? The answer to both is ambiguous. There is no doubt that parties remain the principal visible actor in West European democratic politics. However, the relation between the political programmes they offer the electors and the politics that the winners are actually able to realize are usually very different, not least because governments are constrained by many, including international, factors outside their control. Nonetheless, research has found empirical evidence that parties do make a difference. It confirms that party choices are relevant for the functioning of West European democratic systems: the electorate is aware of the choices available and votes accordingly, rewarding and penalizing parties on the basis of their promises and record in office. There are areas of uncertainty as regards the specific intensity of party influence: for instance it was greater in the social field and less in the economic; greater on pensions policy than on health or education. There was also a link between social democracy and redistributive policies on the one hand, and moderate governments and limits on social expenditure on the other.

Thus parties count, but not alone. They form part of an ensemble of rival organizations that have their say too. The parties' weight depends on a plurality of factors that can change over time. On this basis actual democracy in Western Europe is meaningful in the sense that votes count, even if they rarely decide because rival organizations can offer other resources that counterbalance votes: money still talks in capitalist societies. Finally, as regards talk of new politics and the decline of parties, the evidence is contradictory: if they are declining, the decline is slow and certainly much slower than many have proclaimed.

The answer to the second question can only be conjectural. There has been no political return to the 1930s, despite the economic recessions and the return of mass unemployment; then, in the choice between capitalism and democracy, it was the latter that was abandoned. However, there has been a significant curtailment of social rights as fiscal deficits have mounted. One solution employed by conservative governments in the 1980s was the privatization of public services, substituting provisions for entitlements. At the same time, the coercive powers of the state have been reinforced (police). Hence there has been an increase in the significance of citizens' rights (Charter '88). A reformist policy today is obliged to assert and extend citizens' rights, but this is hardly sufficient in itself, even if it is a first step. To be meaningful, of course, they need to be rooted in a robust civil society, and this requires the development of a civic associationism aimed at demonstrating that the ethically desirable is sociologically possible.

At present, however, a reformist policy is confronted with an almost insoluble problem: north–south relations. Western Europe forms part of the small, wealthy and privileged north which now finds itself virtually surrounded by the enormous poverty-stricken south that naturally wishes to share some of the former's privileges. Western Europe, after building its prosperity and privileges at the expense of the south, is loath to share them. In this perspective, reformist policies are connate with the nation-state. The expansion of the market economy world-wide has not resulted in the general social homogenization that many had hoped; and if it were to do so today, most West Europeans would not want it. In this sense, the EU risks becoming a European fortress which would be a negation of its whole history.

So, whither Europe? 'Nul ne saurait le dire, car déjà les termes de comparaison nous manquent ... la grandeur de ce qui est déjà fait empêche de prévoir ce qui peut se faire encore' (Tocqueville, 1835–40, pp. 8–9).[17]

Further reading

M.J. Crozier, S.P. Huntington and J. Watanuki (1975), *The Crisis of Democracy* (New York: New York UP).

R. Dahrendorf (1988), *The Modern Social Conflict: Essay on the Politics of Liberty* (London: Weidenfeld & Nicolson).

G. Esping-Andersen (1990), *The Three Worlds of Welfare Capitalism* (Cambridge: Polity).

E. Etzioni-Halevy (1993), *The Elite Connection: Problems and Potential of Western Democracy* (Cambridge: Polity).

J.K. Galbraith (1993), *The Culture of Contentment* (Harmondsworth: Penguin).

D. Held (ed.) (1993), *Prospects for Democracy: North, South, East, West* (Cambridge: Polity).

J. Keane (1988), *Democracy and Civil Society* (London: Verso).

J. Keane (ed.) (1988), *Civil Society and the State* (London: Verso).

S. Lash and J. Urry (1987), *The End of Organized Capitalism* (Cambridge: Polity).

C. Offe (1984), *Contradictions of the Welfare State* (London: Hutchinson).

C. Pierson (1991), *Beyond the Welfare State* (Cambridge: Polity).

P. Whiteley (1986), *Political Control of Macro-Economy* (London: Sage).

Notes

Preface

1 To give some idea: the populations (in millions) of the states named are the following: Iceland (0.2), Luxemburg (0.4), Ireland (3.5), Norway (4.2), Denmark (5.1), Germany (79.4) and France (56.4).
2 The fifth largest West European state is Spain with a population of around 38 million, while none of the other states has more than 15 million inhabitants (Holland: 14.6). The Spanish experience is, like that of Portugal, too different to be included in this study.
3 This was truer before the unification of Germany when West Germany's population was 63 million. Today Germany is undoubtedly the dominant state in Europe.

Introduction

1 Rousseau's ideas pose a problem: he is universally considered an advocate of direct democracy. He certainly rejected representative democracy in this famous passage, but he also distinguished between legislation (the people's business) and administration (the ruler's task). However, in other passages, this distinction seems to disappear: on the one hand, it is enough that the people ratify the laws, and, on the other, the ruler's tasks go well beyond simple execution. As regards an attempt at people's government of the modern state, the experience of the citizen-administrator theorized by Lenin in 1917 – for whom the functions of government had 'become so simplified and [could] be reduced to such exceedingly simple operations of registration, filing and checking that they [could] be easily performed by every literate person' (1918, p. 294) – is telling, if not conclusive.

2 This approach found its logical development – namely, the application of classical economic rationality (individual self-interest plus market mechanisms) to party competition for the vote – on Schumpeter's own indication ('Politically speaking, the man is still in the nursery who has not absorbed, so as never to forget, the saying attributed to one of the most successful politicians who ever lived: "what businessmen do not understand is that exactly as they are dealing in oil so I am dealing in votes" ': p. 285) in Downs's (1957) so-called 'economic theory of democracy' (chapter 5 in this book). 'The voter's function is not to decide on policy but merely to choose one set of politicians, who are authorized to decide the policies. This function does not require, nor does it permit, widespread citizen participation. The system is lauded for its efficiency in maintaining equilibrium and providing some degree of consumer sovereignty. Its function is not to promote individual self-development but to meet the demands that individuals, as maximizing consumers, actually have and are able to express' (Macpherson, 1985, p. 95).

3 Even though universal suffrage was introduced in Britain in 1928, the double vote for landowners and university graduates was only abolished in 1948. Similarly, the legislative veto of the House of Lords was severely curtailed in 1911, but still remains suspensive (that is to say for one year) for all matters, except the finance bill.

4 Polanyi thought the crisis of the 1930s (including Nazism) was a direct consequence of this process: 'the origins of the cataclysm lay in the utopian endeavour of economic liberalism to set up a self-regulating market system' (1944, p. 29).

5 The principle of mandating was rejected in Britain long before the extension of the suffrage (Burke's speech to his electors of 1774: Burke, 1987) and in France at the same time as universal male suffrage was proposed (vote of the Constituent Assembly of 1791); moreover, it has never subsequently been accepted, despite the attempts of progressive reformers, like Tom Paine, the Chartists and others. The secret ballot was introduced in Britain in 1873 with the declared objective, according to Bendix (1964), of neutralizing the threatening working class organizations; the provisions for secrecy were intended to isolate the dependent worker not only from his superiors but also from his peers.

6 Pizzorno (1981) has stressed the theoretical significance, at the time (1880–1920), of the recognition that the idea of a direct relationship between the state and the individual was unrealistic and consequently of the need for more or less independent bodies to act as mediator. It was a problem that exercised Marxists (Lenin, Kautsky and Gramsci) and non-Marxists (Mosca, Michels and Weber) alike.

7 In saying this, we have no intention of overlooking the contribution of the conservative authoritarian and paternalistic tradition (Bismarck's *Sozialpolitik* in Germany and the policies of Napoleon III in France and Disraeli in Britain) to the creation of the welfare state: this tradition also opposed the commodification of labour desired by the liberals.

8 This was not a purely hypothetical threat, but a very real one, as progressive governments, like those of Blum in 1936 and Mitterrand in 1982 in France, and that of Fanfani in 1962 in Italy, have known to their cost.

9 This sequence of the historical development of rights is rejected by Polanyi (1944) who maintains that welfare is not a late capitalist development for philanthropic reasons following the era of the absolute exploitation of labour, but the precondition for the commodification of labour.

10 The implications of this statement are considerable. As the Swiss playwright, the late Max Dürrenmatt (1989), observed: 'Marxism failed over man, the rational over the irrational that is part of human nature, not only in Lenin and Stalin, but already in Karl Marx, the founder of this first rationalist religion … Marx believed that humanity endowed with reason would return to reason, by the dialectic of the class struggle immanent in history. The failure of this enterprise and the lack of reflection with which the market economy has been left to take command has allowed it to be said, in the form of a slogan, that the Enlightenment had failed. Thus, overlooking the fact that the Enlightenment itself needed to be enlightened.'

11 In 1947 president Truman told the American Political Science Association that it had a singular responsibility to give the citizens 'a mature understanding' of the essentials of democratic government, understood in liberal societies as they were (inequalities and all) and not democratic societies as they might be (Hoffmann, 1988, p. 142).

12 The treatment of resident aliens, who are now significant minorities in all West European societies, and the social consequences of economic deregulation in the 1980s, suggest that citizenship was even less secure than Marshall supposed. Hindess (1993) has recently argued that 'while Marshall was right to insist on the significance of the principle of citizenship in contemporary political discourse … he is mistaken in his treatment of citizenship as a status that has now been more or less adequately realized' (p. 33). In addition, feminists, like Pateman (1988), have rightly pointed out that Marshall neglected other dimensions of citizenship, particularly the rights of women, but including children, the aged and ethnic groups, because he tended to reduce citizenship to the class system, and these omissions have had important consequences on the position of these groups in Western European societies.

13 Bagehot adds the gloss: 'the dignified parts of government are those which bring it force, which attract its motive power. The efficient parts only employ that power' (1867, p. 61).

14 For a discussion of the concept of civil society in its Gramscian derivation, on which our usage is based, see Bobbio (1976): for a more general discussion see Tester (1992).

15 The Keynesian welfare state with its decommodification of labour has subtly undermined these generalizations: money, for instance, now mediates the relations between state and civil society in a large part of the sphere of reproduction.

16 What Keohane and Hoffmann mean by 'pooling sovereignty' is 'the transfer of states' legal authority over internal and external affairs to the Community as a whole, though not to supranational organs as such' (1991, p. 35).

17 A regulation is directly applicable to all member states and thus automatically becomes part of national law. A directive establishes a framework for national policies; it only becomes effective after member states have enacted legislation implementing it (Andersen and Eliassen, 1993, p. 116).

Chapter 1   Mixed economies

1 The Keynesian system can be defined as a system of general and continuous government guidance of an otherwise individualistic and decentralized market economy.

2 According to *The Economist* of 1 August 1992, the average share of value added capital formation and employment in public sector enterprise in 1988 was: Britain 8 per cent; France 18 per cent; West Germany 12 per cent; Italy 20 per cent.

3 We use this term rather than O'Connor's 'monopolistic' because it is factually more correct.

4 Some argue that a fourth phase opened in 1990 as a result of the collapse of Soviet power, though they have difficulty in defining its characteristics other than suggesting that 'any future international economic order will be the product of political power as much as of economic power' (Mitchell, 1992, p. 195).

5 Britain preferred to remain outside and follow an independent track until 1990.

6 Severe restrictions governing strike action, including the balloting of members, the banning of sympathy strikes, secondary picketing, union fines and the sequestering of their funds for breaches of strike regulations by their members.

7 In a presidential address in October 1993 to the European Economic Association, Mervyn King, the Bank of England's chief economist, demonstrated that 'the greater a country's build-up of consumer debt between 1984 and 1988, the greater the subsequent shortfalls in economic growth between 1989 and 1992 – with the UK experiencing the largest debt build-up and biggest growth shortfall.' In other words, the indebted consumers have spent the last four years retrenching, and consumption in the debt-laden UK and US has traced a pattern markedly below the average of the two previous recessions (*The Guardian*, 4 October 1993, p. 11).

8 When Britain finally decided the time was ripe for entry in autumn 1990, it decided on a sterling/Deutschmark exchange rate that was unsustainable and this further added to the problems of its ailing economy.

Chapter 2   Class, gender and race

1 Understood as the division of society into more or less permanent social hierarchies.

2 The grandfathers of former president Giscard d'Estaing and former prime minister Couve de Murville arrogated titles for their families of dubious authenticity (Giscard's family claimed to be descended from the famous Admiral d'Estaing and added his name to the family surname) during the Third Republic in France. Similarly, republican Italy has been plagued by a plethora of titles – *dottore, cavaliere, commendatore, gran croce* and so on –

despite the formal prohibition in the 1948 constitution (Schnapper, 1971, pp. 142–50). Ardagh (1988a, pp. 153–4) makes similar observations about Germany: (*Graf*, *Herr Professor*, *Oberkirchenrat*, *Oberregierungspräsident*, or even simple *Herr Doktor*).

3 It is a notion that dies hard, if it is true that a British Tory minister, Patrick Jenkin, could declare on the BBC documentary 'Man Alive' in 1979: 'If the good Lord had intended us all to have equal rights to go out and work and behave equally, you know he really wouldn't have created men and women … These are the biological facts of life, that young children really do depend on their mothers.'

4 A 'stigma' has been defined as any identifying characteristic that has a low cost of detection and a high cost of conversion.

5 The figures were taken as the name of a well-known, radical British theatre group in the 1970s.

6 This was not necessarily the case, as John Ardagh (1988b) notes that 'according to one survey, of the 2500 most famous or powerful people in France today, only 3 per cent come from working class homes' (p. 358).

7 As recently as July 1983, for example, the lord chancellor, the chairman of the BBC, the editor of *The Times*, chief of defence staff, the heads of the foreign and civil services and the governor of the Bank of England were all Old Etonians (Sampson, 1983, p. 473); this confirms Scott's (1982, p. 158) argument that the main support of the high degree of social cohesion of the upper classes is 'its system of kinship and educational experience'.

8 For example, the arrival of new personalities in Italy, like the late Raoul Gardini, Carlo de Benedetti, Silvio Berlusconi, Luciano Benetton.

9 Davis (1992) argues, nonetheless, that the capitalist class in Germany 'has more fluidity and less social and political cohesion than in Britain and France' (p. 29).

10 The social and political situation of immigrant workers varies between countries. In France and Germany, they are foreigners without political rights, whose presence in the country is subject to severe administrative control (residence and work permits that have to be renewed every six to twelve months), so that they can be expelled at short notice. In Britain, many are subjects of former British colonies with a British passport, and so enjoy political rights, but newcomers since the Commonwealth Immigration Acts of the 1960s are as severely controlled as in France and Germany. In Italy, traditionally a country of emigration, the problem is very recent and severe controls were only imposed in 1990.

Chapter 3   The forming of civil society

1 Of the kind dear to Adam Smith's 'invisible hand' of the market, much in vogue with Anglo-Saxon neo-liberals in the 1980s.

2 For instance, the famous beer and sandwiches at Number Ten (Downing Street) between the social forces to resolve social conflicts in the 1960s and 1970s, denounced with such vehemence by Mrs Thatcher.

3 For example, *caméralisme* on post-revolutionary official procedures.

4 Even in the United Kingdom where the working class is considered to have made a major contribution to the development of social rights, the state, it is claimed, had its own interest in the promotion of social policy. Pierson (1991, p. 35) notes, for example, that 'concern with the "national efficiency" and physical incapacity of the UK working class to defend the empire against the challenge of the Boers has long been cited as the source of UK welfare reforms at the turn of the century. This view was echoed by Lloyd George who argued in 1917 that "you cannot maintain an A1 empire with a C3 population." '

5 It is worth recalling, in this regard, that the British Isles had, like Germany, an important Catholic minority (in Ireland), most of which was detached from the United Kingdom in 1921 after a bloody civil war.

6 It is ironic in this connection that the collapse of communism signalled by the fall of the Berlin Wall in 1989 has affected the Italian DC as much as the PCI, now the PDS – thus giving substance to Rokkan's hypothesis, despite Hermet's objections. Of course, it is not the only factor in the crisis and dissolution of the Italian DC in 1993–4 (see chapter 5).

7 The concept of the state is still considered by the Anglo-Saxon tradition as 'the metaphysical burden of less happy lands, a symptom of the unfortunate legacy of absolutism, romanticism and nationalism', quoted by Bentley (1908), who dismissed an interest in the state as 'among the intellectual amusements of the past' (p. 263).

8 This was also the view of Enoch Powell: 'We are a parliamentary nation ... If you put us in the jar labelled "democracy" I cannot complain; I can only tell you that you have understood very little about the United Kingdom' (letter in *The Times Literary Supplement*, 1991).

9 Until the 1980s, British passports carried the mention 'British subject. Citizen of the United Kingdom and colonies'!

10 As the verses of the famous song from Gilbert and Sullivan's opera *Iolanthe* (1882) illustrate: 'I often think it's comical / How Nature always does contrive / That every boy and every gal, / That's born into the world alive, / Is either a little Liberal, / Or else a little Conservative!'

11 Already begun by the revolutionaries in 1791 with the famous Le Chapelier law against working class associations and in 1795 with the coup as a political weapon.

12 Caesarism in the French context has recently been defined as 'the assumption of power at a moment of real or alleged national crisis by a figure owing his prestige to genuine or associated military achievements' (Thody, 1989).

13 During World War I Thomas Mann wrote: 'I confess to being deeply convinced that the Germans will never have a liking for political democracy ... and further that the much-maligned *Obrigkeitsstaat* is and will remain the most fitting and congenial one for the German people – basically it is the form of state that they most admire' (quoted by G. Smith, 1979, p. 1).

14 This policy was not started by Bismarck, if it is true that the Prussian minister, Strüenzee had already said in 1798 that 'if the creative revolution was carried out in France from below, in Germany it will be accomplished slowly and from above' (quoted in Hintze, 1902, p. 169).

15 A lesser poet wittily noted at the same time: 'Tre fratelli, tre castelli; / Eccoti l'Italia' (Three brothers, three castles; / Here is Italy for you).

16 Title given by D'Annunzio to a series of poems in the *Laudi* (1889) that evoke many of the city-states with a glorious past (Ferrara, Pisa, Ravenna, Padua, Perugia, Orvieto, Prato, Vicenza) but reduced to insignificance at the end of the last century.

17 Typical were speeches like that of Crispi to his Palermitan electors in 1886: 'You should see the pandemonium at Montecitorio [the Italian parliament] when the time for an important division approaches. The government's agents run through the rooms and corridors to gather votes. Subsidies, decorations, canals, bridges, roads, everything is promised; and sometimes an act of justice, long denied, is the price of a parliamentary vote' (1890, p. 575).

18 In the *Sermons* (CXXX, 5, in Hermet, 1983, p. 89), St Augustine says: 'You are well aware that everybody entrusts himself to his own protector. A man threatens you, you are the client of a powerful man and so you tell your adversary: as long as my lord lives, you will do nothing against me.'

Chapter 4   The changing of civil society

1 For the notion of 'common sense' as understood here, see Allum (1991).

2 The section in which this definition appears is omitted from the English version of Pizzorno's article. The page reference is to the original Italian version.

3 Something very similar, but with more elaborate ideological justification, occurred within the various Catholic parties in Belgium, Germany and Italy, organized on the basis of social categories.

4 As regards the various forms of civic participation, Barbagli and Maccelli (1985) have suggested a useful distinction between 'visible' civic participation (activities intended to influence political life: voting, militancy) and 'invisible' participation (emotional feelings, information). In addition, in the class of visible participation, they distinguish between 'institutionalized' forms and 'non-institutionalized' forms: the latter include 'those forms of behaviour that do not conform to the laws and customs that govern political participation in a given regime' (p. 16), for example boycotts, picketing, factory occupations.

5 'The contented electoral majority' of Galbraith (1992).

6 Raymond Williams in his novel *Border Country* (1960) draws attention to the importance of community relations (as in the chapels of the small Welsh villages). One of the characters in the novel explains: 'The chapels are social organizations, Matthew. The church here is not. I don't mean that their religious professions are insincere, but they could equally, it seems to me, be professions in almost anything – any other system of belief, for instance. What matters, what holds them together, is what their members do, through them, for each other. God, you might say, is their formula for being neighbourly' (pp. 222–3).

7 The values of the Catholic world were those typical of the Counter-Reformation – hierarchical-authoritarian type of society, patriarchal family, doctrinaire education – while those of the communist world were centred on the class struggle, workerism and party loyalty (Stalinism).

8 Attempts to break down the one-way communications system have been made through such things as community radio and open space television programmes, but they remain very much marginal phenomena.

9 An important phenomenon in the post-war period, above all in France and Italy, was party newspapers: *L'Humanité* (PCF), *Le Matin* (PS), *L'Unità* (PCI), *L'Avanti!* (PSI), *Il Popolo* (DC); but also *Daily Worker–Morning Star* (CPGB), *Daily Herald* (Labour). Their sales, however, have fallen dramatically, so much so that party publications are in crisis everywhere.

10 In France, the Chirac government (1986–8) privatized TF1 (Bouygues) and created three new channels (le 5, M6, le 7), so that in 1990 only two out of the seven channels were public; in 1993, le 5 was in financial difficulties and was replaced by a Franco-German semi-public channel Arte. In Britain, there has been a shake-up with the reallocation of the private franchises and, although the BBC will be maintained as a public service, it is not yet clear what changes the renewal of its charter in 1995 will entail. Moreover, there is discussion of the introduction of a fifth channel. Finally, in view of the fact that cable and satellite television are only in their infancy in Europe (Murdoch's BSkyB only started broadcasting in 1990), it is clear that the 1990s will be a period of significant change.

11 The House of Commons was hostile for a very long time to the televising of its debates, and it was only in 1989 that it finally approved the presence of television cameras in the House. Television broadcasts began, on an experimental basis, in January 1990!

12 It is worth noting that the BBC came under intense pressure in the 1980s, particularly in the news and current affairs field. 'Its always fragile independence from government has been challenged by a series of moves, ranging from well publicized attacks on "the impartiality" of its news coverage to police seizures of film, and a government ban on live interviews with the members of a range of named organizations in Northern Ireland, including the legal political party, Sinn Fein' (Golding and Murdock, 1991, p. 21).

13 A sample verse reads: 'Women are irrational, that's all there is to that! / Their heads are full of cotton, hay and rags'! / They are nothing but exasperating, irritating, vacillating, calculating, agitating, maddening and infuriating hags! / Why can't a woman be more like a man? / Men are honest, so thoroughly square; / Eternally noble, historically fair; / Who, when you win, always give your back a pat! / Why can't a woman be like that?'

14 For a discussion of 'news sense' and 'news values' which are the basis of 'journalistic practice', see Hall (1973).

15 The latest macroscopic example of the power of TV was the political candidacy of TV tycoon Silvio Berlusconi and his use of the media in the 1994 Italian elections (details in chapter 5, note 7). It has been variously called 'videopolitics' or 'telecracy'.

Chapter 5   Parties and party sysems

1 Burke's classic definition of a party as 'a body of men united for promoting by their joint endeavours the national interest, upon some particular principle in which they are all agreed' dates from 1770 (Burke, 1987, p. 105).

2 Gramsci was one of the few who appreciated the specific Russian nature of Lenin's organizational schema and strategy. It was for this reason that in the *Quaderni del carcere* one of his constant preoccupations is the search for an alternative communist strategy for Europe.

3 Keane (1988) coins the expression 'the compromise party' for this type of party which, outside the obvious pejorative connotation from his ideological standpoint, seems to capture much of the essence of parties in representative democracies: that of mediation (pp. 106–11).

4 Duverger was wrong when he suggested in 1951 that the mass parties, as he defined them, would dominate the future of the European political systems. The reason, according to Pizzorno (1980, pp. 32–3), lay in the fact that the emergence of mass parties was linked to the social mobilization resulting from political and economic modernization. It is no accident that party mass mobilization slowed down, and even regressed, with the decline in the situation of effervescence and solidarity, linked as the latter is to relatively short periods of collective enthusiasm. The upwards trend of the 1940s became the stagnation of the 1950s and 1960s.

5 In 1986 the left-wing faction (CERES) of the French PS operated a similar ideological revision, as did the Italian PCI which changed both name (to Democratic Party of the Left: PDS) and symbol (from hammer and sickle to an oak) in 1991.

6 Before World War I, de Jouvenel observed: 'Après quelques temps l'élu aura définitivement perdu le contact avec l'opinion publique: il sera un vrai parlementaire' (1914, p. 39).

7 This trend has had its most sensational development to date in the creation by Italian media baron Silvio Berlusconi of his political movement, Forza Italia, two months before the March 1994 elections. It won the largest number of votes (table 5.9) and led to his appointment as prime minister in May 1994. It was an extension of his business empire, being constituted of a series of soccer supporters' clubs and manned by the local sales staff of one of his companies, Publitalia, acting as political cadres and employing unlimited resources and the latest managerial and marketing techniques (such as US-style TV spots on his three private channels). It should be added that this was possible as a result of the exceptional political situation in Italy at the time, that is the institutional vacuum created by the *tangentopoli* (bribesville) scandal involving over 300 MPs, mainly from the DC and PSI, and including four former prime ministers.

8 Down to 55 per cent in 1992 from a peak of 75 per cent in the 1980s.

9 The Conservative Party has always been extremely secretive about the sources of donations. When challenged over the source of unaccounted funds which represent £40 million of the party's declared income of £67.7 million (that is two-thirds) over the last five years, a spokeswoman said it

would always be party policy to keep private the individual donations to the party (*The Guardian*, 26 November 1992, p. 7). But as a member of the reformist Charter movement in the party commented, 'we can be absolutely sure that the interests of party democracy are not enhanced!' (*The Guardian*, 13 March 1993, p. 5).

10 It is claimed that 24 million of the 100 million francs that Mitterrand's 1988 presidential campaign officially cost came from this source (Gaetner, 1992, p. 371).

11 As noted, over 300 MPs, including many former ministers and many of the major party leaders (former prime ministers Craxi (PSI), Andreotti, Forlani, De Mita (DC)), were under judicial investigation when the Italian parliament was dissolved in March 1994.

12 Labour Party about £2 million; Conservative Party about £19 million.

13 This is further evidence that 1968 may represent an ultimate critical juncture.

14 However, these conclusions must be tempered by the following results of Bartolini and Mair's (1990) in-depth research. Firstly, recent electoral volatility has increased 'only with respect to the 1950s and 1960s' and not the inter-war years (p. 61), and so 'fails to display any secular trend over time' (p. 119). Secondly, cleavage volatility 'does evidence a clear secular decline over time at the overall cross-national level, as well as in most individual countries.' They conclude that 'as the Lipset-Rokkan hypothesis implies, levels of cleavage volatility – and cleavage salience – do indeed reach their highest value in the period characterized by the mobilization of the class left and do decline thereafter' (p. 120).

15 But not only post-revolutionary: Armagnacs and Bourguignons, Guelphs and Ghibellines, Catholics and Protestants.

16 As Seiler (1980, p. 45) notes, left–right dualism appears profoundly linked to the French political tradition; but if Duverger adopts it, it is because he has a conception of politics as conflict and integration. However, games theory analysis of coalitions has demonstrated the limits of their dualistic character.

17 Visualized in the difference between the plan of the French National Assembly organized in the form of a hemicycle, where the MPs sit on the left or right of the tribune, according to their political colour, and that of the British House of Commons organized in the form of a square, with the government benches facing those of the opposition.

18 It is worth noting an observation of Quermonne (1986, p. 161): namely, the tradition of continuity of electoral regimes in Anglo-Saxon countries (always single-ballot majority systems) in contrast to a certain discontinuity on the continent – and particularly in France (PR, double ballot).

19 Sartori (1982, p. 200) has explained that Downs furnished him with a model of a centripetal-competitive two-party system; but he was unable to go any further because Downs's assumptions ignored the ideological distance that separated the parties and hence the extent of the competitive 'space'. It was in developing Downs that Sartori formulated the centrifugal-competition multiparty system.

20 For a discussion of the limits of this type of data, see the comments of Daalder (1984, pp. 95–6) and the literature quoted.

21 Almost 50 years, from 1946 to 1994.
22 Not only is the expression 'one-party system' a contradiction in terms but, as Weber (1922) noted, when a party eliminates all its rivals it ceases to be a party and becomes something different: a state agency. When the Guelphs defeated the Ghibellines in Florence in the communal period, 'party statutes were treated as part of the city law. Only enrolled party members could be elected to a city office' (p. 1304). Weber (1921, pp. 99–100) was quite explicit about the parallels with the Bolshevik Party.
23 Georges Marchais announced, on going into hospital for an operation in September 1993, that he was standing down as secretary-general at the next congress; he was replaced by Robert Hué.
24 Germany was really an exception because the KPD was the largest European communist party before its suppression by the Nazis.
25 The present leadership of the party is in the course of reducing the weight of the trade union presence in the party's decision-making processes so as to arrive at the goal of 'one person, one vote', which was approved for candidate selection by a very small majority at the 1993 conference in Brighton.
26 See John Keane's (1988) discussion of the problems of the 'socialist compromise party' (pp. 124ff).
27 This has happened to the PCI since it abandoned democratic centralism and changed into the PDS; a minority reconstituted the old party as Rifondazione Comunista. This is an index that the former is now a social democrat party.
28 Berlusconi's Forza Italia can be seen as an attempt to create a modern conservative party in Italy to fill the vacuum caused by the collapse of the Christian Democrats.
29 Its philosophy can be summed up in the remark of prince Tancredi to justify to his father his participation in Garibaldi's Thousand in 1860 in Giuseppe de Lampedusa's (1958) famous novel, *The Leopard*: 'If we want things to stay as they are, things will have to change' (p. 29).
30 The Lega Nord was an alliance of the various regional *leghe* (and above all of the Lega Lombarda and the Liga Veneta) under the leadership of the leader of the Lega Lombarda, Umberto Bossi, which put up candidates in all the northern regions and some central ones in 1992 and 1994.
31 The special rules for the first all-German elections of December 1990 allowed the PDS (former East German SED) and A90/Greens (East German combined list: Alliance 90/Greens, citizens' initiative movement) to be represented in the Bundestag with seventeen and nine seats respectively on the basis of their vote (11.1 per cent and 6.2 per cent) in the former East Germany.
32 The green members of the Bundestag in 1990 were all elected in former East Germany, under the special rules applying for the first all-German election (namely that the 5 per cent rule was applied separately in both former East and West Germanies).
33 The aim was to simplify the party system with the objective of creating coherent alternating majorities. It functioned to the extent that the right-wing Freedom Pole won an overall majority in the Chamber and a virtual

one in the Senate. The question is whether this heterogeneous electoral alliance can secure stable and coherent government.

34 Craxi-Andreotti-Forlani, after the name of the three leaders who concluded the party accord, which regulated the share-out of the spoils between the parties in the 1980s.

35 As a member of the ERM after Maastricht, a competitive devaluation of the lira – the traditional Italian government manoeuvre – was no longer an overt political option for the Italian government, although the lira, like sterling, was forced out of the ERM on Black Wednesday (16 September 1992), which has the same effect.

36 By 1994 over 300 MPs, including former prime ministers and top party leaders – Craxi (PSI), Andreotti (DC), Forlani (DC), De Mita (DC) – were under judicial investigation for bribery and illegal party funding. Hence, the parliament elected in April 1992 was considered to lack legitimacy by the beginning of 1993.

37 Michalski and Wallace (1992) have commented that 'political parties, in spite of a much increased level of contact at the EC level, have not provided the transmission systems to sell the results of Maastricht or to substitute a definition of wider European concerns for the pull of parochialisms ... They would need a bigger stake in the governance of the EC to bridge the continuing gap between national political debate and the European arena, to confer authority on the executive institutions, to intermediate between conflicting interests and to scrutinize decisions' (p. 26).

Chapter 6   Groups and interest intermediation

1 The annual report of the Chemical Industries Association (CIA), a major industrial association, illustrates its activity thus: 'during the year, the CIA has been in touch with the various government departments, thanks to regular contacts and consultation. This has enabled it to follow and anticipate trends in public opinion, inform politicians, civil servants and the committees, attempting to influence legislation from the initial project to the final statute, cooperating with ministerial departments and public agencies in implementation. Relations with the Department of Trade and Industry, which is the relevant ministry, are very close' (quoted by Grant, 1986).

2 About 55 Labour MPs (or just under 25 per cent) were union sponsored in the 1987–92 parliament.

3 From the 1987 *Register of Members' Interests*, it transpires that a significant proportion (26.7 per cent) of (particularly Conservative) MPs have held company directorships. Also, a significant proportion (34 per cent) have held consultancies for companies or lobby organizations – the word 'consultancy' being a euphemism for representing the client's interests in parliament. Indeed, the practice of large companies employing MPs as consultants in parliament is so widespread that most of them have at least one MP in their employment (Etzioni-Halevy, 1993, p. 189).

4 In 1972 the Devlin Commission on Industrial Relations stated that 'All executive policy and most legislation is conceived, framed, drafted and all but enacted in Whitehall' (p. 5).

5 On the power of capitalists, see Kalecki's famous thesis, discussed in chapter 11.

6 Lloyd's has long had a consortium which has raised its voice over legislation; its current problems, moreover, have given rise to organizations seeking to influence the government.

7 Now heavily hedged in by restrictive trade union legislation, like the Employment Act of 1988 which limits the powers of trade unions and strengthens the guarantees for non-strikers.

8 We should perhaps mention the MRP, the Catholic party founded by Catholics active in the French resistance, but, as noted in chapter 3, the church in France followed a very different political course from that in Germany and in Italy, by not organizing a Catholic movement, so support was less strong. Hence, after initial success in the 1940s, the MRP was unable to resist the rise of Gaullism and was dissolved in 1966.

9 In fact, the National Union of Manufacturers and the National Confederation of Employers' Associations, both created as a result of World War I.

10 'Commissioners prefer to be in contact with manufacturers themselves or their direct representatives. Federations or associations are further away from the "ballgame". The "ballgame"... being the technical regulations, notably those relating to safety or the environment': Perrin-Pelletier, quoted in Andersen and Eliassen (1993, p. 41).

Chapter 7   Government and executive power

1 Otto Hintze (1906) claimed that two phenomena condition 'the real organization of the state. These are, first, the structure of social classes, and second, the external ordering of states, their position relative to each other, and their overall position in the world' (p. 183).

2 Hintze insists on the importance of the European system of states for state form: 'all the empires of ancient times and of the non-European world', he wrote in 1902, 'were despotic in their form of government ... free constitutions emerged only where a number of states existed next to each other on equal terms, the independence of each being recognized by the others ... Such a society of states has always been the exception, if we look at the past of the human race ... it is a phenomenon that emerges only once on a large scale – namely in the European system of states, which owes its rise to a wholly individual historical process' (p. 164).

3 In Britain, there are two kinds of minister: cabinet ministers, who have a seat in cabinet; and ministers of state (equivalent to the French *secrétaire d'état* or the Italian *sottosegretario*), who do not.

4 'Procedure is all the Constitution that poor Britain has' (Sir K. Pickthorn, 1960; quoted by Hennessy, 1986, p. 1). He was referring to Erskine May's

Treatise on parliamentary procedure and the cabinet's secret rule book (*Questions of Procedure for Ministers*) as the basis of British government. Hennessy claims that it is the nearest thing that Britain has to a written constitution on British cabinet government (p. 7).

5 This is no longer strictly true in the sense that EU regulations theoretically take precedence and, where there is a conflict, they have to be incorporated in national constitutional law. Hence there were various constitutional revisions to ratify the Maastricht Treaty in 1992–3.

6 The distribution of seats is as follows: six each for Bavaria, Baden-Württemberg, Lower Saxony and North Rhine-Westphalia; four each for Rhineland-Palatinate, Hesse, Berlin, Brandenburg, Saxony, Saxony-Anhalt, Schleswig-Holstein and Thuringia; three each for Saarland, Bremen, Hamburg and Mecklenburg-Western Pomerania.

7 Article 72 lays down that bills dealing with the budget, international treaties, electoral laws, constitutional laws and delegated legislation cannot be approved in final form in committee.

8 In 1979 twelve select committees, covering the major ministerial departments, were introduced to scrutinize government activity; however, as the Westland affair (1986) demonstrated, the government can muzzle their activity and all they can do is to issue damning reports.

9 The Italian situation is a reflection not only of the micro-legislation resulting from the ubiquity of clientelism but also of the legalism of Italian politics – that is the regulation of political problems by legislation (see Cassese, 1984, pp. 64–5).

10 On the growth of the use of decree laws in Italy in 1980, see Della Sala (1988).

11 Berlusconi's anti-communist propaganda, re-evoking 1948, seems to have worked in 1994 against the PDS-led Progressive Pole, despite the PCI's change of name and status.

12 The only party in a liberal democratic regime to rival the DC was the Japanese Liberal Democrat Party, but it lost power in 1993 as a result of a series of corruption scandals, splits and electoral defeat. Faced with a similar prospect, the DC was dissolved and refounded with a new name (PPI) in January 1994, in a desperate attempt to save the party (chapter 5).

13 Or at least it was until the 1994 elections; whether the new electoral system marks a change, time alone will tell.

14 For some details, see chapter 8.

15 For example, in the sphere of competition policy, the Commission has often ruled that state payments and debt write-offs were forms of illegal subsidies undermining fair competition: for instance, Renault in France, privatization of Rover in Britain.

16 Former prime minister and PSI secretary Craxi appealed to the electorate to desert the voting booths for the beaches so that the 50 per cent turnout quorum would not be reached and the vote would be null and void. However, 62.5 per cent of the electorate turned out on a fine Sunday in June and voted 95.6 per cent in favour of reducing preference votes to one per elector.

17 The Labour Party conference of 1993 approved a motion whereby half the seats vacated by sitting MPs will be contested by women candidates.

18 With the notable exception of Italy where, following the 1994 elections, nearly half are amateur politicians, not to say novices, according to their own admission: see 'Il parlamento delle "matricole" ' in *Il Sole – 24 Ore*, 11 April 1994, pp. 1–2.

19 Under the old PR list system, of course, in force until the 1993 mixed-majority electoral reform.

20 Perhaps because of the generally poor quality of British ministers, as Sir John Hoskyns, ex-head of Mrs Thatcher's Policy Unit, claimed in a public lecture in 1983: 'the general calibre of ministers is normally low. Their irrelevant experience, coupled with the impossible burdens of office, have contributed to thirty years of policy failure' (quoted in Hennessy, 1986, p. 34).

21 This was the general rule in the post-war period. However, in moments of crisis the appointment of non-party and non-parliamentary personnel has been much extended, as with former governor of the Bank of Italy, Ciampi d'Azelio, as prime minister in 1993–4, and including many of his ministers. Time will show whether this extension of ministerial recruitment is a temporary phenomenon or a new departure in the Second Republic.

22 Professor Dror has commented that 'the nature of political competition in democracies emphasizes criteria that have little correlation with qualities needed for some of the main tasks of rulers, especially policy-making ... The game of politics certainly does not assure the high moral fibre of the people who reach the top' (quoted in Hennessy, 1989, p. 485).

23 Lord Croham, former top British civil servant, commented in an interview in 1987 that 'I am absolutely certain that ministers are overloaded even though many ministers do not think they are ... You have to remember that ministers are pursuing about four or five different roles – they are constituency MPs; they are members of the party; they are members of a government; they are policy leaders for a department; and, quite often, they are representatives in international bodies' (quoted in Hennessy, 1989, p. 486).

24 Aneurin Bevan, former Labour minister and leader of the Tribune group, is claimed to have said that 'there are only two ways of getting into the Cabinet. One way is crawl up the staircase of preferment on your belly; the other way is to kick them in the teeth' (quoted in Hennessy, 1986, p. 94).

25 Hans-Dietrich Genscher of the FDP was, of course, foreign minister for even longer (1974–92) but in two different types of coalition: SPD/FDP up to 1982 and CDU/FDP thereafter.

26 Schmidt (1992) claims that as a result of unification, the federal government has increased its power in relation to the *Länder*. This was mainly due to two factors: (1) the increase in the number of *Länder* and their heterogeneity has impeded consensus formation among them; and (2) the centralization of economic policy resulting from the *Treuhandanstalt* (trust fund) policy in combination with the collapse of the East German economy (pp. 3–4). All of this gave the federal government greater room to manoeuvre than previously.

27 It was thought that Fanfani, who held both posts after the 1958 elections, might have similar temptations; hence his position was undermined so that he felt obliged to resign both posts within less than a year.

28 Literally 'five party', the government alliance comprising, in addition to the

DC and PSI, the PSDI, PRI and PLI, which governed Italy throughout the 1980s.

Chapter 8 Public administration and the policy process

1 Significantly in parallel with the professionalization of the armed forces (Howard, 1976).

2 The former became a permanent department whereas the latter did not survive Frank Cousins's resignation in 1966.

3 Usually one, but there may be two, depending on the size of the department.

4 The *parlamentarischer Staatssekretär* was created in 1967 to meet the need felt for a special coordinative link between political and administrative sectors. His specific task in the process of departmental management is to guide the work of divisions and sections according to political criteria of importance and rationality.

5 *Cabinets* 'have become the chief decision-making centres in the ministries, and in some the very source of administrative action: all relatively important decisions are now endorsed by the *cabinet*' (G Thuiller, *Les cabinets ministériels*, 1985, quoted by Bodiguel, 1986, p. 190; also Quermonne, 1991, pp. 64, 80).

6 Quasi-autonomous non-governmental organizations.

7 They were the Mission Interministérielle pour l'Aménagement du Languedoc-Roussillon; the Mission Interministérielle pour l'Aménagement de la Côte Aquitaine; the Mission Interministérielle pour la Protection et l'Aménagement de l'Espace Naturel Méditerranéen; and the Mission Interministérielle pour l'Aménagement de la Corse.

8 *Observer* of 3 July 1994, p. 2; however, the annual cabinet publication, *Public Bodies*, claims that on 1 April 1992 there were 1412 non-departmental public bodies in Britain, excluding the new Next Step agencies (like the Benefits Agency), which are steadily taking work over from the civil service. They included 369 executive bodies, 846 advisory bodies and 66 tribunals, with a staff of 114,000 and a budget of £13.75 billion.

9 'During its eleven years in office, the Thatcher government resorted to the Official Secrets Act of 1911 ... more frequently than any previous government. By 1988, that government had used the Act in at least twenty-four prosecutions, compared with thirty-four in the previous sixty-eight years' (Etzioni-Halevy, 1993, p. 183).

10 Data kindly supplied by Professor R. Gregory and Dr P. Giddings of the Reading Centre for Ombudsman Studies. In their judgement the ombudsman 'has rarely failed to secure remedial action in "justified" cases; and defective administration in Whitehall has certainly not escaped robust criticism when criticism was merited' (RCO evidence to Home Affairs Select Committee, p. 6).

11 *Tribunaux administratifs régionaux* (TAR) in France and *tribunali amministrativi regionali* (TAR) in Italy.

12 Preventive action is restricted to procedural, and not substantive, matters.

13 Former prime minister Harold Wilson, in opposition, was prompted to remark: 'Whichever party is in office, the Treasury is in power' (quoted by Sampson, 1983, p. 213).

14 It has been pointed out that ministries like Treasury, Defence and Interior have privileged access to relevant information in key fields, thus allowing them to make important decisions and control activities.

15 With the introduction of technical qualifications this terminology has lost much of its descriptive meaning.

16 This is a simplification of a complex situation; it is the subject of controversy just how far the changes of the 1970s followed the Fulton Report's recommendations and how far they were disregarded (Ponting, 1986).

17 Until 1976, West German civil servants elected to the Bundestag received 60 per cent of their civil service salary while on leave of absence. Today, like their French and Italian colleagues, they enjoy their civil service pension in addition to a parliamentary one.

18 Mayntz (1984) argues that the statistics on the civil service origin of many German politicians are deceptive, claiming that only 10 per cent of the members of the Bundestag come from the category of higher civil servant and the proportion has lately been decreasing. She concludes that 'the career ladder of the higher civil service does not normally lead to high political office. To aspire to the office of minister the civil servant would do better to renounce his civil service career and become a professional politician' (pp. 190–1).

19 Typical is the judgement of Sidney Pollard (1984): 'the peculiar strengths and weaknesses of the civil service, and of the Treasury in particular, form a powerful contributory cause of our decline' (p. 159); and that of Sir John Hoskyns in two lectures in 1982–3 (chapter 7).

20 Sir Robert Armstrong, cabinet secretary and head of the home civil service, admitted in an interview in 1980 that 'I've only had three days training in my career. That's not a boast. That's a confession' (quoted in Hennessy, 1989, p. 507).

21 'Law is the language of the Italian public sector ... According to a well-known Italian prime minister, a legal culture is essential in that it allows one to use laws against one's enemies and to interpret them for one's friends' (Cassese, 1993, p. 319).

22 They are often isolated and rarely remain for more than brief periods. Recent British examples include Sir Anthony Parsons, former ambassador, as Mrs Thatcher's foreign policy adviser in the early 1980s, and Professor Walters as her economic adviser in the later 1980s. Lord Annan recounted in 1983 that 'if a minister brings a political adviser into his ministry and the adviser does not toe the line, the mandarins cut off his information: he will appear at a meeting and discover that his rivals possess certain important memoranda that mysteriously have never reached his desk. He therefore appears to be badly briefed and loses credibility' (quoted in Hennessy, 1989, p. 512).

23 ENA graduates 1945–89 have supplied 1 president of the republic, 50 ministers (including 3 prime ministers), 70 *députés* and 7 *sénateurs* (Mauss, 1989).

24 Anthony Sampson claims that what was a trickle in the 1960s has become a

flood since the 1970s: 'Lord Roll from the Treasury is now chairman of Warburg's Bank and director of *The Times* and the Bank of England, among others. Lord Hunt, the former secretary of the cabinet, is now London chairman of the Banque Nationale de Paris and director of IBM, Unilever and the Pru. Lord Greenhill from the Foreign Office, Sir Leo Pliatzky from the Treasury and Sir Antony Part from Industry compete with arrays of directorships.' He adds the comment: 'It is when they leave Whitehall that senior civil servants show the full extent of their influence' (1983, p. 204).

25 The British central administration is 'non-executant', that is to say that the task of implementation is generally in the hands of local authorities which have a corps of professional 'local government officers' (chapter 9).

26 For a definition of political community, see the section on national policy styles later in this chapter.

27 This assertion is much contested: it is supported by Richardson and Jordan (1987), but rejected by Hogwood (1987). 'Community', Heclo and Wildavsky (1974, p. xv) write, 'refers to the personal relations between the main political and administrative actors, sometimes in conflict, often in agreement, but always in contact and acting within a shared *framework*.' This term has been redefined and reused by Richardson and others as a metaphor.

28 Not to be confused with 'rational choice' theory linked to the names of Buchanan and Tullock (1962), Niskanen (1973) and others. According to this theory, political phenomena can be analysed in terms of the rational individual who seeks to maximize his personal interest. Thus government decisions are deducible from apparently simple and rigorous propositions. For instance, given the bureaucrat's monopoly position, as regards both the services he supplies and the information he possesses on costs, and given the politicians' electoral interest, Niskanen predicts the abnormal and inexorable expansion of the public sector. And this is what has happened until the last decade. In this situation, the influence of this theory on groups of academics, particularly among conservatives, is hardly surprising, despite the excessive reductionism that it proposes. Since rational choice models are based on the possibility of deducing non-evident consequences over outcomes of the decision process when both the decisional rule structure and the deciders' interests and incentives are known, it is not very useful in situations where these factors are uncertain and ambiguous. Examples of such situations are the process of consensus building, the definition of the political agenda and the strategic redistribution of power; all these are specifically political elements, in the analysis of which the rational choice models have shown themselves to be wanting (Regonini, 1984).

29 Françoise Giroud (1977) herself quotes the example of France, usually considered a model of administrative efficiency. There, half the laws passed by the Assembly in 1973 had not been published in the *Journal Officiel* when she left office at the beginning of 1977. Moreover, the *décrets d'application* of laws approved in 1964 were only being published in 1973 (p. 98)!

30 It is simply a group of actors with a shared interest in and focus on a particular policy sector. It normally extends beyond the state institutions to include interest groups and even commentators. Harrop (1992, p. 274) writes that 'in

health, the health and finance ministries, doctors' associations, insurance organizations and medical administrators form the core of the community' (see section on national policy styles later in this chapter).

31 This is particularly true in states where the upper house is not always of the same political majority as the lower house, like the Sénat in France, the Bundesrat in Germany and even, on occasions, the House of Lords in Britain.

32 In their zeal to regulate university affairs, the German courts (constitutional and administrative) went as far as voiding decisions about capacity calculations made by university academic senates and developing their own capacity calculus; they even substituted their own criteria of enrolment capacity for those of the universities! All this action was justified on the grounds of the need to defend a fundamental right of citizens 'to freely choose their trade or profession, their place of work and their place of training' (article 12(1) of the German basic law).

33 Despite the seriousness of these limits, the British Conservative government has not wished to heed them and has adopted a policy of 'fools rush in where angels fear to tread', introducing a whole series of so-called 'objective' criteria to monitor hospitals and schools. To have an aura of scientific 'authenticity' for credibility, they have to be quantitative, so they are based on such quantitative data as are easily collectable, without too much care as to their accuracy or relevance.

Chapter 9　Subcentral government and centre–local relations

1 Echoed in Tocqueville's (1835–40) famous remark: 'C'est pourtant dans la commune que réside la force des peuples libres. Les institutions communales sont à la liberté ce que les écoles primaires sont à la science; elles la mettent à la portée du peuple' (p. 112).

2 In fact, according to Wheare (1964), 'Germany has only a "quasi-federal constitution"' (p. 26).

3 The relationship is similar to that at the supranational level between the EU and member states (chapter 8).

4 Wales was integrated in the fourteenth century while Scotland was only with the Act of Union of 1707, which permitted it to retain its own legal system.

5 It is usually claimed that the French state extracted in the eighteenth century four times the amount of tax as the English state. However, Lawrence Stone (1994, p. 8) has noted that 'work by Dickson, O'Brien and Mathias has destroyed the myth of the fiscal and administrative differences between a lightly taxed and slackly governed Britain and heavily taxed and tightly controlled continental powers like France, Spain and Prussia.' Indeed, Britain's naval supremacy required an efficient administration (the Admiralty) and significant resources, and all else was subordinated to it. As regards wars in Europe, Britain got other states to fight for it.

6 First internationally propagated by R. von Gneist in his *History of the English Constitution* (London, 1891), quoted by Page (1985, p. 59).

7 By 'clientelism', we refer to a system in which consensus and electoral support are exchanged for protection at the political and administrative level by, if necessary, bending the rules in favour of protected interests (Eisenstadt and Lemarchand, 1981).

8 These figures are for metropolitan France, excluding the overseas territories.

9 The country is divided into parishes, but parish councils exist only in some parts of the country.

10 The situation in Northern Ireland has been ignored to avoid unnecessary complication, given that it is under a special regime owing to the 'troubles'.

11 'Chairs have no formal authority in their own right. They gain their authority in practice from their ability – except in a hung situation – to command a majority on the committee, but their position depends on the committee. Individual councillors have no formal decision-making powers' (Stewart, 1992, p. 7).

12 Comprising some 22 laws and 170 decrees!

13 Corsica was granted a special statute as a special region.

14 Elected *conseils d'arrondissement* with responsibility for some non-essential services were established in the three major cities (Paris, Marseilles and Lyons).

15 It is said that the reforms caused a crisis of identity among prefects, which led to over a hundred of them abandoning the prefectoral corps for new posts in local government, particularly in the big towns (see later in this chapter).

16 In contrast to Britain, all ministries have departmental or regional representatives: general officer for military districts (defence), rector for the academies (education), *procureur* of the courts (justice), treasurer for the departments (finance).

17 For instance, the difference between North Rhine-Westphalia (47,000 km^2 of territory and 16 million inhabitants) and Bavaria (70,000 km^2 and 11 million inhabitants) on the one hand, and the city-states of Bremen (404 km^2 and 660,000 inhabitants) and Hamburg (755 km^2 and 1.5 million inhabitants) on the other.

18 The former are *Stadtstaaten* (city-states) and hold with the latter the distinction of enjoying the status of both *Gemeinde* and *Land*, combining both functions.

19 Not coincidentally, the former British zone of occupation: constitutional reform of local government is currently being prepared in North Rhine-Westphalia, although the outcome is uncertain (Grunow, 1992).

20 This is the level of horizontal cooperation between the *Länder* themselves (excluding the federation). We can add a fourth, that of direct *Länder* – EU relations: particularly significant in this respect has been the setting up of so-called *Land* information offices in Brussels. All of the *Länder* set up such offices between 1985 and 1987 and they have become established as one of the many actors and institutions which have set down roots around the EU institutions in Brussels, and which form part of the increasingly complex system of communications in the EU. At the *Ministerpräsidenten Konferenz* of

7 June 1990, the *Ministerpräsidenten* demanded that the *Länder* be given extensive rights to participate in the negotiations for European Union and that the principle of subsidiarity be included in the Maastricht Treaty in an enforceable manner. Further demands included the question of the creation of a new European council of regions and the right of the *Länder* to bring actions before the ECJ. At the *Bund–Länder Besprechung* of 10 August 1990 the *Länder* representatives met the federal government, which made clear that it could accept three of the four *Länder* demands – the right to bring legal actions, the principle of subsidiarity, and the creation of the European regional council – but rejected the fourth demand, the inclusion of *Länder* representatives in the national delegation to the European Council of Ministers (Paterson, 1993, p. 168).

21 Although the law laid down a period of one year after the coming into force of the law, the definition of the metropolitan areas and cities still had not been defined four years later.

22 The law contains another novelty: article 5 lays down that in all lists of candidates 'neither of the two sexes can, as a rule [*di norma*], be represented by more than two-thirds' of the candidates. This suggests that at least a third of all councillors must be women. However, the jurists have pointed out that the use of the term *di norma* is ambiguous and not enforceable in law. Thus it is to be interpreted as a pious recommendation for more female candidates, with little probable effect.

23 The communal secretary is a civil servant hierarchically dependent on the Ministry of the Interior.

24 The conditional is obligatory in the case of the German Federal Republic, because overall figures are not available (Caciagli, 1991, p. 209).

25 One difference is the duration in office: in some states, the average for local councillors is almost twenty years.

26 This polemic has a long tradition in Britain. Already in the middle of the nineteenth century, before the election of local councillors, J.S. Mill (1861) complained that: 'the greatest imperfection of popular local institutions, and the chief cause of the failure which so often attends them, is the low calibre of men by whom they are always carried on' (p. 274).

27 The rule that English local councils cannot delegate responsibilities to individual councillors, but only to committees, reinforces the role of the latter as the formal decision-making body. In addition, it is claimed that 'the committee system involves all councillors – front benchers and back benchers, majority and opposition – in the work of the authority, giving them information and involvement that many MPs would envy' (Stewart, 1992, p. 9).

28 While it is not infrequent for former Labour councillors to become MPs, or unheard of for Conservative councillors either (prime minister Major was a Lewisham councillor for a few years), it is normal for them to drop their local office, once elected, and concentrate solely on their work in Westminster since 'it is widely held by local and national politicians that it would be impossible to undertake both the role of councillor and that of MP' (Chandler, 1991, p. 89).

29 The greater the number of subcentral authorities, the more difficult an adequate control becomes, because beyond a certain threshold the sheer vol-

ume of numbers renders it virtually impossible, in terms of both time and cost.

30 However, there is a lot of evidence to suggest that economic dissatisfaction was as important as territorial identity in the spectacular electoral success of the Lega Nord in the 1990s (Diamanti, 1993). The SNP won 30 per cent of the vote (and 11 seats) in Scotland in October 1974, but its support has fluctuated since.

31 This is a general strategy that explains the numerous conferences and committees, both global and sectorial, which were set up over the years and through which national associations of local authorities (ACC, AMA in Britain; Association des Maires de France; ANCI, UPI in Italy) enter into dialogue with the central government.

32 It should be noted that the top posts in local government (chief executive and chief officer) are usually recruited not by promotion from within the same authority but by open competition between all authorities, and this is a factor reinforcing national policy integration.

33 The imposition of a penalty in the form of the reduction of the central government grant (representing almost 40 per cent of expenditure) to local authorities which overstepped the limits the government set for the rates (Gibson, 1992).

34 It is claimed that this was owing to the commitment of the basic law to maintaining a 'uniformity of living conditions' ('Einheitlichkeit der Lebensverhältnisse') across the federation which allowed the federal government to make use of its concurrent and framework powers. The result was that the federal government has been able to claim these legislative powers for itself and to marginalize the role of the *Länder* parliaments, and so an ongoing trend towards a more centralized and uniform policy process was established (Jeffery, 1994).

35 Schmidt (1992) now claims that one of the consequences of unification has been to reinforce 'tendencies towards an increase in the importance of the federal government [relative to the *Länder*] in some policy areas' (p. 4).

36 It took almost twelve years for the structural reforms (that is the creation of *communautés* of communes and towns envisaged in the Guichard Report of 1976) to be given legislative form (law 92–125), and then the setting up of new institutions was not made obligatory.

37 See note 15 to this chapter.

Chapter 10   The state and invisible power

1 According to Ardant (1975, p. 135), tax collection was, in the period of state formation, the principal cause of conflict between rulers and ruled.

2 Punctually confirmed in 1870–1 in the Franco-Prussian War, when, after the military defeat which brought down the Second Empire and the proclamation of the republic, the ignoble peace of January 1871 led to the Paris Commune.

3 In the nineteenth century, control of foreign affairs was vested in the sover-

eign, that is the executive, and not subjected to parliamentary scrutiny. In Britain, for example, the foreign secretary sat in the House of Lords and parliamentary questions received a negative reply of 'not in the public interest'.

4 Adolphe Thiers had foreseen this development in a speech to the French Chamber of Deputies in 1866: 'I beg the Germans to reflect that the highest principle of European politics is that Germany shall be composed of independent states connected only by a slender federative thread. That was the principle proclaimed by all Europe at the Congress of Westphalia ... A union of Germany would subvert the balance of power and would endanger the peace of Europe' (quoted in Tugendhat, 1986, pp. 88–90).

5 We need only recall the speech with which president Truman launched the Truman doctrine in 1947 or president Eisenhower's Cold War rhetoric: 'rarely have so many forces of good and evil been gathered, armed and opposed to one another before now in history. Freedom against slavery, light against darkness.'

6 In his 1972 BBC Reith Lectures, Andrew Shonfield (1973) described the EC as 'the purest expression in the international system of what François Duchêne has called a "civilian power" as opposed to a traditional military/political power'.

7 Germany was constitutionally inhibited from deploying its armed forces in conflicts outside the NATO area (see discussion later in this chapter).

8 Pushing Wallerstein's theory to its logical conclusion we arrive at the following paradox: namely that if the state's behaviour really were determined by the world economy, state action would be irrelevant and devoid of interest.

9 The judicial enquiry *mani pulite* into political corruption being carried out by the Milanese investigating magistrates, which has placed over 300 former MPs, and numerous former ministers, under judicial investigation (Allum, 1993).

10 The former commissioner of the French DST, J.-P. Mauriat, claimed that 'in several foreign embassies in France, 40 per cent to 60 per cent of the personnel belongs to the intelligence services' (quoted in *Revue de la défense nationale*, January 1968).

11 For example, the 1917 Bolshevik revelations of the secret Pact of London of 1915 between the Anglo-French allies and Italy to facilitate the latter's declaration of war.

12 A French diplomat has defined the French nuclear deterrent as an 'aerial Maginot line'.

13 Hence US secretary of state Dean Acheson's famous remark in a speech at the US Military Academy, West Point in 1962: 'Great Britain has lost an empire but has not found a role.'

14 It has been pointed out that Britain's nuclear deterrent – which is perhaps the only public justification for considering itself a great power and so maintaining its privileged status within the UN – was an American-built missile system sold exclusively to Britain, and is one of the last remaining visible expressions of the special relationship!

15 Churchill always believed that France should assume the moral leadership of Europe on the basis of a Franco-German association, as he made clear in his famous Zurich speech of 1946.

16 Perhaps because it raises, *inter alia*, painful questions like the vacuousness of
Britain clinging to its world role, instead of recognizing its status as a middle-
sized European power. The foreign secretary Francis Pym, speaking after
the Falklands War, could still state: 'But I do not regard Britain as simply a
regional power which should concentrate on a few areas of clear economic
and political concern to us and avoid involvement in other issues where our
interests do not appear to be so directly engaged. This would be to turn our
back on our history and our traditions, and take an unnecessarily short-
sighted and narrow view of national interest, and to waste the assets built up
by our long years of action on the world stage. We are obviously not a superpower, but we are a world power; and it is not in any sense an anachronism
or an anomaly that we are one of the five permanent members of the security council' (quoted in Spence, 1984, p. 224).

17 It meant the extension of the direct threat to French national territory (the
previous limits) to include the territory on its eastern borders (in practice
West Germany); it was a covert way of reintegrating in NATO's military
structure, in the sense that France participated once again in its long-term
planning.

18 Roger Morgan (1992) has recently defined West German foreign policy in
terms of Churchill's 'three circles': 'those of West European integration,
North Atlantic security commitments and pan-European cooperation'
(p. 107). The question, as he sees it, is whether the Germans' attempts to
reconcile them (or indeed square them) will be more successful in the long
run than Britain's has been.

19 Germany is far and away the largest net contributor to the EU
budget.

20 This was true until the collapse of communism: in 1990 foreign minister De
Michelis came out unexpectedly with the proposal of merging the WEU into
the EC (which angered Britain and the US, while failing to win the support
of other EC partners), and then in 1991 co-signed with his British colleague
a declaration that stressed the role of the WEU as a pillar of NATO
(Merlini, 1993, pp. 240–1).

21 The British Foreign Office was quick to cultivate the new government,
despite the presence of five neo-fascist ministers within it (*The Guardian*, 9
June 1994, p. 22).

22 The troika consists of the previous presidency and the succeeding one and
was introduced to provide greater continuity in policies.

23 The expression was coined by Finer (1962) to indicate the type of military
organization/structure in a state in a given period.

24 Military understood, in this case, as armed forces, police and intelligence services.

25 Certainly, as Edmonds (1988) has pointed out: 'superficially, Lasswell's
hypothesis has proved to be correct, more in kind than degree. The post–1945
world has seen greater armed services and police involvement in the internal
affairs of the state … Security considerations have become paramount in
modern states … The percentage of the world's resources devoted to armed
services in peacetime … has indeed steadily increased. But his ultimate prediction has not finally emerged; armed services, while influential by dint of

their being a specialist corporate body, do not either dominate or control society in the manner envisaged in his garrison state construct' (p. 89).

26 Some 50 per cent of conventional forces and some 80 per cent of nuclear weapons (Stratmann, 1993, p. 451).

27 This reflected Germany's concern to integrate the Warsaw Pact states, for which a North Atlantic cooperative council at foreign minister and ambassador level was set up at the Rome summit. It was hoped that this would ease the development of a dialogue and practical cooperation between these states' armed forces and NATO's military apparatus.

28 It was general de Gaulle in a well-known book (*Vers l'armée de métier*, 1934) who pleaded without success for a small, professional, mechanized army; this failure explains perhaps why, in choosing nuclear weapons in the 1950s and 1960s, he did not raise the question of conscription again.

29 The figures for 1991 are: Britain 4.2 per cent; France 3.5 per cent; Germany 2.6 per cent; Italy 2.1 per cent (Labour Research Department *Fact Sheet* 54.31, 1992).

30 It is true that this was affected by the fact that the bomb did not kill him so that there was no power vacuum in which the generals could act, and hence a different outcome was possible.

31 Ferraresi (1992) notes that 'in the mid 1960s well-known fascists like Pino Rauti and Guido Giannettini constituted part of the brains trust of the defence chief of staff, the highest military authority of the republic born of the resistance' (p. 37).

32 This was confirmed in France when the defence minister, François Léotard, inadvertently admitted that it was the general staff which made decisions about the appointment to the top military posts and that he merely ratified them (*Libération*, of 12 April 1993, p. 11).

33 The fact that West European states spend a greater than average proportion of their annual military budget on equipment and that this proportion rose during the 1980s is testimony to their influence.

34 According to Bobbio, the expression derives from Tacitus. The American writer Bok (1986) has stressed the Indo-European root *arek* (to hold, contain or guard) of the word *arcana*.

35 One of the reasons, suggested by Bobbio, at least during the 'behavioural ascendancy', is that it does not lend itself to investigation by sociological methods, such as social surveys.

36 Anthony Sampson (1983) has commented that the 'fundamental difficulty of all political intelligence [is] that it is very difficult to tell politicians what they do not want to know' (p. 275).

37 The number of defections, infiltrations and double agents in the secret service of the different states is striking: in addition to Guillaume, there was John Felke in Germany; Burgess, Maclean, Philby and Blunt in Britain; Rinaldi and Pazienza in Italy; and Pacques in France. Others include Blake, Bettaney and Prime in Britain, and Tiedge, Rotsch, Luneberg and Hoeke in Germany.

38 Apparently a bugged microphone was installed in the *pavillon* of the Hotel Matignon by the SDECE during the conflict between president Giscard and prime minister Chirac in 1975–6, at least according to the version of the head

of the SDECE given to socialist prime minister Mauroy in 1981 (Hayward, 1983, p. 153).

39 One should mention the close links sponsored by NATO between the US secret services and the British, West German and Italian ones (the French remained more aloof). In fact, of course, the British and US secret services had a prime role in reconstructing the West German and Italian secret services after the war. For instance, the head of the CIA, Allen Dulles, was responsible for inserting the famous Gehlen organization in the BND.

40 In 1991 Stella Rimington, a woman but from a conventional middle class background, was appointed.

41 Police officers, as opposed to constables, in France, Germany and Italy had to have university degrees, and promotion of chief constables from those who started on the beat as in Britain was impossible.

42 It has many parallels, in both structure and substance, with the 'military mind'. For a study of cop culture see Smith and Gray (1985).

43 In most states there are close links between the special corps and political groups (usually right-wing); the most notorious were those between the SDECE and the Gaullist SAC (Service d'Action Civique) in France in the 1960s and the 1970s; those between MI5 and reactionary groups in Britain in 1970s, mentioned in the best-seller *Spycatcher*; or again those between SIFAR/SID/SISMI and Gladio and parallel neo-fascist groups in Italy from the 1950s to the 1990s (Ferraresi, 1992). Moreover, it is perhaps no coincidence that the heads of the Italian secret services, generals De Lorenzo and Micheli, the subjects of parliamentary enquiries into their activities, stood and were elected in the MSI (neo-fascist) lists.

44 John Alderson, chief constable of Devon and Cornwall 1973–82, told the House of Commons Home Affairs Committee inquiry into the Special Branch that 40 per cent of the people on the files of the Special Branch in his force were there because they had outspoken views (Dearlove and Saunders, 1991, p. 247).

45 Former prime minister Edward Heath told the House of Commons in 1988 that: 'I met people in the security services who talked the most ridiculous nonsense and whose whole philosophy was ridiculous nonsense. If some of them were on the tube and saw someone reading the *Daily Mirror*, they would say "Get after him, that is dangerous. We must find out where he bought it"' (quoted in Dearlove and Saunders, 1991, p. 246).

46 Since the market economy is considered a constitutive element of the basic law, the *Berufsverbot* allows all those that defend state intervention in the economy to be branded as opponents of the basic law and, hence, as engaged in unconstitutional activity.

47 The book whose publication the Thatcher government did its best to prevent. As a result of the jury's failure in 1985 to convict senior civil servant Clive Ponting under the Official Secrets Act of 1911 over the Belgrano affair (it accepted the public interest defence), the government resorted, in the *Spycatcher* case, to breach of crown confidentiality to bring unsuccessful actions in the civil courts of Australia, New Zealand and Britain; it won its case only in Hong Kong!

48 The Italian situation is not without its weaknesses. Barile (1987) has pointed out the limits of law 801: 'the only form of control that can condition the secret services in any way is financial accountability. Parliament is expressly denied such accountability in Italy' (p. 42). Evidence becoming public as a result of the *mani pulite* investigations into corruption supports the hypothesis that the principal motivation of the activities of Italian secret service agents was lining their own pockets. He also alludes to a prime ministerial circular, giving directives in the hypothetical situation that secret service agents are called on to give evidence to magistrates: 'The circular seems to invite the agents to claim state secrecy, leaving the prime minister to confirm or not whether secrecy is involved. The publication of this circular in *Panorama* (13 October 1985) led to charges against the editor and subeditor. Many consider such charges as very questionable' (p. 43).

49 However, in November 1993 the government published the Intelligence Services Bill which received its second reading in the House of Lords on 9 December. The bill gives the secret services a statutory mandate and provides a restricted commissioner and tribunal structure to investigate complaints. In addition, it sets up an Intelligence and Security Committee (ISC), comprising six MPs appointed by the prime minister after consultation with the leader of the opposition, to examine the expenditure, administration and policy of the security services (see Gill, 1994, for details and assessment).

Chapter 11   Actual democracy in Western Europe since the war

1 'The counting of "votes" is the final ceremony of a long process, in which it is precisely those who "devote their best energies to the state and the nation" (when such they are) who carry the greatest weight' (Gramsci, 1949, p. 193).

2 Daniel Bell (1988, p. 133) has pointed to Albert Camus as the first writer to use this expression, in an article entitled 'Ni victimes, ni bourreaux' in *Combat* in November 1946.

3 Lipset admits that he took the expression from a book by D. Anderson and P. Davison entitled *Ballots and Democratic Class Struggle* (1943).

4 The analogy between the 'end of ideology' and Fukuyama's 'The End of History' (1989) are obvious. Just as ingenuous are statements like: the USA is 'the last rational form of society' (Fukuyama) or 'the good society in operation' (Lipset), or again that there are 'no contradictions that modern liberalism cannot solve' (Fukuyama).

5 It is a difficult concept, which he developed in his study of Freud. For the latter, the sublimation of sexuality was traditionally repressive; thus any desublimation would only be produced by a lessening of repression. For Marcuse, on the contrary, desublimation had already occurred in advanced

industrial societies, but without liberation: 'for the release of libido is so controlled that sexuality as it were saturates the surface of social life – in the motifs of much advertising, for example – and satisfies men without restoring to them the proper enjoyment of their own sexuality' (MacIntyre, 1970, p. 66).

6　It is worth pointing out, as Maddison (1982) observed, that none of the 'long-wave' theorists has been able to explain the regularity of the phases of capitalism.

7　A declaration confirmed by a statement of British prime minister Harold Wilson in 1968: 'all political history shows that a government's image and its ability to maintain electoral support depend on the success of its economic policy.'

8　In saying this, we must stress that we do not share the assumptions of the public choice school for the reasons given in chapter 8 (note 27), namely that everything is sacrificed on the altar of the formal rigour and internal coherence of the model. Thus, for example, excessive methodological individualism leads to the neglect of complex social group dynamism.

9　In an appendix to Crozier, Huntington and Watanuki (1975, pp. 173–203) a list of disparate proposals was made which went from restrictions on access to higher education and precautionary control of the news media to 'strengthening the institutions of political leadership' and the creation of an institute for strengthening of democratic institutions (p. 187)!

10　We can mention those of Heath 1973–4, of Callaghan 1978–9 and of Major 1992–3 in Britain; of Barre 1977–81, of Fabius 1984–6 and of Cresson and Bérégovoy 1992–3 in France; of Kohl 1992–3 in Germany; of the socialist party in France in the 1990s; and of the traditional parties in Germany and Italy (the latter as a result of the revelation of widespread corruption), also in the 1990s.

11　These developments, and above all the economic changes that have given rise to them (globalization, spatial organization of production), constitute 'the end of organized capitalism' (Lash and Urry, 1987) and the onset of 'disorganized capitalism' (Offe, 1985).

12　Recent events in Italy emphasize the full import of this impact, for good and ill.

13　The criticisms of the results of the policy studies concern the interpretative models used which are generally limited to describing the changes occurring in a number of crucial macro-economic and macro-social variables following public intervention of government party alliances that rarely go beyond a generic distinction between right and left (Calise, 1989).

14　It is worth noting that Esping-Andersen (1990), developing this type of analysis, has recently identified (using empirical data) three worlds of welfare capitalism: (1) liberal welfare (Britain, USA); (2) conservative/corporatist welfare (France, Germany, Italy); and (3) social democratic welfare (Sweden); but he warns that they are ideal types.

15　In the actual political crisis in Italy, what is at stake is not democracy, but merely the best institutional structure for giving it expression, in view of the country's very mixed post-war experience. We should perhaps add that it would be very difficult for an EU state to abandon representative democratic institutions, since it adopted a solemn declaration that they were a condition of membership. A state that abandoned them would at the very least be marginalized, as Greece was under the colonels (1967–73) when it was merely an associate member, if not expelled altogether.

16 It seems that Dahrendorf uses the term 'civil society' with a strongly prescriptive meaning which differs from the descriptive usage in this study.

17 'No one can tell, for already terms of comparison are lacking ... the magnitude of present achievement makes it impossible to forecast what may still be done.'

References

Aberbach J.D., Putnam R.D., Rockman B.A. (1981), *Bureaucrats and Politicians in Western Democracies* (Cambridge Mass.: Harvard University Press).

Adorno T.W. et al. (1950), *The Authoritarian Personality* (New York: Harper Row).

Agulhon M. (1979), *La République au village* (Paris, Seuil, 2nd edn); English trans. *The Republic in the Village* (Cambridge: Cambridge University Press, 1984).

Aiken M., Newton K., Friedland R., Martinotti G. (1987), 'Urban Systems Theory and Urban Policy: A Four Nation Comparison', in *British Journal of Political Science*, 3, 341–58.

Alberoni F. (1968), *Statu nascenti* (Bologna: Il Mulino).

Alberoni F. (1976), *Italia in trasformazione* (Bologna: Il Mulino).

Alberoni F. (1977), *Movimento e istituzione* (Bologna: Il Mulino).

Allum P. (1980), 'Les groupes de pression en Italie', in *Revue française de science politique*, 30, 5, 1048–72.

Allum P. (1991), 'Ideology and Common Sense: A Discussion on Culture and Politics', in *Reading Papers in Politics* n. 2 (Reading: Reading University).

Allum P. (1993), 'Chronicle of a Death Foretold: The First Italian Republic' in *Reading Papers in Politics* n. 12 (Reading: Reading University).

Almond G.A. (1983), 'Corporatism, Pluralism and Professional Memory', in *World Politics*, 1, 245–60; now in *A Discipline Divided: Schools and Sects in Political Science* (Newbury Park, Calif.: Sage, 1990).

Andersen S.S., Eliassen K.A. (1993), *Making Policy in Europe: The Europification of National Policy-Making* (London: Sage).

Anderson D., Davison P. (1943), *Ballots and Democratic Struggle* (Stanford, Calif.: Stanford University Press).

Andrew C., Dilks D. (eds) (1984), *The Missing Dimension: Governments and Intelligence Communities in the 20th Century* (London: Croom Helm).

Ardagh J. (1988a), *Germany and the Germans* (Harmondsworth: Penguin).

Ardagh J. (1988b), *France Today* (Harmondsworth: Penguin).

Ardant G. (1975), 'Financial Policy and Economic Infrastructure of Modern States and Nations', in C. Tilly (ed.), *The Formation of National States in Western Europe* (Princeton, NJ: Princeton University Press).

Aron R. (1962a), *Dix-huit Leçons sur la société industrielle* (Paris: Gallimard); pages cited from English trans. *Eighteen Lessons on Industrial Society* (London: Weidenfeld & Nicolson, 1967).

Aron R. (1962b), *Paix et guerre entre les nations* (Paris: Calmann-Levy); English trans. *Peace and War: A Theory of International Relations* (London: Weidenfeld & Nicolson, 1966).

Aron R. (1964), *La Lutte des classes* (Paris: Gallimard).

Aron R. (1968), *Progress and Disillusion: The Dialectics of Modern Society* (London: Pall Mall).

Ashford S., Timms N. (1992), *What Europe Thinks: A Study of Western European Values* (Aldershot: Dartmouth).

Bachrach P., Baratz M.S. (1962), 'The Two Faces of Power', in *American Political Science Review*, 56, 947–52.

Bachrach P., Baratz M.S. (1963), 'Decisions and Non-Decisions', in *American Political Science Review*, 57, 632–42.

Badie B., Birnbaum P. (1979), *Sociologie de l'état* (Paris, Grasset); English trans. *Sociology of the State* (Chicago: Chicago University Press, 1981).

Bagehot W. (1867), *The English Constitution* (pages cited from edn London: Fontana, 1963).

Baget-Bozzo G. (1982), *Il futuro viene dal futuro* (Rome: Editori Riuniti).

Bagnasco A. (1977), *Tre Italie: La problematica territoriale dello sviluppo italiano* (Bologna: Il Mulino).

Baldassarre A. (1983), 'L'evoluzione dei partiti politici', introduction by J. Raschke, *I partiti dell'Europa occidentale* (Rome: Editori Riuniti), vii–lviii.

Ball A.R., Millard F. (1986), *Pressure Politics in Industrial Societies* (London: Macmillan).

Baran P.A., Sweezy P.M. (1966), *Monopoly Capital: An Essay on the American Economic and Social Order* (New York: Monthly Review Press).

Barbagli M., Maccelli A. (1985), *La partecipazione politica a Bologna* (Bologna: Il Mulino).

Barile P. (1987), 'Democrazia e segreto', in *Quaderni costituzionali*, 1, 29–50.

Bartolini S., Mair P. (1990), *Identity, Competition and Electoral Availability: The Stabilisation of the European Electorates 1885–1985* (Cambridge: Cambridge University Press).

Bayley D. (1975), 'The Police and Political Development in Europe', in C. Tilly (ed.), *The Formation of National States in Western Europe* (Princeton, NJ: Princeton University Press).

Bean R. (1973), 'War and the Birth of the Nation State', in *Journal of Economic History*, 1, 203–21.

Becker J. (1980), 'Il lettore tedesco non vuole pensare', in *L'informazione accentrata* (Turin: Rosenberg & Sellier).

Bell D. (1960), *The End of Ideology: On the Exhaustion of Political Ideas in the Fifties* (Glencoe, Ill.: Free Press).

Bell D. (1973), *The Coming of the Post Industrial Age: A Venture in Social Forecasting* (London: Heinemann).

Bell D. (1988), 'The End of Ideology Revisited', in *Government and Opposition*, 23, 2, 131–50; 23, 3, 321–31.

Bendix R. (1964), *Nation-Building and Citizenship* (New York: Wiley).

Bentley A. (1908), *The Process of Government: A Study of Social Pressures* (Chicago: Chicago University Press).

Bernstein E. (1899), *Die Voraussetzungen des Sozialismus und die Aufgaben der Sozialdemokratie*; pages cited from English trans. *Evolutionary Socialism: A Criticism and Affirmation* (New York: Schoken, 1961).

Berridge G.R. (1987), *International Politics: States, Power and Conflict since 1945* (Brighton: Wheatsheaf).

Bevan A. (1952), *In Place of Fear* (London: Heinemann).

Birnbaum P. (1977), *Les Sommets de l'état: Essai sur l'élite du pouvoir en France* (Paris: Seuil).

Blair P.M. (1991), 'Trends in Local Autonomy and Democracy', in R. Batley and G. Stokes (eds), *Local Government in Europe* (London: Macmillan).

Bloch-Lainé F. (1990), 'Affirmation d'une puissance', in *Pouvoirs* 53 (numéro spécial: *Le Ministère des finances*), 5–15.

Blondel J. (1963), *Voters, Parties: and Leaders. The Social Fabric of British Politics* (London: Penguin).

Blondel J. (1978), *Political Parties: A Genuine Case for Discontent?* (London: Wildwood House).

Blondel J. (1985), *Government Ministers in the Contemporary World* (London: Sage).

Blondel J., Thiebault J.-L. (1991) (eds), *The Profession of Government Minister in Western Europe* (Basingstoke: Macmillan).

Bobbio N. (1976), *Gramsci e la concezione della società civile* (Milan: Feltrinelli); English. trans. in *Which Socialism?* (Cambridge: Polity Press, 1987).

Bobbio N. (1983), 'Introduzione' by E. Fraenkel, *Il doppio Stato* (Turin: Einaudi), ix–xxiv.

Bobbio N. (1984), *Il futuro della democrazia: Una difesa delle regole del gioco* (Turin: Einaudi); pages cited from English trans. *The Future of Socialism* (Cambridge: Polity Press, 1987).

Bobbio N. (1985), *Stato, governo, società: Per una teoria generale della politica* (Turin, Einaudi); pages cited from English trans. *Democracy and Dictatorship* (Cambridge: Polity Press, 1989).

Bodiguel J.-L. (1986), 'The Political Control of Civil Servants in Europe: Some Aspects', in *International Review of Administrative Science*, LII, 187–200.

Bois P. (1960), *Paysans de l'ouest* (Le Havre: Mouton).

Bok S. (1986), *Secrets: On the Ethics of Concealment and Revelation* (Oxford: Oxford University Press).

Bollati G. (1983), *L'Italiano: Il carattere nazionale come storia e come invenzione* (Turin: Einaudi).

Boltho A. (1993), 'Western Europe's Economic Stagnation', in *New Left Review*, 201, 60–75.

Bordogna L., Provasi G. (1984), *Politica, economia e rappresentanza degli interessi* (Bologna: Il Mulino).

Bourdieu P. (1971), 'Reproduction culturelle et reproduction sociale', in *Information sur les sciences sociales*, X, 2, 45–72; English trans. 'Cultural Reproduction and Social Reproduction', in R. Brown (ed.), *Knowledge, Education and Social Change* (London: Tavistock, 1973).

Bowles S., Gintis H. (1986), *Democracy and Capitalism* (New York: Basic Books).

Braudel F. (1979), *Civilisation matérielle, économie et capitalisme* (Paris: Colin, 3 vols); English trans. *Civilization and Capitalism, 15th–18th Centuries* (London: Fontana, 1981–3, 3 vols).

Brittan S. (1977), *The Economic Consequences of Democracy* (London: Temple Smith).

Bryce J. (1921), *Modern Democracies* (London: Macmillan, 2 vols).

Buchanan J., Tullock G. (1962), *The Calculus of Consent: Logical Foundations of Constitutional Democracy* (Ann Arbor: University of Michigan Press).

Bulpitt J. G. (1983), *Territory and Power in the United Kingdom* (Manchester: Manchester University Press).

Burch M., Moran M. (1985), 'The Changing British Political Elite, 1945–1983: MPs and Cabinet Ministers', in *Parliamentary Affairs*, 29, 1, 1–15.

Burch M., Wood B. (1983), *Public Policy in Britain* (Oxford: Robertson).

Burckhardt J.C. (1906), *Weltgeschichtlichen Betrachtungen*; pages cited from English trans. *Reflections on History* (London: Allen & Unwin, 1943).

Burke E. (1987), *The Political Thought of Edmund Burke*, ed. I. Hampshire-Monk (London: Longman).

Burnham J. (1941), *The Managerial Revolution: What is Happening in the World* (New York: John Davy).

Butt-Philip A. (1985), 'Pressure Groups in the European Community', *UACES Working Paper* no. 2.

Caciagli M. (1991), 'Vita e opere di un ceto politico', in *Polis*, 5, 2, 209–16.

Calise M. (1989), *Governo di partito: Antecedenti e conseguenze in America* (Bologna: Il Mulino).

Calise M., Mannheimer R. (1982), *Governanti in Italia: un trentennio repubblicano 1946–1976* (Bologna: Il Mulino).

Calise M., Mannheimer R. (1986), 'Come cambiano i governanti di partito', in *Rivista italiana di scienza politica*, 3, 461–83.

Calleo D. (1978), *The German Question Reconsidered* (Cambridge: Cambridge University Press).

Cassese S. (1980), *Esiste un governo in Italia?* (Rome: Officina Ed.); English trans. 'Is there a Government in Italy? Politics and Administration at the Top', in R. Rose, E.N. Sulieman (eds), *Presidents and Prime Ministers* (Washington, DC: AEI).

Cassese S. (1984), 'The Higher Civil Service in Italy', in E.N. Sulieman (ed.), *Bureaucrats and Policy-Making: A Comparative Overview* (New York: Holmes & Meier).

Cassese S. (1993), 'Hypotheses on the Italian Administrative System', in *West European Politics*, 16, 3, 318–28.

Castells M. (1972), *La Question urbaine* (Paris: Maspéro); English trans. *The Urban Question* (London: Arnold, 1974).

Castles F.G. (1982) (ed.), *The Impact of Parties* (London: Sage).

Catanzaro R. (1988), *Il delitto come impresa: Storia sociale della mafia* (Padua: Liviana).

Cawson A. (1986), 'Corporatism and Local Politics', in W. Grant (ed.), *The Political Economy of Corporatism* (Basingstoke: Macmillan).

Cazzola F. (1988), *Della corruzione* (Bologna: Il Mulino).

Cerroni U. (1979), *Teoria del partito politico* (Rome: Editori Riuniti).

Chandler J. (1991), *Local Government Today* (Manchester, Manchester University Press).

Chapman B. (1959), *The Profession of Government* (London: Allen & Unwin).

Chapman B. (1970), *Police State* (London: Pall Mall).

Charlot J. (1971) (ed.), *Les Partis politiques* (Paris: Colin).

Cheles L., Ferguson R., Vaughan M. (1991) (eds), *Neofascism in Europe* (London: Longman).

Claessens D., Klonne A., Tschoepe A. (1978), *Sozialkunde der Bundesrepublik Deutschland* (Dusseldorf: Dietrichs).

Clark G., Dear M. (1981), 'The State in Capitalism and the Capitalist State', in M. Dear, A.J. Scott (eds), *Urbanisation and Urban Planning in Capitalist Society* (London: Methuen).

Clark G.N. (1927), *The Seventeenth Century* (Oxford: Clarendon Press).

Clausewitz K. (1832–4), *Vom Kriege*; pages cited from English trans. *On War* (Harmondsworth: Penguin, 1968).

Cohen J. (1985), 'Strategy or Identity: New Theoretical Paradigms and Contemporary Social Movements', in *Social Research*, 52, 671–708.

Cotta M. (1976), 'Classe politica e istituzionalizzazione del parlamento 1946–1972', in *Rivista italiana di scienza politica*, 1, 71–110.

Cox O.C. (1970), *Caste, Class and Race* (New York: Monthly Review Press).

Crick B. (1987), *Socialism* (Milton Keynes: Open University Press).

Criscitiello A. (1993), 'Majority Summits: Decision-Making inside the Cabinet and out: Italy, 1970–1990', in *West European Politics*, 16, 4, 581–94.

Crispi F. (1890), *Scritti e discorsi politici* (Rome).

Croce B. (1928), *Storia d'Italia dal 1871 al 1915* (Bari: Laterza); pages cited from English trans. *A History of Italy, 1875–1915* (Oxford: Oxford University Press).

Crompton R., Jones G. (1984), *White Collar Proletariat* (London: Macmillan).

Crouch A. (1986), 'Le origini storiche dei rapporti tra stati e interessi organizzati nell'Europa occidentale', in *Stato e mercato*, 18, 315–45.

Crozier M. (1963), *Le Phénoméne bureaucratique* (Paris: Seuil); pages cited from English trans., *The Bureaucratic Phenomenon* (London: Tavistock).

Crozier M., Huntington S.P., Watanuki J. (1975), *The Crisis of Democracy* (New York: New York University Press).

Curran J., Seaton J. (1988), *Power without Responsibility: The Press and Broadcasting in Britain* (London: Routledge, 3rd edn).

Cutright P. (1965), 'Political Structure, Economic Development and National Security Programmes', in *American Journal of Sociology*, 5, 537–50.

Daalder H. (1984), 'In Search of the Centre of European Party Systems', in *American Political Science Review*, 1, 92–109.

Dahl R.A. (1971), *Polyarchy: Participation and Opposition* (New Haven, Conn.: Yale University Press).

Dahl R.A. (1985), *A Preface to Economic Democracy* (Berkeley, Calif.: University of California Press).

Dahrendorf R. (1964), 'Recent changes in the Class Structure of European Societies', in *Daedalus*, winter, 250–65.

Dahrendorf R. (1965), *Gesellschaft und Demokratie Deutschland*, (Munich: Piper); English trans. *Society and Democracy in Germany* (London: Weidenfeld & Nicolson, 1967).

Dahrendorf R. (1988), *The Modern Social Conflict: An Essay on the Politics of Liberty* (London, Weidenfeld & Nicolson).

D'Alimonte R. (1978), 'Competizione elettorale e rendimento politico: il caso italiano', in *Rivista italiana di scienza politica*, 3, 457–93.

Dalton R.J., Flanagan S.C., Beck P.A. (1984) (eds), *Electoral Change in Advanced Industrial Democracies: Realignment or Dealignment?* (Princeton, NJ: Princeton University Press).

Davis H.H. (1992), 'Social Stratification in Europe', in J. Bailey (ed.), *Social Europe* (London: Longman).

Dearlove J., Saunders P. (1991), *Introduction to British Politics* (Cambridge: Polity Press, 2nd edn).

De Beauvoir S. (1949), *Le Deuxième Sexe* (Paris: Gallimard, 2 vols); pages cited from English trans. *The Second Sex* (London: Cape, 1968).

De Jouvenel R. (1914), *La République des camarades* (Paris: Grasset).

Della Sala V. (1988), 'Government by Decree: The Craxi Government and the Use of Decree Legislation in the Italian Parliament', In *Italian Politics: A Review*, 3, 8–24.

De Lutiis G. (1991), *Storia dei servizi segreti in Italia* (Rome: Editori Riuniti).

Dente B. (1985a), *Governare la frammentazione* (Bologna: Il Mulino).

Dente B. (1985b), 'Centre–Local Relations in Italy: The Impact of Legal and Political Structures', in Y. Mény and V. Wright (eds), *Centre and Periphery Relations in Western Europe* (London: Allen & Unwin).

Deutsch K.W. (1963), *The Nerves of Government* (New York: Free Press).

Diamanti I. (1993), *La Lega: Geografia, storia e sociologia di un nuovo soggetto politico* (Rome: Donzelli).

Dicey A.V. (1885), *Introduction to the Study of the Law of the Constitution* (London: Macmillan).

Di Palma G. (1977), *Surviving without Governing. The Italian Parties in Parliament* (Berkeley, Calif.: University of California Press).

Dogan M. (1967), 'Les Filières de la carrière politique en France', in *Revue française de sociologie*, 4, 468–92.

Dogan M. (1979), 'How to Become a Minister in France: Career Pathways, 1870–1978', in *Comparative Politics*, 1, 1–26.

Donati P.P. (1984), 'Organisation between Movement and Institution', in *Social Science Information*, 4/5, 837–59.

D'Orsi A. (1971), *La macchina militare: Le forze armate in Italia* (Milan: Feltrinelli).

Downs A. (1957), *An Economic Theory of Democracy* (New York: Harper & Row).

Dror Y. (1964), 'Muddling Through – Science or Inertia?', in *Public Administration Review*, 2, 153–7.

Dunn J. (1979), *Western Political Theory in Face of the Future* (Cambridge: Cambridge University Press).

Dürrenmatt F. (1989), *Dokumente und Aussprachen* (Bonn: Bouvier).

Duverger M. (1951), *Les Partis politiques* (Paris: Colin); pages cited from English trans. *Political Parties* (London: Methuen, 1957).

Duverger M. (1955), *Institutions politiques et droit constitutionnel* (Paris: Presses Universitaires de France, 2 vols), vol. I *Les Grands Systèmes politiques*.

Duverger M. (1964), 'L'Éternel Marais: essai sur le centrisme français', in *Revue française de science politique*, 14, 38–40.

Duverger M. (1967), *La Démocratie sans le peuple* (Paris: Seuil).

Duverger M. (1972), *Janus: Les Deux Faces de l'occident* (Paris: Fayard).

Duverger M. (1982), *La République des citoyens* (Paris: Ramsay).

Duverger M. (1986), *Bréviaire sur la 'cohabitation'* (Paris: Presses Universitaires de France).

Easton D. (1953), *The Political System* (New York: Knopf).

Eco U. (1964), *Apocalittici e integrati* (Milan: Bompiani); pages cited from English translation. R. Lumley, ed., *Apocalypse Postponed* (London BFI Publishing 1994).

Eco U. (1980), *Il nome della rosa* (Milan: Bompiani); pages cited from English trans. *The Name of the Rose* (London: Secker & Warburg, 1983).

Eckstein H. (1966), *Division and Cohesion in Democracy: A Study of Norway* (Princeton, NJ: Princeton University Press).

Edmonds M. (1988), *The Armed Services and Society* (Leicester: Leicester University Press).

Eisenstadt S.N., Lemarchand R. (1981), *Political Clientelism, Patronage and Development* (Beverly Hills, Calif.: Sage).

Elias N. (1939), *Über den Prozess der Zivilisation* (2 vols); English trans. *The Civilizing Process* (Oxford: Blackwell, 2 vols, 1984–6).

Enzenberger H.M. (1982), *Politische Brosamen* (Frankfurt: Suhrkamp); English trans. *Political Crumbs* (London: Verso, 1990).

Esping-Andersen G. (1990), *The Three Worlds of Welfare Capitalism* (Cambridge: Polity Press).

Etzioni A. (1967), 'Mixed Scanning: A "Third" Approach to Decision-Making', in *Public Administration Review*, 4, 385–92.

Etzioni-Halevy E. (1993), *The Elite Connection: Problems and Potential of Western Democracy* (Cambridge: Polity Press).

Fabbrini S. (1988), *Politica e mutamenti sociali: Alternative a confronto sullo stato sociale* (Bologna: Il Mulino).

Fabbrini S. (1990), 'Cambiamento politico e qualità della rappresentanza democratica', in *Il Mulino*, 1, 9–33.

Ferraresi F. (1980), *Burocrazia e politica in Italia* (Bologna: Il Mulino).

Ferraresi F. (1992), 'A Secret Structure Codenamed Gladio', in *Italian Politics: A Review*, 7, 29–48.

Finer S.E. (1962), *The Man on Horseback: The Role of the Military in Politics*

(London: Pall Mall; 2nd edn Penguin, 1975).

Finer S.E. (1970), *Comparative Government* (London: Allen Lane).

Finer S.E. (1973), 'The Political Power of Organised Labour', in *Government and Opposition*, 4, 391–406.

Finer S.E. (1975a) (ed.), *Adversary Politics and Electoral Reform* (London: Wigram).

Finer S.E. (1975b), 'Manifesto Moonshine', in *New Society*, 684, 379–80.

Finer S.E. (1980), *The Changing British Party System, 1945–1979* (Washington, DC: AEI).

Fossati A. (1990), 'La nuova legge sull'Ordinamento delle autonomie locali', in *Aggiornamenti sociali*, 9–10, 633–46.

Foucault M. (1969), *L'Archéologie du savoir* (Paris: Gallimard); English trans. *The Archeology of Knowledge* (London: Tavistock, 1972).

Fraschini A. (1992), 'Financing Communal Government in Italy', in *Local Government Studies*, 18, 4, 79–93.

Freeman G.P. (1985), 'National Styles and Policy Sectors: Explaining Structures Variation', in *Journal of Public Policy*, 4, 467–96.

Friedman M. (1962), *Capitalism and Freedom* (Chicago: Chicago University Press).

Freidrich C. (1968), *Constitutional Government and Democracy: Theory and Practice in Europe and America* (Walpham, Mass.: Blaisdell).

Fukuyama F. (1989), 'The End of History?', in *The National Interest*, 16, 3–18.

Furet F. (1978), *Penser la révolution française* (Paris: Gallimard); pages cited from English trans. *Interpreting the French Revolution* (Cambridge: Cambridge University Press, 1981).

Fusaro C. (1991), *Guida alle riforme istituzionali* (Soveria Mannelli, CZ: Rubbettino).

Gaetner G. (1992), *L'Argent facile: dictionnaire de la Corruption en France* (Paris: Stock).

Galbraith J.K. (1958), *The Affluent Society* (Boston: Houghton Mifflin).

Galbraith J.K. (1967), *The New Industrial State* (London: Hamish Hamilton).

Galbraith J.K. (1991), ' "The Revolt in our Time": The Triumph of Simplistic Ideology', in M. Kaldor (ed.), *Europe from Below: An East–West Dialogue* (London: Verso).

Galbraith J.K. (1992), *The Culture of Contentment* (London: Sinclair-Stevenson).

Galli G. (1974), *I partiti politici* (Turin: UTET).

Gambino A. (1988), *L'Europa invertebrata: Passato, presente e futuro di un 'protettorato imperfetto'* (Milan: Mondadori).

Gamble A.M., Wakeland S.A. (1984), *The British Party System and Economic Policy* (Oxford: Clarendon Press).

Garrett S. (1987), *Gender* (London: Tavistock).

Gerschenkron A. (1943), *Bread and Democracy in Germany* (Berkeley, Calif.: California University Press).

Gibson J. (1992), 'British Local Government Finance under the Conservatives', in *Local Government Studies*, 18, 4, 55–77.

Giddens A. (1983) 'La società europea negli anni ottanta. Divisioni di classe, conflitto di classe e diritti di cittadinanza', in G.-F. Pasquino (ed.), *Le società complesse* (Bologna: Il Mulino).

Giddens A. (1986), *The Nation-State and Violence* (Cambridge: Polity Press).

Gill P. (1994), 'Information Control and Change in United Kingdom Security Intelligence Agencies under Major', in P. Dunleavy and J. Stanyer (eds), *Contemporary Political Studies* (Political Studies Association of GB), vol. 1, 170–80.

Giroud F. (1977), *La Comédie du pouvoir* (Paris: Fayard).

Golding P. (1980), 'Gran Bretagna: la battaglia per il centro', in *L'informazione accentrata* (Turin: Rosenberg & Sellier).

Golding P., Murdock G. (1991), 'Culture, Communications and Political Economy', in J. Curran and M. Gurevitch (eds), *Mass media and Society* (London: Arnold).

Goldthorpe J.H. (1980), *Social Mobility and Class Structure in Modern Britain* (Oxford: Clarendon Press).

Gorz A. (1980), *Adieu au prolétariat* (Paris: Galilée); English trans. *Goodbye to the Proletariat* (London: Pluto Press, 1982).

Gourevitch P. (1978), 'The Second Image Reversed: the International Sources of Domestic Politics', in *International Organisation*, 4, 881–911.

Gramsci A. (1949), *Note sul Machiavelli sulla politica e sullo Stato moderno* (Turin: Einaudi); pages cited from English trans. *Selections from the Prison Notebooks* (London: Lawrence & Wishart, 1971).

Grant W. (1986), 'Introduction', in W. Grant (ed.), *The Political Economy of Corporatism* (London: Macmillan).

Green P. (1985), *Retrieving Democracy: In Search of Civic Equality* (London: Methuen).

Grjebin A. (1986) (ed.), *Théories de la crise et politiques économiques* (Paris: Seuil).

Grosser A. (1964), 'The Evolution of European Parliaments', in *Daedalus* 1, 153–78.

Grosser A. (1985), *L'Allemagne en occident* (Paris: Fayard).

Grunow D. (1992), 'Constitutional Reform of Local Government in Germany: The Case of North Rhine-Westphalia (NRW)', in *Local Government Studies*, 18, 2, 44–57.

Guadagnini M. (1983), 'Partiti e classe parlamentare negli anni settanta', in *Rivista italiana di scienza politica*, 2, 261–94.

Gulik L., Urwich L. (1937) (eds), *Papers on the Science of the Administration* (New York: Colombia University Press).

Gurevitch M. (1991), 'The Globalization of Electronic Journalism', in J. Curran and M. Gurevitch (eds), *Mass-Media and Society* (London: Arnold).

Haas E.B. (1958), *The Uniting of Europe: Political, Social and Economic Forces, 1950–1957* (London: Stevens).

Habermas J. (1962), *Strukturwandel der Öffentlichkeit* (Neuwied: Luchterhand); English trans. *The Structural Transformation of the Public Sphere* (Cambridge: Polity Press, 1989).

Habermas J. (1973), *Legitimationsprobleme im Spätkapitalismus* (Frankfurt: Suhrkamp); pages cited from English trans. *Legitimation Problem* (London: Heinemann, 1974).

Hailsham, Lord (1978), *The Dilemma of Democracy* (London: Collins).

Hall S. (1973), 'Determination of News Photographs' in S. Cohen, J. Young (eds), *The Manufacture of News: A Reader* (Beverly Hills, Calif.: Sage).

Hall S. (1984), 'The State in Question', in G. McLennan, D. Held, S.Hall (eds), *The Idea of a Modern State* (Milton Keynes: Open University Press).

Hall S. et al. (1978), *Policing the Crisis* (London: Macmillan).

Ham C., Hill M. (1984), *The Policy Process in the Modern Capitalist State* (Brighton: Harvester Press).

Hamon L. (1977), 'Nécessité et conditions de l'alternance', in *Pouvoirs*, 1, 19–43.

Harrop J. (ed.), (1992), *Power and Policy-Making in Liberal Democracies* (Cambridge: Cambridge University Press).

Hayek F.A. (1944), *The Road to Serfdom* (London: RKP).

Hayward J.E.S. (1983), *Governing France: The One and Indivisible Republic* (London, Weidenfeld & Nicolson, 2nd edn).

Hayward J.E.S. (1986), *The State and the Market Economy: Industrial Patriotism and Economic Intervention in France* (Brighton: Wheatsheaf Press).

Heady B.W. (1974), *The Roles of Politicians in Executive Office* (London: Allen & Unwin).

Heath A. (1981), *Social Mobility* (London: Fontana).

Heclo H., Wildavsky A. (1974), *The Private Government of Public Money* (London: Macmillan).

Heidenheimer A.J., Heclo H., Adams C.T. (1990), *Comparative Public Policy: The Politics of Social Choice in Europe and America* (New York: St Martin's Press, 3rd edn).

Held D. (1987), *Models of Democracy* (Cambridge: Polity Press).

Hennessy P. (1986), *Cabinet* (Oxford: Blackwell).

Hennessy P. (1989), *Whitehall* (London: Secker & Warburg).

Hermet G. (1983), *Aux frontières de la démocratie* (Paris: Presses Universitaires de France).

Hermet G. (1986), *Sociologie de la construction démocratique* (Paris: Economica).

Herzog D. (1971), 'Carriera parlamentare e professionismo politico', in *Rivista italiana di scienza politica*, 3, 515–44.

Hill C., Rhodes R.A.W. (1972), *Intergovernmental Relations in the European Community* (Farnborough: Saxon House).

Hindess B. (1987), *Politics and Class Analysis* (Oxford: Blackwell).

Hindess B. (1993), 'Citizenship in the Modern West', in B.S. Turner (ed.), *Citizenship and Social Theory* (London: Sage), 19–35.

Hinsley F. H. (1963), *Power and the Pursuit of Peace: Theory and Practice in the History of the Relations between States* (Cambridge: Cambridge University Press).

Hintze O. (1902), 'Staatenbildung und Verfassungentwicklung'; pages cited from English trans. 'The Formation of States and Constitutional Development', in M. Gilbert (ed.), *Historical Essays of Otto Hintze* (Oxford: Oxford University Press, 1975), 159–77.

Hintze O. (1906), 'Staatsverfassung und Heeresverfassung'; pages cited from English trans. 'Military Organization and the Organization of the State', in

M. Gilbert (ed.), *Historical Essays of Otto Hintze* (Oxford: Oxford University Press, 1975), 180–215.

Hirschman A. O. (1982), 'Rival Interpretations of Market Society: Civilizing, Destructive or Feeble?', in *Journal of Economic Literature*, 4, 1463–84.

Hobbes T. (1651), *Leviathan* (Harmondsworth: Penguin, 1972).

Hobsbawm E.J. (1975), *The Age of Capital 1848–1875* (London: Weidenfeld & Nicolson).

Hoffmann J. (1988), *State Power and Democracy* (Brighton: Wheatsheaf Books).

Hoffmann S. (1963), 'Paradoxes of the French Political Community', in *In Search of France* (Cambridge, Mass.: Harvard University Press).

Hoffmann S. (1965), 'The European Process at Atlantic Crosspurposes', in *Journal of Common Market Studies*, 4, 85–101.

Hoffmann S. (1974), *Essais sur la France* (Paris, Seuil); English version *Decline or Renewal? France since 1930s* (New York: Viking Press, 1974).

Hoffmann S. (1983), 'Reflections on the Nation-State in Western Europe Today', in L. Tsoukalis (ed.), *The European Community, Past, Present and Future* (Oxford: Blackwell).

Hoggart K. (1987), 'Does Politics Matter? Redistributive Policies in English Cities 1949–1974', in *British Journal of Political Science*, 3, 359–71.

Hoggart R. (1957), *The Uses of Literacy: Aspects of Working Class Life with Special Reference to Publications and Entertainments* (London: Chatto & Windus).

Hogwood B. (1987), *From Crisis to Complacency: Shaping Public Policy* (Oxford: Oxford University Press).

Howard M. (1976), *War in European History* (Oxford: Oxford University Press).

Hume D. (1740), *A Treatise on Human Nature* (Harmondsworth: Penguin, 1969).

Huntington S.P. (1957), *The Soldiers and the State: The Theory and Politics of Civil–Military Relations* (Cambridge: Mass.: Harvard University Press).

Inglehart R. (1977), *The Silent Revolution* (Princeton, NJ: Princeton University Press).

Inglehart R. (1990), *Cultural Shift in Advanced Industrial Society* (Princeton, NJ: Princeton University Press).

Janovitz M. (1960), *The Professional Soldier: A Social and Political Portrait* (Glencoe, Ill.: Free Press).

Janovitz M. (1975), *Military Conflicts: Essays in the Institutional Analysis of War and Peace* (Beverly Hills, Calif.: Sage).

Jeffery C. (1994) 'Failing the Challenge of Unification? The *Länder* and German Federalism in the 1990s', in P. Dunleavy and J. Stanyer (eds), *Contemporary Political Studies* (Political Studies Association of GB), vol. 2, 765–79.

Jessop B. (1978), 'Capitalism and Democracy: The Best Possible Shell', in G. Littlejohn (ed.) *Power and the State* (London: Croom Helm).

Kalecki M. (1943), 'Political Aspects of Full Employment', in *Political Quarterly*, 4, 322–31.

Katz E., Lazarsfeld P. (1955), *Personal Influence: The Part Played by People in the Flow of Mass Communications* (New York: Free Press).

Katzenstein P. (1987), *Policy and Politics in West Germany: The Growth of a Semi-Sovereign State* (Philadelphia: Temple University Press).

Keane J. (1988), *Democracy and Civil Society* (London: Verso).

Kelsen H. (1929), *Vom Wesen und Wert der Demokratie* (Tübingen: Mohr).

Keohane R.O. and Hoffmann S. (1991) (eds), *The New European Community: Decision-Making and Historical Change* (Boulder, Col.: Westview).

Kesselman M. (1967), *The Ambiguous Consensus* (New York: Knopf).

Keynes J.M. (1936), *The General Theory of Employment, Interest and Money* (London: Macmillan).

Kindleberger C.P. (1967), *Europe's Postwar Growth: The Role of Labour Supply* (Cambridge, Mass.: Harvard University Press).

Kirchheimer O. (1957), 'The Waning of Opposition in Parliamentary Regimes', in *Social Research*, 2, 127–56.

Kirchheimer O. (1966), 'The Transformation of Western Party Systems', in J. LaPalombara, M. Weiner (eds), *Political Parties and Political Development* (Princeton, NJ: Princeton University Press).

Kissinger H. (1979), *White House Years* (Boston: Little Brown).

Kissinger H. (1982), *Years of Upheaval* (Boston: Little, Brown).

Khrushchev N.S. (1971), *Khrushchev Remembers* (Boston: Little Brown).

Knapp A. (1991), 'The *cumul des mandats*, Local Power and Political Parties in France', in *West European Politics,* 14, 1, 18–40.

Lampedusa G. di (1958), *Il gattopardo* (Milan: Feltrinelli); English trans. *The Leopard* (London: Collins & Harvill, 1961).

Lane J.E., Ersson S.O. (1987), *Politics and Society in Western Europe* (London: Sage, 3rd edn, 1994).

Lane J.E., Mckay D., Newton K. (1991), *Political Data Handbook: OECD Countries* (Oxford: Oxford University Press).

LaPalombara J. (1964), *Interest Groups in Italian Politics* (Princeton, NJ: Princeton University Press).

LaPalombara J. (1987), *Democracy Italian Style* (New Haven, Conn.: Yale University Press).

Lash S. And Urry J. (1987), *The End of Organized Capitalism* (Cambridge: Polity Press).

Laski H. (1933), *Democracy in Crisis* (London: Allen & Unwin).

Laski H. (1935), *The State in Theory and Practice* (London: Allen & Unwin).

Lasswell H.D. (1935), *World Politics and Personal Insecurity* (New York: McGraw-Hill).

Lasswell H.D. (1941), 'The Garrison State', in *American Journal of Sociology*, 5, 455–68.

Lasswell H.D. (1956), *The Decision Process: Seven Categories of Functional Analysis* (University of Maryland, College of Public Administration).

Lawson K. and Merkyl P. (1988) (eds), *When Parties Fail* (Princeton: Princeton University Press).

Le Cacheux J., Tourjansky L. (1992), 'French Decentralization Ten Years On: Local Government Finances', in *Local Government Studies*, 18, 4, 28–37.

Lee J.M. (1963), *Social Leaders and Public Persons* (Oxford: Clarendon Press).

Lehmbruch G. (1984), 'Concertation and Structure of Corporatist Networks', in J. Goldthorpe (ed.), *Order and conflict in Contemporary Capitalism* (Oxford: Clarendon Press).

Lenin V.I. (1918), *Gosudarstro j revoljuccia* (St Petersburg, Zhizn i Znaniye); English trans. *State and Revolution*, in *Selected Works in One Volume* (London: Lawrence & Wishart, 1969).

Lijphart A. (1971), *Class Voting and Religious Voting in European Democracies* (Glasgow: University of Strathclyde Occasional Paper, n. 8).

Lindblom C.E. (1959), 'The Science of Muddling Through', in *Public Administration Review*, 2, 79–88.

Lindblom C.E. (1970), 'Still Muddling, not yet Through', in *Public Administration Review*, 6, 517–26.

Lindblom C.E. (1977), *Politics and Markets* (New York: Basic Books).

Lipset S.M. (1959), *Political Man* (New York: Doubleday).

Livingstone K. (1988), *If Voting Changed Anything, They'd Abolish It* (London: Collins).

Locke J. (1690), *Two Treatises of Government*, in *Political Writings*, (Harmondsworth: Penguin, 1993).

Lodge J. (1993), 'From Civilian Power to Speaking with a Common Voice: the Transition to a CFSP', in J. Lodge (ed.), *The European Community and the Challenge of the Future* (London: Pinter, 2nd edn)

Loewenberg G. (1967), *Parliament in the German Political System* (Ithaca, NY: Cornell University Press).

Long M. (1980), 'Les Corps', in *Cahiers français*, 194, 40–5.

Lowi T.J. (1964), 'American Business, Public Policy, Case-Studies and Political Theory', in *World Politics* 4, 677–715.

Lowi T.J. (1972), 'Four Systems of Policy, Politics and Choice', in *Public Administration Review*, 4, 290–310.

Luhmann N. (1971), *Politische Planung* (Opladen: Westdeutscher).

Lukes S. (1974), *Power: A Radical View* (London; Macmillan).

Luxemburg R. (1899), *Sozialreform oder Revolution?;* English trans. *Reform or Revolution?* (New York: Pathfinder Press, 1973).

Mabileau M. (1985), 'Les Institutions locales et les relations centre–périférie', in J. Leca, M. Grawitz (eds), *Traité de science politique* (Paris: Presses Universitaires de France, 4 vols), vol. IV, 553–98.

Macintyre A. (1970), *Marcuse* (London: Fontana).

Macintyre A. (1981), *After Virtue* (London: Duckworth).

Macpherson C.B. (1985), *The Rise and Fall of Economic Justice and Other Essays* (Oxford: Oxford University Press).

McCarthy J.D., Zald M.N. (1979) (eds), *The Dynamics of Social Movements* (Cambridge, Mass.: Winthrop).

McGregor Report (1977), *Royal Commission on the Press* (London: Cmnd 6810, HMSO).

McLennan G. (1989), *Marxism, Pluralism and Beyond* (Cambridge: Polity Press).

Maddison A. (1982), *Phases of Capitalist Development* (Oxford: Oxford University Press).

Madison J. et al. (1787–88), *The Federalist Papers* (Harmondsworth: Penguin, 1987).

Mandel E. (1972), *Der Spätkapitalismus* (Frankfurt: Surhkamp); English trans. *Late Capitalism* (London: New Left Books, 1975).

Mandrou R. (1966), *La France au XVIIme et XVIIIme siècles* (Paris: Presses Universitaires de France).

March J., Olsen J.P. (1984), 'The New Institutionalism: Organisational Factors in Political Life', in *American Political Science Review*, 4, 734–49.

Marletti C. (1980), 'Economia dell'informazione e sistema politico', in AAVV, *L'informazione accentrata* (Turin: Rosenberg & Sellier).

Marcuse H. (1964), *One Dimensional Man* (Boston: Beacon Press).

Marsh D., Locksley G. (1983), 'Capital: Neglected Face of Power?', in D. Marsh (ed.), *Pressure Politics: Interest Groups in Britain* (London: Junction Books).

Marshall T.H. (1950), *Citizenship and Social Class* (Cambridge: Cambridge University Press).

Martin D. (1967), *The Sociology of English Religion* (London: RKP).

Martinelli R. (1968) (ed.), *SIFAR: Gli atti del processo De Lorenzo – 'L'Espresso'* (Milan: Mursia).

Marx K. (1852), *Der Achtzehnte Brumaire des Louis Bonaparte*; pages cited from English trans. *The Eighteenth Brumaire of Louis Napoleon*, in *Surveys from Exile* (Harmondsworth: Penguin, 1973).

Marx K. (1867), *Das Kapital: Kritik der politischen Ökonomie*; English trans. *Capital: A Critique of Political Economy* (Harmondsworth: Penguin, 1976, 3 vols).

Marx K., Engels F. (1848), *Manifest der Kommunistischen Partei*; English. trans. *The Communist Manifesto*, in *The Revolutions of 1848* (Harmondsworth: Penguin, 1973).

Mastropaolo A. (1984), *Saggio sul professionismo politico* (Milan: Angeli).

Mastropaolo A. (1993), *Il ceto politico: teoria e pratiche* (Rome: Nuova Italia Scientifica).

Mauss D. (1989), 'Les énarques au gouvernement et au parlement', in *Pouvoirs*, 49, 147–55.

Mayntz R. (1984), 'German Federal Bureaucrats. A Functional Elite between Politics and Administration', in E.N. Sulieman (ed.), *Bureaucrats and Policy-Making: A Comparative Overview* (New York: Holmes & Meier).

Melucci A. (1977), *Sistema politico, partiti e movimenti sociali* (Milan: Feltrinelli).

Melucci A. (1980), 'The New Social movements: A Theoretical Approach', in *Social Science Information*, 19, 2, 199–226.

Melucci A. (1984) (ed.), *Altri codici* (Bologna: Il Mulino); English trans. *Other Codes* (London: Radius-Hutchinson, 1990).

Melucci A. (1989), *Nomads of the Present* (London: Radius Hutchinson).

Mény Y. (1987), *Politique comparée: Les Democraties: États-Unis, France, Grande-Bretagne, RFA* (Paris: Édition Montchrestien 4th edn, 1993); pages cited from English trans. *Government and Politics in Western Europe: Britain, France, Germany and Italy* (Oxford: Oxford University Press, 2nd edn, 1993).

Mény Y. (1992a), *La Corruption de la République* (Paris: Fayard).

Mény Y. (1992b), 'La République des fiefs', in *Pouvoirs*, 60, 17–24.

Merlini C. (1993), 'Italy and Europe', in J. Story (ed.), *The New Europe: Politics, Government and Economy since 1945* (Oxford: Blackwell).

Merquior J.G. (1986), *Western Marxism* (London: Fontana).

Meynaud J. (1958), *Les Groupes de pression en France* (Paris: Colin).

Meynaud J. (1964), *Rapport sur la classe dirigeante italienne* (Lausanne: ESI).

Michalski A., Wallace H. (1992), *The European Community: The Challenge of Enlargement* (London: RIIA).

Michels R. (1911), *Zur Soziologie des Parteiwesens in der Modernen Demokratie*; pages cited from English trans. *Political Parties: A Sociological Study of the Oligarchical Tendencies of Modern Democracy* (New York: Free Press, 1968).

Miliband R. (1969), *The State in Capitalist Society* (London: Weidenfeld & Nicolson).

Mill J. (1825), *Essay on Government*, originally written for the supplement of the *Encyclopedia Britannica*, 5th edn (New York: Kelly, 1967).

Mill J.S. (1861), *Considerations on Representative Government*, in *On Liberty and Other Essays* (Oxford: Oxford University Press, 1991).

Mills C.W. (1956), *The Power Elite* (New York: Oxford University Press).

Milward A.S. (1984), *The Reconstruction of Western Europe, 1945–51* (London: Methuen).

Mitchell J. (1992), 'The Nature and Government of the Global Economy' in A.G. McGrew and P.G. Lewis (eds), *Global Politics* (Cambridge: Polity).

Montesquieu G.-L. (1748), *De l'Esprit des lois*; English trans. *The Spirit of the Laws* (New York: Haffner, 1949).

Moore B. (1966), *Social Origins of Dictatorship and Democracy: Lord and Peasant in the Modern World* (Boston: Beacon Press).

Morgan R. (1992), 'Germany and the New Europe', in C. Crouch and D.Marquand (eds), *Towards a Greater Europe? A Continent without an Iron Curtain* (Oxford: Blackwell).

Morris R.J. (1983), 'Voluntary Societies and the British Urban Elites, 1780–1850: An Analysis', in *Historical Journal*, 1, 95–118.

Mosca G. (1895), *Elementi di scienza politica* (Bari: Laterza, 3rd edn, 1933); pages cited from English trans. *The Ruling Class* (New York: McGraw-Hill, 1939).

Mossé E. (1989), *La Crise...et après: Comprendre la politique économique* (Paris: Seuil), vol. 2.

Myrdal G. (1960), *Beyond the Welfare State* (New Haven, Conn.: Yale University Press).

Naville P. (1971), 'France', in M. Archer, S. Giner (eds), *Contemporary Europe: Class, Status and Power* (London: Weidenfeld & Nicolson).

Nicolson H. (1939), *Diplomacy* (Oxford: Oxford University Press).

Nicolson H. (1954), *The Evolution of the Diplomatic Method* (London: Constable).

Niskanen W.A. (1973), *Bureaucracy: Servant or Master?* (London: Institute of Economic Affairs).

Nugent N. (1991), *The Government and Politics of the European Community* (London: Macmillan, 2nd edn).

Oakley A. (1972), *Sex, Gender and Society* (London: Temple Smith).

O'Connor J. (1973), *The Fiscal Crisis of the State* (New York: St Martin's Press).

Offe C. (1972), *Strukturprobleme des Kapitalistischen Staates* (Frankfurt: Suhrkamp).

Offe C. (1981), 'The Attribution of Public Status Interest Groups: Observations on the West German Case', in S. Berger (ed.), *Organizing Interests in Western Europe: Pluralism, Corporatism and the Transformation of Politics* (Cambridge: Cambridge University Press).

Offe C. (1984), *The Contradictions of Welfare Capitalism* (London: Hutchinson).

Offe C. (1985), *Disorganized Capitalism* (Cambridge: Polity Press).

Orwell G. (1949), *Nineteen Eighty-Four* (London: Secker & Warburg).

Orwell G. (1968), *The Collected Essays* (London: Secker & Warburg, 4 vols).

Owen D. (1972), *The Politics of Defence* (London: Cape).

Page E.C. (1985), *Political Authority and Bureaucratic Power – A Comparative Analysis* (London: Wheatsheaf Books).

Page E.C. (1991), *Localism and Centralism in Europe* (Oxford: Oxford University Press).

Panebianco A. (1982), *Modelli di partito* (Bologna: Il Mulino); English trans. *Political Parties: Organization and Power* (Cambridge: Cambridge University Press, 1988).

Panebianco A. (1986), 'Burocrazie pubbliche', in G.-F. Pasquino (ed.), *Manuale di Scienza della politica* (Bologna: Il Mulino).

Parkin F. (1971), *Class Inequality and Political Order* (London: McGibbon & Kee).

Parry G., Moyser G., Day N. (1992), *Political Participation and Democracy in Britain* (Cambridge: Cambridge University Press).

Pasquino G.-F. (1971), 'Militarismo e professione militare', in *Rassegna italiana di sociologia*, 4, 569–609.

Pasquino G.-F. (1986), 'Partecipazione politica, gruppi e movimenti', in G.-F. Pasquino (ed.), *Manuale di scienza della politica* (Bologna: Il Mulino).

Pateman C. (1988), *The Sexual Contract* (Cambridge: Polity Press).

Paterson W.E. (1993), 'Germany and Europe', in J. Story (ed.), *The New Europe: Politics, Government and Economy since 1945* (Oxford: Blackwell).

Pierson C. (1991), *Beyond the Welfare State?* (Cambridge: Polity Press).

Pincher C. (1978), *Inside Story: A Documentary of the Pursuit of Power* (London: Sidgwick & Jackson).

Pizzorno A. (1966), 'Introduzione allo studio della partecipazione politica', in *Quaderni di sociologia*, 3–4, 235–87; now in *Le radici della politica assoluta e altri saggi* (Milan: Fetrinelli, 1993); pages cited from partial English trans. 'An Introduction to the Theory of Political Participation', in *Social Science Information*, 9, 29–61.

Pizzorno A. (1980), *I soggetti del pluralismo: Classi, partiti, sindacati* (Bologna: Il Mulino).

Pizzorno A. (1981), 'Interests and Parties in Pluralism', in S. Berger (ed.) *Organizing Interests in Western Europe: Pluralism, Corporatism and the Transformation of Politics* (Cambridge: Cambridge University Press).

Plischke E. (1979), *Modern Diplomacy: The Art and the Artisans* (Washington, DC: AEI).

Poggi G. (1978), *The Development of the Modern State* (London: Hutchinson).

Polanyi K. (1944), *The Great Transformation: The Political and Economic Transformations of Our Time* (New York: Holt, Rinehart & Winston).

Pollard S. (1984), *The Wasting of the British Economy* (London: Croom Helm, 2nd edn).

Pombeni P. (1985), *Introduzione alla storia dei partiti politici* (Bologna: Il Mulino).

Ponting C. (1986), *Whitehall: Tragedy and Farce* (London: Hamish Hamilton).

Posner M.V., Woolf S. (1967), *Italian Public Enterprise* (London, Duckworth).

Premfors R. (1981) 'Review Article: Charles Lindblom and Aaron Wildavsky', in *British Journal of Political Science*, 11, 2, 201–25.

Pressman J., Wildavsky A. (1973), *Implementation* (Berkeley, Calif.: University of California Press).

Quermonne J.-L. (1986), *Les Régimes politiques occidentaux* (Paris: Seuil).

Quermonne J.-L. (1990), 'Existe-t-il un modèle politique européen?' in *Revue française de science politique*, 2, 192–210.

Quermonne J.-L. (1991), *L'Appareil administrative d'état* (Paris: Seuil).

Radi L. (1973), *Buongiorno Onorevole* (Turin: SEI).

Rawls J. (1971), *A Theory of Justice* (Cambridge, Mass.: Harvard University Press).

Regonini G. (1984), 'Public Choice: Una teoria per l'analisi delle politiche pubbliche', in *Stato e mercato*, 11, 299–333.

Regonini G. (1985), 'Le politiche sociali in Italia: metodi di analisi', in *Rivista italiana di scienza politica*, 3, 335–77.

Reith J.C.W. (1949) *Into the Wind* (London: Hodder & Stoughton).

Rex J. (1986), *Race and Ethnicity* (Milton Keynes: Open University Press).

Reynolds D. (1992), 'Thawing History: Europe in 1990s and Pre-Cold War Patterns', in C. Crouch, D. Marquand (eds), *Towards a Greater Europe? A Continent without an Iron Curtain* (Oxford: Blackwell).

Rhodes R.A.W. (1988), *Beyond Westminster and Whitehall* (London: Unwin Hyman).

Riccamboni G. (1988), 'La regione Veneto', in ISAP Archivio NS 5, *Le relazioni fra amministrazione e partiti* (Milan: Giuffré), vol. I.

Richardson J.J. (1982) (ed.), *Policy Styles in Western Europe* (London: Allen & Unwin).

Richardson J.J., Jordan A.G. (1987), *British Politics and the Policy Process: The Arena Approach* (London: Allen & Unwin).

Roberts K., Cooke S.C., Semeneoff E. (1977), *The Fragmentary Class Structure* (London: Heinemann).

Rokkan S. (1970), *Citizens, Elections, Parties* (Oslo: Universitetsforlaget).

Rokkan S. (1971), 'Nation Building: A Review of Models and Approaches', in *Current Sociology*, 3, 7–38.

Rokkan S. (1973), 'Cities, States, Nations', in S.N. Eisenstadt, S. Rokkan (eds), *Building States and Nations* (Beverly Hills, Calif.: Sage), vol. 1.

Rokkan S., Lipset S.M. (1967) (eds), *Party Systems and Voter Alignments: Cross-National Perspectives* (New York: Free Press).

Rondin J. (1985), *Le Sacre des notables: la France en décentralisation* (Paris: Fayard).

Rosanvallon P. (1990), *L'État en France de 1789 à nos jours* (Paris: Seuil).

Rose R. (1974), *Problems of Party Government* (London: Macmillan).

Rose R. (1980), *Do Parties Make a Difference?* (New York: Chatham House).

Rose R. (1984), *Understanding Big Government* (London, Sage).

Rose R. (1985a) (ed.), *Public Employment in Western Nations* (Cambridge: Cambridge University Press).

Rose R. (1985b), 'From Government at the Centre to Nationwide Government', in Y. Mény and V. Wright (eds), *Centre and Periphery Relations in Western Europe* (London: Allen & Unwin).

Rositi F. (1984), 'Italia: perché è difficile lo sviluppo di una cultura riformatrice nel campo dei mass media', in G.-F. Pasquino (ed.), *Mass media e sistema politico* (Milan: Angeli).

Roth G. (1963), *The Social Democrats in Imperial Germany: A Study in Working Class Isolation and National Integration* (Totowa, NJ.: Bedminster Press).

Rousseau J.-J. (1762), *Du Contrat social*; English trans. *The Social Contract* (Harmondsworth: Penguin, 1968).

Russett B. (1990), *Controlling the Sword: The Democratic Governance of National Security* (Cambridge, Mass.: Harvard University Press).

Sabatier P., Mazmanian D. (1979), 'The Conditions of Effective Implementation', in *Policy Analysis*, 3, 213–27.

Saint-Simon L. de (1788), *Mémoires* (Paris: Gallimard, 1953, 5 vols).

Salmon T. (1993), 'Union, the CFSP and the European Security Debate', in J. Lodge (ed.), *The European Community and the Challenge of the Future* (London: Pinter, 2nd edn).

Salvati M. (1981), 'Ciclo politico e onde lunghe. Note su Kalecki e Phelps Brown', in *Stato e mercato*, 1, 9–46.

Sampson A. (1983), *The Changing Anatomy of Britain* (London: Coronet).

Samuelson P.A. (1960), *Economics* (New York: McGraw-Hill, 8th edn).

Sani G., Sartori G. (1982), 'Polarization, Fragmentation and Competition in Western Democracies', in H. Daalder and P. Mair (eds), *Western European Party Systems* (Beverly Hills, Calif.: Sage).

Sarre P. (1989), 'Recomposition of the Class Structure', in C. Hamnett, L. McDowell, P. Sarre (eds), *The Changing Social Structure* (London, Sage).

Sartori G. (1957), *Democrazia e definizioni* (Bologna: Il Mulino).

Sartori G. (1964), 'Dove va il Parlamento?' in *Il Parlamento Italiano 1946–1963*, (Naples: ESI).

Sartori G. (1968), 'Political Development and Political Engineering', in *Public Policy*, 27, 261–98.

Sartori G. (1976), *Parties and Party Systems* (Cambridge: Cambridge University Press).

Sartori G. (1982), *Teoria dei partiti e caso italiano* (Milan: Sugarco).

Sartori G. (1984), 'The Influence of Electoral Systems: Faulty Laws or Faulty Method', in B. Grofman, A. Lijphart (eds), *Electoral Laws and their Political Consequences* (New York: Agathon Press).

Sartori G. (1987), *The Theory of Democracy Revisited* (Chatham, NJ: Chatham House, 2 vols).

Sassoon D. (1975), 'The Funding of Italian Political Parties', in *Political*

Quarterly, 46, 1, 94–8.

Saunders P. (1986), 'Corporatism and Urban Service Provision', in W. Grant (ed.), *The Political Economy of Corporatism* (Basingstoke: Macmillan).

Saunders P. (1990), *Social Class and Stratification* (London: Routledge).

Scalfari E. (1969), *L'autunno della repubblica* (Milan: Etas Kompass).

Schmidt M.G. (1992), 'The Political Consequences of German Unification', in *West European Politics*, 15, 1–15.

Schmitter P.C. (1974), 'Still the Century of Corporatism?', in *The Review of Politics*, 1, 85–131.

Schmitter P.C. (1983a), 'Organizzazione degli interessi e rendimento politico', in G.-F. Pasquino (ed.), *Le società complesse* (Bologna: Il Mulino).

Schmitter P.C. (1983b), 'Democratic Theory and Neocorporatist Practice', in *Social Research*, L, 4, 885–928.

Schnapper D. (1971), *L'Italie rouge et noir: Les modèles culturels de la vie quotidienne à Bologne* (Paris: Gallimard).

Schumpeter J.A. (1919), 'Soziologie des Imperialismus', in *Archiv für Sozialwissenschaft und Sozialpolitik*; (1927), 'Die Sozialen Klassen im ethnisch-homogen Milieu', in *Archiv für Sozialwissenschaft und Sozialpolitik*; English trans. *Imperialism and Social Classes* (New York: Kelley, 1951).

Schumpeter J.A. (1942), *Capitalism, Socialism and Democracy* (London: Allen & Unwin).

Scott A. (1990), *Ideology and the New Social Movements* (London: Unwin Hyman).

Scott J. (1982), *The Upper Classes* (London: Macmillan).

Seeley J.R. (1894), *Introduction to Political Science* (London: Macmillan).

Seiler D.-L. (1980), *Partis et familles politiques* (Paris: Colin).

Seymour-Ure C. (1974), *Political Impact of Mass Media* (London: Sage).

Sharpe L.J. (1979), 'Modernising the Localities: Local Government in Britain and some Comparisons with France', in J. Lagroye, V. Wright (eds), *Local Government in Britain and France* (London: Allen & Unwin).

Sharpe L.J. (1981), 'Is there a Fiscal Crisis in Western European Local Government? A First Appraisal', in L.J. Sharpe (ed.), *The Local Fiscal Crisis in West Europe* (London: Sage).

Shils E. (1955), 'The End of Ideology', in *Encounter*, 5, 52–8.

Shonfield A. (1973), *Europe: Journey to an Unknown Destination* (Harmondsworth: Penguin).

Simon H.A. (1945), *Administrative Behaviour* (Glencoe, Ill.: Free Press, 2nd edn, 1957).

Skocpol T. (1979), *States and Social Revolution* (Cambridge: Cambridge University Press).

Smith D. (1980), *The Defence of the Realm in the 1980s* (London: Croom Helm).

Smith D.J., Gray J. (1985), *Police and People in London* (Aldershot: Gower).

Smith G. (1972), *Politics in Western Europe* (London: Hutchinson) (Aldershot: Gower, 5th edn, 1989).

Smith G. (1979), *Democracy in West Germany: Parties and Politics in the Federal Republic* (London: Heinemann) (Aldershot: Gower, 3rd edn, 1986).

Smith S. (1994), 'Political Theory and the New Europe', in W. Carlsnaes and S. Smith (eds), *European Foreign Policy: The EC and Changing Perspectives in Europe* (London: Sage), 1–20.

Spence J.E. (1984), 'British Foreign Policy: Tradition and Change', in R.L. Bothwick, J.E. Spence (eds) *British Politics in Perspective* (Leicester: Leicester University Press).

Stewart J. (1992), 'Internal Management of Local Authorities in Britain – The Challenge of Experience in Other Countries', in *Local Government Studies*, 18, 2, 5–17.

Stone L. (1994), 'Introduction', in L. Stone (ed.), *An Imperial State at War: Britain from 1688 to 1815* (London: Routledge).

Story J., de Carmoy G. (1993), 'France and Europe', in J. Story (ed.), *The New Europe: Politics, Government and Economy since 1945* (Oxford: Blackwell).

Stratmann P. (1993), 'Defence and Arms Control in a new Europe', in J. Story (ed.), *The New Europe: Politics, Government and Economy since 1945* (Oxford: Blackwell).

Streeck W., Schmitter P.C. (1991), 'From National Corporatism to Transnational Pluralism: Organized Interests in the Single European Market', in *Politics and Society*, 19, 2, 133–64.

Sulieman E.N. (1984), 'From Right to Left. Bureaucracy and Politics in France', in E.N. Sulieman (ed.), *Bureaucrats and Policy-Making: A Comparative Overview* (New York: Holmes & Meier).

Sylos-Labini P. (1975), *Saggio sulle classi sociali* (Bari: Laterza).

Sylos-Labini P. (1986), *Le classi sociali negli anni '80* (Bari: Laterza).

Tarrow S.G. (1977), *Between Center and Periphery: Grassroots Politicians in Italy and France* (New Haven, Conn.: Yale University Press).

Tarrow S.G. (1978), 'Introduction', in L. Graziano, P.J. Katzenstein, S.G. Tarrow (eds), *Territorial Politics in Industrial Nations* (New York: Praeger).

Tawney R.H. (1931), *Equality* (London: Allen & Unwin).

Tester K. (1992), *Civil Society* (London: Routledge).

Therborn G. (1977), 'The Rule of Capital and the Rise of Democracy', in *New Left Review*, 103, 3–41.

Therborn G. (1989), 'The Two-Thirds, One-Third Society', in S. Hall, M. Jacques (eds), *New Times: The Changing Face of Politics in the 1990s* (London: Lawrence & Wishart).

Thody P.M.W. (1989), *French Caesarism from Napoleon I to Charles de Gaulle* (Basingstoke: Macmillan).

Thomas J.C. (1980), 'Ideological Trends in Western Political Parties', in P.H. Merkyl (ed.), *Western European Party Systems* (New York: Free Press).

Thompson E.P. (1980), 'The State of the Nation', in *Writing by Candlelight* (London: Merlin Press).

Tilly C. (1975) (ed.), *The Formation of National States in Western Europe* (Princeton: Princeton University Press).

Tilly C. (1978), *From Mobilization to Revolution* (Reading, Mass.: Addison-Wesley).

Tocqueville A. de (1835–40), *De la démocratie en Amerique;* pages cited from English trans. *Democracy in America* (London: Fontana, 1966, 2 vols).

Tocqueville A. de (1856), *L'Ancien Régime et la révolution;* pages cited from English trans. *The Ancient Regime and the Revolution* (London: Fontana, 1966).

Touraine A. (1969), *La Société post-industrielle* (Paris: Denoel); English trans. *The Post-Industrial Society* (New York: Random House, 1971).

Touraine A. (1973), *La Production de la société* (Paris: Seuil); English. trans. *The Production of Society* (Cambridge: Cambridge University Press).

Touraine A. (1978), *La Voix et le regard* (Paris: Seuil); pages cited from English trans. *The Voice and the Eye: Analysis of Social Movements* (Cambridge: Cambridge University Press, 1981).

Touraine A. (1983), 'Analisi critica dei movimenti sociali', in G. Pasquino (ed.), *Le società complesse* (Bologna: Il Mulino).

Tressell R. (1914), *The Ragged Trousered Philanthropists* (London: Richards, 1935).

Trigilia C. (1986), *Grandi partiti piccole imprese: Comunisti e democristiani nelle regioni a economia diffusa* (Bologna: Il Mulino).

Truman D. (1951), *The Governmental Process: Political Interests and Public Opinion* (New York: Knopf).

Tuchman G. (1972), 'Objectivity as Strategic Reality: An Examination of a Newsman's Notion of Objectivity', in *American Journal of Sociology*, 77, 660–79.

Tugendhat C. (1986), *Making Sense of Europe* (New York: Viking).

Urry J. (1981), *The Anatomy of Capitalist Societies: The Economy, Civil Society and the State* (London: Macmillan).

Vajda M. (1976), *Fascism as a Mass Movement* (London: Allison & Busby).

Van Doorn J. (1975), *The Soldiers and Social Change* (Beverly Hills, Calif.: Sage).

Van Doorn J., Mans J.H. (1968), 'United Nations', in J. Van Doorn (ed.) *Armed Forces and Society* (The Hague: Mouton).

Veblen T. (1899), *The Theory of the Leisure Class* (London: Unwin, 1970).

Veblen T. (1915), *Imperial Germany and the Industrial Revolution* (Ann Arbor: University of Michigan Press, 1966).

Veca S. (1990), *Cittadinanza: Riflessioni filosofiche sull'idea di emancipazione* (Milan: Feltrinelli).

Vickers S.G. (1965), *The Art of Judgement* (London: Chapman & Hall).

Von Beyme K. (1979), *Das politische System der Bundesrepublik Deutschland* (Munich: Piper); English trans. *The Political System of the German Federal Republic* (Aldershot: Gower, 1983).

Von Beyme K. (1982), *Parteien in westlichen Demokratien* (Munich: Piper); pages cited from English trans. *Political Parties in Western Democracies* (Aldershot: Gower, 1985).

Wallerstein I. (1974), *The Modern World-System* (New York: Academic Press).

Warner, W. Lloyd (1936), 'American Class and Caste', in *American Journal of Sociology*, LXII, 3, 234–7.

Weber M. (1917), *Parlament und Regierung in neugeordneten Deutschland;* pages cited from English trans. *Parliament and Government in a Reconstructed Germany,* appendix II in *Economy and Society* (Berkeley, Calif.: California University Press, 1978), vol. 2.

Weber M. (1921), 'Politik und Beruf', in *Gesammelte Politische Schriften*; pages cited from English trans. 'Politics as a Vocation', in H.H. Gerth, C. W. Mills (eds), *From Max Weber* (London: RKP, 1948).

Weber M. (1922), *Wirtschaft und Gesellschaft*; pages cited from English trans., *Economy and Society* (Berkeley, Calif.: California University Press, 1978), 2 vols.

Weber M. (1986), *Italia: paese europeo? Un'analisi della cultura politica degli italiani in prospettiva comparata* (Milan: Angeli).

Webman J.A. (1981), 'Centralization and Implementation: Urban renewal in Great Britain and France', in *Comparative Politics*, 1, 127–48.

Welch C.E. Jr (1976) (ed.), *Civilian Control of the Military: Theory and Cases from Developing Countries* (Albany: State University of New York Press).

Wheare K.C. (1951), *Modern Constitutions* (Oxford: Oxford University Press).

Wheare K.C. (1964), *Federal Government* (Oxford: Oxford University Press, 4th edn).

Whiteley P. (1986), *Political Control of the Macro-Economy* (London: Sage).

Widdicombe Report (1986), *The Conduct of Local Authority Business* (London: Cmnd 9797, HMSO), Research, 4 vols (Cmnd 9798–9801).

Wildavsky A. (1959), 'A Methodological Critique of Duverger's Political Parties', in *Journal of Politics*, 2, 303–18.

Wildavsky A. (1964), *The Politics of the Budgetary Process* (Boston: Little, Brown).

Wildavsky A. (1979), *Speaking Truth to Power: The Art and Craft of Policy Analysis* (Boston: Little, Brown).

Williams A.M. (1987), *Western European Economy* (London: Hutchinson).

Williams R. (1960), *Border Country* (London: Chatto & Windus; 2nd edn Hogarth Press, 1988).

Williams R. (1961), *The Long Revolution* (London: Chatto & Windus).

Winkler J.T. (1976), 'Corporatism', in *European Journal of Sociology*, 17, 100–36.

Worms J.-P. (1966), 'Le Préfet et ses notables', in *Sociologie de travail*, 249–75.

Worsley P. (1983), 'One World or Three? A Critique of the World-System Theory of I. Wallerstein', in D. Held et al. (eds), *States and Societies* (Oxford: Robertson).

Wright E.O. (1978), *Class, Crisis and the State* (London: New Left Books).

Wright E.O. (1985), *Classes* (London: Verso).

Wright P. (1988), *Spycatcher* (London: Heinemann).

Wright V. (1978), *The Government and Politics of France* (London: Hutchinson) (Unwin & Hyman, 3rd edn, 1989).

Yeo E. (1981), 'Culture and Constraint in Working Class Movements 1830–1855', in E. Yeo, S. Yeo (eds), *Popular Culture and Class Conflict* (Brighton: Wheatsheaf Press).

Zeigler H. (1988), *Pluralism, Corporatism and Confucianism* (Philadelphia: Temple University Press).

Zincone G. (1987), 'Cittadinanza' in G. Zaccaria (ed.), *Lessico della politica* (Rome: Lavoro), 56–65.

Zincone G. (1989), 'Due vie alla cittadinanza: il modello societario e il modello statalista', in *Rivista italiana di scienza politica*, 2, 223–65.

Zolo D. (1992), *Democracy and Complexity* (Cambridge: Polity).

Index